The Organisation in its Environment

John Beardshaw BSc (Econ)

David Palfreman BA

Fourth edition

Pitman

PITMAN PUBLISHING
128 Long Acre, London WC2E 9AN
A Division of Longman Group UK Limited

Fourth edition first published in Great Britain 1990
Reprinted 1990, 1991 (twice), 1992

British Library Cataloguing in Publication Data
Beardshaw, John
   The organisation in its environment. —4th ed.
   1. Business firms
   I. Title II. Palfreman, David
   338.7

ISBN 0–273–03268–2

Printed and bound in Great Britain

Every effort has been made to trace all the copyright owners of
material used in this book but if any have been inadvertently
overlooked the publishers will be pleased to make the necessary
arrangements at the first opportunity.

Contents

Preface
to the fourth edition

In Tolkien's words this 'tale grew in the telling.' BTEC and our book have travelled far in twelve years.

Those of you familiar with previous editions will immediately notice four new features in this edition. *First*, it has a different size and text layout. This is intended to make the information more accessible; it has grown over the years! *Second*, we have included 'keywords' after the major sections of each chapter. These are intended to provide a summary of the main points covered in each section. *Third*, we have added 'learning activities' to the main body of the text. While the general trend in BTEC studies towards integrated assessment is to be welcomed, there is a still a need for unit based learning to develop the *knowledge, skills and understanding* required for integrated assignment work. The learning activities are designed to be used as part of this process. *Fourth*, at the end of each chapter there is at least one major 'learning project'. These are clearly far more substantial than the 'learning activities' but they are *not* assignments as they stand. They are designed to be used as part of the learning process rather than as part of an assessment package. However, they contain a wealth of additional information which both illustrates and develops the material in the chapters and with suitable development could become part of an assignment programme. This edition also has a new chapter on the EC and the impact of '1992', which will surely become a major theme in both the economy and teaching. Elsewhere the book has been extensively updated but existing readers will find much that is familiar.

Our basic aim remains unchanged. We have endeavoured to provide a structure to which students can relate and a comprehensive source of reasonably integrated information, together with explanations and ideas within which students can pursue their own learning. The expected restatement of the BTEC National Core in terms of 'performance objectives' does not gainsay our aim or the role of a textbook such as this, perhaps quite the reverse. Nevertheless, we would stress that, apart from the order implicit in the BTEC specification and any necessary sequential coverage, the content can be used in any order. It has never been our intention either to attempt a definitive statement of a BTEC course or to suggest a comprehensive assessment programme. Both these objectives lie in the domain of the tutors and their students. Broadly speaking, however, the first three parts of the book are relevant to both units while the fourth is relevant to the second year unit.

'Change' is a theme of the BTEC units and of this book, particularly the change engendered in working methods, patterns and environments by the exploitation of IT. This too has affected us. The first edition saw the demise of two portable typewriters and the consumption of at least one packet of carbon paper and numerous bottles of correction fluid. The text of this edition is now held on six discs and the pages were typeset by one of us (DP) at home using nothing more than a humble 'MacPlus', an off-the-shelf desk-top publishing package and a laser printer. What technology will be available for the 8th edition?

In places we have drawn on work done by Chris Faux for the Workbook which complemented former editions of this book. Our thanks to Chris for his help and co-operation. As ever, our thanks also go to Denise and Hellen for putting up with us and taking more than their fair share of the care of growing families while we were otherwise occupied and generally providing the organisation in our environment.

John Beardshaw and David Palfreman, May 1990

1

The changing environment

CHAPTER OBJECTIVES

After studying this chapter you should be able to:

■ Explain different aspects of change as they affect individuals and organisations;
■ Identify and explain the major factors affecting the environment and how these both cause and are affected by change.

We live in a world of organisations. Consider any aspect of our lives and you will find it is bound up with organisations. We are usually born in hospital, spend a number of years in school and go on to work for a company or the government or, perhaps set up our own business. If we misbehave we may end up in prison. These are all organisations. At the end of this life we are likely to be buried by another organisation – the church or other religious body.

The organisation and change

In the next chapter you will learn that organisations as we understand them today are a comparatively recent phenomenon. They are also constantly subject to a process of *change*. Companies merge, government is reorganised, technological processes are revolutionised, laws are introduced or reformed; even family structures change. The examples are endless. You as individuals must change and adapt, as must organisations and their environment. If you and they do not, failure may well be the result. It is often difficult to disentangle cause from response in this process.

Before moving on to specific factors of the organisation and its environment, e.g. economic and political forces, we want to consider some general ideas about the *nature of change*. Throughout, we will see that the forces of change we examine have two, in some respects, apparently incompatible aspects: they not only *constrain* individuals and organisations but also *enable* them to achieve their objectives. For example, although the motor vehicle has given us traffic jams and pollution, it has also given us freedom to travel largely when and where we want, an idea inconceivable one hundred years ago.

Change is a theme running through this book and we have gathered together general references to it in the index under 'change'.

Change is nothing new

Society has undergone radical transformation throughout history. The Agricultural and Industrial Revolutions, for example, profoundly altered the lives of our forefathers. Change is only new to *us*. As the Old Testament prophet remarked: '... there is no new thing under the sun'.

The pace of change

Change is often perceived as rapid. But is this true? The seeming breakthrough is often the result of many years' work. For example, computers were first designed and built in the early 1940s. It was not until the late 1970s/early 1980s that they truly began to have a profound effect on individuals and organisations. Similarly, it is usually not the invention that is important but the application of it. Indeed, it is often a very long time before a technological breakthrough is used to its full potential, if ever. In addition, by the time it is, further technological development may have rendered it obsolescent. Remember, however, that obsolescent does not mean useless; it means in the process of going out of date. For example, most home computers are obsolescent but their capabilities still far exceed the ability of most of us to use them. Comparing the performance of computers in milliseconds is about as relevant to most of us as comparing the 0–60 mph acceleration times of cars to the family motorist.

Change is not painless

Although economic and technological progress is generally regarded as desirable, to an important minority it is a disaster. Today, no less than in the Industrial Revolution (say 1750–1850), many people and organisations have been permanently deprived of their livelihoods by change. Ecologists, in general, and the 'Greens', in particular, would argue that if the environment has not already been irreparably damaged by the pursuit of progress, it soon will be! Even if change is inevitable, it is not necessarily good.

Expectations of change

People are curiously contradictory about change. They usually favour stability in their personal and professional life, and therefore tend to resist change, yet nevertheless expect their standard of living to improve. This can only happen if there is change and progress. The same argument applies to most organisations.

Better or just newer?

There are two ways of regarding change, technological change in particular. First, we may see it as merely a better way of undertaking existing tasks. For example, handling information more efficiently, producing goods and services more cheaply and to a better standard, distributing goods more swiftly and paying for them more conveniently. Second, we may see technological change as completely innovatory, enabling us to achieve goals previously unattainable or even unconsidered. The possibilities of TV were as unforeseen to your grandparents as the possibilities of genetic engineering may be to you today.

Resistance to change

Above we mentioned that change is often resisted. In the context of organisations, why is this so? The underlying reason is undoubtedly that change often causes a feeling of *insecurity*; that you will end up worse off than you were before, particularly in times of economic recession. This insecurity can be explained in terms of fears in three areas of human need.

(a) Economic needs, e.g. fear of unemployment caused by technology, reduced basic pay, demotion and increased work-pace;

(b) Psychological needs, e.g. resentment of the implied criticism that existing methods are inadequate, fear that the present level of skill required will be threatened and hence job status, dislike of the effort required in re-learning and re-training and fear of the unknown;

(c) Social needs, e.g. unwillingness to disrupt established patterns of family and social life by moving to another part of the country, by shift work and by structural reorganisation of the organisation and resentment at the inability to participate in making and planning the change.

The manifestations of such resistance range from *passive resignation* and loss of interest in the job to *passive resistance*, such as failure to learn, working to rule and absenteeism, to *active resistance* such as disputes and strikes or attempting to avoid change by taking another job.

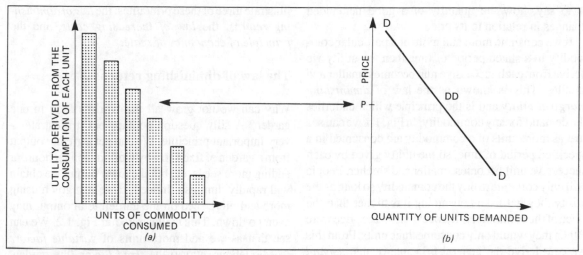

Fig. 1.1 *(a)* Diminishing marginal utility *(b)* The demand curve

Economic constraints

Human behaviour

There are many different aspects of human behaviour: political, social, economic and so on. Let us start our survey of the world of people and organisations with some aspects of human economic behaviour.

First, we assume that people are *maximisers*. They try to gain as much wealth or pleasure as possible. Those things for which people strive, be they goods, services or leisure, are said to give *utility*. Perhaps in a true socialist state people would strive for the greatest good of all but this is not generally true of our society. In saying this we are implying that people are primarily economic creatures and by and large the picture of an *acquisitive* human race seems to hold true. In addition to this we also assume that people are *rational*. That is to say, they will stop to consider which course of action will give them the greatest utility for the least cost. This somewhat unlovely portrait of people is not a suggestion of how the race should be but an observation of how it is!

We also assume that people are *competitive*. This is different from acquisitiveness for it implies that people want to do better than other people. We can also see from this that people are *individualistic*. In a competitive society such as ours, not only are people forced to compete but also the efficient working of the system depends upon them doing so.

In addition to assuming that people generally compete to gain as much utility as they can, we also assume that they do not like work. Work is said to have *disutility* and therefore people have to be paid to encourage them to undertake it. There are people who do like work but in general if people were offered the same money for shorter hours of work they would accept it.

The economic problem

We may speak of the economic problem as being *finite resources* and *infinite wants*. Part of this problem comes from the fact that people's wants are insatiable. Most people seem to think that they would be satisfied if they had just a little more but having attained a little more they discover more things that they want. It would seem that in satisfying one want we create another. For example, a person who does not have a car but wants one would be happy with just any car; having acquired a car, however, they may find they would like a better or bigger one and so on. People do not of course want more of everything: a person can rapidly reach the level of consumption of potatoes that they are happy with and not go beyond it!

Marginal utility and demand

The economic world is, of course, a world of change. Let us start off by considering one of the most fundamental of economic principles, that of *demand*. That is to say, how the quantity of a good demanded changes in relation to its price.

If we consume more and more of a particular commodity in a stated period of time then the utility we derive from each successive unit becomes smaller and smaller. This is known as the law of *diminishing marginal utility* and is the principle which underlies the demand for any commodity. In Fig. 1.1 we can see that as more units of a commodity are consumed in a specified period of time, so the utility given by each successive unit becomes smaller and smaller. People will only continue to buy the commodity so long as the utility they get from consuming it is higher than the price of the commodity. If, for example, the price were P then they would only consume three units. From this we can derive the general principle of the *demand curve* illustrated in Fig. 1.1(*b*), showing that people will only buy more of a commodity if the price is lowered. This is often known as the *first law of demand*.

Ceteris paribus

When considering changes in the economic and social environment, we say, for example, that X causes Y but we can only say this in so far as we are able to *isolate* these factors.

When we state something such as 'more of a commodity will be demanded at a lower price' we should include the phrase *ceteris paribus* (all other things remaining constant) for it may be that other things change at the same time as the price and then it will become impossible to reach any conclusion. In using this expression we are applying *scientific method* and isolating the one effect we wish to discuss. An inability to hold all other things equal when observing the real world is one of the factors which makes the study of the economy inexact.

Constraints imposed by nature

Goods and services are produced by combining resources together. For example, when a person goes out to dig a vegetable patch, the resources of land and labour are being combined.

There are fundamental principles that come into play when we combine resources. What is more, as we change the combinations employed it is possible to

illustrate three of these principles: the *law of diminishing returns*, the *law of increasing costs*, and the *principle of economics of scale*.

The law of diminishing returns

Why can we not grow all the world's food in one garden? A silly question perhaps but it illustrates a very important principle. We can get a greater output from a garden of fixed size by working longer hours or adding more seeds, etc but the *extra* output we obtain will rapidly diminish. Indeed, if we just go on using more and more seed on the garden total output may even go down. This is illustrated in Fig. 1.2. We can see that as we add more units of *variable factors* (seeds, labour, etc) to the *fixed factor* (the garden, output increases rapidly then slows down and finally declines.

The law of diminishing returns will apply to any situation where there is one factor fixed in supply and we change the number of units of other factors added to it.

Have you understood the principle of diminishing returns? Consider the diagram below.

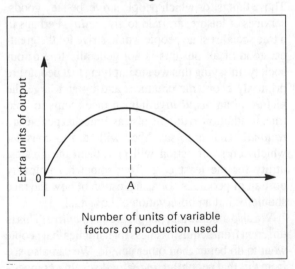

Number of units of variable
factors of production used

1 **At which point is output maximised?**

2 **Over what range of output is diminishing returns experienced?**

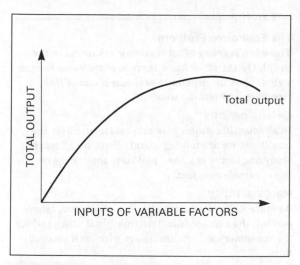

Fig. 1.2 Diminishing returns

The law of increasing costs

The law of diminishing returns concerns what happens to output if one factor remains fixed: the law of increasing costs examines what happens to production, and therefore to costs, as all factors of production are increased.

Let us imagine we are faced with the choice which Hermann Goering gave the German people in 1936: we can produce either guns or butter. Table 1.1 shows a list of alternative possibilities.

Table 1.1 A production possibility schedule

Possibility	Guns (thousands)	Butter (millions of kg)
A	15	0
B	14	5
C	10	10
D	5	14
E	0	15

If we start at possibility C, where we are producing 10,000 guns and 10 million kg of butter, and then try to produce more guns, this involves switching resources from farming to industry. To reach possibility B we have had to give up 5 million kg of butter to gain 4,000 guns. If we want still more guns, to reach possibility A we have to give up 5 million kg of butter to gain only 1,000 guns. Thus, the cost of guns in terms of butter has risen sharply.

It would also work the other way. If we started from possibility C and tried to increase our output of butter, the cost in terms of guns not produced would become greater and greater. Fig. 1.3 shows this graphically. As we move towards either end of the *production possibility curve* we can see that it is necessary to give up a greater distance on one axis to gain a smaller distance on the other axis. Why should this be? It is because while concentrating more and more resources on the output of a particular commodity, the resources we use become less and less suitable. For example, if we tried to produce more and more butter we would inevitably be forced to graze cows on land which was less and less suitable.

Increasing costs have been looked at here from the point of view of society as a whole but any trading organisation could easily become aware of it. If, for example, Ford tried to double the capacity of their plant at Dagenham they would immediately suffer from increasing costs as they would have to pay higher wages to attract labour in from greater distances and higher rents to attract land away from other uses. Increasing costs can therefore come about as a result of the competition for resources. Having looked at the law of increasing costs, it allows us to illustrate another fundamental principle: *opportunity cost*.

Opportunity cost

In the example opposite we looked at the cost of guns in terms of butter. This could be termed the *opportunity*

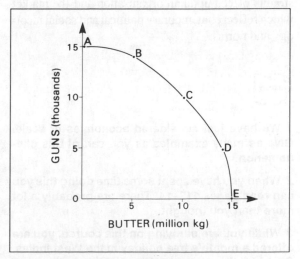

Fig. 1.3 A production possibility curve

cost. The opportunity cost of something is whatever we have to give up in order to produce that commodity. Any movement along the production possibility line AE of Fig. 1.3 will tell us the opportunity cost of guns in terms of butter and vice versa.

Economies of scale

The principles that we have examined so far seem to place limits on our ability to combine resources and produce goods. But just as the world works against us in some things, it works for us in others.

The principle of economies of scale tells us that as we produce a product in large numbers so the cost of producing each individual item may become smaller, i.e. we have become more efficient. For example if a company only produced ten cars a year they would be very expensive but by producing thousands a week the major manufacturers are able to make them more cheaply. This is because they are able to take advantage of better *technology* and *division of labour*. In this case it will mean that as we produce more, the cost of producing a unit will go down instead of up. A time will come, however, when economies of scale are exhausted and unit costs begin to rise again.

Thus, an organisation has to deal on one hand with constraints which govern human behaviour and on the other hand with the constraints placed by nature on production. In addition, there are also the legal constraints placed upon an organisation and the market which reflect contemporary political and social ideology and norms.

1 We have just considered economies of scale. Give as many examples as you can of this phenomenon.

2 When you have spent some time doing this you can read pages 113–14. There are probably a lot more than you thought.

3 While you are studying on this course, you are offered a month's free holiday in the West Indies. Consider the opportunity cost of this holiday.

The legal framework

A contradiction?

We have seen how human behaviour and the natural world both *constrain* and *help* organisations. The legal environment, a framework of rules within which individuals and organisations operate, also does this. Thus, we have two apparently contradictory statements. On the one hand the law *constrains* organisations, preventing them from doing what they want to, e.g. the effect of consumer legislation, and forcing them to do what they might otherwise choose not to do, e.g. requirements laid down by health and safety legislation. On the other hand the law is an *enabling medium* helping organisations to pursue commercial and other objectives. For example, they are able to formulate their policies and determine their responsibilities and liabilities according to known rules of law, benefit from legal protection of their patents and trade marks and acquire resources and sell their products and services through the mechanism of contract law. (We develop the theme of the organisation's use of the law in Chapter 25 and frequently refer to it throughout.)

There is, however, no real contradiction between these two statements. We can explain this quite simply by making a comparison with a game of football. The rules of the game prevent the players from doing certain things but they also enable the game to take place. Without rules, how would the game start and end and how would you determine who had won? In essence the law *regulates* the activities of organisations by providing a framework of rules governing their formation and dissolution; their use of resources and other activities; and their responsibility and accountability to providers of finance, employees, customers and the community in general. It also provides a number of methods of resolving the conflicts which inevitably arise.

Consider how the legal framework affects the activities of the organisation you work for or study in. List as many ways as you can in which the legal framework *(a)* facilitates, and *(b)* constrains those activities.

The framework of rules

The framework of rules consists mainly of Acts of Parliament, although most of the law of contract – the basic law of the market place – is still to be found in the statements of law made by judges. In such spheres as consumer protection, health and safety at work and job security, however, this traditional judge-made law (case law) is neither adequate nor appropriate. Statu-

tory law is far better able to formulate the necessarily detailed framework of regulations required. It can also more effectively take into account the important and often conflicting social, economic and political considerations involved.

Development and change

This legal environment did not materialise overnight – quite the reverse in fact – it has developed over several centuries. As well as representing the social and economic norms of the present, it does, therefore, sometimes reflect the attitudes of the past. It is also subject to a constant process of development and change. Every so often, a case will be decided which significantly alters an existing rule or establishes a new one, usually in response to a particular problem posed to the court. Of greater importance is the constant output of new legislation. Stacked up, an average year's Acts of Parliament and orders made under existing and new legislation would amount to a pile several feet high!

This, however, is very much the *response* to change rather than the cause of it, although an innovatory Act of Parliament will clearly be a force for change itself. We are more concerned with the forces which *cause* change in the legal environment and identifying examples of their effect. So, what are they?

The framework of rules produced since the Industrial Revolution is not just the work of lawyers. It has been shaped by other forces in the environment: by economic theory and practice and by politics and pressure groups. The abuse of commercial, particularly, monopoly power, for example, has led to a need for a comprehensive framework of consumer protection and competition law is necessary to protect the individually weak consumer from the corporate economic might of organisations. The latter have been instrumental in creating a protective framework of planning legislation and employment and labour law designed to encourage and enforce social responsibility in economic activity. Basic philosophical concepts of the law, such as justice and rights of duties, must be considered in these contexts.

The field of employment is a particularly good example of development and change in the legal environment. It also perfectly illustrates the compromise among often conflicting social, economic and political perspectives affecting organisations and economic activity generally. Until the Employment Act 1980 changed the law, an employee who was sacked for not joining a specific trade union where a 'closed shop' agreement was in operation could not sue for unfair dismissal. The Labour government's legislation of the mid-1970s – culminating in the Employment Protection (Consolidation) Act 1978 – declared such a dismissal to be automatically fair. It was hard to accept that this was ever just in the philosophical sense but it arguably made economic and political (with a small 'p') sense. A change of government saw a change of political belief which has been reflected in the law. Today, while closed shops are not unlawful as such, they have absolutely no statutory recognition, this having been systematically removed by the Employment Acts 1980–88. There are no circumstances in which an employee can be lawfully dismissed for not joining a closed shop and such a dismissal automatically entitles the employee to claim compensation for 'unfair dismissal'.

Broadening the example, we could argue for a correlation between the level of economic activity and prosperity and attitudes to employment law. While we are most unlikely ever to see the wholesale taking away of employment rights, a high level of unemployment shifts the balance of power very firmly into the hands of those employers who might be tempted to exploit a person's desire to work. Rather than being formally changed, the law may not be observed. On the other hand, legislation which would appear to strengthen the hand of employers is sometimes not used, for example, the current legislation against secondary picketing. Does this reflect a reluctance to do so on the part of employers for the sake of good long term industrial relations? Alternatively, does it reflect the more basic lack of a need to do so given the comparative weakness of trade unions in times of relatively high unemployment, declining memberships and public support, and a government committed to curbing their powers?

Another feature of employment law in recent times has been anti-discrimination, although the effectiveness and general acceptance of present legislation is another matter. Britain is now a multi-racial society and this fact has to be considered in both political and economic decision-making. To do otherwise would be stupid as it would be dangerous. Similarly, the role

of women has changed and the law as a mechanism for social organisation must accept and reflect this, as must organisations in their attitudes to their female staff.

To what extent do you think the law *(a)* can, and *(b)* has suppressed discrimination in the UK?

Substantive and organic change

It would be quite wrong to see the legal environment as being in a state of constant flux. Indeed one of the characteristics of a stable society is certain legal rules. But the forces of change are always present and over a long period the process of change is clearly evident.

When we consider such changes, we can contrast substantive change with procedural change, and organic change with institutional change. The examples we have used from employment law are examples of *substantive* change, so called because they are changes to the actual rules or substance of the law. *Procedural* change is where the process by which the rules are enforced is changed, not the rules themselves. Examples would be changes in the jurisdiction of the courts or to the procedure to be followed when bringing a court action, some of which may have consequences as important and far reaching as changes in the rules themselves. We can also consider our examples from employment law as *organic* changes. They result naturally from the interaction of the forces which constitute the total environment: social, economic and political – witness the changes in relation to unfair dismissal and the 'closed shop' in particular (*see* Chapter 8). *Institutional* change, on the other hand, is change which is less the result of natural forces and more the result of conscious acts of law reform. The Law Commission, an official body charged with the task of law reform is the most important author of such change.

The processes overlap, of course, Parliament both changes law in response to organic forces and makes conscious decisions to change the law. The Insolvency Act 1985 was a particularly good example of a mixed process. For years insolvency law had developed in a haphazard (and organic!) fashion with statutes being amended by case law being amended by statutes. The business world wanted change. Institutional change took over. In 1982 the Insolvency Law Review Committee reported with a coherent set of proposals (the Cork Report) – so far so good. A White Paper was published in February 1984 and after much debate and amendment (over 1,200 amendments were considered) the Insolvency Act 1985 resulted. While it made important changes, it was a very complicated piece of legislation. As a member of the House of Lords remarked during the debate, 'We would not have got into this confusion had we stuck with the original text, by which I mean the recommendations of the Cork Committee.' Perhaps sometimes you should not interfere. (In fact because it overlapped with the Companies Act 1985 in the area of company insolvency, it was repealed and replaced by the Insolvency Act 1986, although the law remains the same.)

The Companies Act 1989 introduced a *seemingly* important change to the contractual capacity of companies by abolishing the *ultra vires* rule. This rule stated that any contract for a purpose not covered by the objects clause of the company's memorandum of association was void and could not be enforced against the company, a rule at odds with the rest of the EC. However, the *ultra vires* rule had become less and less important over the years thanks to extremely widely drafted objects clauses and a statutory provision last found in the Companies Act 1985 that *any* transaction sanctioned by its directors would bind the company. The 1989 Act was therefore both a recognition of changed commercial practice and a conscious step to bring the UK into line with company law in the rest of the EC.

The evolution of *product liability* is covered in Chapter 17.

The environment at work

It is accepted today that a business organisation owes responsibilities not only to its investors, members, creditors, etc but also to the community in general and it must be accountable to both. Consequently, while the legal environment facilitates an organisation's activities, it somewhat paradoxically imposes constraints and obligations to do this. Without these it would be possible to pursue activities and employ methods which are socially, economically and politically unacceptable. Thus, the law will restrain the

minority to assist the majority. Some examples will illustrate this point.

Investment is vital to the activities of a company and this can best be encouraged by effective legal safeguards against misuse of investments by business organisations. This is achieved through legislation requiring companies to file their memoranda of association and articles of association on formation and information about their activities and financial position annually with the Registrar of Companies for public inspection. In addition, the legal framework imposes sanctions for commercial malpractice, e.g. insider trading – the practice whereby persons such as directors are able to misuse confidential inside information likely to affect the price of the company's securities for personal gain through dealings on a recognised stock exchange. Under the Company Securities (Insider Dealing) Act 1985 insider trading is a criminal offence carrying a maximum sentence of two years' imprisonment.

It is in the interest of economic activity generally that certain limits are placed on the growth of business organisations, particularly through monopolistic practices and mergers which will reduce competition to the detriment of consumers and smaller business units. Private companies are essentially intended to be small businesses and this aim is achieved by allowing a company to restrict its membership and the transferability of its shares by appropriate clauses in its articles of association. On a quite different level the Monopolies and Mergers Commission can investigate monopolies or proposed mergers which would operate against the public interest. These constraints are also part of the legal environment, the simple principle being that since consumers need goods and services as much as business organisations need to produce them, the consumer should not be exploited by them. Thus, consumers are protected against unfair trade practices and the weakness of their bargaining position relative to their suppliers.

Over the years the need to protect the natural environment and local community interests from unplanned or uncontrolled industrial development has become more pressing. The scars left on the landscape by the ravages of the Industrial Revolution are ample evidence of this. The legal environment consequently includes rules regulating land use and development. These attempt to achieve a satisfactory compromise between the legitimate interests of environmentalist and local community lobbies and the resources needed by modern business organisations to produce the wealth necessary to sustain a complex industrial society.

In a somewhat analogous way, the legal environment includes constraints and imposes obligations on a business organisation's use of labour: maximisation of profits cannot be achieved at the expense of the environment or the employee. Thus, reciprocal rights and duties between employer and employee are part and parcel of the legal environment.

Key words

Legal framework

Legally enforceable rules that enable organisations and individuals to pursue their objectives while at the same time putting constraints upon their actions. Its role is to *regulate* activity.

Change

Change in the legal framework is seldom, if ever, a purely 'legal matter'. It is caused and shaped by economic theory and practice, by political beliefs and the activities of pressure groups. The process of change can be both 'organic', the result of evolution, and 'institutional', the result of a conscious decision by Parliament.

The political dimension

Politics, law and economics

You have just read that the legal framework is far from being purely a lawyer's creation. It is formed by an amalgam of forces, one of these being the government and its politics. You will see later that the other constraints outlined in this chapter are, to a greater or lesser extent, affected directly or indirectly by the policy and activities of successive governments.

Because human nature tends to change only very slowly within a society, fundamental economic principles remain unchanging and the legal environment is relatively constant and certain, a government's policy is the least predictable constraint on an organisation's activities. It is true it will have its manifesto and other policy pronouncements but these must be seen in the context of the practical demands and problems of government. Thus, whether because of external or internal pressures, governments tend to modify their policies during their period of office. Because all modern governments intervene in the economy, organisations must cope with an uncertain constraint on their activities and one which will possibly change course drastically every five years.

Government has been a potent force for change not only because the present two party system has tended to result in such marked changes of course but also because it may produce what has been called an 'elected dictatorship'. This is an idea that we explore in Chapter 27 but it basically means that once elected a government is theoretically free to act in any way it likes providing it can avoid being challenged in the courts and continues to have the support of its party in Parliament.

Conflict and consensus

The nature of government and politics is itself also subject to change. The years following the 1939–45 World War were years of general consensus on major issues. There was broad agreement on both the major issues and how they should be approached. In the 1980s increasing conflict and polarisation characterised the relationship between the two major parties.

At one time it looked as though the alliance between the Liberal Party and the Social Democratic Party would form a third force in British politics. Indeed in the 1987 general election their share of the votes (22.6%) far exceeded their share of the seats (3.4%, 22 seats) – thanks to our 'first past the post' system. In other words, their Parliamentary representation did not reflect their support nationwide. Conversely while polling only 42.3% of the vote, the Conservative party formed a government with an overall majority of 102! Subsequent internal division and a merger between the Liberals and SDP to form the Democrats led to a decline in popular support, running at the end of the decade at about 4%. On the other hand, the late 1980s saw a rapid growth in support for the Green Party with policies determined by their views on protecting the environment. Whether support was 'genuine' or just a 'protest' vote against the seemingly invincible Thatcher administration and a Labour opposition still in the process of reshaping its policy and image, the Greens were running at about 5% of the popular vote and polled 20% of the vote in the elections to the European Parliament in 1989. However, because of this 'first past the post' system once again they gained not a single seat in Strasbourg. Cynics commented that this 20% support was indicative of the British response to Europe, i.e. they were far happier to vote 'Green' for Europe – where it did not matter anyway!

A hung Parliament, i.e. one in which no party has an overall majority, would see the power of the smaller parties (Liberal Democrats, SDLP, Ulster Unionists, Scottish Nationalists, SDP) considerably increased. In return for their support they might well demand electoral reform and some kind of proportional representation. This would almost certainly result in a return to consensus politics. The Labour and Conservative parties, for obvious reasons, continue to oppose electoral reform. The 1990s began with a Conservative government looking far less than it had for some time. The Labour party began to look electable and was well ahead in the opinion polls. The story continues.

Another change in politics has been the increasing importance and power of the party leader, almost the rise of a personality cult some would say. Image is all important and policies are slickly marketed to the electorate while in the Cabinet consensus may be more the result of ruthless selection and pressure than genuine agreement. Sometimes the consensus cracks, as it did in the 'Westland Affair' in early 1986, resulting in the resignation of two Cabinet Ministers in quick succession. This change to the cult of the leader and the downgrading of the importance of cabinet government was also well-illustrated by the resignation of Nigel Lawson in 1989. He resigned because the Prime Minister was taking the advice of a private adviser, Professor Alan Walters, rather than that of himself in the Cabinet. Such a practice is more in line with the presidential government of the USA rather than with that of the UK.

List six examples of different types of constraints on the organisation. The first one is done for you:

1 **The law of diminishing returns.**

The international dimension

We are no longer the masters of our own economy, Britain is not able to control the world scene to her own advantage. What influence we have must be exercised through our membership of international organisations such as the EC and the United Nations and through our so called 'special relationships' with America and the Commonwealth Countries. We are not alone of course. President Mitterand of France, for example, found out soon after being elected that it was impossible to pursue an independent, socialist economic policy in the 1980s.

A century ago the position, for the UK, was very different. What caused the change in our fortunes and influence? History tells us that all empires eventually fall to similar combinations of political, economic and social forces to those which ultimately determine a nation's internal affairs. World wars, national aspirations and changing patterns of trade all play their part, but for the business environment two particularly interesting forces for change have been the rise of multinational companies and the switch from coal to oil as the principal world fuel. The most significant force for change in the immediate future will be the impact of '1992'.

Multinational companies

Today there are many multinational companies that are virtual 'city states'. They owe no real allegiance to anyone except themselves, have turnovers which dwarf those of most developing nations and tend to select host countries in much the same way as a shipping line may elect to sail under a flag of convenience. The host country is sometimes, in effect, powerless to control their activities yet so dependent upon their presence that it would probably choose not to if it could. Technological change has meant that such companies have a world strategy; where is the cheapest suitable labour force for example? – no wonder domestic regional development plans are not a roaring success! The activities of multi-national companies are one major cause of the progressive switch of manufacturing, particularly in the 'high tech' industries, to the Pacific Basin. This is rapidly becoming the dominant manufacturing region of the world.

The Environment as an issue

One of the most remarkable features of recent years has been the rise of the Environment as a political issue. As you have seen, in the election to the European Parliament in 1989, the Green Party in the UK polled 20% of the total vote.

It is now realised that the Environment is not a free resource. In previous years it was possible, to some extent, to pump pollution into the atmosphere, rivers and seas and leave them to recuperate naturally. The growing toxicity of our waste products (radioactive waste, CFCs, carbon monoxide etc), combined with the growing number of people on the planet mean that this is no longer possible.

The enormity of environmental issues is so great that it transcends our usual way of looking at problems. However careful we may be we cannot protect ourselves from the pollution of others. World-wide pollution is likely to impose on ourselves and future generations new and unpleasant constraints and to demand new forms of international co-operation to deal with the problems. Unfortunately, most people's understanding of damage to the environment has progressed little beyond being aware of polluted beaches on their holidays.

The influence of oil

Many would say that Britain has not made the best possible use of her oil reserves and, indeed, the pound's value has fluctuated directly as a result of changing world oil prices. But at least Britain was fortunate to have oil and an economy which could just about cope with its presence. Other nations have had their economies completely devasted through no real fault of their own by the once unforeseen rises and subsequent falls in oil prices. Oil rich countries like Nigeria and Mexico, not so long ago apparently set to boom, are now major debtor nations with almost impossible financial problems. Worst hit have been some of the world's poorest countries, Ethiopia for example. Totally dependent on imported oil and powerless to influence its price, their poverty for the foreseeable future has been confirmed; even Bob Geldof and Live Aid could not change this!

What will be the picture when the world's oil reserves run out? Will we consider the anti-nuclear power pressure groups to be incredibly short-sighted, will we see a temporary return of coal as the world's principal fossil fuel (Britain has a great deal of this), or will we see the development of completely new power sources and technologies as the emergent 'Green' forces advocate?

1992

By the end of 1992 there will be a single common market in the European Community with completely free movement of goods, services, labour and capital among the 12 member states. This represents both a great challenge and a great opportunity for business organisations in the UK. Will they meet the challenge, will they seize the opportunity? Indeed, are our businesses prepared for this final stage in the development of the Common Market? Will we become marginalised and parochial behind the English Channel or truly European in our outlook. Will we at last accept that not everybody speaks English!? Time will tell. (We discuss '1992' more formally in Chapter 20.)

Key words ─────────────────────

Consensus politics
When there is broad agreement between political parties about the major issues of policy such as employment, defence and methods to be used to pursue them, then consensus politics exists.

Multinational company
A company producing goods and services in many different countries.

Social change

In this book we tend to concentrate on the economic and legal aspects of life. However, people are not just resources or markets, they are also individuals and families. They both respond to and cause changes in the economy, indeed it is logical to assume that the whole purpose of industry and business is to enable people to achieve better and more rewarding lives.

It is beyond the scope of this book to explain the complexities of modern sociology. We will instead just mention some of the more important changes that have occurred in recent years.

The family

Throughout our history the family has been the most important social unit and also the basis of economic life. In the last 40 years there have been profound changes in family life.

The traditional structure is known as the *extended family*. This is a family consisting not only of parents and children but also of grandparents, aunts and uncles, cousins, second-cousins and so on. Such families lived together, or in close geographical proximity and acted as co-operative and supportive social and economic organisations. Thus, for example, child-rearing was a task which the parents could share with other members of the extended family. Although, obviously, people still have grandparents and aunts and uncles, in many cases they no longer form part of their economic and social lives. Extended families do still exist but are in decline. Nevertheless, among some of the ethnic minorities communities in the UK we can still see the extended family alive and well.

A more typical arrangement today is for a family consisting of just parent(s) and children. This is referred to as the *nuclear family*. It exists separately and is not supported by the other family members. Thus, parents raising young children become more dependent upon social services while at the other end of the age spectrum old people are no longer looked after by their families but become dependent on outside agencies.

The rise of the nuclear family is associated with greater social and geographical mobility, changing social values and changes in educational and social services.

The shape of the family in the UK has also been profoundly modified by divorce. In 1961 there were 27,000 divorces but in 1987 this had risen to 165,000. Divorce brings with it not only social and emotional upheaval but also important economic consequences. For example, as existing families split this creates a demand for extra units of housing. Together with the rise of the nuclear family, this helps to explain why the demand for housing is rising more quickly than can be accounted for by the depreciation of the existing housing stock or by the general increase in population.

The role of women

There has been a tremendous change in the role of women in society. In general we can say that women now have entry to professions which were previously closed to them, even parts of the church, and that there has been a change in the attitude towards the woman's traditional roles as homemaker and child-rearer. Today a young father is likely to have to participate in the business of bringing up his children in a way that was unknown to his father. It is also much more common today to find a woman as head of the household.

These changes have come about partly as a result of changing attitudes and partly as a result of legislation, the two major statutes being the Equal Pay Act 1970 and the Sex Discrimination Act 1975.

Despite these changes, many inequalities still exist. In 1970 the average earnings of women were 56% of those of men. Despite legislation, by 1987 this figure had only risen to 70%. Even in professions where there is apparently equal pay, such as teaching, the average earnings of men are still considerably higher. The percentages quoted above refer only to *full-time* employment. If we took the average earnings of all employed women and compared it with that of men the difference would be much greater. This is because large numbers of women work part-time.

Education

The spread of state education has brought about great changes in society. Although state education can be traced back to the nineteenth century, we may trace modern changes to the Education Act 1944, sometimes known as the Butler Act. This established the tripartite system of secondary education, i.e. the system of grammar, technical and secondary modern schools, with selection at the age of eleven by the 11+ exam. Until the mid-1960s this was the basis of the system of state secondary education. It resulted in progression to higher education for many young people previously disadvantaged by low parental incomes although many held the view that the system was essentially socially and educationally divisive.

This system was to be replaced by comprehensive schools. In 1964 only 4% of secondary students were in the comprehensive system; in 1987 the figure was 86%. Substantial changes are still occurring in secondary education, e.g. the introduction of the National Curriculum in September 1989 for all education from the age of 5.

The form which our primary and secondary education takes is very important not only because of the qualifications which we may, or may not, acquire but also because it helps to form our attitudes and social values (*see* also page 117). Families, incomes and other personal circumstances vary greatly but school is the one great shared experience.

Higher education was substantially expanded as a result of the *Robbins Report*. This recommended extending university provision and many new universities such as East Anglia and Lancaster, were opened as a result. In the 1960s and 1970s higher education was also extended through the establishment of polytechnics. The possibility of people progressing through higher education on the basis of merit rather than social position has led to the creation of a new class of 'upwardly mobile young professionals' (nicknamed 'yuppies'). Despite the impact of the stock market crash in October 1987, the spending power which they possess continues to have significant effects upon the patterns of consumption in the economy, for example, the demand for expensive city housing and consumer durables.

There are, however, serious worries about the current state of education in the UK. Participation rates in further and higher education are much lower than in countries such as Germany and Japan. That is to say, considerably smaller percentages of people receive technician and degree level education. The average production-line worker in Japan, for example, is much better qualified than a comparable Briton and receives far more on-the-job training, particularly in the application and use of high technology equipment (*see* page 144). We should not be surprised, therefore, when we find that the Japanese workforce is much more productive.

Despite the steps which have been taken to rectify these deficiencies, many of the schemes put forward, such as YTS, are often seen as being as much a response to youth unemployment as to genuine educational needs.

Ethnic minorities

One of the most apparent changes in UK society in recent decades is the growth of ethnic minorities. This began with immigration from the West Indies in the 1950s which was actively encouraged to help deal with the shortage of labour at that time. The 1960s saw the arrival of many immigrants from India, Pakistan and Bangladesh. A brake was put on immigration by the Commonwealth Immigrants Act 1962. During the 1970s many people of Asian origin arrived in the UK from African countries whose governments had turned against them. Many of these people were able to claim British citizenship as a legacy of Britain's imperial past in Uganda, Tanzania and Kenya. There has, of course, been immigration of other ethnic minorities such as Chinese and Greek.

Migration is not a significant demographic factor in the sense that it has not substantially altered the overall size of the population. This is because the UK is nearly always a net loser by migration, that is to say, in most years more people leave the country than enter it (*see* page 79). This therefore explodes one myth, i.e. that the UK is being 'flooded' with immigrants. A look at other European countries will show that most have a greater percentage of immigrant population than the UK, with Switzerland leading the way. Large-scale immigration into the UK of people from the New Commonwealth areas have largely ceased. However, the moral claim to come to the UK of several million Chinese UK passport-holders in Hong Kong has been highlighted by the truly dreadful events in Tiannamen Square in the summer of 1989 and the projected return of Hong Kong to China in 1997. Indeed, in December 1989 the Government announced that 50,000 of Hong Kong's key civil servants and business leaders plus their families, some 225,000 people in all, would be given the right to live in the UK. This right was given in the hope that they would *remain* in Hong Kong knowing they could come to the UK if they wished or needed to after 1997 rather than emigrate to the detriment of Hong Kong's immediate future

There is also widespread misconception about the total number of people in the ethnic minorities and their origins. In 1986, whites constituted over 94% of the population. Of the remaining population which constitutes the ethnic minorities, a significant proportion are British born (see Table 1.2).

However, the fact that many ethnic communities tend to be highly concentrated in inner-city areas often gives the impression that they are far more numerous than they are. The different colour and social and religious customs of ethnic minorities also make them very visible.

Table 1.2 Population of the UK by ethnic origin 1987

Ethnic origin	Total (thousands)	Percentage of these UK born
White	53,571	96
West Indian	529	51
Indian	853	36
Pakistani	370	41
Bangladeshi	85	35
Chinese	108	22
African	91	34
Arab	74	14
Mixed	204	78
Other	113	24
Not stated	1,045	74
All origins	56,930	93

Source: Labour Force Survey

Sadly, it must be admitted that the attitude of many people towards ethnic minorities is simply one of racial prejudice. This is made worse in times of economic decline and high unemployment when it is easy to blame all ills on a minority – just as the Nazis did with the Jews in Germany.

The quality of life

For most people the quality of life has improved over the last 20 or 30 years in that they have more leisure time and consume more goods and services. In 1964, 46% of people lived in homes which they owned. In 1987 this had risen to 63%. Over the same period these homes had become stacked with more and more consumer 'goodies' (*see* Table 1.3). Shown in these figures are some of the newer products such as video recorders and home computers. The UK has the highest percentage ownership of these in the world.

A topic which is worth considering is the effect of these new products on social and economic life.

Table 1.3 Services in the home

Percentage of homes with:	1964 %	1986 %
Baths	83	98
Cars	37	65
TV	80	98
Telephone	22	83
Central heating	7	68
Washing machine	53	82
Fridge	34	98
Micro-wave oven	—	23
Video recorder	—	38
Home computer	—	17

Source: General Household Survey 1986

Undoubtedly, videos, like television, have had an adverse effect on more social forms of entertainment such as cinema and football. But they also have more insidious psychological effects in tending to isolate people from one another. The effect of so much interest in home computers could be seen in the same light. We could, however, also argue that it may be a good omen for the future in making Britain a more computer literate society.

We are also a society that now takes more holidays. In 1987, Britons took nearly 94 million holidays. More and more people are going abroad each year. In 1971 only 36% of adults had been abroad on holiday at some time in their life. However, by 1984 this had risen to 66%. No less than 20 million holidays abroad were taken in 1987.

Not all the changes in the quality of life have been good ones. Many people would argue that life is both more frantic and more stressful than it used to be. There has also been a dramatic increase in crime. In 1971, 1.9 million crimes were reported to the police, but by 1987 this figure had risen to nearly 4.5 million, of which 188,000 were crimes of violence.

The Welfare State

After the end of the Second World War in 1945 the British government constructed the Welfare State. This was a series of schemes whereby the general health and well-being of the population was assured. Thus, from the late 1940s all Britons could expect a good standard of health care, old age pensions and education. This was funded from taxation and National Insurance contributions and was in no way related to the ability to pay. At the time this was a revolutionary system and had few, if any, rivals in the world.

People that were brought up in the 1950s and 1960s came to expect that good health care and education were theirs as a right. However, in recent years the Welfare State has been under pressure. First, on an ideological basis some people have begun to question whether or not individuals should not be made more responsible for their own welfare. Second, increasing strains have been placed on the services because of such things as the greater proportion of old people in the community and the increasing cost of medical care. Third, the generally depressed state of the economy has made it more difficult to fund social services while placing increased burdens on them by way of greater unemployment and so on.

Those who have recourse to the welfare services in other European countries such as France and Germany may now be aware that the UK is lagging in these areas. It is no longer true that we lead the world.

The two nations

In 1845 Benjamin Disraeli published his novel *Sybil*, or *The Two Nations*. This described the differences in the community between the rich and the poor. We have become accustomed to seeing the social history of the time since then as an account of how these disparities have been reduced or eliminated.

Many people now fear that a new age of two nations may be with us. There is a widening gap between the 'haves' and the 'have-nots', in particular between the working and the unemployed. What is more there is a distinct geographical basis to this with the south of the country being mainly prosperous while deprivation is concentrated in northern areas. Those at particular risk can be summarised by the acronym YOPS (the Young, Old, Poor and Sick). The problem also manifests itself in the decay of our inner-cities and the growing alienation of the disadvantaged sections of the community. Many would see this alienation, expressed not so much in party political terms but in a general rejection of and non-participation in 'conventional'

society, as the most worrying of all problems.

You should be aware when you are studying the economy or society that it is no longer a harmonious whole. Serious inequalities exist and there are fundamental disagreements about how to cope with the problems. On the one side are those who see the regeneration of the economy as the first priority in order that welfare services may be afforded. On the other side are those who believe that the inequalities must be reduced before it is possible to make progress on economic issues.

Consider your own life and lifestyle and state as many changes as you can which you have experienced as a result of outside influences. For example, how have changes in educational policy influenced you?

Key words ───────────────────────

Welfare State
The conditions on which the government takes a positive attitude towards social welfare, through the promotion and provision of health, education, social security, etc.

Demographic change

Nowhere is the constantly changing nature of the environment more apparent than in demography, that is to say, changes in the size of population, its age structure and its geographical distribution. Also with populations, unlike many other aspects of the economy and society, we have detailed statistics stretching back over a long period of time. The counting of population (a *census*) is just about the oldest statistical exercise undertaken by the human race.

The structure of population

In Fig. 1.4 we trace the growth of the UK population from 1901 to 1991 and show its age structure. You can see that in any particular year the age structure is different from all other years.

It is possible to predict changes in population. There are, of course, unexpected changes but given

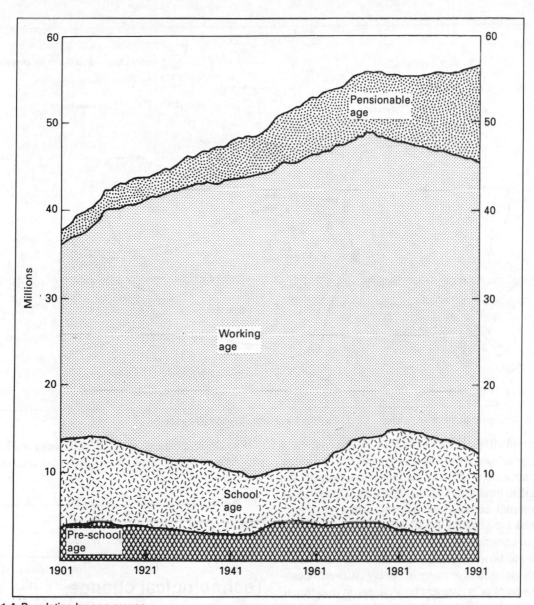

Fig. 1.4 Population by age groups

that there are no great catastrophes we know how the numbers already born will affect the future structure of population. For example, we can predict with accuracy the number of 20 year-olds there will be in 10 years time.

In 1987 there were 13.2 million 15–29 year olds but by 2001 this will have declined to 10.8 million. This will have important effects upon the demand for such things as schools and colleges. It also represents a decline in purchasing power of this age group. This decline in very young people entering the working

population may be regarded as a demographic time-bomb. Businesses are likely to be desperately short of young recruits in the next decade. If, however, you are just starting your career it may be regarded as a factor which will drastically improve your bargaining power.

Where people live

Technology, population and industry interact to produce and to change the shape of towns and villages. Until the 18th century, most people lived in small

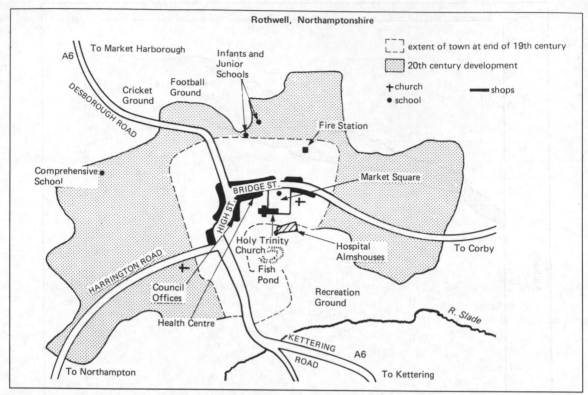

Fig. 1.5 Changing patterns of settlement (From a map by Charles Wynne Hammond)

towns and villages close to their work. The coming of railways allowed people to travel and so communities grew up around railway stations. However, people still had to be able to walk to the station. The arrival of the internal combustion engine filled in the gaps between the separate communities and gave rise to modern conurbations.

We are now beset with different changes, for example, the centres of many of our big cities are decaying. Patterns of settlement now change in response to new stimuli; affluence and mobility have allowed people to choose to live in pleasant surroundings, motorways and airports transform the accessibility of locations.

We have illustrated this with the example of a relatively small community. Fig. 1.5 is a map of Rothwell in Northamptonshire. This is a settlement which has changed from hamlet to village to town and its functions have changed from agricultural centre to market town and then to industry. It is now largely a commuter or dormitory town with its inhabitants travelling to Northampton, Kettering and Corby for work.

If you look at the area in which you live or work can you recognise and explain the different phases of development?

Key word _____

Demography
The study of population characteristics.

_____

Technological change

What is technology?

The usual definition of technology is that it is the *science of industrial arts*. In other words, it is the knowledge that allows us to combine resources to produce the goods and services we want. Consider a simple example. If the job we wish to do is digging a hole, we could use muscle power and a spade or a mechanical digger. Obviously, the mechanical digger represents more advanced technology. You can also understand from this example that the more advanced technology might not necessarily be the best. If, for example, you simply wanted to plant a tree in your garden, a mechanical digger would be somewhat out of place. The best technology is that which is the *most appropriate to our needs*.

Technological revolutions

For most of the human race's history it has used its own muscles and those of animals as power, supplemented from time to time by wind and water power. The changes that constitute what is normally called the *Industrial Revolution* are characterised by the application of steam power to industry. The changes were, of course, much wider than this. They affected agriculture, metallurgy, transport and commerce as well. This underlines the fact that technology is a matter of knowledge as well as of machines.

The changes in industry in the first half of the twentieth century are often referred to as the *Scientific Revolution*. This is because advances in, for example, chemicals, electricity and aeronautics were based upon the application of theoretical sciences such as physics and chemistry to industry. This is in contrast to the earlier advances. These were often made by people with little scientific knowledge. James Brindley, for example, one of the pioneers of the Industrial Revolution, could neither read nor write. Sad to say, some of the major scientific and technological advances of this century were made under the impetus of world wars. Nuclear power and space travel are developments that stem from the 1939–45 War.

The latest changes in our technology are in electronics. The invention of the *silicon chip* and *microprocessors*, and their application not only to industry but also to all aspects of life, can truly be said to be the next revolution. What has been revolutionised is our ability to handle and process information. We may therefore term it the Information Technology (IT) Revolution.

The IT revolution

It is probably true to say that the thing that most sets humans apart from the rest of the animal kingdom is our ability to communicate with each other in a sophisticated way. Language is the greatest creation of humankind. Through language we are able to communicate experiences. Thus, the whole of human knowledge becomes available to individuals. We do not have to experience things directly ourselves to know that they are so. What is more, the body of knowledge developed by one generation can be passed on to the next.

When this depended on the spoken word, it was an imperfect process and the written word and books were extremely rare until the printing process was invented. Indeed, we might see the introduction of movable type in the 15th century by Gutenberg and Caxton as the beginning of the first information technology revolution. However, it was not until the 19th century that the majority of people could read and write. We may pose the question: 'How long will it be before everyone can utilise the present information technology?'

The new technology, however, is more than just a means of communication. We can summarise its chief characteristics as:

(a) Communication. Television, satellite links, electronic mail and word processing are just a few of the examples of the improvements.

(b) Information processing. This ranges from the simple storage and retrieval of data to the complex calculations of astronomy that are literally beyond human capabilities.

(c) Computer aided manufacture (CAM). Microprocessors now help us to control everything from washing machines to industrial robots.

(d) Computer aided design (CAD). Computers now help in the design process. For example, when designing aircraft, computer models can test and evaluate designs infinitely more quickly than the old method of building models and prototypes and then testing them in wind tunnels and on test flights.

(e) Computer integrated management (CIM). We can now use computers in management, not only for such things as stock control but also for more complex tasks such as critical path analysis. (In Chapter 2 we discuss some of the applications of computers in management.)

The impact of technological change

The impact of technological change is all persuasive. At home, at work and at play we continually find examples. Can you imagine how your life would change without television, credit cards, antibiotics and frozen chips?

Work patterns

Perhaps the most significant effect of technology is that it increases production and wealth yet frees us from the sheer hard physical labour which was the lot of our forebears. It is now possible for us to produce the things we need with fewer resources and less labour. But this causes a problem: the lessened demand for labour is not spread equally across society. For many people, it has resulted in unemployment. It remains to be seen whether we shall ever return to the days of full employment which we had in the 50s and 60s or whether millions will continue to be denied work.

Technology has also changed the patterns of work. There is more part-time work and more working from home. Many of the industries associated with the new technology are substantially free from the traditional constraints, such as raw materials and power, that once dictated location. Increased affluence has also created a greater demand for services such as hotels and restaurants, and we now find more people working in these industries.

De-skilling

The new technology has brought a phenomenon called *de-skilling*. By this we mean that machines have taken over human skills. This is particularly true of intermediate skills, thereby increasing the gap between the highly skilled and the relatively low skilled. Banking is a good example. At one time there was a hierarchy of skills: from junior clerical at the bottom, through intermediate skills such as book-keeping, to the higher order management skills. The middle order skills are rapidly being replaced by computers, creating a skill gap between those feeding data into machines and those using and managing it. Similarly in engineering, many skilled crafts have been eliminated. The new technology has, however, brought with it a demand for a new generation of technicians to maintain and service the hardware. It is perhaps a bizarre thought that when a bank has problems with its accounting system it may send for an electronics specialist!

New wants

As well as meeting our economic needs, the new technology has created new wants. Video recorders and home computers are obvious examples; these were unheard of a relatively few years ago. The new technology is also used as a powerful advertising and marketing ploy. Thus, for example, people are led to demand features which they hardly understand, often do not need and cannot evaluate. You can easily double your expenditure on a stereo amplifier to reduce the cross-talk from 60dB to 70dB. Very impressive, but do you know what it means? Could your ears detect the difference? Needless to say many of the 'impressive' features of new technology in consumer goods are never used after the first unsuccessful attempt to do so!

State what is meant by de-skilling. Give three examples of de-skilling other than those given in this chapter.

Technological change in modes of production

The history of technological development has also, largely, been the history of mass production. We have learnt to reduce costs and increase output through *standardisation*. One of the most important developments was the moving production line. With this the workers stay put and the work comes to them. This brought with it the disadvantage of the boredom of repetitive tasks. Recent technological developments have modified this. For example, on a modern robotic production line constant change in models can be programmed into production. As well as this, people are freed from many of the tedious tasks.

Another change is the possibility of working from home. Many secretarial jobs may be performed from home with the aid of word processors, modems and facsimile copiers. One point worth making is that many people still prefer to go to work. This emphasises the important *social function* that working performs for many people.

THE CHANGING ENVIRONMENT 21

The prospect for change

We have looked at both the positive and negative aspects of technological change. We continually face difficult days ahead, especially when we consider the challenges presented by our competitors overseas. It is perhaps appropriate to conclude this part of the chapter with an extract from one of John Maynard Keynes's *Essays on Persuasion*. Although written over 50 years ago it seems just as relevant today as then.

We are suffering just now from a bad attack of economic pessimism. It is common to hear people say that the epoch of enormous economic progress that characterised the nineteenth century is over; that the rapid improvement in the standard of life is now going to slow down – at any rate in Great Britain; that a decline in prosperity is more likely than an improvement in the decade which lies ahead of us.

I believe that this is a wildly mistaken interpretation of what is happening to us. We are suffering, not from the rheumatics of old age, but from the growing pains of over-rapid changes, from the painfulness of re-adjustment between one economic period and another.

Key words

Industrial Revolution
The term used to describe the changes which began in the mid-eighteenth century in the UK involving the application of power to industry and the resultant urbanisation of the population.

Scientific Revolution
Industry in the first half of the twentieth century was transformed by the application of scientific theory to production, e.g. in chemicals, aeronautics etc.

IT Revolution
The changes brought about by information processing by computer and the application of this facility to a wide variety of functions in the late twentieth century.

De-skilling
The replacement of manual and intellectual skills by the application of IT to industry and commerce.

Conclusion

Change is a major theme of this subject and we have, quite rightly, devoted the first chapter of the book to it. Our intention has been to show that every aspect of the environment is constantly changing. 'In this world,' said Benjamin Franklin, 'nothing is certain but death and taxes.'

It is in fact through change that we understand the economy and society. For example, when we study population we do this by looking at how its size and composition have changed and evolved. Similarly, with politics it is with change that we are chiefly concerned. It is necessary for everyone to be able to change and adapt. This is also true for organisations. Their structures, products and services must constantly evolve.

There are some senses, however, in which change is new. In order to understand this compare the great technological achievements of the 19th century with those of our own era. For example, when Isambard Kingdom Brunel built the Great Western Railway he designed every single part of it from the track to the locomotives to the stations. Compare this with space flight. There is no one person who is able to design and build the machines involved. It requires dozens of different types of expertise. The computer specialists cannot design the fuel system and the engineers are unable to comprehend the navigation and so on. We therefore live in a world where we can no longer fully understand our own products and environment. The prospect of fifth generation computers, computers that will be capable of 'thinking' seems likely to widen the comprehension gap.

Yet the problem goes deeper than this. How much do *you* know about quantum physics? In this modern scientific world most people still think in terms of Newtonian physics, i.e. in terms of a theory which was put forward in the late 17th century by Sir Isaac Newton. His views were overturned in the early years of this century. But do you understand the theory of relativity? One of the problems is that much of modern science can only be understood in terms of mathematics. Many of the fundamental ideas of modern physics seem to undermine common sense. This problem can also affect the social sciences. Much macroeconomics, for example, is *counter-intuitive*, that is to say, it seems to run counter to common sense. For instance, when politicians liken the national budget to a housewife's purse they do so in the knowledge that no economist believes this to be true but that the principles involved are often too complex to put across simply.

These problems should not daunt us but encourage us to greater efforts. We study the world of organisations in the belief that through understanding we will be able to increase the wealth and welfare of society and with the conviction that knowledge is better than opinion, analysis better than supposition.

Learning project

Changing employment patterns

Study the table below. This shows the changes in the male:female workforce 1976–87.

(000s)	1976	1977	1978	1979	1980	1981	1982	1983	1984	1985	1986	1987
Workforce	26,110	26,224	26,358	26,627	26,839	26,741	26,677	26,610	27,265	27,797	27,985	28,206
Males	16,270	16,224	16,221	16,224	16,320	16,348	16,257	16,104	16,315	16,548	16,531	16,535
Females	9,840	10,000	10,137	10,404	10,520	10,393	10,421	10,506	10,950	11,249	11,454	11,671

(The workforce is those working plus those claiming unemployment benefit.)
Source: Annual Abstract of Statistics 1989: HMSO

1 Present these figures in a pictorial or graphical manner and describe the main changes observed.

2 What does this information suggest about the changing role of women in society?

3 Account for the changes shown by these statistics.

Further ideas for learning projects

1 The original idea of the Welfare State was that it should provide a safety net without limit and unrelated to ability to pay. How have these aims been modified in the last 20 years and what further proposals for change are there?

2 Prepare a diagram to illustrate the activities of a major multinational company.

3 The organisation for which you work or the college in which you study will almost certainly have undergone major change in both its structure and activities in recent decades. Investigate change within the organisation, perhaps by interviewing one or more of the longer serving employees within the organisation and prepare an informal report:

(a) identifying the main changes that have taken place, and
(b) accounting for those changes.

Your report might include such things as: changes of location, changes in the number of employees, changes in the technology used and changes in markets, and so on.

4 Contrast the policies of the Conservative and Labour Parties on employment law. Identify specific changes which *you* consider should be made to the present framework. Justify these changes.

5 Settlement patterns and areas of industrial and commercial activity in your area will probably have changed substantially in the last 250 years. Working as a group or groups, prepare a presentation/display of these changes giving reasons for them and the social and economic effects on the area.

6 In groups consider each of the following kinds of change: political, social, demographic and technological. Individually prepare a report on what you think will be the most likely developments by the year 2001.

2

Organisations: an introduction

CHAPTER OBJECTIVES

After studying this chapter you should be able to:

- [ ] Define formal and informal organisations;
- [ ] List the characteristics of organisations;
- [ ] State the objectives of different organisations;
- [ ] Define public and private sector organisations;
- [ ] State and explain the main functions in a business organisation;
- [ ] Appreciate different ways of depicting organisations;
- ■ Explain the importance of technology and communication to organisations;
- [ ] Describe the relationship between individuals and organisations;
- ■ Identify causes and symptoms of conflict in an organisation.

Most organisations are surprisingly new. Consider the college at which you are studying. It is doubtful whether it was in existence more than 30 years ago. Consider the local authority which controls it – it is doubtful whether it existed in its present form before 1965. Go back beyond the Second World War (1939–45) and you will find only traces of the now vast apparatus of the Welfare State. Even the most well-established business organisation will seldom have a history of more than a century.

Thus, although we shall trace the origins of organisations we should realise that the 'organisational' society is essentially a 20th century phenomenon. We will also see that it is a constantly changing one. For example, local government was reorganised in 1974 and again in 1986 many industries which were in public ownership in the 1970s became privately owned in the 1980s.

Just like steam engines and computers, organisational forms had to be invented. In the first part of this chapter we will consider how this came about.

The emergence of the modern organisation

Feudal organisation and its legacy

Society has always been organised but for most of history the organisation has been that of tradition and command. This is well illustrated by the feudal system, the form of society which existed throughout Europe in the Middle Ages. Then, for example, the lord of the manor ruled the village and the peasants and serfs worked for him. The feudal system provided a highly organised society but one which was almost devoid of organisations. The most sophisticated organisation of feudal times was the Church. Much of the tradition and custom on which feudal society functioned became embodied in the emergent *common law*. While most other aspects of this society have vanished, it is interesting that some modern legal rights and duties and principles can be traced directly to this era and show comparatively little modification from their original form. When we come to consider the law of property and how it affects organisations we should remember that some of its most fundamental principles are derived from a society which was totally different from the one in which we now live.

The beginnings of a market economy

In feudal society the local community was virtually self-sufficient. It traded only for those things which it could not produce itself. In a process which lasted several hundred years, society evolved from a locally self-sufficient one to a large complex society based upon exchange. Thus, labour became something divorced from social position and was made into a commodity offered for sale. *Land* used to be important because it bestowed power and status – what came to be important was its value. *Capital* had been a static concept of wealth but what became important was its *yield*. Thus, everything was a commodity to be bought and sold. This meant that society began to evolve into a market economy. While we might dispute that we are still in a market economy today, it was undoubtedly the mechanisms of the market which gave rise to many of our organisations.

Different aspects of organisations

When we examine the behaviour and structure of organisations it has been traditional to do this in separate disciplines such as economics, law, management and so on. Indeed, many of the ideas in these separate disciplines are sufficiently complex to demand separate examination when we first consider them. Increasingly, however, we realise that we cannot *evaluate* the organisation's activities in terms of just one subject discipline. Such questions as the siting of a new factory, the raising of the state retirement pension, the compulsory wearing of crash helmets and the siting of a new motorway will have political, social, environmental and even religious aspects. While we may concentrate on the economic or legal aspects, the study of organisations in their entirety presents us with a fuller and more complete picture than any of the individual disciplines.

(Through your assignment work you will develop this inter-disciplinary understanding aided by this book.)

Classification of organisations

Faced with the multiplicity of organisations, it is useful to classify them. There are several ways in which this can be done and one organisation might fit into several classifications.

Formal and informal

Formal organisations may be defined as those which have been established for the express purpose of achieving certain goals, aims or *objectives*. They possess clearly defined *rules* and *structures* and well developed *channels of communication* to help them achieve their goals. This type of organisation includes all businesses, governments, and international institutions. *Informal* (or social) organisations, on the other hand, are those in which social activities are carried on, usually without clearly defined goals, rules or structures. Examples of such organisations include families, friendships and communities.

Formal organisations form the subject of this book. You can see that the distinguishing feature of formal organisations is that they have *stated objectives*, *rules* and *structures*, i.e. characteristics, which are common to all such organisations.

Productive and non-productive organisations

In the UK there are many different forms of formal organisation and they could be classified in several ways. One of the simplest is to divide them into *productive* and *non-productive* organisations.

Productive organisations are all those which are in any way concerned with the production of goods and services. These can be *privately* owned, as is the case with the chemical industry, or *publicly* owned, as is the case with railways. Do not make the mistake of thinking that only those industries which produce physical products such as cars or chemicals are productive; indeed banking, which is a service industry, is one of the UK's biggest export earners.

All the industries mentioned so far *sell* goods and services to the community. However, publicly owned services such as health and education can also be considered as productive organisations, although they do not trade with the public in the usual meaning of the word. We might therefore also divide organisations into *trading* and *non-trading* categories.

Many organisations do not produce any goods and services and may be termed *non-productive*. However, they should not be considered unimportant. The legal institutions (courts of law, etc) of the nation, the trade unions and churches are all examples of non-productive organisations which play an important role directly or indirectly in our lives.

Types of industry

All productive organisations, whether publicly or privately owned, form part of industry. It is often thought that industry just comprises those organisations which manufacture goods or produce raw materials but banking, insurance and retailing are also parts of industry. In government statistics the Standard Industrial Classification (SIC) lists 111 groups of industries. However, industries can be broadly categorised under three headings.

(a) Primary. These are industries concerned with the *extraction of raw materials*, and include agriculture, forestry, fishing and mining.
(b) Secondary. These are industries which are in any way concerned with the *processing* and *manufacturing* of products. They include such industries as iron and steel, motor vehicles and food processing.
(c) Tertiary. These are industries which do not produce goods but supply and sell *services*. For this reason they are often termed 'service industries'. Included in this category are banking, education, tourism and the distributive trades.

In 1988 primary industries accounted for about 7% of the national product, secondary industries about 24% and tertiary industries the rest.

The public sector and the private sector

The organisations which make up the economy may also be divided between the *public sector* and the *private sector*. *Public-sector* organisations are all those which are *owned* and *directed* either directly by the government (central or local) or indirectly through government-created bodies. Examples of public-sector organisations are the Departments of State and the armed forces. In 1988 total expenditure by the public sector accounted for 45.9% of the *gross domestic product*.

The *private sector* of the economy includes all those organisations which are owned and operated by private citizens. This may range in size from very large organisations such as ICI to small local businesses. Organisations in the private sector take a variety of legal forms such as partnerships, companies and co-operatives.

Make a list of those goods or services which you consider are better supplied by public sector organisations rather than by businesses.

Are there any products or services which it is impossible for private business organisations to supply? If so what are they and why is this so?

Problems of definition

Having studied these classifications of organisations, it is apparent that there are no rigid divisions – government owned industries such as railways may nevertheless be run on commercial principles, British Telecom is still 49% owned by the government and so on. To cope with this problem we intend to use the term *trading organisations* to describe all the organisations which exist principally by *selling* goods and services, be they in the private or public sector. In the next chapter we will discuss the various legal forms which trading organisations take. This will include private-sector trading organisations, such as companies, which are normally termed *business organisations* and public-sector trading organisations such as any remaining nationalised industries.

Make a list of the names of 25 organisations in your local area. Make these as different as you can to reflect the diversity of organisations which make

up the economy and society.

For each of the organisations you have named, state whether it is:

(a) productive or non-productive;
(b) in the public or private sector;
(c) in the primary, secondary or tertiary sector of industry.

Characteristics of organisations

We have already mentioned objectives, rules and structures as characteristics which all formal organisations have in common. Eight such characteristics (including objectives, rules and structures) are considered below.

1 Names. All organisations have a name by which they are known. Mr Jones, the local grocer, may trade under his own name but in many cases we shall see that the name and legal personality of an organisation may be quite separate from the people who own it.

2 Objectives. We have already seen that all organisations have objectives – in the case of businesses it is the pursuit of profit. Do not confuse the objective with the method of achieving it. For example, the objective of Ford UK is to make a profit, its method of doing so is to produce and sell cars.

3 Rules. All organisations are governed by rules and regulations. These can be written, verbal or assumed to be known. Generally speaking the larger the size of the organisation the more formal will be the expression of the rules. An organisation may both develop its own rules and have rules imposed on it from outside, e.g. by the government. It is laid down by law, for instance, that all companies must hold an annual general meeting.

4 Structures. Most organisations are basically hierarchical in structure. At the top of the hierarchy is the chief executive, at the bottom the clerks and operatives. Between the two there will be a number of different levels of authority, chains of command, lines of responsibility and channels of communication. As we will see later in this chapter, there are different ways in which we can depict an organisation's structure.

5 Positions. Within an organisation everyone has a role (or position) to fulfil. In a small organisation one person may fill several positions. In a large organisation roles tend to become more specialised, e.g. we would expect to find positions such as marketing manager in a large business.

6 Chain of authority. All organisations have a chain of authority. This enables decisions to be made and jobs and functions to be carried out. The sophistication of a chain of authority will tend to increase with the size of an organisation. If the complexity is too great, however, this may damage the organisation's efficiency and performance.

7 Power. The power in an organisation is usually said to rest with those who have the legal right to take decisions. In the case of a business organisation this is usually the owners, e.g. the shareholders of a company. On the other hand, public corporations such as British Coal are ultimately controlled by Parliament. The power to take decisions is often *delegated* via the chain of authority. For example, the shareholders will appoint a board of directors, they in turn will appoint managers and so on.

8 Records. All organisations have some method of recording their activities. These may range from the minutes of the local Women's Institute to *Hansard* (the publication which records every word spoken in Parliament). There are usually legal requirements to maintain certain forms of record, e.g. for tax-collection purposes.

List ten organisations other than your college and employer that you belong to or are associated with. Consider each of the characteristics listed above for each of the organisations you have listed.

The objectives of organisations

We have said that one of the characteristics of all formal organisations is that they exist to pursue objectives or goals. The objectives which organisations pursue give us another way in which we might classify them. First there are those which exist primarily to make a *profit*, second there are those which exist to direct or administer sectors of the community so as to attempt to *maximise national welfare*, and third there are those which exist to *promote the interests of their members*. The list of organisations given below contains most of the types of organisations which we shall be concerned with in this book. As you work through the list, you should be aware that the distinction between them lies in their chief objectives. For example *business organisations* are of very different shapes and sizes but all have the same chief objective.

Organisations classified by their objectives

1 Business organisations. These are organisations with a variety of legal forms, e.g. sole traders, partnerships and companies, whose object is to make profit. We might distinguish between *industrial* organisations such as manufacturers, *commercial* organisations such as retailers, and *financial* organisations such as banks and insurance companies.

2 Governmental organisations. These are concerned with the running of the country, either at a national or local level. They are controlled by elected representatives.

3 Public corporations. State-owned industries such as coal and railways are run by public corporations. Like business organisations, they may exist by selling goods and services to the community. However they do not exist primarily to make a profit but rather to run the industry in the national interest.

4 QUANGOS (quasi-autonomous non-governmental organisations). These are organisations run by nominated boards, such as regional health authorities, the Training Agency and the Civil Aviation Authority. Almost any public body which is not elected could be described as a quango.

5 Economic interest groups. People or organisations with common objectives may band together; for example the Confederation of British Industry (CBI) promotes the interests of employers, while the Consumers' Association promotes the interests of consumers.

6 Trade unions. Although economic interest groups, they are certainly important enough to be considered separately and they have a special status at law.

7 Legal. The administration of justice presents us with a set of complex organisations and institutions

exercising specialised judicial and quasi-judicial functions.

8 Political. The organisation of political parties is quite distinct from that of government in a democracy. This would not be true in communist or fascist states.

9 Charities. These organisations are normally considered to exist to dispense goods and services to the needy. By and large this is true but the legal form and status of a charity may be adopted to help the not-so-needy – most public schools, for example, are (legally) charities.

10 Mutual help. Some trading organisations, such as co-operatives, are set up with the objective of helping their members rather than making a profit. Building societies, for example, are mutuals.

11 International organisations. Internationally constituted bodies such as the IMF, the EC or even FIFA are now extremely numerous and varied.

12 Multinational organisations. These are business organisations which operate in many countries, e.g. Unilever, BP or ICI.

You can see that all the objectives of these organisations would fit into the three broad categories stated at the beginning of this section. Other types of organisation, such as religious or sporting, might be added to the list but they lie outside the scope of this book.

For each of the different types of organisation listed above, identify at least three examples other than those we may have given you. You should name the organisations rather than give their type. Make your examples as diverse and contrasting as possible. Work in groups or individually.

Objectives of private-sector organisations

It is often assumed that all organisations in the private sector are out to make a profit. A moment's reflection will show us that this is not so; obviously Oxfam is not out to make a profit as its main objective, nor is a trade union, although they will both have a great interest in remaining solvent and even operating profitably. If you examine the private-sector non-business organisations in the list above you will realise that most of them are concerned with mutual help or the advancement of the interests of their members.

A great deal of *The Organisation in its Environment* is concerned with the behaviour of business organisations and we will now briefly consider their objectives and their strategies for achieving them. A detailed consideration of their behaviour forms a greater part of the rest of this book. It should also be understood that individuals within organisations may view these matters differently. Sir Edwin Nixon of IBM has stated that 'One of our goals is to be a technological leader'. This would not find its way into any economic textbook as the objective of a business. It does emphasise, however, how vital technology now is to the survival of many companies.

Profit maximisation in businesses

It is usually assumed that business organisations will always try to maximise their profits. This means that not only will they try to make a profit but they will also try to make as much profit as possible. There are well-established policies to achieve and maintain profit maximisation.

1 Concentration on producing and supplying those goods and services for which demand is increasing.
2 Minimisation of the cost of production by selecting the cheapest possible combination of premises, machinery and labour to use. Thus, if substituting machines for labour is cheaper this will be done despite the social consequences associated with the redundancies which may follow.
3 Maintaining output at the level at which profits are maximised.
4 Where a single organisation is dominant in its own area of activity it can affect the price of the goods it produces by varying the amount it supplies to the market. It is therefore able to adjust either price or output to suit its own profit maximisation objective.
5 Research and development of new products and processes is a vital activity if a business is to survive in a changing environment.

These strategies are considered in much more detail in Parts 3 and 4 of this book.

It is often thought that this pursuit of profit is a unifying characteristic of all business organisations. However, it is possible in large organisations, where

there is a divorce of ownership from management, that there are alternative objectives. There is such a divorce when the directors (managers) of a company have little or no stake in the shareholding (ownership) of a company. Thus, the managers may be able to pursue policies more in line with their own self-interests so long as they are able to make enough profit to keep the shareholders happy. Such objectives are now considered.

Other business objectives

1 Brand leadership/market domination. This may be pursued for the purposes of profit maximisation but this need not be so. Domination of a market may also give stability and security to the organisation. This might be viewed by the managers as more attractive than profit maximisation. Pursuit of this objective may lead a business to pursue a policy of sales maximisation. For example, a business might cut prices and accept losses for a time with the object of driving its rivals out of business. Having achieved this it could then exploit the market.
2 Corporate growth. Growth means increasing power and responsibility for managers, often reflected in higher salaries. Hence, this objective is attractive. However, growth may be achieved at the expense of profit maximisation and therefore may not be in the interests of the owners of the organisation. For example, new and less profitable goods may be produced.

Growth can be achieved by:

(a) expanding existing markets, e.g. through new products and advertising;
(b) diversifying, i.e. extending the product range or activity of the organisation into new areas;
(c) takeover (purchasing control) of other business organisations for either of the two previous purposes.

3 Satisficing. The Nobel prize-winner H A Simon put forward the view that business people may want to 'satisfice', i.e. achieve certain targets for sales, profits and market share which may not coincide with profit maximisation but may rather inflate boardroom egos. Providing that *sufficient* profit is made, managers may seek to expand, for example, their right to exercise personal discretion and obtain perks such as company cars. To achieve this objective, part of the organisation's profit, which could be paid out to shareholders, must be diverted and used to pay for such managerial satisfaction. Since managerial satisfaction pushes up the costs of production and hence the price charged, it is usually associated with organisations which do not operate in highly competitive industries.

We emphasise that these latter three objectives are of a controversial nature and are not accepted by all observers of organisations. It is argued by some that they can all be incorporated into the single objective of profit maximisation, while others go so far as to say that, although attractive, the ideas have little or no evidence to support them.

We could now proceed by accepting that, though there are complications and variations such as we have discussed above, most businesses exist *to make a profit*. This objective certainly characterises most business organisations but some have other central aims which we must briefly consider.

Non-profit maximising objectives

1 Survival. 'Making a profit' implies surplus. Some businesses work at break-even point or below, the overriding aim being still to be in business next year.
2 Loss-making. Not so surprising as it might first sound. A company may be a member of a group which needs a profit-loser to set-off against other companies in the group which are making profits heavily penalised by the Inland Revenue. Ideally, in terms of its output, the profit-loser should be an integral part of the group. For example, although it runs at a loss, it may cost the group even more to buy in its product or service from outside.
3 Making a strictly defined amount of profit. Similarly, some groups of companies limit to the penny how much profit a member company should make so as to maximise group profit.
4 Service. There are organisations structured commercially which do not aim to make a surplus. Their principal objective is their output. Examples are religious companies selling biblical texts, or charitable companies such as Oxfam.
5 Employment. Certain organisations exist almost for the sake of being somewhere for people to spend their time. Socialist co-operatives providing employment for young people are good examples.

Objectives of public-sector organisations

There are a vast range of public sector organisations with an almost equally vast range of objectives. However, we might examine the objectives in terms of what is wanted by:

(a) the *Government*;
(b) those *who operate and work* in public sector organisations; and
(c) the *public*.

When we consider the relationship between the government and the managers of public sector organisations, we may find the conflict we identified above between the managers and the owners of business organisations. That is to say, the government may have one set of objectives, e.g. holding down costs, while the managers may be interested in expanding their jobs and power. Thus, we might also discover 'satisficing' in public sector organisations.

The government will usually state its objectives for public sector organisations in terms of the maximisation of public welfare. It might be thought that governments and the electorate would be as one on this. This is, however, usually not so. A government may see it as its job to restrain public spending while sections of the public may wish to increase it, or vice versa. Governments also have political objectives which affect these organisations, not least among which will be its desire to be re-elected. It is not unknown for a government to prefer its own survival to be maximisation of public welfare!

When we examine business organisations it is usually apparent that employers and employees alike have an interest in the well-being of the business. Thus, there is at least some mutuality of purpose. However, for public-sector organisations this is often not so, for example, their managers may be trying to expand them while a government is trying to restrain their growth. It is not surprising, therefore, that when we consider public sector organisations we shall find much uncertainty about their objectives.

In the 1980s it became fashionable to apply business criteria to public services such as education and health care. In other words, such services are increasingly being expected to improve their productivity and generally give better value for money. An example was the Rayner Report on the National Health Service, where a director of a leading supermarket chain was brought in to oversee the introduction of more cost-effective practices. Whatever the benefits of this, for example, streamlined administration, many people have expressed doubts whether the dispensing of drugs etc, can be treated in the same way as retailing biscuits.

State which five objectives of a business you consider to be the most important. Consider the extent to which they conflict with one another.

Objectives: some practical problems

Clearly, some organisations are more successful than others. A successful organisation can be said to be one that knows what it is trying to achieve and succeeds in doing so efficiently. It follows that if an organisation's objectives and policies are unclear, its management ineffective and its structure cumbersome and inefficient, it is not likely to be successful. We will look at decision-making in Chapter 6 and organisational structure below. Here it is appropriate to consider some typical problems associated with an organisation's objectives, those of business organisations in particular.

Bias

You can begin to find out about a company's objectives from its memorandum and articles of association. These are legal statements of what the company was originally set up to do and include the names of its executives, their functions and how the company is to be run. For our present purpose, however, they are not particularly useful. They are frequently out of date, usually too complex to understand, or establish objectives so wide that the company is permitted to do practically anything!

You may also find objectives in the *directors' reports* and *accounts*. But who wrote them, the directors or the executives directed by them? Their bias *may* be the correct one, but it is only one viewpoint. Employees are part of the organisation, and if their senior convener or shop stewards can be said to speak

for them, what would that person say were the organisation's objectives? No redundancies would surely figure prominently here. We can go on. Would the public relations person agree with either the directors or the senior convener? And who would the chief accountant, the personnel director or the shareholders' spokesperson agree with? An organisation is a complex association of individuals and departments and it would be unrealistic to assume that every individual and each department pursued one common objective. Individuals and departments will have their own objectives within departmental and corporate plans.

By engaging in this sort of research you might be able to identify a collection of objectives but this would be a complex one. Things would not be improved when you tried to make a brief statement of them, as we shall go on to see.

Complexity

If you think that your organisation's objective is to make a profit (the conventional objective of all business organisations), why does it not sell its premises now? The sale would make an enormous profit! You may qualify your statement; a *continuing* profit. OK, do you mean large or small? If you answer a *large* continuing profit, why does it not find something more profitable to do? (An interesting point in relation to the many public service organisations that are now expected to operate 'profitably'.) If you say a large continuing profit in their *field of expertise* (trading), why not deal in heroin? If you say a large continuing, *ethical* profit in their field of expertise, why not crush down the wages and remove the carpet from the executives' floor? If you say .... but the basic point about complexity is now made.

In a large complex organisation, there should be a hierarchy of objectives reflecting its hierarchical structure (see below). The general objectives of the organisation will be restated as objectives for each division or function, for departments within each division or function, for sections within a department down, perhaps, to individuals within each section. In theory, everyone knows exactly what he or she is meant to do and how his or her work relates to the other constituent parts of the organisation. In practice, however, the total model may be too complex to be readily understood and may be ignored for this reason.

Conflict

Very soon after starting to explore an organisation's objectives, you will discover that the objectives of one department, one set of people, or one individual will conflict with another. Some examples will illustrate this. The twin objectives of the sales department will probably be high sales and customer satisfaction, which they are likely to pursue through a policy of providing a wide range of products on time and modified to customer specifications. The production department, probably pursuing the objective of lower unit costs, will want a policy involving economies of scale through standardisation of products, a limited product range and longer production runs. This will clearly conflict with the sales department. The accounts department pursuing the objective of keeping within budgets will follow a policy of careful cost control and be in conflict with everybody!

These conflicts are usually resolved by directives to or from management or not resolved at all – the company may like its people to compete for its own resources because this means they work harder and more effectively. Sometimes they may simply not be recognised as conflicts by those involved.

Lack of clarity

Since few organisations pay strict attention to their statements of objectives in practice, lack of clarity may not be perceived as a problem. Most staff go to work and do as they are told or use their initiative within closely defined boundaries. They usually know what and how much work they are supposed to do but not always what objectives this work goes towards achieving. Some say that this leads to an inefficient organisation. Others argue that it would make little difference to the average employee's work performance if he or she was aware of its objectives.

Some organisations do have corporate plans. These are really an expansion of the process we discussed above under 'complexity' and may suffer accordingly. They detail what the organisation is aiming at over the next, say, five or ten years. From those details a hierarchy of objectives, for example, *targets* and *budgets* can be drawn up. Where they are, departmental managers may receive documents setting them out for their department. Good managers will pass these on so that their staff will know, not just what their job is, but also what they are supposed to be aiming at. In well-run organisations reward systems are established so that reaching targets is worthwhile.

Communication

Although conventional management theory says that people respond well to clear and realistic targets, especially if there is some form of congratulation or reward for reaching them, objectives are frequently not passed far enough down the organisation. They are not effectively communicated. The result is that even though individual employees, be they managers or operatives, know what they are doing they may not be able to relate this to the organisation as a whole. It is perhaps no coincidence that the really successful organisations build a communication system into their structure that ensures that information reaches everyone who should receive it.

Some organisations, however, make a point of communicating their objectives to the general public as well as to their employees. They may do so as a way of promoting their philosophy or simply as a marketing exercise. Reproduced in Fig. 2.1 is a statement of social goals published by Co-operative Retail Services Ltd. It is interesting in that it covers a very wide range of objectives and profitability is an implied rather than an express objective. Needless to say, these objectives, or at least the total commitment to them, are not typical of business organisations generally.

Policies

Objectives and policies

Objectives must be determined before policies can be formulated. Objectives are statements of *what* an organisation is aiming to achieve, policies are statements of *how* this is to be done. Both are determined by senior management and it is the responsibility of executives and their staff to fulfil them. The two terms are often taken to mean the same thing but they are quite distinct, some examples will illustrate this.

If we take your present course of study, the college's prime objective is to enable you to achieve the

Social Goals

The Consumer Co-operative Movement has always been a business with a wider purpose than distributing goods and providing services. Throughout its existence it has sought through the application of co-operative principles to improve the lives of the ordinary men and women who gave birth to, and now own the Movement. It has served the needs of communities for over a century and has constantly striven to achieve its ultimate social purpose – The Co-operative Commonwealth.

In 1985 Britain's biggest Co-op, Co-operative Retail Services, decided on a purpose that will make co-operation as relevant to the twenty-first century as it has been in the nineteenth and twentieth.

To the consumer:

offer high quality goods and services to customers at the lowest possible prices by the efficient management of the Society's human, financial and material resources;

provide consumers with the information necessary for them to choose the best products for their individual needs, and to encourage consumer awareness.

To the members:

by the efficient management of the Society's resources to provide a fair return, with maximum security, on members' investment;

encourage the involvement of members in the democratic control of the Society on the basis of one member, one vote;

provide members and employees with the information necessary to enable them to participate fully in the affairs of the Society;

provide an economic benefit for members trading with the Society;

provide the maximum number of educational, social, cultural, consumer and political activities for members and their families.

To the employees:

encourage employees to play a full role in the democratic structure of CRS and in society generally;

provide broad facilities for training and continued education, thus affording each employee an optimal development of his or her potential;

maintain the best possible working conditions and an exemplary working climate;

pay wages commensurate with the job description and in accordance with performance;

guarantee fair and equal treatment for all employees regardless of sex, race, religion or physical disability;

To Society:

extend the co-operative sector of the economy as a form of social ownership and encourage understanding of co-operative forms of organisation;

give support to voluntary and self-help organisations whose objectives are in sympathy with the ethos of the Society;

meet within the limitations of the resources available, social and community needs which cannot be met sufficiently by other agencies and do not fall within the responsibility of the state;

do everything in its power to protect the environment and ensure efficient use and protection of natural resources;

extend the influence of the Co-operative Movement in public affairs and in society in general;

work towards the maintenance of peace and improvement in international understanding and co-operation.

Fig. 2.1 The 'social goals' of the Consumer Co-operative Movement

criteria for an award, most likely of a BTEC Certificate or Diploma. The policy adopted to achieve this would cover the design of the timetable, the methods of teaching and the programme of assessments. Another example, all high street banks have as one of their objectives the gain of student accounts – the 'poor' unprofitable student of today hopefully becoming the profitable wealthy borrowing customer of tomorrow. The policy to achieve this invariably involves offering inducements: free banking, financial advice, travel vouchers, book tokens and the like. A final example; consider a manufacturing company whose objective is to increase its market share. In order to achieve this it might adopt a policy of price reductions.

Policies are more flexible than objectives. Objectives are the very essence of an organisation; they cannot be changed without changing the organisation itself. Policies, however, can be altered reasonably easily in response to problems and changes in the environment. For example, an organisation's policy on giving credit will be affected by its cash flow situation and its policy on borrowing by interest rates. It is more likely to give credit when it has a healthy cash balance – by giving credit it is in effect making use of the balance to generate sales – and more likely to borrow when interest rates are low – because it is cheaper to do so. This second example illustrates an important point; both objectives and policies, but particularly policies, must be formulated in the *context of the environment*; to be at odds with the environment is a recipe for disaster.

Economic versus social factors

It might be thought that policies are always formulated solely to meet the economic objectives of an organisation. This is not the case. Social responsibilities, e.g. to employees and to the environment, must be taken into account (*see* Chapter 12). Achieving the right balance between financial gain and socially acceptable behaviour is not necessarily easy, different groups expect different and sometimes incompatible things. As you will see later in this chapter, the goals of individuals within an organisation must also be taken into account.

It is generally accepted that the relative importance of financial gain and social responsibility in setting

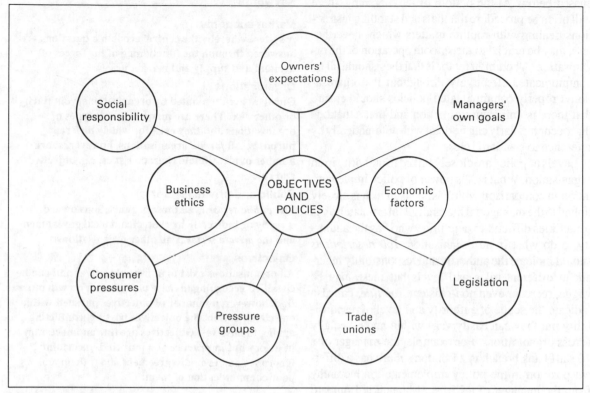

Fig. 2.2 Factors influencing objectives and policies

objectives and formulating policies is to a considerable degree influenced by the size of an organisation. In small business units – typically the owner-manager firm – personal ambition, personal fulfilment and status often provide greater motivation than profit. Social responsibility may be seen as irrelevant or may just not be applicable, for example, there may be no employees. In medium-sized organisations, the profit motive is usually seen as being all important. The personal aspirations that were the original motivation will now largely have been satisfied and overtaken by the desire to make money. Such social responsibility as there is may be enforced rather than voluntary.

In the large organisation, well-established with a firm operating base and a secure market share, social responsibility may be an important factor in its objectives and policies. Consider, for example, the social goals of the Consumer Co-operative Movement reproduced in Fig. 2.1 or the statement in a recent ICI annual report that 'in its dealings with the various groups who make up society, ICI seeks to achieve high standards of behaviour as a socially responsible

company.' You, of course, are free to speculate whether such policies are totally voluntary or whether, over the years, legislation or such matters as employee and consumer protection and health and safety and, recently, growing public awareness of environmental issues have prodded even these organisations in the right direction. Whatever your views on their relative importance, Fig. 2.2 is a summary of the main factors that influence a business organisation's objectives and policies.

Types and levels of policy

As an organisation's objectives can be seen as hierarchical, ranging from the general, e.g. to make a profit, to the specific, e.g. to increase unit sales of item X by 25%, so too can its policies. At the top there will be a number of fundamental, policies which flow from its general objectives, for example, production policies, marketing policies, financial policies and personnel policies. These will broadly coincide with the five traditional functions in a business organisation discussed below. At the bottom of the hierarchy, there will often be procedure manuals and standing instructions dealing with routine matters which, nevertheless, may be crucial to the smooth operation of the organisation. A common factor is that they should all be communicated effectively throughout the organisation. Properly communicated policies should ensure that there is uniformity of action and that situations that occur regularly can be dealt with automatically by reference to standard rules.

Levels of policy are closely linked to authority in an organisation. What is X's power of policy implementation in comparison with Y's? This in turn is closely linked to the managerial hierarchy. Unfortunately, it is sometimes difficult to determine who has the authority to do what in an organisation. *Job descriptions* should indicate the authority and responsibility inherent in different roles and levels but these may be vague, secret or even non-existent. *Job titles* can also indicate the scope of authority and level of responsibility but they can easily vary within and especially across organisations. For example, the manager of a 10 staff bank branch in a London suburb has a different position in the policy implementation hierarchy from the manager of a 250 staff branch in Lombard Street in the City of London. However, in some areas, such as where the branch sales effort will be concentrated and where it will not, the former has more decision-making authority than the branch manager of a major multiple clothes retailer in the West End.

Functions in a business organisation

There are traditionally said to be five major functions in a business organisation.

1 Marketing
2 Production
3 Finance
4 Personnel
5 Administration

Marketing

This function involves:

(a) Finding out what the customer needs;

Keywords

Market economy
A system whereby the central economic questions are answered through the functioning of the forces of demand and supply and market prices.

Organisations
Our lives are dominated by organisations, voluntarily or otherwise. There are many different types of organisations and they exist for widely different purposes. All *formal* organisations, however, share a number of identifiable characteristics, e.g. objectives and rules.

Public and private sector
The *public sector* is all those organisations owned directly or indirectly by central and local government and the *private sector* is all other organisations.

Objectives
All organisations exist to pursue objectives and can be classified according to these objectives. You will often find, however, a number of objectives pursued within one classification, the objectives possibly conflicting among themselves. Objectives are fine and necessary in theory but in practice you may find uncertainty, ignorance and even disagreement about them and poor communication of them.

Policies
Objectives are statements of *what* an organisation aims to achieve, policies are statements of *how* it intends to do this. The policies of a business organisation are influenced by a variety of factors other than achieving economic objectives, e.g. responsibility to the environment.

Profit maximisation
It is assumed that all business organisations seek not only to make a profit but also to make as much profit as possible.

Managerial revolution
The divorce of ownership from control in many large business organisations.

Satisficing
Professional managers may seek to maximise their own welfare (satisfice) rather than maximise profits.

(b) Designing the product or service and specifying its characteristics;
(c) Setting production levels;
(d) Storing the product;
(e) Distributing it to the outlets;
(f) Delivering it to the customer where, when and in

whatever quantity the customer requires;
(g) Monitoring changes in customer demand and tastes *(market research)*;
(h) Informing the customer of the product's existence and qualities *(advertising)*; and
(i) Persuading the retailer or the consumer to choose the product and commit himself to a purchase (selling).

We consider marketing more fully in Chapter 15.

Production

The production function takes raw materials and subjects them to various processes to make or assemble the product. This is done to the designer's plans in amounts specified by marketers and to standards specified by the management. The buying of raw materials at one end of the process and warehousing at the other are often included in the production function.

In manufacturing industry, companies can often be distinguished from one another by their means of production. This ranges from *one-off* production, where the order is for a specially designed, unique product such as a suspension bridge, through *small-batch* production, oil-rigs for example, to *large-batch* production, such as blouses and skirts for a chain-store, and *continuous production* such as chemicals and beer. The method of production will affect the organisation's structure. One-off and small-batch production tend to promote shallow structures, i.e. structures which have simple hierarchies with few levels and flexible rules. The closer the organisation comes to continuous production, the more likely it is to have deep and more rigid structures and rules.

Finance

The four major activities included in this function are: financial accounting; management accounting and management information; budgets and financing the organisation.

Financial accounting

This consists of keeping the books and records; providing the taxation authorities with information; and producing statutory and traditionally required documents such as the annual report, balance sheet, profit and loss account and cash-flow statement.

Management accounting

This is less tradition-bound. It is concerned with the constantly changing picture of movements of money and value around the organisation. Its purpose is to provide figures which are used for planning and decision-making. In other words, it is about *information* and *forecasting*. Most executives (persons who implement the organisation's policy) are included in the circulation of management information documents, among which are often their budgets.

Budgets

Budgets are statements of the resources available over a given future period, say a year. They provide regular, say monthly, information on such things as expenditure and income over- or under-budget. The best way to set budgets is usually with the co-operation of those responsible for meeting them.

Financing

At some time or other, virtually all business organisations will need to borrow or raise finance to continue to trade or to expand. The finance department is concerned with the amounts, the sources (such as loans from banks or share or debenture issues), the methods used and the repayments associated with the raising of such finance.

Personnel

This function is concerned with:

(a) recruiting staff;
(b) deploying them appropriately;
(c) training them to have the skills and knowledge they need to be efficient in their work;
(d) selecting them for advancement and promotion;
(e) wages/salaries and other benefits;
(f) grievances;
(g) discipline; and
(h) the termination of employment – by retirement,

dismissal, redundancy or death.

Many organisations have a *manpower plan*, derived from the corporate plan. This will provide the personnel department with the information and objectives it needs to determine its policies. Alternatively, the personnel executives may instruct the department directly. In turn, the department will provide information to top management and provide support to the line manager (*see* below). The personnel function is covered in more detail in Chapter 8.

Administration

An organisation's administration department *facilitates* the workings of all the other departments. It does this by:

(a) creating and operating systems and rules, procedures and regulations;
(b) implementing decisions and directives;
(c) maintaining channels and lines of communication; and
(d) making changes to take account of alterations to company policy.

While top management will head the function, every executive and many supervisors have some general administrative responsibility. Every employee is subject to its regime. A word often associated with administration is *efficiency*, i.e. the ability of an organisation to pursue its objectives without wasting time, talent or resources.

Line and staff functions

Another way to classify the functions of a business organisation is according to whether they are line functions or staff functions. *Line functions* are those which have direct responsibility for achieving the objectives of the organisation. They are directly concerned with the output of the organisation's product or service. For example, the design office and production and sales managers perform line functions. *Staff functions* primarily provide advice and service to enable line activities to be pursued effectively. For example, a company's computer department, personnel division or equipment maintenance team perform staff functions. Except in their own departments, staff managers would not normally make decisions affecting the organisation's objectives and policies.

While classification into line functions and staff functions will vary from organisation to organisation, of the five functions discussed above, only *production* would be a totally line function.

Depicting organisations

Nearly all organisations are *hierarchical* in structure. This simply means that there are different levels of authority and responsibility within the organisation. Even in co-operatives there are still those who direct operations and those who carry them out. Status and

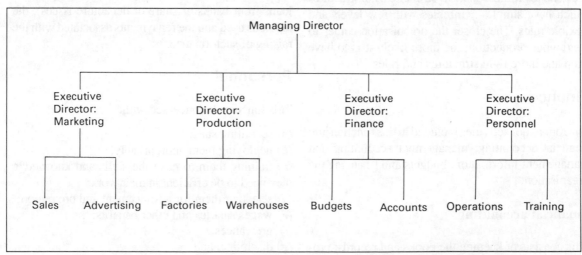

Fig. 2.3 Traditional organisation chart

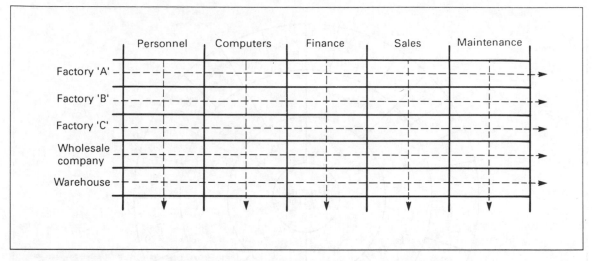

Fig. 2.4 Matrix chart

pay may be the same or similar in such organisations but the hierarchy of functions still exists.

There are various ways of depicting organisations to explain their structure. Some textbooks refer to the result as different types of organisations but you may prefer to think of it as simply different ways of drawing diagrams of the same type of organisation.

Traditional organisation charts

This is perhaps the simplest way of depicting an organisations. Fig. 2.3 is a typical example.

Traditional organisation charts can be extended down to the lowest organisational level. But ask yourself what the lines mean. Do they mean: 'is responsible for', 'has authority over' (downwards) or 'reports to', 'is responsible to' (upwards) and/or 'communicates with' (in either direction). In practice, the lines probably mean all of these. But remember, when drawing or examining traditional organisational charts, never take what the lines mean for granted. The lines connect people and people are individuals, no matter how rigid the rules within which they operate.

Matrix charts

A second way is to consider the organisation as a *matrix*. Staff functions are shown across the top and

line functions down the side; interaction takes place where the functions cross. Look at Fig. 2.4.

Such a diagram does produce a realistic picture of who does what and to whom but, since responsibility is owed to two managers, a cynic might say it perfectly represents one view of the management function: blurring the lines of responsibility!

Concentric circle charts

Some organisations view the traditional organisation chart as too undemocratic and prefer a model which does not appear to make the chief executive so lordly a figure. In these cases, a *concentric circle chart* (see Fig. 2.5) is a good choice. The chief decision-makers are then seen to be *central* rather than *on top*. The managing director appears as the hub and functions move outward in descending order of authority.

The usefulness of charts

In practice, no matter what kind it is, a chart as such makes no difference whatever to the personalities of the people involved and their styles of management. They do, however, tend to make lines of communication clearer, provide a model for reference and a practical starting point for planning organisational changes. In this way they may affect the individuals involved.

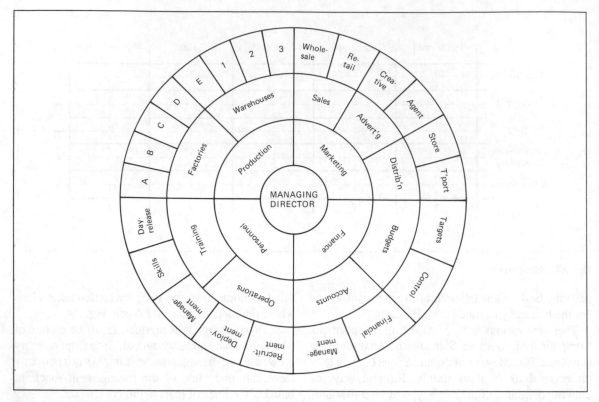

Fig. 2.5 Concentric circle chart

The systems approach

The systems approach is based on the idea that change in any one part of an organisation can affect any other. Furthermore, because this system is said to be *open*, that is, the organisation interacts with its environment, changes in the environment affect the organisation and vice versa. (This was the central theme of Chapter 1.) This interaction applies particularly to its consumer markets. A rise or fall, or an alteration in demand will require the entire organisation to react in order to continue to be able to pursue its objectives, or even to survive. More generally, the systems approach says that it is only by fulfilling the needs of its owners, employees and organisations or individuals with which it deals, e.g. the government, customers, suppliers and creditors, that it will survive and grow.

We have talked above about functions and structure. The systems approach to an organisation combines these two things to some extent, producing a diagram of its structure, how the organisation operates and how it interacts with the environment. Fig 2.6 is a diagram of how it might be used to explain the workings of a typical manufacturing company. To use it as an organisation chart we would have to specify the elements within it in terms of functions and departments. While more sophisticated and complicated in its concept, it does provide a model which better reflects the reality of change, both internally and externally, than the rather static models produced by the other charts.

Technology

At the height of the Industrial Revolution the source of power was steam engines. These were enormous pieces of machinery several storeys high. In order to exploit them fully, large factories had to be built at their sides. Power was then transmitted throughout the factory by a system of pulleys. People at the time believed that the factory itself was as great an invention as the steam engine. They believed that factory organisation, i.e. a large building subdivided into workshops, each super-

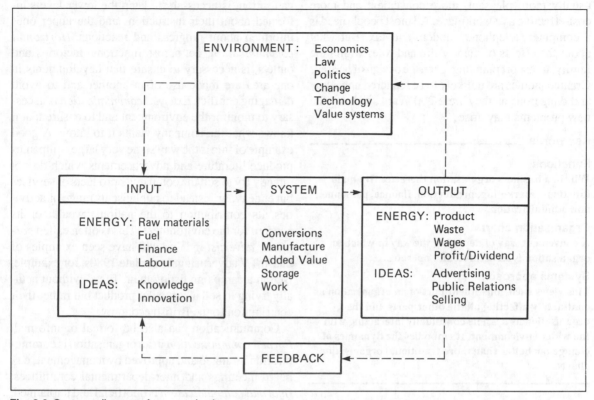

Fig. 2.6 Systems diagram of an organisation

vised by a foreman, could be applied to almost anything. It became the model for schools, hospitals and even prisons. The classroom supervised by the teacher and the ward supervised by the sister are direct descendants of the 19th century factories.

We can see from this that the influence of technology can spread far beyond its industrial applications. It is also apparent that the organisational forms to which it gives rise can survive the technology itself. For example, the general availability of learning resources, such as computers, in most colleges and schools no longer requires teachers to be the main source of information and knowledge. Their role should, perhaps, be as managers of a learning process which is student- not teacher-centred. Is this your experience however?

We should learn from this that it may be dangerous to let technology dictate to us. Rather we should attempt to make technology conform to our needs. Never has it been more important to understand this since we are now experiencing another major change in technology. This was well expressed by Professor Galbraith when he wrote 'The imperatives of technology and organisation, not images of ideology, are what determines economic society.'

Today, thanks to the computer, information is power. Its availability, speed of access to it, its security and control and, above all, our ability to use it are all matters which concern both us as individuals and the organisations for which we work. Without information we cannot usefully function. Quantum leaps in computer capabilities will no doubt continue to amaze us and we must learn to harness them if we wish to stay competitive.

The Industrial Revolution saw the end of the 'Domestic System' – a production system based in the home – and the birth of the factory system. It was in factories that the 'new technology' of the steam engine could be harnessed and, later, it was in offices that information could be gathered, processed and used. The IT Revolution may see a partial reversal of this. More and more people may leave offices and work from home. The modern source of power – the computer – is a portable box and the home environment is usually more pleasant, more convenient and more cost-effective as a workplace. All most people need is a computer, telephone, modem and fax. But what about the effects on family life and roles within the family, transport planning, even the design of houses? Granted, homes are unlikely to be rendered unhealthy and dangerous as they were 200 years ago but what new problems may arise?

Key words

Functions
Within a business organisation there are five main functions: marketing, production, finance, personnel, and administration.

Organisation charts
A convenient way of depicting the way in which an organisation is structured and operates.

Systems approach
This views each constituent part of an organisation as continually affecting all the other parts and the organisation as a whole continually interacting with the wider environment. It embodies the dynamics of change far better than more traditional organisation charts.

Communication in organisations

In very general terms, communication consists of all the processes by which information is transmitted and received. In short, communication links all the parts of an organisation together and is the means by which management co-ordinates its various activities.

Communication warrants a short section to itself for without it no organisation, especially in business, will survive for long. Internal exchange of information and external monitoring and dissemination of it are vital parts of the input and output of a business system. With increasing 'workers' rights', a society which believes more and more in the freedom of information and rapidly improving information technology, keeping people informed of their targets and progress becomes not only more important but also easier. In addition, business organisations face a faster and more complex trading environment and much more sophisticated and better-informed consumers.

Vertical communication, i.e. up and down an or-

ganisation, is necessary to keep the lower levels informed about their instructions and the upper ones informed about progress and reactions. *Horizontal communication*, i.e. across functions, factories and outlets, is necessary to ensure that developments in one area are made use of in another and to avoid damaging conflict. *External communication* is necessary to monitor the environment and to ensure that it knows what the company wants it to know. A good example of this is the way some very large companies produce literature and advertisements which do not directly try to sell the company's products or services but endeavour instead to publicise its range of activities, its contribution to the nation's wealth or its concern for the environment. This is often called *corporate advertising*. You will have seen examples of this in TV advertising. In the late 1980s, for example, BP ran a campaign listing their 'firsts' without actually trying to sell a particular product but rather their contribution to the British economy.

Communication can also be formal or informal. *Formal communication* in an organisation is communication arranged and approved by management, e.g. board meetings and inter-departmental committees. *Informal communication* is unofficial and unplanned, e.g. the company 'grapevine'. Many organisations promote informal communication and play an active part in it in the belief that in some circumstances more or better information can be received and given than through formal channels.

Describe the formal and informal channels of communication within the organisation for which you work or within your college.

Individuals and organisations

For their economic and social lives people function as parts of organisations. From school to college to work, people spend a major part of their waking lives within organisations over which they may have only slight individual control. Thus, it is important that individuals ensure that the organisations in which they function are right for them.

On a wider scale, philosophers since the age of

Aristotle have debated the relationship between individuals and organisations, the relationship between citizens and the state in particular. The *utilitarian* thinkers of the 19th century such as Bentham looked upon organisations as collections of individuals. On the other hand, those who take a more *organic* view see the whole as greater than the sum of the parts. Aristotle argued that it is only through being part of organisations that human beings achieve their full potential.

Interaction of objectives

The individuals in an organisation have their own objectives. These must be compatible with the organisation's objectives if the individuals are to be well-integrated members of the organisation. Individuals also interact with each other. This interaction must be regulated through the organisation's structure to ensure that the organisation's objectives are achieved. Ensuring compatibility and getting the interaction right are both important management functions. We discuss them further below.

On this individual level it should be possible for you to work through the list of the eight characteristics of organisations we discussed above and define them precisely as far as *you* are concerned. You should also realise that many of them – power, rules, etc – also apply to your role in other organisations such as the state. You should ask yourself the question: 'To what extent do the goals of the organisations with which I am concerned coincide or conflict with my personal goals?'

Human needs

If you think about why individuals seek to achieve goals or objectives, it will be so that they can satisfy *needs*. It is therefore relevant to consider briefly at this point what we mean by needs.

The most widely accepted definition and classification of needs is probably that of Maslow, an American psychologist. He divided human needs into five categories.

(a) Physiological or basic needs. These are needs that people must satisfy just to stay alive, for example, the need for food, drink and sleep. The fundamental

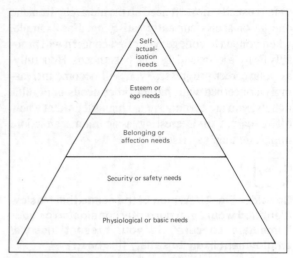

Fig. 2.7 Maslow's hierarchy of human needs

purpose of a wage or salary is to satisfy basic needs. *(b) Security or safety needs.* These are concerned with self-protection and, to some extent, provision for the future. Examples include the need for shelter, warmth and self-defence. In organisations, such needs are reflected in the desire for security of employment, the existence of restrictive practices and the activities of trade unions.
(c) Belonging or affection needs. People need to give and receive friendship – or at least most of us do! We satisfy these needs by having friends and belonging to social groups. Both these things are self-evident in organisations.
(d) Esteem or ego needs. We need to become independent, to acquire possessions, to receive praise from others. Many of us also need to exercise influence or power over others. In an organisation, such needs can be satisfied in a number of ways, for example, by having a position of authority or by occupying a bigger office or having a better chair than other employees.
(e) Self-actualisation needs. These needs are concerned with self-fulfilment, being creative, using your capabilities to the fullest. In an organisation, it is usually only the skilled craftsman, the professional or the manager who can fulfil such needs.

If you think about Maslow's categories carefully, you will see that they form a hierarchy, i.e. people will usually satisfy basic needs before safety needs before affection needs and so on. It follows that the need which is most important to an individual at any one time is usually the next need up the hierarchy from the one he or she is currently satisfying. For example, when you leave college, your first concern will probably be for a job to satisfy your basic needs. Hopefully, as your career progresses, you will become increasingly concerned with higher order needs until, ultimately, you are earning such a high salary that a new office carpet or interesting assignments are more important than pay rises!

Consider Fig. 2.7. Which of the needs that Maslow identified would you currently consider to be your immediate concern? Is your present lifestyle/ employment likely to satisfy this need?

Management by objectives

Management by objectives is a system that attempts to improve the performance of an organisation and motivate, assess and train the individuals in it by integrating their personal objectives with those of the organisation. It clearly implies acceptance of the theory of needs which we discussed above.

Essentially, the process consists of a joint setting of objectives and a joint review of their achievement or non-achievement by managers and their subordinates.

The system has many *advantages*, for example:

(a) The efficiency of the organisation is increased because individuals are clear about their objectives as well as those of the organisation;
(b) Motivation is improved since individuals have shared in setting objectives;
(c) Training needs are better identified;
(d) Communication between manager and subordinate is improved;
(e) Control systems are improved;
(f) Individual performance is appraised (assessed) against very clear objectives and not against subjectively judged personal characteristics.

However, as with any system, it has its *disadvantages*, for example:

(a) It will not work if the organisation is badly organised or managed, where the staff do not have the ability to take part in the objective setting process, or where the traditions or management style of the organisation

are inconsistent with the approach;
(b) It is a complicated, difficult and lengthy process;
(c) It is not appropriate where jobs are highly structured for here there is little room for personal objectives;
(d) It may encourage concentration on short term objectives at the expense of the long term;
(e) It may be viewed as a management weapon of control, i.e. objectives are in reality imposed by management and the performance review becomes inquisitorial rather than constructive.

Management styles

The management grid

There are many different types and styles of management. One way to depict and describe the different styles is to represent them on a grid. On the vertical axis of the grid we put the people orientation of management, i.e. how concerned they are about their workforce. A high value (9) includes such things as wanting to maintain the self esteem of workers and having good personal relations with them. The horizontal axis measures work orientation, i.e. getting the job done.

From this grid it is possible to analyse a manager's

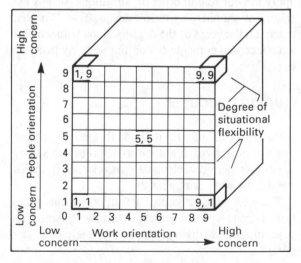

Fig. 2.8 The management grid. A 9.9 style is the ideal manager whereas a 1.1 style shows interest in neither work nor people. (Based on the work of R Blake and J Mouton as adapted by W J Reddin.)

style and give it a value from one of the squares of the grid. The extreme of these management styles are:

1.1 Managers acting as messengers between their supervisors and subordinates. They take little interest in their job or their workers.

9.9 The 'ideal' manager dedicated both to the job and to people.

1.9 The 'country club' manager, easy going and relaxed but shows little concern for the objectives of the organisation.

9.1 The 'autocratic' manager, only concerned with getting the job done.

Square 5.5 is the 'half-way house' approach. The manager performs adequately in both dimensions. The objectives set are usually easily attainable and the manager is moderately autocratic but benevolent.

Research suggests that most managers adopt a 5.5 style and are moderately successful. The most successful managers tend to adopt a 9.9 style but these are rare. However, practising managers see their juniors who adopt a 9.1 style as the most promotable.

A 3-D theory of managerial effectiveness

We can further extend the idea of the management grid by adding a third dimension to it – as we have done in Fig. 2.8. We can take the same basic styles which are described above and add to them the idea of pragmatic flexibility to changing circumstances. Thus, our third dimension is the ability to adapt management style to the demands of the situation.

Participative management

Obviously, it would be good to know which is the 'best' style of management. However, it is quite possible that management should be *situational*, i.e. different styles suit different situations.

Nevertheless some analysts, particularly Rensis Likert, insist that *participative management* is the most effective. In this, effective power in decision-taking is passed to subordinates with senior managers having complete trust in them in all matters. The ideas and opinions of subordinates are actively sought and acted upon. Economic rewards are based on the extent to which they participate in group activities and how well they achieve their objectives. The work done by Likert suggests this is the most successful style of leadership.

Participative management should not be confused with *consultative management*. In this the manager may seek the opinions of subordinates but still retains the power to make important decisions. The management of most colleges provides a good example of the consultative style.

Conflict in organisations

What is conflict?

Conflict is one of those things that is easy to recognise but difficult to define. It can take innumerable forms and depends on the context in which you are considering it. We can, however, exclude *constructive argument* from the definition, for here the exchange of ideas is itself useful and there is always the intention to reach a consensus. We can also exclude *constructive competition*, for this is likely to improve standards and provide stimulus and motivation. But *harmful competition*, sometimes known as 'zero-sum' competition because one individual or group can only benefit at the expense of another, is likely to result in conflict, an example being a fight for resources by departments. Since a long list of examples of conflict is unlikely to help you understand its nature, we are going to explain it in terms of its symptoms, tactics and consequences.

Symptoms of conflict

While considering the symptoms identified below, think of the organisations to which you belong and try to recognise examples of them.

(a) Inter-personal or inter-group jealousies, rivalries or disputes.
(b) Poor communications: both formal and informal and horizontal and vertical.
(c) Resistance to change.
(d) Frequent use of formal or informal arbitration and appeals to higher authority to settle differences

Conflict tactics

Things are really bad when individuals or groups spend a significant proportion of their time 'plotting' to achieve their objectives at the expense of others or even just for the hell of frustrating what that individual or group is trying to do! The following are typical tactics.

(a) Finding flaws in the work of another individual or department and then reporting this to the corporate management.
(b) Line managers refusing to accept the advice of staff managers, particularly where the latter are trying to extend their influence over the former.
(c) Imposing rules or restrictions to increase influence and importance.
(d) Withholding information, thereby weakening the decision-making capability of others while increasing your own influence at the same time.
(e) Presenting information, particularly specialised or technical information, in a distorted or unhelpful way to further your own objectives.

Consequences of conflict

On a regular, institutional basis, conflict is harmful to an organisation. As examples of conflict are innumerable, so the consequences are varied. Nevertheless we can say that in general terms, the consequences are low morale, lack of motivation, a general feeling of frustration at not being able to get things done, ineffectiveness and inefficiency. The organisation will perform badly.

Causes of conflict

Putting aside the many and varied reasons for conflict between individuals, for this is not within the scope of this book, we can identify two general causes of conflict within organisations. The first of these we have already discussed in this chapter: the differences in the value systems (*see* page 32), objectives and policies of different individuals and groups. The second concerns authority, particularly the boundaries and relationships between potentially overlapping spheres of influence. Authority frequently means money, status and power (not necessarily in that order) and it is common for staff managers to exert their influence over line managers' territory and for a department to start 'empire building' by trying to take over the work of other departments.

Resolution and control of conflict

It is futile to hope that conflicts will not arise in organisations; man is by nature competitive and competition easily becomes conflict if not harnessed and channelled.

Typical methods used to resolve and control conflict include:

(a) Establishing rules and procedures for conduct;
(b) Separating employees who clash;
(c) Holding meetings or arranging confrontations where the causes of conflict can be thoroughly aired and the conflict resolved;
(d) Closer management of the area of conflict;
(e) Providing an arbitration facility or establishing a grievance procedure to settle disputes.

Of course, it is better to prevent conflict from arising in the first place. You have already seen that a way to do this is to endeavour to ensure compatibility between the objectives and policies of individuals, groups and the organisation itself. Efficient management, good leadership, effective decision-making and common-sense are also important. These all form part of the process of *co-ordination* within an organisation, that is, the integration of the activities of different sections and departments towards achieving corporate objectives. The structure of the organisation will also play a part. A matrix management structure and the use of inter-departmental teams and committees should promote co-operation while poor communication systems and rigid departmentalisation are likely to hinder it.

Conclusion

You must not think that there exists an ideal form of organisation, a best way of doing things. Some people may advocate that everything would be best provided by private enterprise or, conversely, that everything should be nationalised. Some argue for a matrix structure in organisations while others prefer the more traditional departmental structure. It should be obvious from the variety of objectives we have mentioned that no one organisational form could be expected to suit all organisations. Thus, different objectives demand different forms of organisation. In addition to this, technology takes a hand. Consider, for example, farming and coal mining. Although they are both primary industries, they are very different and the form of organisation which is suited to one is not suited to the other.

Coalition

It is worth ending this chapter by introducing the concept of *coalition*. We have talked about the wide range of objectives found in organisations, and the problems of bias, complexity, lack of clarity and conflict associated with them. So how does an organisation, whatever its type or structure, hold together? Perhaps via *consensus*, which means everybody agreeing on aims. Except on rare occasions this just is not so. Perhaps via *coercion*: the boss tells us all what to do and we do it. However, this does not work well or consistently in our society, as you may have already found out. Perhaps it holds together through *conflict*, where the objectives pursued arise out of the strain of one group pulling against another and winning. But this is no formula for long term harmony and success.

Perhaps by *coalition* is the best way to describe the mysterious process by which organisations operate. In other words, an organisation is an association of people or parties with different but complementary individual objectives who know that these are best pursued together. At any one time the objectives of one party are being met with the reluctant acquiescence of the others. They know that their turn will come.

Key words

Communication
Within an organisation communication links functions and departments and is the means by which activity is co-ordinated.

Human needs
In different situations and at different stages of our life we strive for different things.

Conflict
Conflict is usually a destructive force within an organisation. It is generally caused by differences in value systems, objectives and policies and by the boundaries of authority and influence.

Coalition
Within a large organisation *consensus* is probably more theoretical than real, *coercion* is inefficient and *conflict* eventually destructive. *Coalition* can accommodate a number of different objectives because they are complementary and best pursued in common.

Learning project

A study of an organisation

Using the organisation you work for, study in or which is nominated by your tutor, complete the following tasks.

1 Construct a chart to show how it is organised. (If you work for a very large organisation you may have to restrict your chart to your particular part of the organisation.)

2 By reference to the chart, describe the structure of the organisation.

3 Analyse the line and staff functions of the organisation.

4 Use a different type of organisation chart to represent the structure of the organisation you have chosen.

5 Contrast your organisation with that of a colleague.

6 Analyse the effect of the introduction of the new technology on the structure of the organisation.

7 List as many of the objectives of the organisation you have chosen as you can. Describe the policies pursued to achieve these objectives.

Further ideas for learning projects

1 Make a list of your personal objectives, rank them in order and write down *(a)* what strategies you intend to employ to achieve them, *(b)* how long you consider they will take you to achieve, and *(c)* where you wish

to be in three years' time (in terms of career, education etc) and *(d)* how they relate to the objectives of your organisation/department.

2 (a) For your organisation, draw up a table to show at least three of the following:

- Number of people employed
- Total expenditure
- Sources of income

- Capital employed
- Profit or loss
- Value of turnover
- Issued share capital.

(b) Drawing on the information you will collect, and from any other source, in about 300–500 words describe and assess the position of your organisation within the industry (or sector of the economy).

3

Trading organisations

CHAPTER OBJECTIVES

After studying this chapter you should be able to:

Identify ways of classifying trading organisations;
Explain the concept of legal personality;
List and describe the main forms of trading organisations;
List and evaluate the comparative advantages of different forms of trading organisations;
Assess the role of the nationalised industries in the UK economy;
List arguments for and against privatisation;
Describe the organisation of a nationalised industry.

Introduction

You have probably seldom stopped to consider how, and from what, the goods you consume and the services you use are produced and provided. It is even less likely that you have considered the type of organisation which made, sold or provided them. Manufacturing companies, shops, service agencies and the like are largely taken for granted for they are an accepted part of all our lives. Behind each, however, is an organisation, be it the state (public corporations), a large company, or a single person running a corner shop.

The organisations which trade with the public vary greatly – from ICI to the corner shop, from the British Coal Corporation to the local plumber. It may appear that ICI and the BCC have more in common with each other than they have with the local tradesman. However, in Chapter 2 we saw that ICI and the local plumber have a common interest in that they are both *business organisations*, i.e. they both basically attempt to maximise their profits. The BCC, on the other hand,

is a public corporation and is supposed to operate the coal industry in the public interest. Co-operatives were founded on the idea of self-help by and for their members, while the trading activities of local authorities are primarily intended to provide a service to the community where breaking even is usually more important than profit. We have already distinguished between trading organisations on the grounds of their *objectives*.

In this chapter we are principally concerned with the various *legal forms* which trading organisations adopt but we briefly consider other classifications.

Type of industry

You have seen in Chapter 2 that industries can be classified into primary, secondary and tertiary industries. This is an obvious criterion for classifying trading organisations but it is not, however, particularly useful. For example, manufacturing takes innumerable forms and a single large organisation such as BP may pursue activities in all three fields.

Size

Again, an obvious criterion to use. However, what do we mean by 'size'? Is it the number of retail outlets, the number of employees, the turnover, the share of the market, or profits? Despite the problems, this means of classification is worth pursuing since it can give a good idea of the power, wealth and importance of the largest trading organisations.

In Tables 3.1 and 3.2 you can see lists of the largest organisations ranked by number of employees and turnover respectively. Both illustrate well the mixed nature of the British economy in that four of the largest ten employers in 1988 and one of the ten organisations with the largest turnovers in 1988 were public corporations (often referred to as nationalised industries). The presence of Shell UK (under Dutch control) is indicative of the large numbers of foreign companies which operate in the UK. (Esso UK (under American control) was ranked twelfth.) On the other hand, all of the companies in the lists except the nationalised industries have extensive overseas operations.

Two of the organisations are giants by world standards. The Royal Dutch/Shell Group, of which 'Shell' Transport and Trading is 40%, was ranked eighth to the Japanese Mitsui Group and British Petroleum was ranked thirteenth. Another interesting comparison is employees : turnover. In 1988, 'Shell' Transport and Trading employed 16,731 with a turnover of £22.3bn – ranking second in the UK – and Esso UK employed only 4,480 and yet were ranked thirteenth with a turnover of £5.77bn. Both are *holding* companies and their income comes from the companies under their control. The spectacular rise of Hanson in the turnover rankings deserves a short explanation. Hanson has grown by using its financial expertise in takeovers and mergers, usually using borrowed money – technically referred to as leveraged buyouts.

Table 3.3 shows the top 50 world industrial groupings by country. You will notice here the dominance of Japanese and American companies. (Compare the tables given in Learning Project 4 at the end of this chapter.)

Activity

Update or replace Tables 3.1 – 3.3 from the latest edition of *The Times 1000* (your college or local central library should have it) and account for the changes you observe.

Table 3.1 The ten largest UK employers in 1988 showing 1984 figures and rankings

Rank 1988	Organisation	Employees 1988	1984	Rank 1984
1	British Telecom	242,723	244,592	1
2	Post Office (N)	198,217	201,885	5
3	BAT Industries	172,715	212,822	3
4	General Electric Co	157,262	170,865	6
5	Unilever	155,000	140,000	7
6	British Railways Bd (N)	154,748	207,097	4
7	British Coal Corp (N)	135,900	243,300	2
8	British Aerospace	133,600	75,645	18
9	Electricity Council (N)	131 398	139,740	8
10	ICI	130,400	118,500	12

(N) Nationalised industries

Source: The Times 1000, 1985–86 & 1989–90 Times Newspapers

Table 3.2 The ten largest organisations ranked by turnover 1988 showing 1984 figures and rankings

Rank 1988	Organisation	Turnover (£mill) 1988	1984	Rank 1984
1	British Petroleum Co	33,101*	44,059*	1
2	Shell Tranpt & Trading[1]	22,329*	29,522*	2
3	ICI	11,699	9,909	5
4	Electricity Council (N)	11,366	9,526	7
5	BAT Industries	11,358*	14,426*	3
6	British Telecom	11,071	6,876	9
7	Hanson	7,396	2,382	39
8	British Gas Corp (N)	7,364	6,392	10
9	Shell UK	6,580*	9,608*	6
10	Unilever	6,384	5,859	11

(N) Nationalised industries
* Including sales taxes, excise duties and similar levies
[1] Based on 40% of Royal Dutch/Shell Group

Source: The Times 1000, 1985–86 & 1989–90 Times Newspapers

Table 3.3 Top 50 world industrial groupings by nation 1988

Country	Number in top 50
Japan	16
America	16
West Germany	8
Italy	3
France	2
UK/Netherlands	2
UK	1
Netherlands	1
Switzerland	1

Source: Times 1000, 1989–90 Times Newspapers

Legal status

The most usual way of classifying trading organisations, however, is by their legal status and the way in which they *raise capital*, are *owned* and are *controlled*. These three aspects are vital to the operation of any trading organisation. Their legal status also determines the liability of members for debts, obligations to disclose financial and other information and accountability to individuals and other organisations. On this basis, by far the most numerous type of organisation is the sole trader, accounting for something like 80% of the total. On the other hand, by far the greater amount of business is done by public companies and, of course, by public corporations.

It is clearly unrealistic, however, to divorce the legal status of a trading organisation from its commercial role and economic significance. Indeed, political and sociological perspectives often need to be considered. Nationalisation and regional policy are matters of considerable domestic political importance; multinational corporations can sometimes significantly affect or influence a country's policies or actions and pure economic considerations often have to bow to government policy. Similarly, interactions within and between organisations cannot be ignored and concepts of *power* and *status* will affect the structure of each individual unit. Specific aspects of the organisation's structure, such as the level of automation or the percentage of women employed, may have much more wide-ranging effects.

Nevertheless, the choice between different types of organisation is normally made on the basis of the legal status each type enjoys and the consequences which flow from this. Therefore, a general explanation of the legal status of trading organisations is a firm foundation on which to build a more detailed analysis and comparison of the various types of business unit in which economic, legal, social and political factors can be assessed, and their interaction discussed.

Fig. 3.1 gives a visual indication of how the trading organisations discussed in this chapter relate to one another.

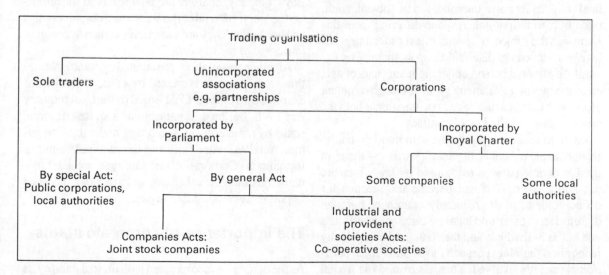

Fig. 3.1 Trading organisations

Corporations and unincorporated associations

Legal personality

Normally, a 'person' means an individual human being but at law the term has a wider and yet more precise meaning. Human personality and legal personality are not one and the same thing. At law the term *person* means an individual, a group of individuals, or even a thing which the law recognises as being the subject of legal rights and duties.

At different times, various legal systems have accorded a degree of legal personality to things other than human beings, e.g. cats in ancient Egypt, church buildings and relics of saints in the Middle Ages and idols in modern India. Under early English law animals were tried for crimes, and even today Admiralty proceedings are taken directly against the ship! Conversely, some human beings have had either only limited legal personality or have been deprived of legal personality altogether. Under modern English law, women, particularly married women, did not enjoy legal equality with men until a variety of Acts of Parliament, passed this century, removed the remnants of inequality. Roman slaves had no directly enforceable rights and outlaws in Norman times were literally outside the law.

The common law (the basic judge-made law of the land) took as its norm the sane, sober, solvent, adult, male human individual. Anyone differing from this norm was the subject of special rules conferring privileges or imposing disabilities upon them. For example, a minor, a person under eighteen years of age, cannot vote in Parliamentary or local government elections but is in a privileged position under both the criminal law and the law of contract.

Early in its development the common law had to recognise the existence of *juristic persons* – the term used to denote persons recognised by law which are not human beings. It had become the practice for office-holders, most frequently church or borough dignitaries, to enter into legal transactions as officials and not as individuals and the common law gradually recognised their legal capacity to do so. The *corporation* eventually evolved. This has resulted in a vital legal distinction between types of organisations; they

may exist as either *corporations* or *unincorporated associations*. Thus, a quite different theoretical concept is added to the commercial differences between types of business unit.

However, you will see that commercial considerations and law cannot be realistically treated as separate matters in this context. For example, the various methods of raising capital began as commercial practices but have now become part of the law which is used to organise and control these practices.

What is a corporation?

A corporation is a group of individuals (*a corporation aggregate*) or one individual (*a corporation sole*) which is regarded at law as being a legal person quite distinct from the individuals or individual who compose it at any particular time. Hence, at law, any event affecting its members does not directly affect the corporation. A company is an example of the former; the Sovereign, bishops and trustees are examples of the latter. The corporation represents the furthest development of juristic personality in English law.

Methods of incorporation

The earliest corporations were created by *Royal Charter*, and while one or two of the oldest existing trading companies were created in this way, e.g. the Hudson Bay Company, charters are now reserved for important non-commercial corporations such as universities and boroughs. They are sometimes known as *common law corporations*.

All other corporations are created by *statute*. Sometimes a corporation is created by a special statute, for example the National Coal Board by the Coal Industry Act 1946, but most organisations acquire corporate status by registering as a company under the Companies Act 1985 after fulfilling the required statutory formalities. Corporations of this type are far more numerous than the other two and are today the most important type of trading organisation.

The importance of corporate status

As the company, incorporated with limited liability, is today the most important type of trading organisation, the consequences of incorporation are of crucial importance to modern commercial activity. Briefly, corporate status is important for five main reasons.

(a) It is convenient for pursuing, managing and protecting the *common interests* of a large number of individuals.
(b) Any event affecting a member, e.g. death or bankruptcy, does not directly affect the corporation because it has its own *separate and permanent existence.*
(c) Corporations may *pursue activities*, within the limits of their powers, in the same way as an ordinary person, although to do this they will have to act through agents because they themselves have no actual physical existence.
(d) Land and other *property* can be owned, used and transferred by the organisation in the same way as by an ordinary person.
(e) The organisation and not its members is *liable for its debts* and other legal obligations.

Unincorporated associations

This term refers to any group of people who pursue an activity in common without having the legal status of a corporation. Such associations may range from relatively informal organisations like local youth clubs, through trading or professional partnerships, to nationally influential bodies such as the Transport and General Workers' Union.

While these associations have no independent legal status, their existence cannot be ignored by the law. In particular, the partnership remains a business organisation of great importance and trade unions have on many occasions played an important role in the development of government economic policy in addition to their day-to-day involvement with industrial and employment law, wage bargaining and labour relations. Indeed, unincorporated associations are sometimes the subject of specific Acts of Parliament and a compromise has been reached between legal disregard for their existence and the practical requirements of business activity and society in general. On the one hand:

(a) the association's *property* belongs to its members jointly and not to the association itself;
(b) *contracts* made on its behalf can only be enforced by or against the individual members who make or

Keywords

Trading organisations
Organisations which provide goods and services to the public, always for profit but not necessarily intending to maximise their profits. Primarily classified according to the legal status, they can also be usefully classified in other ways, e.g. according to the type of industry of which they are part or according to their size.

Legal and juristic persons
A *legal person* is an entity which the law recognises as being the subject of legal rights and duties. A *juristic person* is a legal person that is not a human being. Although basic, these concepts were and still are central to the development of trading organisations.

Corporation
A group of individuals, a company for example, or one individual, for example an office-holder, that the law recognises as being quite distinct from the individuals or individual who compose it at any particular time.

Unincorporated association
A collection of individuals pursuing an activity in common without the legal status of a corporation. Some unincorporated associations, e.g. large partnerships and trade unions, are commercially far more important than many corporations (companies).

authorise them, and;
(c) only those members who have actually committed or authorised *any wrongful* act in the course of the association's activities will incur liability for it. (*See* further page 148 for a trade union's position.)

On the other hand, the law recognises their existence in four important ways.

(a) *Legal proceedings* may be taken by or against one or more members as representing all.
(b) In certain circumstances an unincorporated association such as a trade union may *sue and be sued* as though it were a legal person.
(c) Where property is owned by *trustees* (persons owning property which they must use on behalf of another) for the association, the law recognises and will enforce the association's right to have the property used for its benefit. (A trustee would not, for example, be allowed to sell the property and use the proceeds for his own purpose even though the property is 'legally' his.)
(d) Unincorporated associations may *make and en-*

force rules for their own internal organisation. On a somewhat humble level, a local tennis club will have its own homely 'dos and don'ts' while the relationships among members of a partnership are usually governed by formal articles or a deed. Only where these rules are applied unfairly will the courts interfere.

The development of the business organisation

As society evolved from feudalism to *laissez-faire* and then to capitalism, so the forms of business organisations evolved. The earliest forms were the sole trader and the partnership. The joint stock company (the correct, if little used, term for a 'company') did not become common until the nineteenth century, although its origins are to be found much earlier in the *commercial revolution* of the sixteenth and seventeenth centuries. During this period, the *capitalist system* of production became well established, a system where there was a separation of functions between the capital-providing employer on the one hand and the wage-earning worker on the other.

The joint stock form of organisation developed not from industry but from foreign trade. In order to raise the necessary capital (stock) and spread the risk of early trading ventures, a company form of organisation was adopted. These were called *chartered companies* because they needed a Royal Charter to establish them. Many businesses styled themselves as companies without a charter but this did not constitute a legal form of organisation. At first they were regulated companies, such as the Muscovy Company (1553), which were established for one venture. However, the joint stock company which had a continuous existence and was run by a board of directors and controlled by its shareholders became much more popular. The most important of these early companies was the East India Company. This was founded in 1600 and became a joint stock company in 1660.

Limited liability was first introduced in 1662 but it was only granted to three companies. Dealings in shares took place from the beginning, but the first *stock exchange* was not established until 1778. By this time there was a flourishing capital and insurance market centred on a number of coffee houses in the City of London. The most famous of these was Lloyds. A great speculative boom known as the South Sea Bubble ruined many people and caused the passing of the Bubble Act 1720. This made it illegal to form a company without a charter and this effectively hindered the development of companies for many years.

The building of canals (1761 onwards) required vast amounts of capital and so the joint stock form of organisation had to be adopted. By this time companies were formed not by Royal Charter but by Act of Parliament. The building of railways involved the creation of hundreds of companies and by 1848 their quoted share capital was over £200 million. A few public utilities such as water supply had adopted the joint stock form of organisation but it was not until the mid-nineteenth century that industry began to adopt this form. The development of joint stock banking in England dates from 1826.

It was obviously inconvenient for Parliament to have to establish so many companies and so legislation was passed to enable companies to be set up more easily by *registration*. The most important acts were the Companies Act 1844, the Limited Liability Act 1855 and the Joint Stock Companies Act 1856. The Companies Act 1862 consolidated the previous legislation and was the basis of company organisation until well into the twentieth century.

Throughout the nineteenth century the family business remained the dominant form of organisation in industry. If such businesses sought company status it was usually for the protection afforded by limited liability and not for the purposes of raising capital. It is interesting to note that at this time, when industry and commerce were finding it necessary to adopt the joint stock form of organisation, the government was also finding it impossible *not* to interfere in the economy. That is to say, just as the sophistication of industry and commerce needed regulation through company legislation, so the increasingly complex urban world demanded government intervention to ensure adequate drainage, street lighting, education, etc. It was through the demands of these forces, which could only be met through *legislative law-making*, that Acts of Parliament became the dominant form of law.

Much of the organisation of institutions which evolved at this time, such as hospitals and schools, were modelled on factories. These forms have survived the *scientific revolution* of the twentieth century. We are now beginning to see great changes in our economy brought about by the *information technology revolution*. Perhaps if we are tempted to cling to the forms of organisation of the past we should recall that they originated in the need to exploit large steam engines as a source of power.

How much do you know about your company? Consider it in relation to the information in this chapter so far. What type of industry is it engaged in? How many people does it employ, what is its turnover? Where would it rank if you extended Tables 3.1 and 3.2? It probably is a limited company but it need not be – so what is its legal form and when was it established? What is its history?

You should be able to find information to answer these questions at work but, particularly if you work for a very large company, your college library should have some information, e.g. *The Times 1000* (from which we took our basic information.)

If you are a full-time student, complete this activity using your work experience company or a large local company of your choice.

Different trading organisations

When we look at today's commercial and industrial world it is easy to see a structure dominated by a few giants, the ICIs and BPs of this world. This is, however, a rather misleading picture, for much of the country's wealth is generated by a vast number of small businesses, each often employing only a few people. This was even more true in the past and comments such as 'Britain is a nation of shopkeepers' or 'Britain is the workshop of the world', once appeared almost literally to be true. Today Britain has a diverse economy, consisting of business units of all sizes organised locally, nationally and internationally.

The simplest and most basic trading organisation is the one-man business, i.e. the sole trader or sole proprietor. Commercial development originally started on this basis. However, the combination of a number of factors caused an evolution, markedly more rapid in the eighteenth and nineteenth centuries, from the one-

man business to the corporate commercial giants of today. Principal among these factors were the greater capital resources and expertise available in larger units, business 'enterprise', technical innovations, and the development of a framework of legal principles designed to aid the creation and operation of larger trading organisations.

Clearly, one business unit can be distinguished from another in terms of size, organisation, area of activity, etc, but the basic practical distinction between different units is a consequence of the *legal framework* within which they are owned and operated. All businesses need capital and its contributors take different risks according to the type of organisation in which they invest. You will see that this is a recurrent theme in this chapter.

The sole trader

What is a sole trader?

A sole trader is a business organisation where one person is in *business on his own*, providing the capital, taking the profits and standing the losses himself. Typical areas of commercial activity for the sole trader are retailing and building, i.e. activities which are not usually capital intensive.

Limits are placed on the growth of a sole trader's activities by two main constraints. First, *finance*: economic growth largely depends on the availability of capital to invest in the business, and the sole trader is limited to what he can provide from his own resources and raise from a bank. Second, *organisation*: one man has only limited ability to exercise effective control over and take responsibility for an organisation. As a business growth, a larger and more complicated business organisation will generally replace the sole trader.

Legal status

Sole traders have no special legal status; they are treated in the same way as any other individuals by the law. They alone are responsible for the contracts that they or their employees make in the course of their business and for their debts, while the business premises, stock and goodwill are solely theirs.

Commercial considerations

Sole traders are in a potentially vulnerable financial position. The profits may all be theirs but so are the losses, a great many sole traders are made bankrupt each year. Limited capital resources often make them particularly vulnerable not only to sustained competition from large business units but also to bad capital investments, e.g. a grocer opening a delicatessen in an area which turns out to prefer more mundane food.

It can be argued, however, that sole traders are able to weather a short reduction in consumer spending far better than larger business units. They can adapt quickly to the level of demand and, if necessary, can make personal economies until business improves.

Sole traders remain the most common business units in the UK and they are the backbone of the business structure on which the country depends. Nevertheless, in terms of capital and manpower resources employed, sole traders are of limited importance. In recent years the number of sole traders has decreased. The main reasons for this are:

1 Lack of *capital* to invest in new premises, equipment and materials.
2 Lack of *expertise* in every aspect of the business resulting in inefficiency, e.g. the sole trader may be good at selling but bad at administration.
3 Lack of *advice and guidance* about the operation of the business – consultancy is usually too expensive to be considered.
4 *Competition* from chain stores and other larger business units which are able to benefit from various economies of scale.
5 Changes in *shopping patterns* caused by, for example, an increase in the number of married women working and an increase in car ownership.
6 Increased *overheads* resulting from bureaucratic functions such as VAT collection, imposed by law, which sole traders are often disinclined and ill-equipped to perform. (This is less quantifiable as a reason but still important.)

Yet sole traders survive, there never seems to be a shortage of people willing to invest their money and time in such businesses. In the inner cities, many sole traders now come from ethnic minority groups and most seem to make a good living where 'English' businesses often failed! Why do sole traders survive,

what is their attraction?

As a business organisation they offer attractive advantages when compared with others. The initial capital investment may only need to be very small and the legal formalities involved are minimal. In sharp contrast to companies, they offer financial secrecy, the 'personal touch' (a subjective but often important factor), and the knowledge that sole traders are their own boss and that the profit they make will be theirs. Lastly, perhaps, sole traders are able to alter their activities to adapt to the market without legal formality or major organisational problems. (*See* also page 115.)

The partnership

What is a partnership?

The Partnership Act 1890 defines a partnership as 'the relation which subsists between persons carrying on a business in common with a view of profit'. Many partnerships are very formal organisations, such as a large firm of solicitors or accountants, but two people running a stall in a local Sunday market would almost certainly be in partnership with one another and subject to the same legal rules as a firm of City solicitors with an annual turnover of several million pounds.

Partnerships became common with the emergence of the early capitalist economy, for they were and are still better suited to cope with the demands of modern commercial activity than sole traders who must provide capital, labour and skill themselves. Two or more persons in partnership can combine their resources and in theory form an economically more efficient business unit producing a better return on the capital invested.

The maximum number of members possible in most partnerships is fixed by law at 20. The professional partnerships that may exceed this number, e.g. solicitors, accountants and members of a recognised stock exchange, are often organisations of some size with considerable capital resources and offering economies of scale and the benefits of specialisation. It would be unusual, however, to find a trading partnership consisting of more than five or six partners. Corporate status as a company with limited liability is usually more attractive.

The organisation of a partnership

Partnerships are formed by contract and, within the general framework of the law, the partners may make whatever arrangements they like among themselves. It is usual to set out these arrangements in a formal agreement – Articles or a Deed of Partnership – for this should eliminate uncertainty and dispute between the partners. Where this is not done, the 1890 Act, in particular s.24 which sets out a miniature code, governs the relations among partners.

Membership

No new member may be admitted to the firm without the agreement of all the partners; similarly, no partner may be expelled by the others unless the Articles permit this. If, however, the other partners have a good reason for wishing to expel one partner because of personal deadlock between them, for example, and no power of expulsion is given in the Articles, they may ask the Chancery Division of the High Court to dissolve the partnership. They would then be able to establish a new firm without the unwanted member. Note that the Sex Discrimination Act 1986 prohibits any form of sex discrimination in partnerships and the Race Relations Act 1976 prohibits racial discrimination in a form of six or more partners.

The retirement of partners is usually covered by express provisions in the partnership agreement, e.g. as to notice of retirement and the continuation of the firm afterwards.

Management

Every partner is entitled to take part in the management of the firm but the rights of junior partners to participate in management are often restricted by the Articles. Some firms may have one or more 'sleeping partners' who take no part in the management at all. Day-to-day decisions are taken by majority vote, but any change in the firm's business must be unanimously agreed.

Capital, profits and losses

Under the 1890 Act, all partners are entitled to share equally in the capital and profits of the business and they must contribute equally towards the losses. However, it is not always possible for the partners to provide capital equally and senior partners will generally wish to receive a higher proportion of the profits than junior partners. Consequently, it is common for the Articles to vary the Act and deal with such matters in detail.

Legal status and liability

A partnership does not possess corporate status. Even where it trades under a *firm name* entirely different from the names of its members it has no separate legal existence. Certain restrictions exist upon the name which may be chosen. It must not, for example, deceive the public or represent the business of one firm to be that of another, and the word 'Limited' must not be part of the title.

Many organisations trade under a *business name*, a name other than the registered name of a company or the actual name of a sole trader or the names of all partners in a firm. There is nothing wrong with this providing that it is easy to find out who owns the organisation and who is responsible for its activities. To ensure this, the Business Names Act 1985 requires that all such organisations – be they sole traders, partnerships or companies – must legibly state the names of all persons using the business name on all business letters, written orders, invoices and receipts and written demands for payment. These must give an address where any document relating to the business can be served and accepted. In addition, a notice giving the names and addresses of the person(s) using the business name must be displayed prominently in any place where business is carried on and to which customers have access.

Each partner is the *agent* of the firm and of the co-partners for acts done in the course of the firm's business. As a consequence, the partners incur unlimited personal liability for the debts of the firm. Should the business fail, not only the partnership property but also the personal property of each partner will be sold to pay the firm's creditors. The concept of unlimited liability is a disadvantage common to partnerships and sole traders. It is possible, but uncommon in practice, to form a limited partnership under the Limited Partnership Act 1907 in which one or more, but not all, of the partners stands to lose only the capital they initially contributed if the firm fails. In return they are excluded from the management of the firm. The private company, incorporated with limited liability, is usually a far more attractive alternative to the limited partnership.

The commercial role of partnerships

Quite apart from the rules of professional bodies, which usually prohibit their members from forming a company, a partnership is a business organisation generally more suited to professional people in business together than to manufacturers or traders. In the former, the risk of financial failure is less and consequently unlimited liability is less of a disadvantage. For all but the small trading ventures, or where there are particular reasons for trading as a partnership, registration as a company with limited liability is usually to be preferred.

Keywords

Sole traders
People in business on their own account. This does not mean that they do not employ others, merely that the risk is entirely theirs.

Partnerships
Organisations of individuals (and/or sometimes companies) which carry on a business activity together with the intention of making a profit. The partners share the risk equally and, unless agreed otherwise, play equal roles in management. (Both sole traders and partnerships are unincorporated associations.)

The company

A company (more correctly called a *joint stock company*) may be described as an organisation consisting of persons who contribute money to a common stock, which is employed in some trade or business, and who share the profit or loss arising. This common stock is the *capital* of the company and the persons who contribute it are its *members*. The proportion of capital to which each member is entitled is this *share*.

The need for more capital accounted both for the development of partnerships and later for the development of companies. As soon as it became possible to

do so (by the Limited Liability Act 1855, and the Joint Stock Companies Act 1856 – repealed and consolidated by the Companies Act 1862), many partnerships chose to become registered joint stock companies with limited liability. Today, in terms of capital and manpower resources employed, the company is the dominant form of business organisation.

You may be forgiven for thinking that banks and insurance companies are rather different from other companies. This is not so. They are ordinary companies but subject to specific legislation. Under the Banking Act 1987 no organisation other than an *authorised institution* may accept deposits. Under the Insurance Companies Act 1982 no company may carry on any class of insurance business unless authorised by the Secretary of State. But building societies are not companies. They are registered under and their activities are regulated by the Building Societies Act 1986, an Act which enabled them to increase the range of services they offered, e.g. personal loans.

Legal status

At law a company is a *corporation* which is, as you have seen, a collection of persons which has an existence, rights and duties at law quite separate and distinct from those of the persons who are from time to time its members. This fundamental concept was clarified in relation to companies by the House of Lords (the highest appeal court) in *Salomon v Salomon & Co* (1897). Salomon had incorporated his business as a limited company in which he held 20,000 shares. His wife, four sons and a daughter had one share each. He lent money to his company taking a charge (a right against property) on the assets of the company as security. The company eventually became insolvent and on liquidation the assets were found to be sufficient to satisfy the debt owned to Salomon but insufficient to pay off the unsecured creditors. Despite the commercial reality of Salomon and his company being one and the same, at law the House held them to be quite separate. Therefore, as Salomon was the only secured creditor, he was entitled to all the assets of the company and the unsecured creditors were entitled to none.

Hence, the company's property belongs to the company and not to its members. For the same reason, its members are not liable for its debts, although they stand to lose the money that they have invested when the company is wound up with debts in excess of its assets. A company can only act through human agents (its directors) but they only possess the authority given to them by the constitution of the company. Finally, the company is liable for torts (wrongful acts) and crimes committed by its servants and agents in the course of their employment or authority.

The registered company

The original method of incorporation was by Royal Charter, which was followed in the late eighteenth century by incorporation by special Act of Parliament. Both methods were expensive and elaborate and a simpler method was required to cope with the rapid expansion of business enterprise associated with the Industrial Revolution. This need was met by the Joint Stock Companies Act 1844. This enabled a company to be formed by the registration of a memorandum of association and the payment of certain fees. The present law on registration is contained in the Companies Act 1985.

Legally it is possible to classify registered companies in two ways.

1 According to the limit, if any, of the shareholders' liability to contribute towards payment of the company's debts.
2 According to whether the company is a public company or a private company.

Companies limited by share or by guarantee and unlimited companies

The liability of the members of a company *limited by shares* to contribute to the company's assets is limited to the amount, if any, unpaid on their shares. The vast majority of registered companies are of this type. In companies *limited by guarantee* members' liability is limited to the amount that they have undertaken to contribute to the assets in the event of the company being wound up. Such companies are usually non-profit-making organisations, such as professional, trade and research associations or clubs supported by annual subscription. (Shares are unnecessary in such companies because any profit they make is ploughed back into the company and not distributed among members – shares are the mechanism for this distribution.) As the name suggests, the members of an *unlimited company* incur unlimited liability to contribute to the assets of the company if it is wound up. Unlimited companies are comparatively rare but there has been an increase in their numbers since 1967 because the Companies Act of that year exempted them from the statutory requirement to file accounts with the Registrar of Companies. Hence, they can keep their financial affairs private. Unlimited liability is thus the price of financial privacy.

We have explained limited liability above in terms of liability to contribute to the *assets* of the company because this is what the Companies Act 1985 says. When a company is wound up, its assets are used to pay its debts. If a company is solvent when liquidated, shareholders will get back some, probably all, of their investment. If it is not, their investment goes towards paying its debts, but they do *not* have to contribute more. In other words, limited liability in practice is to be understood as limited liability for a company's *debts*.

Also remember that it is the liability of its *members* that is limited, not the company itself. The company's liability is only 'limited' by its total assets, in the same way as that of a sole trader or partnership.

The principle of limited liability is of considerable economic importance and is fundamental to the financing of business ventures. It encourages investment because it limits the risk that investors take to the amount actually invested. Without limited liability it is likely that none but the safest business venture would ever attract large-scale investment. In particular, the institutional investors, such as life assurance companies and pension funds, would not hazard their vast funds in any speculative venture and would only invest in the gilt-edged market (government securities).

Public and private companies

A *public company* is a company limited by shares with a memorandum of association that states that it is a public company and which has been registered as a public company under the applicable Companies Act. It must have two or more members, a minimum authorised and allotted share capital of £50,000 (in 1990) and it can invite the general public to subscribe for its shares or debentures.

A *private company* is any company which does not satisfy the requirements for a public company. In common with a public company it has two or more members.

The main distinctions between a public and a private company are as follows.

1 A public company can offer its shares and debentures to the public, a private company cannot. In fact, the company and its officers commit a criminal offence if a private company does so.

2 A public company must have at least two directors. A private company need have only one but a sole director cannot also be its secretary.

3 A public company must include the words 'public limited company' or ' plc' in its name, a private company must only include the word 'limited' or 'ltd'.

4 A public company requires a 'business certificate' from the Registrar of Companies before it may do business or exercise any borrowing powers, a private company can commence business as soon as the certificate of incorporation is granted. The 'business certificate' confirms that the company has met the legal requirements in relation to its share capital.

The private company at present is in some respects a transitional step between the partnership and the public company; typically it is a small or family business. In common with a public limited company it possesses the advantage of limited liability, but in common with a partnership it has the disadvantage of only being able to call upon the capital resources of its members, supplemented by possible loans from its bank. Although a private company can make non-public share offers, e.g. through business contacts or its bankers, the ability of a public company to offer shares to the public means that it is more easily able to raise large sums of money to finance major developments.

Since the typical private company is a family business or at least a business run by a small usually close-knit group, the articles of association of most of them will restrict membership and the transferability of shares. In this way the owners ensure that they retain control.

While there are far more private than public companies, in terms of capital, public companies dwarf private companies and they have been responsible for the immense growth in investment this century. The typical public company manufactures cars, gives overdrafts and sells insurance – in other words, there is no such thing as a 'typical' public company.

Forming a registered company

A registered company is formed by submitting to the Registrar of Companies the following documents.

(a) The memorandum of association.
(b) The articles of association.
(c) A statement of the names of the intended first director(s) and the first secretary, together with their written consents to act as such. The statement must also contain the intended address of the company's registered office.
(d) A statutory declaration of compliance with the Companies Act 1985 regarding registration.
(e) A statement of the company's capital unless it is to have no share capital.

The Registrar, when satisfied that the requirements have been complied with, issues a Certificate of Incorporation which brings the company into existence as a legal entity.

Of the documents submitted, the memorandum of association and the articles of association are by far the most important.

The memorandum of association

This regulates the company's *external affairs* and enables a person who invests in, or deals with, the company to ascertain its name; its objectives; whether the liability of its members is limited; and its authorised share capital.

The *objects clause* sets out the purposes for which the company was formed and serves two purposes. First, it enables would-be shareholders to discover what their investment could be used for; and second, once they are shareholders it enables them to prevent the company from entering into transactions which are beyond its powers. However, under the Companies Act 1989 it is possible to register a memorandum which states that a company is to carry on business as a 'general commercial company'. This allows the company to carry on any trade or business whatsoever and gives it the power to do anything which is incidental to or facilitates what it chooses to do, e.g. borrow money. For many companies this would be just a formal recognition of the true position.

Until the Companies Act 1989, s.108 virtually abolished it, a company's activities were subject to the *ultra vires* rule (*ultra vires* meaning 'beyond the powers of'). The rule, as originally applied, meant that a person who had entered into a transaction with a company could only enforce it against the company if the transaction was clearly authorised by its objects clause. Over the years the importance of the rule was significantly reduced by extremely long and wide-ranging objects clauses and a statutory limitation which provided that a company was bound by any transaction sanctioned by its directors. This limitation, originally introduced in 1972, represented a first stage in harmonising UK company law in this respect with the rest of the EC. The Companies Act 1989, completes the harmonisation.

The position now is that the validity of an act done by a company cannot be questioned because it is not authorised by its objects clause. In other words, any transaction entered into by a company can be enforced against it irrespective of what its objects clause says. However, a member of a company can bring proceedings to restrain it from acting beyond its stated powers except where it acts to fulfil a legal obligation already entered into to. (The *ultra vires* rule still applies in a restricted form to companies which are registered charities.)

The name of the company must be stated in the memorandum. Apart from the requirements arising from a company's status as either a public or a private company (*see* above), general restrictions exist preventing a name from being registered which suggests, for example, a royal connection, or which might tend to mislead the public, e.g. a name which closely resembles that of an existing company.

The articles of association

These regulate the *internal administration* of the company, the relations between the company and its members, and between the members themselves. The articles cover such matters as the issue and transfer of shares, the rights of shareholders, meetings, the appointment and powers of directors, and accounts.

A company may adopt the model set of articles contained in Table A of the Companies (Tables A to F) Regulations 1985, or it may frame and register its own.

Operation and control of companies

1 Directors. A company acts through its directors, persons chosen by the shareholders to conduct and manage the company's affairs. Their powers are contained in the articles of association and so long as they do not exceed these, the shareholders cannot interfere in their conduct of the company's business. The directors will normally appoint one of their number as managing director who will be given powers under the articles to make certain decisions without reference to the board of directors.

In respect of the company's money and property, and the powers given to them, directors owe duties to the company similar to those owed by trustees (persons who own property which they must use for the benefit of another) to beneficiaries. When approving share transfers or issuing and allotting shares, for example, they must act in *complete good faith* and they are liable to the company for any breaches of this duty.

Directors act as *agents* of the company in making contracts on its behalf and, as such, they are subject to the general rules of agency. They are, for example, personally liable on the contracts they make if they exceed their authority or do not clearly indicate that they are acting as agents for the company, i.e. they make a contract in their own name.

2 The secretary. Every company must have a secretary. The secretary is usually appointed by the directors.

In the 19th century the company secretary was regarded as a mere servant of the company and in 1902 a 'law lord' in the House of Lords described their duties as being 'of a limited and of a somewhat humble character'. The modern position is different. The secretary is the chief administrative officer of the company with extensive duties and responsibilities. The law now recognises that the secretary has authority to make contracts on the company's behalf connected with the administrative side of its affairs.

3 Control by shareholders. In theory the company is a very democratic organisation, with ordinary shares

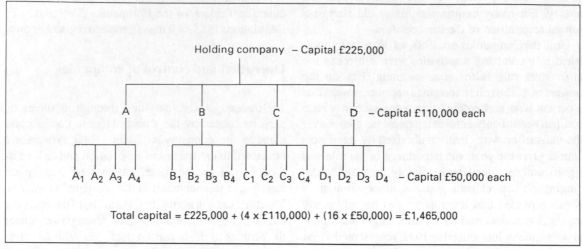

Fig. 3.2 Controlling power of a holding company

giving the right to vote at the company's meetings. Thus, the ordinary members should be able to decide matters of company policy and the composition of the board of directors. For two reasons, however, the reality of the situation is very different. First, it is common for a majority shareholding in a company to be held by a small number of investors or even by one, for example one family or a holding company (*see* below). In such companies the will of the numerical minority of the shareholders prevails over that of the numerical majority. This could be reflected in clashes of interest in such matters as takeover bids or choice of directors. Second, and more commonly, the vast majority of shareholders are either unable or insufficiently interested to attend company meetings, and are content to leave company management to the directors, provided the dividend paid to them is satisfactory.

While in all probability there will always be 'City scandals' e.g. the 'Guinness Affair' in the late 1980s, involving mismanagement or fraud by directors, the trend of the law is towards greater disclosure or information by companies. This should make malpractice more difficult. In addition, the Department of Trade may investigate any company following an allegation by a shareholder of mis-management by the directors.

4 Control by a holding company. It is usually an advantage for companies with similar or complementary interests to group together. The individual companies will still retain their legal and commercial identities and function as separate units but they will be controlled by a central organisation. Sometimes the grouping is not voluntary but the result of fierce takeover battles involving millions of pounds.

This form of extended business units can be created by forming a holding or parent company (a purely financial institution – it does not trade or manufacture itself) to purchase a majority, or sometimes all, of the shares in other companies. By simple mathematical calculations based on Fig. 3.2 you can see that, through a system of subsidiaries, one holding company with a capital of £225,000 can control a commercial empire with a total capital of £1,465,000. Furthermore, a shareholding of £115,000 in the holding company gives effective control of the whole organisation. While £115,000 may represent a fortune to you or me, it is a small sum by the standards of the modern business world. Furthermore, this control of a large group of companies through the ownership of a relatively small part of its total capital is even more exaggerated when different types of shares, e.g. voting and non-voting shares, are considered (see Chapter 10).

Company reports and accounts

The main purpose of company legislation is to *protect investors*, for in practice they have little or no control over their money once it has been invested. Protection is afforded by opening the affairs of companies to public inspection at Companies House. You have already seen that inspection of the memorandum of association and the articles of association enables potential investors to ascertain how, and for what purposes, their money will be used. In the same way a person wishing to deal with the company, for example a bank which is contemplating lending money to the company, may make sure that the proposed transaction is within its objects. Despite the virtual abolition of the *ultra vires* rule, persons contemplating entering into important contracts with a company are likely to want to ensure that the contracts are covered by the objects clause. If they are not, they may insist on the objects being formally amended before the contracts are concluded. In addition, further information can be gleaned from a variety of statutory books (required to be kept under the provisions of the Companies Act 1985) which contain, among other things, details of the company's membership, its directors, and charges over its property.

Every company having a share capital must file an *annual report* in the prescribed form with the Registrar of Companies stating what has happened to its capital in the preceding year, for example the number of shares allotted and the cash received for them. The report must be accompanied by a copy of the audited balance sheet in the prescribed form, supported by a profit and loss account which is a true and fair representation of the year's transactions. These documents are available for public inspection on payment of a small fee. Unlimited companies, however, are exempt from the obligation to file an annual report and their accounts.

In order to harmonise company accounting in the Community, the Companies Act 1981 introduced a new classification of companies for the purpose of accounts and laid down new rules for their form and content. These are now found in the Companies Act 1985.

A *small company* – one with a turnover of less than £2m or a balance sheet total of less than £975,000 or less than 50 employees – is permitted to file only an abridged balance sheet and it does not need to file a profit and loss account or a director's report.

A *medium-sized company* – one with a turnover of less than £8m or a balance sheet total of less than £3.9m or less than 250 employees – may omit details of its turnover and gross profit margin.

These classifications are a recognition that on the basis of resources and organisation it is appropriate to apply different and less onerous requirements to small and medium-sized companies than to large companies. However, a public company, a banking or insurance company, and an 'authorised person' under the Financial Services Act 1986, and groups containing such companies, cannot be treated as a small or medium-sized company.

The directors of a company are under a duty to keep proper *books of account* showing, among other things, receipts and payments of cash, and details of assets and liabilities. The directors incur criminal liability if they fail in this duty.

Keywords

Company
More correctly termed a *joint stock company*, a company is an organisation of individuals who contribute money to a common stock (its capital) which is used in some trade or business and who share the profit or loss arising. It differs from a partnership primarily in that it is a corporation and in that its members incur only limited liability.

Types of companies
Companies are classified either by the nature of their members' liability for their debts, or by whether they are public or private companies. These classifications are not mutually exclusive.

Limited liability
We talk of a company having limited liability but it is the liability of the *members* not the company that is limited.

Memorandum and Articles of Association
Two documents required by the Companies Acts when a company is registered. The *memorandum* regulates a company's external affairs and the *articles* regulate its internal administration.

Directors
Persons who manage a company; they are its agents.

Holding company
A company which holds a majority shareholding in a number of other companies. Frequently a holding company will not actually produce anything itself.

Sole traders, partnerships and registered companies compared

Formation

Sole traders are not really formed, they just exist. As soon as one person starts to manufacture, trade or provide a service by himself he is a sole trader. Partnerships and companies, on the other hand, are both commercial creations but differ considerably in their modes of creation. Partnerships are created by agreement and, while this agreement may be most formal, it may be just as informal. Indeed, there may be no express partnership agreement at all and an agreement can only be inferred from the circumstances. The vast majority of companies are formed by registration in accordance with the Companies Act 1985. This procedure is not necessarily complicated, but it is formal. There is also usually more expense and publicity involved in a company's operation in comparison with that of a partnership or a sole trader.

Legal status

A company exists as a separate legal entity distinct from its members: *Salomon v Salomon & Co.* (1897). In consequence, property belongs to the company and not to its members as individuals and the company's debts and contracts are its own and not its members. Neither partnerships nor sole traders have separate legal identities as business organisations.

Legal status as a *corporation* facilitates dealings with a company's property and, in conjunction with limited liability, encourages investment. A corporation has perpetual succession and anything affecting its members does not affect its own legal position. The death, bankruptcy or retirement of a partner or of the sole trader, however, directly affects the organisation and may bring an end to its existence.

An important feature of modern commerce had been the increasing tendency for sole traders and partnerships to convert their businesses into private limited companies in order to obtain the legal and commercial advantages of corporate status.

Liability of members

Apart from limited partnerships, of which there are few, only registration as a limited company offers liability limited to the amount of their investment to people who contribute capital to the business. This encourages investment, particularly in speculative ventures, and is the principal reason for the dominance of business organisations incorporated with limited liability for their members in today's commercial world. Both a member of a partnership and a sole trader stand to lose virtually all their possessions if their enterprise fails (*see* Chapter 11).

Number of members

A sole trader is clearly one individual in business by himself. A partnership must consist of at least two members but, with certain exceptions, must not exceed 20. A registered company must similarly have a minimum of two members but there is no maximum membership. Note that the EC's twelfth directive on company law would allow, when implemented, *individuals* to form themselves into limited companies as is already possible in some member states.

Two observations based on these figures can be made. First, a small business unit can enjoy the legal and commercial benefits of corporate status as a limited company while still retaining most of the advantages of close co-operation and trust inherent in a partnership. Second, with some exceptions (*see* above), a business unit of more than 20 co-owners must be incorporated.

Transfer of interests

In this respect the greatest difference exists between a sole trader and a partnership. In the former the owner is completely free to sell, or otherwise transfer, his business. In the latter no partner may transfer his share in the firm without the consent of his fellow partners. A member of a company may or may not be free to transfer his shares – it depends on the company's articles of association. It is very probable that most private companies will include such restrictions in their articles in order to retain control within the family or small group. In fact, the management of many private companies will rest with one person, he or she is often virtually the sole owner and its only director. Public companies are legally, if not commercially, free to do the same.

Where interests are freely transferable, flexibility and free movement of capital are given to investors but restrictions on transfer enable a strong common policy to be maintained within a business organisation and encourage trust between its members.

Agency

A great deal of business activity is conducted through agents, i.e. persons who make contracts and dispose of property on behalf of others – their principals. A sole trader may employ an agent but, clearly, he cannot be an agent for himself. Each general partner is an agent of his firm and of his other partners. Therefore, provided the act is within the ordinary course of the firm's business, the act of one partner binds all the others. A shareholder of a company is neither an agent for the company nor for his fellow shareholders unless expressly appointed as such, for example as a director. Thus, the power to enter into transactions binding on the company lies in proportionally fewer hands.

Management

The management of a company similarly lies in fewer hands, for no shareholder, unless he is also a director, can take part in the management of the company. Shareholders can only attempt to influence management through their votes at company meetings. Under the Partnership Act 1890 each general partner can take part in the management of the firm, and a sole trader's organisation is by definition controlled by one person.

Management by directors accountable to the membership at company meetings is the only practicable solution for large (public) companies but control of their activities by the many small shareholders is often more theoretical than real. Therefore, in recent years, *ownership* has been separated from *control* in larger public companies. However, removal of a director from office is a straightforward matter, while the desire to exclude a partner may result in the firm's dissolution.

In the future, greater worker participation in company management is a possibility, but it seems less likely that this step towards industrial/commercial democracy will affect partnerships.

Powers

The powers of a registered company are laid down in the objects clause of its *memorandum of association*. Its internal affairs are governed by its articles of association. Any alteration of either must be in accordance with the Companies Act 1985. Both sole traders and partnerships are more adaptable business organisations. Sole traders are complete masters of their organisations' business activities and any alteration of a partnership's activities is effected by simple agreement among its members.

Formerly, the *ultra vires* rule was, at least in theory, an important constraint on a company's potential actions; it never applied to sole traders or partnerships.

Publicity of affairs

The affairs of sole traders and partnerships are *private*. For example, no annual returns have to be made to any official registrar, and their accounts are not open to public inspection. In contrast, a company's affairs are public, its memorandum of association and articles of association are filed with the Registrar of Companies on registration and its accounts are filed annually. Unlimited companies, however, are exempt from the obligation to file accounts annually and in recent years increasing preference has been shown for partnerships and unlimited companies where financial privacy is of paramount importance. This is because there is a continuing trend towards greater public disclosure of the affairs of limited companies and generally greater government interest in their affairs.

Finance

Economic growth and commercial resilience depend largely on the *availability of capital*. The sole trader must provide capital by himself. A partnership, although financed jointly, also lacks the financial advantages of a public limited company offering limited liability to investors and with access to the capital market. In particular, a company can offer security for long-term loan capital more easily than can sole traders and partnerships. All three business organisations can create mortgages over their property, but only a registered company is able to create a *floating charge* over its property. This offers good security to the lender while still enabling the company to freely use and dispose of the property charged because it 'hovers' over the company's assets and does not attach them specifically to the charge. Only when the charge 'crystallises' (becomes fixed) does the lender acquire rights over specific assets which prevent the company from disposing of them. The ordinary mortgages that sole traders and partnerships can create over their property effectively prevent them from dealing with the property charged without the mortgagee's (lender's) consent.

A bank will often accept the personal guarantees of directors as security for smaller loans to their companies. In similar situations, a bank is usually prepared to make occasional and seasonal unsecured advances to sole traders and partnerships, relying on the reputation of the firm and the financial standing of the parties concerned. In such situations the sole trader or partners are personally responsible for the advance.

Taxation

All three types of organisation pay tax: sole traders and partners will pay income tax under Schedule D on the profits they receive from the business, and capital gains tax on gains from disposal of assets. Companies pay Corporation Tax on both their income and capital profits. Tax liability may often be an important consideration when deciding whether to incorporate a business unit.

Comparative taxation is a specialist's subject and detailed discussion is outside the scope of this book. However, one typical consideration will serve as an example of the 'tax factor'. The tax liability of sole traders and partners is based on the profits made in the preceding financial year. Thus, with inflation or growing profits they will in effect pay tax on an income smaller than they are actually enjoying. A company pays corporation tax on the profits which it actually makes during its accounting period (its own financial year) and is charged at the rate for the financial year in which the profits arose. Therefore, the company's tax liability more realistically reflects the real profit made.

On the basis of the information provided above, summarise the characteristics of sole traders, partnerships and companies by using a box chart. Show the three organisations across the top and the ten characteristics, such as 'formation', 'legal status', down the side. Complete each box with a suitable short comment.

Public corporations

You saw in Table 3.1 that four out of the ten organisations employing the greatest number of people were public corporations – trading organisations owned and controlled by the state. Two public corporations appear in the top ten by turnover (*see* Table 3.2). The role of public corporations in the economy shrank rapidly in the 1980s as a result of privatisations. In 1979 they accounted for 21% of GDP but in 1989 only 10%. Similarly, their share of total investment fell from 18% to 8%.

Legal status

Public corporations are *juristic persons* created either by Royal Charter or, more usually, by special Act of Parliament. They are, therefore, the subject of legal rights and duties and must operate accordingly. Nevertheless, there is no one form of public corporation and the exact status, function, power and method of control of any particular public corporation can only be determined by reference to the statute which created it. However, their legal capacity will be more extensive than that for registered companies. Wide powers are usually granted to the corporation by the relevant creating statute and these in turn are widely interpreted by the courts.

Some public corporations are referred to as *nationalised industries* (*see* page 67). There is, however, no such form of legal entity as a nationalised industry. The name is a carry-over from the days when some industries, such as coal mining and postal services, were directly owned and operated by the government. The GPO, for example, used to be classed as a government department, its employees were civil servants and its head, the Postmaster General, was a minister who represented it in Parliament. This type of nationalised industry ceased to exist in 1969 when the GPO became the Post Office and adopted the public corporation type of organisation.

Ownership, finance and control

In the strict sense public corporations do not have shareholders but, as the government owns the whole of the organisation's capital, you and I – in fact the nation – 'own' the corporations and the government of the day acts as trustee of their assets on our behalf. Any profits the corporations make are ploughed back into the corporations for the benefit of the country as a whole. Our 'dividend' could be said to be a relatively high standard of living and a tax rate lower than it might otherwise be.

Public corporations are mainly financed by the State – it is unlikely that the private sector by itself could or would raise the vast sums which are usually involved. While being financed by the State, each corporation is controlled by a semi-autonomous *board of management* appointed by the government and is theoretically only accountable to Parliament through its annual report to the House of Commons' Select Committee on Nationalised Industries. However, they must operate within a policy framework laid down by Parliament, this being particularly true in respect to their financial objectives.

This method of control means that the Minister of State to whom the corporation is responsible can refuse to answer questions in Parliament about its day-to-day operations, although in practice Ministers frequently interfere in such matters on the grounds of the 'national interest'. We will return to this later.

While it may appear that the appropriate Minister controls the corporation, the case of the British Steel Corporation's accounts (January 1978), when a Commons sub-committee demanded the appearance of the chairman of the board, demonstrates that it is ultimately Parliament which is the controlling force. In fact, as further funds from the public purse for corporations require Parliamentary approval, they are frequently the subject of debate in the House of Commons.

You will find a more detailed account of nationalised industries, their role in the economy, their advantages and disadvantages and their future in Chapter 5.

Co-operative societies

Legal status and background

Co-operative societies date back to 1844 when the first co-operative society was founded in Toad Lane (actually T'Owd Lane), Rochdale.

The object of the first co-operative was to provide cheap, unadulterated food for its members and to return any profit it made to them. In 1990 there were 80 co-operative societies in the UK. Their number has fallen in recent years and is likely to continue to do so as a process of merger and rationalisation is pursued to bring the movement up-to-date in its image and organisation.

The societies constitute a quite distinct form of trading organisation. Each retail co-operative society is registered and incorporated under the Industrial and Provident Societies Acts (not under the Companies Acts) and exists as a juristic person, the subject of rights and duties in the same way as other corporations.

Additionally, they do not fall happily into the conventional division of the economy into the public and private sectors. They are neither nationalised nor state owned on the one hand, nor operated primarily for profit on the other. Their origin and continued existence lies in the notion of *self-help*. As the profits are distributed to its customers, those that use the organisation the most benefit the most from its existence.

Traditionally profits were distributed as dividends (the *divi*). If for example a customer had done £120 worth of business with the society in a year and a dividend of 10p was declared, then that customer would receive a £12 dividend. Thus, most profits went to those who traded most with the society. The *divi* was replaced in many societies in the 1970s with trading stamps which could be traded in at a better rate by members than by non-members. Today profits are distributed in different ways by different societies. Some retain the 'divi', some give trading stamps, and some have introduced member benefit schemes which give discounts and special offers to members only.

Membership, finance and control

A person becomes a member of a co-operative society by buying a share. This provides part of the society's capital and entitles the holder to one vote at the society's annual meeting when its committee of management or board of directors, who control the society, is appointed. It is possible to buy more shares but each shareholder is still only entitled to one vote. This is in sharp contrast to a registered company where shareholders often have as many votes as they have shares. Thus, co-operatives are more democratically run than companies but, as their annual meetings are attended by very few members, their officers are elected and important decisions taken by a small minority of members. This lack of participation is, however, usually to be found in public companies as well.

Shares in co-operative societies differ from those in companies in a number of ways, for example:

(a) shares can be paid for by instalments, not common for company shares;
(b) there is a maximum shareholding, at present £10,000, although the amount of loan capital that the society may raise and the size of the membership is unlimited;
(c) shares are not quoted on the Stock Exchange;
(d) shares cannot be sold, but members can join and leave at any time, i.e. shares can be redeemed at par value; consequently the amount of the society's capital constantly fluctuates.

Capital is also provided by loans, repayable at short notice, from its members. As its members are almost invariably its customers, its customers own the society and can influence its policy by voting in the election of its committee of management or board of directors.

The societies maintain their independence from one another but collectively they have the highest turnover of any retailing group in Britain. In 1863 they founded the Co-operative Wholesale Society (CWS), which is also registered and incorporated under the Industrial and Provident Societies Acts. This organisation manufactures and supplies the member societies with produce for their shops. Today there is hardly a single retail commodity not sold by co-operative societies although food retailing (including dairy operations) is about 70% of their total turnover. In addition, there is the Co-operative Bank, now a member of the Clearing House, a Co-operative Insurance Society and Co-operative travel agencies, optician practices, undertakers and motor dealers. In 1989,

motor dealing accounted for 7% of turnover and travel business 3.7%.

It is worth nothing that the same concept of self-help responsible for the growth of co-operative societies was the origin of building societies.

The co-operative movement

The co-operative movement as a whole has always taken an active interest in politics. At one time many people believed that the movement was a viable alternative to both capitalism and state socialism. The Co-operative Party, founded in 1917, had once achieved some success in returning members to Parliament. Today, the movement has close ties with the 'grass roots' of the Labour Party and frequently sponsors candidates at elections. The Co-operative Union, the movement's spokesman and general adviser, represents its interests by lobbying at both national and local government level.

Other co-operative trading activities

Voluntary buying organisations, such as Spar and Wavyline in the grocery trade, are organised on a co-operative basis. Farmers' co-operatives exist in order that expensive farm machinery can be purchased and used collectively, and produce and supplies bought and sold in bulk. These organisations are not, however, owned and operated as true co-operative societies and are not registered as such under the Industrial and Provident Societies Acts.

The same is true of workers' co-operatives, where the workers are the members and contribute their labour and not capital to the organisation. They receive in return a wage and a share in any surplus profits. Such co-operatives are ordinary registered companies adapted to a co-operative form of organisation and structure. Workers' co-operatives have often been established as a response to economic recession and the decline of traditional industries. For many people, economic change has created the need for alternative forms of employment within alternative forms of organisation. In 1978 the Co-operative Development Agency was established with a brief to help establish viable worker co-operatives. The Co-operative Union provides advice and information and the Co-operative Bank financial support, although commercial viability is still a criterion for making loans available.

Municipal enterprises

While local authorities are primarily concerned with government, they operate a range of trading ventures. Despite the 'right to buy' (*see* page 173) 26% of dwelling houses and flats in the country are rented from local authorities, and this alone makes them important trading organisations. Other activities range from transport services, including docks and harbours, leisure facilities such as swimming pools and golf courses, to more mundane services such as public laundries and crematoria.

In common with public corporations, *profit* is not the driving force behind such activities and many, e.g. the provision of housing, are subsidised from the Community Charge. Local authority housing policy is a highly political issue in many areas. While most people would agree that council houses satisfy a real social need, questions such as subsidies, further investment and development and the purchase of council houses by tenants are guaranteed to cause heated discussion at council meetings. Nor should it be forgotten that, while fulfilling a social need, some council developments, particularly the now discredited high-rise flat blocks, have created their own serious social and, indeed, economic problems.

Local authorities are, of course, corporations, incorporated either by Royal Charter or by special Act of Parliament. They are able to finance their business activities by issuing municipal stock or by raising loans repayable over periods of time varying with the nature of the undertaking and the permanency of its capital assets. Both stock and loans are secured by community charge income and carry fixed (but often highly attractive) rates of dividend and interest. In addition, local authorities can borrow for capital expenditure from the Public Works Loan Board at a preferential fixed interest rate and they often receive government grants and sometimes EC grants.

You and I are able to control the activities of our local authorities by voting at local elections. The elected councils are responsible for overseeing these activities on our behalf, although it is usual to employ professional managers to make all day-to-day business decisions.

Local authority activities are also subject to the *ultra vires* rule. This was spectacularly illustrated in November 1989 when the High Court ruled that speculation on the movements of interests rates (interest-rate swap deals) by Hammersmith and Fulham and over 75 other councils designed to generate income were *ultra vires* the Local Government Act 1972. Put simply, the banks who lent money to the councils to further their speculation could not recover it. The losses were over £100 million in the case of Hammersmith and Fulham alone with a total loss to the banks of between £500 million and £1 billion!

What trading activities are carried on by your local authority? Obtain information from the local town hall or information centre and list them. Which of them do you use/could you use? How do they compare with similar activities carried out by private trading organisations? Explain the comparisons you make.

Keywords ─────────────────

Public corporations
Trading organisations owned and controlled by the state. Some public corporations are referred to as nationalised industries. In the 1980s many public corporations were privatised.

Co-operative societies
Trading organisations based on the idea of 'self-help'. The ideals of the *co-operative movement* extend far beyond retailing.

Municipal enterprises
Local authorities engage in a wide variety of trading activities but profit is seldom the only aim.

***Ultra vires* rule**
An organisation can only act within its legal powers. If it acts *ultra vires* (beyond its powers), its actions can be challenged before a court. Until the Companies Act 1989, the rule was usually associated with companies.

Public corporations and privatisation

When the government owns an industry the legal form it adopts is usually that of a public corporation. These are often termed nationalised industries. In 1976 the

National Economic Development Office (NEDO) defined nationalised industries as those public corporations:

(a) whose assets are in public ownership and vested in a public corporation;
(b) whose board members are not civil servants;
(c) whose boards are appointed by a Secretary of State;
(d) which are primarily engaged in industrial or other trading activities.

You will see from this definition that nationalised industries were those public corporations which *traded* with the public, i.e. they existed by selling their wares to the public in much the same way as a business.

Since 1979 the following nationalised industries have been privatised:

● British Telecom;
● British Gas;
● British Aerospace;
● British Airways;
● British Airports Authority;
● National Bus Company;
● National Freight Corporation.

Although not classified as nationalised industries Britoil and Enterprise Oil were public corporations which were also privatised.

The government also sold off companies in which it held a controlling shareholding. These included:

● The Rover Group;
● Rolls Royce;
● Jaguar;
● Ferranti;
● Cable and Wireless;
● Amersham International;

and numerous smaller companies acquired by the National Enterprise Board during the 1970s. The government also privatised the various Water Boards which were in public ownership.

At the beginning of 1990, plans were being made to privatise the electricity industry. This left the Post Office, British Coal and British Rail as the remaining nationalised industries of any significant size.

There remained many public corporations which were not nationalised industries and which are unlikely to the privatised. Examples of these are the

Bank of England and the BBC.

Choose one of the former nationalised industries listed above and discover as much as you can about it in the five years before privatisation and its history since privatisation. With the aid of tables, compare such things as its turnover, profitability (or otherwise), rate of investment, number of employees and organisational/management structure. What conclusions can you draw from your research?

The privatisation debate

Why privatise?

1 The ideological argument. It would be a mistake simply to see privatisation as a way of the government raising money and thus being able to reduce taxation, or a method by which consumers can be given greater choice. Privatisation is an ideological shift in the way in which society is organised rather than a response to the supposed inefficiencies of the nationalised industries.

The Conservative governments of the 1980s and early 1990s held the belief that the price system is the most efficient way to run the economy and that the price system brings about an optimum allocation of resources. The classical economists, such as Adam Smith, argued that this optimality was brought about by the 'invisible hand' of self interest, i.e. by everyone striving to maximise their own individual benefit, and was regulated by the forces of competition. Competition between businesses, it was argued, protected the consumer from being exploited. Many twentieth century economists, notably Keynes, have disagreed with this view.

In recent years right-wing economists, such as Milton Friedman, have argued for a return to classical values. It is for this reason that they are called the neo (new) classicists. According to this school of thought, the market economy is essentially self-regulating and efficient. Again, according to this view problems such as inflation and unemployment are the result of too much state interference. Thus, in order to have a well-run economy it is essential to reduce the role of the state to a minimum so that the maximum percentage of the economy will be self-regulating.

Thus, privatisation had gone beyond selling-off nationalised industries. The government had forced local authorities to sell council houses, to charge more economic rents for council houses and to sell off some of their other assets. At the beginning of the 1990s the government was moving on to the privatisation of *merit goods* such as education and *public goods* such as public health provision.

This is the philosophical argument for privatisation and a market economy. In addition to this, there are several other points which we will now consider.

2 Crowding out. Those in favour of privatising nationalised industries have argued that they crowd-out investment to other industries. It is said that the enormous demands that they make on the capital market starve other industries of funds. It is also argued that politicians and others who control nationalised industries are not constrained by the economics of the market place. They argue that this makes them inefficient and that this in turn has a bad effect upon the whole economy.

3 The abuse of monopoly power. Some nationalised industries are monopolies and it could be argued that a state monopoly is more disadvantageous to the consumer than a private one. This is because there is no higher authority to protect the consumer's interests. The consumer, therefore, has to tolerate the lack of choice and high prices associated with monopoly with little hope of redress.

4 Bureaucracy. It is argued that nationalisation creates over-large and over-bureaucratic organisations which, therefore, suffer from dis-economies of scale. Evidence of this is the frequent reorganisation of nationalised industries and, often, the splitting of administration into regional boards, etc.

5 Lack of incentive. Although it would not be desirable for nationalised industries to maximise their profits, it could be argued that the lack of the profit motive removes the spur of efficiency which private enterprises have.

6 The problem of declining industries. Those industries which are faced with contracting markets, such as the railways, have a particular problem. The shrinking market forces up their unit costs. A commercial organisation would get round this by diversification. Nationalised industries, however, are prevented from doing this by terms of the Acts which established

them. Thus, they have declining business but are not allowed to branch out into anything else. Indeed, the decision of the Conservative government to sell off the profitable sections of some of the nationalised industries, e.g. British Transport Hotels, worsened the situation for such industries by leaving them only the unprofitable parts of the industry.

7 Political interference. The sound administration of nationalised industries is often undermined by politicians interfering in the industries' policies for short-term political gains. An example of this would be a ministerial order not to raise prices in an attempt to combat inflation.

Arguments for public ownership

There are still many people who believe that the public ownership and control of industries is advantageous. We will now consider some of the arguments which are put forward.

1 The ideological argument. As with privatisation, the most potent argument for public ownership of industries is the ideological one. By force of circumstance the Labour Party has had to shift its stance on nationalisation, i.e. it would be very difficult to re-nationalise many of the privatised industries. However, the socialist idea of public ownership is well summed up in Clause IV of the 1918 Labour Party Constitution. This said that its object was to 'to secure for the workers by hand or by brain the full fruits of their industry and the most equitable distribution thereof that may be possible, upon the basis of *common ownership* of the *means of production distribution and exchange*, and the best obtainable system of popular administration and control of each industry or service'.

2 Economies of scale. There are many industries which are best organised on a very large scale. A good example of this would be electricity. To have several electricity companies supplying electricity to one town would be very inefficient. The nationalisation of an industry should enable it to benefit from all the possible economies of scale and avoid *the duplication of resources*.

3 Capital expenditure. Some industries demand such major investment that only the government is capable of providing the funds. Such an argument was advanced to support the nationalisation of iron and steel in 1967. It might also apply to coal, railways and atomic energy. In addition to capital expenditure, some industries demand large spending on *research and development*. In the case of atomic energy and aircraft it was decided that this could only adequately be met by the government.

4 *Short-termism*. A variation of the argument above is the one concerned with short-termism. Many people argue that British industry is being damaged by the tendency of investors to look for quick returns. This leads to important long term projects being overlooked or starved of funds. In a nationalised industry it may be possible to pursue important long term development projects which would not be possible under the more exacting conditions of private enterprise.

5 *Preventing the abuse of monopoly power*. Where many economies of scale are obtainable, it is quite possible that left to themselves private organisations would become monopolies. This could well be true with industries such as gas, electricity and telephones. Nationalisation can ensure that they are administered in the public interest and not just for private profit, thereby gaining the benefits of large-scale production without the abuses of monopoly.

6 *Control of the economy*. The nationalisation of industries may enable a government to pursue its economic policies on investment, employment and prices through the operation of the industries concerned. For example, it might hold down prices in the nationalised industries as a counter-inflationary measure or, alternatively, invest to create employment in depressed areas of the economy.

7 *Special pricing policies*. The fact that a nationalised industry is usually a monopoly may allow it to change different prices to different customers. This may be for one of two reasons. The first is to *maximise revenue*. In this it would be acting no differently from a private *discriminating monopolist* (*see* Chapter 16). Examples of this can be seen when British Rail offers special fares such as 'Awaydays' or 'Inter-City Savers' to customers. The second is to give *preference to socially needy customers*. A nationalised industry may offer special low rates to customers such as old aged pensioners. Free bus passes for old aged pensioners can be seen as an example of this.

8 *Social benefits*. A product or service may be supplied to the public below cost price where this is considered beneficial. An example of this might be postal services supplied to the more remote parts of the country. Another example is commuter rail fares; these are effectively subsidised because the inconvenience and cost of these customers switching to the roads would be unacceptable.

9 *Strategic reasons*. The government might find it necessary to nationalise an industry considered vital for the defence of the country. Thus, for example, the aerospace industry in Britain was nationalised to keep it in existence (though it was later privatised). The defence implications of nuclear power were also a reason for ensuring that this was a nationalised industry. *Key industries* of less obvious strategic significance, such as iron and steel, coal and transport, might be seen as vital to the defence of the country in times of war.

10 *Industrial relations*. It is argued that nationalisation will improve industrial relations. This argument would seem hard to substantiate. It should be remembered, however, that many of the nationalised industries are *declining industries* and, therefore, problems in industrial relations are to be expected.

Control of nationalised industries

Accountability

So long as there are public corporations, there will remain the problem of how they are controlled and directed. Business organisations in the private sector are controlled, ultimately, by their owners – in the case of companies this would be the shareholders. With nationalised industries the ultimate owners are the whole population. We will now examine the manner in which nationalised industries are held accountable to their 'owners'.

1 *Legal accountability*. Public corporations are corporate bodies and thus stand in the same relation to their suppliers and customers under the law as do other corporate bodies such as companies.

2 *Additional legal restrictions*. Public corporations may only indulge in those activities which are specified in the Act of Parliament which established them.

3 *The minister*. The chairman and board of public

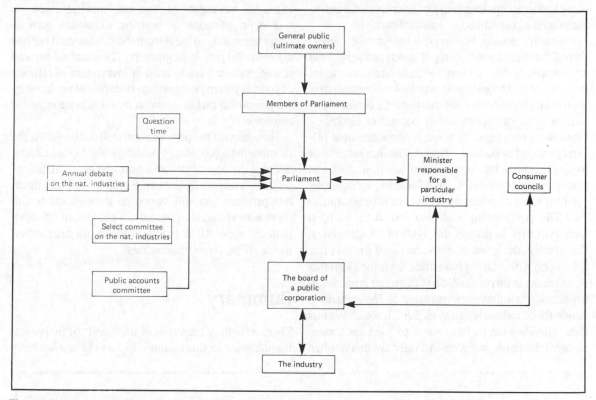

Fig. 3.3 Public accountability and the nationalised industries

corporations are appointed by a minister of state. The minister may also lay down the general policy directives which the board must follow. Ministers are not supposed to intervene in the day-to-day running of public organisations.

4 Parliament. The accounts of nationalised industries are debated by Parliament each year. The accounts are also subject to scrutiny by a parliamentary select committee which may require the chairman of a nationalised industry to appear before it. An industry is also subject to scrutiny by the Public Accounts Committee and by questions from MPs to relevant ministers in Question Time.

5 Consumer councils. The remaining nationalised industries usually have consumers' councils. These usually consist of twenty to thirty people nominated by various organisations such as trade unions. They are unpaid bodies. The councils deal with suggestions and complaints from consumers and advise both the boards and the ministers of consumers' views. Either through ignorance or apathy, consumers have made little use of these councils. In industries where con-

sumers' councils do not exist *consultative councils* are set up.

The public accountability of nationalised industries is summarised in Fig. 3.3.

The chairman and board of the corporation are nominated by the department and minister responsible, the British Railways Board, for example, is nominated by the Department of the Environment. The board is then supposed to operate along the broad lines of the policy laid down by the government but to have autonomy in the day-to-day running of the industry. The activities which any corporation may involve itself in are laid down in the Act of Parliament which established it.

Conclusion

The debate about privatisation has ideological roots. What cannot be doubted is that the privatisations of the 1980s altered the nature of the debate. The extent of privatisations 'moved the goal posts'. The Labour party had to accept that many of the privatised industries could not easily be re-nationalised.

Problems remain, however, whatever the ownership of the industries. Pricing of goods and services is an example of this. To leave British Aerospace to set the price of its aeroplanes is no problem because they are forced to compete with other manufacturers. However, we cannot choose to buy our gas or electricity from other suppliers, they are monopolies now privately instead of publicly owned. This has meant that the government has been forced to enforce special price formulas on them. British Telecom, for example, can only raise its prices by the rate of inflation minus 3%. The government was also forced to set up a Quango, Oftel, to protect the rights of its consumers. Conversely, the government sometimes forced price rises upon nationalised industries. In some cases this was to make them profitable and therefore attractive to investors when they were privatised. The remaining nationalised industries such as British Rail have had their subsidies cut to force them to work on a more commercial basis. In the case of railways this resulted in the UK having the highest rail fares in Europe.

The privatisation of problem industries such as water has removed them from the government but has not made the problems go away. The water supply and sewage systems are in need of investment of billions of pounds just to prevent their collapse. Now that they are privatised this must mean massive price rises for consumers.

How far will the privatisation trail continue? At the moment the advocates of public ownership are reeling under a decade of privatisation and the collapse of socialist systems in Eastern Europe. Will this mean that privatisation will sweep on through the health service and education because of the lack of effective political opposition? Is it possible to run such industries as if they were businesses?

Summary

There are many hundreds of thousands of individual trading units in this country. In this chapter we have

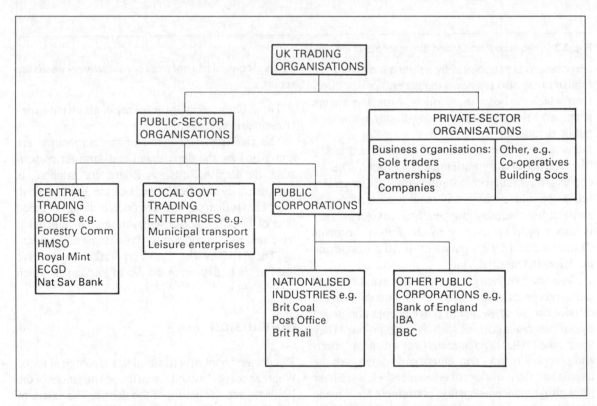

Fig. 3.4 Types of trading organisation.

discussed the legal status and commercial role of the major types of organisations which exist, comparing in some detail sole traders, partnerships and companies. Each type of organisation has its own role to play in the economy and each is regulated by particular pieces of legislation and, to a lesser extent, case law. Law provides a framework in which these various organisations operate and in so far as they produce the nation's wealth, the economy can be considered as a structure of organisations. Fig. 3.4 is a summary diagram of UK trading organisations.

Keywords

Nationalised industries
Public corporations which trade with the public.

Privatisation
The process of selling nationalised industries to the private sector. Whatever other reasons there are for privatisation, in the 1980s the main reason was ideological.

Neo classicists
Modern economists who believe that the market economy is self-regulating and efficient.

Learning project

A local survey

What is the mix of sole traders, partnerships and companies in your local commercial areas? Choose two contrasting commercial streets/areas, preferably one in the town centre and one (probably smaller) out of the town centre and draw a sketch map of each. On it show and label each organisation and choose a suitable method, e.g. colour coding, to identify what 'legal' type of organisation it is. List the organisations separately and categorise them in a suitable way, e.g. retail goods, retail service, manufacturing, etc. Account for and compare the mix of organisations you discover, e.g., relative overheads, customer base, type of community, etc.

Further ideas for learning projects

1 (a) Working in groups discuss the arguments for and against privatisation of nationalised industries.
(b) Working individually prepare a leaflet which clearly communicates the pro *or* anti-privatisation arguments.
(c) Working individually write an article of about 500 words which takes the opposite stance to that you have adopted in *(b)*.

2 Select one nationalised industry and compile a table for the latest year for which you can find figures and for the ten previous years to show *(a)* the number of people it employs; *(b)* the value of its turnover; *(c)* the capital employed; *(d)* its profit or loss.
What changes do you observe? Account for these changes. Do they suggest the industry should be privatised?

3 You and two or three of your colleagues wish to set up in business together. Your combined savings total £20,000, two of you have houses currently valued together at £200,000 with outstanding mortgages totalling £60,000. (Make further assumptions as you consider necessary but clearly state what they are.)
(a) Decide what your business is going to be. (Clearly it should be a small business, e.g. building contractor, retail shop, wine bar, computer software house.)
(b) Decide on a name for your business and design a logo and stationery.
(c) Decide whether to operate as a partnership or as a limited company. Draft articles of partnership or a memorandum and articles of association as appropriate.
(d) Explain the reasons for and the legal and financial consequences of your choice between a partnership and a limited company.

4 The tables on the next page show the world's largest trading organisations in 1971 and 1987. (We have listed more for 1971 in order to show the two top ranked UK companies.)
(a) Account for the changes in the composition of the tables and the relative positions of the companies.
(b) What are the implications of these changes for the British economy?

World's fourteen largest trading organisations 1971

Rank	Organisation	Country	Business	Sales (£mill)
1	General Motors	USA	Vehicle manufacturer	7,755
2	Standard Oil	USA	Oil industry	7,503
3	Ford Motors	USA	Vehicle manufacturer	6,195
4	Sears, Roebuck	USA	Retailing	3,830
5	General Electric	USA	General manufacturer	3,609
6	Mobil Oil	USA	Oil industry	3,349
7	IBM	USA	Business machines	3,103
8	Chrysler	USA	Vehicle manufacturer	2,895
9	Gulf Oil	USA	Oil industry	2,728
10	ITT	USA	Communication equipment	2,632
11	Royal Dutch Petrol Co	Holland	Oil industry	2,629
12	Texaco	USA	Oil industry	2,626
13	British Petroleum	UK	Oil industry	2,614
14	Shell Transport and Trading	UK	Oil industry	2,608

Source: The Times 1000 1972–73

World's ten largest trading organisations 1988

Rank	Organisation	Country	Business	Sales (£mill)
1	Mitsui	Japan	Soga Shosha*	75,310
2	C Itoh	Japan	Soga Shosha*	71,669
3	Mitsubishi	Japan	Soga Shosha*	70,230
4	General Motors	USA	Vehicle manufacturers	69,875
5	Sumitomo	Japan	Soga Shosha*	66,629
6	Marubeni	Japan	Soga Shosha*	65,896
7	Ford Motors	USA	Vehicle manufacturers	58,601
8	Shell Transport and Trading/ Royal Dutch Petroleum	UK/Neths	Oil industry	55,832
9	Nissho Iwai	Japan	Soga Shosha*	51,392
10	Exxon	USA	Crude oil/Nat gas	47,535

*Sogo shoshas: umbrella organisations which provide integrated marketing, financing, transport and information services for their member companies.

Source: The Times 1000 1989–90

4

Demography

CHAPTER OBJECTIVES

After studying this chapter you should be able to:

■ Define and evaluate the concept of optimum population and explain its relevance to the government and the organisation;

■ Describe the present structure of UK population and explain how it came about;

■ List and describe the main factors determining the structure of population;

■ Interpret and represent demographic data found in government and other statistics;

■ State the relevance of the law of diminishing returns to world population growth.

Why consider demography?

The population explosion

Organisations have become complex in the context of rising world population. The impact of the population explosion on all aspects of human life, be they economic, legal, social or political, is so immense as to almost defy analysis. Although we speak of laws, principles, wealth and so on, it is people that lie at the heart of our subject. For the organisation it provides one of its essential resources, *labour*, and also the *markets* for its goods and services. Government organisations must also make their plans on their estimates of changes in the future population. Although it would appear that population growth has stabilised in many western countries, the continuing growth of world population poses some of the most imponderable questions for the future.

Fig. 4.1 shows what is meant by the population explosion. You can see from this graph that the estimated world population was 300 million in AD 1000 and that

this slowly rose to around 728 million in AD 1750. Population then began to rise much more quickly, reaching 3,000 million by 1962 and was estimated to have passed 5,000 million in 1987. Estimates for the year 2000 envisage an increase to 6,200 million. This means that population will have risen over twenty-fold in the last 1,000 years, having been almost static for the previous 200,000 years of human history. Moreover, the majority of this growth will have taken place in 100 years. At the moment estimates of world population are being revised downward. The USA Office of Population believes that world population may only be 5,500 million by 2001. It is unlikely that it will be this small but it demonstrates how uncertain estimates are. Estimates for the year 2050 vary from 8 billion to 14 billion (1 billion = 1,000 million).

State three reasons why you consider that estimates of future population are so unreliable and inexact.

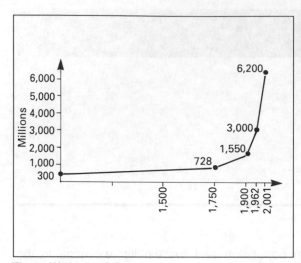

Fig 4.1 World population

Source: based on UN Department of Economic and Social Affairs, Population Division, Figures and Forecasts 1983.

Malthus (1766–1834)

Accurate population figures for Britain started with the first census of 1801. Three years earlier Malthus published the first major work on population, entitled *An Essay on the Principle of Population as it affects the Future Improvement of Society*. Malthus had noted the quickening growth of British population and was also aware of the principle of *diminishing returns* as expounded by Adam Smith and other political economists. Malthus maintained that population would continue to grow in a geometric progression (1, 2, 4, 8, 16, etc.) while world food resources would grow in an arithmetic progression (1, 2, 3, 4, 5, etc.). Since the amount of land on the planet is fixed, this would mean that there would be less and less food to feed each person. This would continue until population growth was halted by 'positive checks' of 'war, pestilence and famine'. This would give more food per person so that population would increase again, thereby causing positive checks to set in again, and so on. Thus, the gloomy forecast of Malthus was that world population would forever fluctuate around the point when most of it was starving to death. This is termed a *subsistence equilibrium*.

For a number of reasons these pessimistic forecasts did not come true in Britain. Through technological improvements, industry and agriculture became more productive, the New World and Australia provided room for expansion and, towards the end of the 19th century, parents in Britain began to limit the size of their families. Moreover, there is a debate in economic history as to whether population growth stimulated economic growth or vice versa.

You must note that the law of diminishing returns cannot be repealed, only offset. When you look at most of the Third World today, you might be forgiven for thinking that Malthus was only too right.

1 **State why Malthus's predictions did not come true for the UK.**

2 **Do you consider his predictions to be true for Third World countries? If so, what should be done to avoid them?**

The rich and the poor

There is a growing disparity between the rich areas of the world and the poor, both in proportional and aggregate terms. That is to say, the poor are poorer than they have ever been before. Population provides one of the major clues as to why this is so. It would appear that in some parts of the world, e.g. in some African countries, however fast the gross domestic product (GDP) grows, population grows faster and therefore the country is poorer in terms of GDP per head.

Asia (excluding the USSR), South America and Africa together occupy about 55% of the land surface of the Earth and have about 70% of its population, whereas Europe, North America and Australasia occupy about 45% of the Earth and have only 30% of the population. By the end of the century it is likely that the first of these two areas will have 80% of the population and the second only 20%. Obviously the poorer areas will need enormous advances in agricultural and industrial techniques to cope with this rise but most of the expertise and the capital is possessed by the richer countries. It is because of this that many people consider that a great fall in the birth rate in the poor nations is the only way out of this cycle of poverty for them. It is possible, however, that continued population growth in poor countries will only increase the bargaining power of the richer nations in world markets, thereby making the problems even worse. This is because so long as the richer nations monopolise technology and capital, they will be able to bargain for higher prices for these while the poor countries are forced to supply their products (chiefly raw materials) at even lower prices.

Factors influencing the size of population

Population is affected by three main influences: the *birth rate*; the *death rate*; and by *migration*, i.e. the net figure derived from immigration and emigration.

Table 4.1 Birth rates

Year	Birth rate (Great Britain)
1871	35.5
1911	24.5
1933	14.4

Birth rates are normally expressed in this manner, that is to say, in 1871 for every 1,000 people in the country 35.5 births took place. This is sometimes called a crude birth rate since it simply records the number of live births, with no allowance being made for infant mortality or other circumstances.

Table 4.2 Death rates

Year	Death rate (Great Britain)
1750	33.0
1851	22.7
1911	13.8

Death rates are normally expressed as the number of people in the country that died in a year per 1,000 of the population. This is sometimes called the crude death rate because it takes no account of the age of the person at death; they could be three months old or ninety years.

Net reproductive rate

By comparing the birth rate with the death rate we arrive at an overall *rate of natural increase or de-*

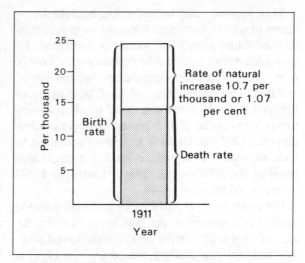

Fig. 4.2 Rate of natural increase in population.

crease in population, excluding migration. One way to illustrate this is to superimpose one bar diagram on another, as in Fig. 4.2. From Fig. 4.2 you can see that Britain had a rate of natural increase of 10.7 per 1,000 per year, or 1.07% in 1911. Today, UK population growth is virtually static. However, if we did the same exercise for India, it would show a high rate of natural increase. Later in the chapter you can see a diagram illustrating the rate of natural increase for the UK for the whole of this century, together with predictions for the future. (*See* Fig. 4.3 page 79.)

Table 4.3 Total period fertility rate

Year	TPFR (Great Britain)
1951	2.16
1966	2.78
1977	1.68
1979	1.86
1981	1.83
1984	1.80
1988	1.83

Source: CSO, Social Trends

Activity

1 Define the terms: *(a)* crude birth rate; *(b)* crude death rate; *(c)* rate of natural increases

2 What, apart from the birth rate and death rate, affects the rate of population increase?

This, however, may be misleading because the increase may be concentrated in the older age groups so that the future increase of society is threatened. To overcome this we can consider the *total period fertility rate* (TPFR). This measures the average number of children born per woman of child-bearing years (defined as aged 15–50) that would result if women survived to the end of their reproductive period. The rate must be 2.0 or above if society is to continue to have the ability to reproduce itself. We might also consider the *fertility rate*. This is births per 1,000 women aged between 16–44.

For example, in 1977 58.8 children were born for every 1,000 women in the population between the ages of 16–44. This, at the time, was the lowest postwar rate. Despite a slight rise to 64.0 in 1979, it declined to 59.6 in 1983. The rate rose slightly in the late 1980s but this was still well below that necessary for the long-term replacement of the population. There has been a similar decline in most Western European fertility rates.

Table 4.4 Fertility rate

Year	Fertility rate (Great Britain)
1900	115
1933	81
1951	72.5
1977	58.8
1979	64.0
1983	59.6
1987	61.7

Marriage and the size of family

Despite a trend towards births outside marriage, 77% of births are to married women, so the number of marriages taking place obviously has an effect upon the number of births. However, until recently the percentage of people marrying has remained fairly constant, around 85%. The age at which people marry may also have an effect. Younger marriages give more potential child-bearing years and, in addition to this, women tend to be biologically more fertile in their teens and twenties. However, age at marriage in the UK has not changed significantly. The most significant factor in British population over the last century

Examine the following statistics, all figures relate to 1985.

	Population (millions)	Area (000 km²)	Birth rate	Death rate
Ethiopia	42.3	1,222	46	19
India	765.1	3,288	45	12
Ghana	12.7	239	49	14
Mexico	78.8	1,973	44	7
Singapore	2.6	1	17	5
UK	56.5	245	13	12
Australia	15.8	7,687	15	7

1 Which country has the fastest rate of population growth?

2 Which country has the greatest/least density of population?

3 What is the rate of natural increase in Mexico?

has been the trend to smaller families. We will examine the reasons for this later, but we can note here the change from the five-to-six child family in 1870 to the present two-to-three child family.

Today, there is also a social pattern to the size of family. Social Class 1 (professional: doctors, lawyers, clerics, etc.) are most prone to have three-to-five children, but Social Class 5 (semi-skilled and unskilled employees) are most likely to have families of six and upwards. Overall, there is an inverse relation between social class and size of family. This is not only true for Britain but also for many other western countries. Ireland, however, because of the influence of Roman Catholicism, continues to have a large average size of family.

Migration

If immigration is compared with emigration, we arrive at a figure of net outflow or inflow of migrants. Demographically, migration has not had a significant effect on the size of population in Britain. On the other hand North America is an area where immigration has been very important and emigration from Ireland has actually been responsible for a decline in Ireland's population. Only on two occasions has Britain been a net gainer by migration. This is illustrated by Fig. 4.3.

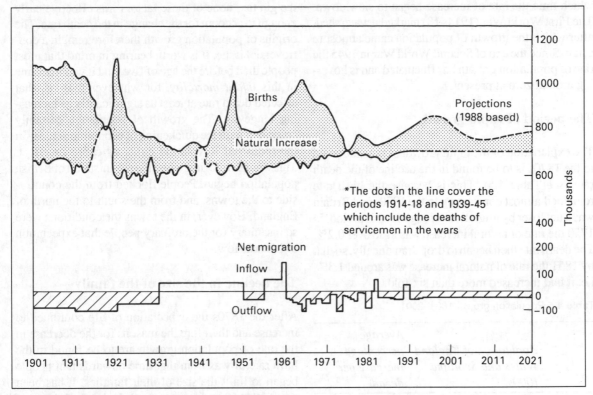

Fig. 4.3 Migration or the natural increase in population

The inflow after 1931 is explained by two factors: first, by people who had emigrated to the colonies returning because of the depression; second in the 1930s there was a large flow of refugees coming from Nazi Europe. Successive waves of immigrants from the new Commonwealth countries account for the inflow in the 1950s and early 1960s. Although the net figure is not significant, the fact that many of the immigrants were from different cultures has posed particular social and political problems. Economically the immigrants have filled a vital role in providing labour for the economy. One factor to be borne in mind is that immigrants are predominantly of working age and therefore swell the ranks of the productive part of society. Balanced against this is the fact that the emigrants which Britain has lost have often been highly trained and dynamic; this has sometimes been called the 'brain drain'.

Activity

We hear a lot about immigration to the UK but emigration is usually greater.

1 **Consider emigration and say:** *(a)* **where emigrants go to;** *(b)* **who are the emigrants?**

2 **Do you consider that emigration helps the UK by reducing population pressure?**

The growth of British population

A census of the total population in the UK is conducted in the first year of each decade – 1971, 1981 etc. A census is usually followed by a more detailed census of 10% of the population five years later. The first census was conducted in 1801 and one was held every ten years thereafter, with the exception of 1941. Calculations and estimates are few and unreliable before 1801 and come from such things as the Domesday Book (1086), the Poll Tax of Richard II (1379), and the *Observations* of Gregory King (1690).

British population grew rapidly up to the 1870s, at

which time the rate of increase began to slow down. The First World War (1914–18) marked a watershed, after which the growth of population came almost to a halt. Since the end of Second World War in 1945 the rate of population growth has fluctuated and is hovering around zero at present.

The period of rapid growth

The explanation of the rapid growth of population up to the 1870s is to be found in the decline of the death rate (*see* Table 4.5). This is because the birth rate remained almost constant up to the 1870s and Britain was a net loser by migration throughout this period. In 1750 the rate of natural increase was little over 0.2%. The death rate then began to drop dramatically, so that by 1851 the rate of natural increase was around 1.3%, i.e. it had increased more than six-fold.

Table 4.5 Population growth 1801–2001

	Population of England Wales and Scotland (000s)	Average percentage increase per decade
1801	10,501	
		13.9
1871	26,072	
		11.5
1911	40,891	
		4.5
1941*	46,605	
		5.8
1971	54,369	
		0.8
1981	54,815	
		1.0
1987	55,355	
		—
1991*	55,941	
		1.4
2001*	57,433	

* = estimate
Source: Annual Abstract of Statistics

One of the main reasons advanced to explain this decline in the death rate is the improvement in medical knowledge and provision, together with the elimination of many epidemic diseases such as plague, smallpox, typhus, typhoid and cholera in the 19th century. In addition to this, there were improvements in diet, housing, clothing and water supply. It has even been argued that the reimposition of the gin tax in 1751 had a significant effect. However, these do not provide an adequate explanation. With the possible exception of

the gin tax, none of these factors was effective early enough to account for the change in the death rate. The origins of population growth therefore remain a controversial issue. It is worth bearing in mind that most people died before the age of five, and it was a decline in this *infant mortality*, for whatever reasons, that affected death rate at least as significantly as increasing longevity. The growth of population certainly coincided with the quickening of economic activity in the Industrial Revolution either as cause or effect. This was also the time when the urbanisation of British population began. People flocked from the countryside to the towns, and from the south to the north of England. However, in the towns the conditions were so insanitary for the ordinary people that expectation of life was low.

The decline in the size of the family

After the 1870s the expectation of life continued to increase and therefore the reasons for the decrease in the rate of population growth are to be found in the birth rate. It was from that time onwards that people began to limit the size of their families. It has been argued that up to this time people had seen children as a source of income and when child labour was forbidden they were discouraged from bearing children. While this argument is of dubious value, it is certainly true that the new Education Acts of 1870 and 1876 increased the cost of bringing up children, i.e. if they were at school they could not be earning. Perhaps it was the decline in infant mortality that caused people to take a different economic attitude towards children. But certainly from this time parents began to want higher standards for their children and realised that limiting the size of their family would make this possible. The new age of Victorian prosperity presented many goods which competed for the income of households and one way to have more income left to buy them was to have fewer children. Doubtless, many people had small families simply because this became the social norm. The emancipation of women and the availability of birth-control also played a part, as did the tendency for people to marry at a later age. It took time, however, for the knowledge and availability of contraception to filter down the social structure.

After 1918 population growth became much slower.

In addition to the influences discussed above, the great economic depression in the 1930s also dissuaded people from having children. Although there has been some increase in the size of the family since the Second World War, it would appear that the smaller family is here to stay.

Population since 1945

Looked at in the long term, the changes in population since 1945 may appear small and to be a continuation of previous trends. However, small aggregate changes may bring with them profound changes in the structure of population, with important consequences for all organisations in the economy. The Second World War, for example, brought large numbers of women into employment and they have stayed there, thereby affecting both production and consumption. Similarly, the 'baby boom' of the late 1940s brought changes in education and public services.

The rise in the birth rate immediately after the War may be partly due to families being reunited. However, there were more significant longer-term reasons. One such reason was people getting married younger. This may be accounted for by increased prosperity and the improved opportunities for married women to work. With increased prosperity it was possible to afford both more consumer goods and children. A larger family became a smaller proportionate burden, especially when the benefits of the welfare state, for example family allowances (1946) and national health insurance (1948), are taken into account. Once again, we should not discount the importance of social fashion in parents' choice of the size of their family.

As predicted, the high birth rates of the late 1940s were followed by lower rates in the 1950s. However, in the 1960s the birth rate began to rise more rapidly than predicted. This was followed by the fall in the birth rate of the late 1970s to the all-time low of 11.6 in 1977. This may have been partly due to the fact that child-rearing became a longer and more expensive task. The school leaving age was raised to 16 in 1972, in addition to which the proportion of students continuing into further and higher education increased sharply. Despite the conditions of economic stagnation people still continued to expect a rising standard of living. This may have been a further motive for limiting the size of the family, or for having no

Table 4.6 The birth rate since 1945 (Great Britain)

Year	Birth rate
1947	20.5
1950	15.9
1955	15.0
1961	17.4
1963	19.2
1965	17.6
1970	16.1
1975	12.3
1977	11.6
1979	13.0
1981	13.0
1985	13.3
1987	13.6

Source: COS and FPIS

children at all. In addition to this, the decline in the birth rate was influenced by a decreasing proportion of people marrying (7.1 per 1,000 in 1981 and 6.9 in 1986) and by an increase in the average age at which people married (26 for men and 24 for women). It is difficult to assess the role of birth control and abortion in this but, certainly, the increased availability and efficacy of birth control must have had a depressing effect on the birth rate. In 1987 there were 166,000 legal abortions in Great Britain, which was the highest number on record. This compared with a total of 748,000 live births. Abortion accounted for the termination of 18% of all pregnancies.

Death rates have declined since 1945 as a result of long-term environmental improvements. In 1987 the death rate was 11.5. Migration has varied as an influence on population. Immediately after the war there was a wave of emigration from the UK with many people going to Canada, Australia and New Zealand. The flow of immigrants from the Commonwealth made Britain a gainer by migration, the net inflow being 97,000 people in the period 1951–61. This has been reversed since the early 1960s and Britain is once again a net loser by migration (*see* Fig. 4.3). The 1970s saw a net outflow of 358,000 people whereas the net figure for the 1980s was close to zero.

The infant mortality rate has declined since 1945 because of improved medical techniques and the introduction of the welfare state. But it is still higher than in some countries, e.g. Sweden (6), and it is unlikely that it will decline much over the next few years.

Table 4.7 Infant mortality (deaths under the age of 1 per 1,000 live births)

Year	Infant mortality
1951	31.1
1971	17.9
1975	16.0
1978	13.3
1981	11.2
1984	9.6
1987	9.1

Source: CSO

Keywords

Demography
The study of population characteristics.

Birth rate
The number of live births in a year per 1,000 of the population.

Death rate
The number of deaths in a year per 1,000 of the population.

Rate of natural increase
Arrived at by comparing the birth rate with the death rate, but excluding migration.

Total period fertility rate
The number of children born per women of child bearing years (15–50).

Migration
The net outflow or inflow of population arrived at by comparing immigration with emigration.

Infant mortality
The number of children which die before the age of one (can also be before the age of four) per 1,000 live births.

The structure of British population

The age and sex distribution of the population

This refers to the number of people in each age group. The most important divisions are 0–15, 16–64 and 65 and over. The relative size of the 16–64 group is important because it is from here that the majority of

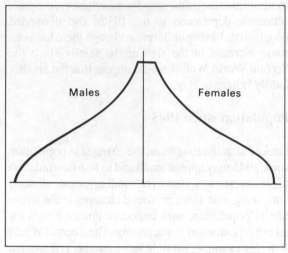

Fig. 4.4 Simplified population pyramid typical of the late 19th century in the UK.

the working population is drawn.

Both age and sex distribution in society can be presented as a pyramid. In a population where there was an even age and sex distribution a smooth pyramid would be the result. The population is divided between men and women and then between age groups at five-year intervals. This is a variant on a histogram. Fig. 4.4 is a simplified diagrammatic representation of a population pyramid for the late 19th century in Great Britain. This smooth and even distribution is brought about because it was a period of population expansion and therefore each new generation was larger than the preceding one. Increasing mortality in the older age groups narrows the pyramid until at the age of 90 there is virtually no-one left. Decline in the birth rate would pinch in the bottom of the pyramid. This is well illustrated by Fig. 4.5.

The number of male births to female births does not usually vary much, with about 105 boys born for every 100 girls. Subsequently, mortality is greater for males in every age group, so that by the age of 85 there are 324 women for every 100 men. There are at present one and a half million more women in the country than men.

The expectation of life also varies. At present a man can expect to live 71.7 years, a woman 77.5. Life expectation has risen continuously since 1901 when men could expect 48.1 years and women 51.8. The discrepancy in the expectation of life of men and women is explained by a number of factors; men work in more

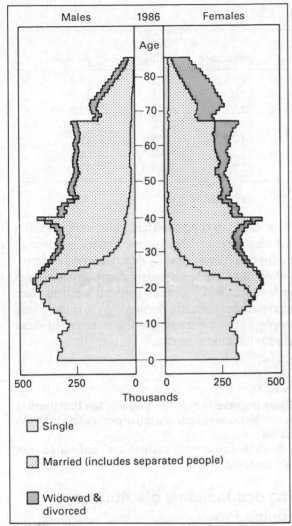

Fig. 4.5 Population: by sex, age and marital status, England and Wales.
Source: Office of Population Censuses and Surveys.

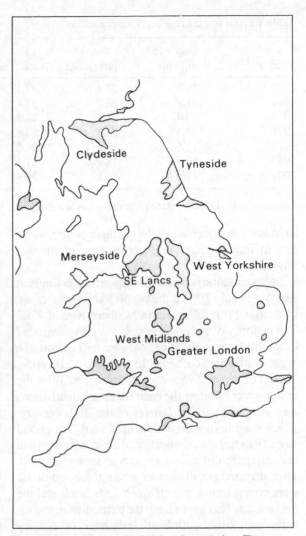

Fig. 4.6 Areas of greatest density of population. The names of the major conurbations are also shown.

hazardous occupations, more men are killed in wars, and men are more susceptible than women to a number of killing diseases such as lung cancer and coronary illnesses. In recent years, however, there has been a growing tendency for women to become more susceptible to diseases which were traditionally associated with men.

Activity

1 **Describe the demographic factors which are responsible for the shape of the population pyramid.**

2 **There are two very sharp steps (around 40 years and 67 years). What accounts for these?**

3 **Study Table 4.8 (on the next page). State three consequences of the fall in the number of children in the 1990s.**

Geographical distribution

The surface area of the UK is 244,104 km² with a population of 56.9 million. This gives a population density of 254 per km², one of the highest in the world. This population is spaced very unevenly, however, (*see* Fig. 4.6) and its distribution is not static. There

Table 4.8 The age distribution of the population

Year	Under 15 millions	percentage	15-64 millions	percentage	Over 65 millions	percentage
1939	10.0	21.4	32.4	69.7	4.2	8.9
1961	11.9	23.4	33.4	65.0	6.1	11.8
1971	13.4	24.2	34.8	62.8	7.2	12.9
1976	13.4	24.0	34.8	62.3	7.6	13.6
1981	11.6	20.6	36.2	64.2	8.5	15.2
1987	10.7	18.9	37.3	65.6	8.8	15.5
2001 (projection)	12.0	20.1	36.9	62.3	10.4	17.6

Source: Social Trends. HMSO (Note: figures are still given as 15-64 rather than 16-64.)

have been many changes during this century, some due to immigration but most because of internal migration.

The population is predominantly urban. In England and Wales only 20% of the people live in rural areas, in Scotland it is 28%, and in Northern Ireland 45%. The majority of the urban population is concentrated in the major conurbations, i.e. Greater London, the West Midlands, South East Lancashire, Merseyside, West Yorkshire, Tyneside and Clydeside. With the exception of London, the basis for these conurbations was the *old staple industries* of the 19th century, which were in turn dependent upon coal. The period since 1918 has seen the decline of these industries and the emergence of new ones such as motor vehicles. This attracted population to where these industries were concentrated; principally the Midlands and the South-East. This gave rise to the phenomenon known as the 'drift to the South-East'. In the later 20th century many of these 'new' industries have declined so that many former areas of prosperity, such as the Midlands, have become depressed. At present the growth industries, such as computer software have tended to be in the tertiary sector. Financial services, for example, have greatly expanded. Despite the fact that these can be decentralised they have, nevertheless, tended to concentrate in the South-East. Thus, the South-East and East Anglia have tended to expand during the 1970s and 1980s leaving the rest of the UK behind.

Another feature of recent years has been the decay of the inner cities. Thus, although the South-East has gained population, London has lost people as they have moved out to the Home Counties such as Hertfordshire, Buckinghamshire and Berkshire. In these Home Counties population has grown more than 30% in the last 20 years. These people remain, however, to a great extent economically dependent on London.

A separate trend has been the depopulation of rural areas such as mid Wales and northern Scotland. Here population has actually declined. As it is the young people who move away, the age structure of these areas is left most distorted.

Study the map in Fig. 4.6. You will see that there is a considerable concentration of population in South Wales.

State three industries which are associated with this concentration.

The occupational distribution of population

This describes the distribution of the *working population* between different occupations. The working population comprises all those people between the ages of 16 and 65 who are working or available for work, and thus includes the registered unemployed. Also included in the figure are those over 65 who are still working. However, housewives not otherwise employed, those living off private means and those unable to work, e.g. the chronically sick, the insane and those in prison, are excluded from the working population.

The working population in the UK represents 49.5% of the total population. In the UK there is a growing tendency for women to work. In 1971, 37% of the working population were women, by 1987 this had risen to 39%. It is this tendency which has been responsible for the growing size of the workforce in recent years. The percentage of women working is the highest figure for any developed country. The reason for this is that many married women entered the working population in the period 1939–45 and this practice has since continued and increased.

It is estimated that by the end of the century 50% of the working population may be women. This picture is modified by the fact that a much higher proportion of women's jobs are part-time.

Table 4.9 Employment and unemployment in the UK (in thousands)

	1971	1979	1984	1987
Agriculture, forestry and fishing	432	368	340	322
Energy and water supply	797	721	630	497
Extraction of minerals and ores other than fuels, manufacture of metal, mineral products and chemicals	1,278	1,143	794	767
Metal goods, engineering and vehicles industries	3,705	3,372	2,595	2,261
Other manufacturing industries	3,102	2,745	2,128	2,117
Construction	1,207	1,248	984	1,009
Distribution, hotels and catering	3,678	4,252	4,323	4,464
Transport and communications	1,550	1,476	1,304	1,345
Banking, finance, insurance and business services	1,336	1,649	1,881	2,328
Miscellaneous	5,036	6,185	6,183	6,700
All industries and services	22,122	23,157	21,162	21,810
Registered unemployed	792	1,295	3,159	2,659

Occupations might be classified as:

(a) primary – extraction of raw materials, agriculture, fishing, etc;

(b) secondary – all manufacturing processes;

(c) tertiary – the provision of services, e.g. finance, education, the civil service and the armed forces.

As a rule, an underdeveloped country would have a large percentage of its total population working and concentrated mainly in primary industries. An advanced economy would have a smaller percentage working population with a larger tertiary sector. In the UK the tertiary sector represents about 68% of the working population. The proportion of the population which is available for work is affected by demographic factors such as the age structure of the population and by other factors such as society's attitude to women working, the school leaving age and the retirement age. These factors have meant that, while the number of people available for work has risen during the century from 32.4 million in 1911 to 36.9 million in 1987, the percentage that are working has, until recently, fallen.

Studying Table 4.9 should convince you that things are changing rapidly in the occupational distribution of the UK population. In recent years there has been a virtual collapse of the manufacturing sector of the economy. This is associated with what is termed the *deindustrialisation* of the economy, i.e. the decline of secondary industries and the rise of tertiary industries. All the industries after 'Construction' in Table 4.9 are tertiary industries. You can see that it is only here that there has been any expansion in employment. Even in this sector, improvements in technology have limited the demand for labour. Another factor limiting employment was the general depression in the economy. You can see that in 1984 21.1 million were employed while 3.2 million were unemployed.

In the later 1980s the economy began to recover. Unemployment declined and employment increased so that the workforce, including the 2.8 million self-employed and the registered unemployed stood at over 28 million.

1 **Study Table 4.9 and identify:** *(a)* **the industry which has experienced the greatest percentage drop in employment since 1971;** *(b)* **the industry which has experienced the greatest percentage growth in employment since 1971 (ignore 'Miscellaneous').**

2 **Account for these changes.**

Demographic constraints

Consequences of the changing structure of population

For the last two centuries UK population has been increasing in size and has been ageing. Most discussion has centred on the consequences of this but now the future of British population seems less certain. It is therefore necessary for us to consider the consequences of the various alternatives.

If population is increasing in size then, other things being equal, there is less land and other resources available per head. In the short term this could lead to a tendency to import more goods, thus worsening the balance of payments. On the other hand there would be an increasing domestic market for goods which could lead to increasing economies of scale. In the 19th century Britain's population growth was accompanied by great technological improvements. Thus, increasing population was attended by increasing prosperity.

A declining population would, other things being equal, lead to more resources being available per head. However, it is possible that, lacking the stimulus of population growth, there would be less incentive to improve technology. This could have an adverse effect on the long-term prospects of the economy.

If the population were becoming younger, then there would be a smaller percentage dependence of the aged and a changing pattern of consumption away from geriatric hospitals and the like to a greater demand for schools, pop records, etc. In addition, a younger population would be more flexible and dynamic and more able to take advantage of technological change. There would also be greater mobility of labour, both occupational and geographical.

Throughout this century up to the 1970s the population of the UK has been ageing but there has been a rising percentage of young people. Consequently, the working population has had to provide for a growing dependent population. This has meant both more schools and more old age pensions. The ageing of the population has also made it less mobile and less able to take advantage of technological change. In addition there has been growing competition for resources such as houses and land. The growth of the tertiary sector has also meant that there is a decreasing percentage of the working population involved in the manufacture of goods. The building of more schools and more senior citizens' homes both make demands on the nation's capital. Although education might be regarded as increasing society's productivity in the long run, services for the old do not do so. When these factors are considered together, they may partly account for the UK's depressing economic growth figures over the last 30 years.

The changing geographical distribution of the population also has economic and social consequences. In an area of declining population it is usually the young and active who move away, leaving a distorted population structure behind them with an even more intractable unemployment problem.

The future structure of population

Although current estimates are being revised downwards, world population continues to increase and there will still be several billion more mouths to feed in the next half-century. However, due to a combination of circumstances demography will actually be working in favour of Britain over the next 25 years. The dependency ratio – the ratio of dependent population to working population – reached a peak in 1974 and is now declining.

Since the mid-1960s the number of births has been declining and the fertility rate has dropped to 56.8. The number of children under 15 has fallen since 1973. Fig. 4.7 shows that the main growth sector for population over the decade 1985–95 is the 25–59 age group and that the fall will be in the 15–24 bracket. We can predict these changes with accuracy because, obviously, the people have already been born. You can also see that the number of people retiring will actually *decline*. This is because of the sharp decline in the birth rate in the 1920s and also because of the number killed in the 1939–45 War. The decline in the number of teens and early twenties is caused by the low birth rate of the mid 1970s. As a result of these factors, dependence will decrease and the average age of the population is likely to fall from the present 33.7 years to 31.5 in 1995.

However, the dependency ratio could be misleading if a larger number of people go on to higher

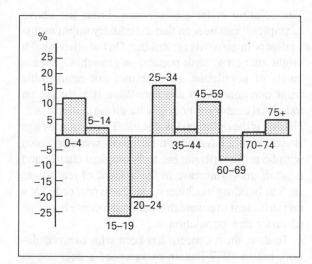

Fig. 4.7 Percentage change in the age structure of the population 1985–1995. *Source:* Annual Abstract of Statistics

education or there is a rise in the number of the very old, since they make the greatest demand on welfare services. Recent work at the Office of Population Censuses and Surveys suggest this will not be so; educational activity, it suggests, has passed its peak and, although it may rise in the late 1980s, it will not reach the levels of the mid-1970s. Similarly, it is envisaged that hospital activity for the very old will decline continuously until the end of the century. It is possible to conclude, therefore, that Britain's dependency burden will decline until the end of the century. This, however, is to see it only in terms of numbers. It is quite likely that the real cost of dependency will rise. In the case of the old aged this may be brought about as more complicated and expensive medical techniques become available. Also, at the other end of the scale, the cost of education is growing as we need to equip or re-equip schools with such resources as computers.

Activity

What effect do you consider that a fall in the average age of population would have upon:

(a) **the pattern of common demand;**
(b) **taxes and public expenditure;**
(c) **job prospects for the young;**
(d) **the dependency ratio;**
(e) **the mobility of labour.**

The relationship of demography to government policy

For many centuries population was relatively stable and people lived in village communities which were in the main both economically and legally self-regulating. Such law as existed was mainly common law. However, under the twin pressures of population growth and industrialisation, the organisational complexity of society has increased and *statute law* is now the dominant form of law. Indeed, nearly all aspects of society are today regulated by legislation.

Education was once the prerogative of the few and was either provided privately or by the church. Today it is obligatory for everyone between the ages of five and sixteen. The raising of the school leaving age has decreased the relative size of the working population. In addition, many people have continued in education long after sixteen. Many employers today are obliged or persuaded to give day-release or block-release to their younger employees thereby, once again, reducing the working population and increasing the size of the vast educational industry. In a technologically-based society, however, it is increasingly important to have trained people. It is also becoming important to educate for leisure.

The *laissez-faire* State of 19th century England believed that health was the individual's responsibility but, as population was crammed into insanitary town life, the Government was forced to introduce public health legislation. It became obvious that public health was indivisible and that disease was no respecter of social class. The State's involvement with health grew and now there exists a welfare state. Today it is considered important not only to provide medical services but to ensure a healthy environment in which prevention is as important as cure. The government's involvement stretches from the provision of hospitals to printing health warnings on packets of cigarettes. On the one hand these measures have increased the size of population, while the provision of free contraception and readily available abortion must have modified demographic trends.

Housing was once entirely the concern of the individual but pressure on resources has meant that the governments have interfered with the market mechanism through Rent Acts, the provision of council houses, and through the provision of tax relief to encourage ownership. The competition for houses has also led to changes in the private sector, with the growth of the building society as one of the most important financial institutions. The crowding together of people has also meant a multitude of planning regulations and controls on building. In an increasingly complex society, a government also has to intervene through such measures as the Health and Safety at Work, etc, Act 1974 and through legislation on prices and incomes. Migration was once a demographic influence but today it has become a social and political problem on which, once again, the government legislates.

Thus, it is possible to see that population is not just the back-drop against which economic and social life is played out, but an all important influence upon individuals, organisations and the Government.

State three aspects of government policy which you consider have an effect upon the size and structure of population.

The concept of the optimum population

The optimum population may be defined as that size and structure of population which is most conducive to the betterment of the wealth and welfare of a society. If a population is too small in relation to resources, *underpopulation* exists; if it is too large, a country is suffering from *overpopulation*. However, it is very difficult to quantify these ideas.

Singapore has turned the seeming disadvantage of overpopulation into an advantage by industrialisation. Conversely, New Zealand has turned the apparent disadvantage of underpopulation to its advantage through agriculture.

The idea of optimum population must, therefore, also depend upon the level of technology, the amount of capital per head and the ability of a population to adapt to change. It is possible to conclude that if population is growing at a greater rate than gross national product (GNP) then there is overpopulation.

The solution is far less obvious. From the above examples it can be seen that the country might industrialise or improve its agriculture. On the other hand it might attempt to limit population growth. Optimum levels of population are therefore not comparable from one country to another. What is right for an industrial country is not right for an agricultural one. Neither is the optimum level static. Two centuries ago Britain would have been disastrously overpopulated with 56 million people but technological change and *capitalisation* (increase in the amount of real assets such as building machinery, etc.) have proceeded at a rate sufficient to ensure that national income has gone up faster than population.

To date, most concern has been with overpopulation, but in 1977 Britain experienced a decrease in population, probably for the first time in peacetime since the Black Death in the 14th century. Many people fear that this may have an adverse effect on the economy, i.e. it might lose the spur to economic growth and the dynamism that population growth provides. While the Green Party may say a stabilisation of economic growth is desirable, industry is now seriously worried about the lack of young people to recruit into the workforce in the 1990s.

Examine the following table and compare it with the table on page 78.
The figures relate to 1985.

	GDP/head $
Ethiopia	110
India	270
Ghana	380
Mexico	2,080
Singapore	7,420
UK	8,460
Australia	10,830

1 On the basis of these figures, comment on the relationship between density of population as the level of prosperity.

2 Using the figures as illustration, comment on the concept of the optimum level of population.

Keywords

Population pyramid
A graphical method of presenting the age and sex distribution of the population.

Age distribution
The number of people in each age group 0–4 years, 5–9 years etc.

Sex distribution
The male-female structure of the population.

Geographical distribution
Where people live.

Occupational distribution
The distribution of the working population between different occupations.

Dependency ratio
The relationship between the non-working (dependent) population and the working population.

Optimum population
That size and structure of population which is most conducive to the betterment of the wealth and welfare of society.

Learning project

The demographic time-bomb

Consider the following article which was taken from *Education Today* by David Johnson in January 1990.

During the 1990s the UK faces an almost unprecedented demographic crisis. It is going to run out of young people.

In the baby boom years of the 1960s, up to 950,000 children were born each year. Thus, in the 1970s and 1980s there were similar numbers of teenagers looking for jobs each year. By 1979 the number of births had dropped to 657,000, a decline of about one third. It does not take much mental arithmetic to work out that in the mid-1990s industry is going to be lacking hundreds of thousands of potential recruits.

Cumulatively, the picture looks even worse. Taking the vital 15-29 years old age group as a whole, there will be about two million less people in 1996 than there were in 1987. By 2001 it will be close to three million less.

This presents severe problems for industry. Where is it to get the hands which it so desperately needs if the economy is to expand as we would wish? Coupled with this is the lamentable state of post-16 education in the UK. It appears that the UK is facing both a shortage of numbers and of skills.

Similar problems are faced by many of our trading partners. Germany, for example, faces the prospect of a declining population although the changes in the East may save it. France has an active programme to encourage childbirth.

Despite a multitude of UK government schemes to encourage post-school education, participation rates in higher education are very low. Nearly three times as many school pupils per thousand of the age group go to university in France, Germany and Japan than in the UK. Expenditure on polytechnics in the UK has been almost static in real terms in the last few years. The government scheme for student loans is hardly designed to encourage young people to continue in full-time education.

At the other end of the demographic scale is the growth in the number of the very old. Although the number of those of pensionable age is not expanding very rapidly, the number of over-85s is. These people are disproportionately expensive to maintain as the costs of medical treatment and the possibilities of ever more sophisticated treatments escalate.

Drastic action is needed by the government to face up to the lack of hands, the lack of skills and the growing burden of welfare services.

Complete the following tasks.

1 Prepare graphs or bar charts to illustrate the fall in the number of young people over the next decade.

2 What likely solutions to the shortage of new recruits in the 1990s are there?

3 Account for the seemingly contradictory factors of continuing high unemployment, (increasing participation rates (% of people working), and the decline in the number of young people.

4 What are the likely affects on the welfare services of the demographic changes described in the article?

5 Describe and evaluate the concept of 'the optimum level of population'.

Further ideas for learning projects

1 Compile a table for the 12 EC nations to show:

- Areas (km²)
- Population
- Income per head

- Birth rate
- Death rate

2 Discuss the view that the size of population is not as significant as its age, sex and geographical distribution.

5

The mixed economy

After studying this chapter you should be able to:

- List the different types of economy;
- Analyse the origins of the mixed economy;
- Describe the different types of government activity;
- Define fiscal and monetary policy;
- Define a nationalised industry;
- State the problems facing the mixed economy.

Types of economy

All societies in the world face the same problem: that of *scarcity*. That is to say there are not enough resources to satisfy all our wants. We do not have to be told that diamonds are scarce but a moment's reflection will show us that potatoes, bread and clothes are also scarce since there are millions of cold and hungry people in the world. Each society has only a limited amount of land, labour and capital (often referred to as *factors of production*) and it has to decide how to make the best use of them to satisfy the *infinite wants* of the population.

This then is the *economic problem* – finite resources and infinite wants. Professor Samuelson says that every society has to answer three fundamental questions – What? How? and For Whom? What goods and services should be produced, how will they be produced, and to whom shall they be distributed once produced? How do countries attempt to solve this problem? We saw in Chapter 2 that an underdeveloped economy tends to function on tradition and command. In advanced economies we see three types of solution.

Free enterprise: capitalism

These are economies in which most of the economic decisions are taken through the workings of the *market mechanism*. Good examples of this type of economy are the USA, Canada and Japan. Often described as free enterprise economies, it might be better to describe them as capitalist for many markets are dominated by large monopolistic organisations.

Collectivism: communism

These are economies where production decisions are taken collectively, for example by state planning committees. Despite the recent changes in Eastern Europe we can still say that examples of this type of society are communist countries such as the USSR, China and Cuba. It should be stated, however, that a state does not have to be communist to be collectivist. Some of the most extreme examples of collectivism can be found in the Kibbutz of Israel. Remember, collectivism does not have to mean centralised state communism.

Table 5.1 Mixed economies

Country	Total government expenditure as a % of GDP				Average annual growth of real GDP (%)	
	1960	1979	1983	1988	1965-80	1980-85
Switzerland	17.2	30.0	30.8	30.9	2.0	1.2
Japan	18.3	31.5	28.1	32.7	6.3	3.8
USA	27.7	33.4	36.9	36.0	2.9	2.5
Canada	28.9	39.3	43.0	47.0	4.8	2.4
UK	32.6	43.6	44.3	44.0	2.2	2.0
France	34.6	45.5	48.2	52.4	4.3	1.1
Germany	32.0	46.3	44.4	47.2	3.4	1.3
Belgium	30.7	50.9	53.5	54.4	3.0	0.7
Netherlands	33.7	59.5	58.3	60.2	3.9	0.7
Sweden	31.1	61.6	61.7	64.5	2.7	2.0

Source: OECD: *Economic Outlook, 1989* and IBRD: *World Development Report, 1987*

The mixed economy: the middle way

All economies are mixed in the sense that even in the most aggressive free enterprise economies the government usually intervenes to provide such things as defence and roads, while on the other hand, in rigorously collectivist economies such as Russia some decisions are still left to private enterprise. However, when we use the term a 'mixed economy' we mean one which is fairly evenly divided between collectivist organisation and free enterprise. The best known example of such an economy is the UK. The extent of government intervention in the economy may be measured by looking at the percentage of the gross domestic product (GDP) which the government disposes of. Table 5.1 shows how government intervention has increased in most countries in recent years. It also shows the UK with rather more government intervention than some of the other advanced industrialised nations such as Japan and the USA, but significantly less than others such as the Netherlands and Sweden.

There is no obvious way to judge what is the best 'mix' for a mixed economy. The doctrines of Thatcher and Reagan were founded on the belief that economies were being strangled by too much public ownership and state interference. A left-wing view might be that there are many decisions far too important to be left to the vagaries of the market. Left-wingers would argue that there is no validity in arguments about promoting competition in the economy which simply replaces

state monopolies with private ones.

Table 5.1 gives no obvious clues. Sweden and Switzerland which have the highest standards of living in Europe lie at opposite ends of the mixed economy spectrum. Conservatives in the UK would claim that improved growth in the UK was the result of restricting the role of the state. On the other hand, Germany's economy, which far out-performed the UK's, moved in the opposite direction.

Before going on to examine the components of Britain's mixed economy we will first trace its origins.

Examine the growth rates shown in Table 5.1. List as many reasons as you can for the observed differences between nations and over time.

The origins of the mixed economy

The decline of the free market

The economy of the UK in the 19th century was one in which people and organisations were in a state of unfettered competition. People believed that the economy would operate best if the government did not intervene in it. Such beliefs were based on the writings of Adam Smith (1723–90) who argued that *competi-*

tion was the best regulator of the economy. The belief that internal and external trade should be left to regulate itself became known by the French expression *laissez-faire*.

It is often thought that free competition is the natural state of the economy. This is not so: it is almost entirely a 19th century phenomenon. Before this time monarchs felt free to regulate the economy as they saw fit. In the 20th century the economy is dominated by the government and by giant business organisations. Only in a few sectors of the economy could truly free competition be said to exist today.

In his book *The Wealth of Nations*, Smith argued that the many taxes and regulations which surrounded the commerce of the country hindered its growth. Business organisations should be free to pursue profit, restricted only by the competition of other business organisations. From about 1815 onwards government began to pursue this policy. Britain, already a wealthy country, grew wealthier still. The success of industries such as textiles and iron appeared to prove the wisdom of Adam Smith. Belief in the free market system became the dominant economic ideology.

However, as the 19th century progressed it became apparent that the free market system had two major defects:

(a) Although efficient at producing some products such as food and clothing, the free market system failed to product effectively things such as sanitation or education.
(b) Competition could easily disappear and give way to monopoly.

It was to combat these two problems that the state began to intervene in the economy. In the case of *(a)* the government did not take a conscious decision to depart from the *laissez-faire* philosophy. Action was forced upon it by the severity of the problems. This is well illustrated by the 1848 *Public Health Act*. In this case cholera epidemics forced the government to promote better drainage and sanitation. In the case of *(b)* there was a more conscious effort to regulate monopolies. This may be illustrated by the measures, which began as early as 1840, to regulate the activities of railway companies.

Thus, the 19th century presents a picture of governments believing in a free market economy but being forced to regulate its most serious excesses.

The effects of the First World War (1914–18)

This thrust upon the government the control of the economy. Until this time the UK's wars had been fought on a free enterprise basis (if we can use the expression) with volunteer armies and little disruption of the domestic economy. Gradually the government had to assume control of more and more of the economy. The railways were taken over, agriculture was completely controlled, the iron and steel industry was directed and conscription was introduced. However, after 1918 the government immediately tried to return to a market economy. In 1921 a depression started in Britain which turned into a world-wide slump in 1929 which the market economy seemed powerless to cure.

The Keynesian revolution

Between 1921 and 1939 the average level of unemployment was 14%; it never fell below 10% and in the worst years was over 20%. Conventional economic theory concentrated on the demand for resources. This held that if there was unemployment it was because wages were too high. Thus, the way to cure unemployment was to cut wages and prices, thereby making people more willing to buy goods and employers more willing to employ people. *Say's Law* further maintained that if the market mechanism was allowed to work it would ensure the full employment of all resources and that this was the natural equilibrium for the economy.

The writings of John Maynard Keynes (1883-1946), an English economist who worked at Cambridge University for many years, are the most important contribution to economic thinking in the 20th century. His views on the economy, however, were so radical that they were not accepted by governments in the 1930s. In his most influential book *The General Theory of Employment, Interest and Money* (1936) Keynes analysed the workings of the economy and put forward his solution to unemployment.

Keynes maintained that it was not the demand for resources which was important but the *level* of total (aggregate) demand in the economy. He said that a fall in the level of demand would lead to over-production; this would lead to the accumulation of stocks (inventories) and people would be thrown out of work in consequence. The unemployed would lose their purchasing power and therefore the level of demand would sink still further and so on. Cutting wages, therefore, would not cure unemployment, it would make it worse.

Since it appeared that the economy was no longer self-regulating there was a clear case for government intervention. Keynes' solution was that, if there was a shortfall in demand in the economy, the government should make it up by public spending. In order to do this the government, would have to spend beyond its means (a budget deficit). In the 1930s this solution was not acceptable. As John Kenneth Galbraith, a Canadian economist, has written: 'to spend money to create jobs seemed profligate; to urge a budget deficit as a good thing seemed insane'. It was, therefore, not until after the end of the Second World War in 1945 that Keynes' ideas were tried.

Socialism

Keynes was a 'conservative revolutionary': his concern was to show not how the capitalist system could be abolished but how it could be modified. Thus, the post-Keynesian capitalist society has been even more successful than its predecessor. The fact that Keynes argued for government intervention in the economy does *not* make him a socialist. *Socialists* are those who believe that the means of production should be publicly owned. Socialism is therefore a different strand in the development of the mixed economy. Although much socialist thinking is based on the works of Marx, socialism in Britain has tended to be constitutional rather than revolutionary. Socialist thinking in Britain probably owes more to *Sidney and Beatrice Webb* and the other great *Fabian* socialist than to Marx and Lenin. Harold Wilson once remarked that British socialism owed more to Methodism than to Marxism.

The effect of the Second World War (1939–45)

From the outset of the war the government took over the direction of the economy. Industries were taken over, labour was directed, food was rationed. Britain

could be said to have had a *centrally-planned economy*. The realisation spread that the government could intervene successfully in the economy. Keynes' ideas at last came to be accepted. Both the major political parties during the war committed themselves to the maintenance of a high and stable level of employment once peace was achieved. This was to be achieved by Keynesian techniques of the management of the level of aggregate demand. The fact that it was a Labour government which was elected in 1945 meant that an element of socialism was also introduced into the economy.

The welfare state

You do not have to be a socialist to believe that everyone is entitled to education, health services and social security. The origins of the welfare state might be traced back to *Lloyd George* and beyond, but its immediate progenitor was the *Beveridge Report* of 1942. This recommended a national health scheme for 'every citizen without exception, without remuneration limit and without an economic barrier'. Beveridge also stated that the basis for comprehensive social security must be the certainty of a continuing high level of employment. A White Paper, *Employment Policy*, was published in 1944 and accepted by both the major political parties. Full employment was to become a first priority for post-war governments.

This policy continued until the late 1970s when inflation began to be seen as a greater problem than unemployment. The mass unemployment of the 1980s placed the whole fabric of the Welfare State under great strain. Not only this but the Thatcher government began to question the assumptions of the Welfare State believing that people should take greater personal responsibility for their welfare.

Opponents of the Thatcher government argued that the measures used to encourage people to work were draconian. Indeed some argued that they were a throwback to the *principle of less* eligibility. This was the the principle of the 1834 Poor Law which established the work-houses which were designed to be so unpleasant that they would force people to work.

In the early 1990s, therefore, the Welfare State was under attack both as an idea and also because of the demographic pressure discussed in the last chapter.

The components of the mixed economy

What emerged from the period of post-war Labour government was an economy which was a compound of socialist ideas, Keynesian management and capitalism. It was truly a mixed economy. Hence, we might summarise the main components of the mixed economy thus:

(a) a free enterprise sector, where economic decisions are taken through the workings of the market;
(b) government regulation of the economy through its budgets, etc.;
(c) public ownership of some industries;
(d) welfare services, either provided by the state or supplied through state administered schemes.

Economic activities take place in the public sector, the private sector or both sectors of the economy. Complete the table below with three further examples.

| Economic activity | | |
Mainly or entirely in private sector	Mainly or entirely in public sector	In both sectors
1 Shoe manufacture	1 Coal mining	1 Armaments manufacture
2	2	2
3	3	3

The monetarist counter-revolution

For many years it appeared that the British and many other economies were moving in the direction of more government control and public ownership. In recent years, however, governments in the UK and elsewhere have tried to reverse this process by privatising nationalised industries and restricting the role of the state. This is associated with the ideas of the monetarist and neo-classical schools of economics. The leading economist in this field is Milton Friedman.

It will be apparent after studying Table 5.1 that this does not seem to have significantly reduced the role of the state. One of the reasons for this is the increased call which the social services are making on the economy, in particular, to finance unemployment benefits and old age pensions.

The remaining sections of this chapter consider the various ways in which the government intervenes in the UK economy.

Management of the economy

The objectives of economic policy

Whatever political party is in power, four main objectives of policy are pursued:

(a) control of inflation;
(b) reduction of unemployment;
(c) promotion of economic growth;
(d) attainment of a favourable balance of payments.

These objectives are not in dispute, they are concerned with the good housekeeping of the economy. Different governments may, however, place different degrees of importance on individual objectives. Thus, for example, a Labour government might place a higher priority on reducing unemployment while Conservatives place the control of inflation first on the agenda. In addition to these generally-agreed objectives, more 'political' economic policies might be pursued such as the redistribution of income.

There are three areas of action in which the government can pursue its economic policies: fiscal policy, monetary policy and direct intervention.

Fiscal policy

This term is used to describe the regulation of the economy through government taxes and spending. The major important aspect of this is the overall relationship between taxes and spending. If the government spends more money in a year than it collects in taxes, this situation is referred to as a *budget deficit*. A deficit has an expansionary, or inflationary, effect upon the economy. Conversely, a situation where the government collects more in taxes than it spends is referred to as a *budget surplus*. A surplus has a restraining, or deflationary, effect upon the economy.

If the government spends more money than it col-

Keywords

What? How? For whom?
These are the three fundamental questions that every economic society must answer. 'What?' is to be produced - 'How?' shall it be produced - 'For whom?', i.e. who will eventually receive the goods and services produced.

Laissez-faire
The belief that the 'What?, How? and For whom?' questions are best answered through the decisions of individuals to the virtual exclusion of collective authority. The term was originally coined by the French writer Quesnay 'laissez faire, laissez passez ...'

Socialism
The belief that the ownership and control of the means of production should be vested in the community and administered in the interests of all.

Capitalism
An economic system which is dominated and the economic decisions taken by the owners of capital.

Ideology
The manner of thinking characteristic of a class or individual. Usually it is the basis of some economic or political system, e.g. Fascist, Marxist or Capitalist, but could also apply to other beliefs, e.g. Christian, Buddhist etc.

Mixed market economy
An economy which is a mixture of capitalism and collectivism.

Collectivism
A system in which the 'What?, How? and For whom?' questions are answered collectively rather than by market forces.

Say's Law
Through the medium of prices, supply will always equal demand. It is not possible, therefore, for there to be unused or idle resources. By extension from this comes the idea that markets and the whole economy are self-regulating and there is no need for government intervention.

Keynesianism
The work and influence of Keynes is so large that it is impossible to define briefly. But to a greater or lesser extent all Keynesians belief that government intervention is necessary for the smooth running of the economy.

lects in taxes, so that it is in deficit, the budget is financed by *borrowing*. The amount of money which the government may be forced to borrow in a year is referred to as the *public-sector borrowing requirement* (PSBR). In the late 1970s and early 1980s the PSBR became very large. However, in the late 1980s the government reversed this situation to a point where budget surpluses allowed government borrowing to be reduced and existing public debt redeemed. It was thus possible to speak of a *Public Sector Debt Repayment (PSDR)*.

Monetary policy

This is the regulation of the economy through the control of the *quantity of money* available and through the *price of money*, that is to say the rate of interest borrowers will have to pay. Expanding the quantity of money and lowering the rate of interest should stimulate spending in the economy and is therefore expansionary, or inflationary. Conversely, restricting the quantity of money and raising the rate of interest should have a restraining, or deflationary, effect upon the economy.

It might be thought that because the government controls the printing of cash, i.e. notes and coins, it is easy for it to control the quantity of money. This, however, is not so because most spending in the economy is not done with cash but with cheques or other means of money transfer in the banking system. The amount of this type of money is determined by the banking system and can only be affected indirectly by the government. The government does, however, have a great effect upon the rate of interest because all other interest rates in the economy tend to move in line with the rates of interest set by the Bank of England. In the late 1980s high interest rates became one of the chief weapons of policy for controlling inflation.

List three recent examples of the application of fiscal policy and three recent examples of the application of monetary policy.

Direct intervention

This expression is used to describe the many different

ways in which the government, through legislation, spending or sanctions, tries to impose its economic policy directly upon the economy. Both fiscal and monetary policy are attempts to *create conditions* in the economy which will cause industry and people to react in a way which is in line with the government's wishes. Direct intervention, on the other hand, seeks to *impose the government's will* directly upon the economy leaving people no choice. A good example of this would be the imposition of a statutory prices and incomes policy.

Provision of goods and services

Many of the things which individuals use are provided either by *central* or *local government*. For example, most people's health care and education is provided by the state. These services are not, of course, free since we pay for them indirectly through taxes. The state also provides many goods and services to the public on a commercial or semi-commercial basis, i.e. they are *sold* to the public. These products, such as rail services and coal, are usually provided by public corporations. (These are considered in the subsequent section of this chapter.)

Many essential services are supplied by the government. These may be controlled directly by *central government*, e.g. social security benefits and motorway construction. Alternatively, the service may be decided upon by central government but administered by local government, e.g. education. Services such as street lighting and refuse collection may be entirely controlled by local authorities. On the other hand, services may be provided by quangos (*see* page 27) set up by the government but which are not regarded as either central or local government bodies. An example of these is the health authorities.

Public goods and merit goods

Those products and services which are provided to the community on a *non-commercial* basis, such as defence and education, are usually termed either *public goods or merit goods*.

Public goods and services

These are products – the benefits of which are indivisible, i.e. the service which is supplied to the public is conferred on all equally well – or equally badly. The most obvious example of this is defence. Everyone in the country benefits equally from the activities of the army, the air force and the navy. Similarly, roads and street lighting are available to all.

Merit goods and services

These are products which are allocated to the members of the public according to their merit (or need). Thus, for example, health services are not given to everyone, only to those who need (or merit) them because of ill-health. Similarly, education is not given to everyone equally. Educational opportunities are only made available to those between the ages of 5–16 and to those whose achievements qualify them for higher education.

1 Give as many examples as you can of goods or services which may be regarded as public goods.

2 In the UK which goods and services are treated as merit goods?

3 Which goods and services that are currently *not* regarded as merit goods do you think should be treated as merit goods? Are there some goods which are currently regarded as merit goods that you think should cease to be so regarded?

Public corporations

The legal form of a Public Corporation has already been examined in Chapter 3. Some of the public corporations are referred to as nationalised industries. Strictly speaking this is a misnomer because to be a true 'nationalised industry' the undertaking would have to be run directly by the government and be headed by a minister. This, for example, was the case with the GPO up to 1969 but in 1969 the GPO was reconstituted as a public corporation, headed by a chairman, and renamed the Post Office.

As you have already seen, there is no distinct legal

form termed nationalised industry but a group of public corporations were commonly referred to as such. Although termed nationalised industries for many years, an agreed definition of them was not worked out until 1976 (*see* page 68). In addition to these there are those public corporations which are not considered nationalised industries. These include the Bank of England, the Civil Aviation Authority and the BBC.

List six organisations which were public corporations in 1979 but which are now Plcs.

Legislation

The government uses legislation to direct the economy less frequently than one might suppose. It cannot, for example, pass a law against inflation or to ensure economic growth. From time to time, nevertheless, it has a statutory prices and incomes policy, for example, but it will not be able to pursue this for very long if it is contrary to prevailing economic forces.

However, the government does legislate on such matters as monopolies and competition, so that certain commercial practices may become illegal. It may also impose planning legislation making it difficult for businesses to locate in certain areas. In recent years there has been an increasing amount of legislation on industrial relations and upon health and safety at work. However, in general the government hopes to *encourage* rather than coerce private enterprise to undertake the desired course. The role of legislation and its interpretation is considered in Chapter 25, while the legislation affecting the business organisation is discussed in Parts 2 and 3 of this book.

The prospect for the mixed economy

We can look at the prospect for the mixed economy in political, economic or technological terms. Considering the economic point of view first, the central problem is the failure of Keynesian management of the economy. Keynes' analysis centred on the *macro-*

Keywords

Public goods
'Goods' such as defence are impossible to supply (charge for) on an individual basis and therefore they have to be provided publicly. It is also the case that consumption of a public good by one person does not diminish consumption by another.

Merit goods
Goods provided not by price but on the basis of merit (need). There is no clear-cut way of saying what should be merit goods and what should not. Typically services such as education are supplied as merit goods.

Monetary policy
Governments can influence the economy by varying interest rates and by attempting to expand or contract the supply of money.

Fiscal policy
Governments can use the amount and manner in which they collect taxes and spend their income to influence the economy.

Prices and incomes policy
The government can try to control inflation by attempting to place limits on rises in prices and wages etc. The policy can be either voluntary or statutory.

Central government
The aspects of government which are controlled by the Ministers of State from Whitehall.

Local government
Those aspects of government controlled by local authorities such as county councils.

economy and was based on the short-term management of demand. This worked reasonably well until the 1960s. But after that time there was a conspicuous failure to solve the twin problems of inflation and unemployment. In recent years governments have tried *micro-economic programmes*, trying to encourage potential growth wherever it can be found in the economy.

Economic policy, however, must function within the political framework. In practice this gives the consumers very little economic choice. However detailed the platform is on which a government is elected, it will only roughly approximate to the wishes of even its own supporters. In addition to this, experience has shown over recent years that governments are often forced into fundamental changes in their policy. Politics also places another constraint upon the mixed economy. At least once every five years the government must seek re-election. It is possible to argue that any major economic policy would take much longer than this to come to fruition and therefore the real welfare of the country is being subjugated to the government of the day's desire for re-election. Thus, politician's are led to ask themselves what most people want while economists would maintain that the correct question should be 'What do people want most?'

It is obvious that technology and, in particular, the IT revolution, is having and will continue to have a very profound effect upon our lives. There are many people, however, who believe that the revolution in technology has also brought about a revolution in economic order and created a new decision-making process. Foremost among the advocates of this point of view is Professor J K Galbraith. Galbraith maintains that power has passed from company directors, shareholders, trade unionists, voters and even the government to the *technostructure*. It is argued that in all advanced states power rests with those who have the high level of skill and information which is neces-

sary to operate in a large corporation or government department. James Burnham in his book *The Managerial Revolution* (1941) argued that the new ruling class would not be capitalists or communists but those who had expert technological skills. The argument is developed in Galbraith's books *The New Industrial State* and *The Age of Uncertainty*. While this is probably an extreme point of view, it cannot be doubted that the new technology, particularly that of the silicon chip, is having a profound effect upon our lives.

Thus, the mixed economy stands poised between the two ideologies of capitalism and collectivism, pulled this way and that by differing political opinions. In addition to this, it has to cope with the rising power of the technocrat both in multi-national corporations and in government departments. We have also seen that demographic changes will also place constraints upon key components of the mixed economy such as the Welfare State. The upheavals in eastern Europe demonstrate that it is not only ourselves who are questioning the principles on which our society has operated for many years.

Learning project

The role of the government

The following passage is taken from the *World Development Report* of the IRBD (World Bank). It is concerned with the role of government in the development of economies, especially in the development of less developed economies.

Read it carefully and then attempt the tasks which follow.

Markets and governments have complementary roles in industrialisation. Markets are adept at dealing with the growing economic complexity that comes with industrialisation, but they are rarely perfect. Government must sometimes intervene to achieve an efficient outcome.

First, governments have to set the rules of the game, which define the use, ownership, and conditions of transfer of physical, financial, and intellectual assets. Irrespective of the type of economy – whether it favours private enterprise or is a command economy – these rules impinge on economic activity. The more they are certain, well-defined, and well understood, the more smoothly the

economy can work. In many developing countries these rules are unclear, interpreted in unpredictable ways, and managed by a cumbersome bureaucracy. This tends to raise the costs of doing business and therefore discourages the transactions that are essential for industrial specialisation.

Governments must continue to be the main providers of certain services that have facilitated industrialisation in the past:

● All governments play a major role in education, especially in providing the basic skills of literacy and numeracy that are vital in a modern industrial labour force. Lack of education, rather than physical assets, is the main bottle-neck in industrialisation.
● Most governments provide the physical infrastructure of industry: transport, communications, and power systems. Although some parts of such systems can be, and are, profitably operated in the private sector in many countries, government provision of large systems in most developing countries is usually the only feasible option.
● Most governments provide economic information and regulation of standards (weights, measures,

safety at work). But there is a limit to the information they can make available in time to be useful, and regulations can often be ineffective or counter-productive.

● Governments in the industrial economies promote scientific and technological research. For developing countries, where it usually makes sense to acquire foreign technology, the arguments for a large government role in industrial research and develop-ment are less compelling. But public support may be justified in some cases.

● State-owned enterprises were established to carry out some of these tasks. Some have performed well, but many have disappointed. Efforts are under way to reform them. Such reforms are high on the agenda for structural adjustment in developing countries.

In addition to these forms of direct participation, governments intervene somewhat less directly in the running of their economies. Trade policy, fiscal incentives, price controls, investment regulations, and financial and macro-economic policies are their instruments. Capital market failures and externalities are the most cited justifications for direct interven-tion. Both concepts have been used, for example, to defend policies toward infant industries.

Suppose a potentially profitable young firm is unable to find the funds to tide it over the period before it becomes financially viable and can recoup its costs. Without government support such firms would not be able to start production. Or suppose that the firm could generate economic benefits to the rest of the economy – for example, in the form of

trained workers who leave and take their skills elsewhere. Again some form of government support is warranted. Import protection is never the best form of intervention in principle, but sometimes there may be no practical alternative.

Different forms of intervention will have different effects on the economy. Indeed, the important question often is not whether to intervene, but how. Quantitative restrictions on imports may be used to protect infant industries, for instance. But they will raise social costs more than a tariff will, such as the efforts of producers to avoid or exploit the controls. Tariffs, however, raise prices to consumers. Subsi-dies to the industry could give the same assistance without raising prices - although not without raising public spending and, possibly, budget deficits.

1 The passage is concerned with industrialisation; de-scribe as fully as you can what this means. The UK is becoming concerned about de-industrialisation. What does this mean and what are its consequences?

2 In the second paragraph the passage discusses the role of the government in that it has to 'set the rules of the game'. What does this mean and how is it accom-plished in the UK? Have there been any major changes in the way this has been done in recent years?

3 The passage identifies five major ways in which gov-ernments have facilitated industrialisation in the past. Briefly state what they are. Go through these five ways and assess the extent to which they are true for the UK.

4 What reasons does the passage put forward for the direct intervention of governments in the economy.

Further ideas for learning projects

1 Examine the likely effect of future demographic changes on the public sector of the economy.

2 Collect evidence from the UK and other economies to assess the impact of rates of investment and size of the public sector on the development of economies.

6

Resources and decision-making

CHAPTER OBJECTIVES

After studying this chapter you should be able to:

- Explain the role of the law in relation to the use of resources;
- Define the law of variable proportions;
- Describe the cost structure of the organisation;
- List possible economies of scale;
- Analyse the organisation's demand for a resource;
- State reasons for the continued existence of the small business;
- ■ Describe types of decisions and methods of effective decision-making;
- Appreciate the importance of value systems;
- Appreciate the importance of information as a resource.

In this part of the book we examine the organisation's demand for and exploitation of resources and technology. Goods and services cannot be produced out of thin air and it is only by acquiring and combining resources that the organisation can produce them. This chapter considers the mainly economic constraints that arise from combining resources, the regulatory role of the law in this context and the importance of effective decision-making and information. Chapter 7 considers technology and its implications and Chapters 8-12 the economic, legal and practical aspects of the main categories of resources. Part 3 of the book deals with the sale of these goods and services both nationally and internationally, once they have been produced.

The role of the law

An organisation's use of resources to make maximum profit is determined by economic forces and not by the law. However, the practical application of economic theory is *regulated* by the law, itself influenced if not determined by politics. For example, the best use of labour might be maximum hours for minimum payment, i.e. wages just sufficient to provide adequate food and other essentials to enable the employee to work at maximum efficiency for the maximum possible hours. Clearly the law does not allow this today, although not so long ago it was precisely what happened.

The ruthless exploitation of economic resources is politically and socially unacceptable and the role of the law is to regulate their use to ensure it remains within acceptable limits. Thus, the law imposes *constraints* on the exploitation of economic resources while remaining an *enabling medium* in relation to economic activity generally. Without suitable constraints it is arguable that business organisations might destroy the very society on which they depend.

The legal framework relating to the use of economic resources is practical and totally lacks any detailed theoretical basis comparable to the economist's Law of Variable Proportions. Such theory as there is originates in political and social philosophy and not in abstract theories of 'justice' and 'rights and duties'. If there is an underlying principle in the law's approach to this subject, it is possibly that economic resources should be exploited and economic activity furthered for the benefit of society generally and not for the benefit of the few. However, gross inequalities still exist.

In Chapters 8–12 you will see the law's regulatory role in relation to each of the factors of production. A brief introduction here will give you a general idea of the areas it covers.

The organisation's relationship with its employees was initially determined by individual contractual arrangements but there has been a progressive superimposition of a statutory framework of rights and duties which are often quite independent of the contract of employment. Trade Unions are also regulated by the law and they enjoy important legal immunities which, although restricted in recent years, enable them to perform their functions and pursue their objectives effectively. The law's interest in land, its occupation and use is now determined as much, if not more, by the interests of the community as by the interests of landowners themselves. You will see in Chapter 9 how planning legislation, the Occupiers' Liability Acts of 1957 and 1984 and the Health and Safety at Work, etc, Act 1974 embody this criterion. The raising, structure and use of finance by a business organisation also takes place within a regulatory framework which varies with the type of business organisation involved. The Partnership Act 1890 and the Companies Act 1985 in particular lay down guides or instructions which partnerships and registered companies must follow. In Chapter 11 you will see the importance of the law as a means of arriving at an equitable distribution of assets to creditors when a business organisation becomes insolvent and is forced into either bankruptcy or liquidation. Finally, information as a resource; information that can easily be exchanged, used and misused is now so widely available in computer data banks that the Data Protection Act 1984 regulates the storage and use of information on individuals. We explain the central role of information later in this chapter.

Taken together, the chapters in this section of the book should help you to appreciate that the reality of business activity does not conform to the neat textbook titles of 'law', 'economics', 'accounts', etc. but is really an amalgam of many disciplines and the product of numerous influences.

Discover how the Health and Safety at Work Act 1974 or the Data Protection Act 1984 have affected your employer or the college at which you study.

Keywords _____

Role of the law
Law regulates business activity. It places constraints on the unacceptable exploitation of resources and markets while facilitating business activity generally.

The organisation's demand for resources

The factors of production

The economic resources of the world have traditionally been divided by economists into four: *labour*, *land*, *capital* and *enterprise*. Some economists have been unwilling to classify enterprise as a separate factor of production, arguing either that it is inseparable from capital or that it is simply a special form of labour. Enterprise, being the organisational ability which combines the other factors together, is, however, very properly a subject for discussion in this book. The factors of production can be separated from each other by considering their special economic attributes or their legal attributes. The legal distinctions arise principally out of a law governing the payments made for factors of production, i.e. *wages*, *rent*, *interest* and *profit*. In this part of the book the economic and legal aspects of the factors of production and the payments for them are considered together. We will now examine some of the principles governing the exploitation of resources and their implications for the cost structures of the organisation.

The derived demand for factors of production

In order to produce goods and services the organisation must use the factors of production. Thus, to produce cars a company must demand land for the factory, capital to build the factory and labour to work in it.

The demand for these factors of production, however, rests on consumers' demand for cars and therefore it is said to be *derived* from this demand. The demand for all factors of production is a *derived demand*.

1 Illustrate the effect upon the market for bricks of an increase in the demand for houses.
2 Illustrate the effect upon the market for greenhouses of a large increase in the price of glass. (If you are uncertain of this, check Chapter 13.)

The theory of distribution

In examining the organisation's demand for resources, we shall see what it is that determines the quantity of a factor that a business will demand and also the price it is willing to pay for it. These are the principles which will determine how much of the national income will go to each factor of production. When we have done this for each factor it will show how income is distributed between the owners of the four factors, i.e. the labourers (or workers), landlords, capitalists and entrepreneurs. As we examine the factors of production and their returns we shall be covering the area of economics known as the *theory of distribution* (*see* Fig. 13.1, page 240).

The law of variable proportions

Technology and change

Change, as we have seen, is a major theme of this book. However, not everything changes all the time. Technology may be evolving but at any given time an organisation is fixed at a certain level of technological development. For example, when an organisation equips itself with a new computer it has opted for a particular model and it is, so to speak, struck with it until it is worn out or obsolete. (*See* page 125).

This is not only true of technological development but also of the organisation's use of resources generally. At any particular time the retailer, for example, is constrained by the size of the shop, the farmer by the area of the farm, the car manufacturer by the capacity of the factory and so on.

Having established this fact we discover that a fundamental economic principle termed the *law of variable proportions* comes into effect. This gives rise of forces which dictate the cost structures of an organisation. Later we will consider how these principles are affected by changes in the level of technology.

Diminishing returns

In order to produce goods and services the organisation must combine the factors of production. As we have seen, however, the amount of certain factors which the firm can employ will be fixed while it will be able to vary others. Suppose we consider a firm of a certain size or a farm of a certain area and to this *fixed factor* the business person adds *variable factors* such as labour and power. Under these circumstances the firm will be affected by the law of *diminishing returns*. That is to say, as the firm adds more and more of the variable factor, e.g. labour, to a constant amount of the fixed factor, e.g. land, the extra output that this creates must, after a time, become less. This means that the amount of resources needed to produce a typical unit of output will vary. It is therefore the law of diminishing returns which gives rise to the law of variable proportions. (It may also be termed the *law of non-proportional returns*.)

The short-run and the long-run

Economists often speak of *long-run* and *short-run* situations; these are not chronological periods of time but refer to the time over which factors of production can be varied. If, for example, we considered a business such as oil refining, the amount of capital equipment cannot easily be varied. If there was a large increase in the demand for oil it would take the oil company a considerable period of time to build a new refinery. In the meantime it could vary the other factors such as the amount of labour it used but it would be limited to its present amount of capital equipment. The period over which the fixed factors of production cannot be changed is referred to as the *short-run period*. The period in which the oil company can build a new refinery, i.e. vary the amount of *all* the factors of production, is known as the *long-run period*.

It is impossible to define these periods in terms of calendar time as they will vary from industry to industry. It may take ten years to build a new power station, whereas a farmer may be able to rent more land and therefore produce more food within twelve months.

As the firm moves into the long-run period it is able to vary all the factors of production and may therefore offset the law of diminishing returns. It may, however, still be subject to the principle of *increasing costs* (*see* page 5).

The marginal physical product

Because of the law of diminishing returns, as factors of production are combined, in the *short-run* various cost structures for any firm will emerge. These are best illustrated by taking a simple example. In Table 6.1 a farmer whose land is fixed at 120 hectares, in the short-run, adds more and more units of the variable factor, labour, in order to produce a greater output of wheat. Obviously, if no labour is used then there will be no output. When one unit of labour is used the output of the farm works out at 2 tonnes of wheat per week (the year's crop divided by 52). If two men are used the output rises to 5 tonnes. The *average product* (AP) per man has risen from 2.0 tonnes to 2.5 tonnes. This does not mean that the second man was more industrious than the first but rather that an 120 hectare farm was too big for one man to work and it runs more efficiently with two. The higher average product therefore applies to both workers. It may have been achieved through *specialisation* and *division of labour*, impossible when there was only one worker.

Trying to obtain more output, the farmer employs a third worker, as a result of which the output rises to 7 tonnes per week. The total has indeed increased but

Table 6.1 Marginal and average products

Number of men employed	Output of wheat tonnes/wk (Q)	Marginal Phys product tonnes/wk (MPP)	Average product tonnes/wk (AP)
0	0		0
		2	
1	2		2.0
		3	
2	5		2.5
		2	
3	7		2.3
		1	
4	8		2.0
		0	
5	8		1.6

when we consider the amount added to total output it is only 2 tonnes, whereas the second worker added 3 tonnes. The amount added to total output by each successive unit of labour is the *marginal physical product* (MPP). If we generalised this principle we could define the MPP as the change in total output resulting from the employment of one more unit of a variable factor.

These figures are illustrated graphically in Fig. 6.1. The MPP curve rises as the benefits of division of labour make the exploitation of land more efficient. Between one and two units of labour, the curve reaches its highest and then begins to decline as diminishing returns set in. At two units of labour the farm is at its most technically efficient and after this its efficiency begins to decline. This is shown by the average product curve declining. When the AP curve is rising the firm is benefiting from *increasing returns*. When the AP curve is going downwards the firm is suffering from *decreasing returns*. The diminishing returns come about because as more labour is employed each successive unit of labour has less of the fixed factor, land, to work with. If it were not for the law of diminishing returns we could supply all the world's food from one farm simply by adding more and more labour to it. Obviously this is not possible.

You will see that the MPP curve goes through the top of the AP curve. This is always so. The intersection of AP with MPP, then, tells us when the organisation is at its optimum technical efficiency. Technical efficiency, however, is not the same as economic efficiency. If, for example, the product we were considering were gold then it might be worthwhile running a very inefficient gold-mine. Eventually, however, because

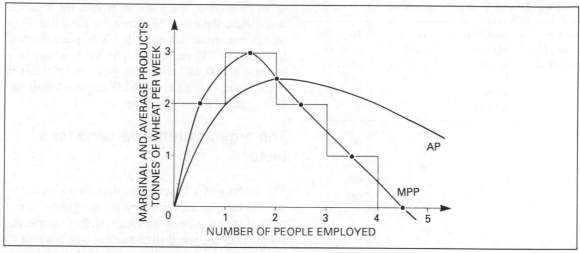

Fig. 6.1 The marginal physical product and average product curves

of diminishing returns, MPP becomes negative when total output falls. No business would be willing to employ more resources to get less output.

You will note that MPP is plotted in a particular manner. In Table 6.1 it is shown as halfway between the units of output. This is because the marginal product is the change in output involved in moving from one unit of variable factor to another. All marginal figures are plotted in this manner. You will also note that in Fig. 6.1 the graph looks like a step-ladder. This is because a whole unit of labour was added. If we could divide up a unit of a factor of production infinitely and, instead of employing 1 man, employ 0.1 of a man, 0.2 of a man, etc, then we would derive a smooth curve for MPP. In Fig. 6.1 this is achieved by joining up the mid-points of the steps. It is usually more convenient to work with smooth continuous curves and this we shall do. Remember, however, the special incremental manner in which marginal curves are built up.

Production and productivity

Production is the total amount of a commodity produced whereas *productivity* is the amount of a commodity produced per unit of resources used. When a firm is improving its efficiency, productivity will be rising. That is to say, if, by better management, more efficient equipment or better use of labour, the firm

manages to produce the same or a greater amount of product with a smaller amount of resources then it has increased its productivity. If, on the other hand, the firm produces an increase in output, but only at the expense of an even greater increase in resources, then, despite the increase in output, its productivity has fallen.

Productivity may be difficult to measure. One of the most common methods is to take the total output and divide it by the number of workers. Another method, used in agriculture, is to express productivity as output per hectare. In the example we have been using, productivity is rising while the AP is rising and falling when AP is falling. Productivity is vital to the economic welfare of both individual firms and the nation. It is only by becoming more efficient that we can hope to compete with other businesses or nations. We have only considered here two factors of production: other considerations, such as capital and the level of technology, are vital in productivity.

Explain the effects of improvements in technology on the market for personal computers. Illustrate your answer with a diagram if possible.
Is what you have described a short-run or a long-run situation? Why?
(Hint – remember *ceteris paribus*.)

Table 6.2 The marginal revenue product

Number of people employed	Marginal physical product (MPP) tonnes of wheat	Price of wheat per tonne (p) £	Marginal revenue product (MRP = MPP x p) £
0		20	
	2		40
1		20	
	3		60
2		20	
	2		40
3		20	
	1		20
4		20	
	0		0
5		20	

The marginal revenue product

The marginal physical product is measured in units of the commodity being produced; in our example it is tonnes of wheat. If this is expressed not in terms of the physical product but the money this product can be sold for, then we derive the marginal revenue product (MRP). Thus, if the second man employed added 3 tonnes a week to output and each tonne could be sold for £20 then the marginal revenue product (MRP) would be £60. So marginal revenue can be calculated as:

$$MRP = MPP \times p$$

where p = the price of the commodity. This applies when the firm can sell more and more of its product at the same price. If, on the other hand, in order to sell more of its product the business organisation has to lower the price of its product, then MRP will be calculated as:

$$MRP = MPP \times MR$$

where MR = marginal revenue, i.e. the change to the firm's total revenue resulting from the sale of one more unit of the commodity.

If in our example we assumed that the firm could sell any quantity of wheat it wished at £20 per tonne, then we could derive the MRP schedule shown in Table 6.2.

These figures are shown graphically in Fig. 6.2. The MRP curve is drawn on the assumption that all other things remain constant; improvements in technology

or an increase in the price of wheat, for instance, would have the effect of increasing the MRP. Suppose, for example, that in Table 6.2 the price of wheat increased to £30 per tonne. The MRP would then increase to £60, £90 and so on. When we plot this in Fig. 6.2, we see that the new MRP curve is higher and to the right of the original one.

The organisation's demand for a factor

The quantity of a factor of production which a firm will demand is determined by the marginal revenue product and the price of that factor. If, for example, the marginal revenue product of a unit of labour were £40 and the cost of that unit of labour was £10, the business would obviously be £30 better off as a result of employing that unit of labour. If the MRP of the next unit of labour fell to £20 but the cost of it remained at £10, the firm would still employ that unit of the factor since it would be a further £10 better off. In other words the business will go on demanding a factor of production while the MRP of that factor is greater than the cost of employing it. This is best understood graphically. Look at Fig. 6.3.

If the wage rate was £30 per person, the best number of people for the firm to employ would be three. The cost of labour would be the area under the wage line,

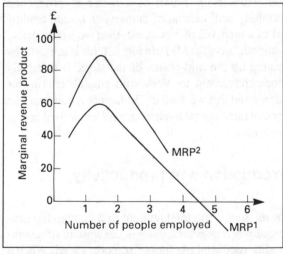

Fig. 6.2 An increase in the marginal revenue product. As a result of an increase in the price of wheat from £20 to £30 per tonne the MRP curve shifts upwards from MRP1 to MRP2.

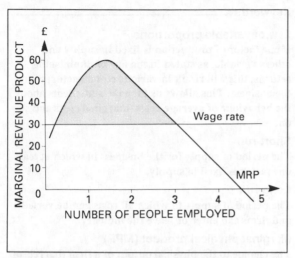

Fig. 6.3 The marginal revenue product and wages. The business employs three people, which is where MRP equals wages rate.

i.e. 3 x £30. The shaded area, above the wage line and below the MRP curve, would be the money that the business could get back over and above the cost of employing the factor. The firm would always be best off by trying to obtain as much of this shaded area as possible. If, for example, the wage rate fell to £10 then the firm would employ four people, but if it rose to £50 it would be best off employing only two. The MRP curve, therefore, shows us that the organisation's demand for a factor of production will vary in relation to the price of that factor. In other words, the firm's MRP curve of a factor is its *demand curve* for that factor.

The equal product curve

There is always more than one way to undertake any particular task. We could, for example, dig a ditch with six men with picks and shovels or employ one person with a mechanical digger. If we considered two resources such as capital and labour there would, therefore, be several combinations of them which would produce the same output. This is illustrated in Fig. 6.4. At point A a *capital intensive* method of production is used employing seven units of capital but only one of labour. As we move down the curve labour is *substituted* for capital. Point C represents a *labour intensive* method of producing the same output – here seven units of labour are used but only one of

capital. Other things being equal, poor countries will tend to use *labour intensive* methods while advanced countries will use *capital intensive* methods.

Achieving the best mix of resources

Achieving the best possible combination of resources for a firm is a case of balancing not just two factors but many. If the firm is to prosper and maximise its profits the mix must be precisely right. We have just seen how a business would go on employing more units of a variable factor up to the point where the marginal revenue product (MRP) of that factor was equal to its price. It would follow, therefore, that if the firm could do this for every one of the resources it employed it would be achieving the best combination of factors of production. Thus, the best profit combination of resources for the firm would occur when

Marginal revenue product of
labour = Price of labour

and

Marginal revenue product of
capital = Price of capital

and so on for any number of factors. In this manner the firm would achieve the most output for the least cost and also maximise its profits.

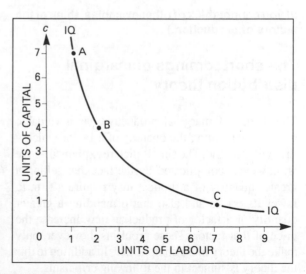

Fig. 6.4 The equal product curve or isoquant. This shows combinations of two factors (capital and labour) which would produce the same output of goods.

These principles may seem a little abstract but they are only common sense. Most business people will know whether they wish to employ another person or another machine without bothering with MRPs and isoquants.

There is no blueprint for the running of a firm because each commercial situation is unique. Two farms side by side would have to be run differently, just as two chemist shops in the same High Street would. Therefore, in every situation the entrepreneur has to work out that combination of resources which is economically correct. If they do it successfully they will be rewarded with profit – unsuccessfully and they will make a loss. Being the person responsible for production decisions you can see that the entrepreneur is one of the most vital cogs in the economic system.

Consider the agricultural industry in the UK and compare it with agriculture in a less developed nation. List three examples of how different methods of production are determined by the different supply situations of the factors of production. The first one is done for you.

1 Agriculture in the UK is capital intensive (lots of machinery etc) whereas capital is scarce in less developed countries.

(If you cannot think of other examples, think of the factors of production.)

The shortcomings of marginal distribution theory

The theory of marginal productivity is a valuable guide in explaining the quantity of a factor which a firm will demand. The simple picture explained above is, however, complicated by the fact that selling a greater quantity of a product may require a firm to lower its prices and also that demanding a greater quantity of a factor of production may increase the price of that factor. These problems, however, only make the theory more complicated. In addition to this the theory is subject to the following criticisms.

(a) *Non-homogeneity.* The theory assumes that all units of a factor are identical. This is not true either of

Keywords

Law of variable proportions
If one factor of production is fixed in supply and others variable, as stated in the law of diminishing returns, this will result in various cost structures for the business. This allows us to make statements about the behaviour of average costs, marginal costs and so on.

Short-run
The period of supply for the business in which at least one factor is fixed in supply.

Long-run
The period of supply in which all costs can be varied and firms can enter or leave the industry.

Marginal physical product (MPP)
The change to the physical output of a firm (barrels of oil, suits of clothes etc) resulting from the employment of one more unit of a variable factor.

Marginal revenue product (MRP)
The change to the total revenue of a firm from the sale of the output resulting from the employment of one more unit of a variable factor (MRP = MPP x p or MPP x MR).

Productivity
Productivity is a measure of the efficiency with which output is achieved. For example, productivity would be improved if a greater level of output was achieved for the same quantity of inputs.

Optimum combination of resources
This is the mix of resources which results in the greatest possible output for the least level of input. It is often determined by the relative prices of factors of production rather than by technological factors.

the quality of a factor or the size of the units in which it is supplied.

(b) *Immobility.* The theory assumes that factors of production can move about freely, both from industry and area to area. In practice there are serious difficulties to the free movement of factors.

(c) *Inheritance.* Marginal distribution theory is also supposed to explain how the national income is distributed between the owners of the factors of production. However, much wealth in the UK is inherited and this is outside the operation of market forces.

(d) *Political-legal.* The value of factors such as land is often determined by planning regulations etc.

(e) *Historical.* The value of factors such as land and

labour is often affected by historical factors such as industrial inertia.

(f) Inflation. Today, when the price of a factor such as labour increases, instead of less of the factor being used it is often possible to pass on the higher costs to the consumer by way of higher prices.

These criticisms notwithstanding, marginal revenue theory is the best aid we have to understanding the cost structures of an organisations.

The cost structure of the organisation

So far in this chapter we have examined production in terms of units of factors of production. In this section we look at the costs of production.

Total cost

Total cost (TC) is the cost of all the resources which are necessary to produce any particular output. It is reasonable to assume that total cost will always rise with output since getting more output always involves increasing inputs. Total costs may be divided into two parts, fixed costs and variable costs.

1 Fixed costs (FC). These are the costs which do not vary directly with output in the short-run. Fixed costs are also known as *indirect costs*. They usually include such things as the cost of land, buildings and capital equipment. These costs will go on even if the firm produces nothing. In the long-run period the business can either increase or decrease its fixed costs.

2 Variable costs (VC). As a firm produces more output, so it needs to add more raw materials, more labour, more power, etc. These costs, which vary directly with output, are called variable or *direct costs*.

You will notice the correspondence between fixed and variable costs and fixed and variable factors of production. As total output increases more slowly once the firm passes its optimum capacity and diminishing returns set in, so total cost will increase more rapidly as a greater quantity of factors of production are required to produce each successive unit of output.

Average (or unit) cost (AC)

Average cost is the total cost divided by the output produced. This may be found by the formula:

$$AC = \frac{\text{total costs}}{\text{output}} = \frac{TC}{Q}$$

Since total cost can be divided into fixed costs and variable costs it will also follow that average cost may be treated in the same way:

$$\text{average fixed costs} = \frac{\text{fixed costs}}{\text{output}}$$

$$AFC = \frac{FC}{Q}$$

$$\text{average variable costs} = \frac{\text{variable costs}}{\text{output}}$$

$$AVC = \frac{VC}{Q}$$

It therefore follows that:

AFC + AVC = ATC (average total cost)

Marginal cost

Marginal cost may be defined as the addition to total cost from production of one more unit of a commodity. In practice, it may be impossible to calculate cost as finely as this so that we calculate marginal cost by the formula:

$$\text{marginal cost} = \frac{\text{increase in total costs}}{\text{increase in output}}$$

$$MC = \frac{\Delta TC}{\Delta Q}$$

Since costs arise from the employment of factors of production it will follow that average and marginal costs will be determined by the same principles which determine average and marginal product. This is illustrated in Table 6.3. Here we use the same figures as we did earlier in the chapter and we assume that the farmer's fixed costs (land) are £40 per week while each unit of the variable factor (labour) costs £30. Here you can see that marginal cost at first falls and then begins to increase. The same is true for average cost; the business is at optimum efficiency at an output of 7 tonnes of wheat where average costs are at a minimum. This is more clearly seen graphically in Fig. 6.5.

Table 6.3 The costs of an organisation in the short term

Number of people employed	Total output of wheat (tonnes/week) (Q)	Marginal physical product (tonnes/week) (MPP)	Average product (tonnes/week) (AP)	Fixed costs (£) (FC)	Variable costs (£) (VC)	Total costs (FC + VC) (TC)	Average fixed costs (FC/Q) (AFC)	Average variable cost (VC/Q) (AVC)	Marginal cost (ΔTC/ΔQ) (MC)	Average cost (TC/Q) (AC)
0	0		—	£40	£0	£40	α	—		α
		2							£15	
1	2		2.0	40	30	70	£20	£15		£35
		3							10	
2	5		2.5	40	60	100	8	12		20
		2							15	
3	7		2.3	40	90	130	5.7	12.9		18.6
		1							30	
4	8		2.0	40	120	160	5.0	15.0		20
		0							—	
5	8		1.6	40	150	190	—	—		—

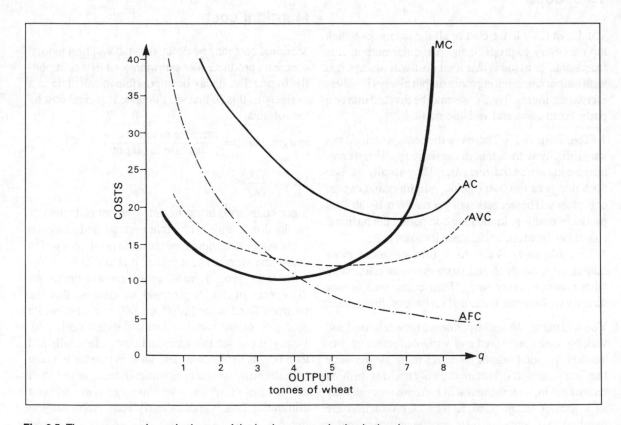

Fig. 6.5 The average and marginal costs of the business organisation in the short term.

Here we see the short-run costs curves of the business. As the MPP curve goes through the highest point of the AP curve, so you can see here that the MC curve goes through the lowest point of the AC curve. In the short run AFC declines continuously as the same amount of fixed costs are spread over a greater and greater output. The behaviour of the average variable cost curve depends upon the MC curve. Look at these now.

The relationship between marginal costs and average cost

The firm's average cost curve is always U-shaped in the short-run. This is because at an output of zero the firm still has to pay the fixed costs and therefore average cost is theoretically infinite. As output increases the fixed costs are spread over a greater and greater number of units of output and therefore average costs fall. This continues until the firm reaches optimum efficiency and then the extra variable costs needed to produce more output rise so rapidly that average cost begins to move upwards.

The average cost curve is always cut as its lowest point by the marginal cost curve. This is because while the marginal figure is below the average it must be pulling the average down but as soon as it is higher it must be pulling the average up. The reasons for this are mathematical rather than economic. Consider a student who must obtain a certain course mark. So far his average is 50% but his next mark (the marginal) is 30%; this will obviously decrease his average. The succeeding mark (marginal) rises to 40% which, although it is higher than the previous mark, will still pull the average down because it is below it. In order to increase the average mark (50%), the marginal mark must rise above it.

It is most important not to confuse marginal costs with average cost. Marginal cost relates to the *increase* in costs from producing one more unit whereas average cost relates to *total* cost which is divided by the *total* output to give the unit cost.

Average costs in the long run

We have already said that the average cost curve is U-shaped in the short term because of the law of diminishing returns. In the long run, however, the

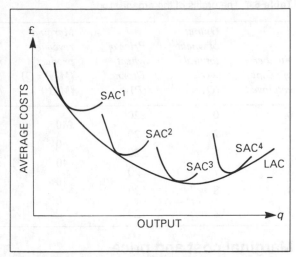

Fig. 6.6 The long-run average cost curve

fixed factors of production can be increased and so get round this problem. What effect does this have on costs? If the firm has already exploited all the possible economies of scale, then all it can do is build an additional factory which will reproduce the cost structure of the first. However, if as the market grows the firm is able to build bigger plants which exploit more economies of scale, it may also be the case that it will benefit from improved technology. These factors will have a beneficial effect upon costs.

In Fig. 6.6 SAC[1] is the original short-run average cost curve of the firm. As demand expands the business finds it possible to build a large plant which is able to benefit from more economies of scale. This is shown by SAC[2]. Eventually, however, this passes the optimum point and SAC[2] also becomes U-shaped. SAC[3] represents a repeat of the process with an even larger plant. It is impossible, however, to go on producing more and more for less and less. This would violate the fundamental basis of economics – scarcity. SAC[4] represents a stage where all possible economies of scale have been achieved and the firm is now suffering from the long-run effects of diminishing returns and the principle of increasing costs. This principle says, you will recall (*see* page 5) that as resources become scarcer they also become more expensive. LAC therefore represents the long-run average cost curve for the firm, and you can see that this also is U-shaped. Such a curve is sometimes referred to as an '*envelope*' curve.

Table 6.4 The profits of the organisation

Number of people employed	Output of wheat tonnes/ week (Q)	Price of wheat £/tonne (P)	Marginal revenue product (MPP x Q) (MRP)	Total revenue (p x Q) (TR)	Total cost (FC + VC) (TC)	Total profit (TR – TC) (TP)	Marginal cost TC/Q (MC)
0	0	£20		£0	£40	£–40	
			£40				£15
1	2	20		40	70	–30	
			60				10
2	5	20		100	100	0	
			40				15
3	7	20		140	130	10	
			20				30
4	8	20		160	160	0	
			0				—
5	8	20		160	190	–30	

Marginal cost and price

So far we have said that the firm will try to equate the marginal revenue product of a factor with the cost of that factor. The MRP, however, depends upon the price at which the product can be sold. In Fig. 6.3 we assumed that the price of wheat was £20 per tonne and we therefore obtained an MRP curve by multiplying MPP by £20. It is now possible to see that the most important consideration is marginal cost. While marginal cost is less than the price the firm will find it worthwhile to go on producing. When marginal cost is greater than the price the firm would do better to contract its output. The firm is therefore going to make most profit by producing that output at which MC is equal to the price at which the commodity is sold.

The relevant information is collected together in Table 6.4. Here you can see that the firm will produce an output of 7 tonnes per week because, if the price is £20 per tonne, this is the only output at which it can make a profit. In Fig. 6.7 you can see that this is the output at which MC = p. You can also see from Table 6.4 that to produce this output will require three units of labour. If you turn back to Fig. 6.3 you can confirm that this was the number of people at which the MRP of labour was equal to its cost.

1 Redraw Fig. 6.7 (on page 113) assuming that the price of wheat rises to £40 per tonne, fixed costs rise to £100 and wages to £50. Determine the best output for the business and how much profit it will make.

2 Wideawake Ltd produces digital alarm clocks which it sells to mail-order warehouses. At the moment it is able to sell any quantity it wishes to produce at a price of £3.50. The figure on the next page shows the present situation with the firm producing output OM.

With the aid of the diagram show the effect of the following.

(a) The cost if Widawake's lease on its factory is increased.
(b) Development in electronics allows Wideawake to produce more efficiently.
(c) The mail-order warehouses are now willing to buy the clocks at £5.00 each.

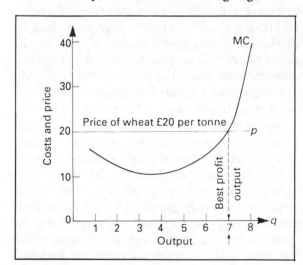

Fig. 6.7 The best profit output for the business organisation. The business makes the most profit by producing the output at which MC equals p.

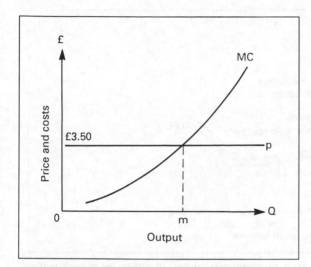

Costs and the scale of production

Several times in this chapter we have referred to economies of scale. These occur when, as a result of producing goods and services on a larger scale, the unit cost of production decreases. Not all industries benefit equally from economies of scale; in some the optimum size of a unit of production is small.

Some of the different types of economies of scale are listed below.

1 Technological. These may occur when a large firm is able to take advantage of an industrial process which cannot be reproduced on a small scale. In some cases it may just be that 'bigger is better', e.g. a double-decker bus is more cost effective than a single decker, so long as you can fill it with passengers. Technical economies are also sometimes gained by linking processes together, e.g. in the iron and steel industry where iron and steel production is carried out in the same plant, thereby saving both transport and fuel costs.

2 Commercial. A large-scale organisation may be able to make fuller use of sales and distribution facilities than a small-scale one. For example, a company with a large transport fleet will probably be able to ensure that they transport mainly full loads whereas a small business may have to hire transport or despatch part-loads. A large firm may also be able to use its commercial power to obtain preferential rates for raw materials and transport. This is usually known as 'bulk-buying'.

3 Organisational. As a firm becomes larger, the day-to-day organisation can be delegated to office staff, leaving managers free to concentrate on the important tasks. When a firm is large enough to have a management staff it will be able to specialise in different functions such as accounting, law and market research.

4 Financial. Large organisations often find it cheaper and easier to borrow money than small ones.

5 Risk bearing. All firms run risks but risks taken in large numbers become more predictable. In addition to this, if an organisation is so large as to be a monopoly, this considerably reduces its commercial risks.

6 Diversification. Most economies of scale are concerned with specialisation and concentration. However, as a firm becomes very large it may be able to safeguard is position by diversifying its products, its markets and the location of production.

As with division of labour the ability of a firm to benefit from economies of scale is not only limited by technology but by the size of the market.

Consider the following industries and activities: dairy farming, oil refining, hairdressing, steel-making, car manufacture, domestic plumbing. State the extent to which each benefits from economies of scale, i.e. a lot, quite a lot, very little, etc. Consider the reasons why this is so.

Internal and external economies of scale

Internal economies of scale are those obtained within one organisation while external economies are those which are gained when a number of organisations group together in an area. Industries such as chemicals and cars provide good examples of internal economies, where the industry is dominated by a few large organisations. Historically, the most famous example of external economies of scale was the cotton industry in Lancashire, where many hundreds of businesses concentrated in a small area made up the industry.

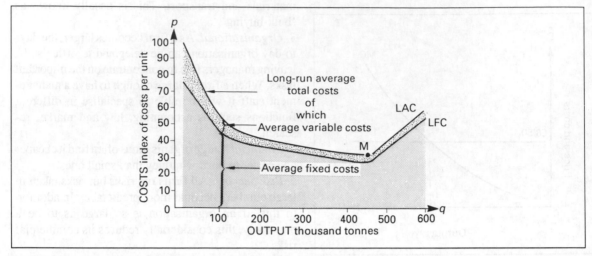

Fig. 6.8 Long run cost curve (ethylene cracker). Point M on LAC curve represents the limit of economies of scale under present technology. *Source*: The Uncommon Market *The Economist*

Long-run average costs: an example

As a firm expands and takes advantage of more economies of scale, so the average cost of a unit of output should fall. An example of this is shown in Fig. 6.8. Ethylene crackers are used in the petrochemical industry in breaking down oil to provide the raw materials for plastics, synthetic fibres, etc. The size of the average plant has grown from about 30,000 tonnes capacity in the 1950s to the present 500,000 tonnes capacity. However, beyond this point *diseconomies of scale* set in the unit costs begin to rise.

You will note that the AFC also turns upwards. This is because this is a *long-run* situation and the capital costs also increase disproportionately beyond the limits of technology. It is typical of an industry in which there are a number of economies of scale to be gained that a high proportion of its costs are fixed costs.

Economies of scale and returns to scale

Where an economy of scale leads to a fall in unit cost because less *resources* are used to produce a unit of commodity, then this is economically beneficial to society. If, for example, a large furnace uses less fuel per tonne of steel produced than a small one, society benefits through a more efficient use of scarce fuel resources. This is termed a *return to scale*. It is

possible, however, for a firm to achieve economies through such things as bulk-buying, where its buying power is used to bargain for a lower price. This benefits the firm because its costs will be lower but it does not benefit society since there is no saving of resources involved. This, then, is an *economy of scale* but not a return to scale.

Diseconomies of scale

We saw earlier in the chapter that the short-run average costs curve of a firm will turn upwards because of the law of diminishing returns. When the long-run cost of an industry turns upwards it is because it is experiencing diseconomies of scale. The typical size of plant will vary greatly from industry to industry. In capital intensive industries such as chemicals the typical unit may be vary large, but in an industry like agriculture the optimum size of firm is quickly reached and beyond this diseconomies set in.

Which of the various types of economies of scale (technical, financial, etc) are the following examples of. The first one is done for you.

1 **38 tonne trucks are made legal in the UK –** *technical.*

2 **Sainsbury's buys Stork Margarine below its usual**

price.

3 Ferranti raises £50m in new loan capital.

4 Shell builds a super-tanker.

5 BAT buys a frozen food company.

6 Marks and Spencer creates a new post of Director of Personnel.

7 GEC buys out Ferranti.

The continuance of small businesses

There are several hundred thousand business organisations in Britain today. However, about half of the total sales in the country are accounted for by the top 100 companies. Undoubtedly one of the reasons for this domination of large companies is economies of scale. It should be remembered, however, that many of these companies are *conglomerates* and may not, therefore, always benefit from economies of scale in the conventional sense. Nevertheless, despite a percentage decline in their importance, small businesses continue. Indeed, one of the features of the economy over the 1980s was the increase in the number of small businesses being set up. This was partly the result of many schemes and incentives from the government. It should also be said that many small businesses also went bust!

Another reason for the continuance of small businesses could be that there are only limited economies of scale to be gained, as in industries such as agriculture and plumbing, but small businesses also survive in industries where returns to scale are considerable. Some of the reasons for this are listed below.

1 'Being one's own boss'. Entrepreneurs may accept smaller profit for the social prestige of working for themselves or the possibility of making a much larger profit in the future.

2 Immobility in factor markets. Labour and other factors may be unwilling or unable to move from one occupation or area to another. For example agricultural workers are often kept in their jobs by 'tied cottages'.

3 Goodwill. A small business may survive on a fund of goodwill where its customers might tolerate higher prices for a more personal service.

Keywords

Fixed costs
Those costs which are fixed in the short-run, e.g. cost of premises – sometimes referred to as indirect costs. In the long-run all costs are variable.

Variable costs
Those costs which vary with output, e.g. raw materials; also called direct costs. Variable costs are zero when output is zero and rise *directly* with output.

Average cost
This is the typical cost of a *unit* of output at any particular level of output. Average cost is calculated by the simple formula:

$$AC = \frac{TC}{Q}$$

Marginal cost
The cost of producing one more unit of output.

Profit maximisation
Any business must maximise its profits by producing at the level of output at which the marginal cost is equal to the price of the product (perfect competition) or, which is the same thing, at the level of output at which the marginal cost is equal to the marginal revenue (imperfect competition).

Economies of scale and returns to scale
The important point is that returns to scale result from increased efficiency in production whereas economies of scale need only result in reduced costs *to the firm*. Thus, both result in lower costs to the *firm* but only returns to scale benefit the *economy*.

4 Banding together. Independent businesses may band together to gain the advantages of bulk-buying while retaining their independence. This is so in the grocery chains such as 'Spar' and 'Wavy-Line'.

5 Specialist services or products. Businesses may provide small specialist services or products, e.g. many small car manufacturers exist making specialist sports cars.

6 Sub-contracting. Many small businesses survive by sub-contracting to larger firms. This is very common in the construction industry.

7 Monopoly. A large organisation may tolerate the existence of small businesses in an industry as a cloak for its own monopolistic practices.

In recent years one of the effects of economies of scale has been to throw people out of work as people are replaced with machines. This has led to unions demanding shorter working weeks to create new jobs and to the government putting a new emphasis on small businesses as a possible source of employment. While new technology may cause redundancies in a stagnant economy, in an expanding economy new jobs would be being created.

The new technology has also had the effect of increasing the number of some types of small businesses. It is now possible, for example, for many office services to be conducted from the home, as we saw in Chapter 1. The standardisation which mass production brings with it has also created a demand for individually produced items, thus revitalising the demand for craftsman skills.

1 List as many reasons as you can why so many new small firms are set up each year.

2 Assess why so many newly established small firms go bust.

3 If you were setting up a new small business, what type of business would you choose and why?

Decision-making

So far in this chapter we have been concerned with factors which must be considered in all decisions relating to the use, acquisition and disposal of resources. Information on such factors is vital to the decision-making process and it is to this that we now turn. We are, as it were, moving from a general picture of the decision-making environment and the theories which influence it to a model of the process itself.

All management is ultimately a matter of making decisions. Decisions must be made on resources, on how to meet customer demands and how to try to influence and respond to the changing forces in the environment. We could have covered decision-making in a number of places in the text; the subject matter may be different but the decision-making process is similar.

Decision-making is all about determining objectives and formulating policies. It is also influenced by the structure, management style and traditions of an organisation. All levels of management and supervi-

sion should make decisions within the scope of their authority and it is a characteristic of poorly managed and unsuccessful organisations that decisions are not made when they are needed or not made at all. A lack of direction and more difficult problems result. In government, failure or unwillingness to make decisions may be reflected in establishing a commission of enquiry; in an organisation in establishing committees and at any level in any organisation in finding convincing reasons for doing nothing. Insufficient information or lack of time for consultation are typical reasons given. Alternatively, some managers make hasty and ill-considered decisions; they do not pay due regard to the circumstances and the possible consequences. Clearly, a systematic approach to all forms of decision-making is required. We consider one possible model a little later.

Levels of decision

Classifying decisions according to level is inevitably something of an artificial exercise because no two organisations are the same in their operation and no two managers will view decision-making in exactly the same way. However, it is useful in that it complements the idea of the organisation having a *hierarchy of objectives and policies* and a *hierarchical structure* (*see* Chapter 2).

Strategic or long-range decisions

These are made by top-level (corporate) management and are concerned with the organisation's overall objectives. They are the essence of *corporate planning*. They include decisions on major capital investments, sources of finance for such investments and product and market choices. The results of such decisions will inevitably take a long time to become apparent.

Tactical or medium term decisions

These are largely concerned with how to use available resources to the best advantage, how to modify policies in the light of changes in the organisation's environment and generally how to ensure it continues to achieve its corporate objectives. Such decisions will be made by the senior management of functions or departments and not by corporate management. Examples include minor capital investment, product modification and amendments to marketing plans.

Operational or short-term decisions

These are taken to put tactical plans into effect and to control activity. They concern the day-to-day activities of the organisation and many will be covered by the procedure manuals and standing instructions that we mentioned in Chapter 2. Such operational decisions are also known as *programmed decisions*; they are taken automatically in a given set of circumstances and require no managerial judgement. It is generally considered good management practice to 'programme' as many decisions as possible.

Operational decisions are made by departmental managers and supervisors. Examples include credit control, stock replenishment and delivery routes.

Consider the organisation in which you work or study, or another organisation with which you are very familiar. Identify who makes the decisions at each of the three levels of decision-making described above. Do you play a part in any of the decison-making processes?

Steps in the decision-making process

The following steps constitute one possible decision-making process. Consider them in conjunction with Fig. 6.9.

1 Observe and recognise the need for a decision to be made. This may seem basic, but is not always done.
2 Define and analyse the problem.
3 Information requirements:

(a) Obtain, store and collate information relevant to the decision. This would be done via the management information system (*see* below).
(b) Evaluate the information for possible bias, lack of objectivity and general comprehensiveness.
(c) Analyse the information to extract the relevant points.

4 Establish criteria for the decision. For example, what would be the most effective solution to the problem and what would be satisfactory.
5 Course of action:

(a) Determine and set out all alternative courses of action.
(b) Analyse the feasibility of the alternative courses of action, e.g. in the context of the resources available and the constraints under which the organisation operates, and reject those that are not feasible.
(c) Calculate the utility, i.e. the usefulness/effectiveness, of each feasible alternative and compare the results with the decision-making criteria.
(d) Select the alternative with the highest utility.

6 Forecast and check all probable outcomes of the selected alternative. What, for example, would be its impact on the organisation as a whole, how would it affect the organisation's public profile. If necessary, go back to *5* if the outcomes forecast are unacceptable.
7 Devise an action plan for the course of action selected.
8 Implement the action plan.
9 Monitor and record progress and outcomes and go back to *1*.

It should be clear to you that decision-making is a looping, evolutionary process, not a linear, 'one-off' activity. One decision leads to another and eventually back to itself for modification in response to feedback. The process outlined above is clearly also sophisticated, not all decisions will involve every step. The organisation may possess all the information it needs and relevant criteria may already have been established. Modifications to the original decision are also unlikely to involve all the stages and operational decisions may involve no more than deciding which standard procedure to use. A simple *decision loop* (*see* Fig. 6.10) shows the main stages and also the central role of information in the process.

Finally, bear in mind that a structured decision-making process will not ensure that a decision is right, only that thought is given to as many aspects of a problem as possible.

Value systems

These deserve a short section to themselves. Value systems are used to describe the way we *interpret*

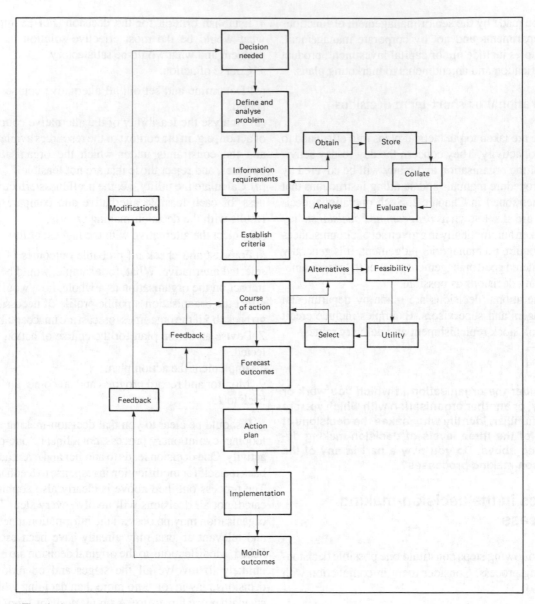

Fig. 6.9 The decison-making process

information. They consist of a mixture of our personalities, attitudes, beliefs and prejudices. Clearly, they can be complex. Value systems also exist in organisations and it is possible to consider them on three levels.

(a) Personal: Likes/dislikes, political beliefs and social attitudes

(b) Departmental: As you saw in Chapter 2; different departments may view problems in different ways.

(c) Organisational: Corporate objectives and policies.

Value systems acts as *filters* through which an individual, a department in an organisation or the organisation itself views a problem. In other words, what is regarded as the best solution to a problem will at least in part depend upon the way the relevant information is interpreted.

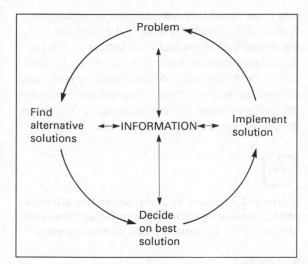

Fig. 6.10 Decision-making loop

Decision-making methods

Decisions can be made by one person alone or by a group of people working together. The method adopted will depend on the structure of the organisation, the relationships and traditions within it and management styles.

It is possible to identify a spectrum of decision-making methods ranging from the *autocratic*, where there is very little if any staff involvement, to the very *democratic*, where the manager may in effect completely delegate this decision-making function. These are explained below. If something approaching *consensus* can be achieved in an organisation (*see* page 45), it will be achieved by the latter method. The former is more likely to be a cause of *conflict* (*see* page 43).

(a) The manager *makes* the decision and *imposes* it.
(b) The manager *makes* the decision and then *persuades* the staff to accept it.
(c) The manager *makes suggestions* and asks for *questions*.
(d) The manager *makes suggestions* and asks for *views* and *other ideas*, which may influence his or her decision.
(e) The manager *explains the problem* and *invites suggestions* for a solution from which *he or she* makes a final decision.
(f) The manager *explains the problem*, the *constraints*

within which it must be solved and then *asks the staff to make the decision*.
(g) The manager *asks the staff to define the problem*, which may require investigation, and then to *find the solution*.

Consider the decision-making methods described above. Which most closely describes the method used in the organisation for which you work? Which method do you think is best or the one which you would be happiest to be a part of?

Information as a resource

You have seen above that information is essential to a properly structured decision-making process. But information is also a valuable resource in its own right. Internally, information on objectives, policies and the general performance of the organisation all help to make it function smoothly, while external information on such things as competitors' plans, demographic trends and relevant technological developments, may be vital to its very survival.

How does an organisation get the information it needs? Much is brought into the organisation through the education and basic training of its employees, a process continued through training and development programmes. Much more is easily accessible through government publications, trade magazines and various computer data banks. Specialised information can be acquired by intelligence units in the organisation or through outside agencies. In fact, so much information is now available, much of it computer based, that the Data Protection Act 1984 now 'regulates the use of automatically processed information relating to *individuals* and the provision of services in respect of such information'.

Operational research

Operational research is the use of mathematical techniques to assist in decision-making. It provides management with *quantitative* information on possible solutions to perceived problems, thereby providing an alternative to experience and intuition in decision-making. If used properly, it reduces the margin of error and therefore the risk. It is particularly useful in such areas as capital investment decisions, production planning and scheduling, stock control and general resource allocation. It cannot be used where the problem involves psychological or sociological elements. It could not be used to solve a problem involving personal motivation or industrial relations, for example.

Two common examples of operational research techniques are probability theory and network analysis. *Probability theory* is used where a large number of factors determine a particular result. So many factors may be involved that the result may appear to be due to chance. If the factors can be quantified, however, mathematical techniques can be used to predict the result of given combinations of factors. *Network analysis* determines the critical elements in a sequence of operations or procedures so that a commercial, industrial or administrative process can be completed in the shortest possible time. The process is represented on a diagram as a series of activities, a *critical path* being formed by joining the elements that are critical to its completion. A completion time is given for each of these elements which, when added together, give the minimum total completion time. (*See* page 129)

Now that computers of one kind or another (remember our comment in Chapter 1 about the excess capacity, even of home computers) are installed in most organisations, many operational research techniques are computer based. A development of them is *computer modelling*, this includes everything from models of the economy to 'what if' financial spreadsheets and computer simulations used in training.

Management information systems

A management information system is a formalised and central system for providing managers at all levels in an organisation with the information they need to make decisions. The amount of information available inevitably means that most systems today are computer based.

Establishing a management information system does not guarantee the provision of the information that may be required, it is true to say that the quality of the output is only as good as the raw data inputted, you

may know the expression 'Garbage in, garbage out'. Neither does it replace managerial decision-making, nor ensure that individual departments or functions operate in consensus rather than in conflict. It merely makes, or should make, decision-making easier and administration more efficient by providing a means of satisfying common information needs. The result should be a more effective organisation.

Discover the nature of and discuss the effectiveness of the management information system which exists in your college or place of employment.

Keywords ───────────────

Levels of decision
Decisions can be classified as either *strategic, tactical* or *operational*. Authority to take decisions at each level will depend on the structure and ethos of the individual organisation.

Decision-making
The complexity of the process will depend on the complexity of the decision to be made. At its simplest it involves identifying the problem, finding alternative solutions, deciding on the best solution and implementing it – all based on the best available information.

Decision-making methods
These can range from the autocratic to the very democratic, depending on the structure of the organisation and the management styles within it.

Value systems
These are ways in which human beings interpret information, react to problems and act as individuals and as members of organisations. Organisations may also have value systems. They consist of a mixture of personality, attitudes, beliefs and prejudices.

Operational research
Information is vital to good decision-making and the techniques of operational research provide *quantitative* information on which to make decisions.

Management information system
A centralised, almost invariably computer-based, system for providing managers with the information they need to make decisions.

Learning project

IMF Furniture

The following figures give the average physical product (APP) information for IMF Furniture. This company manufactures bedside table kits which it sells to chains of discount furniture stores for self-assembly by customers.

Number of people employed	Average product tables/year
0	0
1	1,300
2	1,430
3	1,820
4	2,275
5	2,340
6	2,210
7	1,968
8	1,657

The fixed costs which are allocated to table manufacture in terms of premises, machinery, etc amount to £6,500 pa. At the moment IMF is able to sell all the table kits it can manufacture at £5.00 per kit. At the present, wages and other variable costs amount to £100 per week per employee.

1 Determine how many workers IMF would need to employ assuming it wishes to maximise its profits. Illustrate your answer with a graph. State how many table kits it would produce.

2 Analyse the effects on employment and output if variable cost rise to £200 per worker per week.

3 In your answer to 2 it should be apparent that an increase in variable costs would cause IMF to contract both output and employment. Since the 1939-45 War, real wages have risen and, for most of the period, so have output and employment. Explain how this is possible. Your answer should also consider whether marginal revenue product theory has any relevance to the high levels of unemployment in the 1980s.
(Hints: Improvements in technology, factor substitution, micro economic and macro economic viewpoints.)

Further ideas for learning projects

1 Study Fig. 6.9, the decision-making process. Working in small groups and adapting it as appropriate, apply this to a problem situation which you have to address. This could range from completing assignment work at college, choosing and arranging a holi-day, tackling a problem you currently face at work.

2 Consider how well the economics of the UK motor industry illustrate the ideas of averaging costs explained in this chapter.

7

Technology and processes

CHAPTER OBJECTIVES

After studying this chapter you should be able to:

- Explain the effect of improving technology upon productivity;
- Appreciate the importance of design;
- Define technological leads and lags;
- Analyse organisations and methods (O & M);
- Understand network analysis;
- Distinguish between economic wealth and welfare.

Introduction

In this chapter we will consider various aspects of technology and of processing. As we have been at pains to suggest, it is vital that we understand the nature and effects of technological change because it is only in this way that we may hope to prosper and to grow. However, at the end of the chapter we will pause to consider some of the adverse effects of the unquestioning pursuit of economic growth.

Aspects of technology

The micro-chip and the Spinning Jenny

In 1767 James Hargreaves patented the Spinning Jenny. This was a device which allowed threads to be spun by machine instead of by hand. The first machine spun 12 threads simultaneously but within a few years machines were being built that were capable of spinning one hundred threads, i.e. a machine operated by

one person could do the work which had previously employed one hundred people.

We mention this to point out that the way in which the new technology is replacing jobs and people is nothing new. Indeed, there have yet to be any improvements in modern manufacturing technology comparable in scale with the Spinning Jenny. This is not to say that we should not be concerned with the adverse effects of the technological change upon employment, after all in the first industrial revolution there were great upheavals. For example, gangs of people known as *Luddites* frequently smashed up the new machinery in the vain hope of protecting jobs.

Other lessons can also be learned from the historical comparison. For example, it was frequently the case that adults were completely unable to adapt to the new technology, and so became permanently out of work, while their children laboured in the new factories.

Having pointed out the speed and magnitude of the changes we should also point out that they were slow to affect the whole economy. The full potential of the new processes was only achieved as combinations of technology evolved. For instance, the new *spinning* technology had to wait many years before it was matched by comparable improvements in *weaving*. It is the case today that there are many mismatches in technology with developments in one part of a process outstripping others. This means, of course, that technological innovations may not be fully exploited. To use an example from IT itself; the utilisation of a word processor is usually in practice determined by the speed of its printer, not the word processor itself. In addition to this there is also the inability of people to utilise technology fully.

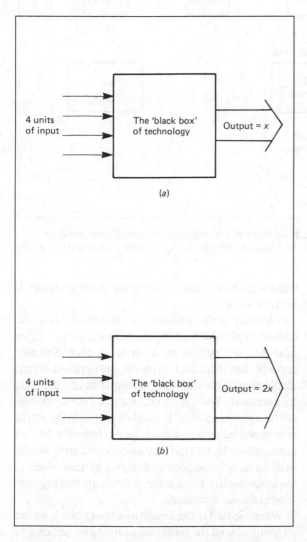

Fig. 7.1 Between (a) and (b) the state of technology improves so that the same 4 units of input or resources are converted through the 'black box' of technology to twice the amount of output.

Technology and productivity

In the previous chapter we considered economies of scale and how they increase productivity. Not all economies of scale are associated with technology; they are also associated with specialisation and with the superior organisation of production.

The place of technology in production has been described as that of *a black box*. By this we mean that all technological devices in some way *convert* energy and materials in such a way as to improve production. This idea is best understood by considering what we mean by an improvement in technology. In Fig. 7.1 *(a)* we consider the input of four units of resources into our black box of technology which *converts* these into *x* units of output. Suppose now that improved knowledge allows us to construct an improved black box. Thus, when we look at Fig. 7.1 *(b)* we see that the same four units of input now produce 2*x* units of output. This is clearly an improvement in productivity which is due to our black box or, technology.

Improved technology nearly always results in *factor substitution*. That is to say, improved machines (capital) are used to replace labour. However, as we explained in the previous chapter, the best combination of factors of production is as much an economic question as a technological one. In other words, it will depend on the relative prices of the factors of production.

An improvement in technology may not necessarily involve economies of scale. For example, a photocopier which produced cheaper or better copies would be improved technology but would not involve larger scale production. Such an improvement would result in a downward shift in the average cost curve without the rightward shift associated with the example in Fig. 6.6. It is possible, of course, that improved technology is only available on a large scale as we explained on page 113.

When a line of production involves various different processes, it is possible that each stage of production may have a different optimal size. For example, a large blast furnace may produce 75 tonnes of pig iron while the steel furnace may only be able to handle 30 tonnes and the rolling mill 50 tonnes. Given these figures, the smallest optimal size for an integrated process would be 150 tonnes. We determine this by taking the lowest common multiple of the individual

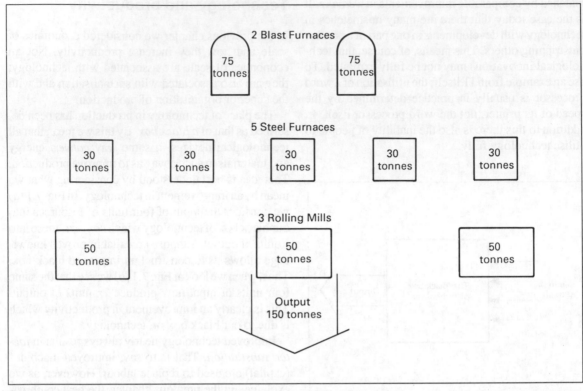

Fig. 7.2 The least optimal size: the smallest size of plant which will keep all the units fully employed is the smallest common multiple of the size of unit, i.e. 2 x 75, 5 x 30 and 3 x 50 all equal 150 tonnes. Any smaller size would leave part of the plant unemployed.

processes involved. In our example this would involve 2 blast furnaces, 5 steel furnaces and 3 rolling mills. (*See* Fig. 7.2.)

The importance of design

It is quite possible for a product to be technically supurb and be a commercial failure. Conversely, some products which are technologically mediocre may turn out to be great successes. One of the reasons for this is design. There are many aspects to design, all of which may prove equally important for the commercial success of a product. We will now consider some of the important aspects:

1 Technical. By this we mean the technical specification of a product. Examples of this could be things such as the fuel injection system for a car, the design of micro-chips for computers, the building plans for a new tower block and so on. While you might think that

these must be the most important aspects of design it is often not so.

2 Relevance to the consumer. To illustrate this point, consider two of the examples we used above. If we take the fuel system of a car it at once becomes apparent that there are two seemingly opposed design requirements: the need for performance and the need for economy. What is correct for one consumer may not be right for another. In nearly every case the actual design will have to be a compromise between the two needs. Other factors too may affect competing needs; in this example the need to design a system which is environmentally acceptable, i.e. on producing low levels of toxic emissions.

When we turn to the design of a tower block we are all familiar with the problems of living or working in buildings which technically speaking may have been masterpieces of design!

3 Style. It is obvious that many products must have a physical appearance which appeals to the consumer.

The style will also have to reconcile appearance with function, utility and economy.

4 Reliability. A product may have excellent design characteristics as far as the first three points are concerned but if it is unreliable it is hardly likely to sell. This was a problem which bedeviled many British industries, especially the motor industry.

Once we have designed a suitable product it is still necessary to sell it. Thus, other skills such as marketing enter into the picture. As an illustration of the points we have discussed, consider the case of the Amstrad and Sinclair computer companies. In the early 1980s Sinclair, led by Sir Clive Sinclair the inventor of the pocket calculator, produced superbly designed personal computers. Amstrad on the other hand, led by Alan Sugar, used rather antiquated technology in the production of its products. However, better marketing and closer attention to the needs of consumers meant that it was Amstrad that succeeded. The humble *Amstrad 8256* still sells in large numbers – you may well use one at college or at home – while you have probably never heard of the superbly designed, innovative *Sinclair QL* PC unless you know someone who has got one. Sinclair, on the verge of insolvency, was taken over by Amstrad in 1986 after which the more successful Sinclair products were effectively marketed and retained a sizeable share of the home computer market.

As a group select a best-selling technology based product such as a computer, hi-fi, video recorder etc. Individually list in order the four features which you think account for its commercial success. Compare the features selected in your group and discuss them in the context of the aspects identified above.

Leads and lags

A *lead* is the technological advantage a business obtains from its adoption of more advanced equipment whereas a technological *lag* is the advantage a business foregoes by not having the most advanced equipment. It is inevitable that businesses will experience both leads and lags.

Let us take an example. A business services com-

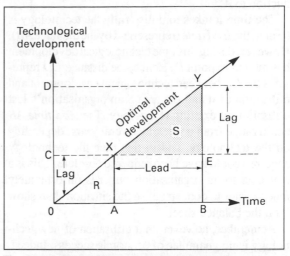

Fig. 7.3 Leads and lags in the utilisation of technology. If an organisation adopts the latest technology at point X, then the shaded area AXEB represents their benefit from it. The shaded areas R and S represent the loss through the organisation's lags in technology.

pany decides to re-equip and invests in a 16-bit computer system. Soon after it has done so, a new generation of 32-bit computers comes on to the market. These are faster, more efficient, have greater capacity and generally are better able to meet the organisation's needs. However, the company cannot afford to scrap its recently acquired system and therefore is failing to utilise all the available technology.

We can represent this diagrammatically. Look at Fig. 7.3. The vertical axis shows *technological development* and the horizontal axis *time*. An ideal situation would be where an organisation was able to exploit fully every relevant technological development immediately, thereby moving along line *OXY*, the *line of optimal development*. However, because of practical constraints this is impossible. Besides the cost involved, considerable periods of time would be lost installing equipment and training staff to use it.

Since this ideal cannot be attained, we can consider an organisation's position in the following way. Point *A* represents an organisation's decision to invest in new technology, say a computer system. It could have bought into the technology right at the start (point *O*) but chose to wait (to point *A*) and therefore reaped the benefit of a move to point *C* on the technological development axis. The area *R* represents the lost utilisation of technology caused by delaying its introduction to *A*.

The time it takes to utilise fully the technology is termed the *lead time* (represented by the distance *AB*). However, during this time technological development has moved to point *D*. Hence, the distance *CD* represents the *lag* between technological development and utilisation of it and the area *S* an organisation's lost utilisation of existing technology. The *lead time AB* could range from a week to several years, depending on the technology, and in this time the technology acquired could have been rendered obsolete. This is a real cost to an organisation but it is unfortunately much easier to conceptualise the situation than show it on the balance sheet.

Remember, however, that utilisation of new technology is no guarantee of economic success. Indeed, many businesses prosper using obsolete technology, e.g. Jacquard silk looms, which were introduced in 1801 are still in use today, while those using or developing the new technology are frequently in trouble, for example the financial problems experienced by such high tech companies as Sinclair and Ferranti. Furthermore, investing in technology which is unnecessary can be an expensive and sometimes disastrous mistake; witness the computers not earning their keep in many organisations.

Investment

In a modern technologically based economy it is necessary that we both develop and implement the best ways of doing things. This implies that we must put adequate resources to investment. Investment, in this context may be divided into two categories: first, the acquisition of new capital equipment; second, investment in the research and development (R & D) of new technology. A problem which afflicts both the British and other economies is that of *short termism*. This refers to the tendency of investors to look for an immediate return on their investments.

To understand the phenomenon of short termism, we must realise that most new investment, by which we mean the purchase of equity (shares), in the UK is in the hands of the insurance companies and the pension funds. These in turn are run by professional managers whose prime concern is to show a better return than their competitors over a twelve-month or even a quarterly period. By its very nature, the majority of pioneering R & D will only pay off, if at all, over a long period. It is essential for the continued well-being of the economy, however, that this type of research takes place. This clearly leaves a role for the government either to fund such investment itself or by tax policies etc to make sure that such research continues.

Construct a graph to show the effect of an improvement in technology on a firm's marginal revenue product (MRP) curve. (*See* Chapter 6.) Explain the relationship between technology and the law of diminishing returns.

Keywords ————————————————

Technology
The science of industrial arts. An improvement in technology allows better use of the factors of production.

Productivity
Increasing productivity means improving the input-output ratio.

Design
Good design is not just technical specification but involves relevance to the consumer, style and reliability. It goes hand-in-hand with technology in determining the commercial success or failure of a product or service.

Leads and lags
A technological lead is the advantage gained from up-to-date technology and a lag is the advantage foregone by using obsolescent technology.

———————————————————————

Processing

What is processing?

Because we have concentrated on technological processes such as the construction of a car we may be in danger of forgetting that there are many other types of processes. As well as the physical construction of a product, a manufacturing company will have to be concerned with many other processes such as purchasing, warehousing, marketing, transport and so on. Indeed, we find that these are as important as the

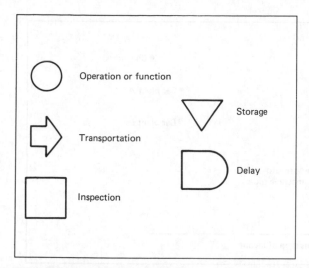

Fig. 7.4 Process chart symbols.

constructional processes involved. For many businesses, of course, there is no product involved because they are in tertiary (service) industries. For these industries the organisation of processes and their exploitation of technology is equally important.

A process, therefore, is any organisation or activity aimed at the production of goods and services. Thus, when you go to renew your library book a process is involved. When you purchase new clothes you are at one end of an extremely complicated process.

Process charts

One way of understanding processes is through *process (or work) charts*. There are standard symbols for analysing processes and displaying them in charts. These are illustrated in Fig. 7.4 and are based on the British Standards Institution recommendations. Fig. 7.5 shows a *flow process chart* of the relatively simple process of a worker checking the accuracy of a component. The numbers inside the symbols record the number of times each particular type of function occurs in the process. In our example there are four transport operations. This is the process chart for the *worker* doing the inspection. The chart for the component itself would look rather different.

Such detailed analysis of processes becomes absolutely essential when we come to computerise operations.

Organisation and Methods (O & M)

The *function* of organisation and methods, commonly known as O & M, is to establish the best forms of organisation, systems and procedures for carrying out any task or series of tasks. It must take into account constraints of all types: financial, physical and human. The principle *objective* of O & M is to eliminate waste: of time, human energy, materials, space, etc. If this is done successfully then productivity will be increased and costs reduced. It is another important objective of O & M to improve the job satisfaction of staff.

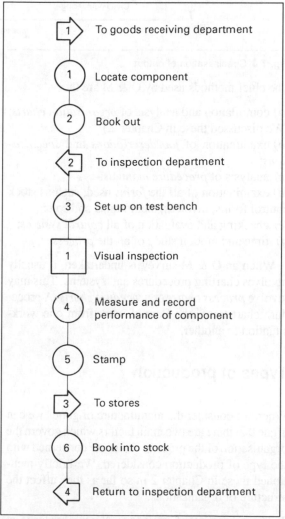

Fig. 7.5 Flow process chart showing a worker going to the goods receiving department, collecting a component, checking it, adding it to stock and then returning to their own department.

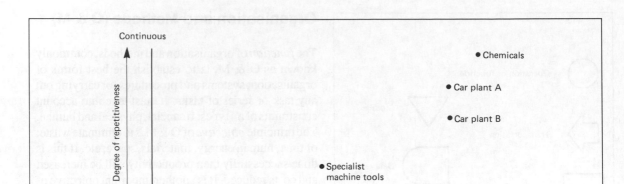

Fig. 7.6 Specialisation of output.

The chief methods used by O & M are the:

(a) compilation and analysis of *organisation charts*; (We discussed these in Chapter 2.)

(b) examination of *job descriptions* and *specifications*;

(c) analysis of *procedure manuals*;

(d) examination of all the *forms* used, such as stock control forms, invoices, memoranda and so on;

(e) checking and evaluation of all *control systems*;

(f) time and motion study of all the *processes*.

When an O & M survey is undertaken, it usually involves charting procedures and systems. This may involve *process charts* or *procedure charts*. A procedure chart traces the flow of work from one work-situation to another.

Types of production

When we consider the manufacture of goods we can argue that there are two main factors which govern the organisation of the process. These are concerned with the type of production considered. We briefly mentioned these in Chapter 2 in so far as they affect the structure of organisations.

1 The uniqueness of production. We might also term this the *degree of repetitiveness* involved. At one end of the scale there is totally unique production, e.g. the building of a bridge, and at the other a continuous

process where all the products are absolutely identical, as with the output of petrol from a refinery.

2 The degree of specialisation of layout. At one end of the scale we have the situation where there is no specialisation, as with the building of a house, when the product remains stationary and the facilities required during its manufacture are brought to it as and when required. At the other extreme we can place highly specialised layouts such as moving production lines.

We can plot these two against each other on a chart. This is done in Fig. 7.6. In the top right-hand corner we would expect to find continuous processes such as the manufacture of chemicals while towards the bottom left we find civil engineering and shipbuilding. You might expect that repetitiveness and specialisation always go hand-in-hand, but this is not necessarily so. In Fig. 7.6 Car Plant A is more old fashioned than Car Plant B. The possibilities of computer control have allowed Plant B to be more specialised than Plant A while at the same time enabling more variation in the models produced.

The importance of time

Time can dramatically alter the costs of a project or product. If you look at Fig. 7.7, you will see that it appears very similar to the cost curves which we examined in the last chapter. However, you will see

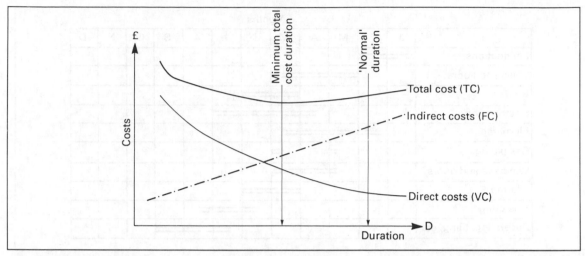

Fig. 7.7 Costs are affected by the duration of the project. Indirect costs tend to rise with duration and direct costs tend to fall.

that on the horizontal axis, instead of output we have the duration (or time) of the project. The duration of a project is likely to vary inversely with the resources applied to it and therefore with the cost associated with its completion. Under these circumstances neither the minimum nor the maximum project duration is likely to be the same as the least cost duration. Reductions in project duration are likely to lead to increases in direct costs (more overtime worked, more resources wasted etc) and reductions in indirect costs such as administration. Conversely, increases in duration are likely to have the opposite effects. In Fig. 7.7 the lowest point of the total cost curve represents the best relationship between duration and costs.

Time scheduling

We may now approach the task of how we best allocate time when organising a task. This depends upon two things:

1 Activity scheduling. When we organise a task we must bear in mind that some activities have to be completed before others can be started. In some cases two or more activities may be dealt with simultaneously. In order to schedule the activities we must identify the key items on a checklist.
2 Time scheduling. A time schedule sets out the items on a check list in the order in which they have to be undertaken and indicates the time required for each item.

One way in which these two forms of scheduling may be combined is in a bar chart. This is illustrated in Fig. 7.8. This indicates when the major tasks in building a house will take place.

Network analysis

We may also look at the problem of time in a more sophisticated way through *network analysis*. This is one of various terms used to describe the best known analytical planning technique. It is also called:

PERT   (programme evaluation review technique),
CPA   (critical path analysis) and
CPN   (critical path networks).

Network analysis is particularly valuable as a method of planning and controlling large and complex projects.

In order to undertake network analysis, we must take the following steps.

1 Construct a network (or arrow) diagram to represent the project to be undertaken. In the diagram each arrow represents an activity. The arrangement of these activities represents the order in which jobs have to be done and the interdependence of the jobs. Where one job depends upon another being done these are known as *sequential activities* and, obviously, one must come after the other in the network. For example, if the

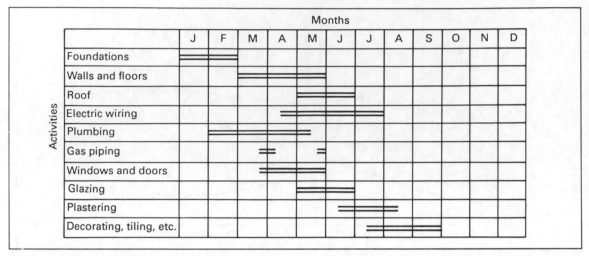

Fig. 7.8 Time schedule bar chart showing the length of time and sequence for major activities in building a house.

project we were considering was wallpapering a room then clearly stripping off the old paper must come before putting on the new! On the other hand, some activities may take place while other activities are going on; these are known as *parallel activities*. For instance, to continue our example, it would be possible for someone to be selecting the new wallpaper while someone else was stripping off the old. At some stage the various activities must come together and this is shown by convergence of the arrows in the diagram.

2 Make estimates of the duration of each activity in the network.

3 Using these estimates, calculate the *earliest* and *latest event dates* for each stage of the project, the earliest finish date for the project and the amount of float (or free) time available for each activity.

A sample network analysis is shown in Fig. 7.9. Each activity is labelled A, B, etc, together with the time in days which is allowed for this activity. The numbers in circles show the various stages which must be achieved. The numbers in boxes alongside the circles show, respectively, the earliest date by which they can be achieved and the latest date by which they must be achieved if they are not to hold up the project. The numbers in brackets record the possible free time which may exist between stages. For example, the earliest date for stage 11 is 28 days while the latest date for stage 14 (the next sequential stage) is 42 days. The estimated time for the process which links these (ac-

tivity Q) is 8 days, thus giving possible free time of up to 6 days.

In practice, of course, it may be difficult to predict with accuracy the duration of activities to be undertaken. Unforeseen factors such as the weather, strikes or delays in the supply of materials may intervene.

 Activity

Prepare a network analysis for a simple task with which you are familiar, e.g. making a cup of tea or preparing a meal.

Keywords _____

Processing
A process is the organisation of any activity aimed at the production of goods or services. It may or may not involve a technological element.

Process chart
A way of representing, planning and analysing a process.

O & M
A study of a task or a series of tasks to determine the most efficient and effective way to achieve an objective.

Network analysis
A production planning technique which uses projected times which a series of connected tasks will take to complete as a basis on which to schedule those tasks.

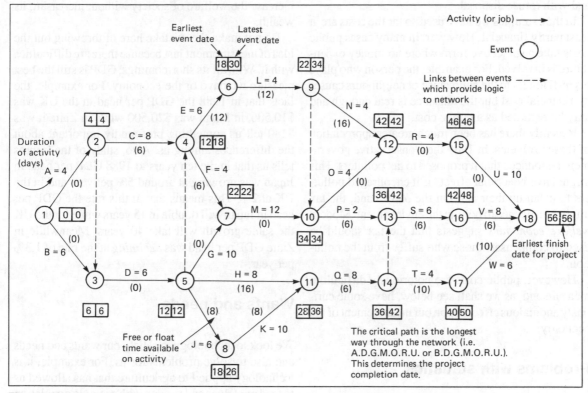

Fig. 7.9 Network analysis

Perspectives on technology

So far we have been recommending technological change unreservedly. In this last section of the chapter we pause to consider whether all technical progress is equally desirable and whether the pursuit of productivity and economic growth might not be accompanied by problems.

Private, social and public costs

When we discussed technological change, we made the implicit assumption that anything which increases productivity, i.e. decreases the unit costs of production, is desirable. This may indeed be so as far as the business itself is concerned but it may ignore some of the wider implications.

When an individual or a business carries out a particular activity *private costs* are incurred. That is to say, the financial cost of the operation. *Social costs* on the other hand are the total cost of that activity to all members of the community. *Public costs* are the difference between private and social costs, or in other words, the costs which an individual's or business' activities impose upon other members of the community. The classic example of public cost is the factory chimney belching out black smoke. The private cost involved is the fuel bill of the factory. But the public costs are borne by the people who live near the factory and who may, for example, have to spend more on soap and detergents than they otherwise would and perhaps have their health ruined.

Almost any activity which has adverse effects upon the environment can be regarded as an example of public costs. Another way of putting this is to say that the production of economic *goods* may also involve the production of economic *bads*. The brewery which sells its beer in cans incurs the cost of packaging but the costs of dealing with the empty cans do not fall on the brewer. They are met by the various public authorities concerned with keeping public places tidy and with refuse disposal.

In the examples we have used so far the costs are at least partly financial. However, in many cases public costs take a subjective form where no money expenditure is involved. For example, the person who plays his hi-fi loudly to the annoyance of neighbours causes no financial cost but the nuisance is real enough and may be regarded as a public cost.

Recently there has been much greater appreciation of these problems. In 1989 the Conservative government announced that it proposed to tax polluters. This might have beneficial effects if it encouraged polluters to clean up their act. On the other hand, the tax might be a licence to pollute the environment. Modern *welfare economics* suggests that the tax should be used to compensate those who suffer from the pollution.

However, public costs are notoriously difficult to measure and, as we shall see below, have some curiously anomalous effects upon our measurement of the economy.

Problems with statistics

One of the most important economic indicators for the economy as a whole is the *Gross Domestic Product* (GDP). This is a measure of all the wealth produced, distributed and consumed in a year. It is commonly known as the *national income*. An increase in the GDP per head is commonly accepted as indicating that the whole nation is becoming better off. However, from what we have said above it becomes clear that many things which affect the *quality* of our lives will be left out. Traffic congestion, air pollution and litter are just three things which detract from our life style. Not only that but where public costs give rise to financial transactions they actually *increase* the GDP. The more money people spend on laundry bills, the more people are employed picking up empty beer cans in parks, the more is spent by sewage disposal authorities, the greater is the GDP.

What we are speaking of here is what economists refer to as the *wealth/welfare connotation*. By this we mean that increasing the wealth of society may not necessarily increase its total well-being (welfare). We can also infer from this that it may be possible to

increase the welfare of society without increasing its wealth.

Do not make the mistake here of throwing out the idea of measurement just because there are difficulties with it. With all its shortcomings, GDP is still the best measure we have of the economy. For example, the facts that in 1988 the GDP per head in the UK was $10,506, in Japan was $20,500 while in Zaire it was $180 tell us something profoundly important about the differences among us. Also, study of the figures tells us that in the ten years to 1988 GDP per head in Japan was growing at around 5% per year and in the UK at 2%. This means that at this rate the GDP per head in Japan will double in 15 years while for the UK the same growth will take 40 years. Meanwhile in Zaire GDP per head was *declining* at the rate of 1.3% per year.

Wants and needs

We look to technology to satisfy our wants and needs and also to solve problems for us. For example, it is technology applied to agriculture that has allowed us to feed ourselves and to cope with growing population pressure. However, there is a distinction between what we absolutely *need* – things which we might term satiable (satisfiable) needs (food, clothing and shelter) – and the insatiable desire for things which we *want* (fashionable clothing, larger houses, fast cars and so on).

One of our problems is that both as producers and consumers we tend to concentrate on the insatiable markets. Why is this so? First, there is no market as dangerous for the business as a satiable one. The ups and downs of agricultural markets demonstrate the point very clearly. The demand for food can never exceed what the consumers can be induced to eat. There are, of course, millions of hungry people in the world but you cannot base a business on the provision of goods for people who cannot pay for them – demand in economics is *need* backed by the *ability to pay*. Concentration on insatiable markets is therefore to be preferred if increasing demand for a product is to be maintained.

A second attraction of a prospectively insatiable market is that it may be rendered truly insatiable by the management of demand. There are two major instruments of the maintenance of insatiability in a market. The first is the stimulation of dissatisfaction by advertising, the second is cultivation of planned obsolescence. To illustrate these points, consider the market for cars. Think for a moment of the car you would *really* like. Then pause to consider that what attracted you was perhaps the fact that it is able to travel much faster than it is legally, or practicably, possible to drive. Also bear in mind that it will probably rust and drop apart very quickly. You will probably have to admit that the car you *want* is not suited to your, or society's, true *needs*. The design of motor cars in the late 20th century is as much a product of marketing as it is of technology.

In a wealthy industrialised economy such as that of the UK we might be able to afford throw-away consumerism but this also affects the rest of the world. Most obviously we are depleting the resources of the World. Less obviously it results in modes of production and products inappropriate to the needs of poor countries. If we continue our cars example, we can see that the poorer countries of the World must use cars designed for the streets of Chicago and Paris on the streets of Bombay and Addis Ababa. An ideal Third World car might well be aluminium-bodied, mechanically very simple with a very low petrol consumption etc. However, the massive size of companies such as General Motors and Nissan prevents Third World countries competing with them and producing the type of car which is really needed. Similarly, convincing very poor people that what they really want is a bottle of *Coca Cola* is surely the most expensive way to buy water that there is!

Perhaps there are the first signs of a change in our approach. As you saw in Chapter 1, in the late 1980s the 'Green Lobby' achieved some political success in the UK after grass roots interest had been growing for a number of years. 'Green' issues became fashionable and attractive to both politicians and marketers. A favourable price differential, based on a lower tax rate, gave lead-free petrol a real boost and the stimulus to car manufacturers to produce cars that could run on it, although in other countries this had been required for some years. On the other hand, detergent manufacturers produced environmentally friendly detergents, often packaged in appropriately green boxes, which

'concerned' consumers seemed happy to pay more for. It remains to be seen whether these are systems of a real change in our attitudes or the latest fashion designed to make us feel better about our largely uncaring exploitation of the environment. 'Green' politicians are certainly interested in rather more than detergents and lead-free petrol!

Keywords

Private, social and public costs
Private costs are the financial costs incurred in an activity. Social costs are the total cost to the community of an activity. When social costs exceed private costs the difference is said to be public costs.

Standard of living
The most common measure of standards of living is income per head. A true measure of standard of living must consider welfare as well as wealth.

Economic 'bads'
When an activity results in pollution etc a negative externality is said to exist. It is possible for there to be positive externalities.

Appropriate technology
The best technology for a society is the one most appropriate to its condition and needs, not necessarily, the most advanced.

Conclusion

The problem of economic society is *optimising*, that is to say, making the best use of resources. Improvements in technology have constantly enabled us to make better use of resources as have improvements in organisations and methods. When we use the word *better* here we are using it in the sense of a smaller amount of resources being used to produce any particular item. This is absolutely essential if we are to compete in world markets. However, there is the danger of *suboptimisation*, that is to say, finding out the best way to do something which should not be done at all. Engineers, the military, governments, businesses and, quite possibly, you and I are all quite busy, not to say good, at this.

Learning project

Automation in banking

Read the following article which is taken from the journal *Banking World* (November 1987) and attempt the tasks which follow.

Britain's High Street bankers today recognise that in their extensive branch networks they possess unrivalled facilities for selling services in an increasingly competitive market-place.

The branch is where customers go to deposit funds and borrow money, the argument goes; the challenge is to deploy premises and staff so that customer relations can be developed and consolidated.

Key to this approach is the use of technology. Two concepts underlie today's branch automation. One is the notion that details of a customer's relationship with the bank - across the board from his current account to his mortgage and his holdings of securities - must be filed under his name and not as a series of separate accounts. The other is that it must be possible to access and manipulate this customer data at any point in the network, through distributed processing.

Much of current data processing work in the banks, therefore, now turns on building customer information files (CIF) using what is known in the trade as *relational database technology*. The big UK banks have a tradition of building their own systems, although Midland has recently broken with this tradition and turned to the US-owned software house, Hogan.

For smaller banks, building societies and other institutions packages are becoming available. A recent entrant to this sector of the market-place has been the CAP group, which has acquired the Systematics franchise from the US.

Customer information files, with transactions entered in real time, will provide up-to-the-minute information. They should allow branch staff to make better informed decisions on credit, rates and charges, when approached by personal and corporate clients. These files can also be used by management, since the date they contain can be used to determine the relative profitability of different accounts, customers and services.

Many of the systems underpinning this new wave of branch automation are based on a relatively new animal, the branch controller (which is in effect a mini-computer). The idea is that interlinked networks of branch controllers can provide the distributed processing on which the relational databases containing customer files can be handled.

The major suppliers take this new market very seriously. NCR, for instance, is supplying branch controllers to run the NatWest network; Midland runs its branches on Nixdorf mini-computers; Lloyds Bank is installing IBM branch controllers. And both NCR and Philips (which supplies Bank of Scotland) have begun to offer mini-computers running on the Unix operating system, in the hope that this will emerge as a standard for the industry.

DEC, now a $10bn company with aspirations to lead the bunch of computer manufacturers behind IBM, was an early player in this game. The company secured a contract in 1983 to supply Barclays with what was its current range of mini-computers, the PDP 11, to build the bank's network of branch controllers.

Since that early success, DEC's profile in the branch banking market-place has been fairly low (although the new Vax mini-computers have been successful in the dealing room market).

Greater power to the branch

DEC is now returning to the branch banking market-place with some gusto, and said so at its recent corporate jamboree in Boston, DECWorld. The founder and president Ken Olsen has imbued the company with his basic philosophy: that computers should allow staff to work across intra-corporate boundaries (as opposed to seeking information from a mainframe at the top of a data processing pyramid). DEC's European marketing chief, Bruno d'Avanzo, states the argument succinctly: 'The bank's computer structure has to be reconsidered, to give the branch greater processing power. And we have the architecture.'

In addition to this basic architecture, banks are devoting increasing resources to two other aspects of technology within the branch.

One is the introduction of self-service terminals, quite apart from cash dispensers, to allow customers to enquire about products and services (and perhaps one day to sign up for loans and insurance policies). These terminals are based on interactive video disk technology; this combines videotex (the display of information which can be called up from a central database) with videodisks (for 'films' demonstrating products and services) and the local processing power of a micro-computer. Lloyds Bank and the TSB are leaders here, running terminals in a handful of branches on a pilot basis.

The other area of current technological development is the application of artificial intelligence to branch banking. This could be the alchemist's stone for the UK banks, now wrestling with the problem of training their staff to sell several hundred products to increasingly sophisticated customers.

The benefits of using expert systems were summed up by Helix Software's Joe St Johanser this spring in Geneva at the IBC conference on retail banking. 'When a bank has a network of a thousand branches, there is enormous cost benefit potential in building an expert system to put an expert in every branch. Each branch has to have a pay-off of only 1/1000 of the cost of software development to produce a net benefit.'

1 What does the articles suggest are the key concepts in banking automation?

2 The article makes reference to 'expert systems'. What do you understand by this expression? Illustrate your response by reference to one system with which you are familiar.

3 Construct a diagram which illustrates the 'intra-corporate' nature of the new systems in banking. (You may find the matrix chart on page 37 a useful starting point.)

4 Explain what is meant by the expression 'deskilling'. Examine the effect of this phenomenon on banking or another industry.

5 The mid-1990s will see a major demographic shock for British industry, i.e. there will be a rapid decline in the number of young people entering the workforce (see page 89). Suppose that you are employed in the corporate planning department of a clearing bank. Prepare a strategy for your head of division setting out a strategy for dealing with the problems which are likely to arise. (You may select a different industry if you wish.)

6 In what ways are developments in the new technology qualitatively and quantitatively different from those of previous industrial and scientific revolutions.

7 Examine the ways in which the new technology may improve customer services.

Further ideas for learning projects

1 As a small group select a task at work or at college. Analyse the task using a flow process chart and determine how the task could be performed more efficiently. Attempt to quantify the savings which would result. Present your procedures and findings as a report.

2 Make a list of the factors which you think contribute to your level of welfare, e.g. good health. To what extent do these equate with your level of wealth? Do you consider that if your level of wealth were to double, so too would your level of welfare. Fully explain your reasons.

3 As a group, arrange a visit to a large-scale manufac-turing or processing plant. ('Processing' can include, say, handling parcels, information – indeed anything where a 'process' is used to achieve a result.) Both before and during the visit, find out as much about the design and organisation of the processes used and represent them as process charts. Prepare a commentary on the stages identified in the process charts.

4 Suggest ways in which the subjective cost of aircraft noise might be estimated.

5 Describe how you might set about assessing the level of welfare in society as opposed to the level of wealth.

8

The organisation and its employees

CHAPTER OBJECTIVES

After studying this chapter you should be able to:

Define labour as a factor of production;
Explain the manpower planning process;
■ Explain job descriptions and personnel specifications;
Appreciate the importance of staff appraisal and training;
Describe the nature and functions of a trade union;
Outline the law relating to trade union activity;
Define a contract of employment;
List the contractual and statutory rights and duties which exist in employment;
State the factors affecting the ability of trade unions to raise wages;
Analyse the effect of collective bargaining on wage rates.

Introduction

While both the traditional view of labour as a factor of production and the Marxist view of labour as the source of all wealth are relevant in the study of the economy, these may seem far removed from the employee and organisation. Of far greater relevance to the individual employee is the work of an organisation's personnel department and the institutional and legal framework of employment and industrial relations. For this reason, this chapter examines not only the conventional economic theory but also such things as manpower planning, training, the law relating to employment and trade union activities, and wage bargaining.

Labour as a factor of production

Economically, labour may be defined as the exercise of human mental and physical effort in the production of goods and services.

This means that, to be classed as the efforts of labour, a person must be in some way concerned with the production of goods or services for sale. If, for example, people work in their gardens, this would not be counted as part of labour. If, however, they perform the same task but the produce is then sold, these efforts become labour. Usually labourers are employed for remuneration although they could, of course, be self-employed.

Labour differs from the other factors of production in that it is human. Thus, we cannot just consider units of labour, we must also consider the personality of the workers.

Likewise we cannot just talk about scrapping labour as we might an unwanted piece of capital equipment. As well as being an economic waste, the unemployment of workers brings social, psychological and political problems.

The supply of labour

The supply of labour in an economy is the *working population*. This will be determined by the age, sex and geographical distribution of the population. These are fully discussed in Chapter 4. The supply of labour is also affected by a population's *leisure preference*. If a population has a very high leisure preference, people will work less and take more time off as wages increase.

Vocationalism also affects the supply of labour. In occupations like the clergy, nursing and teaching, people often work for a low wage because they consider the job worthwhile. People are also influenced by social prestige. Many people consider white collar jobs more 'respectable' than manual work and will settle for lower wages. The supply of labour of some occupations is also affected by job security and prospects for promotion. A job might also be attractive for its fringe benefits such as long holidays, a car or cheap loans.

In considering the supply of labour it is also necessary to consider its quality, how well-trained and educated people are, how healthy they are and how industrious. It is not enough just to hire a worker – it must be the right person with the right skills in the right place.

What is meant by the term 'the working population'? Discover the size of the UK's current working population. What percentage of the working population are men and what percentage are women?

The mobility of labour

The UK is short of labour. This may seem strange when there are long 'dole' queues but it is true in that we lack people with the right skills in the right places. Unemployment and the shortage of labour could be eased simultaneously if there were greater mobility of labour. Labour mobility is of two main types, occupational and geographical. *Occupational mobility* is the ability of a person to move from job to job, e.g. from being a coal-miner to being an engineer. *Geographical mobility* is the ability of a worker to move from one area to another. Surprisingly, in a country as small as the UK, mobility is very low. Mobility also tends to be lower in times of heavy unemployment. People are reluctant to move from the places and people they know when the prospects are uncertain.

The government is making efforts to increase mobility with such things as Employment Training, but it seems fair to say that more is needed if the problem is going to be overcome.

List six reasons why the remuneration (wages and salaries) differ so greatly between different occupations. One reason is given for you.

1 Different amounts of training required. (You may find page 108 useful.)

Keywords

Labour
Only where there is payment is human effort counted as labour. This excludes much hard work, e.g. parents bringing up children!

Derived demand
This is where a product or service is demanded not for itself but for the use to which it can be put.

Mobility of labour
The ease with which people can change the type of job they do (occupational mobility) or where they are willing and able to do their job (geographical mobility).

Personnel management

Personnel management defined

Personnel management can be defined as that part of management concerned with people at work and with their relationships within an enterprise. Its aim is to bring together and develop into an effective organisation men and women who make up an enterprise and, with regard to the well-being of the individual and of working groups, to enable them to make their best contribution to its success.

An alternative definition based on industrial psychology sees personnel management as dealing with people at work with respect to:

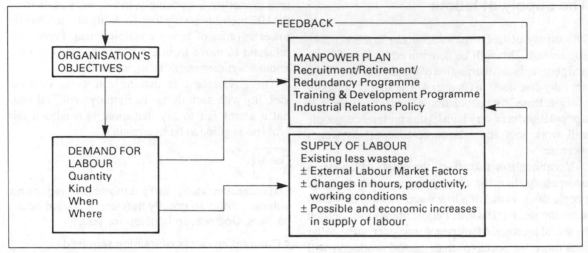

Fig. 8.1 The manpower planning process

(a) Utilisation: recruitment, selection, promotion, appraisal, training and development;
(b) Motivation: job design, pay, benefits, consultation, participation and negotiation;
(c) Protection: working conditions, safety, welfare.

Personnel management is a large and important subject in its own right. In this book we can only give you a selective introduction to it. Our aim is to provide sufficient information for you to understand the term and appreciate its importance in the modern organisation and a basis on which you can make your own observations. Although this section is specifically entitled *Personnel management*, we have covered other aspects of it elsewhere to fit in with the broader perspectives of the book: *Change* and its implications for organisations and individuals in Chapter 1; *Objectives, policies and needs* in Chapter 2; *Safety legislation* in Chapter 9; and *Employment law, Aspects of industrial relations* and *Wages* later in this chapter.

Manpower planning

Manpower planning is concerned with forecasting how many and what kind of employees the organisation will require in the future, and to what extent this demand is likely to be satisfied. It is important to decision-making in a number of areas, for example, recruitment, training, labour costs, redundancy and accommodation.

The organisation's *objectives* determine the man-

power plan. From these its demand for labour can be derived and the plan must then seek to satisfy this demand from the available supply. The planning process must consider a wide range of factors. *Internal factors* include: capital equipment plans; reorganisation proposals; financial limitations; labour turnover and absenteeism; amount of overtime worked; staff appraisal and comparative wage rates. *External factors* include: population trends and local population movements; housing and transport plans; government policies on, for example, training and regional development; and expansion and contraction by other local firms. The planning process can be represented diagrammatically as shown in Fig. 8.1.

Content of the plan

The manpower plan produced would normally include statements on the following points:

(a) changes to existing jobs;
(b) possibilities of re-deployment and re-training;
(c) changes at management and supervisory levels;
(d) training needs;
(e) recruitment, retirement/redundancy programmes;
(f) industrial relations considerations;
(g) accommodation requirements;
(h) feedback arrangements to facilitate subsequent changes to company objectives or the manpower plan.

The type of plan outlined above is *long-term*, say five years. A *short-term* plan covering the next year is more common, partly because it is easier to formulate and partly because many organisations think it better fits in with the changing nature of their business. Essentially, a short-term plan will be formulated by estimating the number of man-hours required to meet the production targets or marketing plan and subtracting the number of man-hours currently available. The result gives the manpower required. This may mean either a recruitment or a retirement/redundancy plan. The period covered is usually too short to formulate a worthwhile training plan.

Some practical problems

Although manpower planning is generally regarded as a 'good idea', a number of factors make it difficult and often inaccurate in practice. For example:

(a) the organisation may operate in an unpredictable or highly competitive industry, making long-term forward planning virtually impossible.
(b) some managers may oppose or be sceptical of the plan.
(c) changes indicated in the plan may be seen as a threat and therefore resisted.
(d) social and economic changes in the environment are difficult to predict with sufficient certainty.
(e) employee records must be complete and up-to-date.
(f) short-term financial considerations may make long-term planning impossible. For example, the organisation may simply not be able to afford the cost of a training programme included in the manpower plan.

Job descriptions and specifications

A *job description* is a broad statement of the purpose, scope, duties and responsibilities of a particular job. A *job specification* is a detailed statement of the physical and mental activities involved in the job, usually expressed in behavioural terms – what the individual does and by what means.

Although job specifications change with the needs of the organisation and the way individuals carry out the jobs, they are vital information in selecting and promoting staff, evaluating jobs and setting performance standards, and appraising staff and designing training programmes. It is common for them to begin with the general job description and then include more detailed statements covering:

(a) major responsibilities and results expected;
(b) routine and non-routine duties under these headings;
(c) working conditions;
(d) equipment and materials used;
(e) contact with other employees;
(f) performance standards.

Performance standards

These are statements of the quantity and quality of the work expected from an employee. They are generally associated with appraisal and training processes, and with payment systems.

Setting performance standards is relatively simple where repetitive physical activity is involved, e.g. units produced per hour. It becomes more difficult where activities are varied or where mental activity is involved. In the latter case it is important to establish objective criteria within the control of the employee. For example, to require sales managers to maintain sales at a given level is objective but to require them to ensure that a product has the largest market share is not because they have no control over the development and marketing policies of present or future competitors.

Personnel specifications

This is an interpretation of the job specification in terms of the kind of person suitable for the job. It is used in the recruitment, selection and promotion processes. Standard criteria are usually used, often the same as those used during a selection interview. One set of criteria appropriate for recruiting new staff, school and college leavers for example, is:

(a) Physical requirements, e.g. age, eyesight, manual dexterity, general appearance;
(b) Attainments, i.e. relevant qualifications and practical achievements through experience;
(c) General intelligence, e.g. the ability to think critically, to analyse and to discriminate, and to possess an inquiring mind;
(d) Special aptitudes, e.g. a particular ability to work

with machines, a flair for design, or the ability to work quickly and neatly;

(e) Interests, often gives a good guide to the type of person an organisation is looking for, e.g. a 'good mixer', capable of working with others;

(f) Personality and temperament, far easier to specify than to judge: some jobs require a bright, enthusiastic person while in others a more steady personality would be suitable. Typical criteria here would include, honesty, resourcefulness, helpfulness, enthusiasm and potential leadership qualities;

(g) Circumstances, e.g. employed/unemployed, distance of home from the proposed place of work.

Remember, however, that it is unlikely that an individual will ever fit a job specification exactly. Indeed, it may sometimes be better to recruit people with useful skills and knowledge and then alter the job to match them.

Consider your own job description. In the light of experience, how does it relate to your actual job? On the basis of the comparison, prepare a job description, job specification and personnel specification which you think reflects the work you do.

Labour turnover

Labour turnover is the movement of people into and out of an organisation. It is expensive, particularly if specialist, i.e. highly trained and difficult to replace staff, leave. For example, it usually results in lost or lower production while a replacement is recruited and trained; recruitment, selection, training and administrative costs; higher overtime payments and possible temporary redeployment of more specialised staff. Thus, personnel policies should aim to keep labour turnover at an acceptable level.

Reducing labour turnover

In general terms, labour turnover can best be kept at an acceptable level by ensuring that staff have job satisfaction and that work groups are cohesive. The importance of recognising individual *objectives*, which we discussed in Chapter 2, is relevant here. More specific action would include investigating abnormally high

separation rates (see below) in particular departments, ensuring that selection procedures are adequate, introducing or improving training programmes, reviewing pay structures, and ensuring that working conditions are adequate.

Measuring labour turnover

1 Separation or wastage rate. This expresses the number of employees leaving (separation) during a given period as a percentage of the average number of employees during that period.

$$\frac{\text{Number of separations during period}}{\text{Average number employed during period}} \times \frac{100}{1}$$

The separation or wastage rate is easy to calculate and is widely used. However, the percentage rate can be distorted by high turnover in a particular type of job or by the usual separation rate associated with newly recruited staff.

2 Labour stability index. This shows the percentage of employees with at least one year's service.

$$\frac{\text{Employees with at least one year's service}}{\text{Number of employees one year ago}} \times \frac{100}{1}$$

Used in conjunction with the separation rate, this shows the extent to which the organisation is keeping its experienced employees.

3 Survival rate table. If an organisation recruited 100 employees during a three-month period, a survival rate table could be constructed recording the rate they leave the organisation. Look at Table 8.1.

Table 8.1 Survival rate

Quarterly periods of service	Number of leavers	% leaving	% staying
First	40	40	60
Second	20	20	40
Third	10	10	30
Fourth	5	5	25
Fifth	3	3	22
Sixth	2	2	20
Seventh	1	1	19
Eighth	1	1	18

Such a table would normally show that employees are most likely to leave soon after they join the organisation. Tables can be prepared on a departmental, age, sex or job basis. A *survival curve* can be drawn by plotting the percentage leaving against quarterly periods of service on a graph.

Staff appraisal

Staff appraisal is a process which judges employee performance taking a wider view than productivity alone. It looks at the past performance of an employee, assessing strengths and weaknesses; considers suitability for promotion; and assesses how performance can be improved or developed, for example, by training, by gaining experience in other jobs and by counselling on weaknesses. The main objectives of systematic staff appraisal are to indicate training needs, determine the future use of staff, decide on merit pay awards, and motivate employees. The process presupposes job specifications which include precisely stated performance standards (*see* above) and there is a close link with the system of *management by objectives* (*see* page 42). In short, appraisal schemes are a means of rewarding, criticising, encouraging and counselling.

Appraisal techniques

The most common technique of appraisal is to use a *rating scale*. It consists of a list of personal characteristics or factors, e.g. knowledge of the job, co-operation with others and initiative, and a scale, usually ranging from poor to excellent in five points, for the manager's assessment of each of the characteristics or factors. Both the factors and the points on the scale should be defined so that judgments are consistent. A section for general remarks and recommended action is usually included at the bottom of the form. Rating scales are particularly suited to groups of staff with similar, routine, jobs. Fig. 8.2 is a typical staff appraisal rating scale.

An alternative method of appraisal is *open-ended* assessment. Instead of assessing predetermined factors against a predetermined scale, both open to interpretation unless the manager is well-trained, it requires the manager to write a few sentences under general headings about employees. In some cases employees also write a short appraisal of their own work and this forms part of the process. An open-ended method is best suited to a job which is relatively unstructured; here it would be difficult to design a suitable rating scale.

Appraisal is too often one-way and even totally secret, with employees not knowing what has been said or written about them and therefore gaining no motivation from the process. *Appraisal interviews* are intended to involve the employees in the process in the hope that they will gain motivation from what is said and written about them and engage in constructive self-criticism.

Some practical problems

Staff appraisal can make a positive contribution to achieving the objectives of both the organisation and its employees. However, it demands well-trained managers who can be objective, who can reconcile their role as 'judge' with the human relation aspects of their job and staff who take a positive, constructive attitude to the process. Unless the purpose of appraisal is properly communicated and understood, it can very easily be seen as a form of inquisition by staff and another exercise in 'paper-pushing' by management. There is also the view that it is unnecessary since good management involves continuous appraisal and constructive criticism of subordinates' work.

Activity

Either individually or in a small group, use Fig. 8.2 to conduct an appraisal of your own abilities and identify your strengths and weaknesses. On the basis of the results, identify your training needs which will rectify your weaknesses and exploit your strengths.

Training

If an organisation is to respond to challenges and technological change it needs a properly trained workforce. Training not only enables the organisation to make better use of its labour force by improving job skills and influencing attitudes, it also motivates employees by giving job satisfaction, often increased earning power, management recognition of attainment and opportunities for promotion. This is, of course, an ideal situation, these results will not be achieved if the training is perceived as irrelevant or purposeless.

Staff Appraisal Form

Name ....   Department ....

Job ....   How long in dept ....

Date of birth ....   How long in company ....

Please tick the ratings you think appropriate, after reading carefully the definitions of the factors and grades. You should add any general remarks in the space provided at the end of the form. Base your judgment on the requirements of the job and the employee's performance in the job.

1   **Knowledge of job**
(Present knowledge of job and of work related to it.)

Knows only routine repetitive work. Will not learn ....

Knows most jobs but relies on others for special knowledge ....

Good knowledge of practically all aspects of the work ....

Complete grasp of all aspects of the work ....

2   **Accuracy**
(Standard of work compared with standard expected, degree to which work must be checked.)

Work is inaccurate; requires constant checking ....

Careless at times; requires frequent checking ....

Usually accurate; requires occasional checking ....

Accurate except on very difficult jobs ....

Accurate on all jobs ....

3   **Speed of work**
(Speed at which work is accomplished in relation to the standard expected in the job.)

Very slow; always fails to meet requirements ....

Slow; often below requirements ....

Average speed; meets requirements as a rule ....

Above average speed; usually exceeds requirements ....

Fast; always exceeds requirements ....

4   **Co-operation**
(Ability to work with others at all levels; readiness to try out new ideas and methods; responds when asked for a special effort.)

Difficult to work with; often touchy and unco-operative ....

Occasionally difficult to work with ....

Normally co-operative; raises few difficulties ....

Always tries hard to co-operate; easy to work with ....

Co-operates extremely well with others at all levels ....

5 Initiative

(Resourcefulness; ability to work without detailed instructions; readiness to offer ideas and suggestions about work.)

Requires detailed supervision; waits to be told ....

Requires frequent supervision; asks for instructions ....

Requires occasional supervision; sometimes offers ideas ....

Rarely requires supervision; resourceful, offers ideas ....

Never requires supervision; has many ideas, solves problems
unaided ....

Training needs

(Suggest any training courses or in-company experience which might improve the employee's performance.)

Promotion potential

The employee is an excellent promotion candidate because

The employee is a good promotion candidate because ....

The employee is a border-line promotion candidate because ....

The employee is unlikely to be promoted because

General remarks

General rating

Assess employee's job performance in his/her *present* job:

☐	☐	☐	☐	☐
Poor		Average		Excellent

Signed .... Position .... Date ....

Countersigned .... Position .... Date ....

Fig. 8.2 Staff appraisal form

Most organisations will give their new employees some form of basic training or induction and many will run routine training programmes (of which your present course of study may be part). More specific training programmes are often the result of change, for example, the installation of new equipment, a change in working methods or the introduction of a new product. Other reasons include, labour shortages, promotions and transfers, safety and improvements in performance.

There is considerable evidence that, as a nation, the UK does not invest in training, retraining and updating at anything like the level of our major and often more successful competitors. In a research study, *Adult Training in Britain* conducted by IFF Research, 14 hours training per employee per year was the average, while in West Germany 30 to 40 hours was considered good practice. The report also found a positive correlation between training and industrial and commercial performance, high-performing companies being twice as likely to train employees as low-performing companies. The problem appears to be not so much one of attitudes towards training, as a problem of translating attitudes into action.

Designing a training programme

As with any other process, a training programme should be carefully planned and supervised. If it is not, it is certain to be wasteful and may totally fail to achieve its objectives.

Within the overall context of the manpower plan, the following stages are frequently followed in the design of a training programme.

(a) The job is analysed and defined.

(b) Performance standards are established.

(c) Employee attainment is assessed against the performance standards.

(d) The training gap, ie. the difference, if any, between *(b)* and *(c)* is considered to identify training requirements.

(e) Training programmes are devised to meet the identified needs.

(f) The training programme is implemented and records kept.

(g) The results are checked. If successful, the trainees should have achieved the specified performance stan-

Keywords ———————————————

Personnel management
Is concerned with people at work and their relationships with and within the organisation.

Manpower planning
An organisation must forecast its future labour requirements and training needs. Manpower planning is the term used to describe this forecasting.

Job description
A statement of the purpose, scope, duties and responsibilities of a particular job. From it is derived a *job specification*, which describes the actual activities involved, and a *personnel specification* which identifies the skills and other attributes required.

Labour turnover
Although a certain level of labour turnover is inevitable, if not monitored and controlled it can be highly damaging to an organisation.

Staff appraisal
Often viewed as an undesirable personal inquisition, but when conducted objectively and constructively should result in better identified training needs, better matching of staff to jobs and higher staff motivation.

Training
Training (and re-training) is equipping people with the right skills for the right job. Training is necessary to make the best use of and motivate a workforce, particularly where technological change both threatens traditional skills and offers new opportunities. It is generally agreed that the UK does not invest sufficiently in training – but little appears to be done about it!

———————————————————

dards. This may be relatively simple if straightforward physical tasks are involved but difficult if management performance is being assessed.

(h) The training should be evaluated to assess its cost-benefit, that is, its costs in comparison with the financial benefit gained through improved employee performance, and for possible modifications to the programme to make it more cost-effective.

Are you management material?

On the assumption that you one day wish to have a 'management' post, it is perhaps relevant to conclude this section on training by briefly considering some of the factors that an organisation is likely to consider when selecting existing employees for management development programmes. Typically, these will be:

(a) Motivation and job satisfaction;
(b) Ambition;
(c) Management skills, e.g. administration, perception of opportunities and an ability to persuade and influence;
(d) Initiative and determination;
(e) Achievement of objectives in a job;
(f) A desire to earn more money;
(g) Good inter-personal skills;
(h) The ability to accept change;
(i) A willingness to be geographically mobile;
(j) The ability to take a broad view of situations and problems and to be realistic.

Consider the factors above. How do you rate *your* potential?

Trade unions: an introduction

What is a trade union?

Broadly speaking, a trade union is an organisation consisting wholly or mainly of workers, whose principal purposes include the regulation of relations between workers and employers or employers' associations (Trade Union and Labour Relations Act 1974). With a few exceptions trade unions are unincorporated associations but they resemble corporate bodies in certain important ways, i.e. they are allowed to make contracts and may be sued in their own names. In addition, simplified procedures exist for transferring the property of 'listed' trade unions (*see* below) to new or continuing trustees (by which it must be held) when new trustees are appointed or a trustee retires.

In 1988 there were 354 trade unions with a total membership of about 10.5 million. Individual membership ranges from the 1.3 million of the giant Transport and General Workers' Union to the 17 members of the Sheffield Wool Shear Workers' Union. In 1989, 78 trade unions were affiliated to the TUC. Trade unions are collectively (and often individually) a very powerful pressure group to be consulted and considered in any political or economic decision taken by the government or business organisation.

It is likely that your experience of trade unions and your image of them will have been coloured by media coverage and family views. You must now try to be objective. Consider the facts and then decide for yourself whether the trade union movement is the champion of the downtrodden worker or a confounded, legally-protected nuisance, interfering with the economy, with damaging consequences. Whether this chapter will form, change or confirm your views, one thing is certain: trade unions are an integral part of our modern industrial society.

Types of union

Several different types of union may be recognised. These are not hard and fast distinctions: a union might belong to more than one category.

1 Craft or skill unions. These occur where the members have a skill in common like the United Pattern-makers Association (UPA).
2 Industrial unions. The members of these unions all work in the same industry although they may have very different jobs, e.g. the National Union of Railwaymen (NUR).
3 General unions. The members of general unions may be in many different industries and occupations. They are often unskilled or semi-skilled workers. The largest union in Britain is a general union, the Transport and General Workers' Union (TGWU).
4 Company unions. These occur when all the employees of one company form a union. These are practically unknown in the UK but common in the USA where, for example, you would find a union of Ford Workers. Probably the banks' staff associations, or the single union agreements arrived at by some of the Japanese firms recently established here, are the nearest thing to them in the UK.
5 White collar unions. Since 1945 the white collar workers, who were previously almost completely non-unionised, have joined trade unions. The National Union of Teachers (NUT), the Association of Scientific, Technical and Managerial Staffs (ASTMS) and the Banking, Insurance and Finance Union (BIFU) are good examples.
6 Professional associations. Although they would strenuously deny that they are trade unions, some

professional associations like the British Medical Association (BMA) and the Inns of Court exhibit many of the features of trade unions. Certainly the two mentioned above are successful in pay bargaining to an extent which would disgrace many trade unions!

It is certainly possible to argue that there are too many trade unions in Britain and that this is a cause of endless demarcation disputes. On the other hand it is argued that some trade unions are too big and wield too much power.

External relations

The Trades Union Congress (TUC)

Founded in 1868, the Trades Union Congress is one of the oldest of trade union institutions. It is really just a talking shop as its decisions are only morally binding upon its members, although it has the power of expulsion. The TUC meets once a year to elect the general council of the TUC. The secretariat of the TUC is small and works on a shoe-string budget, and is headed by the General Secretary. The TUC has always been overtly political, in fact its first title back in 1868 was the 'Parliamentary Committee' when its object was to try to influence government.

The International Labour Organisation (ILO)

The ILO, established in 1919, is just about the only survivor of the many institutions which were set up alongside the League of Nations in Geneva. It now operates under the auspices of the UN and its task is to try to improve working conditions throughout the world. It has no power to compel governments and so it must proceed by persuasion. It is of valuable assistance to less developed countries who are trying to establish systems of industrial relations. One of the most important functions of the ILO is to publish economic statistics and reports. The *ILO Yearbook* is a valuable source of international statistics.

The European Community (EC)

Wide differences exist between unions in the EC. In general, unions in the rest of the EC tend to be fewer and larger than in Britain. In Germany the sixteen unions are based on industrial grouping. Ironically the highly stable system of industrial relations in Germany was designed, after 1945, mainly by British trade unionists, notably Ernest Bevin. Unions in Germany are apolitical while elsewhere unions may have a religious affiliation, e.g. in the Netherlands, or may be Communist-led, as some are in France and Italy. Therefore wide differences need to be overcome if European industrial relations are to be harmonised. Many of the European unions meet in the *European Confederation of Free Trade Unions*.

Not only do unions differ but the structure of wages in the EC also differs. This is because of differences in taxation and social security payments.

Trade union finances

The bulk of a trade union's income comes from contributions from members. Most unions in Britain have very low subscriptions, often as little as 10p per week. The unions also draw income from their investments. Investments make the unions dependent upon the well-being of the capitalist state, which may seem a strange state of affairs for overtly socialist organisations. The NUR became the most famous union investor when it purchased fine art and antiques as investments for its pension fund.

A union's expenditure falls under four main headings. First there are *administration costs* and the salaries of its full-time officials. Another type of expenditure is *pensions and sickness benefits*. Before the advent of the Welfare State, these were one of the most important of the union functions. The pension fund is usually kept separate from the union's other finances. The *strike fund* is another aspect of union finance. It is a reserve of money kept to pay workers if there is a strike and, again, is usually kept separately.

Finally there is the money the trade unions pay to support the Labour Party. Legally this must be raised by the unions as a separate *political levy* from which members may *contract out* if they wish. The levy is seldom more than 1p or 2p per week but is politically contentious as some unions make it difficult for people to contract out. Under the Trade Union Act 1984, a resolution to establish a political fund must be passed at least every ten years by a ballot of all the union's members. The ballot must be secret, by voting paper and must not cause the members voting to incur any direct cost. Some argued that the ballot requirement was not about freedom of choice but merely a thinly disguised attack by a Conservative government on the Labour Party's main source of income, the assumption being that votes would go against the political funds. Whether or not this was so, the ballots that have been held so far have resulted in large majorities in favour of maintaining political funds. And, indeed, if everyone who contributed to the financial support of the Labour Party in this way voted Labour we would always have a Labour government!

Trade union functions

It is widely believed that unions exist solely for the purpose of obtaining more pay for their members. While this may be one of the most important functions they have many others.

1 Pay bargaining. Unions are concerned to achieve a rise in the real wages of their members as well as the money wages. Actual earnings are not only determined by the wage rate but also by the hours worked, overtime rates and bonuses. Because of this, a 1% rise in the wage rate tends to bring about a rise in earnings greater than 1%. This tendency of earnings to rise faster than wage rates is known as *wages drift*.

2 Conditions of work. It is important not only to have a safe and healthy workplace but also to have a good working environment. Many people believe that unions have not been sufficiently concerned with this aspect.

3 Financial benefits. Unions frequently offer pensions, sickness benefits and insurance to their members. In the early days of trade unions this was one of their most important functions but most of this task has now been taken over by the state.

4 Training and conditions of entry. Many unions regulate the supply of labour to an occupation by insisting on entry qualifications such as apprenticeships. While this may ensure an adequately qualified work force it is also used to push up wages.

5 Security. Everyone is familiar with the slogan 'one out, all out'. Unions will often fight strenuously for job security.

6 Participation in public bodies. As representatives of labour, trade unions sit on many bodies as diverse as the Monopolies Commission, the National Economic Development Council (Neddy) and the Food Hygiene Advisory Council.

It is unfortunate that industrial relations in the UK are still a 'them and us' situation. In a mixed economy the management of the economy and of industry should be a partnership. The 1974–9 Labour government brought in new legislation giving trade unions wider powers. The Health and Safety at Work, etc, Act 1974 obliges management to consult with unions on health, safety and welfare at work and to give union representatives adequate time to inspect the premises and carry out other duties connected with health and safety. The Employment Protection (Consolidation) Act 1978, as well as giving greater job security, obliges employers to give union officials time off for their duties. Under the Employment Protection Act 1975 employers are obliged to consult with unions on redundancy.

It was thought that in some industries the labour force was so weak and badly organised that it was necessary to set up wages councils to redress the balance. At one stage, over three million workers were covered by wages councils. However, the Conservative Government of Margaret Thatcher believed that the statutory minimum wages laid down by them were a restriction on the labour market and a cause of unemployment. Therefore, the Wages Act 1986, while retaining existing councils, limits their powers to setting basic minimum hourly rates and removes employees under the age of 21 from the scope of their regulations.

Many occupations have special institutionalised pay-bargaining procedures, such as the *Whitley Council* which decides nurses' salaries.

ACAS (the Advisory, Conciliation and Arbitration Service), set up by the Employment Protection Act 1975, is known for its intervention in many disputes such as the teachers' pay claim and the ambulance men's dispute, both in early 1990. Despite some failures, ACAS has had many successes in bringing peaceful conclusions to industrial disputes.

The demands of trade unions, however, go beyond current legislation: many are looking for industrial democracy. This could mean worker directors, profit-sharing or co-ownership. The *Bullock Report* 1975 recommended worker directors but so far the proposals have not been acted upon. The participation of workers in the running of industry should not be looked on with horror; it can be very successful, as experience in Sweden has shown.

Discover which union(s) is active in your place of employment – you may or may not already be a member. Find out as much as you can about the union, its size, structure, benefits offered to members etc. Do you contribute to a political fund? Do you know for what purposes it is used?

Trade unions and the law

The basic framework

The present legal framework within which trade unions operate is to be found mainly in the provisions of the Trade Union and Labour Relations Act 1974, as amended by the Employment Protection Act 1975, the Trade Union and Labour Relations (Amendment) Act 1976, the Employment Acts 1980, 1982 and 1988 and the Trade Union Act 1984. Despite their name, certain important sections of the Trade Union and Labour Relations Acts 1974 and 1976 apply equally to employers' associations, namely the provisions relating to legal status, accounting duties (all trade unions and employers' associations, whether listed or not, must keep proper accounts and submit an annual return about their activities, including their accounts, to the Certification Officer) and 'listing' with the Certification Officer.

Under the 1974 and 1975 Acts, the Certification Officer is responsible for maintaining a list of all trade unions within the legal definition (*see* page 145). Listing is essential if a trade union is to be granted a *Certificate of Independence* and it gives certain rights to tax relief. An *independent union*, of which there were 220 in 1988, is one which is not under the domination of control of, or subject to financial or material support from, an employer. The Certification Officer determines any dispute as to independence. Recognition as being independent is essential in con-

nection with many collective and individual rights under current employment legislation.

The Employment Acts of 1980, 1982 and 1988 and the Trade Union Act 1984 were the Conservative government's counter to the increased power given to trade unions under the previous Labour government's employment legislation (the 1974 and 1976 Acts) and policies. Depending on your point of view, they can be seen as either a politically motivated attack on trade unions and an unwarranted interference in their internal affairs or as a reassertion of individual freedom.

The 1980 Act makes available public funds for secret ballots for such things as electing officers, calling or ending a strike or amending rules and gives the Secretary of State wide-ranging powers to issue codes of practice 'for the purpose of improving industrial relations'. The 1982 Act, among other things, brings legal immunities for trade unions into line with those for individuals - so that trade unions become liable to pay damages if they organise industrial action in contravention of the Act (their immunity is thereby greatly reduced), and restricts lawful trade disputes to disputes between workers and their employers.

Under the 1984 Act, strike action is lawful only if sanctioned by a secret ballot of members and it puts strict limits on secondary action. The first provision is designed to promote greater union democracy, the second, protection of innocent third parties who may not be involved in the dispute in any way. The Act also provides that every voting member of the principal executive committee of a trade union must be elected by ballot at least every five years. This includes voting members who are members by virtue of holding a union office. Electing general secretaries for 'life' has been the practice in some powerful and, some would say, politically aggressive unions, e.g. the National Union of Mineworkers.

The Employment Act 1988 enhances the statutory rights of trade union members against their unions and supplements the union election provisions introduced by the 1984 Act. For example, members are able to obtain a court order against their union preventing it authorising or endorsing industrial action unless the balloting requirements have been met and they may not be disciplined for failure to take part in a strike even where they have. The Act establishes a 'Commissioner for the Rights of Trade Union Members' who has the power to assist trade union members in taking certain legal actions against their unions, e.g. to ensure statutory balloting requirements are met. The Act also removed the last statutory recognition of closed shop agreements (*see* page 151).

The Employment Bill published at the end of 1989 proposes the complete abolition of the closed shop by making it unlawful not to employ a person because he or she will not join a union – a pre-entry closed shop. (Some 1.3 million jobs were at the time covered by pre-entry closed shops.) However, it gives workers the right *not* to be dismissed for being union members, a right proposed in the EC's 'Social Charter'. The Bill also aims to outlaw secondary action and unofficial strikes. In the former case it proposes to remove all union immunity from civil action. In the latter it proposes that when industrial action is organised by any union official it must be put to the test of a secret ballot or be specifically repudiated by the union concerned.

Whatever the pro- or anti-union arguments, perhaps the criteria on which these Acts are judged should include whether or not they lead to an improvement in industrial relations and economic performance generally. The indications are that they are going to have no more success than previous attempts to control industrial relations by law. Surely *consensus* rather than *conflict* should be the way forward. The question is how to promote it.

There are five main aspects of the legal framework which directly affect the relationships between trade unions and other organisations: collective agreements; the legal immunities and privileges enjoyed by trade unions; picketing; closed shop agreements; and union-only labour and recognition practices.

An unavoidable problem with any book which deals with such a dynamic branch of the law as industrial law is that it is out of date almost as soon as it is published. What major changes have taken place in industrial law since this edition was published? Update the text. Do you consider that the changes were politically motivated?

Collective agreements

Over two-thirds of all employees have their rates of pay and other terms of their employment decided by collective agreements between their unions and their employers. Under the Employment Protection Act 1975 an employer has a duty to disclose to a recognised trade union, on request, information for collective bargaining purposes. 'Recognition' in this context means an agreement between the employer concerned and the union that the union has a certain status.

Collective agreements are vital both to the individual employee, whose bargaining power in such matters is negligible, and to industrial relations generally. However, under the Act these agreements are not presumed to be legally enforceable unless they are in writing and expressly state that the parties to the agreement intend it, or a specific part of it, to be so. It follows that a union is not liable for strikes that occur in breach of a collective agreement.

It is arguable that with some 75% of all strikes being unofficial, the legal framework of collective bargaining does not reflect the tremendous changes in the economy and industrial relations that have occurred over the last half century. The problem is not collective agreements themselves but how to ensure that unions have sufficient control over their members to enforce a collective agreement once it is made. The problem has become more pressing in recent years because a handful of workers taking unofficial strike action in an industry vital to the economy can cause immense harm and disruption. In addition some people would argue that a small minority of trade unionists use trade disputes to further their own political ends. Should these activities increase, or even continue, they may eventually call into question the legal status of collective agreements. As you have seen, the legislation of the present Conservative Government has already restricted the extent of trade union immunity at law and imposed rules relating to their internal affairs. It remains to be seen whether the proposals in the Employment Bill 1989 will prove effective in curbing unofficial strikes, particularly the more 'spontaneous' ones.

Legal immunities and privileges

Possible liability

In pursuing what most people regard as legitimate trade union activity, trade unions and their members can easily commit three *civil* offences (torts). *First*, it is unlawful to induce (persuade) another person to break a contract to which that other person is a party, or to procure (bring about) a breach of contract. For example, the tort would be committed by a union official calling a strike or by calling upon union members in one organisation to boycott another, say, by refusing to deliver supplies to it. *Second*, a conspiracy is committed when two or more people combine together to commit an unlawful act or a lawful act by unlawful means, e.g. by organising a boycott of an organisation to force it to employ only union labour. *Third*, the tort of intimidation can be committed by threatening to call a strike.

On the assumption that a union should have the right to call its members out on strike, or threaten to do so, extensive immunity from liability for the above torts is plainly necessary. Without it, a union could be sued for the loss a strike caused to the organisation(s) against which the strike was called. This would mean that union funds necessary to sustain striking members and finance its other activities would always be at risk.

Statutory immunity

Immunity is given by the Trade Union and Labour Relations Act 1974, as amended by the Employment Act 1982, to *'acts done wholly or mainly in furtherance or contemplation of a trade dispute.'* A trade dispute covers, for example, disputes over terms and conditions of employment, recruitment of workers or termination of employment, and disputes over allocation of work. A strike called for political reasons is *not* a trade dispute within the Act; for example, one called in protest against government policies. Secondary action, that is, action against organisations that are themselves not party to a dispute, is only protected if it directly interferes with the supply of goods or services to and from the organisation with which there is a dispute.

In recent years there has been a growing body of opinion, reflected in the policy of the Conservative Government, that the tactics employed by some trade unions in industrial disputes are unacceptable. On this premise, the Trade Union Act 1984 now requires a trade union to hold a secret ballot of its members *before* calling a strike or instigating other industrial

action. If it does not do so, it loses its legal immunity. This means that an organisation could seek an injunction to call off the strike against the trade union or sue for damages. Injunctions were issued against the National Union of Mineworkers during the Coal Strike of 1984–5 and against the National Union of Seamen in 1988 and both were heavily fined for contempt of court for their failure to do so.

The ballot requirement is seen by trade unions as a completely unwarranted and hostile political interference in their internal affairs. On the other hand, supporters of the measure argue that it makes trade unions more democratic, e.g. by stopping a decision being taken by a show of hands at a mass meeting or a call of action which is unsupported by the union's rank and file. At one time such a measure was invariably seen in party political terms and would have been unlikely to long survive the election of a Labour government. Now, however, the position is not so certain. The Labour Party of the late 1980s was far less willing to concede to trade union demands in their policy-making than at the beginning of the decade.

Where the statutory immunity does not apply, a trade union will only be liable, however, where the act in question was authorised or endorsed by a *responsible person* of the union, e.g. the principal executive committee or the president or general secretary. If a trade union is sued successfully, the size of its membership determines the amounts of damages that may be awarded. For example, the limit is £10,000 for a union with less than 5,000 members, increasing to £250,000 for a union with 100,000 or more members. These limits apply to each individual claim, they are not global limits for each unlawful incident.

Other possible liability

Conduct protected by the Act may be actionable on other grounds. For example, union members may be both sued and, under the Conspiracy and Protection of Property Act 1875, prosecuted for actions amounting to assault and battery and criminal damage. Thus, while they have immunity from *civil action* for all loss and damage they cause purely because they were lawfully on strike, they are not immune where their acts give rise to a course of action quite independent of their strike action. For example, a line is drawn between damage to plant and machinery consequential to lack of maintenance during a strike and deliberate sabotage, and between reasonable argument and threats of physical violence during a picket.

Furthermore, the 1974 Act provides that a trade union (or employers' association) may be sued, without any limit on an award of damages, for negligence, nuisance or breach of duty resulting in personal injury, or for torts connected with the ownership, occupation, possession, control or use of any property, provided that these torts do not arise from an act done wholly or mainly in contemplation or furtherance of a trade dispute.

Picketing

What is picketing?

Picketing consists of communicating information or peacefully trying to persuade someone to work or not to work in the context of a possible dispute between management and workers or in support of a dispute already in progress. The Trade Union and Labour Relations Act 1974, as amended by the Employment Act 1980, states that it is only lawful for persons to picket at or near their own place of work or, if they are officials of a trade union, at or near the place of work of a member of that union whom they are accompanying. If the trade dispute is caused by, or leads to, the dismissal of employees, those ex-employees may picket their former workplace.

Secondary picketing

Since people may only picket at their own workplace, an injunction can be issued against anyone who engages in *secondary picketing*, i.e. picketing at any workplace other than their own, e.g. their employer's supplier. Furthermore, an action for damages may be brought against them if they cause material loss by interfering with other peoples' contracts of employment. This provision against secondary picketing was introduced to prevent mass pickets, where hundreds, or even thousands, of people, most of whom would not be directly involved in the dispute, might join picket lines to support the workers in dispute.

Numbers

The Act does not limit the number of pickets. In theory, the police can still control the number of pickets because picketing by large numbers may obstruct the highway – there is no right to stop vehicles for example – or be likely to cause a breach of the peace. Both situations are criminal offences entitling the police to take action. Clearly, the law should not deny employees the right to picket peacefully but this right should (arguably) be regulated in the context of the social and economic cost to the community. The Employment Act 1980 represents the present Conservative Government's attempt to reconcile these sometimes potentially conflicting values. However, the mass picketing seen during the Miners' Strike of 1984–85, the Wapping Printing dispute of 1986 and the Seamen's Strike of 1988 would seem to indicate that the legislation is unlikely to succeed. Undoubtedly, the police are put in a very invidious position; whatever they do will anger one vociferous faction or another. But one thing is certain – it is very difficult to arrest several thousand people for obstructing the highway! Whatever future changes there may be in the law on picketing, the main problem will continue to be one of enforcement.

What arguments can you put forward *(a)* for and *(b)* against the present law on picketing?

Closed shop agreements

A controversial aspect of trade union law is the provisions relating to union membership agreements (closed shops) by which a person may be required to join a specified union, or one of a specified number of unions, in order to hold a particular job.

From a legal point of view, closed shops are important in relation to unfair dismissal. Under the Employment Act 1988, it is automatically unfair to dismiss an employee for a reason relating to non-membership of a union, irrespective of whether the closed shop is supported by a ballot. (Before the 1988 Act, a closed shop agreement was enforceable if supported by a ballot of the workforce.)

Trade unions have argued that changes made to the closed shop rules by the present Conservative Government are aimed at weakening trade union organisation. An opposing argument is that they merely restore freedom of choice to an employee. On the one hand, closed shop agreements have some advantages in industrial relations generally, e.g. consultation is made easier and more effective, and the possibility of inter-union disputes is lessened. On the other hand an individual employee's freedom to choose whether or not to belong to a trade union is removed, sometimes in a situation where the job to which the closed shop agreement relates is the only suitable employment available.

Whatever your own views are it is clear that the closed shop is something of a lost cause, its last statutory recognition having been removed by the Employment Act 1988 (*see* page 159). Furthermore the Labour Party announced in December 1989 that it no longer subscribed to the idea of the closed shop, arguing that this was in accordance with its acceptance of the EC 'Social Charter' which confers other more specific and valuable rights on workers. As noted above, the Employment Bill 1989 proposes its complete abolition.

Union-only labour and recognition practices

The Employment Act 1982 outlaws any requirement in a commercial contract about trade union membership or recognition. Thus, a contract for the supply of goods or services *cannot* specify that the whole or part of the work shall be done by union (or non-union) labour. It is also unlawful to refuse to include organisations in tender lists or to offer or award contracts to them because they do *not* employ trade union members or recognise, negotiate or consult with trade unions or trade union officials.

Somewhat ironically for a government committed to individual freedom, this provision of the 1982 Act undermines free collective bargaining, i.e. such clauses may not be inserted in contracts even if both parties wish to. Many people see it as part of the government's overall plan to lessen trade union influence on wage levels. In addition, it aids its policy of *privatising* public services by tying the hands of trade unions and

employers likely to oppose it such as Labour-controlled local authorities.

Employers' associations

Just as employees have formed and joined trade unions to protect their interests, so employers have formed and joined organisations to protect their interests, often against trade unions. The latter are usually far more powerful than individual employers. Unlike trade unions, they are associations of organisations and not people. Although there are far more employers' associations than trade unions, only a few are well known, e.g. the Confederation of British Industry (CBI), the Engineering Employers' Federation, the National Union of Farmers, and the Association of County Councils.

The basic role of employers' associations is to represent employer interests in dealings with trade unions. They will, for example, encourage employers to bargain on wage rates through their association rather than individually in order to stop 'leap-frogging' negotiating tactics by trade unions. However, they also have an important role in disseminating information on technology and markets to their members.

The Confederation of British Industry (CBI)

In comparison with the Trades Union Congress (TUC), established in 1868, the CBI has a short history, being established in 1965 by royal charter. It has the following principal objectives.

1 It provides for British industry the means of formulating, making known and influencing general policy with regard to industrial, economic, fiscal, commercial, labour, social, legal and technical questions, and to act as a national point of reference for those seeking industry's views.
2 To develop the contribution of British industry to the national economy.
3 To encourage the efficiency and competitive power of British industry and to provide advice, information and services to British industry to that end.

From these objectives you can see that the CBI's functions are far wider than industrial relations alone.

Keywords

Trade unions

There are a variety of types of trade unions but they share the common purpose of regulating the relations between workers and employers or employer's associations.

Political levy

Traditionally the trade unions have supported the Labour Party and are its main source of funds. These funds are raised through the *political levy* which, by law, must be supported by a ballot of members and from which members can contract out.

Trade union law

More correctly called *industrial law*, this is found in a number of Acts of Parliament which in the 1980s were being enacted almost annually. Trade union law has always been political with a capital 'P'.

Independent union

One which is not under an employer's control. A Certificate of Independence from the Certification Officer confers important rights on the unions and its members.

'Social Charter'

An EC declaration of basic rights, some directly concerning workers, which can be viewed as either a welcome statement of basic standards or as 'socialism by the back door' – depending on your political opinions.

Collective agreements

Agreements between unions and employers determining rates of pay and other conditions of employment.

Trade dispute

Under current legislation, the existence of a 'trade dispute' is the key to trade union protection from legal action by employers damaged by industrial action.

Picketing

Picketing is a traditional tactic used by trade unions. It consists of attempting to persuade someone (usually) not to work in the context of trade dispute. Secondary picketing is where the action is taken at a workplace other than you own or that of your employer's supplier.

The closed shop

Essentially an agreement between an employer and union(s) that all employees *must* belong to one or more designated unions. Closed shops – were finally laid to rest in the 1980s.

Employers' associations

In some ways the opposite of trade unions, these are associations of organisations rather than individuals formed to protect their members' interests – often against powerful trade unions.

Employment law

Some background

There can be very few contracts in which such inequality in bargaining power exists between the parties as in a contract of employment (a general theme developed in Chapter 25). Only the superstars of the entertainment and sporting worlds, exceptionally able technicians, managers and the like are able to dictate their terms. However much unions and other organisations may negotiate national salaries, conditions of employment, pensions, etc, reality for the rest of us is ultimately a simple choice: accept the employers' terms or lose your job. Such a situation is the legacy of *laissez-faire* but it does not follow that an economy controlled entirely by the state would necessarily produce a better choice, or any choice at all. Indeed, it is arguable that while the basic social right to work might be better protected, conditions of service, pay, choice and variety of employment would be far worse.

The harshness of this stark choice is mitigated in reality, of course, by the power of the trade unions and by an elaborate system of national insurance and welfare benefits. Thus, no-one is actually likely to starve. However, it does justify the state intervening to lay down certain basic terms to be embodied in all contracts of employment.

In the late 19th and early 20th centuries certain implied terms in employment contracts were established by judicial decisions, e.g. a mutual duty of care owed between employer and employee, but a comprehensive legislative framework of employment law is somewhat surprisingly a very recent creation, a product of the 1970s. Even so, there is such diversity in employment that only generally accepted rights and duties can be laid down; specific contractual terms are still (theoretically) the subject of negotiation between individual employers and their employees.

Employment law is far from being purely a lawyer's subject; many different influences affect its principles and practices. It is often a politically emotive subject; trade unions can exert tremendous influence in both particular and general issues, diverse pressure groups are active in furthering their causes at both grass-roots and policy-making levels and the media is guaranteed to get maximum mileage from a controversial or unusual 'employment story'. Remember, too, that while the right to work is a generally accepted social right, there is no corresponding legal right. Critics of the present welfare system might argue quite the reverse, i.e. that there is a legal right not to work in so far as a person is legally entitled to enough money from the state for a tolerable existence without working.

In the 1980s the number of people out of work rose alarmingly. Although the numbers dropped substantially at the end of the decade, official figures showed that 2.4 million people were still unemployed in the UK in 1989 (as against over 3.3 million in 1986). Figures in other Western countries were also very high. Many traditional industries are contracting and even where there is expansion, the increasing use of computer-based technology means that not as many employees are needed as in the past. It is highly unlikely that we, as a country, will in the foreseeable future return to the full employment that existed in the 1960s. It would seem that in the future the necessary workforce may be much smaller than it is today. This will mean that accepted concepts of work and leisure will have to change.

These changes will almost certainly speed up the move towards employment in service jobs instead of in manufacturing and, perhaps, the introduction (perhaps even enforcement) of maximum working hours. Indeed, it is highly likely that your (grand)children, working an average of 20 hours a week or less, will consider our hours and conditions of employment, and the whole recently created framework of employment protection, as outmoded and unacceptable as we now consider the dreadful conditions endured by workers in the not-so-distant past. In our eyes the state failed to protect even the workers' basic social right to a dignified existence. But will our (grand) children view the monotony of the production line and the tyranny of the VDU to be equally deplorable and the work alienation they may cause to be economically unacceptable?

Government policy

Employment law tends to suffer more from politically inspired changes than many other matters. The Conservative Party tends to repeal, or substantially amend, what the Labour Party introduces and vice versa. Although this may not be the best way to go about regulating such an important matter, it probably is inevitable under the two-party system.

The present Conservative Government's policy is to remove, as they see it, major legislative restraints on the labour market. It is the Government's view, for example, that the unfair dismissal legislation inhibits employers taking on new labour and that wages councils reduce employment by fixing wages well above market price. It sees the answer in legislative curtailment of trade union power, some restriction of employment protection rights (the qualifying period for unfair dismissal has already been increased from one to two years and it plans to increase the minimum requirement in terms of hours worked, (*see* page 158) and in restricting the powers of wages councils. In its view this should lead to a more flexible, realistically paid labour force. In turn this should mean a more open labour market, increased profits and a reduction in the length of dole queues. Part-time and temporary employment is bound to increase and government-sponsored training schemes, with little or no employment protection, are probably a permanent feature of the labour scene for the foreseeable future.

Whatever the merits or demerits of the policies, the media will ensure that it is difficult to take an objective view.

Contracts of employment

What is a contract of employment?

A contract of employment is a *contract of service*, i.e. a contract under which a person puts his or her labour at the disposal of another in return for the payment of money or other remuneration. The relationship created was traditionally called that of master and servant, but today 'employer and employee' is a more realistic label. However, the traditional term is still commonly used at law, and the term 'contract of service' is still used in modern statutes.

A contract of employment (service) must be distinguished from a contract for services, i.e. a contract where the relationship of employer and independent contractor arises. For example, if a business organisation wished to paint its premises and arranged for a specialist firm to do the work, a contract for services would exist. If, however, their own maintenance section did the work, the painters would be employed under a contract of employment. In a contract for services the employer is able to tell the independent contractor what to do but not how to do it, while in a contract of employment the employer (master) is theoretically able to do both.

At one time the test for a contract of employment was control of the employee, or perhaps more realistically, the right to control, and this corresponded with the now rather outmoded terminology of master and servant. Today, however, the 'control test' cannot realistically be applied to organisations employing thousands of people, particularly where many of the employees are highly skilled or professionally qualified. A number of tests have been put forward to replace the traditional control test but it would seem that a simple commonsense appraisal of the facts of each individual case cannot be bettered. In fact it can only be in a very few situations that the nature of the contract is open to dispute.

However academic or legalistic the distinction between contracts of service and contracts for services may become, the distinction is fundamentally important. Two examples will illustrate this well. Employers are liable for the wrongful acts (torts) of their employees, enabling any person injured by a wrongful act to seek redress from the employer as well as the employee. (This is the principle of *vicarious liability* and we discuss it further on page 156.) Conversely, employers are not generally liable for the wrongful acts of independent contractors. The employee's statutory protection against unfair dismissal, the statutory right to redundancy payments and the statutory obligations imposed on employers, all contained in the provisions of the Employment Protection (Consolidation) Act 1978, only apply to persons employed under a contract of employment. These important provisions are all considered below.

It is worth noting, before we proceed, that the relationship which results from a contract of employment has changed a great deal over the years. The law once allowed masters to sue anybody who injured their servants; in fact it recognised that masters had a kind of property right in their servants. Such a concept is quite unacceptable today and the relationship is now recognised to be essentially contractual. However, in an era of comprehensive employment legislation and collective agreements between powerful unions and vast organisations, you must remember that in real terms the scope of individual employees' contracts with their employers is very limited.

Terms of employment contracts

With a few exceptions a contract of employment requires no special form: it can be written, totally verbal or implied from the conduct of the parties. One of the exceptions is a contract of apprenticeship: this must be in writing. Under the Employment Protection (Consolidation) Act 1978, however, employers are required to give detailed written information to their employees of the terms of their employment within 13 weeks of their employment commencing. For an organisation with a great number of employees it would be unnecessarily onerous and expensive to give this information to employees individually and employers fulfil this duty by referring employees to a reasonably accessible document, e.g. a collective agreement, which contains the required information. Such documents are frequently displayed on works' notice boards.

The information which must be supplied relates to the parties to the contract, the date employment began, pay, hours of work, holidays, incapacity for work, pensions, the notice required by the employee to terminate the contract and employees' job titles. A statement must also be included which specifies any disciplinary rules, the person to whom application for redress of grievances may be made and the grievance procedure available to employees. A written statement of any change in the terms must be provided within one month of the change.

If you are employed you should have a contract of employment. Consider the terms of your contract in the context of the information above and below this activity.

Rights and duties in employment

The rights and duties which arise from and in connection with contracts of employment are a combination of the express terms of each individual contract, terms implied into them by the common law and by statute, collective agreements and a number of statutory rights enjoyed by employees which exist quite independently of their contracts.

Employers' contractual duties

1 To pay wages. The duty to pay wages is obvious but strictly speaking it only arises if there is an express or implied agreement to pay them. The amount paid again, strictly speaking, depends on the individual contract but collective agreements on wages are now the norm.

2 To provide work. You saw earlier in this chapter that there is no legal right to work as such, but following the decision of the Court of Appeal in *Langston v Chrysler UK* (1974), it may be that the law will recognise the principle that employers are under a duty to provide work for their employees. If this were so, suspension on full pay could be a breach of contract.

3 To take reasonable care of their employees at work. The common law recognised that employers were under a duty to take reasonable care for the safety of their employees but today all the important specific aspects of this duty are governed by statute. These will all eventually be regulated by statutory instruments made by the Secretary of State for Employment under the Health and Safety at Work, etc, Act 1974. (We discuss the general duties imposed by this Act in the next chapter in the context of the responsibilities owed to employees and visitors through the occupancy of premises.)

Should employees suffer injury at work and wish to claim damages from their employers, they may sue:
(a) on the principle of *vicarious liability* – an employer is liable if employees injure one another while acting in the course of their employment;
(b) on the basis of the employer's own personal *negligence* in relation to the provision of adequate plant, premises and machinery, competent staff and a safe system of work with adequate supervision and in-

struction; or
(c) because there has been a *breach of statutory duty.* To succeed here, employees must show that they were included in the class of persons for whose benefit the duty was imposed and that they have suffered the type of injury which the Act was passed to prevent.

In any action for damages by employees against their employers, the employees' own conduct will be taken into account. If they are found to have been partly to blame for their own injuries the damages awarded will be reduced: Law Reform (Contributory Negligence) Act 1945. However, the Courts accept that the repetitive nature of modern industrial employment reduces employees' awareness of their conduct. Furthermore, as the Employers' Liability (Compulsory Insurance) Act 1969 requires employers to insure against liability for injury to their employees, public policy dictates that it should be they who pay, even though the employee was partly to blame for his own injury.

4 To indemnify employees. This duty is owed to all employees who incur expense and liability in the proper performance of their duties.

If employers are in breach of any duty, employees injured by it are entitled to claim damages at common law.

The employee's contractual duties

1 To obey his employer. Employees are bound to obey the lawful instructions of their employers which are within the scope of their contracts of employment.

2 To exercise care and skill. Employees are expected to perform their contractual duties with reasonable care. Should their employers be held liable to third parties as a result of a breach of this duty, employees can be made to indemnify their employers for the loss they incur. In most cases, however, it is not worthwhile for employers to seek this indemnity.

3 To act reasonably. Employees' dishonesty or incompetence always justify their dismissal; whether disobedience, laziness, rudeness etc., also justify dismissal depends on the circumstances of each particular case.

4 To act in good faith. Employees must not allow their own interests to conflict with those of their employers. There are two main aspects of this duty.

First, they must not disclose *confidential information* to third parties, e.g. trade secrets; second, they must not make a *secret profit* out of their appointment. Employees who accept secret commissions from suppliers with whom they place orders for their employers would be an example of a secret profit.

Employees' statutory rights

We mentioned earlier that employees enjoy a number of rights in employment which exist *independently* of the contract of employment. Many of these rights were created or extended by the Employment Protection Act 1975 and are now found in the Employment Protection (Consolidation) Act 1978 and, in the case of statutory maternity pay, in the Social Security Act 1986. They include a right to:

1 Guaranteed daily pay (£11.85 at present) for five days in any three-month period when no work is available, e.g. through lay-offs caused by external strikes;

2 Be paid normal wages when a health hazard requires their suspension from work under the provisions of an Act of Parliament, e.g. the Health and Safety at Work, etc, Act 1974, or a code of practice; (In both *1* and *2* many employees would not be entitled to payment under the terms of their contracts.)

3 Paid maternity leave and a right to re-engagement within 29 weeks of giving birth (*see* page 160);

4 Paid leave in order to fulfil certain trade union duties, and a right to unpaid leave to take part in trade union activities or public duties; (This right is subject to certain limits regarding time and amount as the case may be.)

5 An itemised pay statement showing details of gross pay, deductions and net pay;

6 A written statement upon request giving the reason for dismissal.

Termination of employment contracts

In practice, contracts of employment are nearly always ended by notice or by summary termination. At common law either side may lawfully terminate the contract by giving reasonable notice, or summarily (without notice) where the other side has committed a serious breach of contract. In particular, termination by notice used to put employees in a very weak position – workers are usually more easily replaced than work – and the present situation must be considered in the light of the statutory protection from arbitrary dismissal that the employee now has and the wider political effect of exercising legal rights of dismissal to the letter. Employers would be very foolish to risk confrontation with the might of a trade union by unlawfully dismissing employees – quite apart from the latter's legal rights. Indeed, it is a fact of industrial life that it may be better not to sack an employee where there is legitimate cause in order to avert a possible damaging unofficial strike – whatever legislation there may be against it. In short, legal rights and duties must be considered in the light of the economic and political realities of each particular situation.

Termination by notice

At common law you have seen that the contract can be terminated by giving reasonable notice: the more senior the employee and/or the longer the service, the longer being the period of notice required. By the Employment Protection (Consolidation) Act 1978, *minimum* periods of notice are laid down but even here the concept of unfair dismissal (discussed below) must be considered because a lawful dismissal may still be 'unfair'. Conversely, the Act does not affect the employers' common law right to dismiss employees summarily without notice for misconduct.

Table 8.2 Periods of notice

After continuous employment for:	Period of notice
4 weeks up to 12 years	1 week
2 years up to 12 years	1 week for each year
12 years or more	12 weeks

Employees who have been employed continuously for four weeks are required to give their employers one week's notice.

These periods can be increased by the contract of employment but they cannot be decreased. Either side may, however, waive the right to notice or accept payment in lieu. If the contract specifies a longer period than the statutory minimum, the latter is irrelevant. Indeed at common law reasonable notice may be held to be longer than the statutory minimum. In *Hill v C A Parsons Ltd* (1972), for example, the Court of Appeal thought that a chartered engineer, who had been employed continuously for 35 years, was entitled to at least six months' notice and possibly a year.

Summary termination

The contract may be terminated without notice in two cases. First, by either side where the contract gives an express right to do so; and second, by one party where the other has committed a serious breach of contract. It is always a question of fact, to be decided in the circumstances of each case, whether a breach is sufficiently serious to justify summary termination but an employee's incompetence, dishonesty or wilful disobedience is usually considered sufficiently serious.

Statutory intervention

The common law provided little help to employees who were wrongfully dismissed; they were not generally entitled to a hearing before dismissal and an award of damages was limited to their loss of earnings in the period of notice to which they were entitled. Dismissal by notice was generally lawful no matter how arbitrary and their circumstances after dismissal were not considered.

Such a situation is unacceptable today and Parliament has created the quite separate concept of *unfair dismissal* (applicable whether dismissal is lawful or unlawful) with its own system of remedies and a system of *redundancy payments* following loss of employment. The systems recognise the weakness of individual employees vis-à-vis their employers and their rights to financial compensation for loss of employment. The compensation takes into account the disruption caused by the loss of work and the possible difficulties in obtaining comparable employment.

Unfair dismissal

This is governed by the Employment Protection (Consolidation) Act 1978 as amended by the Employment Act of 1980 and 1988.

The concept is based upon the right to *job security* in which employed status is more important than the terms of the contract. Under the Act employees with at least two years' continuous service at a minimum of 16 hours a week or five years at between 8–16 hours a week can challenge their dismissal before an industrial tribunal, irrespective of whether or not they were in breach of contract and irrespective of whether they were dismissed summarily or by notice.

The burden of proving that the dismissal was fair was originally on employers but since the Employment Act 1980 the tribunal looks at the facts presented by both sides in reaching its decision. In practice this will probably not make much difference because the Tribunal will still be looking to see that:

(a) the reason for the dismissal was fair; and
(b) that it was reasonable in the circumstances for that reason to cause dismissal.

To be 'fair', the reason must relate to the employee's capability or qualifications, conduct, redundancy, a legal restriction which prevents the employment, e.g. a lorry driver who has lost their licence as a result of conviction for a motoring offence, or some other substantial reason, e.g. the employee has asked to be dismissed.

In cases involving the dismissed employee's conduct, a commonsense approach is adopted. Most people, for example, would agree that unpunctuality would be a reason for dismissal but would not expect to be dismissed the first time they were late. Where the employee's conduct would not justify a summary dismissal, the tribunal would expect that the employer had given verbal and then written warnings so that the employee was fully aware that their conduct would lead to a dismissal if it did not improve. How many warnings have to be given will depend on the circumstances. Someone who is persistently late may receive a verbal warning and then several written warnings before the final warning and dismissal. On the other hand, someone who has been caught fighting at work may receive a final written warning immediately. Many firms have a disciplinary procedure which states what warnings will be given before dismissal.

The statute declares certain reasons to be *automatically unfair*. These include dismissal for joining a trade union or taking part in its activities and dismissal on grounds of pregnancy, unless the employee is incapable of doing her job or her continued employment would infringe the health and safety legislation. Conversely, certain reasons for dismissal are automatically considered to be *fair*, e.g. in order to safeguard national security and because the employee was on strike or locked out by the employer unless the dismissal was selective, i.e. only some employees still on strike at the time were locked out or dismissed. This last reason shows that the legislation is not intended to interfere with the legitimate exercise of economic sanctions by either side in a trade dispute. Dismissal for *not* joining a trade union is automatically unfair. The former exception to this – where a valid union membership (closed shop) agreement existed – was removed by the Employment Act 1988.

Remedies for unfair dismissal

These are also contained in the 1978 Act, as amended. An industrial tribunal may order an employee's *reinstatement* (s/he is given back the job and treated as if the dismissal had never taken place), or *re-engagement* (s/he is given a new job by the employer), or it may make an award of *compensation*.

An award comprises two elements: a *basic award* made regardless of loss and calculated on a similar basis to redundancy payments (*see* below) based on age (with the difference that years of employment below the age of 18 also count), length of service and rate of pay; and a *compensatory award* based on the loss the employee has actually suffered through the unfair dismissal. The maximum weekly pay for calculating the basic award is (at present) £172 and the maximum compensatory award is (at present) £8,925. The award can be reduced if the employee has unreasonably refused an offer of reinstatement or because of conduct before the dismissal which was not necessarily known or cited as a reason at the time. Additional awards (maximum 52 weeks x £86) can be made if the employer fails to reinstate/re-engage the employee and/or the unfair dismissal was discriminatory based on sex or race.

These formulae give the usual following maxima (as at 1990) in an unfair dismissal claim:

Maximum basic award	
(20 weeks x 1.5 x £172)	£5,160
Maximum compensatory award	£8,925

Normal maximum	£14,085
Maximum additional award	
(52 weeks x £172)	£8,944
Total	£23,029

Redundancy

Under the redundancy payments provisions of the Employment Protection (Consolidation) Act 1978, redundancy occurs when employees are dismissed because their employers have discontinued or intend to discontinue the business for which they were employed, or because the need for their particular services has diminished or is expected to diminish. The payments are intended to compensate employees for the loss of their jobs through no fault of their own. Thus, if a person is dismissed for a good reason, or unreasonably refuses a comparable job, they are not entitled to a redundancy payment.

To be entitled to a redundancy payment employees must be under the age of 65, if a man, or 60, if a woman, and have worked continuously for the same employer for either:

(a) two years at not less than 16 hours a week; or
(b) five years at not less than 8 hours a week (in effect part-time employees).

The Government plans to change the present entitlement rules for redundancy and unfair dismissal to 20 hours and 12 hours respectively.

The calculation of payments is based on age, length of service and final earnings.

For each year employed between:

ages 18-21	half a week's pay
ages 22-40	one week's pay
ages 41-65	(men) one-and-a-half weeks' pay
ages 41-60	(women) one-and-a-half weeks' pay.

The maximum length of reckonable service is 20 years and the maximum reckonable weekly earning is £172. Thus, the maximum payment possible at present is £172 x 1.5 x 20 = £5,160. Some redundancy payments are higher than the maximum entitlement under the Employment Protection (Consolidation) Act 1978. These are, however, usually the result of negotiation between the employer and strong trade unions.

Employers must make contributions to a redundancy fund operated by the Secretary of State for Employment, from which they will receive a 35% rebate of any redundancy payments they make provided they give advance notice of the redundancy to the Secretary of State. The Employment Protection Act 1975 requires employers to consult the unions representing their employees about possible redundancies and notify the Secretary of State where they propose to make redundant more than 100 employees at one establishment within 90 days, or more than ten employees within 30 days. It also entitles individual employees who have been given redundancy notices to reasonable time off from work to look for new employment or to arrange for retraining before the dismissal takes place.

Update the figures relating to guaranteed payments and awards for unfair dismissal and redundancy. (The *New Law Journal* or *Law Notes* are two publications which you are likely to have in your library which will contain this sort of information.)

Other statutory protection of employees

Much has already been said about Government intervention to regulate employment and protect employees. In particular we have discussed the terms implied in employment contracts, the protection against unfair dismissal and the right to compensation on redundancy contained in the Employment Protection (Consolidation) Act 1978. In addition, however, other legislation gives important protection in more specific situations.

Discrimination

The Race Relations Act 1976 makes it unlawful to discriminate on the grounds of colour, race or ethnic or national origins generally and Part 2 of the Act deals specifically with employment. It provides that it is unlawful to discriminate on these grounds in the recruitment, terms of employment, opportunities for promotion, training or other benefits and dismissal. A complaint under Part 2 of the Act is dealt with by an industrial tribunal which may award compensation and order steps to be taken to stop the discrimination. There is also growing Parliamentary pressure to introduce age discrimination legislation, e.g. in job advertisements and promotions. One such private members bill was debated in the House of Lords in 1989.

The Equal Pay Act 1970, the Sex Discrimination Act 1975 and the Employment Act 1989 taken together require that men and women (regardless of marital status) are treated equally as regards pay for equal or equivalent work, recruitment, training, promotion and dismissal. The exception under the 1975 Act is where sex or marital status is a genuine occupational qualification, e.g. as a model. The 1989 Act brings UK law on sex discrimination into line with the EC equal treatment directive by making the prohibition on discrimination in the 1975 Act the starting point and retaining only those discriminatory provisions considered by the government to be suited to present day conditions, e.g. regulations preventing a pregnant woman working in environments which might endanger her unborn child. The Sex Discrimination Act 1986 provides that employers may not set different compulsory retirement ages for men and women working in comparable employment.

Unfortunately, this is one area where the law is often powerless to fulfil its purpose effectively. Women remain underpaid in comparison with men partly because they tend to work in jobs that are badly paid, e.g. shop work. It is virtually impossible to change attitudes and expectations by legislation.

The Employment Protection (Consolidation) Act 1978, as amended, gives a woman who has been absent from work because of pregnancy the right to return to work in the job in which she was employed, under the original contract of employment and on terms no less favourable than those which would have been applied had she not been absent. The right is subject to a number of conditions. In particular, it must be exercised by the end of the 29th week after the birth, she must have been employed until 11 weeks before the expected birth date and at the time have had two years' continuous employment; she must also have notified her employer in writing of her intended absence, the expected week of the birth, and her intention to return to work.

The Rehabilitation of Offenders Act 1974, designed to enable offenders to make a fresh start, provides that after certain periods convictions become 'spent' and need not be disclosed to an employer. Dismissal on discovery of a spent conviction would be 'unfair' under the Employment Protection (Consolidation) Act 1978.

National insurance and industrial injuries

Both these important aspects of the welfare state are now regulated by the Social Security and Housing Benefit Act 1982 and the Social Security Act 1985. The National Insurance scheme provides for contributions to be paid by both employers and employees and for benefits to be paid in certain situations, e.g. sickness, unemployment, maternity, retirement and death. The *statutory sick pay* scheme, for example, involves *employers* paying a weekly sum for a maximum of 28 weeks to employees who become ill and subsequently recovering the amounts paid by deductions from the employers' National Insurance contributions.

The industrial injuries provisions of the Acts entitle any person in insurable employment to benefits if they suffer personal injury caused by an accident in the course of their employment. Benefits are of three types: injury benefit, payable for a maximum of six months while the claimant is unable to work; disablement benefit, the amount and form of payment depending on the degree of disablement; and death benefits.

Based on your experience, assess the extent to which the letter and/or the spirit of anti-discrimination legislation is followed.

Employment law in perspective

Employment is vital to most people's social and economic existence and, whether we like it or not, we all spend a great deal of our lives working. The legal framework of employment law reflects this. Today there exists a comprehensive set of regulations designed to ensure that employees' social rights and needs are equated with the economic forces which dictate the actions of their employers. Some of you may consider that the legal framework unduly favours employees, others that the social cost of unemployment and the economic power of large organisations

justifies even greater employee protection.

Whatever your personal political views might be, most commentators would agree that, under the Conservative government of the 1980s, UK employment law became increasingly at odds with European and international developments. Published in May 1989, the EC's 'Social Charter' was criticised by the Government as being 'socialism by the back door' and it remained opposed to it. (For further detail, *see* page 352). Conversely, the Labour Party embraced the 'Social Charter' whole-heartedly arguing that it would enshrine basic workers' rights in the law throughout the EC. Cynics did however comment that it offered the Party a convenient way out of credibility problems caused by largely giving up traditionally very open and general support for trade unions – support which was seen as an electoral liability. The 'Social Charter' could be promoted (at worst) as the acceptable face of European Socialism.

The ILO's (*see* page 146) observations in 1989 were very specific. It condemned the government for dismissing workers at GCHQ (a top secret communication establishment) in 1984 for refusing to give up their union membership and expressed concern at the restrictions imposed on unions by the Employment Act 1988 to discipline and expel members, particularly those who refuse to take part in lawful industrial action. It also expressed concern about the ban on unions indemnifying members for any penalty which may be imposed on any individual for an offence or for contempt of court – in short for restricting the autonomy of trade unions to make their own internal rules.

The ILO also called for widened definitions of a trade dispute, protected secondary action and legislation protecting striking employees from dismissal. In general terms it concluded that the balance between the 'rights' of the individual had been emphasised at the expense of those of trade unions. It also expressed the view that the huge amount of employment legislation in the 1980s had produced a framework which was too complex and that the government should 'codify, clarify and simplify its legislation concerning industrial relations.'

Employment is a subject which perfectly illustrates the need to arrive at a workable amalgam of social consciousness, economic reality and political possibility. Law as a concept has taken a back seat in the creation of the legal framework but law as a social process is crucial to the operation and enforcement of the framework.

The organisation must concern itself with trade union and employment law: indeed, there are economic and legal penalties for not doing so. Average employees, however, know little if anything about employment law and are generally apathetic about trade unions. They are, naturally, most concerned about the contents of their pay packets but it is very likely that they are equally ignorant of the factors which determine the amount of their wages. To obtain a full picture of the organisation and its employees we must also discuss the factors which determine the level of wages.

Keywords

Contract of service
The correct legal term for a contract of employment; a contract where people put their labour at the disposal of others in return for some form of remuneration. The existence of the contract gives employees important statutory rights and makes their employer legally liable for their actions.

Rights and duties
In employment law these are of two kinds: those that arise from the contract of employment itself and those that are conferred or enforced by legislation, e.g. redundancy rights.

Unfair dismissal
Legislation gives employees the right not to be 'unfairly dismissed'. A complaint of unfair dismissal does *not* depend on the employer having acted in breach of contract but simply that the employer has terminated the contract in circumstances that are 'unfair' within the meaning of the legislation. Statutory compensation awards are available for unfair dismissal.

Redundancy
Redundancy occurs where an employer no longer intends to carry on the business or no longer requires the services of the employee. Quite apart from any contractual severance terms, statutory payments have to be made to employees who are made redundant.

Discrimination
A range of Acts of Parliament protect employees from various types of discrimination. Whether or not legislation is an effective method of promoting equality (different from preventing discrimination) is another matter.

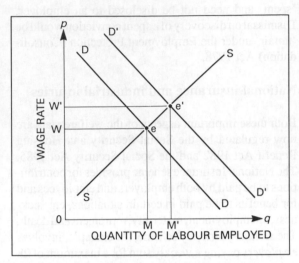

Fig. 8.3 The determination of the wage rate

The determination of wages

The demand and supply of labour

The wage rate will be determined by the interaction of the organisation's demand for labour and the supply of labour forthcoming. In Chapter 6 we saw that an organisation's demand for a factor of production is the marginal revenue product (MRP) curve of that factor. The supply of labour, you will remember, is determined by such things as the size and age distribution of the population (*see* Chapter 4). Without interference from the government or trade unions the wage rate will be determined by these forces of demand and supply. This is illustrated in Fig. 8.3 (*see* also pages 245–50). Under these circumstances it is unlikely that the supply of labour will vary much from year to year. The wage rate in a business is therefore more likely to be the result of changes in demand. The movement of the demand curve from DD to D'D' could have been brought about by either an improvement in technology or a rise in the price of the product being produced (*see* page 106). Although improving productivity is one of the most certain ways of increasing wages, there is little that trade unions can do about it. They therefore tend to work by affecting the supply of labour. (Trade unions may, of course, be involved in agreements with employers to increase productivity.)

1 With the aid of a diagram, assess the effect of the government's imposition of minimum wage legislation, e.g. wages councils, on an occupation, that is, the wages are made higher than they would be in a free market situation.

2 Illustrate the circumstances under which the imposition of such wage legislation might lead to *less* wages being paid – a task for the ambitious.

Restrictive labour practices

A most effective way for trade unions to increase their members' wages is to restrict the supply of labour to a particular occupation. This can be done by *closed shop* practices (*see* page 151). These are not always aimed at increasing wages but have certainly been used for this purpose in some industries, e.g. printing and film-making. As you saw earlier, however, closed shops are now, at least 'legally', a virtual thing of the past. The supply of labour to an occupation can also be limited by enforcing long *apprenticeships* or *training periods*. Another method is *demarcation*, where particular tasks in a job may only be done by members of a particular union, for example plumbers not being allowed to do joiners' jobs in a particular factory. Demarcation or 'who does what' disputes were a frequent cause of unrest in British industrial relations, especially in the shipbuilding industry. The 1980s saw a virtual end to these disputes under the combined pressure of anti-closed shop legislation and high unemployment. However, such disputes still did occur as with the Wapping dispute in the printing industry when printers accused electricians of taking their jobs.

Fig. 8.4 shows that the effect of restricting the supply of labour is to increase the wage rate from W to W' but it also means that the quantity of labour employed declines from OM to OL. Thus, while some workers are receiving higher wages other people are unable to obtain jobs. This kind of practice is not restricted to trade unions; the Inns of Court run a most effective closed shop which restricts the supply of labour to the Bar, thereby keeping out many young lawyers who might like to become practising barristers. This not only has the effect of driving up barris-

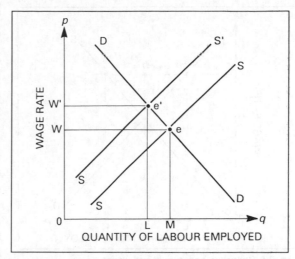

Fig. 8.4 The effect of restrictive practices upon the wage rate

ter's fees but also contributes to the delays which bedevil the administration of justice.

If you are employed, attempt to answer the following questions.

1 How many people are employed in your industry?

2 Is employment expanding or contracting?

3 To what extent is your occupation affected by geographical and occupational immobility of labour?

4 Are there any restrictive practices in your industry?

Collective bargaining

Working people learned long ago that to ask employers individually for a wage rise was a good way to lose a job. Trade unions therefore negotiate on behalf of all their members and if agreement is not reached they may then take action collectively to enforce their demands. The collective bargaining strength of a trade union varies enormously from industry to industry. This is affected by factors such as the percentage of trade union members in the work force, their organisation, the law and by general economic conditions. The National Union of Mineworkers seemed invin-

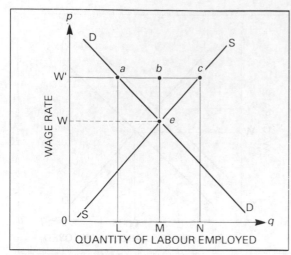

Fig. 8.5 Collective bargaining and wages

cible in 1974 but in 1984 it was a different story. Certainly the bargaining power of many workers is very weak.

Fig. 8.5 illustrates three possibilities. Which one occurs will depend upon the strength of the union. Here successful collective bargaining has raised the wage rate from OW to OW'. As a result of this the employer would like to employ less labour (OL instead of OM) – this is position *a*. However, the strength of the union may be such that it is able to insist that the organisation retains the same number of workers as before. This is position *b*, where the wage rate is higher but the quantity of labour employed remains OM. As a result of increasing the wage rate more people would like to work for this organisation. In an extreme case the union may be able to insist that the organisation moves to position *c* where the wage rate is OW' and the quantity of labour employed is ON. If the organisation is pushed into this position it may be forced to close down since *ac* represents a surplus of labour which it would not choose to employ if it were not forced to. Such *featherbedding* and *overmanning* has occurred in a number of British industries. Such practices have declined greatly in recent years as a result of the generally hostile economic conditions and changes in trade union law. The printing unions such as SOGAT, which for many years dictated to newspaper proprietors, found conditions drastically changed in 1986 as Rupert Murdoch made 6,000 unemployed when he moved his printing operation from Fleet Street to Wapping.

Factors affecting bargaining strength

The ability of a trade union to raise wages will be influenced not only by its collective bargaining strength but also by several economic factors which we list below.

1 The price of the final product. If the demand for the product being made is such that it is not sensitive to changes in price (inelastic, *see* page 259), the organisation will be able to pass on the cost of increased wages to the consumer. Conversely, if the demand for the product is sensitive to price changes (elastic) it will be difficult to pass on the cost of increased wages and consequently difficult for unions to gain wage rises.
2 The proportion of total costs which labour represents. If labour costs make up a large proportion of total costs this will tend to make it more difficult for them to obtain pay rises. On the other hand, if the labour costs are only a small proportion of the organisation's other costs and more especially if the worker's task is vital this will tend to make it easier to secure a wage rise. This is referred to by Professor Samuelson as 'the importance of being unimportant'.
3 Factor substitution. If it is relatively easy to substitute another factor of production for labour, e.g. capital, this will mean that as unions demand more wages the business will employ fewer workers. In Britain since the 1939–1945 War rising labour costs have encouraged employers to substitute capital for labour wherever possible. This is well illustrated by the changes in technology in Fleet Street.
4 The level of profits. If an organisation is making little or no profit then the effect of a rise in wages could well be to put it out of business. Conversely, high profits would make it easier for unions to obtain higher wages and job security. In recent years high profits have often had the effect of stimulating wage claims.
5 Inflation. Not only does inflation stimulate bigger wage claims but it may also make it easier for an organisation to pass on increases in wages to the consumer.

If trade union activity were successful in the national sense it would increase the proportion of the national income going to wages. Despite all the struggles of trade unions this is not so. The portion of national income going to wages now is not significantly different from that of 60 years ago. The proportion fluctuates round 60–65% depending upon the general level of economic activity: that is to say, when there is a slump it decreases and when there is a boom it increases.

1 Go through points *1–5* in this section and assess their importance to your wage or salary now and over the next ten years. For example, in point *3* 'factor substitution', is it possible that a machine could do your job as well (or better) as you?

2 If you are a full-time student, you might like to consider how these points affect your lecturers or education in general.

Strikes

The withdrawal of labour is the ultimate union weapon. The word 'strike' is very emotive and many people believe strikes are the cause of Britain's economic difficulties. It is more likely, however, that rather than being a cause, strikes are a symptom of Britain's industrial malaise.

Rather than expressing opinions, it is better to examine the facts. Statistics on strikes vary greatly from year to year but many countries often have a worse record than the UK, especially Italy and the USA. This is small comfort when we compare ourselves with the excellent industrial relations of the Germans and the Japanese. This section concentrates on general features because of the wide variations in figures from year to year. Up-to-date figures on industrial disputes are published monthly in *The Department of Employment Gazette*.

In the late 1970s strikes were certainly worse than for many years. A number of reasons might be identified. The economy was stagnant and this made it very difficult for wage earners to obtain *real* increases in their earnings. On the other hand, inflation meant that, unless large wage claims were made, real income would decline and the rapid and continuing inflation encouraged unions to make exorbitant wage claims. The combined effects of inflation and incomes policy spread strikes to previously trouble-free groups such as hospital workers, firemen and ambulance crews.

There were also several protracted strikes for union recognition. It should be remembered, however, that good industrial relations do not make good television and that we always see the very worst side of industry's troubles on TV.

The vast majority of strikes are for increased wages. Sympathetic strikes, i.e. one union striking to support another, and political strikes are very uncommon in Britain. There was an exception to this in the years 1971–4 when many unions took action against the Industrial Relations Act 1971. In 1979, 29 million days were lost through strikes. This total was the highest since the General Strike of 1926, and it was partly as a result of opposition to the Labour government's pay policy in what became known as the 'winter of discontent' (1978–9). However a far greater number of days was lost in the autumn of 1979 because of the series of weekly one-day and two-day strikes called in the entire engineering industry. In the early 1980s the number of days lost through strikes fell rapidly. This may be partly attributable at least to rising unemployment.

Despite this, the 1980s saw a number of protracted strikes. For a number of reasons, several of these are particularly worth noting. First, the *Miners' Strike 1984–85* was at least as much a political confrontation as an economic one. The Government, however, was well prepared and succeeded in dividing the NUM. After almost a year, the Government's victory was virtually absolute. Second, the *Teachers' Pay Dispute of 1985–86* illustrated the problems which beset those in the public services. It was also symptomatic of the general run-down of public services. Third, the *Fleet Street Dispute of 1986* illustrated the devastating effect that new technology can have on employment. Fourth, the dispute in the docks and in shipping in 1988–89 demonstrated the increased power which legislation was having upon the industrial scene.

It is the large protracted strikes that attract most attention but most strikes are short-lived, with 65% of strikes lasting less than one week. Britain is, however, bedevilled by unofficial strikes. These outnumber official strikes by about 20:1 but on the other hand official strikes tend to last about three or four times as long as unofficial ones. Unofficial strikes may be a symptom not only of bad relations between employers and workers but also between the union bureaucracies and their members.

With some notable exceptions, the number of days lost through strikes was low in the 1980s compared with previous decades. As well as the effect of rising unemployment mentioned above, this was also a result of the Government's structured attack not only on trade union power but also on working conditions generally. (We have examined the changes in trade union law in some detail.) Moreover, it is debatable whether the absence of strikes is necessarily evidence of a better climate in industry. Despite these changes, most people would agree that better industrial relations are essential if there is to be greater economic prosperity. This will take a great effort from employers, unions and government.

Before leaving the subject of the employee and his wages, we must consider the law relating to their payment.

The payment of wages

Under the Wages Act 1986 employees no longer have a *right* to be paid in cash, a practice which had become outmoded in any case. Employers now have the right to pay employees by cheque or, more usually, by crediting the employee's bank account. Payment in cash can, of course, still be agreed.

All deductions from pay must be authorised by legislation, e.g. income tax and National Insurance deductions, or by a written contract of employment.

In the not-so-distant future the need to use cash may almost disappear; even today it is possible to pay for virtually anything you need with a credit card. The technology already exists to take this a stage further and to debit a person's bank account, or perhaps some other monetary fund, at any point of payment. This would completely eliminate the transfer of cash and any intermediate accounting stage such as a credit card company or shop account. If the technology were to be exploited, the present methods of paying wages and the legal rules regulating them could become completely obsolete.

Keywords

Restrictive practices
Methods by which free competition is reduced by the action of trade unions and producers.

Collective bargaining
The actions of trade unions in negotiating with employers on behalf of all their members on matters such as pay and conditions.

Factor substitution
The reduction in the use of one factor of production, e.g. labour, and its replacement by another, e.g. capital.

Learning project

Strikes over the years

Study the table below and complete the tasks which follow.

Working days lost through strikes in the UK (000s)

1967	2,783	1978	9,391
1968	4,719	1979	29,051
1969	6,925	1980	11,965
1970	10,908	1981	4,244
1971	13,589	1982	5,276
1972	23,923	1983	3,753
1973	7,145	1984	27,135
1974	14,845	1985	6,399
1975	5,914	1986	1,923
1976	3,509	1987	3,545
1977	10,378		

1 Using the figures in the table, draw a graph to show the number of days lost through strikes 1967–87.

2 Annotate the graph with important events, e.g. Miners' Strike.

3 Identify and explain any connections between the figures and changes to legislation on industrial law.

4 In what industries are strikes most prevalent and why?

5 Discover whether there appears to be any connection between plant size, ie. the number of employees on-site, and the tendency to strike.

Further ideas for learning projects

1 Analyse the changing structure of the UK working population over the past 15 years. Consider:

(a) its total size;
(b) the level of unemployment;
(c) its composition in terms of men and women;
(d) the proportion of full-time and part-time work.

Explain the observed changes as fully as possible and illustrate your findings with tables and graphs.

2 Consider your own employment or, if you are a full-time student, that of a friend or member of your family. What changes do you foresee in its manpower require-ments over the next five years? Using the contents of a manpower plan outlined in this chapter, prepare a manpower plan to meet those perceived changes.

3 Write an article of about 1,200 words suitable for inclusion in a student paper *either* in support of restrictions on trade union activities *or* in favour of reducing the restrictions. (Remember: your article should not be based purely on personal opinion – you need some facts – and you need to adopt a style which is likely to get it published, attract and hold the attention of the reader.)

9

Land and other property

CHAPTER OBJECTIVES

After studying this chapter you should be able to:

■ Define land in the legal and economic senses;
■ State and explain the differences between freehold and leasehold estates in land;
■ Outline how title to land is transferred;
■ List and evaluate the factors determining land use;
■ Describe the responsibilities arising from occupancy of land;
■ Analyse the concept of rent.

What is land?

All organisations use land. In this chapter we begin by considering the legal and economic meanings of land and later we consider the income derived from land and the factors which determine site value.

Definitions

Economically, land may be defined as the space in which to undertake economic activity. Although all economic activities do not use land in the way which, say, farming does, every activity must have a 'space' in which it can take place. Included within the definition of land are whatever *natural resources* the space possesses. Land therefore includes mineral wealth, timber, climate, position, and topography. Since fishing is an economic activity it is possible to regard the sea as 'land'.

At law the term land embraces not only the visible surface of the earth but also, in theory, everything above and below the surface and rights over land. When the term is used in Acts of Parliament it is defined by the Interpretation Act 1978 as including

'buildings and other structures, land covered with water, and any estate, interest, easement, servitude or right in or over land'. Hence, legally, we can say that land includes minerals, buildings, fixtures in buildings, reasonable rights in the airspace above the surface and rights over another person's land such as a right of way.

While a lawyer's definition of land may appear superficially similar to that of an economist, and indeed to some extent they are complementary, economists and lawyers view land from different perspectives. The economist views it as a *resource* and is therefore interested in its *utility*; the lawyer is primarily concerned with its *ownership*, the *transfer* of ownership, *restrictions* upon its use and the legal *obligations* arising from its occupancy. And yet, these perspectives are also complementary. It is very much the idea of land as a resource which accounts for the detailed and often technical framework of rules and regulations regardings its use and the legal responsibilities arising from it. Similarly, although ownership of land and its transfer are usually less complicated than most people imagine, it is perhaps the resource value of the land concerned which often requires and explains the professional role of lawyers in the transaction.

Practically, it may be difficult to separate land from other factors of production; theoretically, however, it possesses two attributes which distinguish it. First, it is fixed in supply. Since we have already observed that the sea may be land it is obvious that there is only a finite amount of planet. However, although the total amount of land may be fixed, the *effective* area of land may be varied. In the nineteenth century, for example, the introduction of railways and steamships opened up the mid-west of America, thereby effectively increasing the world's supply of grain-growing land. Similarly, the effective supply of land to any particular use may be altered by a change in price, e.g. if the price of building land increases, more land will be switched from agriculture, thereby increasing the effective supply of building land.

The second unique feature of land is that it has no cost of production. Although an individual may have to pay a great deal for land, and society may devote a lot of resources to its exploitation, the land itself has always existed and in that sense has no cost of production. In this sense an alternative definition of land might be that land is all the free gifts of nature.

We mentioned earlier that, at law, land consists of more than the surface of the earth. Indeed, in so far as rights over water and its use are included in land law, land also includes water in a lawyer's definition. Ownership of land and rights over it have always been important to English law and an idea of the sophistication of the law's development can be gained by considering first the concept of fixtures and second rights in the airspace above property.

Fixtures are things which at law have become part of the land or building to which they are attached. Whether the objects are fixtures, however, may be a question of some nicety. For example, in *Berkley v Poulett* (1976) pictures fixed in the recesses of the panelling of rooms, a marble statue of a Greek athlete (weighing half a tonne and standing on a plinth) and a sundial resting on a stone baluster outside a house, were held not to be fixtures which passed to the purchaser of the house. They were chattels personal (*see* below) and accordingly the seller of the house was entitled to remove them. In deciding such cases the courts look at the degree to which the object in question is attached to the building (the greater the annexation the more likely it is to be a fixture) and, more importantly, the purpose of the annexation. If the intention was to permanently improve the building, and not merely to enjoy the object, it is a fixture. Hence, fitted cupboards in a house and permanent installations in a factory are fixtures, while pictures hung on walls and moveable machinery are not.

Rights in airspace can be illustrated by two cases. In *Kelsen v Imperial Tobacco Co Ltd* (1957) an advertising sign which projected over the plaintiff's land was held to be an actionable trespass, while in *Bernstein of Leigh (Baron) v Skyviews & General Ltd* (1977) the court rejected the view that a landowner's rights in the airspace above his property extend to an unlimited height. In that case an action for trespass had been brought after an employee of the defendant had allegedly flown over the plaintiff's land in order to photograph his house. Normally, of course, legislation – the Civil Aviation Act 1949 – prevents any action being brought in respect of aeroplanes playing over a person's land and interference by space vehicles is verging on the realms of fantasy. However space law – in some ways the exact opposite of land law – must surely become important in the future.

Land and other property

Our legal system classifies property as either *real or personal*, the former comprising only freehold interests in land and the latter everything else, including leasehold land. (Freehold and leasehold are explained below.) Freehold and leasehold interests in land are in fact treated in much the same way and it is usual to refer to leaseholds as *chattels real* to distinguish them from *chattels personal*, i.e. other forms of personal property (*see* Fig. 9.1).

These somewhat strange sounding categories are a legacy of the very rigid procedural rules which the common law courts (the Royal courts) developed early in our legal history. If a person's freehold land was wrongfully taken from him, not an infrequent occurrence in those days, he could recover the actual land by bringing a *real action* in the common law courts. If, however, he was dispossessed of anything else it was not possible for him to recover the actual property. He was only entitled to a *personal action* for money compensation against the person who had taken it. The concept of the leasehold interest devel-

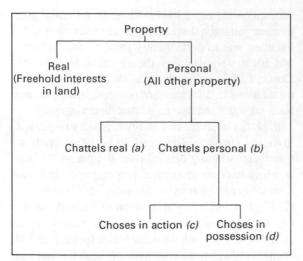

Fig. 9.1 Types of property. (a) Leasehold interests in land. The word 'chattel' is a linguistic corruption of 'cattle', the ownership of which is still regarded as a measure of wealth in some societies. (b) All other personal property: 'pure personality'. (c) Property which does not physically exist and which consequently cannot be effectively protected by physical means, only by legal action, e.g. patents, copyrights, goodwill of a business. 'Chose' – old French legal term for 'thing'. (d) Property with a physical existence – it can be physically possessed and protected, e.g. this book, clothes.

oped later than the freehold, by which time legal procedure had become so rigid that the real action available to a freeholder could not be adapted to a leaseholder's claim. In time, however, a remedy developed which enabled a leaseholder to recover his land if he had been wrongfully dispossessed.

Already you can see that a knowledge of legal history is necessary to fully appreciate our system of land law. In fact, the concept of ownership as applied to land is still based on ideas dating back to William the Conqueror and the Normans' feudalism! Fortunately, however, the present system can be described and explained in general terms without more than a few passing references to the past. Nevertheless, it is a remarkable fact that it was not until the Law of Property Act 1925 that our system of land law made any real concessions to complex industrial society. Even today land law may be criticised for being unnecessarily old-fashioned and complicated both in principle and practice, the Land Registry (where proof of title to most land is held), for example, is not even computerised. Law in practice often seems to presup-

pose the existence of lawyers and it can be argued that in land law lawyers have created a system which in effect they alone can understand and from which, despite the abolition of the solicitors' monopoly on conveyancing, comes a large proportion of their income.

Be this as it may, three main reasons can be put forward to account for land law's complexity.

1 Land is *permanent property* and therefore a variety of interests, effective at the same time or consecutively, may exist over it. For example, A may 'own' Number 1 High Road, but may let it to B who sub-lets to C, each of whom may have mortgaged it to different mortgagees. In addition there may be a variety of rights over the land on which Number 1 High Road stands (*see* below). In contrast, other forms of property, such as goods and shares, are normally the subject of absolute ownership only.

2 History: land law has its origins in feudal society (*see* page 23) and no major attempt was made to reduce its accumulated complexities until the Law of Property Act 1925.

3 Land is the one *finite economic resource* and its use is a subject of public concern. Thus, there are a variety of statutes, such as the Town and County Planning Act 1971, by which the State imposes restrictions on a person's use and exploitation of his land.

The ownership of land

Since the Norman Conquest in 1066 all land in England has been theoretically owned by the Crown and the same has been true of the rest of Great Britain for many centuries. The most that anyone else can own is one of the two legal estates which now exist: a freehold estate or a leasehold estate. An *estate* is a measure of a person's interest in a particular piece of land in terms of time. In the olden days it was held on a certain *tenure*, originally the provision of goods or services of some kind and later the payment of a sum of money. We still have tenancies and rents, of course, but these are very different from the original feudal ideas of tenure which have now almost entirely disappeared.

A legal estate is an abstract idea and is quite separate from the land itself. It can be bought or sold, transferred by gift or by will, without affecting the actual land itself or the possession of it. It is possible, for example, to buy the freehold of a large block of flats without in any way affecting the rights of occupation of the many tenants in the flats.

When the property market is buoyant this divorce of the legal estate from the land itself is one factor which allows large profits to be made from the buying and selling of this purely abstract concept. Some people would argue that this is a quite proper benefit to be gained from the law's recognition of private property rights. Others would argue that this is a reason why land, a fundamental social and economic resource, should be nationalised. They would allow, perhaps, absolute ownership of houses and other buildings built upon it. In such a question political beliefs are all-important.

Freehold land

All land in this country is now held on freehold tenure (free as opposed to unfree in the olden days) which for all practical purposes amounts to absolute ownership. A freeholder may, for example, dispose of his estate to anyone he pleases. Nevertheless, there are important restrictions upon the rights of freeholders to do as they please with their land. At common law the law of torts prevents them from using their land in a way which would cause an actionable nuisance to their neighbours, and their right to develop land is restricted by the Town and Country Planning Acts.

Before 1925 there was a variety of freehold estates which the common law recognised but since the Law of Property Act 1925 only the fee simple absolute in possession is recognised as a legal freehold estate. All the former freehold estates can now only exist as equitable interests in land behind a *trust* – an arrangement whereby property is held by one person (a trustee) who must use it for the benefit of another (a beneficiary).

The words used in the term *fee simple absolute in possession* have the following meanings.

Fee – an estate of inheritance, i.e. one that may be inherited or which may pass by will.
Simple – the inheritance is not limited to a particular class of the estate owner's heirs, for example males only or the offspring from a particular marriage. (An estate where the inheritance was limited in this way

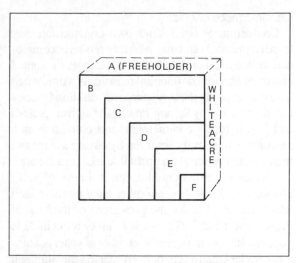

Fig. 9.2. Creation of leases

was known as a 'fee tail'.)
Absolute – not subject to any conditions, as a 'life estate' would be for example.
In possession – takes effect immediately. This includes not only the right to immediate possession but also the immediate right to rents and profits where the land is leased to a tenant.

Leasehold land

As you have seen, all land in this country is held on freehold tenure but the estate owner may create from his freehold an estate of limited duration: a leasehold. This can be illustrated diagrammatically: look at Fig. 9.2. The *freehold* of Whiteacre is owned by A. He leases it to B for 99 years (the head lease) for £5,000 a year. B in turn leases most of it to C for 90 years at, say, £5,500 a year and so on down the chain until a small part is let to F. Alternatively, the *whole* of Whiteacre could be sub-let a number of times, leaving F as the last sub-lessee and the present occupier. Yet again, B could transfer (assign) his lease to C who transfers it to D etc. Here there only ever exists the one lease. In all three cases, the right to occupy the land normally reverts back to A (the freeholder) when the (head) lease expires, i.e. at the end of 99 years. The points to note from this are first, that a leaseholder is usually able to sub-let his land and, second, provided each successive sub-lease is for a shorter period, a number of legal estates can exist at any one time over the same piece of land.

Confusing, or is it? Your own organisation may lease its premises and may possibly sub-let accommodation in excess of its needs. The lease was invented centuries ago for commercial reasons (at a time when land was virtually the sole source of wealth and money could be raised by selling its use for a given period) and it still fulfils commercial functions. Land as a resource is frequently acquired by buying a lease and high rents in return are a profitable source of income.

Technically a leasehold estate is a *term of years absolute*, and it is the only other legal estate in land which can exist under the provisions of the Law of Property Act 1925. The words *terms of years* include not only leases for a specific number of years but also those for less than a year or from year to year, although short leases are commonly referred to as tenancies. *Absolute* means that the estate is not subject to any conditions.

To create a legal estate, the Law of Property Act 1925 requires a lease for more than three years to be made by deed but a lease which takes effect in possession (immediately) for a term not exceeding three years at the best rent which can be reasonably obtained may be created orally or in writing.

The essential features of a leasehold estate are that:

(a) it gives the right to *exclusive possession*;
(b) it is for a *definite term*, i.e. the start of the term and its duration are fixed or can be determined (this is the essential distinction between a lease and a freehold for the latter is of unlimited duration);
(c) it creates the relationship of *landlord and tenant*.

At the end of the lease the land reverts to the freeholder. However the common law position is clearly socially and politically unacceptable. Varying degrees of protection have been given by statute to both domestic and commercial tenancies. A brief summary of the protection given to domestic tenancies is given here and commercial tenancies are considered more fully below.

Statutory intervention

The subjects of 'landlord and tenant' and 'housing' in general are regulated by detailed statutory provisions, many of which reflect the political philosophy of the present government. In a book such as this, we can only give you an outline of this detailed legal framework.

The Leasehold Reform Act 1967 give a leaseholder of a house, originally let for 21 years or more (a long tenancy) at a low rent and held for at least five years, the right to enforce a sale to him of the freehold in payment of the value of the freehold interest in the site. This is known as *leasehold enfranchisement*. Alternatively he may ask for a 50 year extension of the lease. However the Act only applies to houses (not flats) of less than £200 rateable value (£400 in Greater London) as at March 1965. Under the Landlord and Tenant Act 1987 tenants of residential flat blocks must be given first right of refusal to acquire their landlord's interest in the premises, i.e the freehold or head lease, where he wishes to dispose of it.

A tenant under a long tenancy of a flat or a house (to which the Leasehold Reform Act 1967 does not apply) at a low rent is protected by the Landlord and Tenant Act 1954. Many other tenancies, of both furnished and unfurnished property, are currently protected by the Rent Act 1977. However, under these Acts the statutory protection only applies to the tenant's personal right of occupation. Furthermore, these Acts, as amended by the Housing Act 1988, only give one right to succeed to a statutory tenancy on the death of the tenant: either to a spouse or to any other member of the family, provided in the latter case he or she had been living with the protected tenant for two years before the death. This is obviously a much lesser right than that acquired under the Leasehold Reform Act 1967.

The Housing Act 1988 provides for the phasing out of the protection afforded by the Rent Act 1977. Under the 1988 Act *new* private sector tenancies will be *assured tenancies* and all protected tenancies under the 1977 Act will be converted to assured tenancies on the death of the protected tenant. While an assured tenancy cannot be ended except by a possession order from the court, a market rent can be charged. The statutory fair rent provisions of the 1977 Act do *not* apply, only the option of applying to a rent assessment committee to determine what a reasonable *open market rent* might be. Possession orders are awarded on either mandatory (compulsory) or discretionary grounds. Examples of the former are where the landlord requires the property as his home and where possession is required for demolition or reconstruction of the property. An example of the latter is where the landlord offers the tenant suitable alternative accommodation.

The 1988 Act also introduces the *assured shorthold tenancy*, a fixed term of at least six months. The intention is to encourage landlords to make property available for letting by allowing them to recover possession at the end of the tenancy without having to establish a statutory ground, merely by giving two months notice.

This current legislation is therefore intended to increase the supply of private rented accommodation by making it more attractive for landlords and prospective landlords to bring existing and new property onto the private sector market. It seeks to do this by freeing the market from statutory restrictions on rents and making it far easier for landlords to recover possession.

Do you consider it right that the rented housing market should be freed from statutory restrictions? Give your reasons.

The Housing Act 1985 covers a *secure tenancy*, i.e. that of a dwelling house let as a dwelling by a local authority, a housing action trust or other listed body, to an individual, or individuals jointly, who occupies it as his or her only or principle home. A landlord can only recover possession with a court order made on one of a number of statutory grounds listed in the Act. There is, however, no statutory control of the rent that may be charged. (Rent is fixed by a combination of political and economic factors.) One right of succession to the tenancy is given: to the spouse or a member of the family who has occupied the dwelling as his or her principal home, in the latter case for at least 12 months before the tenant's death.

The 1985 Act codifies the rights and protections of a secure tenant, including the right to take in lodgers, the right to sub-let part of the dwelling house with the landlord's consent, the right to carry out landlord's repairs, and recover the cost from the landlord, and make improvements with the landlord's consent and the right to be consulted by the landlord concerning matters of housing management.

Such rights are hardly controversial but the same cannot be said for the tenant's 'right to buy' under the 1985 Act. A secure (local authority) tenant of at least two years' standing has the right to buy the freehold (house) or a long lease (flat) of his dwelling from the local authority and a right to a loan, subject to status, from the local authority to do so. Substantial discounts on the market value of the property apply. In 1987 there were 141,530 sales under the 'right to buy' scheme.

The 'right to buy' clearly seeks to further the Conservative aim of a property-owning democracy. However, to the Labour Party it represents a wrongful selling-off of public assets to the detriment of those who will be in need of public housing in the future. It is certainly likely to be the better houses and flats which will be bought first and by the better-off tenants. Would you, however, deny somebody the right or chance to own his or her own home, particularly when they have been living in the property they seek to buy for a number of years? It is worth noting here that some of the local authorities who are ideologically most opposed to the 'right to buy' were in the late 1980s some of the keenest sellers! Selling their housing stock offered a way to generate income to meet cash crises caused, so they maintained, by central government policy towards them. It remains to be seen whether the 'right to buy' will survive a change in government, whenever that may be.

Further politically contentious provisions are found in Part IV of the Housing Act 1988. With the tenants' consent, these provide for the 'privatisation' (transfer) of public sector estates to private sector landlords approved by the Housing Corporation, e.g. housing associations. Once transferred, existing tenants cease to be 'secured' and become 'assured'.

The aim of the legislation is to encourage local authority tenants to transfer to private sector or housing association landlords and thereby reduce the role of local authorities in the provision of social housing. They should ensure everyone is properly housed, so the argument goes, but not necessarily by them. Under the 1988 Act, the local authority can be *compelled* to transfer their property to a private landlord; under the Housing and Planning Act 1986 it can take the initiative in a *voluntary* transfer, again with the consent of the tenants.

Critics of the system see this whole procedure as a wrongful selling off of public assets and the letting loose of market forces in an area where they are completely inappropriate. Social housing they argue can only be provided by the public sector. It remains to be seen what will happen.

In 1961 there were 5.3 million dwellings available to rent in the private sector, in 1987 there were 2.7 million. Ironically, the decline is itself partly an unfortunate (but perhaps inevitable) consequence of giving security of tenure to tenants of private rented accommodation in previous landlord and tenant legislation. The 1988 Housing Act aims to make it possible for responsible landlords to secure a reasonable return from rented property while not taking away the existing rights of tenants. If this is achieved, the supply should increase.

The policy of successive Conservative governments in the 1980s was to promote home ownership, especially through the sale of council houses. Unfortunately this did not relieve the chronic shortage of housing, the only thing which would do this would be the building of substantially more dwellings. Whatever the reasons, 69,000 families were classified as homeless in 1981 but 107,000 families in 1987. The government claimed that the 1988 Act would help to solve this problem but the housing action group *Shelter* claimed that it would make even more families homeless. (*See* the learning project at the end of this chapter.)

Where do you stand on the 'right to buy' and 'privatisation' issues? Discuss the issues in a group and write a short article of about 750 words, suitable for a college paper, in support of or in opposition to the 'right to buy' and 'privatisation' policies.

Interests in land

Although there are only two legal estates in land, there are a considerable number of interests in land. The distinction between an estate and an interest is that the former is a right to the land itself while the latter only gives a right to some claim against the land of another.

Such interests are either legal or equitable. *Legal interests* are rights against the land itself and are therefore enforceable against the 'whole world' but an *equitable interest* only gives a right against the person who granted it. Therefore, before the property legislation of 1925 a purchaser of a piece of land was bound

by any legal interests which existed over it but was not bound by equitable interests unless he knew of them. If he did it was considered unfair for him to be allowed to disregard them.

A national system for the registration of many of the possible interest in (unregistered) land (*see* below) was established by the Land Changes Act 1925 (now replaced by the Land Changes Act 1972) and the old rules about notice no longer apply to registrable interests. Protection of such an interest now depends solely on its registration. The system applies mainly to equitable interests – these are the more vulnerable of the two types – but some important legal interests are also registrable, e.g. a legal mortgage of unregistered land (*see* below) which is not supported by a deposit of the title deeds with the mortgagee. Technically this is known as a *puisne* (pronounced 'puny', meaning lesser) *mortgage* and is a common security taken by a bank for an overdraft. Typically a *puisne* mortgage would be a 'second mortgage' given to a bank or building society intended to release the capital tied up in a house or business premise where the property is already mortgaged, and the deeds deposited, with another bank or building society.

The most important legal interests are: easements (a bare right over the land of another), e.g. a right of way; profits (the right to take something from the land of another), e.g. fishing or shooting rights; a right of entry held by a landlord in respect of a lease, e.g. to inspect the property or to effect repairs; and a legal mortgage, i.e. a right to the property of another as security for a debt.

The 1925 property legislation converted all the old legal estates and interests, except the fee simple absolute in possession and the term of years absolute, into equitable interests and hence there is a variety of them, e.g. life tenancies and future freehold interests. The latter cannot be legal estates despite their freehold nature because they are not 'in possession' as required by the Law of Property Act 1925. Equitable interests of this nature must be created behind a trust but there are others, e.g. a restrictive covenant, which need not.

A *restrictive covenant* is an agreement whereby one person promises to restrict the use of his land for the benefit of another's adjoining land. A typical covenant is that land shall not be used for the purpose of trade. If the covenant is registered, it will bind any subsequent purchaser of that piece of land.

Title to land and its transfer

Land, or more correctly, estates in land, can be bought and sold by contract in the same basic way as any type of property. However, due to the way that our land law has developed and the miscellaneous interests which can exist over it, considerable formality and complexity is often encountered in the transaction.

Proof of title to land is evidenced in one of two ways, depending upon whether title to it is unregistered or registered. Title is registered when it has been investigated by the state and entered on the Register at one of a number of local land registries. If the title is *unregistered*, title is proved by a collection of deeds and documents (the title deeds) which show a good 'chain of title' dating back 15 years and concluding with the right of the present owner. If the title is *registered*, proof of title is an entry on the register at the appropriate Land Registry, as evidenced by a land certificate. A registered title is guaranteed by the state. The system of land registration now covers most of the country and with time unregistered land will become rare. As you can imagine, the system of registration of title greatly simplifies the whole process of proof of title and its transfer, although many would say it is still unnecessarily slow and complex.

Title to *unregistered land* is transferred by an appropriately drafted deed of conveyance in the case of freehold land and by a deed of assignment in the case of leasehold land. Title to *registered land* is transferred by a short simple Land Registry form. The transaction is in two stages. First, the *contract of sale* which binds the parties to the transaction but does not actually transfer title to the land. (By the Law of Property Act 1989, the contract must be in writing; in practice the buyer and seller each sign a copy of the contract which are then exchanged.) Second, the *transfer of the legal estate* in return for the balance of the purchase price (the completion). This must be by deed (a document which is signed, witnessed and delivered) and usually takes place one month after contracts have been exchanged.

Restrictions on the use of land

There is an old saying that an 'Englishman's home is

Keywords

Land
Land is an economic resource and organisations are primarily interested in its utility. To utilise land it must be owned and, frequently, occupied. Economic theory determines its utility and legal rules regulate its ownership, occupancy and use.

Real and personal property
Real property is freehold land. *Personal property* is every other type of property including leasehold land.

Freehold and leasehold estates
An *estate* is a measure of a person's interest in land in terms of time. A *freehold* estate is the greatest right it is possible to own in land. For practical purposes, it amounts to absolute ownership. A *leasehold* estate is created from a freehold and gives the right to exclusive possession for a specified period of time.

Statutory intervention
In the 1980s a number of fundamental changes to landlord and tenant law were made by legislation. These changes – inspired by political beliefs – were intended to increase the amount of private rented accommodation available and shift the provision of social housing away from the local authorities towards private landlords.

Leasehold enfranchisement
The right of certain lessees of houses to buy the freehold estate from its owner or to the grant of a 50 year extension of the lease.

Interests in land
A right to a claim against the land of another short of actual occupation. Such interests are frequently valuable, e.g. mortgages.

Proof of title and its transfer
If registered, proof is by an entry on the Land Register; if unregistered by a collection of deeds and documents showing a good chain of title dating back 15 years. Transfer is in two parts, a contract of sale binding, the buyer and seller to the transaction, and transfer by deed of the legal estate itself.

his castle'. Sociologically this may be true in so far as it reflects primitive territorial instincts and legally it is true in that the protection of private property rights has always been a fundamental principle of the common law but today a variety of direct legal restrictions are placed upon a man's use of his land. These may be grouped under three headings:

1 restrictions imposed and enforced by the *common*

law (the basic judge-made law which originated in custom);

2 restrictions enforceable in *equity* (the body of rules which originated in the jurisdiction of the Lord Chancellor and the Court of Chancery);

3 restrictions imposed by the *state* through government policy in the form of *legislation*.

Restrictions at common law

These may be further subdivided into those which result from an agreement and those which do not.

Restrictions arising from agreement

You have seen that title to land is transferred by deed and it may be that the purchaser of the freehold estate will make a covenant (a promise contained in a deed) not to use the land for a particular purpose. Similarly, on the grant of a lease, the lessee (the tenant) may accept restrictions on the use of the property, e.g. not to use it other than as a dwelling house. Reinforcement of existing covenants or imposition of further restrictions, e.g. not to grant leases without the mortgagee's (the lender's) consent, are usually to be found in mortgages.

Other restrictions

An important branch of the common law is the Law of Torts. A tort may be defined as a legal wrong against an individual which gives a right of action at civil law for damages (*see* Chapter 25).

The modern law of torts restricts a person's or an organisation's use of its land in three ways; first by the tort of *trespass*. You saw in *Kelsen v Imperial Tobacco Co Ltd* (1957) that it is possible to trespass in the airspace above a person's land and a person or organisation must be sure that any structure on their land does not encroach on to adjoining land, either on the surface or above or below it. The two other restrictions are imposed by the tort of *nuisance* and the rule in *Rylands v Fletcher* (1865) – a development from the tort of nuisance.

Nuisance is usually defined as 'an unlawful interference with a person's use or enjoyment of land or some right over, or in connection with it' (Professor Winfield). The essence of the action is in the words of Lord Denning, a former Master of the Rolls (head of the Civil Division of the Court of Appeal), in *Miller v Jackson & Another* (1977), 'the unreasonable use by a man of his land to the detriment of his neighbour'. Hence, in *Bland v Yates* (1914) a landowner was liable for an unusual and excessive collection of manure which attracted flies and caused a smell and in *Nicholls v Ely Beet Sugar Factory Ltd* (1936) the defendant was liable for the interference with fishing rights caused by discharging factory waste into a river. Therefore any organisation must bear in mind the rights of neighbouring landowners. Ironically it is not so much large manufacturing organisations which may transgress the law in this respect – their activities are mainly confined to industrial estates where the law allows activities which would not be permissible elsewhere – but small units operating in predominantly residential areas, e.g. smells or heat from restaurants, fumes from dry-cleaners or noise from industrial out-working. In the London garment industry, for example, a considerable amount of production is in out-working homes.

From these examples you can see that the restrictions imposed on land use are not purely legal matters but encompass general environmental issues. A somewhat unusual case which illustrates these wider issues, albeit in a humble setting, is *Miller v Jackson & Another* (1977). Mr Miller was a 'newcomer' to the village of Burnopfield in Yorkshire. He bought a house on a new estate adjoining a cricket ground which had been used for the last 70 years by the village cricket club. He brought an action for damages for the interference with his use and employment of his property caused by balls being 'hit for six' on to his property and for an injunction (a court order) to prohibit cricket being played on the ground in the future. In the event an actionable nuisance was proved and damages were awarded. However an injunction was not granted and the village club was able to continue as before.

The case itself is perhaps the unfortunate consequence of, and least important issue involved in, a much wider problem. The village community had been disturbed by the planners and developers whose motives and interests were rather different from those of the villagers. The newcomers felt their property interests threatened by the village cricket club and the villagers felt their long-standing leisure activities threatened by the newcomers. Once created, such tension in a small community is slow to disappear. Even though damages were awarded but an injunction withheld – arguably a compromise – the law was still patently inadequate in solving the problem. Nor could it be expected to, it had been presented with a clash of interests to which there was no real solution available to the Court. The situation was the work of neither the 'newcomers' nor the villagers; the relevant decisions had been made elsewhere and it was arguably these which should have been on trial.

So far we have considered the tort of nuisance in relation to individuals. Where it affects the public in general, however, it may be the subject of criminal proceedings (a public nuisance) and some important examples are now the subject of legislation, e.g. the Clean Air Act 1956 and the Noise Abatement Act 1960.

The essence of the rule in *Rylands v Fletcher* (1965) is that landowners are strictly liable, i.e. whether at fault or not, for damage caused by the escape of 'dangerous things' likely to do harm which they brought or artificially stored on their land. The case itself concerned the escape of water from a reservoir.

Non-natural use of the land is an alternative but complementary explanation of the principle. This reasoning reconciles economic activity with the accumulation of dangerous things, for the land use of the area is a major factor in determining liability under the rule. The criteria to be applied are perhaps unreasonable risk to the community and public policy. In practice the rule is seldom invoked. Disasters of the magnitude of the chemcial explosion at Flixborough some years ago are normally settled out of court (was it 'non-natural use' anyway?) and lesser damage potentially within the rule is usually the subject of insurance claims.

Restrictions in equity

You have seen earlier in this chapter that a restrictive covenant is an equitable interest in land which restricts the use of the land of another. The concept originated purely as an agreement between the parties to the transfer of the legal estate of a particular parcel of land. Enforcement of the covenant against subsequent purchasers of the land depended upon notice of it.

However, since the late nineteenth century restrictive covenants have been considered as rights existing over one piece of land (the *servient tenement*) for the benefit of another piece of land (the *dominant tenement*). Thus, they can now only be enforced against a purchaser of the land to which the convenant applies by a person who occupies land that benefits from the convenant. Additionally, it is a cardinal rule that a restrictive covenant will only be enforced if it is *negative* in nature. Any convenant which entails expense to perform properly is not negative, e.g. a covenant prohibiting industrial use is negative but a covenant not to let premises get into disrepair is essentially positive, despite its wording.

Restrictive covenants are far more likely to affect domestic land use or small business units than large organisations, the latter mainly having to concern themselves with statutory planning control. Indeed, state intervention in land use has reduced the importance of restrictive covenants because the amenities of an area may now be preserved by statute and there may be little incentive to enforce private covenants. However the statutory system complements rather than supersedes them. Covenants entitle landowners to take direct action to protect their interests rather than having to rely on their planning authorities and they can cover far more particular restraints than the more general curbs imposed by legislation. Clearly, organisations must ensure that they infringe neither the private system of restrictive covenants nor the public system of planning control in any of their activities. It is to the public system of planning control that we now turn.

Restrictions imposed by the state

State planning controls do not affect the ownership of estates or interests in land, only its *use*. In this way the often opposing interests of the individual and the state are reconciled. Such controls are necessary for there are ample legacies of unplanned or ineffectively controlled urban development in most large cities. Sometimes entire developments appear as environmental scars on the landscapes: Peacehaven, a speculative development situated on the south coast, is commonly considered a prime example.

In the past under the common law landowners could

develop their land as they wished, provided they did not infringe their neighbours' common law rights (*see* above). The 19th century *laissez-faire* philosophy in government, law and economics was conductive to speculative, profit-oriented development. While there were important examples of social consciousness in urban and industrial development before 1900, e.g. Robert Owen's development at New Lanark, the concept of planned development belongs to the 20th century. Since the middle of this century the state has attempted to play an active role in planning, for land is now considered a far too scarce and valuable natural resource to be left purely in the hands of private interests.

The present statutory controls are to be found in the Town and Country Planning Act 1971-4, under which local planning authorities are responsible for the routine administration and the Department of the Environment for overall control of the system of regulation. The Local Government, Planning and Land Act 1980 shifted some planning functions from country to district council level, e.g. applications for planning permission. The essence of planning legislation is *development*, defined by the 1971 Act as building, engineering, mining or other operation in, on, over or under the land, or any material change in the use of any building or other land.

Under the legislation applicants must obtain planning permission to develop land from the local planning authority or from the Secretary of State for the Environment on appeal, having first notified their intentions to those owning interests in the property and advertised their application where the proposed development is likely to offend their neighbours. These provisions enable objections to the application to be lodged. Each local planning authority maintains a register of applications and their results. In 1981 a scale of fees was introduced for planning applications in an attempt by the the government to recover some development control costs. Any individual or organisation contemplating the purchase of land in an area likely to be the subject of a development application should check the register before going ahead with the purchase.

Such control is necessary if regional imbalance in the level and type of economic activity, with its attendant social problems, is to be ameliorated. Enforcement and stop notices, backed by possible criminal proceedings, are issued if development is carried out without the required permission.

To supplement the main planning legislation, the Local Government (Miscellaneous Provisions) Act 1982 gives local authorities powers over a wide range of topics. These include the control of street-trading, take-away food shops, demolitions, disturbances on educational premises, even 'sex shops'. In addition, there are a variety of other controls under the Town and Country Planning Acts, including: tree preservation orders, preventing the cutting of trees; regulation of advertising on land; and the 'listing' of buildings of special or historical interest, preventing their alteration or demolition.

An interesting example of this last restriction, also illustrating the possible financial consequences of a preservation order, is *Amalgamated Investment v John Walker & Sons Ltd* (1976). The parties had made a contract for the sale of land near the Thames on which stood a disused warehouse. The purchasers intended to redevelop the site for office use and had obtained an Office Development Permit (since abolished) to this end. The vendors were aware of this. Unknown to either party, a civil servant in the Department of the Environment had already decided to add the warehouse, somewhat arbitrarily as it happened, to a list of protected buildings which would prevent the proposed redevelopment. The building was actually listed the day after the contract was made. On the facts there were no grounds on which to set the contract aside even though the property as a protected building was only worth £200,000 while the contract price was £1,500,000! An amendment to the Town and Country Planning Act 1971 by the Local Government, Planning and Land Act 1980 now enables an application to be made to the Secretary of State for a certificate guaranteeing that no listing will occur within a five year period when planning permission has already been granted for the extension, alteration or demolition of an existing building.

The development of land is also subject to other statutory controls designed to ensure that minimum standards of design and construction are adhered to. The Public Health Acts enable the Secretary of State for the Environment to make bye-laws regulating such matters as the construction, materials, sanitation and size of rooms of new buildings. The Health and Safety at Work, etc, Act 1974 (considered in more detail below) indirectly affects development by enacting regulations designed to maintain and improve existing standards of health, safety and welfare at work.

In the mid-1970s the then Labour government passed the Community Land Act 1975 and the Development Land Tax Act 1976. These introduced a new and more far-reaching form of government intervention in planning and development in general and were interesting as attempts to tax and control what economists would term *economic rent* (*see* page 190). The subsequent Conservative Government's Local Government, Planning and Land Act 1980 repealed the Community Land Act and Development Land Tax was abolished in the 1985 Budget.

A completely different form of restriction on land use is the activity of pressure groups (considered more fully in Chapter 27). The environmentalist and 'green', lobby have become increasingly more vociferous and effective. Individual groups of protesters have scored resounding successes both in persuading local authorities or the government to significantly change their plans and, in some cases, in preventing development altogether. The success of the opposition to plans to build the third London airport at either Wing in Buckinghamshire or Maplin in Essex are notable examples in recent years. Protesters were less successful in the case in Stansted Airport. Battles are still to be fought over the dumping of nuclear waste at various locations. The Government's abandonment of expanding its nuclear programme in 1989 was more a response to economic rather than political pressure but, clearly, the anti-nuclear pressure groups saw it as a great victory.

An interesting sociological fact is that it is usually what can be described as 'middle class interests' which are most successfully protected, the simple reason being that 'middle class' protesters have both the financial means and the necessary expertise to fight the 'system'.

Organisations are mainly concerned with statutory restrictions on land use and clearly these are here to stay, the only real argument being the extent to which these restrictions and the methods are employed. Land is a finite resource and while some may protest at the limits placed on private rights, it seems reasonable to argue that the social and economic consequences of unplanned development or excessive private gain justify putting the community first.

Draw a diagram similar to Fig. 9.6 (*see* page 190) to illustrate the restrictions which the law imposes on the occupier of land. Fig. 9.6 illustrates only those restrictions normally classified as 'occupiers' liability' – your diagram should include the other restrictions imposed by common law, equity and statute.

Keywords _____

Covenant
At law, means a promise contained in a deed. Covenants frequently restrict the use to which land can be put.

Tort
A legal wrong against an individual which entitles the injured person to claim damages. The torts of trespass, nuisance and *Rylands v Fletcher* restricts an organisation's or an individual's use of their land.

Planning legislation
A framework of planning and development controls on land enforced by the state.

Pressure groups
A group of people pursuing a particular objective; the activities of pressure groups can sometimes be an important factor in determining how land is developed or whether it is developed at all.

The organisation and its use of land

The location of industry

Land is not a homogeneous commodity. It differs greatly in its contents and its position. There are, therefore, many factors which affect the attractiveness of a site to an organisation. We examine these below in two groups: those occurring spontaneously in the economy; and those engineered by the government. We might imagine that organisations weigh all the possible advantages and disadvantages carefully and site their business so as to minimise their costs. It is doubtful whether this is ever really so. Historical accident might play a big part in location. For example, William Morris started car manufacture in Oxford because that was where his cycle shop was.

Equally businesses tend to be gregarious and will often site their organisation where there are a number of others. However, no-one will begin a business or site a new factory without considering some of the following factors.

Non-government influences upon site value

1 Raw materials. Extractive industries must locate where the raw materials are and this may in turn attract other industries, e.g. the iron and steel industry being attracted to coalfields. Engineering industries were then often attracted to the same location. Thus, around Glasgow there is the Lanark coalfield; this attracted the iron and steel industry which in turn attracted shipbuilding. Today, when many raw materials are imported, industries frequently locate at ports.

2 Power. The woollen industry moved to the West Riding of Yorkshire to utilise the water power from Pennine streams. In the 19th century most industries were dependent upon coal as a source of power. Since coal was expensive to transport, they tended to locate on coalfields.

Today, most industries use electricity, which is readily available anywhere in the country. This means that the availability of power is not now an important locational influence. An exception to this is the aluminium smelting industry which uses vast quantities of electric power. The industry is therefore centred on countries where there is much cheap hydro-electric power, such as Canada and Norway.

3 Transport. Historically transport was a vital locational influence. Water transport was the only cheap and reliable means of transporting heavy loads. Most industries, therefore, tended to locate near rivers or the coast. Canals and later railways allowed industry to spread to other locations. Today access to good transport facilities is still a locational influence. This is illustrated by the town of Warrington in Cheshire, which has experienced a renaissance in its industrial fortunes partly as a result of its location at the intersection of three main motorways.

Max Weber, a famous economic historian and sociologist, developed a theory on the location of industry. Weber maintained that industrialists would try to minimise their transport costs. This meant that if a commodity *lost weight* during manufacture the industry would tend to locate near to the raw materials,

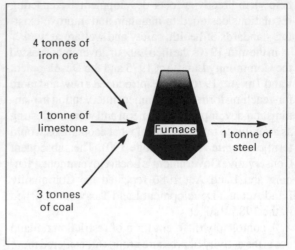

Fig. 9.3 Weight loss

whereas if it *gained weight* during manufacture it would tend to locate near to the market. Steel is an example of a commodity which loses weight during manufacture. To manufacture steel near to the market would mean transporting several tonnes of raw materials but only selling one tonne of finished product. This is illustrated in Fig. 9.3. Brewing is an industry in which the product gains weight during manufacture. It is therefore more economic to transport the hops, barley and sugar to near the market, where water is added and the brewing takes place. Traditionally, brewing was a widely dispersed industry although in recent years it has become more centralised. Weber's theory is modified by the value of the commodity. Whisky, for example, is so expensive that transport costs are only a small percentage of the price and are therefore not a locational influence.

4 Markets. Service industries such as catering, entertainment and professional services have nearly always had to locate near their markets. In the 20th century many more industries have located with respect to markets so that today it is one of the most important locational forces. Goods which are fragile and expensive to transport, such as furniture and electrical goods, are better produced near where they are to be sold. The ring of consumer-goods industries around London is adequate testimony to the power of the market.

5 Labour. It might be thought that the availability of cheap labour would be an important locational influence. It does not appear to be so. The existence of a

Table 9.1 Regional disparities in the UK

Percentage unemployed by region	1951	1961	1971	1981	1986	1989*
North	2.2	2.5	5.9	14.9	16.4	8.9
Yorks & Humberside }	0.7	1.0	4.0	11.9	13.5	6.9
East Midlands			3.1	10.3	10.7	4.9
East Anglia }	0.9	1.0	3.1	8.8	9.0	3.2
South East			2.0	7.7	8.7	3.6
South West	1.2	1.4	3.4	9.5	9.9	4.1
West Midlands	0.4	1.4	4.0	13.2	13.6	5.9
North West	1.2	1.6	4.1	13.5	14.6	7.8
Wales	2.7	2.6	4.7	13.9	14.4	6.9
Scotland	2.5	3.1	6.0	13.5	14.5	8.6
Northern Ireland	6.2	7.5	8.0	18.9	18.1	14.4
United Kingdom	1.3	1.6	3.5	10.6	11.2	5.9

* (December)
Sources: Regional Trends and Employment Gazette, both HMSO

pool of highly skilled labour may be a locational influence but increasingly manual skills can be replaced by automated machinery. An exception to this may be 'footloose' industries. These are industries which are not dependent upon other specific locational influences and are therefore attracted to cheap labour. An example of this is electronic component assembly, although organisations in this field have tended to locate in the suburbs to utilise cheap female labour rather than moving to areas of heavy unemployment.

6 *Industrial inertia.* This is the tendency of an industry to continue to locate itself in an area when the factors which originally located the industry there have ceased to operate. An example of this is the steel industry in Sheffield, although this may be partly explained by external economies of scale and the existence of skilled labour.

7 *Special local circumstances.* Such things as climate or topography may affect the location of an industry. The oil terminal at Milford Haven is located there because of the deep-water anchorage available. A further example is provided by the market gardening industry in the Scilly Isles, located there to take advantage of the early spring.

8 *Sunrise industries.* This is the name given to industries which are associated with the 'new technology'. They could be regarded as 'footloose' industries since

they are relatively free from apparent locational constraints. However, many of them have become concentrated in the so-called 'Software Valley'. This is the area either side of the M4 stretching from Slough west towards Bristol. Reasons that have been suggested for this concentration, apart from the natural gregariousness of business people, are the good communications and, more importantly, the fact that freed from other obvious constraints, business people have opted to live and work in the pleasant environment of Berkshire and Oxfordshire.

Governmental influences on the location of industry

The old staple industries such as iron and steel, shipbuilding and coal-mining have been in decline for most of this century. These tended to be heavily concentrated in the coal-mining areas. The operation of free market economies seemed powerless to alleviate the economic distress of these areas. This has meant that since the 1930s the government has brought in more and more measures to try to attract industry to these areas. Table 9.1 shows the disparities that exist.

1 Study the information in Table 9.1. Present this

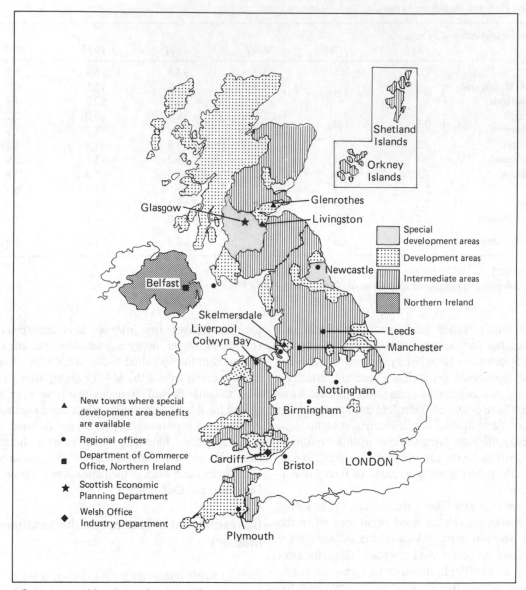

Glasgow
Glenrothes
Livingston

Shetland Islands

Orkney Islands

Newcastle

Belfast

Special development areas
Development areas
Intermediate areas
Northern Ireland

Skelmersdale
Liverpool
Colwyn Bay
Leeds
Manchester

Nottingham
Birmingham

▲ New towns where special development area benefits are available

● Regional offices

■ Department of Commerce Office, Northern Ireland

★ Scottish Economic Planning Department

◆ Welsh Office Industry Department

Cardiff
Bristol
LONDON

Plymouth

Fig. 9.4 Government aid to the regions as defined in 1971. Reproduced by permission of the Department of Industry.

as a bar chart. What changes do you notice in the pattern of regional unemployment?

2 For the region in which you live or work, examine the figures and then give as full an explanation of them as possible, paying particular attention to expanding and declining industries.

There are today so many legislative controls and financial inducements that the government must be considered the most important locational influence upon industry. It is possible to identify four main ways in which the government tries to influence the location of industry.

1 Financial incentives. Financial incentives to encourage organisations to move to depressed areas started with the Special Areas Act 1934. After the 1939–45 War various Acts increased regional assistance. The Industry Act 1972 designated large areas of the country as Special Development Areas (SDAs), Development Areas (DAs) and Intermediate Areas (IAs), all of which qualified for financial assistance.

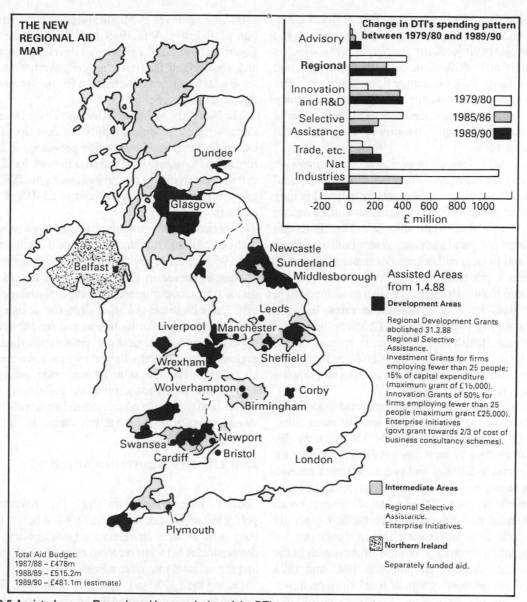

THE NEW
REGIONAL AID
MAP

Dundee

Glasgow

Belfast

Newcastle
Sunderland
Middlesborough

Leeds

Liverpool   Manchester

Wrexham   Sheffield

Wolverhampton   Corby

Birmingham

Swansea   Newport

Cardiff   Bristol

London

Plymouth

Total Aid Budget:
1987/88 – £478m
1988/89 – £515.2m
1989/90 – £481.1m (estimate)

Change in DTI's spending pattern between 1979/80 and 1989/90

Advisory

Regional

Innovation
and R&D

Selective
Assistance

Trade, etc.

Nat
Industries

-200   0   200   400   600   800 1000
£ million

1979/80
1985/86
1989/90

**Assisted Areas
from 1.4.88**

Development Areas

Regional Development Grants
abolished 31.3.88
Regional Selective
Assistance.
Investment Grants for firms
employing fewer than 25 people;
15% of capital expenditure
(maximum grant of £15,000).
Innovation Grants of 50% for
firms employing fewer than 25
people (maximum grant £25,000).
Enterprise Initiatives
(govt grant towards 2/3 of cost of
business consultancy schemes).

Intermediate Areas

Regional Selective
Assistance.
Enterprise Initiatives.

Northern Ireland

Separately funded aid.

Fig. 9.5 Assisted areas. Reproduced by permission of the DTI

These are illustrated in Fig. 9.4.

Successive Conservative governments in the 1980s drastically reduced both the amount of regional aid and also the extent of the areas which could receive aid. This is illustrated in Fig. 9.5. Northern Ireland continued to receive considerable assistance.

The situation illustrated in Fig. 9.5 is based on the Co-operative Development Agency and Industrial Development Act 1984. This designated two types of region: *Development Areas* (DAs) and *Intermediate*

Areas (IAs). The reasons for these changes were the Government's desire to economise on regional aid and partly because it believed that regional aid distorts and damages the development of industry.

Manufacturing and some service projects which create or increase capacity in DAs are eligible for financial support. This consists of *Regional Development Grants*. The grant is 15% of the cost of the project or £3,000 for each new job created, whichever is the greater. Firms in both DAs and IAs may apply for

Regional Selective Assistance. This regional assistance consists of Capital Project Grants towards the capital cost of projects, the Training Scheme, which is a grant of up to 80% of the cost of training staff, and the Exchange Risk Guarantee Scheme which covers firms against the exchange risk on foreign currency loans, i.e. against the danger that a fall in the value of the pound might require the firm to repay the loan at an inflated cost.

Financial assistance is available on a nationwide basis for certain projects. There is, for example, special finance for small firms and grants for new technology investment projects. Financial assistance for the regions is also available from the EC. The European Development Fund provides grants both to private firms and to local authorities. For example, Sony UK received a grant towards the cost of setting up its television plant in Bridgend. The European Investment Bank gives loans at advantageous rates. Between 1973 and 1983, Britain received £2,550 millions from this source. British Rail, for example, received a loan of £69 million towards the cost of building high speed trains. Grants are also available for special purposes such as energy development.

A development in 1980 was the introduction of *enterprise zones.* These are small areas of inner cities, averaging in size approximately 150 hectares. By 1988 there were 17 such zones in England, three each in Scotland and Wales and two in Northern Ireland. Firms setting up in enterprise zones get a stream of incentives: no rates; 100% capital allowances on all commercial and industrial property; and generally less bureaucracy and fewer planning regulations.

2 Legislative controls. A number of Acts such as the Town and Country Planning Acts 1947 and 1971 erected an elaborate system of restrictions on development outside the regions. However, in 1981 the government suspended nearly all these provisions preferring to rely on market forces. Thus, to all intents and purposes, planning regulations are the same throughout the country. The exceptions are Enterprise Zones and the Industrial Development Corporations where regulations are less strict.

3 Direct Intervention. The government can place orders for goods and services in development areas or encourage nationalised industries to do so. In addition to this it could decentralise Government developments such as it did when the Inland Revenue administration was moved to Middlesbrough. The Distribution of Industry Acts 1945 and 1950 allowed the government to build factories in development areas and lease or sell them. Today the government may lease a factory to an organisation for two years, rent free, if it creates enough jobs.

The New Towns Act 1946 and the Town Development Act 1952 brought a number of new towns into existence, the first of which was Stevenage in Hertfordshire. In August 1981 the government decided to curtail the activities of new towns and eight of the new town corporations were to dispose of £140m of their assets (see page 68).

4 Persuasion. Information about the regions is provided both centrally and regionally. The Local Employment Act 1960 set up development councils in depressed regions. However, in 1965 the whole of the UK was divided into eleven regional economic planning councils. Each of these is responsible for devising an economic strategy for its region and for publicising opportunities in the region. Advertisements placed by regional planning councils and by new town corporations are a familiar sight in our newspapers. The Department of Industry provides information and advice both from its headquarters in London and from its regional offices (*see* the towns' names in Fig. 9.5).

How effective is government policy?

There is little evidence to show that government policy had much success up until 1963. After that date there was a more aggressive regional policy. The discrepancies between regional rates of employment and the national rate were narrowed.

During the 1970s and especially during the 1980s, the picture was complicated by the overall surge in unemployment. However, it was clear that vast regional imbalances existed. Not only this but previously prosperous areas of the country such as the West Midlands became depressed. This was caused by the decline of previously prosperous industries such as motor vehicles. This in turn was partly due to general depression in the economy but also due to the impact of imports upon manufacturing industry.

Recovery in the late 1980s still left profound regional imbalances. By 1990 many industries in prosperous areas were experiencing shortages of skilled labour while in some areas of Northern Ireland rates of up to 40% unemployment of adult males were recorded. Whether the government's policy of leaving the solution to market forces forces would work in the long-run remained to be seen.

1992 adds a new dimension to the problem. Studies of the likely effects of the Single Market suggest that it is likely to *increase* regional differences. Thus, those in prosperous areas such as SE England and Northern Germany will be better-off while those in the depressed areas such as Scotland and Northern France will become worse-off.

Study the information in Table 9.2.

Table 9.2 Index of GDP per capita

Region	1979	1989
North	93.0	91.4
Yorkshire and Humberside	95.4	91.3
East Midlands	98.6	95.7
East Anglia	94.0	101.2
South East	113.4	115.0
South West	91.6	93.8
West Midlands	96.4	92.3
North West	95.4	96.0
Wales	88.4	88.8
Scotland	96.9	97.3
Northern Ireland	77.5	74.8
United Kingdom	100.0	100.0

Source: Regional Trends: HMSO

1 What do these figures show about the effectiveness of Regional Policy in the 1980s?

2 Over the period shown the index GDP/capita of the East Midlands fell from 98.6 to 95.7 compared with the national average. Does this mean that a typical person in the East Midlands was poorer in 1989 than in 1979? Explain your answer.

3 In 1989 only two regions had above average incomes. How is this possible or is there a mistake in the figures?

4 Do the figures imply that an average person in the South East was 15% better-off than the national average? If not, why not?

5 What additional information would be useful in answering these questions and where would you find it?

Costs and benefits of regional policy

In the financial year 1989–90 the government spent only £513 million on regional aid. However, in addition to this large amounts were spent on job creation schemes which were heavily concentrated in the regions. It is difficult to estimate the cost to the government of creating genuine jobs in the regions. A government inquiry in 1977 into the building of two petrochemical plants in Scotland revealed a cost to the government of £1 million per permanent job created. The De Lorean car plant in Northern Ireland had by 1982 cost the government £74 million and had created 2,500 jobs, thus giving a cost of approximately £30,000 for each job created. This is a wide variation, but both schemes seem costly. The reason for this is that government policy up to the 1980s tended to create capital intensive schemes rather than labour intensive ones. Policy in 1986 limited assistance to £3,000 per job created. The government has stated that it wishes to stimulate more small firms but the owners of such firms frequently complain that the 'red-tape' surrounding regional aid often prevents them from obtaining assistance.

Against the financial cost of the government of the creation of employment we must set social security benefits which will not have to be paid out, the income tax which the workers will pay and the extra jobs that are created via the employment multiplier (*see* page 387).

The most important criticism of regional policy is that it tended to create inefficient units of production. For example, Chrysler (now Peugeot) were persuaded by the government to build a new factory at Linwood outside Glasgow rather than in Coventry where they would have preferred to build it. Car engines were made in Coventry, transported to Scotland to be put into car bodies and then transported south again to be sold. The closure of the Linwood plant in 1981 requires little further comment. While the creation of inefficient plants may be tolerated within the economy as a way of coping with unemployment it has very bad consequences for our external trade because it destroys our competitiveness.

However, if we look at regional policy in the context of the whole economy there are several points to be borne in mind. First, although organisations might choose to locate in the South East, they often ignore the very high social costs in these areas. Housing, for example, is in very short supply in the South East and is consequently extremely expensive, while elsewhere in the country houses stand empty. Second, as aid is put into the regions it should regenerate the areas to such an extent that their recovery becomes self-sustaining. Third, the lessons of the 1930s also teach us that there is a great danger in concentration. Diversification is a good safeguard against changes in demand, even if it is slightly less efficient.

Consider the area in which you live.

1 What sort of industries and businesses might be tempted to establish themselves there and why?

2 List three factors which would discourage businesses from establishing in your area.

3 What measures would do most to encourage new businesses or the expansion of existing ones?

Keywords _____

Land

In the economic definition, land includes all the free gifts of nature but not anything built on it nor improvements made to it. The legal definition is much wider.

Location of industry

Today a location is more likely to be affected by economic factors such as markets and irrational factors such as gregariousness than it is by the factors such as access to raw materials and to power which were formally important.

Regional policy

In trying to reduce regional disparities the basic dilemma of policy is whether to take work to the workers or workers to the work.

Occupancy of land and its responsibilities

An occupier or owner of land or premises owes important duties to anyone who comes on to his land: to visitors, under the Occupiers' Liability Act 1957; to trespassers, under the Occupiers' Liability Act 1984; and to employees, primarily under the Health and Safety at Work, etc, Act 1974.

Responsibilities to visitors

The Occupiers' Liability Act 1957 states that an occupier of land or premises owes a *common duty of care* to all his visitors. Premises are defined as including 'any fixed or movable structure, including any vessel, vehicle or aircraft' and not just land and buildings. A visitor is anyone who enters on land with permission, and the common duty of care is defined in s.2(2) as '... a duty to take such care as in all the circumstances of the case is reasonable to see that the visitor will be reasonably safe in using the premises for the purposes for which he is invited or permitted to be there.'

The meaning of an *occupier* under the Act has been interpreted as being the person in *control* of the structure. Therefore, an owner out of possession is not generally liable if the premises are occupied by someone else. However, exclusive possession is not necessary to establish *control*. This was illustrated in *Wheat v Lacon & Co Ltd* (1966), where the manager of the defendant's public house was allowed to take paying guests in the upper part of the premises occupied by himself and his wife. This part was quite separate from the licensed premises. A guest was injured on the staircase leading to the upper floor. The facts posed the Court with an interesting problem. Physically the defendants did not *occupy* the upper part but the whole premises were theirs and public policy would be best served by making them responsible for it all. Although, on the facts, it was decided that the common duty of care had not been broken, the defendants were held to have enough residual control of the upper floor, particularly as it was occupied by a manager and not a tenant, for them to be occupiers within the meaning of the Act. As a result of this interpretation, organisations cannot escape the responsibilities of occupancy merely because they are not in actual physical occupation and control of the premises. The public interest is clearly best served by this approach.

If an organisation employs an independent contractor to undertake work on the premises, the organisation, as occupier, is not liable for any injury caused to visitors by the independent contractor's shoddy work, providing the organisation exercised reasonable care in choosing the contractor and checked the work (if that was possible) after it was finished.

In relation to the common duty of care, the Act provides that an occupier can expect children to be less careful than adults (therefore extra care is required), and a person to be aware of dangers normally associated with their work. An electrical contractor called in to repair faulty equipment, for example, is expected to realise the dangers of and to take his own precautions against electric shocks and other injuries from the defective equipment.

Limiting Liability

Whenever an individual or organisation is in a position of potential legal liability, there is a natural tendency to try to limit, or preferably exclude, that liability altogether. This has been true of liability under the Act. Until 1977 it was possible for the occupier and visitor to make a contract which limited the former's liability under the Act for any kind of injury. In addition, it was possible to employ the simpler expedient of displaying a notice restricting or more usually excluding liability. (A straightforward warning notice, indicating danger, is just one *possible* way of satisfying the common duty of care.) Since the Unfair Contract Terms Act 1977, a person cannot by contract or by notice exclude or restrict his liability under the 1957 Act for death or personal injury arising from negligence in connection with the occupancy of premises used for the *business purposes* of the occupier. An exclusion of liability for other loss or damage must satisfy the requirement of *reasonableness*.

This important provision strengthens an individual's rights against organisations without unjustly imposing a burden upon them. Any actual liability of this kind is almost invariably met through an insurance claim and, as insurance premiums are related to claims made, the financial burden is spread among the business community in general.

Very often an organisation will lease or sub-let office or other commercial space on terms entitling its tenant to permit other people to enter and use the leased premises. The lease will usually limit the organisation's responsibilities towards the tenant under the Act. This is reasonable, both the landlord and tenant have roughly equal bargaining power. But what, however, is the responsibility of the organisation to its tenant's visitors? Under the 1957 Act, the organisation cannot reduce its obligations to visitors who are not parties to the contract (the lease) to a level below that of the common duty of care. This is particularly applicable to common staircase, lifts and passengers.

Under the Defective Premises Act 1972, a landlord under an obligation to repair or maintain the premises let owes a duty to all persons who might reasonably be expected to be affected by defects in the state of the premises to take reasonable steps to ensure that such persons and their property are reasonably safe.

Responsibilities to trespassers

An occupier of premises, whether used for business purposes or otherwise, clearly cannot be expected to owe the same standard of care to a person who should not be there in the first place as he owes to a visitor. This situation is governed by the Occupiers' Liability Act 1984.

Under this Act, an occupier of *business premises* owes a duty to 'persons other than his visitors' if *(a)* he is aware of the danger or has reasonable grounds to believe that it exists; *(b)* he knows or has reasonable grounds to believe that the other is in the vicinity of the danger concerned or that he may come into the vicinity of the danger; and *(c)* the risk is one against which, in all the circumstances of the case, he may reasonably be expected to offer the other some protection. In such circumstances, the occupier must take such care as is reasonable in all the circumstances of the case to see that the other person does not suffer injury on the premises because of the danger concerned. The duty can be discharged by taking reasonable steps to give warning of the danger. One consideration here, of course, would be the type of trespasser involved – a burglar compared to a child who innocently trespasses.

Besides owing a lesser duty of care, an occupier's

position in relation to trespassers differs in two further ways to his position in relation to lawful visitors. First, he incurs no liability in respect of loss of or damage to property. Second, he can probably exclude or restrict his duty by a suitable notice. This is because the Unfair Contract Terms Act 1977 (*see* above) does not apply to the 1984 Act.

Responsibilities to employees

Great Britain was the cradle of the Industrial Revolution and it is all too easy to allow the technological and industrial achievements of that period to obscure the harsh realities of working conditions in those not so distant days. A 14-hour day was commonplace and conditions were quite simply appalling. The social cost to the ordinary man and woman of Great Britain's emergence as the world's foremost industrial nation in the 19th century was extremely high. Even today coalminers can justify their relatively high wages by the fearful conditions and accident rate that they still have to endure.

Over the years social consciousness about the plight of the usually exploited worker grew and with it began to develop the concept of the employers' responsibility to provide a minimum standard in working conditions for their employees. Today we largely take such ideas for granted and via a whole range of statutes we have come a long way from the Factories Acts of 1802 and 1819, and the Coal Mines Act 1842, to the Health and Safety at Work, etc, Act 1974. The Acts of 1802 and 1819 forbade the employment of *children under nine* in cotton mills, and limited working hours to *twelve a day* for persons under sixteen; the 1842 Act prevented *women and girls and boys under ten* being employed underground. Fortunately, this is history to us and it is perhaps just as well that the physical strain, squalor and degradation endured by the early industrial worker is virtually unimaginable.

The Health and Safety at Work, etc, 1974

This Act is the most recent landmark in the evolution of the responsibilities owed by an employer/occupier to employees. At present much of the previous relevant legislation, and subsidiary regulations made under it, still remains in force but repeal, amendment, revision and updating by regulations made by the Secre-

tary of State for Employment, under the enabling powers contained in the Act, will eventually see the effective disappearance of previous landmarks in health and safety at work legislation. Two such examples are The Factories Act 1961 and The Offices, Shops and Railway Premises Act 1963. The major requirement of the former is that dangerous parts of machinery must be securely fenced. The latter contains general requirements relating to cleanliness, overcrowding, heating, ventilation and lighting, the occupier of premises being responsible for ensuring that the Act is obeyed. However, the owner will be liable for those parts of the premises covered by the Act but not included in the occupier's leases, e.g. stairways. The 1963 Act does not apply, among other places, to premises where self-employed persons work.

Besides the subject matter inherent in the short title of the 1974 Act, the 'etc' covers other aims such as protecting people from risks created by people at work, controlling dangerous substances and preventing their unlawful acquisition and use, and controlling the escape of fumes into the atmosphere.

The Act lays down a number of *general duties* with which employers, employees, controllers of premises and designers, manufacturers, importers and suppliers of articles for use at work must comply. It is an offence punishable by a maximum penalty of £1,000 fine to fail to discharge these duties. However, there is no civil liability under the Act for breach of the general duties. After consultation with the Health and Safety Commission (one of two corporate bodies established by the Act), the Secretary of State has power to make Health and Safety Regulations to achieve the Act's objectives. These may repeal, modify or give exemption from existing statutory provisions and may exclude or modify the general duties. *Civil liability* exists for breach of these health and safety regulations.

The five *general duties* are as follows.

1 It is an employer's duty to ensure so far as is reasonably practicable the health, safety and welfare at work of all his employees. For example, the provision and maintenance of plant and systems of work that are safe and without risks to health and, more generally, the provision of a working environment that is without risks to health.
2 It is an employer's duty to conduct his undertaking in such a way that so far as is reasonably practicable,

Keywords

Common duty of care
Owed under the Occupiers' Liability Act 1957, this is the minimum duty of care an occupier of land or premises owes to another person lawfully on their land.

Occupier of land
For the purposes of the Occupiers' Liability Act 1957, this is the person who is in *control* of the land or premises, not necessarily the actual occupier. Liability for breach of the common duty of care is thereby imposed on the person usually better able to pay.

Excluding liability
The Unfair Contract Terms Act 1977 severely restricts occupiers' (and others) ability to exclude liability caused by their negligence.

Liability to trespassers
Under the Occupiers' Liability Act 1984, an occupier of *business premises* owes a limited duty of care to trespassers.

Health and Safety
All business organisations owe important general health and safety duties to their employees under the Health and Safety at Work, etc, Act 1974.

non-employees are not exposed to risk.

3 A duty is imposed on a controller of premises made available to persons other than his employees to take measures to ensure so far as is reasonably practicable that the premises and the entrances and exits are safe for those using the premises.

4 A duty is imposed on anyone who designs, manufactures, imports or supplies an article for use at work to ensure, so far as is reasonably practicable, that the article is safe and that adequate information on its use is supplied.

5 A duty is imposed on an employee to take reasonable care at work for the health and safety of himself and others who may be affected by his conduct at work, and to co-operate with his employer to enable his employer to carry out his duties.

In most cases the duties are *absolute*. In other words, the breach of the general duty itself is the offence, no intent nor negligence is required and no defence to the charge is available.

The duty of enforcing the Act and previous relevant legislation lies with the other corporate body established by the Act, The Health and Safety Executive.

Failure to obey notices to comply with the provisions of the Act and regulations made under it is punishable with a maximum fine of £1,000 on summary conviction or by imprisonment for up to two years or a fine, or both, on indictment.

The importance of the Act can be judged by the fact that it applies to *all* persons at work; employers, the self-employed and employees alike (with the exception of domestic servants in private households), and about 5 million people were given legislative protection for the first time, e.g. those employed in education, medicine and leisure industries. In addition, the Health and Safety (Youth Training Scheme) Regulations 1983 extended the provisions of the Act to trainees on government sponsored training schemes. The Act also protects the health and safety of the general public who may be affected by work activities.

Restrictions: more or less?

In this section we have discussed the responsibilities which follow from the occupancy of land. Remember that employees are also visitors within the Occupiers' Liability Act 1957 and any specific responsibilities owed to them by their employers as occupiers of land and premises are in addition to their general responsibilities.

Some of you may feel that the restrictions imposed by the state on the use of land, and the duties owed by occupiers are basically necessary in essence but grossly excessive in extent. Others may think that they strike a reasonable and workable compromise between the often opposing interests of the state and the individual. A small minority may believe in one of the two extremes; either complete freedom from any State-imposed restrictions and duties, or complete nationalisation of land.

A summary diagram of this topic is to be found in Fig. 9.6.

Are you aware of health and safety policy at your workplace or your college? A health and safety officer should be responsible for implementing the agreed policy. Discover as much as you can about health and safety issues which affect you and your place of employment or college.

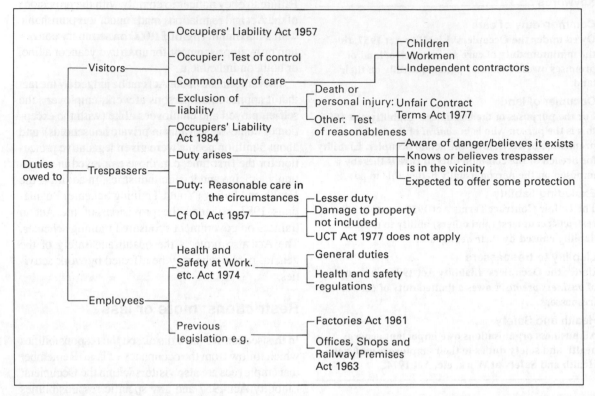

Fig. 9.6 Occupancy of land and its responsibilities.

Rent: its theory and practice

Different types of rent

The term rent can be used in four different ways; it is important not to confuse these.

1 Commercial rent. This is rent in the legal sense and is used to describe the payment made for the use of buildings or land.

2 Hire charge. People often think of renting a TV or a car but actually this is really hiring or leasing.

3 Rent. The payment made for the use of land as defined in the economic sense. In practice, however, land is frequently 'mixed up' with other factors of production and it is difficult to ascertain precisely how much is being paid for the land and how much is being paid for the capital (buildings, etc) on it.

4 Economic rent. This is the payment made to *any* factor of production over and above that which is necessary to keep the factor in its present use. For

example, a soccer star may earn £1,000 a week because his special skills are in great demand. If his skills were not in great demand it is possible that he would be willing to work as a footballer for £200 a week, for there is little else he can do. In which case £800 of the £1,000 is a kind of *producer's surplus* or *rent of ability*, for it is not necessary to keep his skills in their present use. This payment can therefore be described as an *economic rent*.

Economic rent and transfer earnings

The concept of economic rent is derived from the ideas of David Ricardo, a political economist of the early 19th century. In developing the idea Ricardo made two assumptions. First, that the supply of land is fixed; and second, that land has only one use and that is growing food. If this were the case, the supply curve for land would be a vertical straight line as in Fig. 9.7.

The demand for land, or any other factor, is a *derived* demand for it is demanded, not for itself, but

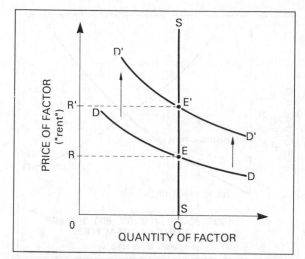

Fig. 9.7 Economic rent. All factor earnings are economic rent because whatever happens to the price the quantity supplied remains the same.

for what can be produced with it. In Ricardo's time the demand for land was very high because Napoleon's Continental System had cut off European grain from the British market. The result of this was that landlords were able to charge very high rents for the land on which to grow grain. Ricardo argued that this did not create more land, so that landlords were receiving more money but not supplying anything more. Conversely, the demand for land might fall, in which case the rents would decrease but the supply of land would not. From this Ricardo concluded that rent fulfilled no purpose and was a *producer's surplus*. Although Ricardo's assumptions were incorrect, he did manage to construct the theoretical extreme of the supply of a factor of production. In Fig 9.7 you can see that the supply curve is vertical and that, therefore, the factor earning is determined by the demand curve. The increase in demand from DD to D'D' increases the price but not the quantity of land. Theoretically demand could decrease until the price (rent) was zero without the quantity supplied decreasing. Thus, all the earnings made by this factor, be it land or anything else, are over and above that which is necessary to keep it in its present use and are therefore *economic rent*. (See page 241–8 for demand and supply curves.)

Ricardo also argued that rent was *barren* since, however high it was, it produced no more of the factor. To some extent this is true but high rents do have the function of making us exploit scarce resources more

sensibly. For example, when land was very cheap in the USA it was ruthlessly exploited. This resulted in the 'Dust Bowl'. High rents for land mean that farmers are anxious to preserve the fertility of land and look after it carefully.

In practice, if a factor's earnings decline there comes a time when that factor will transfer to some other use. The payment which is necessary to keep a factor in its present use is described as a *transfer earning*. If we assume that a firm employs people at a fixed wage agreed with the trade union, then we could represent the supply of labour as a horizontal straight line. In other words, the firm must pay that amount or no-one will work for them. This would mean that in this case all the workers' earnings could be regarded as transfer earnings. This is illustrated in Fig. 9.8.

Most factor earnings are a composite of economic rent and transfer earnings. In Fig. 9.9. the firm requires a work-force of 500. In order to attract this many workers it must pay a wage of £20 a day. If we consider the 200th worker, however, it appears that he or she would have been willing to work for a wage of £9. He or she is, therefore, receiving £11 a day more than is necessary to keep them in their present employment. This is, therefore, economic rent. One could make a similar division of the earnings of the workers until one reaches the 500th worker where all of the £20 is necessary to attract him or her to the firm. Thus all the shaded area is economic rent while the area beneath it

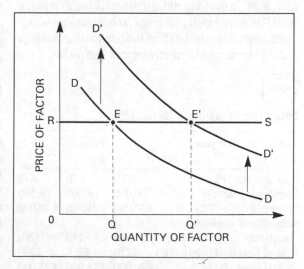

Fig. 9.8 Transfer earnings All factor earnings are transfer earnings because whatever the demand the same price must be paid for the factor of production.

is transfer earnings.

It is possible to consider more than one transfer for a factor. For example, in the centre of London a site might earn £500 per square metre as an office but only £400 per square metre as a cinema, in which case the owner of the office site is earning an economic rent of £100 per square metre. If, however, the site reverted to agriculture it might only earn £20 per square metre, in which case the economic rent would be £480. The amount of economic rent and the amount of transfer earnings, therefore, depend upon the transfer considered.

Are the transfer fees of footballers an example of transfer earnings, economic rent or both? Explain your answer.

Quasi-rent

If we consider a machine that is recovering £500 a year above its operating cost, then in the short run we could consider this as economic rent since it is £500 more than is necessary to keep capital in its present use. However, in the long run the machine must recover not only its operating cost but also its replacement cost if capital is going to remain in that use. If, for example, the replacement cost of this machine was £500 per year, then, in the long run, all the machine's earnings would become transfer earnings. Those earnings which are economic rent in the short run but transfer earnings in the long run are correctly termed quasi-rent.

Study the following information.

Farm costs (per year) and profits	Farm A	B	C
Price per unit (P)	£10	£10	£10
Output per year (Q)	10,000	9,000	9,500
Operating costs (VC)	£30,000	£25,000	£30,000
Area of land employed (hectares)	120	140	200
Rent of land per hectare (FC)	£250	£230	£200
Capital costs (FC)	£20,000	£18,000	£25,000
Total profit per year	£20,000	£14,800	£0
Profit as a % of turnover	20.0	16.4	0

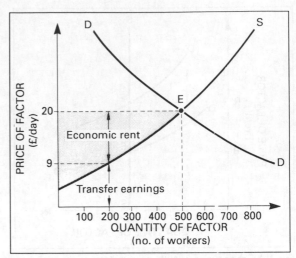

Fig. 9.9 Factor earnings. A composite of economic rent and transfer earnings. The wage is £20; therefore the 200th worker's pay is £9 of transfer earnings and £11 of economic rent.

1 From these figures identify any economic rent.

2 What variations in economic rent might be observed if farm A were to be compared with farm B and then with farm C?

3 Identify any quasi-rent illustrated by these figures.

4 How would your answers to 1 and 2 differ if it became possible for the land involved to be developed as residential building land?

(This is quite a difficult activity. You may find it necessary to consider 'short-run shut-down' conditions (see page 281).)

Rent and taxes

Henry George, a 19th century economist, hit on the idea that if rent were a surplus which could be removed without affecting the distribution of resources, then all taxes could be raised from rent. This idea was very popular with those who did not derive their income from rent! The idea is not feasible, however, because George's argument only works for economic rent and we have seen how difficult this is to quantify.

From time to time governments have, however, tried to tax economic rent. In 1947 the government introduced *development charges* under the Town and Country Planning Act. This was soon repealed but the

Land Commission Act of 1967 introduced a *better-ment levy* of 40%. This was abolished by the Conservative Government in 1970. In 1985, the Conservative Government abolished development land tax which had been introduced by the Labour Government in 1976.

Put forward two arguments for and two against the proposal that there should be a tax on the capital gain made on the transfer of land and property.

Keywords _____

Economic rent
The payment made to any factor of production over and above that needed to keep it in its present use.

Transfer earnings
The payment made to a factor to keep it in its present use.

Quasi rent
Those earnings which are economic rent in the short-run but transfer earnings in the long-run are correctly termed quasi-rent.

_____

The legal agreement under which rent is paid for the use of land and premises is called a *tenancy*. Since many business organisations rent their premises, business tenancies and the obligations imposed by them are subjects of considerable practical importance to them.

Tenancies of business premises

A constantly recurring theme in this chapter has been the intervention of the state in land ownership, its use and the consequences of occupancy. This again is so with tenancies of business (commercial) premises. Until 1915 there was no intervention of any substance by the state in any kind of tenancy. In that year a 'war economy' necessitated legislation restricting rises in rent and mortgage interest. Before 1915 landlords and tenants had been free to strike whatever bargain they wished.

The present law relating to rent and security of tenure of business premises is contained in Part II of the Landlord and Tenant Act 1954. The Act applies to all property occupied by a tenant for the purpose of any trade, profession or employment. There are, however, certain exceptions, e.g. tenancies of farmland, tenancies under the Rent Act 1977 or Housing Act 1988 (these Acts regulate tenancies of dwelling houses but cover a house used for both domestic and business purposes, e.g. taking in paying guests, and mining leases, among others.

In any landlord and tenant situation, the tenant is the more likely to be in the weaker position and to a greater or lesser extent needs the aid of legislation to redress the balance, the two key matters of concern being protection against eviction and control of rent. Thus, the basic aim of the 1954 Act is to allow the tenant to conduct his business in the premises indefinitely, subject to the landlord's legitimate rights when the tenancy expires or the tenant abuses his tenancy. Initially commercial tenancies are unrestricted in their terms but any renewal is controlled by the courts.

Security of tenure

A tenancy of business premises can only be terminated in accordance with the Act. While the tenant may give notice to quit or surrender the lease at any time, a landlord must be given between six and twelve months notice. However, if the tenant does not wish to give up possession and he applies in the proper way, the Court is *bound* to grant him a new tenancy unless the landlord successfully objects on one of seven specified grounds. For example, failure by the tenant to fulfil his obligation to keep the premises in good repair; persistent delay in paying rent; because the premises are part of larger premises and the landlord could obtain a substantially greater rent if the property was let as a whole and not in parts; and because the landlord has the firm intention to occupy the premises for his own business or residential use.

A new tenancy granted by a court will be for a maximum of 14 years but there is no limit on the number of applications that a tenant can make under the Act.

Control of rent

A distinction is drawn between the original tenancy and any subsequent tenancy granted under the Act. As you have seen, the former is unrestricted in its terms and hence there is no limit on the amount of rent that may be charged and no power to secure its revision.

Under the latter, the rent is assessed on an open market basis and a rent revision clause can be included in the tenancy. Both the rent and the other terms of the tenancy can be decided by the Court in the event of a dispute between the parties.

Compensation for eviction and improvements

A tenant who is evicted in accordance with the Act is not entitled to any compensation unless the statutory ground on which the landlord successfully objected to a new tenancy being granted was for his own benefit, e.g. he intended to occupy the premises himself. In such cases, compensation equivalent to the rateable value of the premises is payable, this being doubled if the tenant has been in occupation for 14 years or more.

A tenant must give his landlord three months notice of his intention to make improvements and he can only recover compensation for them when the tenancy ends if they add to the letting value. In addition he must claim at the right time and in the right way. Compensation is never payable if the landlord successfully objected to the improvements or effected them himself in return for a reasonable increase in rent.

Keyword

Security of tenure
Tenants of business premises are given security of tenure by the Landlord and Tenant Act 1954.

Conclusion

Running through this chapter has been the theme of the organisation's ownership and use of land. However, the legal and economic concepts involved extend beyond land as a natural resource and can be applied to other property. It may seem that economic rent is an abstract concept, but it is interesting to note that when it is clearly discernible, as in the case of a soccer star, consequences more usually associated with land result. In the example, the soccer star becomes treated as though he were a 'possession' and he is the subject of personal and commercial restrictions and he may even be leased.

The organisations must use land as a resource. The law both facilitates and controls, even frustrating the organisation's exploitation of this resource. For example, government intervention giving security of tenure to tenants of business premises protects them from the unbridled workings of the market mechanism.

From the beginning of legal history, governments have always interfered in the use of land to a greater or lesser extent. Today, however, the interference has extended so far that it could be argued that the economist's theories and the lawyer's definitions have been to some extent superseded by the effects of government policy.

Learning project

Changing patterns of tenure

Read the short extract from *The Daily Telegraph* below and study the table and complete the tasks which follow.

In 1987, 63 per cent of households owned their own homes, compared with 52 per cent in 1981 and 49 per cent in 1971.

Most of the rise has been attributable to an increase in the proportion owning with a mortgage, particularly during the 1980s, rising from 27 per cent in 1971 to 30 per cent in 1987.

Around one-fifth of households renting from a local authority had considered buying their homes but most had taken no active steps towards purchase.

The proportion of council home households fell from 34 per cent in 1981 to 26 per cent in 1987.

Among those, the proportion headed by someone aged 65 or over increased between 1981 and 1987, although the actual number stayed the same.

Related changes included an increase in those renting council homes who were economically inactive, from 42 per cent in 1981 to 55 per cent in 1987, and a fall in the proportion who were economically active in the skilled or semi-skilled groups, from 43 per cent in 1981 to 37 per cent in 1987.

	1971	1975	1979	1983	1985	1986	1987
Owned outright (%)	22	22	22	24	24	25	24
With mortgage (%)	27	28	30	33	37	38	39
Rented with job or business (%)	5	3	3	2	2	2	3
Rented from local authority (%)	31	33	34	32	28	26	26
Rented from housing assoc. (%)	1	1	1	2	2	2	2
Rented unfurnished (%)	12	10	8	5	5	5	4
Rented furnished (%)	3	3	2	2	2	2	2

1 Construct a composite bar graph using the figures from the table above. (If it is available to you at college, update the table from the *General Household Survey*, published by HMSO.)

2 Using the table and your graph, identify the major housing trends and account for them.

3 Assess how recent legislation is likely to affect future figures.

4 How have changing family patterns affected the demand for housing. (If you need to, refer back to Chapter 1.)

5 With the aid of a diagram, explain the effect on the market for owner-occupied houses of restrictions placed upon the rents charged by private landlords.

6 Under what circumstances might changes in the housing market affect the demand for consumer durables?

7 The article points out the substantial increase of people owning their homes with a mortgage. What is a mortgage? Why did this increase occur?

8 What reasons can you suggest for the 20% of local authority tenants who had considered buying their homes not taking active steps towards doing so.

Further ideas for learning projects

1 Prepare a leaflet suitable for distribution to tenants of a local authority which encourages tenants to take advantage of the 'right to buy' scheme under the Housing Act 1985 *or* seeks to persuade them not to be tempted by any proposed 'privatisation' offers under the Housing Act 1988.

2 Planning disputes receive frequent coverage in local newspapers. Collect information on one such dispute from newspapers and elsewhere and write a report which summarises the arguments on both sides. If possible, follow the dispute through to its conclusion.

10

The financial resources of the organisation

CHAPTER OBJECTIVES

After studying this chapter you should be able to:

- Explain the different meanings of capital;
- Describe the ways in which different organisations raise finance;
- State the ways in which a company issues shares and debentures;
- List the different forms of share and loan capital;
- Calculate the return on invested and loaned finance;
- Explain the factors which determine the rate of interest.

Capital, wealth and finance

Types and forms of capital

The accumulated resources of the economy such as roads, houses, factories and the stocks of raw materials may be described as the country's *wealth* or *capital*. The definition of a *capital* or *producer good* arises not out of its intrinsic nature but out of the use to which it is put. For example, if we consider a commodity such as a potato, to the household it is a consumer good but if used by the farmer to plant for next year's crop then it is capital because it is being used in the production of further wealth. Similarly, a can of beans is a consumer good once it reaches the shopping basket but it is a producer good while still on the shelves of the supermarket since it is part of the capital of the business. There are some goods, such as oil tankers or tractors, which are invariably capital goods; this is because they are used only for the purpose of supplying other goods and services.

All organisations must use capital goods when they are producing goods and services. Capital goods can be classified under two main headings.

1 *Fixed capital* which comprises such things as buildings and machines, i.e. items which continue through several rounds of production.
2 *Working or circulating capital,* i.e. items which are used up in production such as raw materials.

Which of the following are capital (or producer) goods and which are consumer goods.

(a) A Mercedes-Benz tractor;
(b) A Qualcast hover-mower;
(c) 500 pairs of Levi Jeans;
(d) Two kilos of McCain Oven Chips.

In each case say how you decided which category the goods belonged to.

The organisation can acquire capital goods either by buying them, often with the aid of hire-purchase or trade credit, or by leasing them. Leasing of capital is becoming much more widely used since it offers tax advantages to the business.

The term 'capital' is in fact used in two senses, either to describe *capital goods* or to describe *financial resources*. In this latter sense we may distinguish between invested finance (*share capital* in the case of a company) and the loaned finance (*loan capital*) of an organisation. This is the way most people think of capital. Share and loan capital are the legal forms of capital and they illustrate the way in which an organisation is owned and controlled (*see* below).

It is important to realise that capital goods represent *real wealth*, while shares, debentures, money, etc, are not wealth but a legal claim upon it. This distinction may not be important to the individual but it is vital to the economy as a whole. If these paper forms of capital were real wealth then the country could solve all its economic difficulties by printing more money.

Where does capital come from?

As we have already seen, capital goods are not necessarily different from consumer goods but are rather used for a different purpose. If, for example, we have a stock of potatoes then we can consume them all or consume some and plant some. In this way we hope to have more potatoes next year. In the same way, an organisation is faced with the choice of distributing all its profits or *ploughing them back* into the business in the hope that this will enable them to make even more profit in the future. This is the old familiar idea of 'no jam today for more jam tomorrow'. In other words capital is *formed* by doing without now and using the resources so freed to create more wealth in the future.

The output of capital goods

Each year the economy produces new capital goods: roads, factories, machines, etc. However, each year some of the existing capital of the country wears out. Thus, it is necessary for the economy to produce new capital goods to replace those which wear out. The sum total of all capital goods produced is referred to as the *gross output of capital*. When capital *depreciation* has been allowed for we arrive at a figure for the *net output of capital*. *The National Accounts* ('The Blue Book') records all the output of capital goods in one year. This output is termed *capital formation*, while the depreciation of capital is referred to as *capital consumption*. For an economy to become wealthier, capital formation must exceed capital consumption.

Since capital is vital to the growth of an economy, the rate of capital formation is important if we are to

improve our living standards. It is not the case, however, that any capital formation will produce more economic growth. It would be of little use today, for example, to produce more steam locomotives. Even if the capital equipment constructed is superb it can still be rendered useless by such things as bad labour relations or lack of training in its use. The former has been illustrated in the coal-mining industry where the opening of automated pits has been opposed by the miners, the latter frequently by poor utilisation of IT potential.

Suppose that a country's gross capital formation in 1989 was $30.2bn but capital consumption amounts to 42% of this. In 1990 the gross capital formation is only 92% of the 1989 figure but capital consumption rises to 46%.

What is the net output of capital in 1990 in dollars?

The rich and the poor

The factor which separates the rich nations of the world from the poor is the possession of capital. Since capital is formed by going without now to produce more for the future, it is relatively easy for the richer nations to become even richer since they can forgo current consumption of some goods and still have a high standard of living. However, if a very poor country is living near to subsistence level, it is impossible for them to depress living standards to form capital since this would result in mass starvation. Imagine an economy such as Ethiopia which is so poor that everyone must spend all their time working in the fields to produce sufficient food just to keep them alive. Under these circumstances it will be impossible for the population to turn aside from agriculture to build roads or factories which might increase their living standards since they will have nothing to live on while they do so. It is very difficult indeed for poor nations to break out of this cycle of poverty.

Even for a country such as Britain it is important to realise that we cannot hope to keep pace with our competitors while we are devoting less than 15% of the national income to capital formation and countries such as Japan, France and Germany are devoting 20% and Japan 30%.

Activity

List three factors which you think would be significant in determining a country's rate of growth other than the rate of investment.

Keywords _____

Capital goods
Any product which is used in the production of further goods, for example, corn planted in fields to produce more corn.

Capital formation
Capital is formed by forgoing current consumption.

Financing the organisation

Sources of finance

If an organisation wishes to raise finance there are a number of sources from which this might come.

1 Ploughed-back profits. An existing business might be able to finance new investment from retained profits. This is one of the most important sources of finance today.
2 The public. Finance might be raised by selling shares to the public or by persuading them to make loans.
3 The government. Some finance may be available from the government or the EC but in recent years this has become more restricted.
4 Institutions. An organisation might acquire the finance from banks, insurance companies and other financial institutions (*see* page 415–7).

Smaller businesses will usually have to raise finance through personal contact, either with friends and colleagues or the bank manager. Banks are in fact the main external source of loan capital for the small business and to whom, of course, the interest must be paid. Security is nearly always required for the loan. Large companies will need to draw finance from a variety of sources.

Banks are, of course, in the business of providing finance. Besides the traditional activities such as granting loans and overdrafts, available to all customers, banks provide a range of financial services to their business customers. *Factoring* and *leasing* are two further ways in which finance can, in effect, be provided by banks to business organisations. Most non-retail businesses supply their goods or services on credit. This requires an accounting system capable of efficient credit control: monitoring payments, sending out reminders and statements, vetting new customers and periodically reasessing the credit rating and facilities of existing customers. A number of specialist companies, many under the direct or indirect control of banks, offer a *factoring service*. In return for a service charge, they take over the credit control function in the business.

The fullest factoring service is *factor finance*. Here the factor buys the book debts, i.e. the money the business is owed, paying the business a proportion of their value immediately and the remainder when the debt is collected. This improves the liquidity position of the business as funds previously tied up in debtors, or at least a proportion of them, are released as cash immediately. Increasing use is being made of this facility as an alternative to a bank overdraft as a source of working capital finance. Interest is charged on the amount advanced until payment is obtained from the debtor. This is additional to the charge for the parallel debt administration service. If a debt cannot be recovered, the factor providing the finance will normally assume responsibility for the debt and will not reclaim from the business any money advanced against the debt. This is known as *without recourse* factoring.

Factor finance is similar in operation to *invoice discounting* which has been available for many years. Under this system, a business can sell an invoice at a discount to a third party who then collects the funds on his own account. The major difference is that under an invoice discounting arrangement the party buying the invoice is not in control of the accounting system of the business whereas a factor is.

Many businesses today lease at least some of the capital assets that they use. *Leasing* is an arrangement whereby one party obtains on a long term basis the use of a capital asset which belongs to the other party. The lessee pays a regular rental to the lessor but never becomes the owner of the asset. An *operating lease* is usually offered by the supplier of the assets that are to be leased. The lessor not only supplies the goods but undertakes to service and repair them. Such leases are common for photocopiers, word processors, computers and other sophisticated or technical equipment. *Finance leases* have developed as a method of providing finance for the supply of fixed assets to businesses. They provide an alternative to more traditional loan schemes. Thus, instead of lending a business funds with which to purchase an asset, the leasing company buys the asset in its own name and leases it to the business. The principal distinction from an operating lease is that the lessor's chief interest is in providing the finance rather than in supplying the asset. Banks are heavily involved in finance leasing.

Leasing is a good way of financing the acquisition of capital assets because it does not absorb any of the lessee's own liquid assets, leaving working capital available to finance sales. Nor does the lessee have to worry about depreciation of the asset or about making provision for replacement when it wears out. The rental payments will be set at the outset, helping with the forward planning of the cash budgets of the business. A significant advantage of leasing over lending is that the lessor does not have to check the client's financial stability in such detail as a lending banker. The assets remain the lessor's and he can reclaim them if the business fails.

State five possible sources of finance available to a business wanting to expand its operations.

Finance for trading organisations

Different organisations obtain their finance in different ways, and different rules accordingly regulate the return to its contributors. We will now consider in turn the financial resources of the various types of trading organisations discussed in Chapter 3.

Sole traders

You have seen that a sole trader is a business organisation where one person is in business on his own. He alone is responsible for the organisation's financial capital and consequently he alone is entitled to any income from its use.

In common with the other forms of business organisation, a sole trader will need to raise loans when ploughed-back profits are insufficient to finance future capital development. The principal sources of loan capital are banks. In nearly all cases a bank will require security for its advance and this will usually be provided by a mortgage over the sole trader's house or business premises. Alternative securities that could be offered would include a mortgage of stocks and shares or a life assurance policy, or a guarantee of the advance by a third person. Unsecured temporary overdrafts may sometimes be available to a reputable sole trader who is a trusted customer of the bank.

Partnerships

Contribution of capital by each partner is an essential feature of a conventional partnership, although the partners need not contribute capital equally. Therefore, in common with sole traders, partnerships basically generate the finance that they require from within their own organisation. The Partnership Act 1890 provides that, subject to an agreement to the contrary, a partner is not entitled to any interest on his capital contribution until the profits of the firm have been ascertained.

A partnership raises loan capital in much the same way as a sole trader with mortgages being possible over the partnership property in addition to the separate property of individual partners. In addition, a partner may make a loan to his firm quite separate from his capital contribution; such loans, in the absence of an express agreement on the matter, earning interest at 5%.

Companies

1 Shares and debentures. Companies raise finance by issuing *shares* and *debentures*. While both result in the same thing – money which the company can use to pursue its economic activities – there are a number of differences between them. Primarily, debentures acknowledge and secure loans to the company while shares are evidence of part ownership of the company and investment in it. Thus, debenture-holders are the company's creditors while share-holders are its members. Debentures normally provide for repayment and they are usually secured by a mortgage over the property of the company; a shareholder's investment is only completely repaid if and when the company is wound up while solvent. Consequently, the latter involves greater *risk*. An important commercial difference is that dividends on shares can only be paid out of profits and therefore presuppose a profitable year's trading but the interest on debentures may be paid out of capital. Hence, a debenture-holder receives payment for the loan he makes irrespective of whether the company makes a profit or a loss.

Debentures are usually issued to raise temporary finance up to the limit specified in the company's articles of association. Debentures may be either *redeemable* or *irredeemable*. The former are repayable at or after a specified date and they are usually issued when the need for finance is temporary or when interest rates are high and likely to fall. Conversely, the latter are not repayable until the company is wound up or it defaults in the payment of interest due. They will usually be issued when longer term finance is required or when interest rates are low and likely to rise.

Many companies will also have overdrafts with their banks and these accommodate fluctuations in their cash flow. The amount and duration of the overdraft will depend largely upon the reputation of the company. The directors of small companies often give their personal guarantees, usually supported by a mortgage of property or perhaps a cash deposit, as security for the debt to the bank.

2 *Types of shares.* There are three main types of shares and they are distinguishable according to the voting rights and rights to receive dividends and repayment of capital which their holders enjoy.

(a) *Preference shares.* The holders of preference shares receive a dividend in priority to other shareholders but it is usually only a fixed rate dividend. Preference shares are presumed to be *cumulative*, i.e. if in any one year the dividend cannot be paid it is carried forward and added to the dividend for the following year and so on. In many cases, preference shareholders are also entitled to repayment of capital in priority to other shareholders should the company be wound up.

(b) *Ordinary shares.* The precise rights of ordinary shareholders depend on a company's articles of association but normally they are entitled to attend and vote at meetings and to receive a variable dividend according to, and from, the profits remaining after the preference shareholders have received their dividend. If the company is wound up they are entitled to share in the surplus assets after all debts have been dis-

charged and shareholders repaid. Ordinary shares are the *risk-bearing* shares because they have the greatest potential for either profit or loss.

Preference shares do not normally give voting rights and their holders are not entitled to share in the surplus profits of the company unless they hold *participating* preference shares. On liquidation they do not share in the company's surplus assets unless its articles expressly give them this right.

(c) *Deferred shares.* These are now rare but they are still sometimes issued to promoters (those persons who actually form and set the company going) or employees of the company. No dividend is paid to a holder of deferred shares until dividends have been paid to both preferential and ordinary shareholders. However, after these prior payments, all the surplus profit is distributed as dividend to the deferred shareholders.

3 *Stock and debenture stock.* Fully paid-up shares may be converted into *stock*. There is, however, no advantage in doing this today and the holder's investment in the company remains the same, merely being expressed in different terms. For example, 1,000 £1 shares can be converted into £1,000's worth of stock.

The essential difference between stock and shares is that the former is expressed in terms of money and can be transferred in fractional amounts, e.g. £51.25 worth (although the articles of the company usually provide that stock can only be transferred in round sums), while the latter are units, e.g. 10, 50 or 100 shares, and can only be transferred as such.

Debenture or *loan stock* is borrowed finance consolidated into one debt in the same way as shares may be consolidated and converted into stock. It is usually issued for short periods and it avoids the expense and formality involved in a public issue. Institutional investors such as banks, insurance companies and pension funds are the usual buyers. Debenture stock differs from debentures in the same way that stock differs from shares, i.e. it may be transferred in fractional amounts. Debenture stock may be convertible into ordinary shares. This gives the investor a choice between fixed but secure interest on the loan stock, and the possibly better but less certain return (dividend) paid to shareholders.

4 *Authorised, issued and paid-up capital.* The company's memorandum of association will state the amount of *authorised (or nominal) capital* which its

directors may issue. However, the authorised capital need not all be issued and the shares need not be fully paid. Hence, in a company whose memorandum of association states that its authorised capital is £50,000, of which only £40,000 has been issued at 75p per £1 share, the *authorised* capital is £50,000, and *issued* capital is £40,000 and the *paid-up* capital is £30,000.

It is quite common for a company not to issue all its authorised capital at once but to issue part at a later date, either by direct invitation to the public or through an issuing house or by a rights issue or bonus issue to its existing shareholders (*see* below).

5 *Alteration of share capital.* The members of a company may either *increase* or *alter* its share capital by resolution in a general meeting of the company. Increasing the share capital is self-explanatory, and alteration occurs where the company either consolidates its shares, e.g. converts every four 25p nominal shares into a single £1 nominal share; or sub-divides its shares – the reverse process; or converts shares into stock; or cancels unissued shares. Any increase or alteration of the share capital must be notified to the Registrar of Companies.

Share capital can be *reduced* by a resolution of the company confirmed by the court. A reduction of the share capital might be used either to reduce the liability of its shareholders to contribute unpaid capital in respect of their shares, e.g. by reducing 50,000 £1 shares on which 50p per share has been paid to 50,000 50p shares, each fully paid, or to return paid-up capital in excess of its needs, e.g. where a company has issued 50,000 £1 shares fully paid and reduces its capital to 50,000 50p shares fully paid by repaying 50p per share.

Confirmation of the court is necessary because a reduction in share capital adversely affects the company's creditors, i.e. they are deprived of funds which otherwise would have been available to them in winding-up. Banks in particular would be affected where they had made a loan on the security of the company's shares because the value of their security would automatically be reduced. Consequently, before confirming the resolution the court must be satisfied that the creditors will not suffer through the proposed reduction in share capital.

6 *Capital gearing.* The make up of the company's financial resources we refer to as its *capital structure.* The proportion of loan capital to share capital in a

A company has an authorised share capital of 1,000,000 shares with a par value of £1 each. These have all been issued but are only half paid-up. Suppose the company, after tax, makes £400,000 profit of which it retains £100,000 for investment.

How many pence dividend per share will the shareholders receive?

Would your answer be different if the shares were fully paid-up?

company is referred to as the capital gearing of the company. If there is a small proportion of share capital to loan capital, the capital is said to be *high geared*, because a small number of ordinary shares (giving voting rights) controls a large amount of capital. Conversely, if the company's capital is mainly shares, with only a small proportion of loan capital, it is said to be *low geared*.

Generally speaking it is to the company's advantage to have at least some of its capital as loan capital because this gives two benefits.

(a) *Reduced tax burden.* Since debt interest can be claimed against corporation tax this will reduce the amount of tax the company has to pay.

(b) *Increased growth.* Because the company retains more of its earnings it will require a smaller cash sum to pay the *rate* of dividend on each share. This could result in more money being available for ploughing back into the company or it could be used to pay a higher dividend on each share.

7 *The ownership of shares.* The General Household Survey of 1989 estimated that 20% of Britons owned shares. In 1979 this figure was only 9% but partly as a result of 'privatisation' this increased rapidly in the 1980s. However, many of the new shareholders had a small number of shares, such as the many thousands who own shares in British Telecom. Despite this increase, the percentage of all shares owned by individuals continues to decline. In 1963 private individuals owned 60% of all shares but by 1986 this had fallen to only 22%. Individuals have preferred to put their money into life assurance and pension funds and it is these *institutional investors* which own 60% of all shares. Despite the success of the Government encouraging the individual ownership of shares, the percentage of British industry owned by private investors continued to decline.

Public corporations

The initial capital of a public corporation is provided by the Government and authorised by Parliament but once established it can raise loan capital on its own security in much the same way as other trading organisations if ploughed-back profits are insufficient to finance future development.

Tax-payers receive no actual dividend from the government's investment on their behalf but they may benefit by transfers to the Exchequer fund, lower prices and even the occasional cash refund, as happened with the rebate on telephone charges from British Telecom in 1982. Conversely, they have paid higher prices as the Government 'fattened-up' industries for privatisation, as with electricity in the late 1980s.

Co-operative societies

While there are basic differences in formation, economic objectives and organisation between co-operative societies and companies, they raise finance in similar ways, i.e. through issuing shares and from loans. However, as you have seen, shares in co-operative societies differ from shares in companies in important ways and loans to companies are usually from banks and not from their members, as with co-operative societies.

Shareholders receive a dividend on their investment but it is paid and calculated in a different way from company dividends. Traditionally it took the form of cash payment – the 'divi' – directly calculated according to the amount of business that a member had done with the society. Today the return on investment from some societies still takes this form but in others it takes the form of 'special offers' to members or the greater value of co-operative societies' trading stamps to a shareholder than to a non-shareholder. In this last case the dividend is still, however, directly related to the amount of business the shareholder does with the society.

Municipal enterprises

The concept of financial capital seems somewhat out of place in the context of local authorities but it is as necessary to their trading activities as it is to joint stock companies.

In relation to their finance, a distinction can be drawn between a local authority's trading services, e.g. public transport, which are supposed to be profit-making, and its other services. The former may be run on the principle that they should be financially self-supporting, the full cost being met by the charges made. The initial finance required for trading services comes from the issue of municipal stock and from loans. Both are issued on the security of the local authority poll tax income and carry fixed rates of dividend and interest respectively. The latter, which may in fact involve an element of trading, e.g. a leisure centre, are financed from the poll tax and by central government through the local authority support grant in some cases. Poll tax payers and central government receive no direct financial return on their investment but local authority loan stock usually offers the investor an attractive rate of interest.

Raising finance for companies

The public are invited to subscribe for shares or debentures through a document known as a *prospectus*, defined by the Companies Act 1985 as 'any prospectus, notice, circular, advertisement or other invitation offering to the public for subscription or purchase any shares or debentures of the company'. The prospectus will set out the objectives and past performance of the company and other information designed to prevent investors from being misled. A copy of the prospectus must be delivered to the Registrar of Companies by the company or issuing house before the prospectus is issued.

The subscription can be handled in one of three ways.

1 By the company directly inviting the public to subscribe for its shares or debentures through the issue of a *prospectus* and press advertisement. In contract law (*see* Chapter 17) this is an *invitation to treat* and not an offer to sell its shares. By their applications for shares it is the prospective investors who make the contractual offer. The applications are considered by the company's directors and the contract to take shares is complete when the letter of allotments are posted to the applicants.

2 By an *offer for sale* made through an *issuing house* such as a merchant bank. In this method the issuing house will subscribe for the shares or debentures itself and then resell them at a higher price direct to the public. This method is usually preferred to a direct invitation to the public from the company, particularly for companies too small to be quoted on the Stock Exchange. In contrast to direct invitations by the company, the issue of a prospectus by an issuing house is a contractual offer to sell.

3 *Placing*, by which an issuing house may subscribe for the shares or debentures itself and then invite its clients, e.g. insurance companies and pension funds, to purchase from them at a higher price. Alternatively, without subscribing, they may act as the company's agents in selling the securities offered receiving a commission called *brokerage* for their services. Placing is a popular method of raising finance for a small public company where the amount is too small to warrant either direct invitation to the public or an offer for sale.

Underwriting

To guard against the possibility that not all the *shares* will be bought, the issuing house may engage *underwriters*, e.g. banks, issuing houses or stockbrokers, who guarantee to buy any shares that the public do not take up. This is important for if the minimum subscription is not received no shares may be allotted.

False statements

Should the prospectus contain false statements of fact which induce people to subscribe for shares, misled investors may rescind the allotment of shares and reclaim any money paid to the company for them. They may also bring civil actions for damages against the person(s) responsible for the false statement. In addition, it is a criminal offence either to issue a form of application for shares which does not comply with the requirements of the Companies Act 1985 or to make a false statement in the prospectus, unless any person responsible for it had reasonable grounds to believe the statement to be true.

Special methods of issue

Shares are usually sold at a fixed price. This is the *par value* of the share. It is possible, however, for them to be *sold by tender* in which case the company may obtain more or less than the par value. In addition to these procedures for selling shares to the general public, there are two ways by which the company could issue shares to existing shareholders.

1 Bonus or scrip issues In this case the shares are *given* to existing shareholders and therefore no additional finance is involved. They are usually issued as a special method of dealing with undistributed profits.
2 Rights issues These involve the sale of shares to existing shareholders at less than the market price. Therefore additional finance is raised.

Paying for the finance

Debentures have a fixed rate of interest. That is to say, in return for a loan of £100 the debenture holder will receive a guaranteed rate of interest. Some shares, for example, preference shares, may have an income stated on them but by and large their income will depend upon the *dividend* declared by the company. When the company has paid all its costs including taxes, and after it has retained some profits to finance growth, it distributes the rest of its earnings as a dividend on the par (or face) value of each share. If a share is bought on the Stock Exchange it will almost certainly be at a price other than its par value, e.g. a £1 share may be bought for £2. This, however, will not affect its earning capacity. If, for example, the company has declared a 10% (or 10p) dividend per share then it is 10p that the owner of the share will receive. Since he paid £2 for it the effective return to him is not 10% but 5%. This principle also applies to the return on debentures.

The Stock Exchange

The Stock Exchange is not involved with the issue of shares, it is only concerned with the sale and transfer of 'secondhand' shares. Thus, when shares are bought on the Stock Exchange they do not bring money to the company concerned but to the shareholder who has sold them. The Stock Exchange is important to the new issue market, however, since the ease with which shares can be resold encourages people to invest because they know they can easily turn their shares back to cash. In addition stock jobbers may be members of the Stock Exchange and may sell the new shares they have recently acquired to other brokers on the Exchange. In addition to the Stock Exchange there is also the USM (the Unlisted Securities Market) which deals in the securities of companies too small to be quoted on the Exchange. There is now also a 'third tier' market in even smaller companies.

On 27 October 1986 significant changes occured on the Stock Exchange. Collectively these changes are known as the 'Big Bang'. Two types of changes were introduced simultaneously. First were changes in the rules of operation and ownership and second were the changes in technology and methods of operation.

Changes in rules

1 Dual capacity dealing. Before October 1986 there was a strict division between *jobbers*, who had no contact with the public, and *brokers* who dealt with the public and made deals with the jobbers, i.e. the brokers bought and sold shares from the jobbers. After 1986 a member of the Exchange could undertake both jobs. This raised the problem of a possible conflict of interest. For example, a member of the Exchange might be *making a market* in a company's shares, i.e. buying and selling the shares, producing research information on the company etc, while on the other hand they could, in their other capacity, be buying shares for customers who are members of the public. You could argue that such an Exchange member might not give unbiased advice to clients. In theory the client is protected by 'Chinese Walls', that is to say that the broking and jobbing sides of the business are kept entirely separate.

2 Abolition of fixed commissions. From 1912 onwards there was a fixed commission on all dealings. That is to say, whichever stockbroker a member of the public dealt with, the same percentage commission would be charged on all sales and purchases. This practice was abolished in October 1986. It was argued that this would lead to greater competition and lower commissions but, on the other hand, that brokers might also charge higher commissions to certain customers. For example, small investors with only a few pounds to invest might find themselves discriminated against. This fear seems to have been borne out because, following an initial enthusiasm to attract

small investors, many dealers began to impose minimum commission on deals which were higher than previous commissions on small deals.

3 The ownership of firms. Up to October 1986 stockbroking firms had to be owned by members of the Exchange. After this date it became possible for firms to be owned by outside businesses. This meant, in effect, that companies such as banks were able to take over stockbroking firms, thereby giving their customers direct access to the Exchange. As examples of this, Credit Suisse acquired Buckmaster & Moore, while Barclays acquired the jobbers Wedd Burlacher Mordaunt as well as the brokers de Zoete & Bevan.

Technology and organisation

October 1986 saw the introduction of new technology to the Stock Exchange. Previously deals (buying and selling) were done face-to-face on the Stock Exchange 'floor'. Since October 1986 dealers have kept to their office and dealt from the VDU screens in front of them. SEAQ (the Stock Exchange Automated Quotation System) is a composite screen network showing the latest prices of over 3,500 domestic and international securities.

It was anticipated that the new system of dealing would eventually displace the old Stock Exchange floor. As it turned out, the floor was made obsolete within a matter of weeks. Firms found it more convenient to deal from their offices. They then realised that they could deal from anywhere and began to move some of their operations out of London. An example of this was Credit Suisse Buckmast and Moore which, although keeping its offices in London, established telephone dealing in Coventry.

The floor of the Stock Exchange was unused and became the centre for LIFFE (London International Financial Futures Exchange) and the Traded Options markets.

Despite the introduction of SEAQ the system was still very similar to that which preceded it. The deal was simply done electronically rather than face-to-face. In 1990, however, it was proposed to introduce the TAURUS system of 'on the screen' dealing. In this system the Stock Exchange's computer acts as go-between. In other words, it acts as the stock broker used to. Under this system a dealer is actually trading with the computer; it is a 'paperless' transaction.

The Crash of 1987

Almost exactly a year after Big Bang came the Great Crash. Share prices plummeted in New York, London and Tokyo. It says much for the present system that this did not create the chaos which the Great Crash of 1929 created even though the 1987 crash was greater. However, the attempts by governments in both the UK and the USA to restore confidence by cutting interest rates created inflation and the need for very tight monetary policies at the end of the decade.

Calculating the return

Economists and accountants might disagree on the proportions of a share's earnings which might be called profit and that which might be called interest. To the owner of the share, however, the important thing will be how much the share is earning. Shareholders may obtain income from their shares in two ways; first, from the *dividend* declared by the company. This will be expressed as a percentage of the par value of the share. Second, they could gain income by selling the share for more than they paid for it. Since dividends vary from share to share and the price of a particular share may vary from day to day, various methods of expressing the shares earnings or potential earnings have been devised. This is so that the shares of one company may more easily be compared with the shares of a different company. The different ways of expressing this are listed below.

Yield

This gives a simple measure of the return to capital expressed as a percentage of the shares' current market price. If, for example, a company declared that it would pay a dividend of 15% on each £1 share in the company but the current market price of each £1 share is £2.50p then the yield is not 15% but 6%. This can be worked out in the following manner.

$$\text{yield} = \frac{\text{par value x dividend}}{\text{market price of share}}$$

In our example:

$$\frac{1.00 \times 15}{2.50} = 6\%$$

Keywords

Factoring
A method of raising finance whereby a company's book debts, i.e. the money the company is owed, are bought by a factoring company, which may also take over the credit control function in the business.

Leasing
An arrangement whereby one party obtains on a long term basis the use of a capital asset owned by the other party. Photo-copiers and computer systems are examples of assets often leased rather than purchased.

Shares
Shares represent an investment in a company of which the shareholders become members and part-owners. The rights of shareholders depend upon the type of shares they hold.

Debentures
Debentures acknowledge and secure loans to a company. Debenture-holders are creditors of the company. (Both shares and debentures raise finance for a company.)

Capital gearing
A highly geared company is one which has a high proportion of loan capital to share capital.

Institutional investors
Organisations such as pension funds and life assurance companies which together account for 60% of UK share ownership.

Prospectus
A document which a company must issue by law when it wishes to raise money by inviting the public to subscribe for its shares and debentures.

Dividend
The distribution of a company's profits to its members based on the par (face) value of its shares.

Stock Exchange
A market place for 'secondhand' shares.

Big Bang
The name given to the introduction to the Stock Exchange in 1986 of computer dealing and changes in the rules on ownership and dealing.

Price/earnings (P/E) ratio

The yield of a share may not be a good guide to its earning capacity. The P/E ratio is the relationship between the market price of the share and total earnings, i.e. all profit, not just the declared dividend. The

P/E ratio can be expressed as

Market price of share
——————————————
　　Earnings

If the company has a share capital of £100,000 and its total profits or earnings are £50,000 then its earnings are 50% or 0.50. If the market price of the shares is £2.50 then the P/E ratio will be

$$\frac{2.50}{0.50} = 5$$

This is a ratio, not a percentage.

Dividend cover

Since 1973 the complexities of corporation tax have made the calculation of the P/E ratio somewhat problematic. A new measure of the earnings of shares has arisen and that is dividend cover. This relates the net after-tax profits of the company to the declared dividend. If, for example, the profits of the company were £50,000 after tax had been paid and £20,000 was distributed in dividends, then the dividend cover would be 2.5.

There are thus several ways of looking at the earnings of a company. Anyone contemplating the purchase of shares in a company should take care to look at the financial position of the company in as many different ways as possible.

The nature of interest

What is interest?

Interest is the payment made for the use of capital. As far as individual lenders are concerned it is the *price* they receive for hiring out their money. All interest payments are expressed as a percentage per annum. It is important to distinguish between *lending* money and *investing* money. The main distinction is that money lent is repayable whereas money invested is not. If, for example, someone buys a share in a company, even if it is a fixed interest preference share, he is acting as an investor since his money is not repayable. If on the other hand he is a debenture holder or the money is placed on deposit in a bank he is a lender since it is repayable.

The payment made for the use of money is *pure interest* only when no risk is involved. If a person lends money to a major bank or the Government the risk is virtually non-existent and therefore we could regard all that payment as interest. If, on the other hand, money is lent to a less certain business organisation then, although the payment for it may be termed interest, it will in fact involve some consideration for the uncertainty involved. The rate of interest is also affected by the period of time for which the money is lent. Generally speaking, the longer money is lent for, the greater the payment the lender will expect.

Why pay interest?

As with any other factor of production, an organisation employs capital for the product which it creates. Imagine that the owner of a barren hillside in Scotland invests £100,000 of capital in it by planting and growing trees on it. The trees take 25 years to grow, at the end of which time they are sold for £250,000. Thus, in return for the investment the forester has received £150,000 or £6,000 per annum. This income resulting from the employment of capital is referred to as the *net productivity of capital* and is normally expressed as a percentage. In our example it would be 6%. Organisations are willing to pay for the use of capital, therefore, because it enables them to produce goods and services in the same way that the employment of labour does.

Ultimately the payment of all interest must rest upon the net productivity of capital since, if capital did not produce enough to pay the rate of interest, organisations would cease to employ it.

It is possible for the *real rate of interest* to be negative, that is to say that there may be times as, for example, in 1980 when the rate of inflation was above the rate of interest. This, therefore, devalues people's savings.

What effect do you consider such a situation would have upon (a) savings, and (b) investment? This is a difficult point and the answer is not at all obvious. When you have attempted the problem read page 403.

Moral and political attitudes to interest

Since the time of Aristotle the taking of interest on money has been condemned. It was argued that the person who received interest was obtaining 'something for nothing' and was living off the efforts of other people. The medieval church condemned the taking of interest as the sin of *usury*. Marxist opposition to interest is based on the idea that since capital must have been created in the first place by the efforts of workers, any income that accrues to it must belong to the workers and not to the capitalist. In recent years we have become aware of the Muslim opposition to the principle of interest because it is specifically condemned by the Koran. Banks founded and run on Islamic principles have been set up to circumvent these objectives.

It is apparent from the example we used above that interest is not 'something for nothing'. Capital produces a *net product* in the same way that labour produces a *marginal product*. The payment of interest is therefore necessary to compensate the owners of capital for the loss of the net product which they might otherwise have received themselves. Interest is also necessary to encourage people to forgo current consumption in order to make the formation of capital possible. The ownership of capital is a political question beyond the scope of this book. You should realise, however, that in Britain today, the state is the largest capitalist. The ownership of the means of production by the state does not mean that economic principles can be ignored. For a nation, as for an organisation, capital must be directed towards those schemes which show the highest net productivity if it is to prosper. An economy ignores this principle at its peril.

The rate of interest

Although the rate of interest is related to the level of net productivity, it is not the same thing. There are many different rates of interest in the economy, e.g. deposit rate, base rate, Treasury bill rate and so on. There are also short term interest rates and long term interest rates. There is, however, disagreement about how rates of interest are determined. Some of the more important ideas are discussed below.

The loanable funds theory

The classical view of the interest rate was that it was determined by the demand and supply for loanable funds. The interest rate was therefore an *equilibrium price* (*see* page 246). Thus, the rate of interest was more than just the cost of borrowing, it equated investment and saving in the economy. If, for example, there was a great demand for funds this would raise the rate of interest which would in turn encourage more people to save. The weakness of this argument is that it does not take into account the other uses to which people might put money other than saving and investing.

The liquidity preference theory

Keynes argued that if we regarded the supply of money as being fixed at any particular time then the interest rate would be formed by the interaction of the supply of money with the economy's desire to hold cash. He identified three motives in the demand for money.

1 The transactions motive. This is money held for carrying on everyday business. Receipts and payments of money do not coincide. If, for example, you receive a salary then your income comes in monthly instalments but you have to spend money every day. Both the individual and the organisation, therefore, will have to hold money in hand or in current account deposits in banks to cope with these day-to-day payments. The proportion of income which is retained for the transactions motive will depend both upon the frequency with which income payments are received and upon the level of income.

2 The precautionary motive. This refers to money retained to cope with unexpected eventualities. For example, an organisation might be faced with an unexpected rise in its costs or the individual might have to cope with something like a breakdown of his car. The amount of money retained for the precautionary motive is also closely linked to the level of income and for all practical purposes we may link the two motives together.

3 The speculative motive. This is money held in expectation of a speculative gain. To understand this

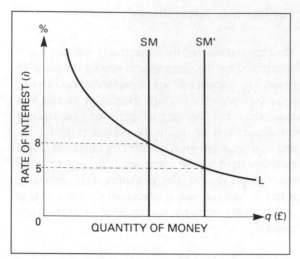

Fig. 10.1 The determination of the rate of interest. The rate of interest is determined by the interaction of liquidity preference (L) with the supply of money (SM). An increase in the supply of money (SM') leads to a fall in the rate of interest.

fully it is necessary to appreciate that the price of securities and the rate of interest vary inversely with one another. If, for example, a £100 bond has a guaranteed income of £5 per year (i.e. a rate of interest of 5%) then should the interest rate rise to 10% it will only be possible to sell that bond for £50 since it only generates a payment of £5 per year. Conversely, if the interest rate fell to 2.5% the earning capacity of the bond would raise its price to £200.

Keynes also believed that investors had a concept of *the normal rate of interest*. If the rate of interest was below this then people would retain cash since interest rates were low and bonds were expensive. They would also retain cash because they expected the interest rate to rise, thereby making bonds cheap and the interest on them greater. Conversely, if the rate of interest was high then people would put their money into bonds because they were cheap and their earnings were high. They would also put money into bonds because they expected the rate of interest to fall which would mean that they would then sell the bonds at a higher price.

For these reasons the liquidity preference curve (so called because it shows the community's demand for cash, or its *liquidity*) slopes downward showing that when the rate of interest is low there is a high liquidity preference, i.e. a large amount of assets are kept in cash form.

If we assume, like Keynes, that the supply of money is fixed then the rate of interest will be where the liquidity preference curve intersects with the supply of money. This is illustrated to Fig. 10.1. Here L is the liquidity preference curve and SM the supply of money. If the supply of money increases to SM' you can see that this has the effect of decreasing the rate of interest from 8% to 5%. Shifts may occur in the liquidity preference curve as a result of such things as changes in income, changes in consumers' tastes and expectations about the future.

With the aid of a diagram similar to Fig. 10.1, demonstrate the likely effects of *(a)* a rise in consumers' incomes, and *(b)* a rise in the speculative demand for money.

A modern view of the rate of interest

Today we do not believe, as the classical economists did, that the rate of interest entirely determines investment, neither do we believe, as Keynes did, that it has little effect upon investment. Keynes believed this because he was primarily concerned with short term interest rates and the other determinants of investment (*see* page 382). If the rate of interest remained high for a long period, however, it would depress consumption, for example by making hire-purchase expensive. It follows that if people were not consuming then business would have to cut back on investment.

As Keynes argued, business expectations of the future are one of the prime determinants of investment. If they are optimistic, businesses will tend to invest irrespective of the rate of interest. High rates of inflation may cause lenders of funds to look for higher rates of interest but constantly rising prices may also make it easier for organisations to pass these increased costs on to consumers. Keynes believed that the money supply was determined by the government. For different reasons, so did the Conservative government of 1979, although it spectacularly failed to control it. After years of attempts to control the money supply, the government turned to controlling the interest rate as its chief weapon of policy in the late 1980s. It would therefore seem fair to conclude that government policy is also one of the chief determinants of the the rate of interest. Thus, we can conclude that the interest rate is the result of the interaction of several forces, i.e. government policy and the money supply, liquidity preference and business expectations.

Keywords

Yield
The effective earnings of a security expressed as a percentage of its current market price as opposed to the stated rate of interest or dividend.

Interest
The payment made for the use of capital. It is always expressed as a percentage.

Demand for money
This is the amount of a person's or a community's

assets which are held as money, i.e. in cash and in bank accounts

Conclusion

This chapter has examined the organisation's demand for financial resources and the payments it will have to make for them. It is important to realise, however, that each organisation is one among many. Therefore investment and the demand for funds must be seen in the context of the whole economy. Thus, the picture will only be complete when we have studied the determinants of savings and investment in the whole economy – this is done in Chapter 22.

Learning project

Wiltown Engineering Ltd

The following information was taken from the financial pages of national newspapers on Wednesday 24 January 1990.

1 Study the information in the table below and then define and explain the various headings to the columns, using numerical examples where possible.

1989-90 high	low	Stock	Price	Yield	P/E ratio
191	130	Abbey Nat	177 + 1	5.8	7.22
360	242	THF	266 + 3	4.3	16.23
£11 1/2	793	Bass	£10 3/8	3.6	11.37
366	228	Smith (WH)	325 – 2	4.3	12.01

The table on the next page presents financial data about Wiltown Engineering Ltd. It shows the interim results for the six months to 28 March 1990. The

figures for the same periods last year are given for comparison as are the figures for the last full year.

At the time these results were published the company's share capital consisted of 50 million £1 ordinary shares and there had been no change in this for the two previous years. The current market value of the shares at 28 March 1990 was 749 pence.

Having studied the information complete the following tasks.

2 Calculate the yield, dividend cover and P/E ratio for the year ended 27 September 1989 assuming that the price of each share was 749 pence.

3 Explain the term capital gearing and demonstrate whether Wiltown is a high or low geared company.

4 Comment upon the financial position of Wiltown. You should include an assessment of the present stock market valuation of the company, the likely effect of these figures upon that valuation and Wiltown's vulnerability or otherwise to takeovers.

Further ideas for learning projects

1 Draw up a prospectus for a projected new software company.

2 Prepare a table to show:

(a) GDP per capita;
(b) gross domestic investment as a percentage of

GDP;
(c) average annual growth rate;

of a selection of nations to demonstrate any connection there may be between investment, growth and the level of income.

Wiltown Engineering Ltd Unaudited results of the first 26 weeks of the company's financial year are as follows	26 weeks ended 28 March 1990	26 weeks ended 28 March 1989	Year ended 27 September 1989
	£ million	£ million	£ million
Turnover	298.0	253.0	497.4
Profits before taxation	36.0	26.0	54.0
Taxation	3.8	2.4	2.8
Profit after taxation	32.2	23.6	51.2
Dividends	12.4	6.6	17.8
Retained profit	19.8	17.0	33.4
Earnings per share	128.8p	94.4p	204.8p
Fixed assets	602.4	578.2	584.6
Net current assets	64.6	83.2	85.8
	667.0	661.4	670.4
Term loans	(64.8)	(66.2)	(67.4)
Represented by equity	602.2	595.2	603.0
Net assets per share	2408.28p	2380.8p	2412.0p
Dividends per share	*Interim 1988*	*Interim 1987*	*Total 1987*
Inclusive of tax credits	64.8	36.0	82.4
Net of tax	49.6	26.4	71.2

S Williamson
Chairman and Managing Director

11

The risk factor

After studying this chapter you should be able to:

- Define the role of the entrepreneur;
- Analyse the concept of optimum resource allocation;
- List the types of industrial property which a business organisation may own;
- Describe the methods by which industrial property may be protected;
- List the sources of profit;
- State the objectives of taxing profits;
- Outline the process of bankruptcy and company liquidation.

Labour, capital and natural resources do not naturally form themselves into a wealth-making combination. Someone must make the decision not only *what* to produce but also *how* and *when* to produce. The people who undertake this task are providing a very special service because they must in so doing take a *risk*. In this chapter we discuss the nature of this risk and the consequences of taking it both successfully and unsuccessfully. We term this decision-making and organisational factor *enterprise*, and the person who supplies it the *entrepreneur*.

The importance of risk-taking

The role of the entrepreneur

Entrepreneurs are the people who run a business organisations; they are not necessarily the capitalists. The capitalist might be a group of people (stockholders) who have lent money to the business but who may have never visited it. The capital could, however, have easily come from banks, from the government or from the entrepreneurs themselves. The entrepreneur's function is to *organise* the business. In order to produce goods and services it is necessary for someone to take a risk by producing in anticipation of demand. That is to say, since it takes time to produce goods the entrepreneur must predict what the demand is going to be when the goods are produced. Entrepreneurs differ from the other people involved in business in that the amount of money they make is uncertain. The workers, the capitalists and the landlord will all have to be paid an agreed contractual amount if the business is not to go into liquidation. However, since there is no way in which you can contract to make a profit, entrepreneurs will make a loss rather than a profit if they are unlucky or unwise.

In organising production entrepreneurs carry out three main functions.

(a) They *buy or hire* the resources (labour, raw materials, etc) which the business requires.
(b) They *combine* the resources in such a way that goods are produced at the lowest cost.
(c) They *sell* the products of the business in the most advantageous way possible.

We assume that entrepreneurs will always try to maximise the profits of the business and also that they will act in a rational and sensible manner. We discuss these assumptions more fully in the next part of the book.

The role of profit

Since goods must be produced in anticipation of demand it is essential that someone takes the risk of doing this. In a mixed economy many production decisions are taken by the government but there are still many more taken by private persons. Entrepreneurs do not act from a sense of public duty but out of a desire to make profit. Adam Smith argued that the 'invisible hand' of self-interest guided the economy to the best possible use of its resources. He argued that to produce profitably the business would not only have to produce the goods which people wanted but also it would have to produce them at minimum cost in order to compete with its rivals. Profit acts not only as an incentive to encourage businesses to produce but also as an indicator. If, for example, profits are high in one particular line of business, this indicates that people want more of that good and encourages more firms to produce it. Also, if one firm in an industry is making more profit than another this could indicate that its methods are more efficient. Other firms will therefore have to emulate this greater efficiency or go out of business.

Thus, profit acts as an incentive to firms to encourage them to take risks, as a measure of efficiency and as a spur to the introduction of new products and processes.

Risks in the large firm

In a small firm it is easy to identify the entrepreneur; this may not be so in a large firm. While the board of directors may be the most obvious risk-taker, many of the senior and middle management may have to make decisions which in a small firm would be considered to be a task for the entrepreneur. In a large firm therefore, the *entrepreneurial function* may be spread among many people and be hard to identify. It may also be the case that when a large company is run entirely by managers and not by profit earners they may be less interested in maximising profits and more interested in such things as the growth of the company, their own job and status, and security. They may therefore act more as *risk-avoiders* rather than risk-takers.

When a company is in a monopoly position the profits it earns may be more a return to its power in the market than to any risk taken.

Mixing resources

The successful running of any business, whether it is a farm, a vehicle manufacturing company or a bank, depends upon using the *right mix* of resources. This is essentially a commercial and managerial problem rather than a technological one. You can produce a technically superb product such as a Rolls Royce and still go bankrupt. It is a commercial problem because the supply, and hence the prices of resources, differ greatly from place to place. A British farmer who tried to grow wheat in a manner which is successful in Canada would rapidly come to grief. In Canada land is plentiful and cheap, whereas farming in Britain depends upon getting as much as possible out of a limited area. This simple but fundamental point is often misunderstood. Many projects in less developed countries have come to grief because they have copied the techniques of advanced countries. If labour is cheap and plentiful it is better to use a process which exploits that. Many people laughed at pictures of the Chinese building reservoirs by moving earth in wicker baskets but if labour was cheap and plentiful and capital equipment expensive and imported, then wicker baskets were the better way. This would provide work and wages for the workers while an imported earth-moving plant would make them unemployed and benefit the country from which the plant was imported. (*See* pages 107–8).

Activity

The figure on page 213 shows a production function for Kleervu Ltd. It shows the number of picture frames which can be produced each day with various combinations of labour and capital. For example, if two units of labour and two units of capital were employed, then the output would be 564 frames per day.

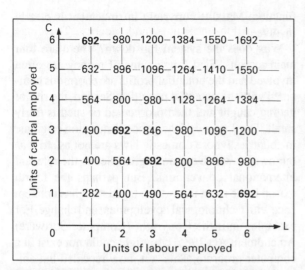

Kleervu Ltd: production function relating output (picture frames) to various combinations of inputs of capital and labour.

1 If capital costs £20 per day and labour costs £30 per day, what is the best (least cost) combination of labour and capital for this firm to employ if it wishes to produce an output of 692 frames per day?

2 Suppose that capital costs were to increase to £40 per day and the business still wished to produce 692 frames per day. What would now be the best combination of labour and capital?

3 You will have realised from the above problems that a change in *relative* factor prices causes the business to *substitute* more of the cheaper factor. Since the 1939–45 War there has been a considerable increase in the *relative* cost of labour. Using the example of the industry in which you work (or another with which you are familiar), describe five ways in which the change in relative costs has resulted in factor substitution. For example, in the banking industry, the introduction of ATMs (automated teller machines) is an instance of substituting machines (capital) for labour.

Keywords _____

The entrepreneurial function
The taking of *risk* in producing goods and or services in *anticipation of demand* for an uncertain return.

Industrial property

What is industrial property?

Great Britain has a record of significant 'firsts' in the history of technology, from the Spinning Jenny to the Hovercraft. Indeed, a talent for invention and development is a considerable economic resource, although the UK has often been guilty of failing to exploit it. The exploitation of inventions (*innovation*) is a form of *enterprise* and the financial rewards from it can be considered as part of the proceeds of enterprise – in an economist's terms, a risk successfully taken. Such enterprise benefits the economy and is to be encouraged. Therefore, it deserves and requires protection at law.

An analogous situation arises if a business organisation earns a reputation for quality, service, etc, in its particular sphere of economic activity. The financial returns from this reputation are also proceeds of enterprise and the right to benefit from this reputation similarly deserves and requires protection.

Inventiveness and reputation are abstract concepts and cannot be physically possessed or protected. However, the right to benefit from them is protected through the ownership of *industrial property*, a generic term encompassing copyrights, patents, trademarks and goodwill. Such intangible property is clearly very different from land, buildings, cars, etc but, as you saw on page 170, personal property includes the intangible as well as the tangible and both are capable of being owned. The various types of industrial property are known as *choses in action*, i.e. property which does not physically exist, and which consequentially cannot be effectively protected by physical means, only by legal action.

Thus, through the concept of industrial property, individuals and business organisations are able to protect their right to benefit from inventiveness, business reputation and hard-work, i.e. their *enterprise*.

Protection of industrial property

As economic activity becomes increasingly diverse and complex, the protection of business interests against unfair trade practices becomes increasingly necessary. A line must be drawn between fair competition, no matter how damaging, and business practices that can be considered unethical. Originally the common law adequately controlled trade practices through the tort of *passing off* but only goodwill and, to a lesser extent, trade-marks are now in practice protected by common law actions. In general, industrial property has additional and more specific statutory protection today and the role of the common law is relatively unimportant.

The relevant statute usually makes interference with these forms of industrial property a tortious act. In addition, as the Trade Descriptions Act 1968 makes it a criminal offence to apply 'a false trade description' to any goods, or to supply any goods to which such a false trade description has been applied, infringement of rights in certain types of industrial property can lead to prosecution. However, although the scope of the criminal law is wide, civil proceedings are usually preferred by a trader whose rights are infringed

Of course, such protection applies to the UK, but what of protection within the 'Single European Market' and world-wide? A System of European patents exists and a system of Community trade marks is under consideration. An agreement on harmonising copyright law, although under discussion, is probably some way off although all member states, as well as many others, are members of the Berne Copyright Convention. In the wider international dimension, an owner of industrial property receives substantial, but by no means total, protection through other similar conventions.

No matter how comprehensive this protection may seem, it is often painfully inadequate. Records and video and audio cassettes are pirated in thousands, articles and books are photocopied by the ream, designer clothes and well-known brand names are copied by the container load and fake character merchandising is extremely easy. Commercial piracy is big business. Yet it does not stop here. Most of us have been guilty at home of infringing copyright law at some time or other. In fact, a survey conducted in 1984 concluded that 84% of blank audio tapes purchased in the UK were used to record music. Of these recordings, 70% were copied from records and 21% from the radio. ('What's wrong with taping a friend's LP?', you may ask). Although no precise figures exist for video cassettes, it is reasonable to assume that recording TV programmes off-air for viewing later is their main function. Massive copyright infringement is clearly involved.

Why does the system fall down? There are four main reasons. First, huge sums of money are often involved and the potential profits are enormous compared with the potential penalties. Second, the risk of getting caught and then prosecuted or sued is fairly small. Third, many of the goods in question originate in countries whose domestic laws are not as strict as our own or which are not signatories to the relevant international conventions. But perhaps the fourth reason is the most important: legislation has not kept pace with technological development and change. For example, until the Copyright (Computer Software) Amendment Act 1985, copyright could not exist in a computer program. This Act, now repealed but embodied in the Copyright, Designs and Patents Act 1988, extended the protection of copyright to a program's originator. The Semiconductor Products (Protection of Topography) Regulations 1987 protects the topography (design) of 'chips'. A topography right arises automatically – there are no registration requirements – in respect of original topographies and gives exclusive rights to commercial reproduction, exploitation and importation of the product for ten years from the end of the year of its first commercial exploitation or 15 years from its creation.

In some cases, however, the law is simply unable to cope with the problem. For example, no law could ever stop the 'illegal' copying of audio and video cassettes for non-commercial use. And yet the property rights of copyright holders must be protected. One solution considered by the government was to impose a levy on the retail price of blank audio and video cassettes, the proceeds of which would go to the copyright holders. In the event, the Copyright, Designs and Patents Act 1988 did not include such a levy, although it is the approach likely to be taken in any future EC regulations. However, it does enable a person who has issued copyright work in a copy-protected electronic form to sue for breach of copyright any person who makes, imports, sells or publishes any information about devices to circumvent the copy-protection. As the recording industry and manufacturers gradually switch from analogue to digital recording technology, a technology which preserves quality in numerous generations of copies and therefore makes effective legal protection even more important, copy protection will almost certainly become more practical and more important.

Interestingly enough, computer software companies have often preferred to use the protection of licences rather than copy protection to protect their interests, partly because circumventing the copy protection may be easy, given the sophistication of modern PCs and their users, and partly because it is simply more cost-effective. You may be familiar with the 'shrink wrap' licence under which the person who opens the package containing the terms of the licence as to the use of the program contractually accepts them. Besides containing terms limiting the purchaser's rights against the software company, e.g. for damage arising out of the use of the program, it will state that the program is licensed, not sold, to the purchaser and although allowing limited back-up copying, will prohibit other copying, modifying or transferring of the program. Such an approach is impractical for the 'home taping' problem.

Types of industrial property

Copyright

The term copyright means the exclusive right of an author, painter, composer, etc to profit from the printing, selling or copying of his original work. It is regulated by the Copyright, Designs and Patents Act 1988. There is no system of registering copyrights with some government organisation, copyright is acquired simply by bringing a work into existence. If you look in the front of this book, for example, you will see that we own the copyright in the text, our ownership being signified by the symbol ©. Under it you will see the basic prohibition against reproducing any part of it in any way.

Copyright in literary, dramatic, musical and artistic works lasts for 50 years after the author's death. Copyright in artistic works which are industrially exploited, e.g. a piece of sculpture or a piece of furniture by a renowned designer, lasts for 25 years from the end of the year in which the articles were first marketed.

Infringing a copyright is a tort of strict liability (*see* page 457–8). The owner may seek an injunction, delivery up of the infringing articles and damages or an account of profits for the infringement. In addition,

they are treated as though they are the owner of the illegal copies and therefore are entitled to damages for conversion, often the full retail value of the articles.

Registered industrial designs

In addition to copyright, an industrial design can be *registered* at the Patent Office under the Registered Designs Act 1949. Registration gives the proprietor the exclusive right to profit from the manufacture of articles to the design. To be registrable, the design must be new or original and an application for registration must state the features of the article which the proprietor considers to be novel. A search through the register of earlier designs is made before the claim to originality is accepted. Registration is for a period of 25 years.

Design, for the purposes of the 1949 Act, relates to those features of the article which appeal to the eye. The design of an article which is determined solely by its function or construction cannot be registered. This, however, is extremely rare. The design of nearly all manufactured articles will contain some element which is determined by artistic and not functional or constructional criteria. Typically the Act would cover the shapes of new electronic equipment, furniture, and shapes and designs for packaging, including the Coca-Cola bottle.

The Copyright, Designs and Patents Act 1988 introduces the idea of *design right* in an original design. Whereas a registered industrial design concerns visual appeal, a design right does not. It arises automatically, i.e. it does not arise by registration, and can apply to any aspect of the shape or configuration (whether internal or external) of the whole or part of an article. Protection of the design right lasts for 15 years. However, where function dictates the design, e.g. for spare parts such as car exhaust systems, the design cannot be registered. Furthermore, a 'licence of right' must be granted to a person who wishes to manufacture the protected article during the last five years of the protected term. This last provision is designed to safeguard competition and the public interest. If the parties fail to agree on the terms of the licence, they are settled by the Comptroller-General of Patents, Designs and Trade Marks.

The 1949 Act gives the proprietor of a registered industrial design the right to a civil action in the High

Court against any person who, without permission, makes or imports, or sells or hires, or offers for sale or hire any article which infringes the design. Such an infringement entitles the proprietor to damages or an account of profits (compensation for the profit lost), the amount being assessed in terms of either lost royalties or lost orders, depending on whether others were licensed to manufacture the design or the proprietor manufactured it himself. In addition, the court may grant an injunction preventing further infringement and order the delivery up or destruction of the articles which infringe the registered design. Similar action is possible by the owner of a design right under the 1988 Act.

Patents

A patent may be defined as the exclusive right to exploit an invention for commercial gain. Should anybody else wish to make or make use of the patented article they must either buy the patent from its proprietor or use it under licence and pay a royalty to him.

Under the Patents Act 1977, as amended by the Copyright, Designs and Patents Act 1988, an invention may only be patented if:

(a) the invention is new;
(b) it involves an inventive step, i.e. a step not obvious to a person skilled in the particular field to which the invention relates;
(c) it is capable of industrial application;
(d) it is not a scientific discovery or theory, an artistic creation, a mental process (including a computer program), a method of presenting information or an invention likely to lead to offensive, immoral or anti-social behaviour and does not relate to an animal or plant or a process for their production.

Applications for Patents under this Act are made to the Comptroller-General of Patents who has jurisdiction to decide questions concerning the entitlement to a patent, although he may refer the matter to the court if he considers this to be more appropriate in the circumstances. Once granted, a patent continues in force for twenty years and can be renewed on payment of the prescribed fee. A European Patent, effective throughout the EC, can be obtained through the European Patent Office under the Act.

Inventions made by employees of a business or-

ganisation in the course of their normal duties usually belong to the business organisation but, on application to the Comptroller-General or to the High Court, they are entitled to compensation if the invention is of outstanding benefit to their organisations.

Patents are generally infringed by making, using, importing or disposing of a patented article, or using or offering for use a patented process for commercial use without the proprietor's consent. If a patent is infringed, the Act gives its proprietor:

(a) the right to bring civil proceedings in the High Court for an injunction against the defendant restraining him from any act of infringement;
(b) the delivering up or destruction of articles infringing the patent;
(c) damages or an account of profits derived by the defendant from the infringement; and
(d) a declaration that the patent is valid and has been infringed by the defendant.

It is a criminal offence to falsify the register of patents or to make a document falsely representing to be a copy of an entry in the register, or to make an unauthorised claim of patent rights or that a patent has been applied for.

It may be that a business organisation uses a secret process or mode of manufacture insufficiently original to patent, or which they do not wish to patent. The term *trade secrets* can be applied to such things, and they will be accorded a certain degree of protection at law (*see* below).

Trade-marks

A basic sales technique is to encourage consumers to identify goods with a particular manufacturer. Sometimes this is done through an advertising slogan or distinctive packaging but usually a registered trade-mark is employed. Indeed, some names which are trade-marks have become so well-known that they are acceptable everyday English, e.g. Gramophone and Hoover.

There are three main types of trade-marks:

1 the manufacturer's name (a trade name) written in a distinctive way, e.g. Coca-Cola;
2 a specially made up trade name, e.g. St Michael, Kodak; or

3 a brand symbol, e.g. the Levis jeans trade-mark depicts two horses trying to rend a pair of their jeans. Other well-known symbols include the Bass Charrington triangle and HMV's dog listening to an old-fashioned gramophone.

In 1986 Coca-Cola tried to register the patterning and shape of their bottle as a trade-mark, not merely the visual representation of it. They failed. Under UK law a trade mark is something which is *applied* to goods, goods themselves canot be registered as a trade mark. The House of Lords stated that a protective law should not bcome a source of monopoly, i.e. registering the bottle as a trade mark would have given the company a perpetual trade mark monopoly over the distinctive shape. However, the proposed EC trade-mark system *would* permit the distinctive shape of goods to be registered.

Trade-marks can be registered under the Trade Marks Act 1938 providing they satisfy certain criteria. In particular they must not suggest fictitious patronage, e.g. by using the word royal in their name, nor convey, nor suggest a particular meaning which can be identified with the goods, e.g. a trade name such as Good Value would not be registrable.

The Trade-Marks Act 1938 entitles the proprietor of a registered trade-mark to bring a civil action for infringement of his monopoly right. He may:

(a) seek an injunction to restrain further infringement;
(b) claim damages or an account of profits derived from the unlawful use of the trade mark; and
(c) demand an order for the delivery up of the infringing articles or other action to prevent them constituting an infringement, e.g. obliteration of the offending trade-mark.

Injunctions are more readily granted to restrain infringement of trade-marks than damage to other industrial property because a trade mark means little unless the proprietor's sole right to its use can be enforced quickly. For example, in March 1986 an injunction was granted against the makers of 'Oxbridge Marmalade' on the application of the proprietors of 'Frank Cooper's Oxford Marmalade' forbidding the former to trade under the 'Oxbridge' name. The judge was of the opinion that there was a 'clear risk' that products bearing the names Oxford and Oxbridge might be confused.

In addition to the statutory right of action, the proprietor of a trade-mark may bring an action in tort for passing off. This is considered below.

Goodwill

Goodwill can be said to be the economic benefit which arises from a business organisation's connections or reputation. In business the term is well understood but at law it is, according to Lord Macnaughten (in a 1901 case), 'a thing very easy to describe, very difficult to define. It is the attractive force which brings in custom. It is the one thing which distinguishes an old-established business from a business at its start.' As such, goodwill can be a very valuable business asset and it may be worth as much as the business premises and stock. Goodwill is usually associated with sole traders, partnerships and small private companies having personal contact with its customers, not with large public companies.

Unlike the other forms of industrial property discussed above, goodwill does not receive specific statutory protection. This is mainly because its whole concept is rather subjective and very difficult to define. In this case the more flexible protection afforded by the common law (the tort of passing off and by an action for breach of contract) is more suitable.

1 Passing off. A business commits the tort of *passing off* where either deliberately or innocently, i.e. with no intention to deceive, it falsely represents its goods or its services to be those of another. It protects traders from having the appearance of their goods copied to the extent necessary to protect the public from being deceived. In *Reckitt and Colman Products Ltd v Borden Inc and Others* (1990) the House of Lords held that to succeed in an action for passing off the plaintiff must establish three points. First, a goodwill attached to the goods or services in question in the mind of the purchasing public by association with a distinctive identifying get-up; second, a misrepresentation by the defendant to the public (intentional or otherwise) leading or likely to lead the public to believe that the goods or services offered were those of the plaintiff; and third, damage caused by the misrepresentation. The case was based on appearance of products alone and did not involve, as most previous successful passing off actions had, an intention to deceive. It may mean that the copying of simple but distinctive features becomes less widespread.

If the court finds that the tort has been committed, the plaintiff is entitled to an award of damages or an account of profits to compensate him for the financial injury suffered through the defendant taking his customers and through any loss to his business reputation or goodwill. As an addition or an alternative to damages, the court may award an injunction forbidding the continuance of the unfair trade practice or, in the case of an infringed trade-mark, the delivering up of infringing articles or the removal of the offending mark. In the *Reckitt and Coleman Case* it was held that the manufacturers of 'JIF Lemon' juice had established a proprietary right in the particular get-up of their product – yellow plastic containers resembling lemons which they had used since the mid-1950s. Over the years JIF had acquired a substantial reputation and goodwill in the JIF get-up. Consequently they obtained injunctions against a number of other companies to prevent them from marketing lemon juice in similar containers. (The case can be distinguished from the apparently very similar Coca-Cola case mentioned above in that appearance protected by a trade mark would give a legally enforceable monopoly, something which the law is reluctant to grant, while a successful action for passing off merely prevents a similar get-up of goods to the extent that the public are deceived by it. In other words, registering a Coke bottle or a Jif lemon as a trade mark would totally prevent another producer from using a similar design, whether or not customers are deceived, while passing off prevents a producer doing this *only* where the public are deceived. The courts are far happier to protect this lesser right.)

The tort of passing off now mainly protects the property right of a trader in the goodwill of his business rather than rights in the other forms of industrial property we have considered above. For example, it is committed by: marketing a product and claiming it is made by the plaintiff; using the plaintiff's trade name, although purely descriptive names such as vacuum cleaner are less likely to receive protection than purely fanciful names; imitating the appearance of the plaintiff's goods; and selling the plaintiff's inferior goods, e.g. seconds or rejects, as perfect goods – in one case an injunction was issued to stop used Gillette razor blades from being sold as genuine blades. In addition, while a person can use his own name in business,

despite injury to another business with the same or similar name, he may possibly commit passing off by doing so. However, in this last situation, the plaintiff must show that consumers have learnt to associate his name with particular goods and that the use of the defendant's own name on similar goods is very likely to mislead consumers into believing the defendant's goods are those of the plaintiff. (In the case of a limited company, the Companies Act 1985 provides additional protection because the Department of Trade can require a company to alter its name if it is too similar to that of an existing one.)

While passing off primarily protects goodwill, the Trade Marks Act 1938 expressly preserves the right to bring a common law action for passing off if a statutory action for infringement of a trade-mark is not available, e.g. through want of registration. Similarly, the common law would allow an action for passing off that had been committed by infringing a patent in the unlikely event of the statutory action being unavailable or declined. Conceivably, an action for passing off could also be used to protect a copyright or patent if, by their infringement, the defendant falsely represented his goods or his services to be those of another in a manner likely to deceive the public.

2 *Other torts.* Two other actions in tort also protect property rights in the goodwill of a business. First, *slander of title* is committed where the defendant falsely asserts that the plaintiff's goods are either not his to sell or that he has no right to sell them, e.g. denying an auctioneer's authority to sell and thereby causing him to lose custom and damaging his reputation. Second, it may be possible to bring an action in tort for a *breach of confidence* for the unauthorised use of information given in confidence, e.g. trade secrets, which damage the goodwill of a business.

3 *Breach of contract.* An action for breach of contract arises where one party to a legally enforceable agreement does not fulfil the obligations imposed upon him by the contract. Through a suitably drafted contract, both the goodwill and trade secrets of a business can be protected in certain circumstances.

When a well-established business is sold it is usual to sell the goodwill along with the business premises and stock. In the absence of an agreement to the contrary, it will be implied in the contract of sale that: *(a)* the seller may set up a similar business in competition with the purchaser but he may not use the old name nor represent himself as carrying on the old business;

(b) the seller may not canvass his former customers but he may otherwise publicly advertise his new business.

A purchaser of the goodwill can further protect himself by expressly including a term in the contract preventing the seller from setting up a competing business for a certain time and/or within a certain area. Goodwill can be similarly protected from possible damage by former employees through an analogous term in their contracts of employment preventing them from working for a competing business for a certain time and/or within a certain area. They must, however, have been employed in a capacity in which they dealt with customers who in consequence might possibly follow the former employee to his new employment. Such restraints have been applied to a wide variety of employees, e.g. a solicitor's clerk, a tailor's cutter-fitter and a milkman.

Trade secrets can also be protected by suitable terms in a contract of employment which prevent an employee with knowledge of them from working for a competitor for a certain time and/or within a certain area. If an employee disclosed his employer's trade secrets during his employment this would be a breach of his contract of employment and would almost certainly justify summary dismissal.

While contractual terms may be used to protect the goodwill and trade secrets of a business, any contract which unreasonably restricts a person's freedom to carry on his trade, business or profession as he chooses (a contract in restraint of trade) is presumed to be void on the grounds of public policy. To enforce such a restraint the purchaser of the goodwill or the owner of the trade secrets must show the restraint to be reasonable and in the interests of both the parties themselves and those of the public in general. For example, the area and duration of the restraint must be no wider than is necessary for the proper protection of the property interest and the community must not be deprived of a necessary and useful service or skill. Thus, a restraint on the vendor of the goodwill of a hairdressing salon in a small town which prevents them establishing a new business in the same town in competition with the purchaser of the goodwill would probably be upheld if the town were adequately served by other hairdressing salons. Also to be considered is the firmly estab-

lished rule that a restraint on a former employee is far less likely to be upheld than that on a vendor of a business. The reason for this different treatment lies in the inequality in bargaining power which exists between the parties to a contract of employment while the vendor and purchaser of a business are presumed to bargain from positions of roughly equal strength.

For each type of industrial property disussed above, find and describe four different examples. Try to make your examples as different from each other as you can. (You may find difficulty in identifying examples of registered industrial designs.)

Keywords

Industrial property
An umbrella term covering a range of intangible but valuable commercial property rights such as patents. By protecting industrial property rights, the law ensures that organisations can benefit from their enterprise.

Copyright
The legal right of authors etc, to profit from their work . . . so don't be tempted to photocopy this book!

Industrial design and design right
An original *industrial design*, a visual concept, can be registered at the Patent Office under the Registered Designs Act 1949. A *design right*, nothing to with visual appeal, arises automatically with no need to register under the Copyright, Designs and Patents Act 1988.

Patent
The exclusive right to exploit an invention for commercial gain.

Trade-mark
A name or symbol used by manufacturers to make their goods or services identifiable to customers.

Goodwill
Valuable but difficult to define, goodwill can be said to be the economic benefit which arises from an organisation's connections or reputation.

Passing off
The tort of passing off is committed where one person falsely represents their goods to be those of another. Because other forms of industrial property are largely protected by statute, passing off now primarily protects goodwill.

Profits

The accountant's view of profit

To the accountant profit is essentially a *residual figure*, i.e. the money which is left over after all the expenses have been paid. Even so, we might talk of profits before tax or after tax, distributed or undistributed. Without a clear understanding of company taxation it is difficult to explain these figures properly. Accountancy is often regarded as an exact study but in arriving at a figure for profit the accountant will have to exercise his judgement in *estimating* many figures in the accounts. For example, estimates will have to be made in arriving at figures for the value of stock, debts and assets. These calculations are made all the more difficult today when the accountant must also estimate the effects of inflation. It is therefore possible for a company to have a healthy-looking balance sheet but to be near to insolvency, or to appear to be making virtually no profit at all but to be very sound.

It is often the case that an organisation owns some of the resources it uses; for example, it may have the freehold on its premises. In these circumstances it is essential to its effective running that these are costed and accounted for as if they were rented. We develop this point below.

There is a considerable element of estimation in determining the profits of a business; estimates will have to be made, for example, of the value of its stocks and debts. It is possible, therefore, for a business either to over- or underestimate its profits.

Explain fully the reasons why a business would wish to:

1 Overestimate its profits when it is in a 'shaky' position;

2 Underestimate its profits when it is sound.

The economist's view of profit

It is possible for a business to make an accounting profit but an economic loss. This is perhaps best explained by taking a simple example. Imagine the case of a solicitor who works for himself in premises he owns. At the end of the year he finds he has made £25,000 above the running costs of the practice and he therefore regards this as profit. The economist, however, will always enquire about the *opportunity costs*, that is to say what else he could have done with his resources of capital and labour etc. We may find on examination that he could have rented the building out for £6,000 p.a., that the capital involved would have earned £2,000 interest if invested elsewhere and that he could have earned £19,000 working as a solicitor for the local council. Under these circumstances he could be £2,000 p.a. better off as a result of closing down his practice and placing his resources elsewhere.

Economists also have a view of the *normal profit* for an organisation. Normal profit is that amount of profit which is just sufficient to keep a firm in an industry. That is to say, even though a firm may be making a profit in accounting terms, if this is very small the entrepreneur will not consider it worthwhile and will close down. The amount of profit which is considered normal will vary from industry to industry and from area to area. Since this profit is necessary to keep the firm in business, economists regard this as a legitimate cost of the business. Once the cost of this profit has been met any profit remaining is described as *super-normal profit*.

Sources of profit

Profits might be regarded as simply the reward for running a business organisation well but in fact there are several different ways in which profits might arise.

The returns to other factors

As we saw above, much of what is commonly called profit is really the *implicit cost* of other factors of production. Thus, the owners of a corner shop might say they made £40,000 profit but in fact £20,000 is payment for their own labour, £4,000 is rent for the shop which they own and so on. This principle can apply to any size of organisation.

The return to innovation

One way to look at profit is to see it as the reward for bringing new products or processes to the market.

This has a special name: *innovation*. Innovation is the application of invention to industry. It is often the innovators who are remembered rather than the inventors. For example, James Watt, George Stephenson and Guglielmo Marconi were all people who made a commercial success of existing inventions. If someone is enterprising enough to bring in a new product or process and it is successful, then for a time they will make a large profit. This will disappear after a while when competitors can copy the process.

In recognition of the importance of innovation, the state rewards the entrepreneur with a limited legal monopoly of it in the form of a *patent*. However, the Competition Act 1980 provides that if a report of the Monopolies Commission shows that an anti-competitive practice which operates against the public interest involves the use of a patented product or process, the Minister may apply to the Comptroller-General for variation of the patent rights.

There are of course many more unsuccessful inventors and innovators than successful ones.

Explain the difference between *invention* and *innovation*.

What inventions and/or innovations were the following responsible for?

- Charles Babbage
- Sir Henry Bessemer
- Christopher Cockerell
- Clive Sinclair
- Henry Ford

The return to risk

Profit can also be said to be the reward for a risk successfully taken. Profits arise, therefore, because the future is uncertain. This would certainly include the innovator's profit because this can be viewed as the reward for the risk of bringing in a new product.

To a certain extent all the factors of production may earn a profit from uncertainty. For example, when a young person decides to train as a lawyer he or she is taking a risk that society will later wish to buy their services. The person who trained as an engineer runs the risk of being replaced by an automated machine. We saw in the previous chapter how the payment made to a debenture in a risky business contained an element of profit. In all these cases, if the risk is taken successfully then the person receives a reward, if unsuccessfully a loss. In other words profit can be both positive and negative.

We might distinguish between:

(a) a speculative risk, where a broker or similar person buys shares, bonds or commodities in expectation of a favourable change in their price;
(b) an economic risk, where an entrepreneur anticipates the demand for goods and services and supplies the product to the market.

Businesses do not, of course, go around looking for risky products. In fact, they tend to try and avoid risk as much as possible. Indeed, many risks may be avoided by *insurance*. But so long as uncertainty remains in the world, someone, be it the entrepreneur or the state, will have to assume the risk of supplying goods to the market.

Suppose that a self-employed solicitor, who works in premises that she owns, finds that at the end of the year she has made £20,000 above the running costs of her practice, which she therefore regards as profit.

1 Explain whether or not this £20,000 should be regarded as profit. Describe circumstances under which, despite this income, the solicitor could be regarded as making an economic loss.

2 Suggest reasons why the solicitor might be willing to work for the £20,000 a year despite the fact that she would be better off in alternative employment.

The return to monopoly power

Where a company has reached a dominant position in the market it may reap a rich reward without taking very much risk. However, it is not only entrepreneurs who might benefit from monopoly power. A trade union might use its monopoly power in a wage market to obtain a greater reward for its members. Similarly, any factor which is earning an *economic rent* could be regarded as making a monopoly profit (*see* page 190).

We would distinguish, however, between the situation where a monopolist deliberately *contrives a scarcity* to drive up the price of their product and a situation where the scarcity occurs *naturally* (*see* Chapters 16 and 17).

The role of risk-taking and of the entrepreneur is fundamental to the working of a free enterprise economy. During the 1970s, this was modified by the Government's unwillingness to let major businesses go bust. Examples of this are the rescues of Rolls Royce and BL (British Leyland). However, with the arrival of a Conservative government in 1979, this policy was reversed. This was well illustrated by the collapse of Laker Airways. The demise of Laker also demonstrated many of the less savoury features of capitalism. The true victims were the customers who had paid their fares but who, as unsecured creditors, lost their money while Freddie Laker himself retained his personal wealth. After the collapse, it was argued that the large airlines such as BA and Pan Am had in fact conspired to drive Laker out of business. The consequences of the abuse of monopoly power and the need for government action are discussed more fully in Chapter 16.

Government policy towards profits

The problem

Profits present the Government with social and political problems of taxation and control. Although profits represent a much smaller share of national income than wages, the Government may have very special reasons for controlling them. For example:

(a) fairness – if the Government is trying to impose a policy of pay restraint on the economy then it cannot expect wage restraint if it is not willing also to restrict profits;
(b) monopoly profits – when an organisation makes large profits as a result of its monopoly power, the Government will need to regulate the situations.

Methods of control

The Government has two main options if it is trying to eliminate excess profit.

Price control

By forcibly holding down the price which a firm wishes to charge, the Government can reduce or eliminate profit. There are two circumstances in which this might be the appropriate policy. First, the Government might wish to do this as part of a policy to restrain prices. Thus, for example, the newly privatised industries such as British Telecom had special price restraints placed upon them. Such restraints might persuade workers and trade unions to be more restrained in their pay demands. Second, irrespective of prevailing economic conditions, price control would be one of the best ways of dealing with monopoly profit. Taxing monopoly profits does not alleviate the misallocation of resources involved in the prices and output policy of the monopolist. We will see later (Chapter 16) that it is often the practice of monopolists to restrict output to drive up prices. This not only results in high profits but also in plant being run below capacity and hence inefficiently.

Taxation

The government has a number of fiscal weapons which it uses, depending upon how the profits arise and how they are paid. The earnings of a company are taxed by *corporation tax*. However, the company will usually incur less tax if it ploughs profit back into the business rather than distributing it. On distribution the profit may also become subject to *personal income tax*. Profits which are made from the sale of shares, commodities, property, etc, are taxed by *capital gains tax*. The rate of tax is much higher if it is a short-term capital gain rather than a long term gain.

It is only companies who pay corporation tax whereas anyone may be subject to capital gains tax.

The consequences of profit control

The control and taxation of profit presents problems to any government. Although price controls may be appropriate to a monopoly situation and may be politically expedient, elsewhere it runs the risk of forcing the firm into a loss and so driving it out of business. Since profits are the return to enterprise, high profits could be regarded as the reward to a very successful business. By removing this profit the Government will take away the incentive for firms to seek new opportunities and to take new risks. Under these circumstances the removal of profits could have a disastrous effect on the economy. Alternatively, the firm may find it possible to pass taxes on to consumers by way of higher prices, in which case the object of the Government will have been defeated. If the business is an exporter, high taxation may have the effect of making its products uncompetitive abroad.

Another problem of company taxation is that it encourages what Keynes termed 'the double-bluff of capitalism'. This is where companies are not taxed on the profits which they plough back because capitalisation will be to the advantage of the economy. The ploughing back of profits will, however, lay the foundation for even larger profits in the future. Undistributed profits also improve the dividend cover, thereby forcing up the price of shares and making capital gains for their owners.

Sharing the profits

In the previous chapter you saw that some form of capital is necessary for any economic activity to be possible and also how interest is payment for the use of capital. In this chapter you have already seen that profit, from which this interest may be paid, is the return to enterprise. Thus, the different types of investment and loans which comprise an organisation's financial capital must now be considered in relation to profit and risk.

Sole traders take all the profits from their enterprise and, under the Partnership Act 1890, the partners in a firm share profits (and losses) equally unless there is an agreement to the contrary. The members of a company share its profits according to the nature of the shares that they hold and the dividend agreed by the board of directors. While public corporations and municipal enterprises may operate at a profit, the concept of profit in its accepted sense is not really applicable to these organisations. The proceeds of enterprise are better viewed in their cases as community benefit, not as cash returns to the tax-payer or rate-payer. Similarly, any profit made by members of co-operative societies must be viewed rather differently from profit derived from membership of companies

because the profit obtained in the former case is less applicable to risk than to the amount of business done with the society.

The sole trader or partner might feel that their risk is greater than that taken by a member (shareholder) of a limited company since sole traders and partners are potentially liable for all the losses of their organisations while the member stands merely to lose their investment. However, someone who had invested £50,000 in a company which became totally insolvent might not agree! Nevertheless, it is true to say that no matter how great the investment, the risk involved in membership of a limited liability company is finite and calculable. It is impossible to say which form of business organisation is potentially most profitable.

Within a company the risk factor varies according to the type of shares held by the members. It is greater for ordinary shares than for preference shares, particularly cumulative preference shares, because the latter are entitled to a lower but more certain dividend than the former. In addition, they often have priority in the repayment of capital on liquidation.

A shareholding in a co-operative society involves a lower risk than investment in a company. The dividend paid to co-operative society members is in effect fixed but secure and the shareholding can be redeemed from the society at any time. In real terms, however, the risk factor involved in holding shares in co-operative societies or companies, being a member of a partnership or a sole trader mainly depends on the individual enterprise. The risk factor is low in running an established corner shop, being a partner in an established firm of solicitors or buying shares in ICI or Marks and Spencer. Conversely, the risk factor is higher in opening a new shop or forming a partnership and still higher in investing in a purely speculative company, e.g. a speculative mining operation. While they do not necessarily end up insolvent, an estimated 80% of new business units go out of business within three years.

So far we have discussed the risk factor in relation to the finance of an organisation which is generated by its members but it also applies to loan capital. In theory the contributors of loan capital only receive interest but the different returns they receive in different types of business units is determined largely by the risk factor involved, i.e. the higher the risk factor, the higher the rate of 'interest'. In addition, there is always the danger that they may lose their money and the contributors of loan capital will try to minimise this aspect of the risk factor. Some loan capital for business organisations is provided by banks and they will always take a mortgage over the organisation's property or other suitable security, e.g. a director's guarantee supported by, say, a charge on his home. A partner who advances money to his firm receives some security in so far as he will be repaid on the firm's dissolution before the partners are entitled to receive back the capital they contributed.

Finally, it must always be remembered that a significant proportion of profit goes to the state in the form of taxes. While there will always be argument about their best form and rate, taxation is clearly necessary to the continued existence of our mixed economy and our society in general.

Consider the case of Megasoft Plc, a software company which relies heavily on the export market. Assess the degree of risk which each of the following may be taking:

(a) an ordinary shareholder of Megasoft;
(b) a preference shareholder of Megasoft;
(d) an employee of Megasoft;
(d) Megasoft's bank.

Keywords

Profit
The return to the factor of production known as 'enterprise'. It is a non-contractual payment and can be either positive or negative.

Role of profit
Profit fulfils a vital allocating function in the economy, redistributing resources from one use to another, rewarding efficiency and punishing inefficiency.

Optimum combination of resources
That which gives the greatest output for the least cost.

Sources of profit
Profits can be a disguised return to other factors of production, a reward for innovation or for a risk successfully taken, or a return to monopoly power.

Control of profit
Taxation or restriction of prices charged may both have the undesirable effect of discouraging enterprise.

The failure of a business

Why businesses fail

Failure is always a possibility in any business enterprise and you have seen above that loss can be attributable to a risk unsuccessfully taken. Its consequences can be disastrous not only for the person or organisation involved but also for its creditors (those to whom it owes money), its employees, its suppliers, other persons or organisations engaged in the same or complementary economic activity and even the local community.

There are perhaps seven main reasons why businesses fail.

1 Poor management, for example, 'one-man' rule in small businesses or an unbalanced, unstructured or incompetent management team in a large business.
2 Accountancy failings, for example, presenting an unrealistic picture of the organisation's assets, poor analysis of financial information or inefficient accounting systems.
3 Failure to respond to change: economic, social or technological, for example, changes in consumer tastes and preferences.
4 Constraints, such as the activities of pressure groups or trade unions, e.g. restrictive working practices or opposition to new technology.
5 Excessive capital gearing, i.e. too high a proportion of loan capital employed in the business, the interest on which becomes an excessive financial burden.
6 A project which is too ambitious and which deprives the rest of the business of resources.
7 Economic recession, leading to a fall in demand for the goods and services produced by the business.

Above we have listed *reasons* for the failure of a business; what should we consider in order to *predict* the likely failure of a business? Clearly its past performance, the strength of its balance sheet, and the value of its shares are the obvious criteria. But it would seem that there can be other, apparently more unlikely, indicators. In 1989 an accountant at Price Waterhouse, a leading City accountancy firm, produced a list of nine indicators for its auditors to bear in mind. Based on experience, it was suggested that if more than five were present, the business was likely to be in trouble!

- Fish tank in the boardroom;
- Company yacht, or plane;
- Beautiful new offices;
- Firm's flagpole appears;
- Fountain in the forecourt;
- Founder's statue in reception;
- Directors who use military titles;
- New, fast-talking managing director arrives;
- Boss too friendly with the bank manager.

This list may appear flippant, but it apparently worked!

Compare the likely effects of a drastic fall in profits on a company whose capital structure is:

(a) high geared
(b) low geared.

Terminology

The term bankrupt is often applied to any person or organisation which is insolvent, i.e. where liabilities exceed assets, but this blanket usage is incorrect. Sole traders and partnerships are made *bankrupt* but registered companies are *wound up*, i.e. go into *liquidation*. Public corporations do neither – the tax-payer meets any debts they cannot pay themselves! There is, in fact, an important distinction between bankruptcy and liquidation, the former always entails insolvency but the latter does not. Liquidation or winding-up is the process by which a registered company ends its legal existence and this need not be through business failure. For example, it is common for the members of a private company who wish to retire to wind up the company as a more practical alternative to its sale.

Insolvency legislation and its aims

Whatever the reason for the failure of a business, its consequence must be regulated by using the law. In 1987 there was a total of 11,439 notified company liquidations and 6,994 bankruptcies, plus 404 individual voluntary arrangements. (These terms are explained below). Yet again, the construction industry came top of both the liquidation and bankruptcy leagues.

The primary aim of the insolvency legislation is to secure a fair distribution of the available assets among creditors so that fraud or secret arrangements cannot prejudice some to the benefit of others. Additionally, bankruptcy law aims to free debtors from hopeless situations so that they can start afresh. However, as you will see, bankruptcy deprives a person of almost all his possessions so that no-one will resort to it merely to avoid the inconvenience of being in debt. In contrast, the failure of a company registered with limited liability does not usually mean total financial ruin for its members. They only lose their investment and any further liability is limited to the amount unpaid, if any, on their shares.

The law regulating the insolvency is contained in the Insolvency Act 1986 and the delegated legislation made under it. This Act completely rewrote the law on individual insolvency as it had existed since the Bankruptcy Act 1914. It introduced new and more streamlined procedures to cope with a changed business environment and swept away concepts and approaches which were perhaps better suited to the insolvency of the local corner shop than to large unincorporated business organisations or individuals trying to make a living in a fiercely competitive business environment. It also introduced greater commonality with company insolvency.

Individual insolvency

There are two aspects to the legal framework under the 1986 Act: the *bankruptcy process* and *voluntary arrangements*.

Bankruptcy

Bankruptcy proceedings begin with a *petition* for a bankruptcy order. This can be brought by debtors themselves, if they realise that their financial position is hopeless, or by a creditor, or creditors, owed at least £750. A creditor must allege that the debtor is either unable to pay, or has no reasonable prospect of paying, the debt or debts specified in the petition.

There are two basic *consequences* of the petition being presented. First, with exceptions, any transaction with the debtor in the time between the petition being presented and the bankruptcy order being made, is void and any property transferred by him is recoverable and goes to augment the property available to meet the debts. Second, legal action cannot be taken against the debtor while the proceedings are pending. In other words, his property is protected for the benefit of the creditors generally, an individual creditor is prevented from recovering an unfair share.

If satisfied that the debtor is unable to pay his or her debts, or has no reasonable prospect of doing so, the court will make a *bankruptcy order*. This makes the debtor an *undischarged bankrupt*. Title to the bankrupt's property vests in (is transferred to) their *trustee in bankruptcy* when they are appointed and unsecured creditors (those who did not take, say, a mortgage over the debtor's property as security for a loan) lose their rights of action against the debtor, they can only prove for the debts owed to them in the bankruptcy. It is important to remember that nothing in the bankruptcy process or any voluntary agreement entered into (*see* below) can prevent secured creditors from realising their security, e.g. selling a mortgaged property, to obtain repayment.

The immediate effect of the bankruptcy order is to make the *Official Receiver*, an official of the Department of Trade and Industry, the receiver and manager of the bankrupt's property pending the appointment of a trustee in bankruptcy. The Official Receiver must investigate the bankrupt's conduct and affairs and, if necessary, make a report to the court and summon a meeting of creditors. The bankrupt has 21 days to provide the official receiver with a *statement of affairs* setting out details of debts and assets.

The official receiver may also apply to the court for a public examination of the bankrupt where he thinks that it would serve a useful purpose, e.g. where a considerable amount of money is involved or where the bankrupt has been guilty of fraudulent or reckless behaviour.

Bankruptcy *commences* with the day upon which the bankruptcy order is made and continues until the bankrupt is discharged. This occurs, subject to an application to the contrary by the official receiver, after two years in the case of summary administrations (*see* below) and after three years in other cases.

As an alternative to making a bankruptcy order on a *debtor's petition*, the court can appoint an *insolvency practitioner* to inquire into and report to the court on the debtor's willingness to purpose a *voluntary arrangement*. The Act is intended to encourage the making of voluntary arrangements in order to avoid the full, and perhaps unnecessary, effects of bankruptcy. However, this procedure can only be followed where the debts are small (at present below £20,000) and the value of the assets is above a minimum amount (at present £2,000). On the basis of the report, the court may either make an interim order (*see* below) or make a bankruptcy order and issue a certificate for a *summary administration*, a simplified procedure not involving the official receiver.

Voluntary arrangements

Debtors can enter into binding *voluntary arrangements* with their creditors in advance of and as an alternative to bankruptcy. The arrangement will take the form of either a *composition* of their debts – basically creditors agree to take a proportion of what is owed to them in full satisfaction – or a *scheme of arrangement* of their affairs – basically an arrangement as to how and when the debts outstanding are to be paid.

A voluntary arrangement begins with the debtor making an application for an *interim order*. This prevents a bankruptcy petition from being presented and any other legal action from being taken against the debtor. The order is initially effective for 14 days and in that time the *nominee* (a qualified insolvency practitioner) named in the petition must prepare and submit to the court a report on the debtor's proposals and whether or not a *meeting of creditors* should be called to approve them. Provided they had notice of it being held, approval of the proposals by the meeting binds all the debtor's creditors to the scheme or composition whether or not they attended and voted. On its approval, the nominee becomes the *supervisor* of the scheme or composition. Any voluntary arrangement can be changed into a bankruptcy by the court on the application of the supervisor or a creditor.

Company insolvency

Liquidation

There are two methods of liquidation: compulsory winding up and voluntary winding up.

In a *compulsory winding up* the company is wound up by the court. It usually occurs where the company is unable to pay its debts, e.g. where a creditor to whom at least £750 is owed presents a petition after having made a proper demand for repayment which remained unsatisfied for three weeks. In addition, the Secretary of State for Trade has certain powers to present a winding-up petition in order to protect the public interest.

When the winding-up order is made the company ceases to be a going concern. Any disposal of property or any transfer of its shares after the order is made is void unless sanctioned by the court.

The Official Receiver collects the assets of the company and asks all members whose shares are not fully paid up to contribute the amount they owe. The assets are then applied to discharge the company's liabilities..

In a *voluntary winding up* the process of liquidation begins at the company's own initiative after a resolution to this effect has been passed by its members. Whether they or its creditors control the liquidation is determined by the company's financial position. If it is insolvent, the liquidation is controlled by the creditors who are able, therefore, to appoint a liquidator of their choice. The liquidator's functions are to settle the list of contributories (those members whose shares are not fully paid-up), collect the company's assets, discharge its liabilities to creditors and, where the company is solvent, redistribute the surplus to its members according to the rights attaching to their share of the company's capital.

When winding up is complete, compulsory or voluntary, the company will be dissolved – its legal existence ended. Following a compulsory winding up, an order may be made by the court to this effect but more usually it is dissolved by asking the Registrar of Companies to strike its name off the Register. In the case of voluntary winding up, the liquidator submits his account to a final general meeting of the company – also a creditors' meeting if the company was insolvent – and within one week files a copy with the Registrar. Three months after this the company is regarded as dissolved.

Administration order

The Insolvency Act 1986 introduced two new procedures as alternatives to liquidation, at least in the first instance. The first is the *administration order*, similar in its effect to the interim order in an individual insolvency which we discussed above. Essentially the order is intended as a 'rescue' mechanism for companies in serious financial difficulties. The idea was imported from American Bankruptcy Law and, although there are mixed feelings about its success there, the possibility of avoiding the usually damaging social and economic consequences of liquidation arguably justifies its introduction.

The court can make an administration order on the petition of a company's directors or creditors where the company has become, or is likely to become, unable to pay its debts and making the order would either promote the survival of the company, or lead to a voluntary arrangement being agreed (*see* below), or secure a better realisation (sale) of the assets than would a winding up. The making of the order prevents the company from being wound up and, generally, prevents any legal action from being taken against the company in respect of its debts. The administrator, who must be a qualified insolvency practitioner, basically takes over the management of the business and, if necessary, can reorganise it. Within three months of his appointment he must send his proposals for the company to all its creditors and present them to a creditors' meeting. If approved, they are put into effect; if not, the company is put into liquidation.

Voluntary arrangements

The second new procedure is the *voluntary arrangement*, again, very similar to that available in the insolvency of an individual or partnership. The idea is that the company is provided with a way of coming to terms with its creditors by agreeing a composition of its debts or a scheme of arrangement for its affairs with the minimum of formality and involvement by the court. After all, it may be in the interests of the creditors to see the company survive. In the short term there may be too few assets to provide an acceptable part repayment of debts. In the long term a wound-up company is one less customer. Similar considerations also apply, of course, to creditors agreeing to administration orders. A proposal for a voluntary arrangement can be put to a company's creditors by the liquidator, if the company is in liquidation; by the administrator, if an administration order is in force; or by the directors in any other case. A qualified insolvency practitioner must act in relation to the proposal and he is known as the *nominee*. The proposal must be put to a meeting of creditors and, if approved, is implemented with the nominee becoming the *supervisor* of the arrangement. If the scheme is unsuccessful, the supervisor can apply to the court to have the company wound up or made subject to an administration order.

The consequences of insolvency

Social and economic consequences

In terms of immediate consequences, bankruptcy is more disastrous to individuals than liquidation (through insolvency) is to the members of a company. The latter lose only their investment but the former will lose virtually all their property. However, the failure of a large company can have far-reaching social, economic and even political consequences, quite apart from the larger financial losses likely to be involved. It will almost invariably mean redundancy for its employees with perhaps limited prospects at best for their immediate re-employment, although much will depend on the area and the age, skills and qualifications of those made redundant. This in turn will affect the social structure of the immediate locality, possibly even causing migration of the young and middle-aged to more prosperous areas in search of jobs. It will certainly damage morale both on the micro-level of the family units affected and on the macro-level of economic activity (*see* page 377). It may even result in the government taking political decisions to encourage and direct investment to the area in order to provide alternative employment.

Activity

Prepare a file of newspaper cuttings/photocopies to illustrate the failure of a business organisation, preferably one in your local area or one which 'hits' the headlines. Using the material you have collected, assess the impact of the failure on:

(a) the owners of the organisation;
(b) its employees;
(c) its customers and suppliers;
(d) the industry;
(e) the public interest.

The rights of creditors

The rights of creditors in liquidations of insolvent companies and in bankruptcies of individuals and partnerships are very similar. The position depends upon whether the creditor is secured, has preferential status or is unsecured. A *secured creditor* is one who has a right against some of the debtor's property as security for the debt owed to him. A mortgage of a house or business premises is a typical example. As discussed earlier, neither the liquidation nor the bankruptcy process prevents a secured creditor from realising their security, usually by selling it. Thus, they are not really involved in the insolvency process at all, although they are to pay any surplus realised over to the liquidator of the company or trustee in bankruptcy.

The claims of *preferential creditors* have priority over unsecured creditors when the assets are shared out. The Insolvency Act 1986 lists the preferential creditors. Not surprisingly, the State features prominently in the list. Preferential status is given to claims for unpaid income or corporation tax, social security contributions (both for a year before the insolvency), and for VAT (for the six months before). Unpaid wages and salaries also have preferential status although, at present, this only covers the four month period before the insolvency and up to a limit of £800 per employee – not a great deal!

Unsecured creditors, e.g. trade creditors, only get paid after secured and preferential creditors have been paid in full. Often they get paid nothing at all when they are perhaps the creditors least able to stand the loss. Included, of course, would be consumers who have paid for goods or services which have not been and will not be provided. To protect themselves, suppliers of materials frequently insert *retention of title clauses* into their contracts. These are often referred to as *Romalpa Clauses* after a legal case involving a company of that name. Such clauses basically provide that ownership of the goods supplied does not transfer to the buyer until the seller has been paid in full. If the company goes into liquidation or insolvency proceedings are taken against a sole trader or partnership, the goods covered by the clause do not form part of the debtor's property and cannot be sold to pay off the debts. They can be reclaimed by the seller.

Available assets

Basically, all property owned by the insolvent company, partnership or individual can be realised (sold) to repay the creditors. In addition, four types of property can be *recovered*.

1 Preferences. A preference is made when a company, partnership or individual does anything which, in the event of the company's or that person's insolvency, has the effect of putting a creditor in a better position than they would have been in had that thing not been done. A simple example would be paying a debt to one creditor and not to another. However, to recover the money or other property transferred, it must be proved that *(a)* the debtor was insolvent when the preference was made, *(b)* that the company, partnership or individual was influenced by a 'desire' to improve the debtor's position, and *(c)* the preference took place in the six months (usually) before the insolvency proceedings were started.

2 Transactions at an undervalue. These are transactions where a gift of property is made or where what is given in return (the *consideration* in contract law) is worth substantially less than the property transferred. An individual transferring property to another member of his family is a good example. However, no intention to benefit the other party need be shown, it is enough that the transaction occurred.

Once again the transaction must have been entered into when the debtor was insolvent and within two (companies) or five (individuals and partnerships) years of the insolvency proceedings.

3 Transactions defrauding creditors. These are transactions at an undervalue entered into for the purpose of putting assets beyond the reach of creditors. Making such a transaction is a criminal offence.

However, a person who buys property from a seller who acquired it through either a preference, a transaction at an undervalue, or a fraudulent transaction gains a good title to it, i.e. he can keep it, provided he bought it in good faith and for value (gave something of value – consideration – in return) without knowing the circumstances.

4 Extortionate credit transactions. A credit transaction is extortionate under the Insolvency Act 1986 if, having regard to the risk accepted by the person providing the credit, it requires grossly exorbitant payments to be made or otherwise grossly contravenes the principles of fair dealing. If the debtor entered into such a transaction within the three years before the insolvency proceedings, the court can set it aside or vary its terms. If any property was used as security for repayment, the lender's rights can be taken away and the property becomes available for distribution among the creditors generally.

Unavailable assets in bankruptcy

It is in nobody's interests, certainly not those of the creditors, who one day hope to be repaid, for bankrupts to be deprived of all means of supporting themselves and looking after their families. Thus, certain property is not available to creditors. The most important are *(a)* personal income necessary to support the bankrupt and their family, *(b)* the family home and *(c)* trade and personal property. This last category covers tools, books, vehicles and other equipment necessary for their personal use in their business and such clothes, bedding, furniture and household equipment and provisions as are necessary for satisfying the basic domestic needs of the bankrupt and their family. However, where the value of an asset in this last category exceeds the cost of its replacement, the trustee can claim it and purchase a suitable replacement. For example, traders used to making deliveries in new Volvo estates would probably find themselves delivering in second-hand vans and individuals used to living in houses full of valuable antiques would probably find themselves living in more conventionally furnished homes!

Penalties and disqualifications

Bankruptcy involves a debtor in business and financial ruin but the liquidation of an insolvent company may have little personal effect on its directors. Indeed, it would be quite possible to shelter behind the *veil of incorporation* and use the process of voluntary liquidation as a device to end an unsuccessful business

Keywords

Bankruptcy and liquidation

Both are terms for insolvency – a sole trader or partnership is made bankrupt, a company goes or is put into liquidation.

Voluntary arrangement

An alternative to bankruptcy or liquidation – very similar rules apply to both situations – where insolvent debtors come to private arrangements with their creditors, agreeing either to repay all debts according to an agreed plan or make part payment which is accepted in full satisfaction by the creditors.

Interim orders and administration orders

The former applies to bankruptcy, the latter to liquidation. Both protect insolvent debtors and their property from court action by creditors for a short period of time in the hope that arrangements can be agreed with creditors that will prevent bankruptcy or liquidation from taking place.

Compulsory and voluntary winding up

A *compulsory* liquidation is initiated by creditors, almost invariably because a company cannot pay its debts; a *voluntary* winding up is initiated by the company itself – the company may not necessarily be insolvent.

Secured creditors

Creditors who have rights against a debtor's property as security for the debt, e.g. a bank.

Preferential creditors

Under the Insolvency Act 1986, certain classes of creditors have priority over all others except those that hold security. Examples include the Inland Revenue for a years' unpaid tax and employees for unpaid wages and salaries.

Available assets

The term used to describe those assets of a bankrupt or a company in liquidation that are available to pay off the debts. They include not only the property owned at the time of the bankruptcy or winding up order but also certain types of property which were formerly owned and which can be recovered, e.g. property that was the subject of a *preference*.

venture without involving its owners in great financial loss, particularly if the company's assets are few and its capital small. Furthermore, there is nothing to stop the same people starting a 'phoenix' business by buying an off-the-peg company or opening up as a partnership and commencing the same or similar economic activity the very next day, conceivably from the same premises. Alternatively, equally unscrupulous business people could use voluntary liquidation as a means of avoiding future onerous and expensive obligations after having made a large initial profit, e.g. after sale service or a guarantee.

To help prevent this from happening, the Company Directors Disqualifications Act 1986 gives the court power to disqualify a person from acting as a director of another company or from taking part in the formation or management of a company for up to 15 years. This power can be exercised where, for example, the person is convicted of a serious criminal offence in connection with the company, has persistently failed to comply with the Companies Act 1985, has been guilty of fraudulent trading, i.e. the business of the company was carried on with the intent to defraud creditors, or where they have been a director of an insolvent company and the court considers them unfit to be concerned in a company's management. A person who acts as a director while disqualified can incur *personal* liability for the company's debts.

Another 'disqualification' relates to the use of an insolvent company's name. It is a criminal offence under the Insolvency Act 1986 for a director of a company which has gone into insolvent liquidation to be involved in the management of any other company using the same or a similar name within five years of the company's failure. Once again, personal liability for debts can be incurred, this time for the debts of the new company.

A bankrupt also suffers disqualifications and can incur penalties. The Act makes it a criminal offence for an undischarged bankrupt to (a) act as a director or take part in the management of a registered company without the court's consent, (b) obtain credit or (at present) £250 without disclosing their status, or (c) engage in any business under a name other than the one in which they were made bankrupt without disclosing that name to all persons with whom they enter into any business transaction.

These provisions undoubtedly make it more difficult for people to set up 'phoenix' businesses but, unfortunately, there will always be a few with the ability and inclination to exploit a legal framework's loopholes and deficiencies in principle and procedure for their own ends. Corporate personality, while clearly fundamental to modern economic activity, can be used unfairly by the few.

Learning project

Insolvencies in England and Wales

Study the table below and complete the following tasks.

1 Update the the table above.

2 Using the figures from the table, construct

(a) a composite bar chart, or (b) a combined graph to show the number of insolvencies over time.

3 What trends do you notice from your bar chart or graph? Account for them.

Individual and company insolvencies in England and Wales: 1976–1987

	1976	1977	1978	1979	1980	1981	1982	1983	1984	1985	1986	1987
Bankruptcies	7,108	4,403	3,826	3,456	3,986	5,075	5,700	7,032	8,229	6,778	7,155	7,427
Liquidations	5,939	5,831	5,086	4,537	6,890	8,596	12,067	13,406	13,721	14,898	14,405	11,439

Source: Department of Trade and Industry

Further ideas for learning projects

1 Draft a restraint on an employee or the vendor of a business dsigned to protect trade secrets, goodwill etc.

2 Prepare a report which advances arguments for and against increasing the taxation of profits.

3 Construct a flow diagram of the bankruptcy and voluntary arrangement processes.

12

Responsibility, accountability and resources

CHAPTER OBJECTIVES

After studying this chapter you should be able to:

■ Explain the business organisation's responsibilities which arise from the use of resources;
■ List the different groups to which a business organisation is accountable for its economic activities;
■ Identify and explain the basis on which business organisations are accountable;
■ Evaluate the wider environmental issues which pose new problems of responsibility and accountability.

In this part of the book we have discussed the use of resources by organisations. You have seen how their use is determined by a combination of economic principles and social and political considerations embodied in a regulatory framework of law. Thus, the use of resources gives rise to economic and social responsibilities encouraged or enforced by legal or political accountability. It is now generally accepted that trading organisations have a wider responsibility than that owed merely to their shareholders etc. For example, aerosol and refrigerator manufacturers have had to acknowledge their responsibility for damage to the environment, i.e. to the ozone layer, and change their methods of manufacture. In the last part of the chapter we shall deal with this wider problem of environmental responsibility.

Economic responsibility

The primary economic responsibility owed by com-

panies, partnerships and sole traders (the three main types of business organisations) is to make a profit, for it is from this profit that contributors of their financial capital receive a return on their investment or loan. (Rather different economic criteria apply to municipal enterprises, public corporations and co-operative societies.) Profit is equally important to create and secure market confidence in their activities. Without this confidence invested finance would be endangered and economic recovery or growth would have to be financed by expensive loan capital. Ultimately the result could be takeover by another business organisation or insolvency.

Social responsibility

The economic responsibility to make a profit cannot nowadays be considered in isolation from the wider social responsibilities that organisations owe to their employees, the community and the natural environment. Indeed, social responsibility is now expected from all organisations. Businesses are expected to provide goods and services which reflect the needs of consumers and society in general, e.g. energy-saving devices, and anticipate future needs. Local authorities are expected to provide services and preserve and improve the environment at an acceptable cost. Teaching institutions are expected to produce students with skills and knowledge useful to both the individual and society.

The profit-maximisation objective of *business organisations* is not easy to reconcile with social responsibility and in the past the latter was largely ignored. Today, however, social responsibility is in the main voluntarily accepted as an important factor in determining objectives and formulating policies. Indeed, companies often make a virtue of necessity by promoting products as being environmentally friendly and reducing social responsibility to a marketing ploy. Nevertheless social and environmental responsibility is now encouraged and sometimes enforced by far greater political and legal accountability, e.g. the Consumer Protection Act 1987. We now turn to aspects of this interrelationship.

While control of resources is largely in the hands of a few, the partial reconciliation of economic and social responsibility has meant that profits from the use of resources are shared somewhat more fairly. In particular, investors receive a good return, employees are better paid and enjoy greater job security and society as a whole benefits from the enormous tax payments made to the Exchequer by business organisations. To whatever extent the profit motive has been reconciled with social responsibility, it is due to a combination of changes in socio-economic philosophy, the divorce of management from ownership in large business organisations, the power and influence of trade unions, the activities of pressure groups and the imposition of legal and political accountability upon business organisations.

It is now probably accepted by most people that a business organisation's economic activity should not profit its owners at the expense of the employees and the community in general. Thus, a framework of employment law (stipulating minimum standards in working conditions and protecting a person's employed status) and planning law (protecting the natural environment and the community from unplanned and antisocial use of land) are accepted constraints upon a business organisation's activities in general and profit maximisation in particular. The ethical behaviour of business organisations is also a matter of major public concern. Pressure groups are increasingly better organised, more articulate and more proficient at using the 'system' and the media, be they environmentalists concerned about pollution or the mismanagement of natural resources, or conservationists trying to stop development or save wildlife. Management must take their views and possible actions into account when setting objectives and formulating policies.

The divorce of management from ownership in large business organisations (sometimes called the *managerial revolution*) has come about as a result of their increased size, the emergence of the company as the dominant form of business organisation and the need for specialised technical skills in management. Gone are the days when the owner-manager reaped all the profits from this relatively small but profitable organisation. Today, the managers of large public companies do not usually own them and the profits made by small business units, where owner-management is still possible, must be shared more fairly among those responsible for its generation. While small businesses vastly outnumber large, the latter have the greater effect on the socio-economic environment. Conventional management theory states that management divorced from ownership is far more likely to consider social responsibility in decision-making, providing profits are sufficient to satisfy shareholders and to safeguard its own continued employment. Any increase in worker participation in management will arguably see further reconciliation between the profit motive and social responsibility.

In theory, business organisations are neither responsible nor accountable to trade unions but responsibility to employees is in practice very largely responsibility to trade unions. The provisions of the Health and Safety at Work, etc, Act 1974 are a good example of this. Despite the much lower political profile of trade unions in the late 1980s, caused by a government openly hostile to them, trade unions have tremendous influence with business organisations over conditions of employment and wage rates. In some ways the sanctions which a powerful trade union can impose may be more effective than formal legal accountability should a union consider that a business organisation has acted against the best interests of its members. With governments more sympathetic to their views in power, trade unions have often had great influence in political and economic policies at national level.

Social accounting

Some organisations, particularly those with a high political profile such as local authorities, make a regular, systematic assessment of their activities in so far as they affect society. This is usually known as *social accounting* or a *social audit*.

The exercise will typically cover environmental issues, recruitment and personnel policies and community involvement. It may be extended to include an analysis of the expectation of every group with which it interacts, for example, customers, suppliers, investors and employees. Job advertisements which emphasise that the employment is an 'Equal Opportunities Employer' or advertisements which emphasise its concern for the environment are common examples of the process. The purpose of the exercise is to establish an 'environment' which is to the benefit of all. It can, of course, be an extremely effective marketing or propaganda exercise as well. There is nothing necessarily wrong with combining the two objectives.

Consider the organisation in which you work or study. Identify specific ways in which it endeavours to pursue its activities in a socially responsible fashion.

Find out whether it has a 'Mission Statement' or a similar document which states its objectives. Obtain a copy of this and critically evaluate it and suggest changes.

Accountability

Legal or political accountability cannot ensure that business organisations will fulfil their economic responsibilities to their members and other contributors of finance. However, it can ensure that economic activity is pursued according to standards designed to protect the interests of investors, creditors, employees, the environment and the community in general.

Political accountability

Political accountability is associated mainly with public corporations and municipal enterprises, the former being accountable to Ministers of State and ultimately to Parliament and the latter to the appropriate local authority or other local government organisations. However, an element of political accountability can be employed by the government to encourage private enterprise to abide by its policies. In the late 1970s, for example, the government attempted to enforce voluntary pay codes by threatening any business organisation which broke them with the loss of its government contract – the 'black list'. In foreign affairs the legal penalties imposed for breaking the economic sanctions against Rhodesia (now Zimbabwe) were used by successive governments as a means of reinforcing what was essentially political accountability.

The Westland Affair in 1986 raised other aspects of political accountability. Westland are helicopter manufacturers who exist primarily on defence contracts. When they got into financial difficulties they proposed a link-up with the American Sikorsky Corporation. This appeared to be a straightforward commercial arrangement. However, it created a political storm when a section of opinion led by Michael Heseltine, the then Defence Secretary, pressed for the business to remain in European hands if it had to pass out of British hands. The pro-European camp argued that they had a right to a voice in the future of the business since the company existed mainly on public money. The subsequent confusion resulted in the resignation of both the Defence Secretary and the Secretary of State for Trade and Industry, Leon Brittan.

Although the Westland rescue eventually went through, it raised a question in the public's mind about the extent to which a public company is always free to dispose of its assets as it sees fit. Later in 1986 it was a major factor in causing the government to abandon the proposed sale of Land Rover to the American company General Motors and in 1989 the strategic implications of possible foreign takeovers of important defence contractors were again raised by the

Plessey and Ferranti affairs. It is clear, therefore, that when a company is seen as being significant to the well-being or even the image of the country a degree of political accountability must enter into its dealings.

Legal accountability

In the private sector of the economy all organisations are legally accountable for their economic activities to their contributors of finance, be it invested or loaned; to their employees; to the state; and ultimately to their customers.

To investors and creditors

This is reflected in the Partnership Act 1890 by the duty to keep proper books of account and the right to inspect them and the right to take part in the management of the firm. Companies are accountable to their shareholders through the annual general meeting required by the Companies Act 1985 at which the shareholders can, in theory, exercise control over the running of the company. All creditors are able to take legal action to enforce payment of sums owing and secured creditors, i.e. those whose loan is covered by a security such as a mortgage, can in addition realise their security if repayment of the loan is unforthcoming. If the business becomes insolvent, both the business and its management are legally accountable for their activities under the Insolvency Act 1986.

To employees

Accountability at law to employees is imposed by the law of contract and the law of torts at common law and by the comprehensive statutory framework of rules regulating contracts of employment, job security and working conditions. Such accountability is necessary to ensure that social responsibilities are fulfilled. Employees are, of course, in turn accountable to their employers through their contracts of employment. Besides such duties as obedience and good faith, this accountability is reflected in the *staff appraisal* programmes that many firms now run. If you recall from Chapter 8, appraisal in a sense involves accountability to yourself in that it assesses the attainment of your own work objectives.

To the state

Business organisations are legally accountable both directly and indirectly to the state. Direct legal accountability is found in the general duty to obey the law and in a number of specific obligations, e.g. the duty to pay taxes, to abide by planning legislation, to provide safe working conditions for employees and to supply information required by law to state officials such as the Registrar of Companies. In so far as the state imposes sanctions for all infringements of the law, whether these directly harm the state or solely an individual, all business organisations are indirectly accountable at law to the state for all their activities.

To consumers

The sale of goods and services to consumers for profit is the ultimate purpose for which business organisations acquire and use resources. The law of the market place – contract and consumer law – makes all business organisations legally accountable to consumers and to the state (primarily through the courts and the Office of Fair Trading) for failure to meet the standards of quality and behaviour required by law and for much of the damage that this failure may cause. The business organisation's markets and clients are the twin themes of the next Part of this book, and the law of the market place is considered in detail in that Part.

List six ways in which you think the accountability of business organisations could be improved to the advantage of the consumer.

Key words

Responsibility
In the context of using resources, responsibility refers to an organisation's acceptance of a duty to use those resources for the benefit of both its owners (economic responsibility) and the wider environment (social responsibility).

Accountability
The political and legal processes by which responsibility in the use of resources is enforced.

The environment

The environmental problem

Economists have long recognised the problem posed by the fact that the environment is a free resource. This arises because in most cases it has been impossible to charge for the use of the environment and users are therefore left unaccountable for the way they use it. You cannot, for example, charge people to breath! This, however, has meant that people have felt free to exploit the environment by discharging their waste products into it. Tall factory chimneys were one early attempt to deal with the problem – by spreading the pollution far and wide! The seas have also long been regarded as a free resource and this has led to over-fishing and pollution. In the early 1990s the Japanese 'wall of death' fishing techniques are denuding the South Pacific of all marine life. (This is a system whereby 50 kilometre long nets are dragged through the seas by a dozen boats ensnaring all living creatures.)

Other resources – land, capital, labour, etc – can be charged for, and consequently various types of accountability have arisen. These include actions for breach of contract or for injury to person or property rights. The recognition of such rights gives rise to actions by individuals, organisations, the government and even the EC.

Within a society, where people have to live in harmony with their neighbours, social responsibility is also a very real constraint upon the exploitation of the environment. In this respect our ancestors were often greater conservators of their environment than we are of ours.

One of the major problems posed by the environment is that it lies outside societies in that it is an international issue and we do not have an 'international society'. At law it would be very difficult for Norwegians, for example, to seek compensation for damage caused by 'acid rain' from power companies in other countries such as the UK. Similarly, while most people can agree that over-exploitation of the sea is a mistake, they are not willing to forgo their 'right' to this 'free resource'.

The Third World dilemma

When we come to consider the problem of the environment in the context of Third World countries, additional problems are revealed. Consider the problem of CFCs which are slowly destroying the World's Ozone Layer. It is easy for rich countries to find (more expensive) alternatives for aerosol propellants and new gases for use in refrigerators but Third World countries might argue that they only want cheap fridges, after all the rich countries have had them for years! Similarly, it is impossible to convince a starving peasant in Brazil that the rain forest should not be burnt down to make more room for crops – after all we cut down our natural oak forests generations ago – not only to create space for agriculture but to build the ships with which many of the Third World countries were conquered, colonised and exploited!

Third World countries can also argue reasonably that most of the environmental pollution has been caused by the last three hundred years of economic development in the industrialised nations. Hence, since it is the industrialised nations which caused the pollution and because only they can afford to, *they* should do something about it. Thus, if the industrialised nations want the Third World to become more conservation-minded, they should not only clean up their own act first but also give substantial aid to the poorer nations to help develop them.

The sad fact of the matter is that because of the debt of the Third World, it is they which send large amounts of money to the developed world each year not *vice versa*.

Future generations

Exploitation of the environment also poses problems when we consider future generations. It is impossible for future generations to hold us responsible for the damage we cause. Unfortunately people have an enormous current consumption preference, i.e. they prefer to spend their income now – or at least in their lifetime. While some people are willing to make enormous sacrifices for their children, they show little willingness to do this for the children of others and for those as yet unborn – particularly for those on the other side of the World and belonging to a completely different culture. We are, however, passing pollution to future generations; some toxic waste will still be damaging the environment 10,000 years from now. People are aware of the hole in the ozone layer but have they yet understood that it possibly means skin cancer for all their grandchildren?

It is against this problem that we realise that governments or other agencies must intervene to make people accountable for the damage to the environment and to limit it.

Solutions

It is obvious to all that what is needed is world-wide environmental protection agencies but this seems impossible to achieve. The natural starting point would seem to be international organisations such as the UN but its policies often seem impossible to enforce; in other words, nations are frequently willing to give lip-service to a policy and then be unwilling to implement it. It is perhaps ironic that pressure for conservation is coming not so much from governments and interna-tional agencies but from organisations such as the Green Party – which refuses even to elect a leader. Unfortunately it will probably take more environ-mental disasters such as Chernobyl to persuade the human race that the environment is not in practice a 'free resource' and to accept and formalise responsi-bility to, and accountability for its use. With this will have to come enforceable duties on present and future generations to care for the environment in the same way as people owe duties to care for their property and that of others and for the use of other resources for which they actually have to pay.

Keyword

Environmental problem
The environmental problem poses questions quite different in kind from other problems facing organisa-tions and governments. It is not merely international but global and affects rich and poor alike. It particu-larly affects the Third World which, given its present economic development, is forced to pollute the environment merely to survive.

Learning project

Delta-T

Read the following extract from an article by Alexandra Buxton in *The Guardian* of 20 November 1989 and answer the questions which follow.

Achieving growth while maintaining the ethical and democratic principles on which it is based is always a problem for an expanding worker co-op, especially if it is a high technology business.

Delta-T, based in Burwell, near Newmarket, designs and manufactures scientific instruments for environmental monitoring and plant sciences. More than 75% of the co-operative's sales, often handled through agents, is overseas – many of the products going to Third World countries which desperately need to improve their agriculture.

Alistair Philips, a qualified electronics engineer with more than 17 years' experience, is a member of Delta-T. Three years ago he headed a team of 11 in a Cambridge computer firm; he took a substantial cut in salary to join Delta-T and is one of several members who could easily find better paid jobs locally.

'We choose to work at Delta-T because we value people more highly than money, and ethical trading more highly than making a fast buck,' says Mr Philips.

'It's amazing how much of people's potential is brought out when they work in a supportive environ-ment.

'Our products and sales policy is to encourage a high level of individual commitment. We do not, for example, sell to the military or to South Africa and we state this in our catalogue.'

Delta-T owes its existence to Edmund Potter, a Cambridge engineering graduate, who had spent several years in the kind of firm where the 'boss drives a Porsche and owns a whacking great house', before launching on his own in 1971.

In a reversal of the usual pattern, Mr Potter began with a strong idea of how he wanted to work but not knowing what to make.

'Being socialistically inclined, I had this notion that decision-making and profits should be shared. It's what I call non-authoritarian self-management.'

The majority of co-op members, though having an equal hand in the running of the company and offering a number of skills, specialise in a certain area, be it development or production, sales or administration.

Nevertheless, members are encouraged to try other aspects of the business. Sometimes people who have been taken on to fill a particular role end up in another. Participation in decision-making involves numerous committees and meetings, something new members find daunting, and meticulous attention is paid to sharing more menial tasks.

Delta-T's membership of 25 – and growing – makes it large in terms of the 'new wave' of co-ops which emerged in the 1970s. Inevitably, as the group has grown, there have been problems, nearly always to do with communication. The informal exchanges over a cup of tea which sufficed when the co-op comprised less than 10 people, began to fall apart when it approached 20.

'When there were just a few of us, we could reasonably hope to reach a consensus but in a larger group there's bound to be a divergence of views. I'm glad to say we discovered a wonderful thing called voting. The important thing is to stop a discussion before it drives everyone mad, and count the hands.'

Delta-T's members contradict the stereotype image of a worker co-op as something bound up with lentils, beards, and sandals. However eccentric it may be in mainstream management terms, the company is technically innovative, commercially successful and well-organised.

Each year a proportion of the revenue goes into its 'Socially useful Fund' and is divided between various good causes; in 1988 this amounted to £19,000.

This summer the co-op has invested roughly £200,000 in doubling the size of its premises. A modern extension now abuts the original building – a picturesque barn surrounded by willows – to form a sheltered courtyard where, in fine weather, meetings can be held.

While acknowledging that growth is vital, Mr Potter fears that expansion could encourage the 'creeping rot of complete conventionality', at the cost of some of the principles that members hold dear.

1 What are the advantages and disadvantages of worker co-operatives highlighted in the article?

2 In what ways is the co-op run on 'ethical' principles?

3 From the article, what do you understand by the phrases 'making a fast buck', 'non-authoritarian self-management', and the 'creeping rot of complete conventionality'?

4 What problems is the co-op likely to face if it continues to be successful?

5 Do you think the principles on which the co-op is run can retain staff and ensure continued success in the long-term? Give your reasons.

Further ideas for learning projects

1 Working as a group(s) select a current 'environmental issue', preferably one which is relevant to your geographical area and/or the organisation/industry in which you work.

Research the issue and prepare an illustrated presentation or report on it. Your presentation should cover, as a minimum, the following aspects:

(a) the origins of the issue(s);

(b) scientific evidence both in support of and against the activity(ies) causing the problem;
(c) the costs – private, public and social – both of removing the problem and of carrying on as at present;
(d) the forms of accountability which have or have not been used to stop the problem.

2 Identify and discuss arguments for and against policies of positive discrimination in employment.

13

The price system

CHAPTER OBJECTIVES

After studying this chapter you should be able to:

Define and evaluate the concept of the optimum allocation of resources;
State the defects of the price system as a method of allocating resources;
Define the basic laws of supply and demand;
List the five main determinants of supply;
Describe the consequences of interfering with the price mechanism;
Analyse changes in the equilibrium price.

How the market functions

Allocating resources

In Part One of this book we looked at different economic systems such as collectivism and capitalism. In Part Two we examined how organisations utilise resources in a mixed economy. In this chapter we examine the determination of the prices of consumer goods. If we put the two together, the demand and supply for consumer goods and the demand and supply for factors of production, we obtain a picture of the *price system*, i.e. a method of allocating resources based on free market prices. This is illustrated in Fig. 13.1. This shows the critical importance of prices as the connecting, or communicating, mechanism between households and business organisations.

Any economy is interested in achieving an *optimum allocation of resources*, i.e. the best possible use of scarce resources. This is not, however, simply a measure of technical efficiency. If we considered any commodity, for example shirts, it would be possible to envisage a much more efficient system of production

in which we concentrated on one design and one colour. However, a best use of resources should also be judged by whether it gives people what they want and clearly people are not content to wear identical clothing. Therefore, an acceptable economic system must take account of this.

Consumer sovereignty

It is often said that the 'consumer is king', meaning that the consumer decides what is to be produced by being willing to spend his or her money on those particular goods. It is probably more accurate to say that there is joint sovereignty between the consumer and the producer because the producer's behaviour and objectives will also have a great influence on the market.

The price system is also said, by some people, to be democratic in that every day consumers 'vote' for what they want to be produced by spending their money. Although this is true to some extent, it is considerably modified by the fact that money votes in the economy are unevenly distributed. Thus, those

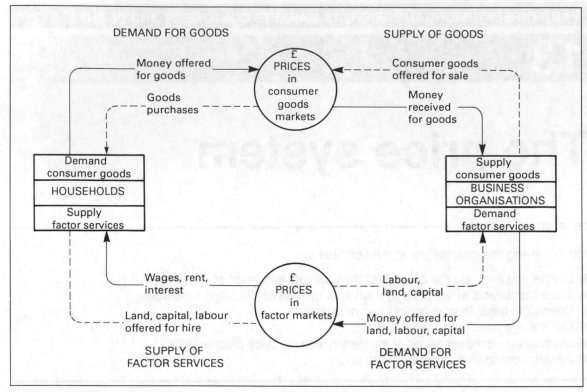

Fig. 13.1 The price system

Economic demand and social need

In this chapter we will see something of how demand and supply help us to deal with the economic problem. Prices are a method of rationing out the scarce goods and services in the economy. The price system provides one answer to the three vital economic questions: *what* shall be produced, *how* shall it be produced and *who* will receive the goods when they have been produced. In many ways the price system is a remarkably efficient mechanism: there are no unsold stocks of goods left rotting; there are no long queues waiting for goods that are in short supply.

There are some commodities, however, which the price system is not so good at producing; things like medical services, defence and education are usually better provided on a community basis. The state also usually intervenes to prohibit or control the sale of certain goods such as dangerous drugs and firearms.

with a high income have more voting power than those who are poor.

Today there is also a great deal of legislation surrounding manufacturing processes, e.g. to prevent organisations from discharging toxic waste, and to impose minimum standards of manufacture. This may increase prices but it is considered better to have safer products made.

The fact that income is unevenly distributed also means that the price system is inequitable. There may be no queues outside the foodshops but nevertheless people may be hungry or starving and simply not have the money to buy food. This is not a problem which is confined to poor nations. Indeed, recent reports in Britain have suggested that many children suffer from malnutrition and each year many old people die of hypothermia because they cannot afford to heat their homes. People of all political persuasions agree that the State should intervene in the running of the economy to ensure social justice. The basic political argument is therefore between those who believe that the price system is basically sound and that the government should intervene by levying taxes to finance old age pensions, defence, etc, and those who wish to see the State taking a bigger part in the direct running of the economy.

1 Consider your own resources and how you allocate them, i.e. how you spend your money. How would this allocation change if:

(a) your real income were to double;
(b) you won £20,000 on premium bonds?

2 Explain with examples the extent to which your lifestyle is supplemented by your consumption of *public goods* and *merit goods*.

Demand

Market demand

The demand for a commodity is the quantity of the good which is purchased over a specific period of time at a certain price. Thus, there are three elements to demand; *price*, *quantity* and *time*. This is the *effective demand* for a good, i.e. the desire to buy the good backed by the ability to do so. It is no use considering people's demand for the good if they do not have the money to realise it.

Other things being equal, it is usually the case that as the price of a commodity is lowered so a greater quantity will be demanded. This is because of the *law of diminishing marginal utility*. The law states that over a specific period of time as more and more units of a commodity are consumed the additional *satisfaction*, or *utility*, derived from their consumption will decrease, other things being equal (*see* page 3). For example, if you have had nothing to drink all day, the utility of a glass of water would be very high indeed and in consequence you would be willing to pay a high price for it. However, as you proceeded to drink a second, third and fourth glass of water the extra utility derived from each would become less. In this case, you might have been willing to pay a great deal for the first glass of water but, as you continue to consume, the price you would be willing to pay would decrease. This would be because you would be deriving a smaller utility from each successive glass. This helps

to clear up the puzzle of why we are willing to pay so little for bread, which is a necessity, and so much for diamonds, which have little practical value. The answer is that we have so much bread that the extra utility derived from another loaf is small whereas we have so few diamonds that each one has a high marginal utility. Thus, this principle helps to explain why more of a good is demanded at a lower price. The extra sales come from existing buyers who buy more and new buyers who could not afford, or who did not think the good was worth buying at, the higher price.

Price effects and income effects

As the price of one commodity falls relative to the price of other goods, people usually buy more of the cheaper good. If, for example, carrots become cheaper than cabbages, people will tend to eat more carrots and less cabbage. This is known as a *price* or *substitution* effect.

If the price of a commodity falls or the prices of commodities in general fall, then the amount of money required to buy them will be less. This leaves the consumer more of his income to spend. If he buys more of that or another commodity this is known as an *income effect*.

The demand curve

The following data is a hypothetical *demand schedule* for wheat. It illustrates the *first law of demand*. This is that, other things being equal, more of a good will be demanded at a lower price.

Table 13.1 The demand schedule

	Price of wheat (£ per qtr tonne)	Quantity of wheat demanded (qtr tonnes per week)
A	50	10
B	40	17
C	30	25
D	20	35
E	10	50

Such information is usually expressed as a graph called a demand curve. As you can see in Fig. 13.2, the graph marked DD slopes downwards from left to

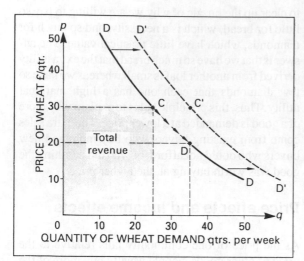

Fig. 13.2 Changes in demand. The movement from C to D is an extension of demand. The movement from C to C' is an increase in demand. If the price is £30 and the quantity demanded is 25 qtrs then the total revenue is £750.

right, and this is almost invariably the case. The relationship between price and the quantity demanded is an inverse relationship since as price *goes down* the quantity demanded *goes up*. If the price is lowered from £30 per qtr to £20 per qtr then the quantity demanded grows from 25 qtrs to 35 qtrs. This can be shown as a movement down the existing demand curve from C to D. This is termed an *extension* of demand. Conversely, if the price of the wheat were raised, this could be shown as a movement up the curve. This is termed a *contraction* of demand. An extension or contraction of demand is brought about by a change in the price of the commodity under consideration and by nothing else.

If there were a failure of the potato crop, people would wish to buy more wheat even though the price of wheat has not fallen. This is shown as a shift of the demand curve to the right. In Fig. 13.2 this is the move from DD to D'D'. As a result of this, at the price of £30, 35 qtrs are demanded instead of 25; we have moved from point C to C'. A movement of the demand curve in this manner is termed an *increase* in demand. If the curve were to move leftwards, for example from D'D' to DD this would be termed a *decrease*. An increase or decrease in demand is brought about by a factor other than a change in the price of the commodity under consideration.

List the factors which you think might bring about an increase in the demand for cars. You have been given the first one.

1 A rise in consumers' incomes.

Total revenue

The total revenue is the total sales receipts in a market at a particular price. In Fig. 13.2 you can see that if the price were £30 per qtr then the quantity demanded would be 25 qtrs per week. Consequently the total revenue would be £750.

Total revenue = Price x Quantity

If the price were lowered to £20 per qtr, the total revenue ($p \times q$) would be £700. You can see that, graphically, the total revenue can be represented as the area of a rectangle drawn under the demand curve.

Consumers' surplus

Consider Fig. 13.3. Here the price in the market is £3 per kg and at this price the quantity demanded is 50 kg. However, we can see from the demand curve that, had the price been £7, there would still have been a demand of 10 kg. Some people derive such a high

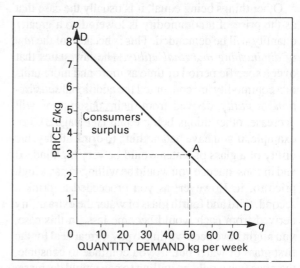

Fig. 13.3 Consumers' surplus. Shaded area is the utility derived but not paid for by those who would have been willing to pay more than the market price.

utility from the consumption of this good that they would be willing to pay this high price. If we consider the market price of £3 we could then argue that the people who would have been willing to pay £7 are receiving £4 worth of utility for which they are not paying. A similar exercise would be carried out for a price £6 and £5 and so on. This excess utility is referred to as a *consumers' surplus*. It would be very good for suppliers if they could charge consumers different prices according to the different utilities they derived from the goods. This, of course, is not possible, so that if suppliers wish to sell 50 kg they must set their price to sell the 50th kg not the first one.

The following information concerns the weekly demand for cartons of chocolate mousse in the MDF supermarket chain. As you can see, demand varies inversely with price.

5,000 cartons @ 60p
7,500 cartons @ 45p
9,000 cartons @ 36p
10,000 cartons @ 30p
10,500 cartons @ 27p

(You will probably need to draw the demand curve to answer the questions which follow.)

1 How many cartons would be bought if the price were:

(a) 42p
(b) 33p?

2 What would the total sales revenue (TR) be if the price were 33p?

3 MDF takes over a smaller supermarket chain and can now sell 50% more cartons at each price. However, it now sells them in packs of four. What is the total sales revenue if the price is £1.26 per pack of four?

Supply

Market supply

By supply we mean the quantity of a commodity that suppliers will wish to supply at a particular price. This is illustrated by Table 13.2. As you can see, the higher

Keywords

The optimum allocation of resources
The situation where it would not be possible to make anyone better off without making someone else worse off.

Consumer sovereignty
Consumers have the ultimate power in the economic system because they can choose to buy or not to buy. However, this position is seriously compromised by monopoly power, government interference and consumers' ignorance.

Market demand
The *quantity* of a product or service which is bought at any particular *price* over a specified period of *time*.

Effective demand
The desire to buy a product backed by the ability to do so.

Price effect
People buy more of a product if it becomes cheaper relative to other products.

Income effect
As a product becomes cheaper it has the effect of making consumers better off in real terms. This causes them to buy more of that or other products.

Demand curve
A graph showing the relationship between the price of a product and the quantity demanded.

Extension of demand
More is demanded *because* the price has been lowered – a movement down the existing demand curve.

Increase in demand
More of a product is demanded because a change in some factor other than the price of the product has caused people to buy more of it – a rightward shift of the demand curve.

Total revenue
The total sales revenue from a product at any particular price. Given by the formula TR = p x q.

Consumers' surplus
The excess of the amount consumers are prepared to pay for a product (rather than go without it) over the amount they actually pay. Graphically it is represented by the area beneath the demand curve but above the price line.

the price, the greater the quantity which suppliers will wish to supply. If the price decreases, there will come a price (£10) at which suppliers are not willing to supply because they cannot make a profit as this point.

Table 13.2 Quantity of a commodity supplied at a particular price

	Price of wheat (£ per qtr tonne)	Quantity of wheat suppliers will be willing to supply (qtr tonnes per week)
A	50	40
B	40	34
C	30	25
D	20	15
E	10	0

A greater quantity is supplied at a higher price because, as the price increases, organisations which could not produce profitably at the lower price find it possible to do so at a higher price. One way of looking at this is that as price goes up less and less efficient firms are brought into the industry. A good example of this is provided by North Sea oil. Britain's oil costs four or five times as much to extract as oil from the Middle East. The low prices of the 1950s and early 1960s would certainly not have allowed Britain to extract the oil profitably but as the price rocketed in the 1970s it became a lucrative trade for Britain. Conversely, when prices dropped in the 1980s it left very narrow profit margins for British companies but profits remained good for the Arab nations.

When asked why more is supplied at a higher price, students frequently reply 'because increased profits can be made'. This you can now see is not so. The organisations which could make a profit at the lower prices do indeed make more profit but the extra supply comes from the marginal firms which are now brought into the industry. Conversely, these marginal firms will be the first to leave the industry if prices fall. Thus, we can conclude that more is supplied at a higher price because at a higher price increased costs can be incurred.

The supply curve

If we take the information from Table 13.2 and plot it as a graph we obtain a supply curve. This is illustrated in Fig. 13.4. As you can see, the supply curve slopes upwards from left to right. This is a direct relationship, i.e. as price *goes up* the quantity supplied will *go up*. If the price increases from £20 per qtr to £30 per qtr

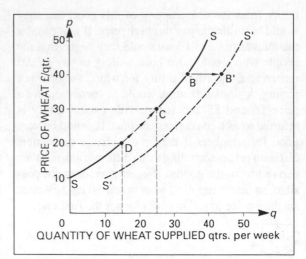

Fig. 13.4 Changes in supply. The movement from D to C is an extension of supply. The movement from B to B' is an increase in supply.

then the quantity suppliers are willing to supply grows from 15 qtrs to 25 qtrs. As with the demand curve, this movement along the supply curve from D to C is called an *extension* of supply. A movement down the curve would be called a *contraction* of supply. As with demand, an extension or contraction is brought about by a change of the price of the commodity under consideration and nothing else.

If the weather were very favourable then farmers would supply more wheat, not because the price had increased but because the harvest had been better than expected. This would have the effect of shifting the supply curve to the right. This is shown as the move from SS to S' S'. Previously, if the price was £40, 34 qtrs would be supplied, after the shift, 44 qtrs are supplied. This movement B to B' is called an *increase* in supply. Conversely, a shift of the curve to the left is termed a *decrease* in supply. An increase or decrease in supply is brought about by a change in a factor other than the price of the commodity under consideration.

Regressive supply curves

Supply curves usually slope upwards from left to right. Sometimes, however, they change direction, as in Fig. 13.5, and are said to become regressive. For example, this might be the case with the supply of labour. In coalmining, where the job is extremely unpleasant, it has often been noticed that as wage rates

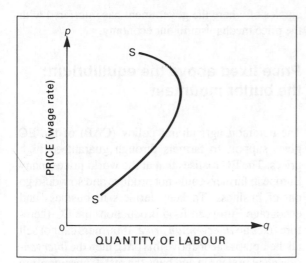

Fig. 13.5 A regressive supply curve. As price continues to rise, less is supplied because suppliers are content with their level of income, and use the increased price to finance increased leisure.

have been increased miners have worked shorter hours. This is because the miners are taking the increased wage rate as increased leisure instead of as money.

The determinants of supply

The behaviour of organisations in the market and the economy is the subject of the greater part of this book. More particularly, the prices and output policy of organisations in the private sector is examined in Chapter 16. In this section of this chapter we simply note the factors which may influence the supply curve.

The most important determinant of supply is *price*. A change in the price of a commodity will cause a movement up or down the existing supply curve. A change in any of the other determinants of supply, which may be termed the *conditions of supply*, will cause a shift, left or right, to a new supply curve.

An important condition of supply is the price of the *factors of production*. A fall in the price of raw materials, for example, would have the effect of moving the supply curve rightwards. The large fall in oil prices in 1986 had this effect upon many industries. The supply of a commodity is also affected by the *price of other commodities*. If there is a rise in the price of barley, this will tend to decrease the supply of wheat as farmers plant more barley. It would be fairly easy for a farmer to do this but economic theory often

assumes that business people in any field can alter production rapidly in this manner. This is obviously unrealistic; it would not be possible for an organisation producing shoes to change and produce cars simply because the price of cars is rising. It is the case, however, that there are often rapid transfers on the Stock Exchange in response to such changes.

Changes in the *level of technology* also affect supply. An improvement in technology allows us to produce more goods with less factors of production. This would, therefore, have the effect of shifting the supply curve to the right.

Some people would also maintain that the *tastes of producers* also affect supply. This is best illustrated in the case of the supply of labour, e.g. in nursing. There, because the suppliers of labour have a vocation they often tolerate low wages and poor working conditions.

Demonstrate the effect on the supply curve of the following situations.

1 The world supply of oil following a war in the Middle East.

2 The supply of North Sea oil as a result of a war in the Middle East.

3 The supply of computers as a result of greater economies of scale in their production.

4 The supply of butter as a result of an outbreak of foot-and-mouth disease.

5 The supply of tomatoes as a result of a good summer.

6 The supply of bread as a result of a rise in the price of wheat.

7 The supply of whisky as a result of increased excise duty.

Equilibrium prices

The formation of an equilibrium price

If we bring the demand and supply curve together we will see how a price is determined in the market

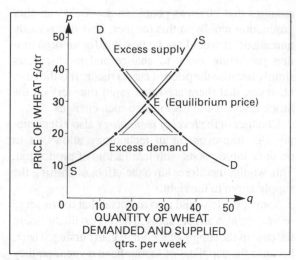

Fig. 13.6 The equilibrium price. At the price of £30 per qtr the quantity which is offered for sale is equal to the quantity people are willing to buy at that price.

situation (*see* Fig. 13.6). As you can see, when the price is £30 per qtr the effective demand for wheat is 25 qtrs per week and this is also the quantity which suppliers will wish to supply. This price is termed the *equilibrium price* since, having arrived at it, there is no tendency for it to change. If the price was higher, for example £40, then suppliers would try to sell 34 qtrs but buyers would only be willing to purchase 17 qtrs. There is an *excess supply* of 17 qtrs. In order to get rid of the surplus, wheat suppliers will have to lower their prices. Conversely, if the price were £20 then buyers would like to purchase 35 qtrs but suppliers would only be willing to sell 15 qtrs. There is an *excess demand* of 20 qtrs. Suppliers will therefore put up their prices to ration out the scarce wheat. The excess demand will have pushed up the price. Thus, there is only one equilibrium price. At any other price there is a tendency to move towards the equilibrium.

Equilibrium prices *ration* out the scarce supply of goods and services. There are no great queues of people demanding the best cuts of meat at the butchers. A price of £10 per kg of fillet steak ensures that only the better off or those who derive great utility from beefsteak buy the meat. It might appear iniquitous to some people that even a small house in London costs £85,000. But if we do away with price as a rationing mechanism we only have to put something else, perhaps equally unacceptable, in its place.

In this section of the chapter we examine two ex-amples of where the government has interfered with the price mechanism in our economy.

Price fixed above the equilibrium: the butter mountain

The common agricultural policy (CAP) of the EC gives support to farmers through guaranteed high prices. The EC realises that at the world prices many European farmers could not produce and so would go out of business. To keep farmers in business and encourage European food production, the EC there-fore fixes an *intervention price*. If farmers cannot sell all their output at or above this price then the *intervention agency* steps in and buys the rest. Consumers are prevented from buying food more cheaply from non-EC countries by the *variable import levy*. Thus, the price of most agricultural products is fixed above the equilibrium price.

Probably the most notorious consequence of this is the 'butter mountain' – the surplus butter production which the EC has to buy up and store because it cannot be sold at the *target price*. In 1989 this amounted to 200 thousand tonnes of butter. In addition to this the EC had bought and stored 1,000,000 tonnes of skimmed milk powder which is enough skimmed milk to keep the whole of the EC supplied for over five years! This is explained in Fig. 13.7. Here the free market price is

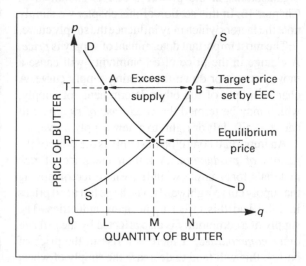

Fig. 13.7 The butter mountain, created by the EC setting the target price above the equilibrium price.

represented as OR. At this price the quantity demanded and supplied is OM and there is, therefore, no excess demand or supply. The target price fixed by the EC is OT (at some times the EC price has been over three times the world price). European housewives are not, however, prepared to pay that price. Thus, the demand contracts to OL, whereas, encouraged by the high price, European farmers apply ON. This, therefore, leaves a quantity of LN to be bought by the intervention agencies, thereby creating the butter mountain. The proportions are greatly exaggerated in this diagram. The excess supply is in the region of 20% but this still amounts to an awful lot of butter!

This method of supporting agriculture is wasteful because it creates surplus food. It is often sold outside the EC at a loss as in 1985 when a large tonnage of butter was sold to the Russians at 40p per kg. Thus the European consumer is paying higher prices in the shops to subsidise Russian consumers. The system is also inequitable since it is poorer families who spend a higher proportion of their budget on food. They are therefore giving a greater proportion of their income to support farmers' incomes and are getting less food as a result of it. Despite attempts to eliminate them, EC farm surpluses remain, not only in dairy products, but also in wheat, wine, olive oil and so on. The practice of selling-off surpluses to the Russians may be justifiable in narrow economic terms, i.e. it is better to receive a few pence per kilogram for the butter than pay the cost of storing it until it rots, but its morality seems highly dubious when the EC refuses to release surpluses to help relieve famines in Africa. The previous British system of supporting agriculture was to give subsidies to farmers. This resulted in more being produced but it was sold at a *lower price*. Although this was still inefficient, since the subsidies had to be paid for by taxes, it had the desired effect of supporting farmers, giving low prices to consumers and creating no excess supply of the good.

Price fixed below the equilibrium: rent control

Since the 1914–18 War there have been several Acts of Parliament which have tried to fix the price of accommodation. These have usually had the laudable motive of trying to ensure reasonably low rents for

Activity

The following information defines the demand and supply curves for 'Daybreak Eggs'.

Price pence/dozen	Quantity demanded dozen/week	Quantity supplied dozen/week
80	1,000	3,400
70	1,600	2,400
60	2,200	1,400
50	2,800	400
40	3,400	—

1 Determine the equilibrium price and quantity of 'Daybreak Eggs' and state them clearly.

2 What is the total sales revenue (TR) at the equilibrium price?

3 Suppose that the EC as part of the Common Agricultural Policy (CAP) were to guarantee a minimum price of 70 pence per dozen for eggs. What are the effects of this policy likely to be?

4 Suppose that in the original situation, as a result of a successful advertising campaign, the demand for eggs increases by 50% at every price. What is the new equilibrium price and quantity of 'Daybreak Eggs'?

tenants. Through inflation, the effect of fixing rents was that in many cases the rent was way below the equilibrium price. As you can see from Fig. 13.8 the effect of this was to create excess demand. The supply of houses for rent contracted as landlords sold their homes rather than lease them at low rents. The number of people who wished to rent became greater. In Fig. 13.8 LN represents the amount of excess demand. Those who occupied rented accommodation were pleased with the low rent and were naturally very unwilling to move, thereby worsening the situation. The fact that until recently landlords have not legally been able to put up prices has frequently led to black market payments such as 'key money' despite it being illegal to demand such payments.

In addition to this there are those living in council houses. Despite increases in rents they remain below the free market equilibrium price. In this case another rationing mechanism comes into play: the housing lists of local authorities.

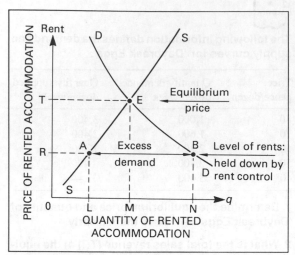

Fig. 13.8 Rent control. Artificially low rents bring about less supply but a greater demand and therefore an excess demand for rented accommodation.

Changes in the equilibrium price

In the previous section we examined the consequences of interfering with an equilibrium price. Prices frequently change, however, as a result of market forces. In this section we examine the four basic changes that are possible in the equilibrium. It is important when considering these changes to stick to the rule of *ceteris paribus* (*see* page 4), i.e. we must keep all other things equal and only consider the effects of one change at a time.

Fig. 13.9 demonstrates the four basic changes. This illustrates all the variations that are possible unless regressive demand and supply curves are considered. You will see that an increase in demand brings about an extension of supply, an increase in supply brings about an extension of demand, and so on. This will take time to come about and there may be several transitional stages before the new equilibrium is reached. However, having reached a new equilibrium, there is no further tendency to change.

Activity

Study the diagram in Fig. 13.9 which shows the effects on equilibrium price and quantity of various changes.

Which one of the diagrams *(a)*, *(b)*, *(c)* or *(d)* best

Keywords

Market supply
The *quantity* of a product which is supplied at any particular *price* over a specified period of *time*.

First principle of supply
Other things being equal, at a higher price producers will wish to supply a greater amount because at a higher price increased costs can be incurred.

Supply curve
A graph showing the relationships between the price of a product and the quantity supplied.

Extension of supply
More is supplied *because* the price of the product has increased – a movement up the existing supply curve.

Increase in supply
More of a product is supplied because of a change in some factor other than the price of the product – a rightward shift of the supply curve.

Determinants of supply
Supply is determined by the price of the product, the price of factors of production and the price of other products. It is also determined by the state of technology, the tastes of producers and by external factors such as the weather.

Equilibrium price
The price at which the wishes (or intentions) of buyers and sellers coincide.

Excess demand
If the price is *below* the equilibrium price, consumers will wish to buy more than suppliers are willing to sell.

Excess supply
At prices *above* the equilibrium price, suppliers will supply more than the consumers are willing to buy.

Price floor
A government imposition of a price set *above* the equilibrium price, e.g. the CAP. The result is excess supply.

Price ceiling
The government intervenes to fix the price *below* the equilibrium. The result is excess demand.

illustrates the effect on the market for:

1 Tomatoes, as a result of a very poor summer;

2 Pork, as a result of a large rise in the price of lamb;

3 Personal computers, as a result of a large rise in the price of microchips;

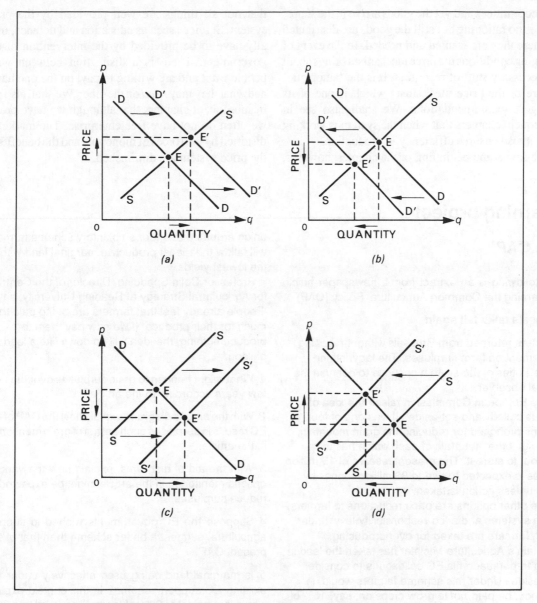

Fig. 13.9 Changes in the equilibrium price. *(a)* Increase in demand results in more being bought at a higher price. *(b)* Decreases in demand results in a smaller quantity being bought at a lower price. *(c)* Increase in supply results in more being supplied at a lower price. *(d)* Decrease in supply results in less being supplied at a higher price.

4 Sales of Flora margarine, as a result of a successful advertising campaign to promote it;

5 Cars, as a result of a fall in the price of petrol;

6 Ice cream, as a result of a very cold summer;

7 Diamonds, as result of a revolution in South Africa;

8 Daz, as a result of a large rise in the price of Persil?

Conclusion

The price system lies at the heart of the free enterprise economy. In the price system there are no state planning committees and yet the goods arrive in the shops; there is no rationing but still the goods are distributed to where they are wanted and needed. In the event of changing conditions the price mechanism brings about the necessary shift of resources. It is the 'automatic' feature of the price mechanism which is one of its strongest recommendations. We shall also see in subsequent chapters that when the system is working well, it also ensures efficiency in production.

We saw at the beginning of the chapter, however, that not all things are well provided by the price system. Services such as education and defence, usually have to be provided by the intervention of the government. There is a distinction between what people *want* and are willing to pay, on the one hand, and what they may *need* on the other. We shall also see in subsequent chapters that although we have prices we often do not have free enterprise. The market is distorted by the forces of monopoly and the benefits of the price system are diminished.

Learning project

The CAP

The following is an extract from a newspaper article concerning the Common Agricultural Policy (CAP).

Brussels talks fail again

Ministers returned from Brussels without reaching agreement on farm surpluses. The labyrinthine complexities of the system continue to confuse the casual observer.

The European Commission raised the idea of what is called 'land set-aside'. It was one of four options proposed for reducing the grain mountain, and with it the mountain of cash which has to be paid out to store it. The present reserve of 15 million tonnes is expected to rise to 80 million tonnes by 1991 unless action is taken.

The other options are price reductions to farmers, quota systems and a 'co-responsibility levy' under which farmers are taxed for over-producing.

Britain's Agriculture Minister has taken the lead in trying to persuade his EC colleagues to consider 'set-aside'. Under this scheme farmers would, in essence, be paid *not* to grow crops on, say, 10% of their acreage.

The NFU favours a compulsory scheme. The union argues that under a voluntary scheme farmers will fallow their least productive marginal land with the lowest yields.

Professor Colin Spedding, Director of the Centre for Agricultural Strategy at Reading University, says 'People already feel that farmers are being paid too much for their produce. If we now pay them to produce nothing, the idea will go down like a lead balloon.'

1 What might happen to grain surpluses over the next few years according to the article?

2 With the aid of a diagram, explain how the CAP of the EC results in surpluses such as that of grain mentioned in the article.

3 With the aid of diagrams, explain how the various options mentioned in the article might be expected to reduce surpluses.

4 Suppose the EC governments wished to support agriculture, suggest a better scheme than that of the present CAP.

5 Is marginal land being used effectively under the existing EC support scheme? In this context explain why a 'set-aside' of 20% of land will not lead to a 20% drop in output.

Further ideas for learning projects

1 In an informal report, analyse the effects of the recent changes in legislation governing private rented accommodation. (You will probably need to refer to Chapter 9 to complete this project.)

2 In 1973 crude oil cost around $5 per barrel, in 1980 around $40 and in early 1990 around $18. With the aid of demand and supply diagrams analyse and explain these changes. Consider the effects of these changes on the UK economy.

3 Discuss the merits of extending the price mechanism to higher education.

14

Aspects of demand

CHAPTER OBJECTIVES

After studying this chapter you should be able to:

- Define market demand and evaluate its importance to the business organisation;
- List and describe the determinants of demand;
- Calculate the elasticities of demand;
- Analyse the effect of sales tax on the market.

What determines demand?

The market as a mechanism and the market as 'demand'

In the last chapter we saw how the market functions as a mechanism for allocating goods and services in the economy. Left to itself the price mechanism can answer the three fundamental questions of economics: *what* shall be produced; *how* shall it be produced; and *for whom*? The price mechanism, then, is a means of communication between the very disparate organisations which make up the economy. Most organisations, however, are not interested in the market mechanism from this point of view. The thing which concerns trading organisations is the market for their particular product, that is to say how much of their output they can sell and for how much. In this chapter we examine markets from this point of view.

Price

We fully discussed the relationship between the price of a good and the demand for it in the previous chapter. We may note here that price is the single most important factor in determining the demand for a good. It is interesting to note that there are a few exceptions to the *first law of demand*, i.e. where a rise in the price of a commodity *causes* more of that commodity to be demanded. We will now consider three such examples.

1 Goods demanded for their price ('snob value'). With some expensive items, such as a Rolls Royce or Chanel perfume, the consumer may buy the commodity because it is expensive, i.e. the price is part of the attraction of the article and a rise in its price may render it more attractive.

2 An expectation of a further change in price. You may observe a *perverse demand* relationship on the Stock Exchange; a rise in the price of a share often renders it more attractive causing people to buy it and vice versa.

3 Giffen Goods. Robert Giffen, a 19th century statistician, was studying the economy and noticed that a rise in the price of potatoes caused more to be bought but when the price went down, less were bought. In other words, the normal demand relationship appeared to be back-to-front.

For a Giffen effect to take place two conditions are necessary. First, the the product considered must be an *inferior good*, i.e. something which people would prefer less of if they were richer – in the case of potatoes they might prefer more meat, cheese etc.

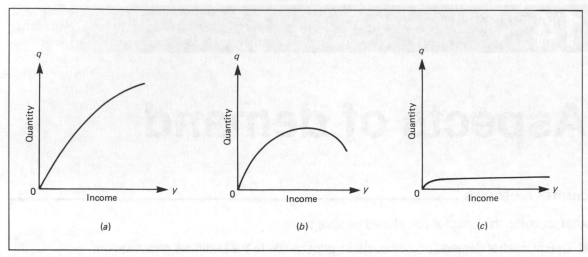

Fig. 14.1 Income and demand. *(a)* Normal goods *(b)* Inferior goods *(c)* Inexpensive foodstuffs, e.g. salt.

(Inferior goods are more fully explained below.) Second, households must be spending the majority of their family budget on the inferior good. In Ireland in the mid-19th century, for example, peasant families might have weekly incomes of less than £1 per week. Consider what might happen if the price of potatoes fell by 50%. Households would now be better off in real terms (income effect) and therefore be able to afford small amounts of better foods and thus need less potatoes. However, when the price of potatoes rose again, households had to switch back to living entirely on potatoes because it was the only foodstuff that they could afford enough of to stay alive.

Thus, you can see that the demand relationship is back-to-front (perverse) because dropping the price caused less to be bought and vice versa. Remember, it is necessary to have very peculiar circumstances to get a Giffen effect. Potatoes cannot be said to be a Giffen good today because for this to be true the average family would have to spend £150 a week on potatoes! You must look to very poor Third World countries to observe Giffen effects.

Income

Since *effective demand* is the desire to buy a good backed by the ability to do so, it is obvious that there must be a relationship between the demand for an organisation's product and the consumer's purchasing power. Purchasing power is usually closely linked to

income. The nature of the relationship between income and demand will depend upon the product. A rise in income is hardly likely to send most consumers out to buy more bread whereas it might cause them to buy a larger car. If the demand for a commodity increases as income increases it is said to be a *normal good*. Conversely, if the demand for a product goes down as income rises, then it is said to be an *inferior good*. There are some products, for example salt, which tend to have a constant demand whatever the level of income. These three possibilities are illustrated in Fig. 14.1.

You will note that the demand for the inferior good behaves like the demand for a normal good at low levels of income. All inferior goods start out as normal goods and only become inferior as income continues to rise. Cotton sheets might be considered an inferior good if you substituted silk sheets as you became very wealthy. In other words, the goods are not intrinsically inferior, it is the commodity's relationship with income which is inferior. It is, however, commodities such as bread and potatoes which are usually termed inferior, since here the relationship of *market* demand with the community's income is inferior, whereas the demand for a product such as cotton sheets is not.

The price of other goods

In marketing its products any organisation is aware that it is competing for a share of a limited amount of

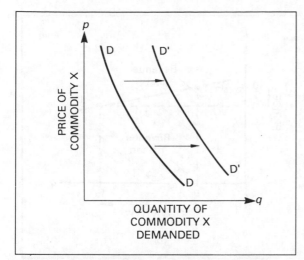

Fig. 14.2 A shift in demand. An increase in demand brought about by a change in the conditions of demand, e.g. a fall in the price of a complement, a rise in the price of a substitute, a rise in income if commodity X is a normal 'good', a fall in income if commodity X is an 'inferior good', a change in taste in favour of commodity X, or a successful advertising campaign.

households' incomes. In this sense all demands are interrelated. However, there are two particular interrelationships of demand which may be observed; these occur when goods are *substitutes* one for another or are *complementary*. Examples of substitute commodities would be tea and coffee, or butter and margarine, where one consumes one or the other. The case of complementary or *joint* demand is illustrated by commodities such as cars and petrol, or strawberries and cream. In all these cases there is a relationship between the price of one commodity and the demand for the other. If, for example, the price of cars were decreased this would cause more cars to be bought and hence an increase in the demand for petrol.

Other factors influencing demand

When discussing the factors influencing demand we must remember the rule of *ceteris paribus*. That is to say, for example, we can only conclude that a fall in the price of a complementary good such as cars would increase the demand for petrol if we state that all other things remain equal. If, for example, incomes decrease at the same time it would be impossible to come to any conclusion.

The factors we have discussed above, i.e. price, the price of other goods and income, are to a certain extent quantifiable. There are numerous factors which can influence demand, many of which it would be extremely difficult to quantify. However, as we stated in the last chapter, it is possible to conclude that if we change any of the determinants of demand other than price, i.e. any of the *conditions of demand*, we will cause an increase or decrease in demand (*see* Fig. 14.2). You will remember that the effect of this is to shift the demand curve rightwards or leftwards.

Suppose that you own a business which imports and markets personal computers from Japan. What would you expect the effect of the following factors to be on your sales over the next 12 months?

(a) **Real personal disposable incomes rise by 2.5%.**
(b) **The external value of the pound falls by 15%.**
(c) **Amstrad start a major advertising campaign for their products.**
(d) **The Chancellor of the Exchequer reduces direct taxes but increases VAT.**

We list below some of the other factors which may influence demand.

1 Tastes, habits and customs. These are extremely important determinants of demand but rather intangible and difficult to evaluate. We can say, however, that if a product comes more into favour with consumers then an increase in demand will occur and this will shift the demand curve rightwards.

2 Changes in population. Demand is obviously influenced by the number of people in the economy and the age, sex and geographical distribution of the population.

3 Seasonal factors. The demand for many products, such as clothing, food and heating, is influenced by the season.

4 The distribution of income. It is not only the level of income which influences demand but also the distribution of income. A more even distribution of income might increase the demand for hi-fi equipment but decrease the demand for luxury yachts.

5 Advertising. A successful advertising campaign would obviously increase the demand for a product. Advertising might also be aimed at making the de-

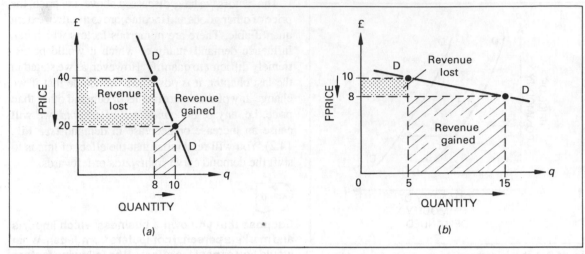

Fig. 14.3 Elasticity of demand. *(a)* Inelastic demand. *(b)* Elastic demand.

mand for a product less elastic (*see* below).

6 *Government influences.* The Government frequently influences demand: for example by making it compulsory to wear seat belts, it increased the demand for them.

Students are often tempted to say that supply is a determinant of demand; this is *not* so. Supply influences affect demand only via the price of the commodity (*see* page 249). Similarly, indirect taxes on commodities, e.g. VAT, or subsidies, are supply influences since they affect the costs of production (*see* page 260).

Measuring demand

Price elasticity

So far we have said that if price is lowered, other things being equal, a greater quantity will be demanded. Thus, the demand curve slopes downwards from left to right. If, however, an organisation is going to cut its prices then it would be advantageous for it to know how much more was going to be demanded. A cut in price might cause a lot more to be demanded or not very much more. This is illustrated in Fig. 14.3.

In Fig. 14.3 *(a)* you can see that a relatively large drop in price from £40 to £20 results in demand growing by a relatively small amount, from eight to ten units. Thus, demand is not very *responsive* to

Keywords _____

Determinants of demand
Demand is determined by price, consumers' incomes, the price of other goods, and other factors such as tastes and advertising.

Perverse demand
Demand may increase with price and vice versa in the case of Giffen goods, where a further change in price is expected, and where the goods have 'snob value'.

Normal goods
Those goods for which the demand increases with consumers' incomes.

Inferior goods
Those goods for which the demand decreases with consumers' incomes.

Complements
Products which are demanded together, e.g. gin and tonic. This situation can also be termed *joint demand*.

Rightward shift
The demand curve for a product would shift rightwards as the result of a fall in the price of a complement, a rise in the price of a substitute, a rise in income if it is a normal good or a fall in income if it is an inferior good, or a change in taste in favour of the commodity.

changes in price. We term this an *inelastic demand*. However, in Fig. 14.3 *(b)* a relatively small fall in price causes a proportionately much greater rise in demand. In this case demand is *responsive* to changes in price. Here the demand is said to be *elastic*.

Activity

Consider the list of products below and for each decide whether the demand for it is elastic or inelastic. Give reasons for your choices.

- Salt
- Domestic gas
- Package holidays
- A 'second car'
- Tea

- Cigarettes
- Beer
- Chanel perfume
- Oxo cubes
- Household furniture

The criteria we have discussed above are somewhat vague but elasticity can be categorised precisely by looking at total revenue. If the price of a commodity is lowered and the total revenue ($p \times q$) increases then demand is elastic. Conversely, if the price of the commodity is lowered and the total revenue ($p \times q$) decreases then demand is *inelastic*. There is also an in between case where if the price is lowered and this causes just enough more to be demanded so that total revenue ($p \times q$) remains unaltered then demand is unitary. These principles may be summarised as follows:

(a) demand is *elastic* where:
    price decreases – total revenue increases
    price increases – total revenue decreases
(b) demand is *inelastic* where:
    price decreases – total revenue decreases
    price increases – total revenue increases
(c) demand is *unitary* where:
    price changes (+) or (–) – total revenue constant.

This is illustrated in Fig. 14.3.

You can see from this why elasticity of demand is of crucial importance to a business organisation. If, for example, four of the five major car manufacturers in the UK announced price increases while the fifth announced a price decrease, can you determine from the above principles which categories of elasticity they thought existed for their products?

Activity

Explain how the value of price elasticity of demand will affect the success of the following actions.

1 Cinema owners increase the price of admissions in order to increase their receipts;

2 London Regional Transport reduces tube fares to attract more customers and increase its receipts.

It might be thought that elasticity could be judged from the slope of the demand curve. In Fig. 14.3 the steep curve is inelastic demand and the one tending towards the horizontal is elastic. But the appearance of the curve is *not* a reliable guide. It is only at the extremes that it is possible to reach a definite conclusion about the category of elasticity simply by looking at the curve. These extremes are illustrated in Fig. 14.4. Where the demand curve is vertical (Fig. 14.4 *(a)*) there is no elasticity at all and demand is said to be perfectly, or absolutely, inelastic. Conversely, where

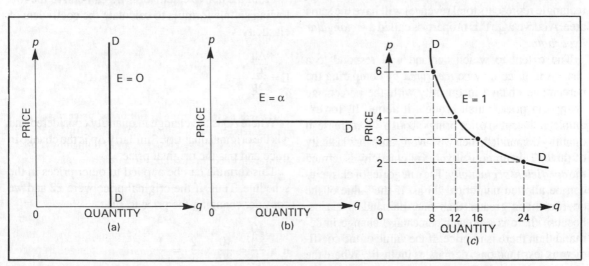

Fig. 14.4 The limits of elasticity. *(a)* Totally inelastic demand. *(b)* Perfectly elastic demand. *(c)* Unitary demand.

Table 14.1 Demand schedule

Column	Price of commodity £/kg (1)	Quantity demanded kg/week (2)	Total revenue £s (3)	Category of elasticity (4)
A	10	0	0	
B	9	10	90	
C	8	20	160	Elastic
D	7	30	210	
E	6	40	240	
F	5	50	250	Unitary
G	4	60	240	
H	3	70	210	Inelastic
I	2	80	160	
J	1	90	90	

the demand curve is horizontal demand is said to be perfectly, or infinitely, elastic (*see* Fig. 14.4 *(b)*). Unitary demand poses a difficult problem. A demand curve which has unitary elasticity along its whole length must have the property that, whatever the price, the total revenue remains constant. Thus, whatever point on the demand curve we choose, the value we get when we multiply the price by the quantity, i.e. the total revenue, must be constant. You can see in Fig. 14.4 *(c)* that if the prices is 6 then the quantity demanded is 8 and therefore the total revenue is 48. If we choose the price of 4 then the demand is 12 and therefore the total revenue is 48 and so on.

Another way to put this is to say that any rectangle we draw under the demand curve (remember that the rectangle represents total revenue) will have the same area. A curve with this property is called a *rectangular hyperbola*.

The extent to which demand will respond to a change in price may be *measured by* comparing the percentage change in quantity with the percentage change in price which brought it about. If, for example, a 1% cut in price brings about a 3% increase in quantity demanded, then we have a value for elasticity of three. This numerical value of elasticity is termed the *coefficient of elasticity*. The categories of elasticity can be allotted numerical limits. If the value of the coefficient is greater than one, demand is elastic, because there is a greater percentage change in demand than there is in price. If the value of the coefficient is less than one, demand is inelastic. Where the value of the coefficient is exactly one, elasticity is

unitary because the percentage change in quantity is equal to the percentage change in price thereby leaving total revenue unchanged. We therefore work out the value of the coefficient (E) by the following formula.

$$E = \frac{\% \text{ change in quantity}}{\% \text{ change in price}}$$

We can illustrate this by considering the demand schedule in Table 14.1.

Suppose that the organisation which markets this commodity is selling it at £8 per kilo, then it might consider what the effect would be if it lowered the price to £7. You can see from column *(2)* that the quantity demanded would grow from 20 kg per week to 30. A 12.5% cut in price has therefore brought about a 50% growth in demand. The percentages involved here are very simple to work out and you can probably calculate them in your head but we need a formula if the figures are not so straightforward. We can write out the above calculation as:

$$E = \frac{\% \text{ change in quantity}}{\% \text{ change in price}} = \frac{\frac{10}{20} \times \frac{100}{1}}{\frac{1}{8} \times \frac{100}{1}} = 4$$

In this case the coefficient is 4 and since this is greater than 1, demand is elastic. You can confirm this by checking the change in total revenue in column *(3)*. Here a cut in price has resulted in an increase in total revenue, so demand is, indeed, elastic.

From the above calculation we can derive the following simple formula to calculate the coefficient of elasticity:

$$E = \frac{\frac{\Delta q}{q}}{\frac{\Delta p}{p}}$$

Where Δq is the change in quantity considered and q is the original quantity. Similarly Δp is the change in price and p is the original price.

This formula can be applied to other prices in the schedule. Thus, if the original price were £2 and we consider changing the price to £1:

$$E = \frac{\frac{10}{80}}{\frac{1}{2}} = \frac{10}{80} \times \frac{2}{1} = \frac{1}{4}$$

Thus, the coefficient is less than one and demand is inelastic. If the value of the coefficient is 1/4, this tells the seller of the commodity that if they cut their price by 1% it will result in only a 1/4% more being bought. The elasticity of demand should be unitary where total revenue is maximised. In our example this is at a price of £5 per kg. This we can confirm by calculating the coefficient at that price:

$$E = \frac{\frac{10}{50}}{\frac{1}{5}} = \frac{10}{50} \times \frac{5}{1} = 1$$

The demand schedule of Table 14.1 is presented as a demand curve in Fig. 14.5. From this you can see that although the slope is constant, i.e. it is a straight line, the elasticity changes along its whole length. We have already seen evidence of this from the calculations we did above. In fact, at each point we choose the elasticity will be different. If we start at point A we can determine the value of the coefficient as infinity. The value then drops until it reaches 1 (unity) at point F, half way along the length of the demand curve. It finally reaches zero at point K when it hits the horizontal axis. You can check that this is correct by calculating the coefficient at various points.

1 The following information represents the demand and supply for product X.

Price of X £	Quantity of X per week Supplied	Demanded
70	100,000	40,000
60	80,000	50,000
50	60,000	60,000
40	40,000	70,000
30	20,000	80,000
—		90,000

(a) **What is the coefficient of elasticity of demand at the equilibrium price?**
(b) **If there were only one company supplying product X, would there by any advantage in it increasing its prices?**
(c) **Explain how you would set about measuring the elasticity of supply.**
(d) **If possible, calculate the coefficient of elastic-**

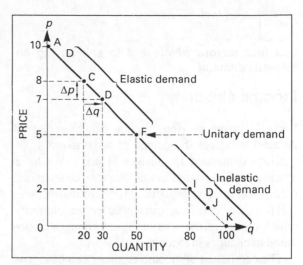

Fig. 14.5 Elasticity of demand. One demand curve can have all three categories of elasticity.

ity of supply at the equilibrium price. In what way does this differ from the value for demand and why?

2 Consider what the value of elasticity of demand for Giffen goods would be. What other products might have a similar value?

The factors which determine the degree of price elasticity are as follows.

1 The number of substitutes available. The greater the number of substitutes, the greater the elasticity will tend to be.
2 The percentage of income spent on the good. If a purchase takes up a large percentage of income, for example buying a car, this tends to make the demand more elastic.
3 Durability. Durable goods, for example cars and furniture, usually have a higher elasticity of demand than perishable goods, such as food.
4 The number of uses for the commodity. If the same product can be put to many different uses this tends to increase the elasticity of demand for it.

Thus, cigarettes, which have no substitute, occupy a relatively small proportion of a person's income, have no durability and only one use, therefore have a very low elasticity of demand. In addition to this, cigarettes are addictive. You will note here that the product does not have to be a necessity to have an inelastic demand.

List four factors which lead to salt having an inelastic demand.

Income elasticity

We said in the previous section that elasticity of demand measures the degree of responsiveness of quantity demanded to changes in price. We have already made the point in this chapter that there is a measurable relationship between demand and income. It is possible, therefore, to calculate *income elasticity* which measures the relationship of changes in demand to changes in income.

The coefficient of income elasticity can be calculated as:

$$Ey = \frac{\% \text{ change in quantity}}{\% \text{ change in income}} = \frac{\frac{\Delta q}{q}}{\frac{\Delta y}{y}}$$

where y = income.

If an organisation is selling a normal good such as cars it might expect that as incomes rise so would the demand for cars. In this case an increase in income (+) has brought about an increase (+) in demand. The value of the coefficient is therefore positive. If, however, the organisation sells inferior goods such as potatoes, then as income rises (+) demand will decrease (–). The value of the coefficient will therefore

be negative. For some goods, such as salt, the demand may not vary at all with income and in these cases there is zero income elasticity. These possibilities are illustrated in Fig. 14.6 (*see also* Fig. 14.1).

List the following in the order of their responsiveness to increases in income: video recorders; cigarettes; petrol; beef; foreign holidays; salt; potatoes.

Cross elasticity

Where there is a relationship between the price of one commodity and the demand for another and it is possible to measure this, it is termed the *cross elasticity of demand*. There is, therefore, a coefficient of cross elasticity and this may be calculated as:

$$Ec = \frac{\% \text{ change in quantity of commodity B}}{\% \text{ change in price of commodity A}} = \frac{\frac{\Delta qB}{qB}}{\frac{\Delta pA}{pA}}$$

In the case of complementary commodities a fall in the price of one should increase the demand for the other. For example, an oil company might expect an increase in demand for petrol as the result of a fall in the price of cars. In this case the value of the coefficient would be negative since a decrease (–) in the price of cars has brought about an increase (+) in the

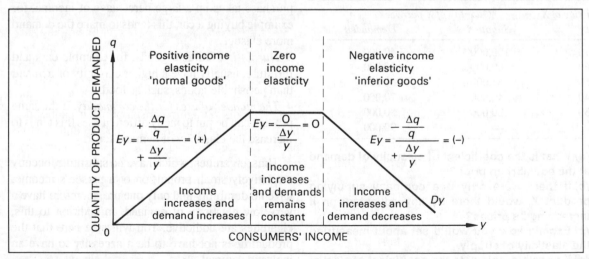

Fig. 14.6 Income elasticities

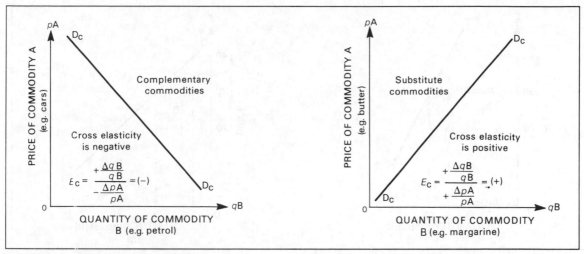

Fig. 14.7 Cross elasticities of demand

demand for petrol (*see* Fig.14.7).

Conversely, if an organisation were selling a commodity for which there were a substitute the opposite would be the case. For example, a margarine company might expect a decrease in the demand for its product as a result of a fall in the price of butter. In this case a decrease (–) in the price of one product has led to a decrease (–) in the demand for the other and the value of the coefficient is therefore positive (*see also* page 252).

Activity

Consider the demand for petrol. List three pairs of products which are complements and three which are substitutes.

Elasticity and tax revenues

We have already explained that elasticity of demand is of great importance to a trading organisation. If an organisation knew that the demand for its products were inelastic it might be tempted to raise its prices, whereas it might be tempted to lower its prices if it believed the demand were elastic. (A simple observation of this is complicated by changes in the general price level brought about by inflation.) The Chancellor of the Exchequer is also concerned with the elasticity of demand for the products on which he levies indirect taxes such as VAT and Customs and Excise duty.

Activity

Explain under what circumstances you would expect to observe a Giffen paradox in the world today.

In Fig. 14.8 a tax of £10 per unit is levied on the commodities. This raises the price to £30 per unit. In (*a*) this raises a tax revenue of £100,000 (10 x 10,000), whereas in (*b*) the tax revenue is £30,000 (£10 x 3,000). If, instead of a £10 tax, the Chancellor were to impose a £20 tax you can see that where the demand is inelastic the tax revenue would now be £180,000, whereas where the demand is elastic tax revenue would only be £20,000. Thus, in the latter case, increasing the tax has decreased the tax revenue. This is because where demand is elastic, increasing the price through higher taxation discourages sales to such an extent that less tax revenue is raised. When the Chancellor imposes an indirect tax on a commodity it can therefore be with the object of either raising more money *or* discouraging consumption: it cannot do both. This point is illustrated by excise duty on tobacco. Chancellors have frequently said that they are raising the tax on tobacco to discourage smokers. However, since the demand for tobacco is extremely inelastic it is to be doubted whether the government means this but rather is using this argument to legitimise the increasing of an already very high tax.

It is commonly believed that it is only the consumer who pays indirect taxes. This is not always so. The

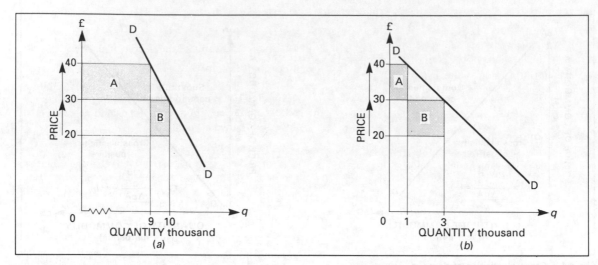

Fig. 14.8 Revenue from an indirect tax. *(a)* Inelastic demand. (b) Elastic demand. A = revenue gained by raising the tax; B = revenue lost by raising the tax. Only if A is greater than B will raising the tax be worthwhile.

incidence of taxation depends upon the elasticity of demand for the product. This is demonstrated in Fig. 14.9.

Indirect taxes have the effect of moving the supply curve of the commodity vertically upwards by the amount of the tax. In Fig. 14.9 this is the move from SS to S'S' where the amount of the tax is shown by the arrows. The equilibrium price increases from E to E'. The price does not go up by the full amount of the tax because part of the tax has been absorbed by producers who are worried about the effect increased prices would have on their sales. The greater the elasticity of

demand, the greater the percentage of the tax the producers will absorb. If, therefore, the tax on tobacco is increased, most of the increase is passed on to consumers. This is because the demand is very inelastic. However, if the tax were increased on cars, more of it would be absorbed by the motor trade because the demand is more elastic.

In 1983 the Chancellor raised the excise duty on cigarettes but was surprised to find that the tax revenue from their sales fell. With the aid of a diagram explain why this was so.

There are two ways of imposing an indirect tax. First, it could be a *specific* or *unit* tax, where the tax is the same per unit of a commodity irrespective of its price. In Britain, the most important unit taxes are the excise duties on tobacco, alcohol and petrol. The other method is to levy a tax by the value of the commodity, this – being known as an *ad valorem* tax – is VAT.

Conclusion

We have now finished our survey of demand and supply and you should be able to explain the importance of price as a method of distributing goods and services. In addition, you should be able to use the techniques of demand and supply curves and the

Fig. 14.9 The incidence of an indirect tax

measurement of elasticity to analyse market situations.

In the next three chapters we are going to look at some of the physical characteristics of markets in more detail and later at the framework of law that regulates them.

Keywords _____

Elasticity of demand
This measures the degree of responsiveness of the quantity demanded to changes in price.

Elastic demand
A fall in price increases total revenue and a rise in price decreases it.

Inelastic demand
A fall in price decreases total revenue and a rise in price increases it.

Unitary demand
Any change in price leaves the total revenue unchanged.

Coefficient of elasticity
The numerical value of the degree of elasticity.

Income elasticity
Measures the degree of responsiveness of the quantity demanded to changes in consumers' incomes. It is positive in the case of normal goods and negative in the case of inferior goods.

Cross elasticity of demand
Measures the degree of responsiveness of the quantity demanded of the good to changes in the price of another. The value of cross elasticity is negative in the case of complements and positive in the case of substitutes.

Incidence of tax
The distribution of an indirect tax between producers and consumers depends on the elasticity of demand for the product.

Learning project _____

Personal income, goods and services

Study the information contained in the figure on the next page. This shows indices of the sales of various categories of household goods and services. It also shows personal disposable income (PDI), i.e. people's incomes after deducting income tax and national insurance contributions.

All figures are in *real* terms, i.e. the effects of inflation have been discounted. First make sure that you understand what an index is and why all the graphs pass through 100 in 1985.

1 Describe the patterns of expenditure which the graph shows.

2 Use this information to comment upon the concept of income elasticity of demand.

3 The index of PDI was 103.7 in 1986 whereas that for household expenditure on tobacco was 97. From this information calculate the income elasticity of demand for tobacco. Does this suggest that tobacco is an inferior good or could this value be explained some other way?

4 What would be the effect on the index for tobacco if the Chancellor were to significantly increase the tax on cigarettes?

5 What reasons account for the large increase in the index for TV and video?

Further ideas for learning projects _____

1 Examine the effect of the availability and cost of credit upon consumers' expenditure.

2 Compare the effects of increasing excise duty with those of increasing VAT.

3 Conduct a survey of the price of ten products in ten different local retail outlets. Explain the observed differences (and similarities) of the prices paying particular attention to the concept of elasticity of demand. Present your findings in the form of a short report using tables and other appropriate means to illustrate your findings.

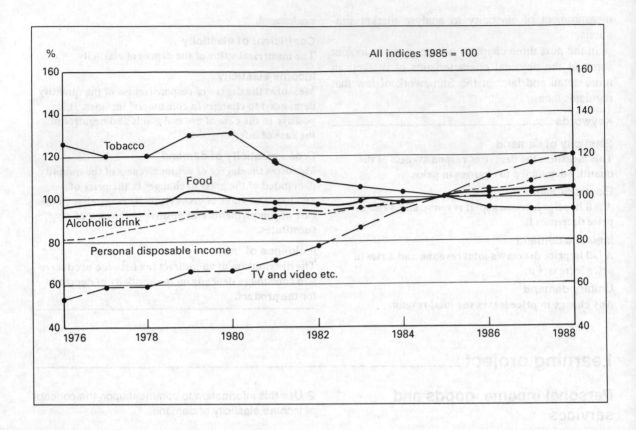

15

From producer to consumer

CHAPTER OBJECTIVES

After studying this chapter you should be able to:

■ Describe different market places;
■ Identify the different activities involved in marketing;
■ Appreciate the importance and cost of marketing in both the public and private sectors;
■ Describe the function of advertising;
■ Analyse the inter-relationship among the components of the chain of distribution.

Distribution

Market places

In previous chapters we have discussed the market as a *mechanism* and as *the demand* for a particular commodity. However, when people think of the word market in the sense of market place, somewhat different concepts are involved. In this sense a market is any means by which buyers and sellers are brought together. This may be directly, as in a street market such as Petticoat Lane, or indirectly, as for example, by computer screens, fax and telex machines in foreign exchange markets. A market can be local, national or international. Which it is will depend upon the nature of the commodity, the state of communications and upon government restrictions. Some of the main types of market are listed below.

1 Retailing. Goods and services are sold to the final consumers; usually through shops.
2 Wholesaling. Commodities are sold to retailers for resale to consumers. As well as general wholesalers, there are specialist markets such as Billingsgate for fish and Smithfield for meat.

3 Commodity markets. Since Sir Thomas Gresham built the Royal Exchange in 1571, London has had important commodity markets where raw materials are bought and sold both for use in the UK and abroad. Indeed, Britain remains the world centre for many of these trades. There are about 40 commodity trade associations which make up the *British Federation of Commodity Associations*. The following are examples of these markets.

(a) The London Commodity Exchange at Plantation House: markets in rubber, cocoa, jute and sugar.
(b) The Tea Auction Room in Plantation House: markets for both tea and coffee.
(c) The Baltic Exchange: markets for coarse grains, oils and oil seeds.
(d) Hatton Garden: market for gem stones and industrial diamonds.
(e) Beaver House: market for furs.

There have been commodity markets outside London such as the Manchester Royal Exchange and the Bradford Wool Exchange.
4 Shipping and insurance. London remains a world centre for both shipping and insurance services. These are centred on Lloyds. Shipping services are also sold

on the Baltic Exchange.

5 Financial Markets. There are many national and international financial markets in London (*see* Chapter 23).

(a) The money market; loans made for very short periods, i.e. money 'at call or short notice.'

(b) The discount market; dealing in bills of exchange, both Treasury bills and commercial bills.

(c) The capital market; dealing with the provision of capital both to government and industry.

(d) The new issue market; dealing with the raising of capital through the issue of new stocks and shares.

(e) The stock market; dealing in the sale and purchase of previously issued stocks and shares.

(f) The foreign exchange market; dealing in the sale and purchase of foreign currencies.

Trading is carried on in the markets in very different manners, some of which are listed below.

1 Auctions. Sales of easily standardised commodities such as tea or grain are carried out by auction. London is also a centre of the auction market for antiques and works of art.

2 Private deal. This is where a broker concludes a deal with a trader on behalf of a client, having approached several sellers to obtain the best terms. This is the practice, for example, on the Stock Exchange and the Baltic Exchange.

3 Ring trading. This is the practice on the Metal Exchange where the forty members of the ring sit in a circle bidding for one consignment of metal at a time, until the five minute limit is announced by the ringing of a bell. The problems of the commodity market in tin made news in 1986 when the price collapsed and the market ceased trading.

4 'Sights' market. The seller shows his commodity, asks a certain price and if this is not met he withdraws it from the market. This is the case in the sale of diamonds. The sellers of diamonds have frequently acted as a *cartel* to restrict the flow of diamonds to the market and thereby raise their price.

5 'Spot' markets. This is where the goods are sold for immediate delivery and could have been sold by any of the above methods.

6 'Futures' markets. In this case the goods are purchased 'forward'. That is to say, they will be supplied at the agreed price at some time in the future. This is often the case with commodities such as metals, grains and sugar. This gives the seller the certainty of an agreed price and the buyer the possibility of a speculative gain if prices rise. It also gives rise to much speculative dealing as the futures themselves are bought and sold many times. Not just commodities but also financial assets are traded on the London International Financial Futures Exchange (LIFFE).

You can see that there are many different ways in which goods can be bought and sold. Indeed, in international trade *barter* is re-establishing itself. Countries are directly swapping goods to avoid the uncertainties brought about by changes in exchange rates. This is known as *counter-trade*. Counter-trade has become quite popular with Third World and Eastern Bloc countries because of the uncertainty of the value of their currencies.

We will now proceed to look at the physical methods by which goods are transferred from producer to consumer.

Channels of distribution

The most direct channel of distribution is when the manufacturer sells directly to the customer. This may be the case, for example, with very expensive equipment such as aircraft or, alternatively, with individually customised items such as bespoke tailoring. There are often, however, one or more intermediate stages between the manufacturer and the customer.

There are, of course, many different ways in which finished products can reach the customer and the product may pass through many different hands before being sold to its eventual owner. Fig. 15.1 summarises some of the more common channels of distribution.

Wholesaling

Wholesalers frequently play a key role in the *chain of distribution*. It is often said that wholesalers do nothing for the money they receive and that, consequently, they make the price of goods unnecessarily high. Wholesalers do, however, perform several useful functions. First, they *concentrate* stocks of different goods in one place. This allows manufacturers to make one bulk delivery instead of several small ones. The goods are then *split* as the wholesaler breaks them down into smaller consignments for retailers. This is

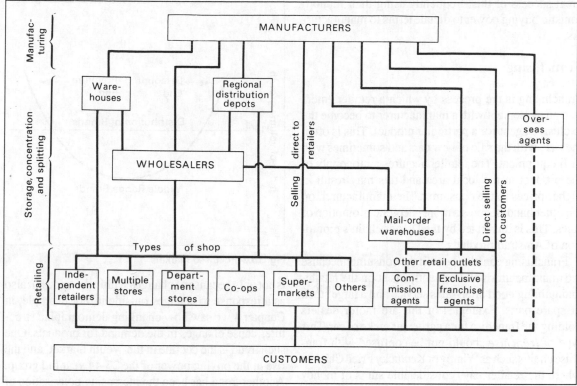

Fig. 15.1 Channels of distribution

a more efficient use of *transport* since manufacturers are able to send full loads of the same good to wholesalers and wholesalers are then able to send full loads, made up of many different products, to retailers. It is also convenient for retailers to be able to do their 'shopping' in one place. Wholesalers are also able to develop an *expert knowledge* of the market and advise retailers on how demand is changing. They also perform a valuable service in *holding stock* although they will, of course, charge for the risk involved. If the demand for products is regular and predictable, as for example in foodstuffs, the wholesalers' margins are likely to be small. On the other hand, if wholesalers hold very specialist stock which may not be demanded for months or years, for example specialist ironmongery, they are likely to look for higher margins. If wholesalers do not demand immediate payment for goods they are also acting as suppliers of *trade credit*.

There have been, however, many successful examples of wholesalers being eliminated. On the other hand customers should treat carefully offers of 'straight from the manufacturer prices' and 'discount warehouses' – these are frequently just alternative forms of retailing. It is not unrealistic to assume that wholesalers survive because they fulfil some useful function. There is a danger of course that a wholesaler might be able to 'corner' the market in a product and reap monopoly profits.

Types of shop

There are many different types of shops. Some of the more common types are shown in Fig. 15.1. They are not mutually exclusive categories. Co-ops operate supermarkets and there are multiple department stores such as the John Lewis Partnership plc. Over the past twenty years multiple stores and supermarkets have grown in importance while the independent retailers', department stores' and the co-ops' share of the market has declined. The large retail groups frequently undertake their own wholesaling. This was pioneered by the co-ops when they set up the CWS but today it is multiples like Marks and Spencer who have made a great success of this, frequently using their monop-sonistic buying power to dictate terms to manufactur-ers.

Franchising

Franchising is the process by which a retailer enters into an agreement with a manufacturer to become the exclusive agent for a particular product. This is often the case with the sale of new cars and sometimes with hi-fi equipment. The retailer acquires a monopoly of the product in the local area and this may result in higher prices to the consumer. The manufacturer, on the other hand, secures a more energetic promotion of sales. This is illustrated by the Dixons chain's promo-tion of Amstrad products.

Franchising can also benefit the consumer because the manufacturer will frequently insist on the retailer maintaining good after-sales service and a large stock of spare parts. Examples of this are motor dealers holding the franchise for a particular make of car. This type of *franchise* should not be confused with fran-chise chains such as Wimpy or Kentucky Fried Chicken where the retailer pays considerable sums of money for the use of the franchise.

Mail order

The mail-order business was pioneered in the USA where most of the people could not reach a city. In recent years the mail-order business has become more important in the UK although in 1987 it still only accounted for 3.5% of all retailing. The mail-order order house usually acts like a department store, selling well-known brand names. The mail-order catalogue is often backed up by local commission agents. Sales have often been helped by the instant credit available to customers through the catalogue. The mail-order business in Britain has traditionally been strongest among the lower income groups but in recent years mail order has tended to move up market, with many articles being sold through colour supple-ment advertisements and often being paid for by credit card.

Changes in markets

The retail market is in a constant state of change. This

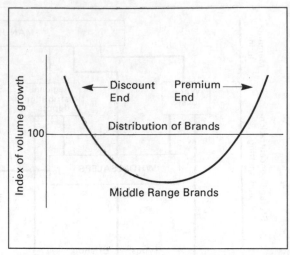

Fig. 15.2 Polarised markets

is not only because of changes within the trade but also as a response to changes outside it. For example, in Chapter 4 we saw how changing demographic struc-tures cause changes in the demand for products. One such trend is the decline in the 'youth market' and the rise in the buying power of the 25-44 year old group. Another trend has been the increasing polarisation of markets. That is to say, there has been a growth in the 'discount' end of the market, e.g. house brands in supermarkets and, at the other extreme, in the 'pre-mium' end of the market where people are prepared to pay for high quality/high cost brands. However, the middle-range brands have suffered a decline. This is illustrated in Fig. 15.2.

Study Fig. 15.2. Where on the curve of the distribu-tion of brands would you place the following prod-ucts? They can be anywhere on the curve.

(a) **Sainbury's washing powder**
(b) **Persil**
(c) **Allison's Wholemeal Bread**
(d) **Esso 4-star**
(e) **BMW 535i**
(f) **Ford Escort**
(g) **Bernard Mathew's turkey roast**
(h) **Rolex watch**
(i) **Levi jeans**
(j) **Dunhill cigarettes**

Transport

The producer of a good must, almost invariably, use some form of transport to deliver the product to the consumer. The importance of the different forms of transport within Great Britain can be gauged by studying Table 15.1.

Table 15.1 Transport of goods within Great Britain

Mode	Quantity of freight carried million tonnes)		Share of total tonne kilometres (%)	
	1966	1984	1966	1984
Road	1,641	1,542	57.9	58.0
Rail	217	141	20.4	8.8
Coastal shipping	53	145	20.2	27.7
British waterways	8	3	0.2	0.2
Pipelines	31	83	1.2	5.3
Air freight	0.1	0.1	0.1	0.2
Total	1,950.1	1,914.1	100.0	100.0

You will see from Table 15.1 that road tonnage has declined. At the same time the real GDP of the economy increased by 80%. State three reaons which might explain this apparent contradiction.

The picture is modified by the value of the goods which are transported. Air traffic, for example, looks to be of very little importance but many of the most valuable and important cargoes travel by air.

There have also been some unusual developments in the pattern of transport. For many years the tendency was for more and more goods to be transported by road. However, this has been modified by two factors. First, North Sea oil and gas have stimulated the use of pipelines and coastal shipping. Second, the decline in manufacturing industry has decreased the total tonnage transported.

For most normal purposes road transport continues to gain ground against rail. The great advantage of road transport is its convenience and flexibility. The suppliers of goods must decide between owning their own transport and hiring transport from road hauliers. To some extent this is governed by the size of the company and by the type of transport required. A frozen food company, for example, would usually have its own fleet of refrigerated trucks. Business organisations frequently find road to be cheaper than other modes of transport. Society, however, may not find this so. In 1988-89 the accounting cost of building and maintaining roads was £6,049 million. There are also social and private costs by way of damage to buildings through vibration and damage to the environment through air pollution. We must also take account of the road accidents. In 1987, for example, 311,473 people were killed or seriously injured in road accidents. It would take 66 years of rail accidents to equal one year of road fatalities.

Rail transport in Britain is nationalised and frequently criticised for the losses it makes. It is, however, a quick and efficient means of transporting passengers. It is very efficient as a transporter of cheap bulky goods such as iron ore and is vital for the distribution of mail and newspapers. It has the disadvantage that it only operates between fixed points and goods nearly always require another form of transport to complete their journey.

Two important developments in transport have been containerisation and pipelines. Containers are more important in overseas than in domestic trade. In 1984 Britain exported 94.6 million tonnes of goods by sea and imported 194.4 million tonnes.

Despite all our advances in technology, water transport still remains the cheapest way of moving goods from A to B. Britain makes much less use of internal waterways than most of her European neighbours. The greatest expense in transport is often in loading and unloading and it is because of this that containers have been so successful. Producers will not always want the cheapest form of transport. Commodities such as diamonds are usually transported by air, while for perishable goods speed is all-important. In general, however, manufacturers will always want to minimise their transport costs. Society, however, must weigh the total advantages and disadvantages of one form of transport against another.

Redraw Fig. 15.1. In each box give an example of the type of shop etc. For example, Selfridges is a department store.

Finance

The availability of finance has an important effect on both sides of the market. As we pointed out in Chapter 11, organisations produce in anticipation of demand. During the process of manufacture they must therefore have the resources to finance their operations. This can either come from their own resources, from trade credit or from outside sources.

While it is always readily accepted that income is a major determinant of demand, it is not so obvious that credit may also have an important effect. Today many expensive consumer durables such as cars are bought with the aid of credit. The general availability and price of credit, i.e. the rate of interest, therefore affects demand. The importance of the interest rate in affecting demand was well illustrated by the high rates of the late 1980s and early 1990s. High mortgage rates left many people with much less to spend and this badly affected the demand for such things as furntiture.

State five effects that the growth of credit cards has had upon the pattern of distribution. The first one is done for you.

1 **Growth of sales by telephone.**

We have seen that a market is not usually a producer selling directly to a consumer, between them are transport, shops, wholesalers, finance houses and so on. Despite this, we should not lose sight of the fact that all markets are controlled by the prices which people are willing to pay for goods.

Marketing

Introduction

Marketing is a commercial discipline that organisations have developed in trying to identify and respond to the needs of their customers, be they individuals or organisations, be those needs commercial or social. It is a broad discipline, one that is far easier to describe than to define.

To some people, the whole idea of marketing is

Keywords _____

Wholesaler
A trader who concentrates stocks, splits them into smaller consignments and organises distribution to retailers.

Commodity markets
The organisation and institutions associated with the sale of commodities such as cotton and cocoa in large amounts.

Futures markets
The buying and selling of commodities and financial securities at an agreed price at some date in the future. Also called forward markets.

Franchise
An agreement whereby a business obtains the use of the name and services of a manufacturer. For example, Ford may grant a franchise to only one garage in an area.

somehow disreputable, it becomes associated with, for example, plastic boxes which cost more than the product they contain, high-powered salesmanship and insincerity. Perhaps you might be forgiven for thinking this at first. However, you must remember that the basis of marketing is identifying and satisfying the *needs of customers*. Put in its very simplest terms, there is absolutely no point in producing something that nobody wants or in producing something everybody wants and then not telling anybody! Be it a manufacturer who has produced a new cold water, environmentally friendly detergent for energy saving washing machines or a college that is offering retraining programmes in response to changes in skill needs, the organisation must market its products or services. Marketing therefore needs to be understood and practised, not justified.

But what is marketing? Our aim is to answer this in general terms. A detailed discussion is outside the scope of this book but after reading this section you will have a foundation to build upon in your course work and, perhaps, further or option studies.

Definition

Peter Drucker, one of the founding fathers of modern management, defined marketing as: '... the whole business seen from the point of view of its final result, that is, from the customer's point of view'. This certainly conveys its breadth and its customer orientation but it does not help to specify what is included under this umbrella function.

The British Institute of Marketing defines it as '... the management process responsible for identifying, anticipating and satisfying customer requirements profitably.' This begins to indicate the content. We could also substitute the word *effectively* for profitably when we are dealing with the provision for social needs. We would hardly talk about providing health and medical services *profitably*, at least, not in the public sector.

Needs and wants

We have said that marketing is about satisfying *needs*. It is also about creating *wants*. Needs exist quite independently of marketing. For example, a company may have a need for a better management information system. The marketer's role is to identify that need and then to create a want (a market demand) by persuading the potential customer that their computer system for example, will satisfy that identified need. Often, however, the want is already in existence in that the potential customer has already identified a need and decided that, say, a computer will satisfy it. Here, the marketer's function is to translate the general want into a specific want for that organisation's product or service.

What is involved in marketing?

An organisation should draw up a *marketing plan*. This will have four key elements, traditionally known as the 'four Ps'.

1 Products. This will involve consideration of the existing products, possible future products, and the products of competitors.
2 Place. What distribution channels are/will be used.
3 Promotion. What methods are/will be used to communicate with the potential customers.
4 Price. What is/will be the total cost to the customer.

The marketing plan will be implemented through a number of fairly standard marketing techniques; to these we now turn.

Marketing research

This involves a wide range of activities and we will concentrate on just a few.

1 Market research. The purpose of this is to identify the *total demand* available in the market and how this is likely to change. Thus, it will not only involve research into potential customers but also into the activities of competitors, their market shares, ruling market prices and general factors affecting or likely to affect the market, e.g. demographic and social changes.
2 Consumer research. This takes market research one stage further and looks in detail at the buying behaviour and general habits of specific groups of customers. The objective is to build up a profile of the potential customers in terms of the factors that determine the likelihood of them purchasing the product or service.
3 Product research. As the name suggests, this aims to discover what products or services the market requires, the specification and performance expected of them, and the price that the market is prepared to pay.
4 Distribution research. The organisation needs to know the most cost-effective method of getting its product or service to the customer at the time, place and in the quantity that the *customer* requires.
5 Promotional research. The market must be informed of the product or service. What are the best methods of doing this? When? How much will they cost? How is the effectiveness of existing promotional activity to be assessed? Promotional research aims to answer such questions.
6 Forecasting. As you have seen, all marketing research is about forecasting future conditions and markets. A range of forecasting methods are available and all deal with one or other of the elements of uncertainty that exist in business. Methods can range from blind guess-work to sophisticated statistical analysis. Unfortunately, all methods are subject to a great deal of uncertainty because the world is an ever changing place. The cost of forecasting must also be borne in mind. It must be considered in relation to the potential sales of the product. The following are some of the methods used.

(a) Historical projections. With these the business attempts to build on past trends and project them into the future. This may consist of simply drawing a line

on a graph and projecting it forward. More sophisticated statistical techniques include moving averages and exponential smoothing.

(b) Experimental research. This includes test marketing, e.g. trying a new product in one part of the country, and experimenting with product design and price.

(c) Surveys of buying intentions. This is what most people think of as market research. It consists of asking a number of people their intentions and then using the data obtained to predict demand in the whole market.

(d) Leading indicators. These are events that predict other changes. For example, *The Financial Times* index of the leading 500 shares usually moves 12-18 months before there is a corresponding increase or decrease in national income. Such indicators are useful to the government in its running of the country and can also be useful to individual businesses if they can discover leading indicators that are relevant to their situation.

(e) Analytical methods. We can also attempt to forecast the future by using analytical models. The most sophisticated of these are econometric models of the working of the whole economy. The government uses these to predict such things as the rate of inflation and economic growth.

(f) Technological forecasting. In any high technology economy forecasting of likely changes and future needs in technology cannot be avoided. For example, planning for electricity generation is a very long term affair. Decisions have to be made now on the likely demand in 20 or 30 years time. The present arguments over different types of power stations, particularly nuclear power stations, are adequate testimony to the disagreements that can arise in technological forecasting.

Market segmentation

These days it is not usual for a firm to market one (identical) product to a total market. It has become necessary to *segment* markets. Segmentation means breaking down mass markets into segments on the basis of social class, age, lifestyle, income, etc. Thus, the firm might take an essentially similar product and, through product differentiation, make it appear attractive to particular segments of the market.

We might also consider *niche marketing*. This involves supplying specialised products or services for very closely defined groups, e.g. gourmets, left-handed people, vegetarians, and so on.

What forms of market segmentation does your organisation use? On what basis is this done?

Promotion

Many people think that marketing is just about promotion but you must first have market information on which to base it. Promotion is also an umbrella term involving advertising, promotions and public relations.

All promotion is, however, aimed at:

Attracting ... **Attention**
Arousing   ... **Interest**
Creating a ... **Desire**
Prompting ... **Action**

1 Advertising. Advertising involves selecting the best media in which to advertise, e.g. radio, TV, newspapers, and making decisions on the nature, design and frequency of the advertisements. (*See* further below.)

2 Promotions. These are usually short intensive activities to boost an ailing product or launch a new one. Typical examples include: price cuts; free gifts or special offers; and special advertising.

3 Public relations. This is more subtle and consists of making sure that the public and the press are fully informed of the organisation's activities and intentions. Typical methods used include personal lobbying, lunches and dinners and securing editorial coverage in the trade press.

What marketing research and promotional techniques are used by your employers for their goods and services.

Product management

Existing products have to be managed to ensure that they remain profitable. Often they must be modified as a response to customer feedback or changes in technology. New products or services must be developed to ensure the organisation's survival in the face of competition and market and technological change. Existing products must be rationalised to eliminate those that are obsolete and unprofitable.

Market management

This largely parallels product management but in respect to the market(s) for the organisation's products and services. Existing and successful markets must be maintained by ensuring that the organisation responds to changes in customer needs, competition and technology, and that its promotional activities remain appropriate.

Markets may have to be modified or rationalised if they were incorrectly identified or if they cease to be profitable. New markets may be identified to take their place.

Sales management

Clearly, this covers all aspects of the selling operation, for example, the size of the sales force, its training, and the monitoring of results.

Physical distribution management

The responsibility here is to ensure that the product gets to the customer at the right time and place, in the right quantity and in the right condition. Hence, it covers warehousing, stock control, channels of distribution, methods of transport, e.g. road/rail, own vehicles/contractor, and the associated administration.

Marketing costs

All the techniques and functions we have discussed above have a cost; the *marketing cost*. This is a legitimate cost to the business and often forms a substantial part of the final price of a product or service. To some extent, the marketing costs reflect the imperfections of the market (*see* Chapter 16). That is to say, where large companies divide the market between them they often spend vast sums on marketing. Even monopolies advertise.

Consider razor blades as an example. The cost of packaging and advertising is several times the cost of production. Thus, when you buy a razor blade, you are mainly buying the marketing. The same is true of expensive perfumes. A bottle sold for £10 may well have a production cost of less then £1. The rest is the cost of marketing and profit.

On the other hand, where there are hundreds of firms competing for a market, competition is more likely to be in straightforward economic terms, i.e. on price and quality. For example, greengrocers do not advertise extensively, they merely display prices in their shops. However, you should not draw the conclusion from this that marketing costs are necessarily wasteful. If you consider some of the products you use or possess that give you most pleasure, designer clothes, a personal stereo system, a car for example, they are all very much creations of the marketing industry.

Marketing in the public sector

The remaining nationalised industries exist by trading and they therefore have the same need for marketing as private sector businesses. What, however, of the rest of the public sector?

We have seen earlier that the government provides both public goods and services, such as roads and defence, and merit goods such as health and education. Although the government does not have competition in the usual sense, its goods and services must still be marketed. This may not appear obvious at first but remember that marketing includes determining the size of the demand (market), its distribution, character, etc. For example, the likely demand for such things as school places, hip operations and so on must be predicted. Small changes in the birth rate can rapidly upset the best laid plans for education. So the government will use many of the standard 'commercial' techniques of marketing and forecasting. It also uses straightforward advertising techniques for a variety of purposes.

These include:

(a) Informing, e.g. telling people about their rights under new legislation;
(b) *Promoting good practice*, e.g. safety in the home and at work;

(c) Making people aware of government services, e.g. social security benefits;
(d) Selling, e.g. National Savings Securities.

1 Collect examples of the government or your local authority publicising the availability of such things as social security benefits. How successful do you think they are as forms of marketing?

2 We tend to think of selling in terms of retailing. However, there are many other types of sales, for example, sales of airliners, steel girders, coal, computers, office furniture, insurance underwriting and advertising. Describe the methods by which non-retail sales are promoted. To what extent are they different from the methods used in retailing.

Advertising

One of the most obvious aspects of marketing is advertising. We mentioned this briefly above but we must now consider it in more detail. The normal commercial meaning of advertising is that it is any action by a firm to promote the sales of its products or services, the aim being to increase the number of consumers who prefer its products to those of its competitors.

1 Informative and persuasive advertising. Informative advertising is, as its name suggests, a simple announcement of information to the public. This is done by both trading and non-trading organisations. Many job advertisements may be regarded as purely informative.

Persuasive advertising is that which appeals to people's emotions rather than to their rationality. In reality most advertisements tend to be a mixture of the informative and the persuasive.

2 Corporate advertising. Here the organisation is promoting itself rather than its products. Such advertisements are quite common on TV, those for BP for example. The purpose here is to promote the image of the company itself, often through publicising its contribution to the economy or its concern for the environment, although it may spin off into extra sales.

For each of the following, suggest three examples which best illustrate these various types of advertising.

(a) Persuasive advertising
(b) Informative advertising
(c) Corporate advertising

3 Advertising and propaganda. There may also be undertones of political propaganda suggesting that such large capitalist companies serve the nation well. On occasions, advertisements placed by companies are more overtly political. This is most likely to be the case when there is a government in power that appears to be unsympathetic to the needs of big business.

It can be argued that advertisements also put out a more subtle form of propaganda through the way of life they show as desirable. In recent years legislation and the advertising industry's own efforts have tried to make advertisements more truthful. Occasionally the government intervenes to prohibit some advertisements, for example, cigarette advertising on TV is illegal.

However, legislation cannot protect us from the general materialistic image portrayed in advertising. Advertisements suggest, for example, that you will be a happier, more successful person if you use a particular deodorant or drive a particular car. We do not have the same level of exposure to images suggesting that we might be happier and healthier if we spent more on education and health care. In this, however, we are touching on the whole question of the ethics of our economic and political system, something that you may like to think about.

There are said to be six aspects of advertising. These are:

(a) The advertiser
(b) The agency
(c) The media
(d) Public relations consultants
(e) Mailing services
(f) Freelance services.

Explain each of these terms giving examples.

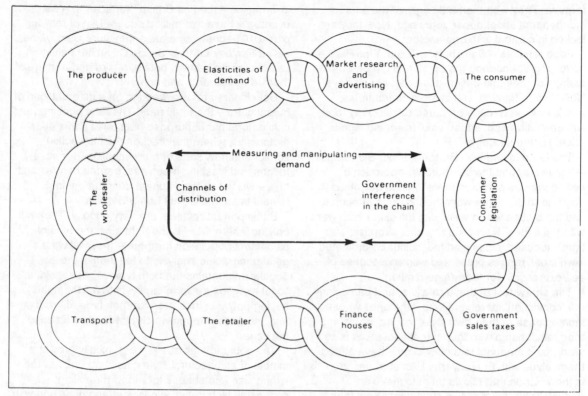

Fig.15 3 From producer to customer: the chain of distribution. The chain stretches down the left hand side of the diagram from the producer to wholesaler and so on, before reaching the consumer. Across the top of the diagram the producer tries to assess and manipulate consumers' demand.

Keywords

Marketing
Marketing is the process of identifying, anticipating and satisfying customer requirements profitably and/or effectively.

'Four Ps' (of marketing)
A marketing plan will concern itself with *products*, *place*, *promotion* and *price*.

Forecasting
Forecasting future conditions and markets is the essence of marketing research.

Promotion
Promotion is concerned with attracting *attention*, arousing *interest*, creating a *desire* and prompting *action*. It embraces *advertising*, *promotions* and *public relations*.

Advertising
The publicising of goods and services in order to increase sales.

Learning project

Changes in retailing

Read the following article – adapted from various articles appearing in the late 1980s – and attempt the following tasks.

Shopping is a war zone at the moment. The multiple retailers, local authority planners, even the Government, are piling into a fight about where you spend your shopping pound.

The national chains – Sainsbury's, Burton's, Next, John Lewis – have always fought to find a winning formula. They won the battle against the small independent shopkeeper years ago. Now they are locked in combat with one another.

Food retailers – Sainsbury's, Tesco, Fine Fare – have long abandoned the 5p off and Green Shield stamps of their pile-it-high-and-sell-it-cheap days. Now they're fighting with in-store charcuteries, exotic fruits and ready prepared dinner-party food. Differentiation and 'added vale' (meaning higher prices) is the strategy.

The famous chains – Burton's, Next, Storehouse – have scrapped the blunderbuss approach of selling various manufacturers' brands of clothes. You had to do all the work then, picking through to find the blouse which went with the skirt which went with the shoes. Now it's a rifle shot exercise, with tightly focused, closely edited, colour co-ordinated 'own label' ranges presented with accessories of self-expression for today's generation.

The shrewdest of these retailers, and particularly the 'conviction' merchandisers – the ones whose innate sense of their *own* style and standards and their relationship with their target audiences is so vivid that it amounts to a conviction – have armed themselves with the powerful Exocet of *design*. This is the weapon that allows them to make an unmistakable pre-emptive statement about their shop which shows at a glance *who* they're for. It's called 'market segmentation'.

The discerning top 40% is now spoilt for choice, as retailers dream up more and more specialist shops to cater for every 'niche whim'. They compare shops on nuances of quality, design and image, not price.

The 'have-nots' – the old, the unemployed, the young mums on a budget – have low disposable incomes and little access to credit – except the expensive HP kind. No one's investing in new shops for them.

There is currently over 40 million square feet of retailing development in the planning pipeline for Britain, much of it in the form of out-of-town regional shopping centres. There are five waiting for planning consent round the M25 alone.

In the new centres, acres of landscaped car parking will surround a million or more square feet of shopping in spectacular environments, with vaulted roofs, marble finishes, luxuriant planting, wall-climbing lifts, 'food courts' and entertainment. They are designed to become *destinations*. The proposed regional centres all plan to offer *something* to do to pull shoppers in. The Metro Centre near Gateshead

in Tyneside – the first British megacentre – will eventually have two million square feet of retailing, plus a 101-screen cinema, a miniature Disneyland called Fantasy Land, a Space City where children can play video games, hotels, a lake and a range of themed restaurants and cafés.

Developers are also working on a different kind of megacentre – the retail park. They are pushing to cluster together in purpose-built retail parks near motorways, where they reckon their collective impact and new sorts of merchandise – furniture, fridges and washing machines, garden centres and toys – will widen their appeal from the original female base and attract family outings.

But important retailers are very choosy. They will only go where there is the right size and type of catchment population for them – they will want a geodemographic analysis to tell them if the population contains the right type of household; a 'local expenditure zone' analysis to tell them the buying power in their area for their type of product, and 'isochronic' maps which plot journey times to the centre.

The poor old high street – organically grown; a jumble of architectural styles; its shop units all the wrong size and shapes for modern retailing; congested with traffic; windswept and dirty, and with minimal parking – stands less and less of a chance.

There are growing signs that the UK is already over-provided with retail space. Some of the specialist retailers in the high street are already concerned about being on the treadmill of redesigning their shops every three or four years.

The funny thing is that when you ask people to tell you about their most memorable shopping experience, they inevitably cite this little country town, with a marvellous baker, an ironmonger who sells nails in bags not blister packs, a *proper* dress shop run by real individuals who know exactly what suits you, and perhaps a children's shoe shop where comfortable types spent ages measuring up and having time to chat.

1 Define the following terms.

(a) Market segmentation;
(b) Niche marketing;
(c) Geodemographic analysis;
(d) Isochronic mapping;
(e) Destination place;
(f) Local expenditure zone analysis.

2 Assess the importance of design in the modern

retailing environment.

3 Assess the importance of the cost and availability of credit to retail sales. (Note: Figures on this appear in the *Annual Abstract of Statistics*.)

4 What are the consequences of the changes in retailing for the 'have-nots'? Do these have any implications for government policy?

5 Organise a visit to a regional shopping centre near to you (*see* map). Write a report which analyses it in terms of:

(a) Its location and accessibility;
(b) Car parking
(c) The shops located there;
(d) Other facilities (restaurants, entertainment, etc);
(e) Which sections of the population it is designed to attract.

Further ideas for learning projects

1 Design a market research questionnaire for a product of your own choice.

2 Write an article for a newspaper criticising the effect of advertising on society.

3 Obtain copies of at least three daily newspapers for the same day. (You should include one 'quality' paper and one mass circulation tabloid.) Analyse the advertisements according to the following criteria.

(a) What is being advertised?
(b) Who is the advertisement aimed at?
(o) What techniques are being used? Present your findings to contrast the difference between newspapers and between products?

4 Working either as a group or individually, undertake a survey of the following products.

(a) 200 gramme (7oz) tin of tuna steak;
(b) Standard white sliced loaf;
(c) Packet of 'Mr Kipling' apple pies;
(d) Packet of Persil; (Make sure you select the same E size.)
(e) Half a pound of tomatoes;

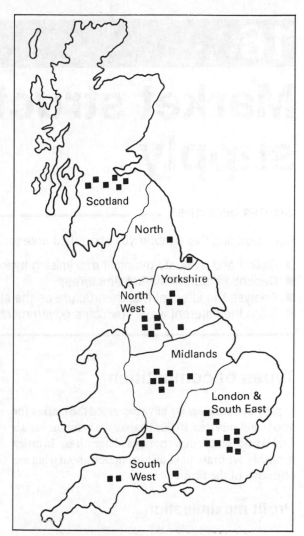

Location of existing and proposed shopping centres of over 500,000 square feet in Great Britain.

(f) 8oz jar of Nescafé Gold Blend;
(g) 8oz jar of 'house brand' instant coffee.

Add other products of your own choice to the list.

Sample the price of these products in six different retail outlets and explain the observed similarities and differences in prices. For example, why is there such a big difference in the price of cans of tuna? Is there a geographical basis to price differences?

16

Market structure and supply

After studying this chapter you should be able to:

■ Define and evaluate the profit maximising hypothesis;
■ Describe different market structures;
■ Analyse the effect of market structure on the allocation of resources;
■ State the different ways in which a government might deal with monopoly.

Types of competition

In previous chapters we have examined the market for goods and services. In this chapter we examine how a firm's prices and output policy is determined. In order to do this, we must make an assumption about what the objective of the firm is.

Profit maximisation

It is usually assumed that business organisations will always try to *maximise their profits*. This means that not only will they try to make a profit, but they will also try to make as much profit as possible. This assumption is given the somewhat grand title of *the profit maximisation hypothesis*. In general, this is a realistic assumption. However, profits are often regarded as the return to a risk taken; a business may try to minimise the risks it takes and in doing so it could therefore be accepting lower profits. It is certainly true that many business people are interested in stability and will be willing to tolerate slightly less profit if that profit is stable and predictable. (For a full discussion of this *see* pages 27–31.)

Although, obviously, markets can be very different, we find that, economically, they can be classified under a few main headings. These are based upon the *type of competition* existing in the market in which the firm is operating. These vary from the situation where there are thousands of firms competing to the situation where there is no competition (monopoly). The different types of competition result in different prices and output policies for the business.

The perfect market

For a state of perfect competition to exist in an industry, the following conditions have to exist.

(a) A large number of buyers and sellers of the commodity, so that no one person can affect the market price through their own actions.
(b) Freedom of entry and exit to the market for both buyers and sellers.
(c) Homogeneity of product, i.e. all the goods being sold would have to be identical.
(d) Perfect knowledge of the market on the part of both the buyers and the sellers.
(e) It must be possible to buy or sell any amount of the commodity at the market price.

It is obvious that all these conditions cannot exist in one market at once. There are, however, close ap-

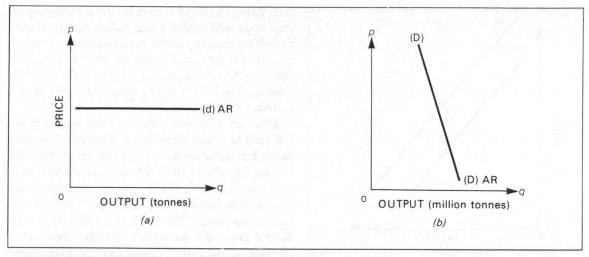

Fig. 16.1 The demand curve under perfect competition. *(a)* The demand curve for the individual business organisation's product. *(b)* The industry demand curve.

proximations to perfect competition, e.g. the sale of wheat on the commodity market in Canada. In this situation there are thousands of sellers and ultimately millions of buyers and it is relatively easy for farmers to enter or leave the market by switching crops for, once graded, one tonne of wheat is regarded as identical with another. In addition to this, when wheat is sold on the commodity market, both sides have a good knowledge of the market and it appears to farmers that they can sell all they want at the market price although they are, individually, unable to influence it. The perfection of the market is, however, flawed by farmers banding together in co-operatives to control the supply, by widespread government intervention in agriculture and by some very large buyers in the market. For instance, in recent years the USSR has bought millions of tonnes of wheat on the North American market to make good the shortcomings in its own domestic output.

Although perfect competition does not exist, we continue to examine it because it represents the ideal functioning of the free market system. Thus, although we cannot eliminate all imperfections in the market, we may try to minimise them as an engineer may try to minimise friction in an engine. If there were perfect competition, the individual firm would *appear* to face a horizontal demand curve for its product. If it raised the price of its product it would no longer be on the demand curve and would sell nothing. Conversely, it would have no incentive to lower its prices since it

appears to be able to sell any amount it likes at the market price. The organisation is thus a *price taker* and its only decision, therefore, is how much to produce (*see* Fig. 16.1). The price may of course change from day to day, as it does in the case of wheat, but to the farmer the demand curve always appears horizontal. The industry demand curve will remain a formal downward sloping one; indeed the world demand curve for wheat is fairly inelastic, large changes in price bringing only relatively small changes in demand.

Give three examples of firms in an industry which you think are price takers rather than price makers.

Imperfect competition

All markets are, to a greater or lesser extent, imperfect. This is not an ethical judgement upon the organisations which make up the markets. There is nothing morally reprehensible about being an imperfect competitor, indeed, this is the normal state of affairs. It could be the case, however, that firms contrive imperfections with the object of maximising their profits to the detriment of the consumer. We discuss this later in this chapter and also in the next chapter.

All imperfect competitors share the characteristic that the demand curve for their individual firm's

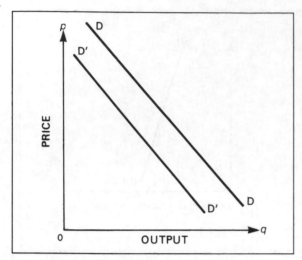

Fig. 16.2 The demand curve for an individual organisation's product under imperfect competition. The first has some choice over price or output but can also be affected by competitors. The decrease in demand from DD to D'D' could have been brought about by a fall in the price of a competitor's product.

product slopes downward. That is to say, if the firm raises its prices it will not lose all its customers as it would under perfect competition. Conversely, it can sell more of the product by lowering its prices. In addition to this, it can be affected by the action of its competitors. In Fig. 16.2, for example, the decrease in demand DD to D'D' could have been brought about by competitors lowering their prices. If, for example, Ford were to drop the prices of their cars by 5% it would probably bring about a substantial decrease in demand for Vauxhall cars. This would not be so in the case of perfect competition. If, for example, Farmer Jones were to cut the price of his wheat by 5% it would scarcely affect the sales of the thousands of other farmers who make up the market.

It is possible to distinguish several types of imperfect competition. These distinctions arise, chiefly, out of the different numbers of firms which make up any particular industry and the consequent differences in market behaviour in the short run and the long run.

Monopoly

This, literally, means a situation where there is only one seller of a commodity. This is the case in the UK with Tate & Lyle, who have a virtual monopoly of cane sugar and Joseph Lucas which has an almost complete monopoly of the manufacture of electrical components for cars. Legally speaking an organisation may be treated as a monopoly under the Fair Trading Act 1973 if it has more than 25% of the market.

There are, of course, some state monopolies in the UK such as British Coal. Since, however, their economic behaviour is not usually governed by the profit making hypothesis, their behaviour is not discussed here (*see* Chapter 3). The recent privatisation of nationalised industries such as British Telecom has reduced the number of industries for which this is true. Special provisions have been imposed upon privatised industries to guard against them exploiting their monopoly position.

Oligopoly

Oligopoly means a situation where there are only a few sellers of a commodity. There are several industries in the UK dominated by a few large firms, e.g. the production of detergent is almost entirely divided between Proctor & Gamble and Unilever. Banking also presents an example of oligopoly. The major clearing banks dominate high street banking having very similar contractual terms as well as rates of interest etc. In some cases these firms might *legally* be described as monopolists rather than oligopolists.

Oligopolists might produce virtually identical products and compete with each other through prices. It is more common, however, for them to compete through advertising and *product differentiation*. In the case of detergents, for example, although all the products are basically similar, there is a proliferation of brands and heavy advertising but very little price competition.

Many industries in the UK are oligopolistic. For the three industries listed below, give the names of three of the companies which dominate the industry concerned.

(a) **Detergents**
(b) **Motor Vehicles**
(c) **Instant Coffee**

Monopolistic competition

When there are a large number of sellers producing a similar but differentiated product then a state of monopolistic competition is said to exist. This might be the case in the supply of a commodity like shirts, where essentially similar items are supplied by many different firms at widely differing prices with a lot of product differentiation by way of colour, style and material. Such an industry is also characterised by the frequent entry and exit of firms.

It is called monopolistic competition because, due to imperfections in the market, each organisation has a small degree of monopoly power. If, for example, Benetton can convince the public that their shirts are better than those of their competitors, then they have, as it were, created a small monopoly for their own product. The *branding* of goods is an attempt to break the *chain of substitution* by which one commodity can be substituted for another. When a consumer enters a shop and asks for a bar of chocolate, a shirt or a tube of toothpaste by its brand name, then the manufacturers have succeeded in their designs and may be able to reap the reward of their monopoly. Some advertising and branding is so successful that people use brand names without realising it, e.g. Thermos, Hoover and Vaseline.

State five industries in the UK in which the largest five or fewer firms account for 90% or more of the output of these industries.

It is paradoxical that under perfect competition very little competition is visible since there is no advertising and promotion of products, whereas under all types of imperfect competition rivalry between organisations is only too obvious. Even monopolies advertise. Tate and Lyle, for example, not only promote their product but extol the virtues of free competition. It is a case, as Professor Galbraith wrote in *The Affluent Society*, of competition being advocated 'by those who have most successfully eliminated it'!

List the following types of competition

● Perfect competition
● Monopolistic competition
● Oligopoly
● Monopoly

For each state:

(a) **The number of producers and degree of product differentiation;**
(b) **In which industries you would find each type;**
(c) **The degree of influence over price which the firm has;**
(d) **The chief marketing methods.**

Market behaviour under perfect competition

Marginal revenue

In Chapter 6 we examined the cost structure of organisations. Before considering how the prices and output policy of a firm is determined we need to consider only one more concept, that is marginal revenue (MR). If, for example, a farmer can sell any amount of his product at £5 per kg then the demand schedule for his product would be like that in Table 16.1.

Table 16.1 Demand schedule

Demand for commodity (kg per week)	Price of commodity (£/kg)	Total revenue (£s)	Marginal revenue (£s)
0	5	0	
1	5	5	5
2	5	10	5
3	5	15	5
4	5	20	5

Thus, each time the farmer sells another kg his total revenue increases by £5. This increase to his total revenue is termed the marginal revenue. Under perfect competition marginal revenue is the same as price because the producer can sell more of his or her output without lowering the price. Thus, the demand curve and the marginal revenue curve are the same thing. This is not the case with imperfect competition. If producers wish to sell more of their output they must lower their price to do so. Thus, under imperfect competition the marginal revenue curve slopes down-

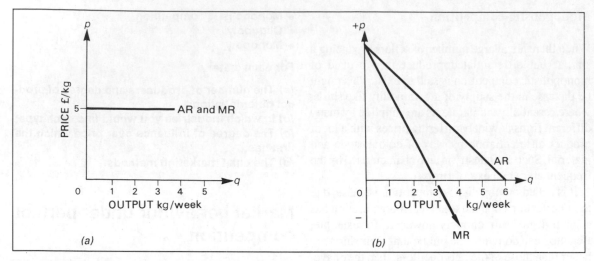

Fig. 16.3 The marginal revenue curve: two possibilities. *(a)* Perfect competition. MR and AR curves are identical because the price is constant. *(b)* Imperfect competition. The MR curve descends twice as quickly as the AR curve, bisecting the horizontal axis.

wards beneath the demand curve. These two possibilities are illustrated in Fig. 16.3.

As imperfect competitors continue to lower their prices there comes a time when it is no longer worthwhile. The extra demand they acquire is not sufficient to offset the drop in the price and so their total revenue decreases. At this point marginal revenue will become negative and the MR curve will cross the horizontal axis. (You might like to consider the relationship between MR and elasticity; what, for example, is the elasticity of demand when marginal revenue is zero?)

Since marginal revenue can be both positive and negative, it is best to define it as the *change* to total revenue resulting from the sale of one more unit.

You will note that in Fig. 16.3 the demand curve is labelled AR. This stands for *average revenue*. This is the usual practice when considering the price and output policy of firms as it brings it in line with the other terms being used such as average cost (AC) and marginal revenue (MR).

Suppose a firm can produce 100 units of product X and receive a total revenue of £500 or expand its output to 101 units and receive £505.

(a) What is the marginal revenue from the sale of the 101st unit?
(b) What is the market price of product X?

Output and profits in the short run

Under perfect competition the firm is a *price taker*, i.e. it has no control over the market price. It can only sell or not sell at that price. Therefore, in trying to maximise profits the firm has no pricing decision to make, it can only choose the output which it thinks most advantageous. For example, in a freely competitive market a farmer could choose how much wheat to plant but could not control the price at which it would be sold when harvested.

The best profit position for any business organisation would be where it equated its marginal revenue (MR) with its marginal cost (MC). If the cost of producing one more unit (MC) is less than the revenue the producer obtains for selling it (MR), then they can obviously add to their profit by producing and selling that unit. Even when MC is rising, so long as it is less than MR the business organisation will go on producing because it is gaining *extra* profit. It does not matter if the *extra* profit is only small, it is nevertheless an *addition* to *profit* and, if producers are out to *maximise profits*, they will wish to receive it.

This is illustrated in Fig. 16.4 where the most profitable output is OM. If the business produced a smaller output (OL) then the cost of producing a unit (MC) is less than the revenue received from selling it (MR). The business could therefore increase its profits by expanding output. The shaded area represents the

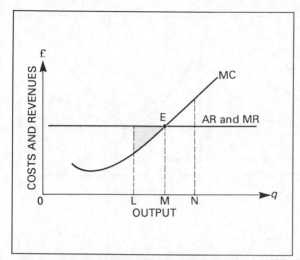

Fig. 16.4 Perfect competition: the short run. The organisation maximises its profits by producing the output at which MC = MR.

extra profit available to the producer as output is expanded. At point E (output OM) there is no more extra profit to be gained. If the firm were to produce a larger output (ON) then the cost of producing *that* unit (MC) would be greater than the revenue from selling it (MR) and the producer could increase profits by contracting output back towards OM. Thus, the output at which MC = MR is an *equilibrium position* for the producer, i.e. the one at which the firm will be happy to remain if it is allowed to (*see* page 245). Imagine that a farmer has produced a crop of apples. They now have to harvest them and send them to market. Since apples are highly perishable they will continue sending apples to market while the extra cost (MC) incurred in doing so (labour, transport, etc.) is less than the money to be got for selling them (MR). As soon as the cost of getting them to market is greater than the money the farmer received for them will cease to do so, even if it means leaving the apples to rot.

Define normal profit. Explain the conditions under which a higher than normal profit can exist under perfect competition (*see* page 220).

Shut-down in the short run

In the above example, the cost of planting the apple trees and of renting the land for the orchard could be regarded as *fixed costs* (FC) since the farmer can only shed these costs by going out of business. That is to say, these costs cannot be varied in the short run. Other costs, such as maintaining the trees, harvesting the crop and transporting it to market, can be carried in the short run and can therefore be described as *variable costs* (VC). This being the case, it is apparent that if the price of apples was so low that the farmer could not recover all the costs they would still continue to sell apples in the short run if they could cover variable costs. In other words, if the money they are getting back from the sale is greater than the cost of picking and selling them, it would appear that in the short run they will produce, ignoring fixed costs.

Conversely, if the cost of harvesting, transport, etc, was greater than the sales revenue, the farmer would obviously minimise losses by closing down immediately and saving the expenditure on variable costs.

Thus, we can conclude that a firm will continue to produce and sell its product in the short run, even when it is making a loss, so long as it is covering its variable costs because in this way it is minimising its losses. In the long run, of course, all costs must be covered if the firm is to remain in the industry. This conclusion is true for all types of firm, not just for those operating under perfect competition.

Consider the case of an apple grower who is able to rent a 100 hectare orchard for £26,000 per year. In addition to this he must pay other capital costs of £2,600 per year. When it comes to harvest time casual labour can be hired at £56 per week. The average quantity of apples which each labourer can pick is 4,800 apples (400 dozen) per week. In addition to this, other direct costs (VC), such as packaging and transport, amount to a further 3 pence per dozen.

1 State the absolute minimum price per dozen which the apple grower will be willing to accept in the short-run. Give reasons for your answer.

2 Suppose that the apple grower finds that it takes 5 labourers 5 weeks to harvest the complete crop. If all other costs and productivities stay the same as above, what is the minimum price per dozen the apple grower will look for to remain in the industry in the long-run? Give reasons for your answer?

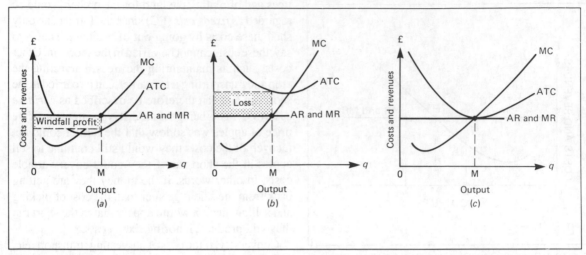

Fig. 16.5 The long run equilibrium of the firm under perfect competition. *(a)* Windfall profits attract new firms to the industry. This lowers the price and eliminates the abnormal profit. *(b)* The firm is making a loss and in the long run will leave the industry. *(c)* The firm is just recovering normal profits; this is the long run equilibrium of the firm, where MC = MR = AR = AC.

Output and profits in the long run

In the short run the firm will choose to produce at the output where its marginal revenue is equal to its marginal cost. This is true whether the firm is making a profit or a loss, so long as it is covering its variable costs. However, in the long run all costs must be covered and it is therefore necessary to consider the total costs (TC) of the organisation. It is most convenient to consider total cost as average total costs (ATC). In this way it may be compared with AR and MC. The MC curve always cuts the ATC curve at the lowest point of the ATC curve (*see* page 111). When we consider the firm under perfect competition three possibilities exist, i.e. this intersection of MC and ATC must occur at a level higher, lower or equal to the price at which the commodity is being sold. These three possibilities are illustrated in Fig. 16.5. This demonstrates that only *(c)* can be a long run situation. Before going any further with this explanation, you should recall the idea of *normal profit* (*see* page 220), that is, the minimum amount of profit a firm will require to remain in an industry. You will remember that since this is necessary to keep the firm producing it is considered as a legitimate cost of production and is therefore included within the ATC.

In all three diagrams in Fig. 16.5 you will see that the firm produces output OM, i.e. the output where

MC = MR, because at this output it either maximises its profits or minimises its losses.

In *(a)* the average revenue (price) is higher than average total cost. This means that the firm is making an above normal profit. Under perfect competition this is often described as *windfall profit* since it is not a profit which has been contrived by the firm. It arises because the price is unexpectedly higher than anticipated. However, this situation will not continue in the long run because, under perfect competition, there is freedom of entry and exit to the industry and these high profits will attract new competitors into the industry who will compete the profit away.

In *(b)* average total cost is at all times higher than average revenue. It is therefore impossible for the firm to make a profit. Although the firm may produce in the short run (*see* above), it is impossible for it to continue in the long run and it must therefore close down unless there is a favourable change in the market.

Neither *(a)* nor *(b)* can be long run situations but in *(c)* we see that the ATC curve is just tangential to the AR curve. At a greater or lesser output the firm would make a loss but at output OM it is just receiving normal profit. The situation represented in *(c)* can continue in the long run because the firm is just recovering enough profit to keep it in the industry but not sufficient to attract other competitors to take that profit away.

Thus, we can see that under perfect competition the

long run equilibrium for the organisation is one where:

$$MC = MR = AC = AR$$

The average business person is hardly likely to look at the running of their business in this way. Profit maximisation is arrived at by practical knowledge of the business and by trial and error. The concepts of marginal cost, average revenue, etc, allow us to rationalise the principles that are common to all businesses. Although the business person may not be familiar with words like marginal revenue, they will nevertheless be used to the practice of making small variations in output and price to achieve the best results and will thereby be using a marginal technique to maximise profits. By this we mean that they will be unlikely to double output or price but rather that they will try small adjustments. For example, a business might try a 10% cut in price and see what effect that has upon sales and profits.

Consider the information in the table below which relates to the output of company X.

Output Units per week (Q)	Total Cost (£)
0	580
1	700
2	800
3	880
4	1,000
5	1,200
6	1,480
7	1,840
8	2,280

Suppose that company X can sell all the output it wishes at a price of £240 per unit.

1 Determine and explain the profit maximisation output for company X.

2 Consider the long-run effects upon company X of the following price changes.

(a) Price falls to £160 per unit.
(b) Price increases to £320 per unit.

3 Is it true to say that in all cases Company X will produce at the output at which MR = MC.

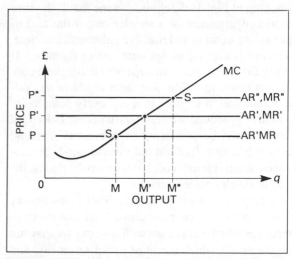

Fig. 16.6 The supply curve under perfect competition

The supply curve

No matter how the *market price* changes, the demand curve always appears to be a horizontal line to the individual firm under perfect competition. Therefore as price goes up or down the firm always tries to equate price with marginal cost in order to maximise its profits. In Fig. 16.6 as price increases from OP to OP' to OP" the firm expands output from OM to OM' to OM". This, therefore, shows how the firm varies output in response to changes in price – in other words, it is a supply curve. Thus, we may conclude that under perfect competition the firm's MC curve, above AVC, is its supply curve.

The optimum allocation of resources

The importance of the idea of perfect competition is that it represents the ideal working of the free market system. The fundamental problem of any economy, you will remember, is to make the best use of scarce resources. If we look at the model of perfect competition, we will see how it relates to this. In its long-run equilibrium the firm is producing where MC = AC, i.e. at the bottom of the average cost curve. At this output, costs, that is to say the quantity of resources needed to produce a unit of the commodity, are minimised.

Looking at Fig. 16.5 *(c)* you can see that if the firm produced a greater or a smaller output the cost of producing a unit would rise. In equilibrium, therefore, the firm is making an optimum use of resources. If every firm in the economy operated under these conditions it would follow that there would be an optimum allocation of resources and every commodity would be produced at a minimum unit cost. Indeed, all firms would be producing to consumers' demand curves and therefore not only would goods be produced at a minimum cost but they would also be the goods which people wanted.

We have already seen that this view of the economy is subject to two major criticisms. First, that the commodities which people are willing to pay for may not be the goods which are most useful to society, and second, that income in the economy may be unevenly distributed, meaning that an efficient system may not be socially just (*see* Chapter 13).

Competition is, however, also important as a political idea. When right-wing parties advocate increasing the amount of free competition in the economy it is in the belief that this would lead to a more efficient use of resources. Even trade unions have advocated 'free competition' in wage bargaining. Free competition in our economy is something of a myth in that markets often tend to be dominated by large organisations with a great deal of monopoly power. In the same way, 'free collective bargaining' is dominated by large powerful unions. It is imperfections of the market which are the rule rather than free and unfettered competition.

Market behaviour in imperfect markets

Maximising profits in an imperfect market

Any organisation will obviously make most profit where there is the biggest possible difference between its costs and its revenues. This does not mean, however, that it will seek either to minimise its costs or to maximise its revenues; instead it will seek the best relationship between the two. Table 16.2 illustrates the costs and revenues of a firm operating under

Key Words _____

Perfect competition
A market structure is perfectly competitive if: there is a large number of buyers and sellers each with an insubstantial share of the market; they produce a homogeneous product; there is perfect knowledge of the market; and there is freedom of entry and exit to the market.

Imperfect competition
All market structures are to a greater or lesser extent imperfect since there can never be perfect knowledge, complete freedom of entry and exit, etc.

Monopoly
A situation in which there is only one seller or producer of a commodity. Legally it refers to anyone with more than 25% of the market.

Oligopoly
There are only a few sellers of a commodity.

Monopolistic competition
A situation in which there are many sellers of a similar but cost differentiated product.

Marginal revenue
The change to total revenue from the sale of one more unit of a commodity.

Short-run short-down
In the short-run a firm will continue to produce so long as its revenues are above its variable costs. In the long-run all costs must be covered.

Profit in perfect competition
The firm maximises profit by producing the output at which MC = p (MR). It may make abnormal profit (or loss) in the short-run but in the long-run makes only normal profit.

Optimality
If all firms were producing under conditions of perfect competition there would be an optimum allocation of resources.

_____

conditions of imperfect competition. Here you can see that the best possible profit position is where the output is 4 units and the price is £48. At this point MC = MR. You will note that this is not the output at which revenues are maximised (this is 5 units where TR = £200), nor average cost minimised (this is also 5 units where AC = £24).

In the previous section we saw how a firm maximises its profits where MR = MC. If we construct the relevant graphs from the above figures we will see that

Table 16.2 Costs and revenues of a firm under conditions of imperfect competition

	Output units per week (q)	Average revenue £/unit (p)	Total revenue (p x q) (TR)	Total cost £ (TC)	Total profit (TR − TC) (TP)	Marginal cost $(TC^n - TC^{n-1})$ (MC)	Marginal revenue $(TR^n - TR^{n-1})$ (MR)	Average cost (TC/q) (AC)
A	0	80	0	58	−58			∞
						12	+72	
B	1	72	72	70	+2			70
						10	+56	
C	2	64	128	80	+48			40
						8	+40	
D	3	56	168	88	+80			29.3
						12	+24	
E	4	48	192	100	+92		MC = MR	25
						20	+8	
F	5	40	200	120	+80			24
						28	−8	
G	6	32	192	148	+44			24.6
						36	−24	
H	7	24	168	184	−16			26.3
						44	−40	
I	8	16	128	228	−100			28.5

this is so. The MR and MC curves do, indeed, cross at an output of 4 units. Under perfect competition the MR curve slopes down below the AR curve because the firm must lower its prices in order to sell more. This is illustrated in Fig. 16.7. In the same diagram we can see that when the output is 4 the price (AR) is £48 and that at this output the average cost (AC) is £25. This firm is therefore making £23 profit on each unit. Since the firm is selling 4 units, the area of the shaded rectangle represents the amount of profit that this business is making (£92).

You will recall from the previous section that normal profit is included in the costs of the firm and therefore the profit discussed above is all *abnormal profit* (also called *excess profit or monopoly profit*), i.e. all of this profit could be eliminated without forcing the firm to leave the industry. How has this abnormal profit been made? The answer is by selling a restricted output at a higher price. Under imperfect competition, in order to sell more the firm must lower its prices. Therefore there must come a time when the price is so low that profit is eliminated. It is not so surprising then that a firm finds its best profit position

before this point. This idea is often unintentionally illustrated by bad harvests where the lack of supply forces up prices and farmers find themselves much better off, even though they are selling less produce. Abnormal profit is usually, however, considered a *contrived profit* – a return to the *monopolistic power* of the organisation. Earlier in this chapter we referred to the diamond market, where supply is often deliberately restricted to increase the profits of diamond producers.

As a result of imperfect competition, consumers are paying more for products than they might and yet this is not the most serious consequence. You will also observe from Fig. 16.7 and Table 16.2 that the product is produced at a higher average cost than it need be. In our example average cost is minimised at an output of 5 (where AC = £24). It would therefore seem that imperfect competition leads to an inefficient use of resources. This is the most important criticism of it.

Thus, we can conclude that to maximise its profits the firm restricts its output and thereby raises the price of its product. In so doing it moves backwards up its AC curve, producing fewer goods at a higher cost.

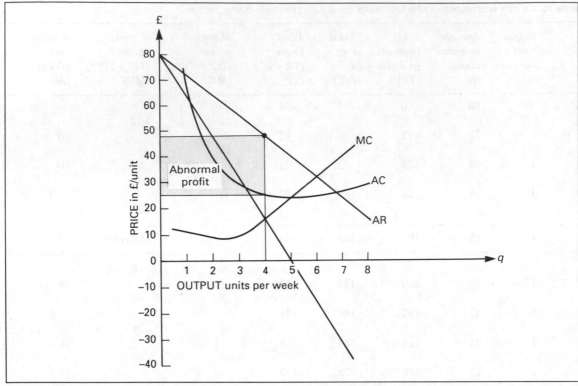

Fig. 16.7 The equilibrium price and output of the firm under imperfect competition: the short run. Profit is maximised at an output of 4 units and a price of £48, where MR = MC. Profit = (AR − AC) x q = £92.

This situation can only continue if other firms are prevented from entering the market and competing for this profit. In other words this is a short run situation. What happens in the long run will depend upon the type of imperfect market we are considering.

Monopoly

A monopoly is a firm which, for one reason or another, enjoys freedom from competition. In the long run there is no-one, therefore, to come into the market and compete for the monopolist's abnormal profit. The long run equilibrium of the monopolist is therefore like the short run.

Monopolists may, however, choose not to maximise their profits as fully as they might for:

(a) fear that the government may intervene;
(b) respect for the community's welfare;
(c) fear that they may attract competition from overseas.

Oligopoly

Oligopoly, the situation where the market is dominated by a few large firms, is hard to analyse. The most practical implication is, however, that oligopolists realise that if they were to co-operate and have a common prices and output policy a greater total amount of profit could, as a result, be made from the market. Such a policy would amount to setting up a *cartel* or price-fixing ring. Since these are usually illegal, some industries have resorted to *information agreements* or *market sharing*. For example, the construction companies in an area might get together and take it in turns to submit the lowest tenders for contracts. Virtually all such arrangements are now illegal and the law relating to them is discussed in the next chapter.

Although agreements between organisations to exploit the market may be illegal, it is possible to see that in many oligopolistic markets price competition is avoided. If, for example, we consider the detergent market, we can see that Proctor & Gamble and Unilever

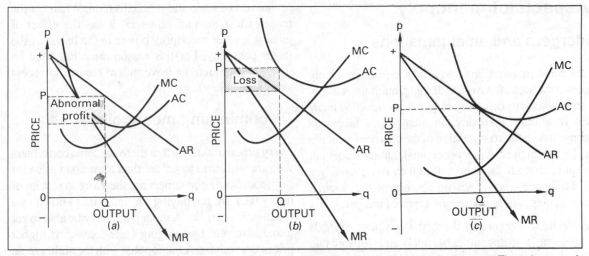

Fig. 16.8 The equilibrium price and output of the firm under monopolistic competition: the long run *(a)* The existence of abnormal profit attracts new firms to the industry which lowers the price and eliminates the profit. *(b)* The firm makes a loss at all levels of output and in the long run will leave the industry. *(c)* The long run equilibrium where the firm just recovers normal profit.

prefer to compete by product differentiation and advertising rather than by price cutting wars with each other.

One consequence of oligopoly can be that a firm appears to face a kink in the demand curve for its product. This arises because, although its competitors will allow it to put up the price without interference, the moment it brings its prices down below the ruling market price they will respond by lowering their prices. Thus, the elasticity of demand for the firm's product is much greater above the ruling market price than below it.

Barriers to entry protect monopolist and other imperfect competitors. For the following explain what are the barriers to entry.

(a) **Motor vehicle industry**
(b) **Microcomputers**
(c) **The legal profession**

Monopolistic competition

In situations where there are many competitors in an imperfect market, if one firm is seen to be making high profits other businesses will be encouraged to enter

that line of production and compete the profit away. The situation is therefore similar to that of perfect competition. This is illustrated in Fig. 16.8. In *(a)* the average cost curve is below the average revenue curve and abnormal profits are being made. Since there is free entry to the market, other firms enter and compete this profit away. In *(b)*, however, AC is above AR at all points and the firm is making a loss and will, in the long run, leave the industry. The long run equilibrium is therefore *(c)* where the AC curve is tangential to the AR curve and the firm is only receiving normal profits.

For example, a company manufacturing shirts might accurately predict a new fashion trend and for a short while be able to exploit its monopoly of that design of shirt. But other companies will soon be able to copy this and price competition between the firms will compete the excess profit away.

You will note in *(c)* that, unlike perfect competition, the company does *not* produce at the lowest point of average cost. It is still the case, however, that it produces where MC = MR. Thus, even though the company is not making abnormal profits, it is still producing a restricted output at a higher unit cost. It follows that in all types of imperfect market the organisation, in following its own interest of profit maximisation, is likely to bring about an inefficient use of resources.

Aspects of monopoly

Mergers and amalgamations

Business organisations frequently acquire monopoly power through takeovers and amalgamations. A *takeover* is when one company acquires a controlling interest in another company. In many cases takeovers happen with the co-operation of the company which is being taken over. A *merger* or amalgamation does not require that all the shares are taken over; usually a *holding company* is set up to control the original companies. There are several types of merger.

1 Vertical merger. In these the business expands 'backwards' to its sources of supply and 'forwards' to its markets. A good example would be an oil company which controlled everything from the oil well to the filling station.

2 Horizontal merger. In this the business expands and integrates with other businesses involved in the same activity. An example of this was the merger of the discount stores MFI and Comet.

3 Mergers of diversification. Businesses frequently spread out into other fields to diversify their risks. One of the most famous examples is Unilever which produces a wide variety of products from soap to sausages.

There are several reasons for mergers, the two most important being the following.

1 Economies of scale. This is where the larger company is able to make better use of resources. For example, GEC, is hoping to achieve more economies of scale having taken over Ferranti.

2 Market domination. The object of the merger is to eliminate competition and so allow the company to maximise profits, no economies of scale need to be involved. It is this type of merger which frequently attracts the attention of the Monopolies and Mergers Commission.

Take-overs sometimes involve 'asset-stripping'. This occurs when a company takes over another and then sells off its assets to raise cash. British Aerospace did this both with its take-over of Royal Ordnance and the Rover Group.

Desirable economic consequences can frequently follow the creation of a larger company as a result of economies of scale and rationalisation. Whatever the reason for a merger, however, it has the effect of placing greater monopoly power in the hands of the larger company. For this reason there has been an increasing amount of government control in recent years (*see* below).

Discriminating monopolists

Every producer knows that there are some consumers who are willing to pay more than the market price for the good. Some consumers are therefore in receipt of utility they are not paying for and this is known as a *consumer's surplus*. A monopolist may be able to eat into this surplus by charging some consumers higher prices than others. A monopolist with the ability to do this is known as a discriminating monopolist. Two conditions must be present for this price discrimination to take place.

1 The monopolist must be able to separate the two markets; this may be done geographically, by branding or by time. The suppliers of personal services such as doctors and lawyers also often charge different prices for the same service.

2 The two or more markets so separated must have different elasticities of demand, otherwise the exercise could not be worthwhile.

Fig. 16.9 shows how the monopolist might set about increasing profits by price discrimination. The manufacturer, in this case of a drink, maximises profits by equating MR with MC and therefore sells 2,000 bottles a week at £8.00 each. However, the entrepreneur realises that many customers are willing to pay more than £8 for a bottle (market B). The firm therefore puts some of the drink in bottles labelled 'Highland Royal de Luxe' and sells it as a high-class product. At the cheaper end of the market there is a great deal of elasticity of demand (market A). Here the price is dropped to £7.20 1,500 bottles labelled 'Glengrottie' are sold. The way in which marketing strategy is decided is by taking the MC for the combined market and equating it with the marginal revenues for the two separate markets. This shows the output to sell in each market. By tracing that output up to the demand curves in the separate markets you can see the price which would be charged. In our example the firm collects £800 a week extra profit because it is able to convince

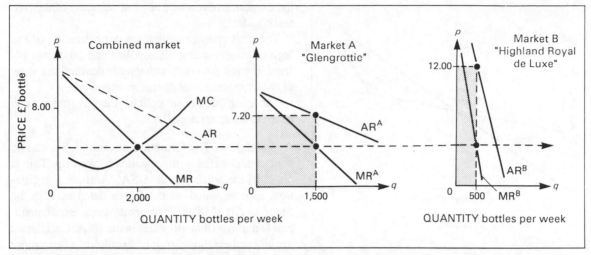

Fig. 16.9 The discriminating monopolist divides output between two markets. *(a)* Combined market without price discrimination. Price = £8, quantity = 2,000, total revenue (p x q) = £16,000. *(b)* Separate market A with price discrimination. Price = £7.20, quantity = 1,500, total revenue £10,800. *(c)* Separate market B with price discrimination. Price = £12.00, quantity = 500, total revenue = £6,000. Total revenue from markets A and B = £16,800. This is £800 greater than in the combined market. Since the output is the same, costs must be the same and therefore this extra revenue must all be extra profit.

customers, by branding and advertising, that one bottle of drink is better than the other. Price discrimination is fairly widespread. The following are examples of some of the types of price discrimination.

1 Geographical. Goods are sold at different prices in different countries. This was illustrated in 1977 when the Distillers Company was ordered by the EC to cease selling the same brand of whisky at one price in the UK and at a higher price in the rest of Europe.

2 Branding. Many manufacturers sell the identical product at one price under their own brand name and at a lower price branded with the name of a retailer. For example, many famous manufacturers sell some of their output more cheaply under the 'St Michael' label of Marks and Spencer.

3 Time. Many public monopolies sell the same product at different prices at different times. Example of this are off-peak electricity, 'Saver' returns on British Rail and 'stand-by' flights by British Airways.

4 Dumping. This is a variation on geographical discrimination but in this case the manufacturer 'dumps' surplus output on a foreign market below cost price. This often has the object of damaging foreign competition. Examples of this in Britain are Russian cars and cameras and Korean shoes and clothes. The EC has to resort to dumping to get rid of excess agriculture

products.

Consultant doctors are often said to operate price discrimination by working in both private practice and the National Health Service. Patients might find, however, that they receive more prompt and personal service in the private sector and feel this is worth paying for.

There are considerable differences between the prices of cars in the UK and in other EC countries. Assuming that this is greater than can be accounted for by transport costs, taxes etc, explain why this is so.

Give reasons for the continued existence of this phenomenon despite intervention by the EC.

Mark-up pricing and break-even charts

Although an organisation's behaviour may be governed by concepts such as marginal revenue and marginal cost, in practice they may be very difficult to determine, especially when a large organisation is marketing a variety of products. In these circumstances they often try to base their prices on average or

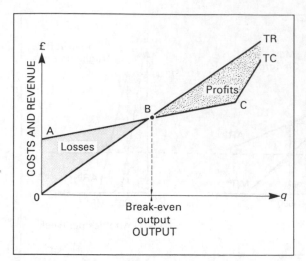

Fig. 16.10 A break-even chart. If the price is fixed, TR is a straight line. Profits or losses are the vertical distance between the two curves. B is the break-even point at which losses turn into profits.

unit cost. To do this they must make assumptions about the future volume of sales and likely average cost at that output. This having been done, a *mark-up* of, say, 10% is then added for profit. This fascinatingly simple theory seems realistic but stops tantalisingly short of telling us why the average mark-up should be 40% in one industry and 5% in another.

You should take careful note that this is the way the organisation may try to determine the right price for *itself* but the consumers may or may not be willing to pay the right price or buy the right quantity. Prices in the market are still determined by the forces of supply and demand. Monopolists have greater power, of course, to impose their wishes on the market. If an organisation sets its prices in this manner then we can draw up a *break-even chart* to demonstrate its profits and losses. In Fig. 16.10 the TR curve is a straight line because price is constant. TC is a normal total cost curve; costs turn upwards very sharply after point C when the firm passes optimum capacity.

This way of looking at profits is much closer to the accountants' view than most of the economist's ways of looking at the market.

Governments and monopoly

In any free enterprise economy governments will usually have legislation concerned with monopolies, since the existence of monopolies is a negation of the free market ideal.

The next chapter includes a consideration of the legislation governing monopolies and consumer affairs. The last part of this chapter is devoted to a view of the economic considerations involved.

There are three basic policies the government can adopt towards monopolies.

1 Prohibition. The formation of monopolies can be banned and existing monopolies broken up. This is basically the attitude in the USA. 'Anti-trust' legislation, as it is called, in the States dates back to the Sherman Act of 1890. There are nevertheless a considerable number of monopolies in the USA. Legislation against actions 'in restraint of trade' has been more vigorously prosecuted against unions than against big business.

2 Take-over. The government can take over a monopoly and run it in the public interest. Although many industries and companies have been taken over by governments, it has not usually been done with the object of controlling a monopoly.

3 Regulation. The government can allow a monopoly to continue but pass legislation to make sure that it does not act 'against the public interest'. This is basically the attitude of the British government.

The attitude of a government towards a monopoly will partly be influenced by the way in which the monopoly arose. Some monopolies are *spontaneous*: they arise naturally out of the conditions of supply. For example, Schweppes have a *natural* monopoly of Malvern Spa water because they control the spring from which it comes. Other monopolies are *contrived*, that is to say a business or group of businesses have deliberately set out to create a monopoly. Some of the origins of monopoly power are listed below.

1 Natural. This arises out of the geographical conditions of supply. For example, South Africa has an almost complete monopoly of the western world's supply of diamonds.

2 Historical. A business may have a monopoly because it was first in the field and no-one else has the necessary know-how or customer goodwill. Lloyds of London's command of the insurance market is largely based on historical factors.

3 Capital size. The supply of a commodity may involve the use of such a vast amount of capital equipment that new competitors are effectively excluded from entering the market. This is the case with the chemical industry.

4 Technological. Where there are many economies of scale to be gained it may be natural and advantageous for the market to be supplied by one or a few large companies. This would apply to the motor vehicle industry.

5 Legal. The government may confer a monopoly upon a company. This may be the case when a business is granted a patent or copyright. The right to sole exploitation is given to encourage people to bring forward new ideas.

6 Public. Public corporations such as the Post Office and British Rail have monopolies.

7 Contrived. There is nothing much a government could or would wish to do about breaking up the monopolies discussed above. When people discuss the evils of monopoly, however, it is not usually the above forms of monopoly they are thinking about but rather those that are deliberately contrived. Business organisations can contrive to exploit the market either by taking over, or driving out of business, the other firms in the industry (*scale monopoly*) or by entering into agreements with other businesses to control prices and output (*complex monopoly*). It is this type of monopoly that most legislation is aimed at.

The government's regulation of monopoly will depend upon the technical conditions of supply existing in the industry. In the 'normal' monopoly situation, illustrated in Fig. 16.11, monopoly legislation should be aimed at marketing the monopolist produce at point F where AC = AR. At this point the price is OS and the output ON. All monopoly profits have been eliminated and the public is obtaining the largest output for the lowest price that is compatible with the monopolist remaining in the industry. In this instance the government could also consider breaking up the monopoly into smaller units.

In some industries, however, especially those involving a great deal of capital equipment, such as chemicals and motor vehicles, it could be that the larger and more monopolistic a business organisation is the more it is able to take advantage of economies of scale. The industry is said to have a flat-bottomed average cost curve.

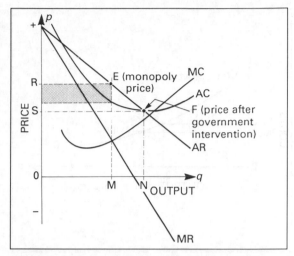

Fig. 16.11 Government intervention in monopoly. The monopolist would choose to produce at point E making maximum profit. Government policy aims to compel the monopolist to produce where AC = AR thus eliminating abnormal profit (this is still not the lowest point of AC).

With the aid of a diagram, explain why a government might still be unhappy with a monopoly situation, even if all the excess profits were taxed away?

In Fig. 16.12 the national market for cars is 2 million per year. In our example production is divided between two companies, Kruks and Toymota. Toymota has a bigger share of the market (1.1 million) and, because of the economies of scale to be gained, the long-run average cost curve (LAC) of the industry is downward sloping. This means that Toymota's average costs (£4,000) are lower than Kruks (£4,800). In the price-conscious car market this means Toymota will sell even more cars, gaining a bigger share of the market and leaving Kruks with a smaller share and even higher costs. In this situation Kruks will eventually go out of business and Toymota will have a complete monopoly. This could be to the public's benefit if continuing economies of scale mean even cheaper cars.

The end result of such a situation is therefore monopoly or some form of oligopoly. This is very much the case in the motor industry, which is dominated by a small number of very large firms. Medium-sized firms have tended to disappear. Jaguar, taken-over by

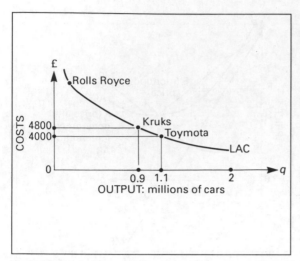

Fig. 16.12 Long run average cost curve

Ford, was one in a long list of companies which were submerged in larger ones. Earlier examples include Armstrong Siddley, Wolsley, Humber and Singer. However, companies producing a very small output of specialist and expensive cars still exist, e.g. Rolls Royce and Lotus, because they are not very concerned about unit costs.

In such an industry it would not be economic sense to break up the monopoly. Indeed, it has been observed that in the UK the Government has often promoted the formation of monopolies in these sorts of industries. In these circumstances the Government's options are limited either to taking over the industry or regulating its prices and output. Although the choices are very clear in theory, in practice it is often very difficult to acquire enough information to judge what is happening in an industry.

1 State three industries that, in your view, are subject to economies of scale. What is likely to be the size of firms in those industries?

2 Suppose that the long-run average cost curve in these industries slopes downwards continuously to the right. What does this mean and what will be the consequences for the likely number of firms in the industry?

Key Words

Profit maximising equilibrium
Firms always maximise profits by producing the output at which MR = MC.

Mergers
The joining together of two different firms.

Discriminating monopoly
A situation where the firm is able to sell the same product at two (or more) different prices.

Spontaneous monopoly
A monopoly naturally arising out of the conditions of supply.

Contrived monopoly
A monopoly deliberately created by merger and amalgamation.

Inefficiency
All types of imperfect competition are to a greater or lesser extent inefficient.

Control of monopolies
The Government may attempt to control monopolies by banning them, by taking them over or by regulating their prices and outputs.

Flat-bottomed average cost curve
When, in the long-run, there are more and more economies of scale to be gained this results in a flat-bottomed AC curve. This usually leads to a situation of monopoly or oligopoly.

Conclusion

In this chapter we have attempted to show that however dissimilar markets may be in their physical attributes, their market behaviour is governed by the same fundamental economic principles. The model of the market is modified by Government intervention, by way of taxes, legislation and the Government's own production of goods and services. In the next chapter, we consider the legal framework of the market place.

Learning Project

Garfield Procter

You are acting as assistant to the Sales Director of Garfield Procter, a company which manufactures detergents and soap products. The Sales Director requires you to prepare a report for the Sales Planning Board. In this report you are asked to recommend the best price and output for 'Gleam', a dishwasher rinse-aid manufactured by Garfield Procter. It will be necessary to justify your recommendation with charts, diagrams and figures where necessary. You should also outline alternative strategies open to Garfield Procter.

Garfield Procter is one of four major companies dominating this line of business. As well as selling Gleam under its own brand name in its distinctive blue plastic dispenser packs Garfield Procter is considering a suggestion from a major supermarket chain that it should pack for them under the supermarket's own house-brand name.

The present price of Gleam is £1.00 and the Sales Director estimates that if the price were to be cut to 80p Garfield would be able to capture one-third of the total UK market for rinse-aids which is estimated at 1,800,000 for the coming year. However, other directors are concerned about the effect such a cut would have upon profit margins. Market research has discovered that the product is held in high esteem by customers who

Garfield Procter Unit Costs of 'Gleam'

Output (packs per year)	Average fixed costs (pence)	Average variable costs (pence)
200,000	92.498	27.489
300,000	68.334	25.018
400,000	56.248	26.251
500,000	49.003	30.994
600,000	44.168	37.449
700,000	40.713	45.001

are willing to buy it even at relatively high price levels. Research suggests that even at a price as high as £1.40 sales of 300,000 a year could be anticipated.

The table on this page shows the estimated unit costs of production of Gleam at various levels of output for the coming year. Using the information and the estimates of the Sales Director and the Market Research Department prepare a formal report for submission to the Sales Director. As well as your recommendation for the best price and output policy, remember to recommend other strategies. You should also consider Garfield Procter's possible response to the approach by the supermarket chain. You should take account of competition law in your report.

Further ideas for learning projects

1 Compare the economist's view of profit with that of the accountant.

2 Present a case study of one industry which has been investigated by the Monopolies and Mergers Commission.

3 Devise a strategy for the revitalisation of the British motor industry.

4 Compile a table of the greatest profit earners in the private sector of the UK economy.

17

Law and the market place

CHAPTER OBJECTIVES _____

After studying this chapter you should be able to:

Define a contract;
State and explain the elements of a valid contract;
Explain why inequality in bargaining power exists between business organisations and their customers;
List the statutes by which this inequality is lessened;
Describe the roles of the administrative agencies of consumer protection;
Outline the legal remedies and sanctions, and the administrative action by which consumer and competition law is enforced.

The law of contract

What is a contract?

A contract is simply *an agreement which the courts will enforce*. Contract law consists of *legal rules* governing the enforceability of obligations arising from voluntary agreements between individuals or organisations.

The practice of contract law reflects its commercial origins and an agreement will only be enforced if it is also a *bargain* that is intended to create *legal relations* between the parties. Each side must give something of value for what they receive from the other; a mere agreement where one party receives without giving anything in return is not enforceable. To this basic principle there is one exception – an agreement made by deed. This is a historical legacy which you are unlikely to encounter in normal business transactions.

When an organisation enters into a contract with another party it is the final step in a process of negotiation. This may have taken many weeks to conclude in the case of a large complicated transaction. Not only the organisation's legal department or its solicitors will have been involved but also its executives and financial advisers, for such a contract may involve important questions of policy, procedure and financial prediction. Alternatively, the contract may have been an ordinary retail sale or a contract for the provision of a simple service, in which case the customer and possibly the organisation's employees may have been only vaguely aware that they were entering into a legal relationship involving well-defined and important rights and duties.

Make a list of all the different types of contracts you have entered into personally or on behalf of your employer or someone else over the last week.

The need for contract law

Contract law is central to all aspects of business activity, whether in its basic form or applied to, say,

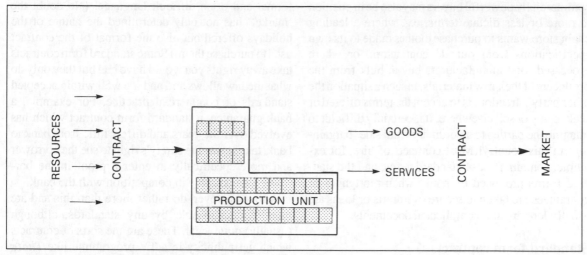

Fig. 17.1 The role of contract law

agency or contracts for the sale of goods. In short all business organisations pursue their objectives by entering into voluntary agreements with other organisations and individuals. Resources are acquired and products and services sold by making agreements complying with a set of rules which must have the force of law to ensure the smooth operation of commercial activity. We can represent this role of contract law in a diagram.

Too often the law is viewed as a constraint upon a person's activities. Justifiably, this may be so in the the case of the criminal law, where society prohibits a particular activity or action, or the law of torts, where the law protects the legal rights of individuals and organisations, but the law of contract should be viewed as a *facilitating medium* enabling an organisation to operate. It cannot be viewed realistically as a medium of constraint, automatically involving sanctions for anyone who becomes involved with it. However, unless society wishes to have a commercial world in which there are no rules and no protection for the weak, some constraints in the law of contract are clearly necessary. Employment and consumer contracts are good examples of where the state has intervened in commercial contracts reducing the parties' freedom to bargain (*see* below).

Thus, the law of contract provides a framework around which a business organisation can build its activities and with which it can regularise its operations, both externally in its dealings with its customers and other organisations and internally with its own employees.

Before we leave these introductory thoughts, it is important to realise that the vast majority of commercial transactions never result in any dispute or court action. They run their course according to their contractual terms. Even where there has been a clear breach of these terms by one of the parties, wider commercial considerations, e.g. the time, cost, hassle and publicity involved, may mean that the injured party takes no legal action. Again, there is little point 'suing a man of straw', i.e. someone with assets insufficient to meet a debt; hence the provision for 'bad debts'. A breach of contract has to be seen in perspective. The advantages of taking legal action must be weighed against its disadvantages: a legal remedy versus financial and general commercial considerations.

Freedom to bargain

Whatever the exact nature of the contract, the parties to it are free to negotiate with each other and conclude a voluntary bargain, stipulating and agreeing to the terms which they wish the contract to contain. The courts will uphold the bargain, good or bad, provided the essential elements required of a contract exist and it does not infringe other basic contract rules.

However, in many contractual situations this freedom to bargain is more theoretical than real. Sellers are often only willing to supply their goods and services on their own standard terms of business and commercially powerful buyers may also be in position to more or less dictate terms, e.g. where a leading chain store wants to purchase clothes made to its own specifications from outside contractors, or where processed food manufacturers buy in bulk from the producers of their raw materials. In such a situation the other party's freedom is to accept the terms offered or seek to buy or sell elsewhere. It is certainly difficult to imagine the parties to an ordinary retail sale 'bargaining' in this country! Most contracts of hire, for example, contain a list of standard terms, and the standard forms produced by banks when mortgages or guarantees are taken to secure overdrafts or loans are usually lengthy and complicated documents.

Standard form contracts

These are contracts where the terms are predetermined, they are not subject to negotiation between the parties. They are not new, the standard terms found in policies of insurance and bills of lading evolved over a long period of time to best represent the commercial interests of all involved. Such standard form contracts, or at least the terms, are of *general application* in the particular area of economic activity.

Many business organisations, however, design and use their *own* standard form contracts so that they can do business on the terms they prefer; frequently they will do business on no other. This, of course means they do business on the terms that are most advantageous to them – legally, commercially and administratively. For example, it enables procedures to be standardised, which means saving time with fewer staff errors. Indeed, the use of such contracts is also to the other party's advantage in so far as the transaction is usually simplified and they know in advance its terms, and therefore their rights and obligations, and can plan accordingly. The disadvantage, if any, will be in the terms themselves. Such standard form contracts – known as *contracts of adhesion* – are of more modern origin and differ from the older type in that they have not been the subject of negotiation and evolution over the years.

The vast majority of both types of standard form contracts are completely unobjectionable. Those used by the major holiday tour operators, i.e. their booking forms, are models of clarity and show that legally binding agreements do not have to be couched in very formal and often difficult language. (No doubt the 'market' has not only determined the nature of the holidays offered but also the format of the contract used to purchase them.) Some standard form contracts take away rights you would have had but they only do what the law allows and and are well within accepted standards of commercial practice. For example, a bank guarantee, a standard form contract which has evolved over the years and differs little from bank to bank, takes away the surety's right to sue the borrower and more specifically to enter a proof in the borrower's bankruptcy in competition with the bank.

A few, however, do rather more than this and are morally questionable by any standards, although (usually) quite legal. These are the sorts of contracts which get publicity in a TV programme like *That's Life*. One programme described how a firm had sold some very expensive bathroom suites, the various outlets from which did not comply with by-laws; in fact anybody fitting them would have committed a criminal offence. No mention (of course) was made of this in the showroom but the standard form contract made it the purchaser's responsibility to check whether the suites complied with the relevant regulations. Consequently, people who bought the suites had no right to a refund when they found they could not get the suites fitted.

In the provision of utility services such as electricity, gas and water standard form contracts are invariably used and the inequality in bargaining power is even more evident. Be they in public or private ownership, the organisation controlling the supply has a monopoly on it. You have to accept their terms or go without.

Consider the list of contracts you made earlier. In which of them, if any, did you or, perhaps, the other party, have any freedom to negotiate its terms?

Statutory intervention

The courts have always been aware of such basic inequalities in bargaining power and have to some extent lessened the harshness of their effect by, for example, restricting the effect of exclusion clauses (*see* below), Parliament, however, has only comparatively recently entered the arena of consumerism with a range of statutes designed to redress the balance in favour of the consumer. Continuing with our example of *standard form contracts*, the Unfair Contract Terms Act 1977 subjects any exclusion clause in such a contract to a test of *reasonableness* (*see* below).

Before this intervention, the *laissez-faire* rules of contract law were often exploited by the stronger party. Most frequently this was done by including a term in the contract comprehensively excluding their liability or limiting the other party's rights in the event of a breach of contract. 'Guarantees' which in fact excluded a buyer's rights under the Sale of Goods Act 1893 (now the Sale of Goods Act 1979) in return for the seller's own less extensive promises to rectify faults, and blanket exclusions of liability for negligence were two of the most common.

Sellers occasionally would go further – possibly some still do – and would tacitly accept that they were in breach of contract but would refuse to do anything about it. As you will see later, consumer legislation often requires consumers to take the initiative against sellers. While their task is now easier, many consumers with a legitimate complaint may be unwilling to become involved with the law for the sake of a few pounds.

To some extent lawyers are to blame for creating a legal system which deters people from looking to the law for compensation. However, in recent years the state has increasingly intervened to help the consumer, both by protective legislation and by simplifying the legal process. This combination of state aid and individual initiative in consumer law will be discussed and assessed later in the chapter.

It is likely that you or a member of your family will have entered into a standard form contract quite recently. This may have been a signed written document or a verbal contract which incorporated a printed statement of terms. Examples would include a holiday booking form, a credit sale agreement, a loan agreement – in fact an almost endless list. It is highly probable that your employer buys in resources and sells products and services through standard form contracts.

Obtain copies of at least two such contracts and identify the clauses which protect the interests of

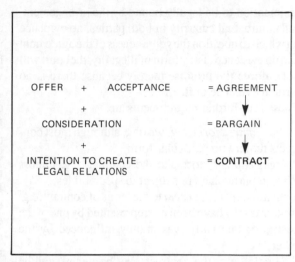

Fig. 17.2 The essentials of a contract

the party whose contract it is. Do you consider these clauses to be 'fair'?

The elements of a valid contract

Having discussed the central role the law of contract plays in the legal framework within which a business organisation operates, we can outline the elements of a valid contract.

A valid contract has three essential features.

1 The *agreement*, consisting of one party making an offer which is accepted by the other.
2 The *bargain*; there must be an element of exchange, the law requiring what is called 'consideration'.
3 The *intention to create legal relations*.

These features are represented diagrammatically in Fig. 17.2

In addition there are four other requirements which, although not essential features as such, will effect the validity or enforceability of the contract should it be defective in one or more of these respects (*see* below). To cite a specific example, by a very old statute – the Statute of Frauds 1677 – a guarantee (a promise to answer for the debt of another) is only enforceable at law if there is *written evidence* of the guarantee; verbal evidence, no matter how conclusive, is not enough. Thus, even though there is a definite agreement, consideration (the granting of, say, a loan in return for the promise to answer for it), an intention to be legally bound by the arrangement, full contractual capacity in both parties, no evidence on which to question the genuineness of the agreement and no evidence of any form of illegality, the court will not enforce the promise merely because there is no written evidence of it.

These four further requirements are:

1 the *required form*, e.g. writing, although most contracts require no particular form;
2 *legal capacity* to make the contract, e.g. minors who, in particular, are subject to special rules;
3 *genuineness of consent* to the terms of contract, e.g. the terms may have been misrepresented by one of the parties or one party was unduly influenced by the other;
4 *legality*, e.g. the contract may be against public policy such as where an employment contract restricts employees' rights to accept freely other employment on leaving their current employer.

In the rest of this chapter we discuss each of these requirements in turn and cite a number of cases. There are two reasons for citing these cases: first, they illustrate the situations we discuss; second, and more importantly, most of contract law is derived from cases and any dispute arising from the contract would be resolved in court by reference to decisions in similar cases. The cases we describe are all well-known and their principles apply to all fields of business. Remember, however, that such well-known cases either laid down a principle which to us now seems self-evident and/or were clear-cut and often extreme situations. Many contractual problems encountered today are, of course, often more involved although, ultimately, a simple rule of law will probably be applied to settle the dispute once the exact nature of the dispute has been determined and all the evidence and arguments have been heard.

Void, voidable and unenforceable

Agreements which fail on one of these four further requirements are either void or voidable or unenforceable. We need to explain each of these terms.

A *void* contract is a contradiction in terms since it has never been a contract and is, therefore, without legal effect. Despite this, it is a useful term to describe a situation where the parties intended to enter into a contract, and apparently did so, but legally or physically the agreement can have no effect. In *Strickland v Turner* (1852), for example, an annuity was void because neither party to it knew that the person on whose life the annuity was taken out had already died!

A *voidable* contract can be rejected by the 'innocent' party but it is perfectly valid until it is rejected. For example, if your consent to the agreement was obtained by fraud, other misrepresentation or by the exercise of undue influence, you have the right to rescind (set aside) the contract when you realise this. However, because the contract is valid until avoided subsequent events may prevent you rejecting. For example, in *Lewis v Averay* (1971) a rogue obtained a car from L by posing as a famous actor whose cheque book and studio pass he had stolen. The sale was clearly voidable for fraud. He then sold the car to A posing as L. In an action by L to recover the car from A, it was held that when A bought the car in good faith and for value from the rogue, A obtained good title to it. The contract of sale between L and the rogue had ceased to be voidable and L could not recover the car.

An *unenforceable* contract is perfectly valid and therefore property or money transferred under it can not be recovered. However, it is not enforceable because the necessary legal evidence of it is missing. Thus, if you fail to fulfil your obligations, the other party can not compel you to do so. We have already mentioned that a guarantee requires written evidence of its terms to be enforceable.

The agreement

Offer

The law requires that one party must make a *definite offer* to the other, although the offer need not be expressly stated but may be made by implication. An automatic car park, for example, is an implied offer to motorists that they may park their cars inside in return for a specified payment. Acceptance of the offer here would be, in most cases, taking the ticket from the entry machine or, at the very latest, driving through the barrier.

Once an offer is accepted by the person to whom it is addressed then, subject to the other contractual requirements, a binding agreement comes into being. Although most offers are made to individual people, an offer can be made to a specified group or even to anyone who receives notice of it – the 'world at large'. In *Carlill v Carbolic Smoke Ball Co* (1892), for example, the company offered to pay £100 to anybody who used their 'smokeball' (a patent medicine) in the way prescribed and still caught influenza. When sued by Carlill, who used the 'smoke-ball' and caught influenza, the company unsuccessfully argued *inter alia* (among other things) that they could not be held to their promise because they had not made the offer specifically to Carlill.

Invitation to treat

An offer must be distinguished from an *invitation to treat*. This is an invitation to enter into negotiations or to make an offer which may or may not result in the conclusion of an agreement. Many organisations advertise or display their products and while these may be interpreted by the man in the street as 'offers' to sell goods or provide services, at law no offer is made. Hence, in *Pharmaceutical Society of GB v Boots Cash Chemists (Southern), Ltd* (1952) a prosecution under the Pharmacy and Poisons Act 1933, which made it an offence to sell any listed poison 'unless the sale is effected under the supervision of a registered pharmacist', failed because it was held that selection of an item from a self-service display did not amount to a sale. The display was an invitation to treat. The customer had made the offer by selecting the article, the defendants had accepted it and completed the sale when a pharmacist approved the transaction near the cash-desk. At law, therefore, the sale took place according to the provisions of the Act.

The case of *Gibson v Manchester City Council* (1979) is well worth mentioning at this point because it illustrates the idea put forward on several occasions already in this book that law should neither be seen nor studied in a vacuum. In 1970 the Council had a policy of selling council houses to existing tenants. In February 1971 the plaintiff received a letter from the Council stating that the Council 'may be prepared to sell the house to you at the purchase price of £2,725 less 20% = £2,180 (freehold)' and inviting him to make a formal application. This he did. However, before formal contracts had been exchanged the local government elections in 1971 brought a Labour controlled council to power and the policy of selling council houses was

reversed. The Council decided only to complete the sale of those homes on which formal contracts had been exchanged. This did not included the plaintiff's house. Nevertheless, Gibson maintained that he had a binding contract with the Council. The House of Lords decided, however, that the Council's original letter to him was an invitation to treat and that his application to purchase was the offer. This offer the Council had clearly rejected.

All organisations require land as a fundamental economic resource. You have already seen that land became a complicated concept at law and considerable formality attaches to its sale and transfer as a consequence. A series of cases show that the courts are generally unwilling to acknowledge the existence of an offer to sell land unless the clearest evidence of this intention exists. In *Harvey v Facey* (1893) a telegraphed reply giving the lowest cash price at which the defendant was willing to sell his property was held not to amount to a definite offer to sell and in *Clifton v Palumbo* (1944) an 'offer' to sell a large estate for £600,000 was held to be merely a statement of price. However, in *Bigg v Boyd Gibbons Ltd* (1971) the Court of Appeal found that the parties had concluded a contract to sell the property in question, even though only the names of the parties, the property and the price were certain. These aspects, however, are the essential features of the agreement in a contract for the sale of land.

Termination of the offer

At any time after the offer is made it can be revoked (withdrawn) by the offeror (the person who makes the offer) provided the revocation is communicated to the offence (the person to whom the offer is made) before the latter has accepted the offer. Although the offeree incurs the responsibility of deciding whether the notice is reasonable, the decision in *Dickinson v Dodds* (1876) clearly shows that it is not necessary for the offeror to communicate the revocation personally. In that case, an offer to sell a house to the plaintiff was held to have been effectively revoked after the defendant sold it to a third party and the plaintiff was informed of this by a fourth. The plaintiff had received sufficient notice of the defendant's revocation.

Where the offeror revokes the offer the offer terminates through the positive act of one of the parties involved. This is also the case where the offeree accepts or rejects the offer that was made to them. However, an offer can terminate in other ways. The offeror may have specifically stated that the offer was to remain open for a limited period and it will automatically terminate if not accepted within that time limit. If no time limit is stated, it is a question of fact whether the offer still exists after a given time has passed.

Offers are sometimes made subject to a condition that must be fulfilled before any acceptance of the offer creates a binding agreement: a condition precedent. It is normal when buying a second-hand car to want a valid MOT certificate for the car and therefore X might say to Y: 'I offer to buy your car for £600 provided it passes its MOT test.' Should the car not pass, X's offer to buy terminates.

In *Financing Ltd v Stimson* (1962) a more difficult situation arose. The defendant alleged the existence of an implied condition precedent. He had signed an 'agreement' to buy a car which he had seen at a dealer's premises from the plaintiff on hire-purchase terms. The 'agreement' stated that the plaintiffs were only to be bound when they signed it. The defendant paid the first instalment and took the car away but, being dissatisfied, returned it two days later. The car was then stolen from the dealer's premises and recovered badly damaged. In ignorance of all these events the plaintiffs signed the 'agreement'. On discovering what had happened they sold the car and sued the defendant for breach of the 'agreement'. The Court of Appeal held that the 'agreement' was in fact an offer which had been made subject to an implied condition that, until it was accepted, the car would remain in substantially the same state as when the offer was made. The defendant's offer had therefore terminated before it was accepted by the plaintiffs.

Acceptance

The agreement is completed by the offeree accepting the offer which has been made to him. Just as the offer must be firm and certain, so must the acceptance. No agreement results from 'I'll think about it' or 'I might buy that.' Legal obligations must be definite and only a complete acceptance of the offer will result in an enforceable agreement.

The same is true where the offeree wishes to have a second opinion before committing himself to a contract. For example, when a second-hand car is offered for sale, a potential purchaser might say 'I'll buy it providing it passes a garage inspection'; this is not a definite acceptance. Such conditional acceptances are also common when the offeree does not wish to be legally bound until a formal contract is drafted. The phrase 'subject to contract', which solicitors invariably include in preliminary correspondence relating to the sale of land, operates as an express denial of any binding agreement.

Should the offeree wish to try to vary the terms of the offer it is a question of fact whether the proposals amount to a counter-offer and a rejection of the original offer or merely a request for information which would still allow them to accept the offer in its original form. In *Hyde v Wrench* (1840) a reply to an offer, quoting a lower price for the land that the defendant wished to sell, was held to be a rejection of the original offer preventing the plaintiff from subsequently accepting the offer at the original price. In *Stevenson v McLean* (1880), however, S requested further information from M on the method of payment and delivery after he had received M's offer. M then sold to a third party. In ignorance of this sale S accepted the offer on the original terms. On the facts it was held that the request for information did not constitute a counter-offer and rejection of M's offer. S was therefore entitled to damages for breach of contract.

In some agreements there is no express acceptance; the offeree does not say 'I accept' but the existence of a firm acceptance can be gathered from the circumstances. In *Brogden v Metropolitan Rail Co* (1877), Brogden had supplied coal to the Company for a number of years without any formal agreement and at length the parties decided to put their dealings on a more formal footing. A draft agreement sent by the Company was amended and approved by Brogden and then returned. The Company's agent did not complete the formalities required but both sides began to deal with each other according to the terms of the draft. Brogden had not accepted the draft because he had added a new term by his amendment and it was up to the Company to accept or reject this. However, the subsequent conduct of the parties could only be explained on the basis that the draft had been agreed by both sides. On the facts a binding contract existed.

Certainty in the agreement

There must be *certainty* in the agreement reached by the parties. The law will not enforce vague agreements. In *Loftus v Roberts* (1902), an agreement where an actress was engaged at 'a West End salary to be mutually arranged between us' was held to be unenforceable because the salary, an important term in the agreement, was clearly too vague. Similarly, in *Scammel v Ousten* (1941) an agreement to buy a motor van on the 'usual hire-purchase terms' was too vague because at the time there were no usual hire-purchase terms which could have been implied into the contract.

The law recognises, however, that there are a number of ways in which vagueness can be rectified and will enforce agreements that can be made certain. For example:

(a) terms may be implied into the agreement by Acts of Parliament, the courts or by trade custom to give it certainty;

(b) the parties to the agreement may have had dealings with each other before and it may be possible to remove any uncertainty in the agreement by referring to these previous dealings;

(c) the agreement itself may provide a way to remove the uncertainty. In *Foley v Classique Coaches Ltd* (1934), a provision to submit disputes to arbitration overcame the uncertainty in an agreement to supply petrol 'at a price to be agreed by the parties in writing from time to time'. However, in *May v Butcher* (1929) an arbitration clause did not rectify the uncertainty where the date of payment, the delivery period and the price had still to be agreed. In truth there was no concluded bargain and the law would not recognise an agreement to agree. An arbitration clause can only operate after a bargain has been concluded.

Communication of acceptance

It is not enough merely to accept the offer, the acceptance must be communicated. Usually this is done verbally or by letter.

In this context it has long been established that re- maining silent in response to an offer is not an acceptance of it. If the law were otherwise, contractual liability could be imposed on an unwilling person by merely stating that his silence was acceptance of the offer. (This is also the theory behind the Unsolicited Goods and Services Act 1971 – *see* below.) However, in the offer the offeror may expressly or by implication waive the need to communicate acceptance. In *Carlill v Carbolic Smoke Ball Co.* (1892) the company argued that Carlill had not communicated her acceptance but it was held that the nature of the offer implied that it was unnecessary to do so. Her conduct was her acceptance.

The *post* is a basic form of communication in business and special rules relate to postal acceptance of offers. Normally an acceptance by post is complete as soon as it is posted, provided it is properly stamped and addressed. Once posted, the acceptance cannot be withdrawn but an offeror will be bound by a postal acceptance even if it is never delivered. In contrast, a postal revocation of an offer is only effective when actually brought to the offeror's attention. The postal rule is an exception to the general rule and cannot apply where the terms of the offer specify actual communication or communication within a time limit. In *Holwell Securities Ltd v Hughes* (1973), for example, the proper construction of an option to purchase property 'exercisable by notice in writing to intending vendor at any time within six months from the date thereof', was that the notice had to be delivered to him personally and a properly posted letter which never arrived did not amount to an exercise of the option.

The offer may itself specify the way in which it is to be accepted and the method amounts to a term of the offer. The courts, however, allow some flexibility and where the requirement is not obligatory they will accept another method that is equally good. For example, in *Yates Building Co Ltd v R J Pulleyn & Sons (York) Ltd* (1975), a letter exercising an option was held to have been wrongly rejected even though it was sent neither by registered post nor recorded delivery as requested. The requirement was not obligatory and the letter sent was equally effective. Where the offeror does not stipulate any particular method of communication, the effectiveness of the method chosen depends upon the facts of the case. An offer by telegram, for example, implies a similar method of acceptance.

On 1 January Jack writes to his hill-walking friend Jill offering to sell her his car for £2,500, knowing that she has been looking to buy such a car. He states that he must have an answer by 10 January at the latest because he needs the money to buy another car on the 11 January. Jill writes back, her letter arriving on the 3 January, saying that the price was rather more than she could afford to pay at once and would he accept payment in two equal monthly instalments. Jack does not reply to this letter and Jill fails to contact him by telephone because he is spending time with his new ball-room dancing partner Buster. Jill wants the car and manages to put together Jack's asking price. She writes accepting Jack's offer on 8 January, her letter arriving on 10 January. On 9 January Jack sells his car to Buster for £2,000 and informs Jill of this after her letter has arrived.

Jill is not pleased and wishes to take legal action against Jack for breach of contract, maintaining that he was under an obligation to sell the car to her.

Consider the strength of her case.

The bargain

The nature of consideration

A contract is a bargain and a bargain involves an element of exchange: each side must give and receive something of value. Goods in exchange for cash is a simple and perfect example. Therefore, the law will only enforce a promise when it has been bought by the person who wishes to enforce it. Consideration is the price of this promise. An agreement in which consideration is present is nearly always an enforceable bargain. More formal judicial definitions of consideration exist but they often serve merely to cloud the essential simplicity of the concept. Even so, over the years the law has evolved a series of requirements which must be fulfilled before the proposed consideration will be acceptable.

Consideration must move from the promisee

The consideration must be provided by the person to whom the promise was made and who wishes to enforce the promise. In other words, only the parties to the contract can generally acquire rights and obligations under it. Thus, a third party (a stranger to the contract) cannot generally enforce a contract. This is known as the doctrine of *privity of contract*. In *Tweddle v Atkinson* (1861), for example, T married X's daughter and X and T's father agreed with each other to pay £100 and £200 respectively to T to provide for the couple. The contract expressly gave T the right to enforce their promises against them. T's father paid but X died before his payment was made. T sued his executor, A, for the £200. His action failed despite having been given the 'right' to enforce the contract because he had not provided consideration for X's promise.

Consideration must not be past

The consideration must not precede the promise that it supports. In *Re McArdle* (1951), a father's will left his house jointly to his children. One of the children and his wife still lived with the mother and the wife had made substantial improvements to the house. The other children subsequently agreed to contribute towards the cost of these. An action to enforce the agreement failed because the improvements preceded the promise to contribute towards them.

Exceptions to the rule exist. If a person asks another to do something for them in a way which raises the presumption that they will be paid, a subsequent promise to pay will be enforceable. In *Re Casey's Patents, Stewart v Casey* (1892), a promise to give a one-third share of the patent rights, in return for services which the plaintiff had already performed in promoting the patents, was enforced. The services had been requested and it was clearly understood that they were to be paid for.

A statutory exception exists in the Bills of Exchange Act 1882 s.27. This states that in relation to bills of exchange, 'an antecedent debt or liability', i.e. a previous or existing liability, is 'valuable considerations'. A bill of exchange contains a promise to pay a specific sum of money and many bills, particularly cheques (the most common type of bill of exchange), are drawn to settle existing (past) debts. Thus, the consideration given for the promise contained in the bill is past, e.g. payment by cheque for goods delivered a week ago. In short, the consideration precedes the promise. Clearly, however, this exception is necessary in order for bills of exchange to fulfil their function as a method of payment. It is also a good example of the needs of commerce and industry affecting the rules of contract law. (If in *Re McArdle* (1951), for example, the other children had given the wife a cheque, she could have enforced the promise of payment contained in it.)

Consideration must be of some legal value

Consideration must be *sufficient* but it need not be commercially *adequate*. For example, a person could sell his car for £1.00 and the law would not question the bargain that the parties had struck, provided that the bargain was not defective in any other respect. It is up to the parties to reach their own bargain, the law does does not question their commercial judgment. In *Chappel v Nestlé* (1960), for example, N offered for sale a record of 'Rockin Shoes' for 7.5p plus three wrappers from their chocolate bars. C owned the copyright in the tune and brought a successful action for breach of copyright when N paid the statutory 6.25% royalty on the 7.5p received for each record. The court held that the wrappers, while being of little or no commercial value to N, were part of the consideration for the record and therefore royalties were payable on them as well!

Consideration is said to be *insufficient* where the person providing it is merely fulfilling an *existing legal duty*. This may be either a contractual duty or a public duty. In *Stilk v Myrick* (1809) two sailors deserted their ship and the master, unable to recruit replacements, promised the rest of the crew that they would share the wages of the deserters if they would complete the voyage home. This they did but they were held to be unable to enforce the master's promise. In *Collins v Godefroy* (1831), C was under a public duty to give evidence in court for G and accepted G's promise to pay him six guineas (£6.30) for doing so. C could not recover the sum because he had provided no consideration, he had merely fulfilled his public duty.

This principle was refined by the Court of Appeal in relation to contractual duties in *Williams v Roffey Bros & Nicholls (Contractors) Ltd* (1989). Here RB&N were the main contractors for the refurbishment of a block of flats and had contracted W to do the carpentry work. RB&N became worried that W would not complete their work on time and offered W extra money to do so because their own contract contained a penalty clause. W sued for this extra payment and RB&N pleaded lack of consideration. It was held that W was entitled to payment. The principle behind the decision is that where a promisor obtains a benefit through the contractual performance, obtaining that benefit can amount to consideration for an extra payment provided the promise was not obtained by economic duress or fraud. (*Stilk v Myrick* (1809) still applies where no benefit is secured as a result of the promise.)

It follows, of course, that if you exceed your duty you provide consideration for a promise of payment. In *Glasbrook Brothers v Glamorgan CC* (1925), GB wanted to protect their mine during a strike. GCC, the police authority, were under a public duty to provide protection but had a discretion as to its exact form. GCC were prepared to offer only a mobile force but subsequently agreed to provide a permanent guard in return for £2,200. The payment was held to be enforceable because on the facts GCC had done more than the law obliged them to do. In *Hartley v Ponsonby* (1857) the scope of the contractual duty of a group of sailors was at issue. They had been offered extra wages to continue working a ship after the crew had become so depleted that continuing the voyage was dangerous. On the facts, their original contractual obligation had been discharged by the changed circumstances and they were free to enter into a new contract. The extra wages could therefore be recovered.

A somewhat different problem arises where a person pays or promises to pay part of a debt in return for the creditor promising to forgo the balance. Here it is a question of avoiding an existing duty, not enforcing extra payment. It is not uncommon for a business organisation to be in a position where it has to forgo the balance of a debt to avoid liquidity problems. By the time the full debt is recovered a crisis could have arisen. This means that a firm might be forced, indeed even willing, to accept £500 in payment for a debt of £750 in order to pay its own overheads and thereby stay in business. This economic truth, coupled with an almost traditional reluctance on the part of business people to resort to legal action, has resulted in a divergence of theory and practice. At law the balance can be recovered because the debtor has provided no consideration for the creditor's promise; they have not even fulfilled the legal obligation that they were already under. In *Foakes v Beer* (1884) the House of Lords confirmed the rule when Beer sued Foakes for the interest owed to her on a judgment debt. The House rejected Foakes' argument that, in return for this payment of a lump sum and the balance of the judgment debt in instalments, she had agreed to take no further action on the matter.

To this rule a number of exceptions were laid down in *Pinnel's Case* as long ago as 1602. Payment of a lesser sum amounts to consideration where, at the creditor's request, it is paid at an earlier date or at a different place. The debt is similarly satisfied where the debtor gives or does something else which may be worth more or less with the creditor's consent. In each of these cases the debtor has introduced a new element into the transaction, giving the creditor something other than that to which they were entitled. The exceptions make commercial sense: an earlier payment of less might solve an acute cash-flow problem, while payment at a different place may be convenient (particularly so in olden days), and if the creditor wishes to take payment in kind, e.g. goods instead of money, a contract is after all a private bargain between two or more individuals.

A more modern exception exists where it would be unfair for the promisor who agrees to accept less to go back on his word. This exception emerged in the *High Trees Case* (1947) and is known as *promissory* or *equitable estoppel*. In 1939 the plaintiffs had leased a block of flats to the defendants. In January 1940 they agreed in writing, but without the defendants providing consideration, to accept only half of the rent due under the lease because the war had caused many of the flats to be unoccupied. From 1940 to 1945 the defendants paid the reduced rent. However, when the flats were again full in 1945 the plaintiffs brought an action claiming that they were entitled to the full rent not only for the future but also from 1940, thereby seeking to go back on the written agreement. To test their claim they sought payment of the full rent for the last two quarters of 1945. On the facts, the actual claim succeeded because the agreement was intended to be a temporary arrangement which would cease to operate when conditions changed, as they had by mid

1945. However, the judge was of the opinion that had the claim been pursued right back to 1940 the plaintiffs would have failed because they would have been estopped (prevented) from going back on their promise, even though the defendants had given nothing in return.

The application of the principle of promissory estoppel, to prevent the promisor going back on his word, is at the discretion of the court and subsequent cases show that it can only be used as a defence against a person seeking to enforce their original contractual rights and never as the basis for a legal action. A promise can only be enforced where consideration has been given for it. It is unresolved at present whether promissory estoppel merely suspends the promisor's original rights or whether it extinguishes them entirely. If the former is the case, promisors can reassert their rights by giving adequate notice of their intention to do so. For example, if a buyer has waived a contractual delivery date they would subsequently be able to take back their promise and exercise their right to reject delivery after giving the seller a reasonable ultimatum.

Another situation where payment of less is full satisfaction for a greater sum owed is to be found in insolvency law. Debtors may make compositions (as they are called) with their creditors under which their creditors each agree to take a proportion of what they are owed. They are bound by the composition because any action to recover the balance would amount to fraud against their fellow creditors.

Finally, the performance of an existing duty is sufficient consideration where the duty is owed to someone other than the promisor. This was illustrated in *The Eurymedon* (1974) where the defendants, who damaged goods while unloading them from a ship, were held to have provided sufficient consideration by unloading the goods, a duty that they already owed to the shippers, to take the benefit of a promise from the plaintiffs to treat them as exempt from any liability for damaging the goods.

Activity

Kylie is going on holiday for a month and asks her neighbour Jason to look after her four pet Siamese cats while she is away. Jason is somewhat reluctant to do so because the previous month they have badly savaged his pet pit-bull terrier that he

has been given the previous Christmas. Nevertheless he agrees, after explaining that it would mean he will have to cancel his planned annual fly-fishing weekend.

On Kylie's return Jason explains that the cats have been quite a handful and that she needs to collect her last two weeks' post from the local Post Office.

Kylie is full of remorse and promises to pay Jason £100 for his time and trouble.

After six weeks she still has not paid him. Can Jason enforce her promise?

The intention to create legal relations

The existence of a definite bargain between the parties still does not mean that an enforceable contract exists. The law requires that the parties must have intended their bargain to be legally binding. In effect this requirement is more apparent than real for every commercial agreement is presumed to be legally binding unless the contrary is proved by the person who disputes the presumption. In the event of a dispute the question is decided by looking at the facts of the case. In *Carlill v Carbolic Smoke Ball Co* (1892), for example, the defendants had advertised that they had deposited £1000 with their bankers as evidence of their good faith. This deposit was held to be sufficient indication that their promise was not intended to be a 'mere puff' but a statement upon which they expected to incur legal liability. It is possible, however, to expressly exclude legal liability in a commercial agreement by including a suitably worded clause – an 'honour clause' – in which the parties declare that their agreement is not to be binding at law.

In contrast, social and domestic agreements are not presumed to be legally binding and if one of the parties wishes to enforce such an agreement they must prove the required intention. This is done by producing evidence to show that the social agreement is in reality a commercial arrangement or that the domestic relationship has ceased to exist. In *Merritt v Merritt* (1970) an agreement between a wife and her husband, by which he promised to pay £40 a month to her and to transfer the matrimonial home into her sole name in return for her paying the outstanding mortgage payments, was legally binding because the domestic relationship had ended when the husband had left his wife to live with another woman.

Further requirements

The presence of an 'agreement', a 'bargain' and an 'intention to create legal relations' are the essential requirements of a valid contract but four other factors have an important bearing on its validity and enforceability. These factors may be termed, as you saw earlier, 'form', 'contractual capacity, genuineness of consent' and 'legality'. They can best be considered, perhaps, as possible legal defects in the bargain the parties have struck.

Form

It is a common and understandable misconception that contracts have to be written, or at least recorded in writing, for in a great many transactions one or both of the parties signs a written contract or receives a written receipt. This practice is seldom based on legal requirement but on the practical needs of administration. Within an organisation records must be kept, accounts filed and sent, stock turnover monitored and generally a whole host of internal functions either directly depend on, or are fueled by, written records of the organisation's transactions.

Legal requirements as to form are comparatively few and the most formal document known to English law, the deed – a document that must be signed, witnessed and delivered but no longer sealed (Law of Property (Miscellaneous Provisions) Act 1989) – is only commonly required in contract law where a lease of land is granted for more than three years. Even here an enforceable agreement to grant a lease, as distinct from the grant itself, need only be by a signed written contract containing the terms and this for many purposes creates the same rights between the parties.

In recent years a requirement that certain contracts must be written has proved effective in consumer protection and all consumer credit agreements covered by the Consumer Credit Act 1974 are required to be in writing. A regulated agreement which fails to satisfy the statutory requirements can only be enforced against the debtor on the order of the court. The Law of Property (Miscellaneous Provisions) Act 1989 now requires a contract for the sale of land to be in writing – something which was normal anyway.

Finally, under the Statute of Frauds 1677 a contract of guarantee (a promise to answer for the debt of another) must be evidenced in writing, i.e. the creditor must have documentary evidence of it although the guarantee itself can be given orally. In practice of course, commercial guarantees, such as those given by directors to their company's bank as security for a loan to their company, are invariably very formal *written* contracts.

Contractual capacity

Traditionally, the law took as its norm the sane, sober, adult human male and anyone or anything else either had to be protected from society or suffered disabilities within it. Today most of the disabilities have gone but special rules exist concerning the contractual capacity of minors.

A minor, a person under 18 years of age, can only be *bound* by contracts for 'necessaries' (basically food, clothing, lodging and other things without which it would be unreasonable to expect a person of that age to live) and contracts of employment that are to his or her advantage, for example those containing an element of education or training such as articles of apprenticeship.

Contracts under which minors acquire interests in subject matter of a permanent nature which involve recurring obligations, e.g. a lease or a partnership agreement, are binding on them *unless* they avoid them while they are still under eighteen or within a reasonable time after becoming eighteen. All other contracts entered into by minors are *unenforceable* against them although they may ratify such contracts on reaching eighteen, thereby becoming bound by the contract.

Genuiness of consent

An agreement where one of the parties did not freely and fully consent to the terms will generally not be enforced. An agreement obtained by actual or threatened unlawful force (duress), or by the use of unfair pressure may be set aside by the party who was unable to exercise a free will. The former is highly unlikely but in the latter, more common case, certain well-defined confidential or fiduciary relationships give rise to the presumption that unfair pressure or undue

influence, as it is termed at law, has been exerted. Such relationships include solicitor/client, doctor/patient and parent/child. In other relationships undue influence must be proved. However, for the court to set aside the contract the weaker party must show that the stronger party took advantage of the situation to their financial benefit. It will not be set aside merely because a confidential relationship was proved to have existed.

Similarly a contract is voidable (capable of being set aside) where one party has misled the other by misrepresenting, either fraudulently, negligently or innocently, the true facts.

Undue influence and misrepresentation both entitle the injured party to rescind (to set aside or cancel) the contract but they will lose this right if they subsequently confirm the agreement after appreciating the true facts, if they delay too long before seeking to rescind, or, in certain circumstances, where other people have become involved and have acquired an interest in the property.

Occasionally, where one or both parties to a contract make a mistake the contract will be void and a total nullity. But most types of mistake have no effect at all. For example, the law will not assist an organisation which mistakes the quantity of goods it requires or underestimates the time required to complete an order. Where, however, the mistake prevents any agreement being reached at all, or where an agreement is reached which lacks any foundation because of the mistake, the contract will be void. The former situation can possibly arise in a contract of sale where the seller mistakes the identity of the buyer or, more likely, where the buyer and seller are at cross-purposes as to the subject-matter of the sale, the seller wishing to sell X but the buyer wishing to buy Y. In the latter situation the effect of a mistake is very limited. The contract will only be void if, without the knowledge of either the buyer or seller, the intended subject matter of the contract ceased to exist for the purposes of the contract before the agreement was concluded. This could happen where the seller's agent has already sold the goods to another buyer or where they have been physically destroyed.

Legality

All contracts must be within the law. Illegality is an

umbrella term in the law of contract, covering contracts which involve actual criminal acts, e.g. an organisation allowing an employee to include his tax liability in his expense account, thereby defrauding the state, to contracts which merely offend public policy. A contract in which a person restricts his future freedom to carry on his trade, business or profession as he pleases comes into this latter category. An example would be a contract of employment containing a term which prevents an employee from working for a competitor of her employer for a certain period and/or within a certain area after leaving her job. You may, perhaps, have such a provision in your own contract of employment but the point is that the restriction will be upheld if it can be proved to be reasonable and necessary for the protection of your employer's legitimate trade interests. A further example where such a restriction may be justified is where an established shop is sold with its goodwill and the vendor agrees not to open a similar shop within a certain area and/or time.

In all cases those aspects of the contract which are illegal or tainted with illegality are void but where the contract merely offends public policy, the offending parts may be severed from the whole and the rest enforced. Employees whose contracts contain unlawful restraints of trade can still enforce the payment of wages owed to them although their employers cannot enforce the clauses in which the unreasonable restraints are contained.

Such then are the essentials of a valid contract. Its concepts underlie all aspects of business law and it exists as a medium through which an organisation can pursue its activities. The essential simplicity of the main concept should never be forgotten; it is a bargain struck between two parties who, as in all spheres of social activity, must observe certain rules so that commercial activity may continue with the minimum of disruption, dispute and uncertainty.

Breach of contract

We made the point at the start of this chapter that of the many millions of contracts that are entered into each year it is only a very small minority that are not performed according to their terms. There is not much that can go wrong when you use a bus or a train or buy the weekly groceries is there? What, however, happens when a contract is broken? You will see in Chapter 25 that the breach gives rise to *strict liability*. But what does this mean in practice? What remedies are available to the 'injured party'?

We start with the rule that any breach of contract, no matter how minor, entitles the injured party to *sue for damages*. The amount, or *quantum* of damages, is the financial loss incurred; the purpose of an award is to put the parties in the position they would have been in had the contract been performed according to its terms. For example, if a supplier fails to supply, the buyer's loss would be assessed in terms of any higher price paid for the materials elsewhere, the cost of the delay caused, e.g. loss of profit and operating costs, and general management and administrative expenses.

Where there has been a breach of a major term, such as a failure to supply or a failure to meet quality specifications in a manufacturing contract (a *condition* as opposed to a *warranty*, to use the correct terminology) the injured party is entitled to reject (*repudiate*) the contract instead of or in addition to bringing an action for damages. The terms implied by the main pieces of consumer legislation such as the Sale of Goods Act 1979 (with which we deal later) are contractual *conditions*.

An award of damages is the usual remedy sought when a contract has been broken. Business is about money, a breach of contract usually causes financial loss and the purpose of the action is to compensate the party who has been caused such loss. Occasionally, however, money is inadequate compensation, the subject matter of the contract may be unique and by definition financial compensation cannot provide a substitute. In such situations the court has the power to order specific performance of the contract, i.e. that the contract be performed according to its terms. A contract for the sale of land is the best example of where *specific performance* might be awarded if one of the parties has failed to fulfil their obligations.

Select two of the contracts in the list you made earlier and consider each of them carefully in the light of the text above. Specifically:

1 Who made the offer to whom, how and what exactly was it? Was there an invitation to treat?

2 How was the offer accepted?

3 What were the express terms of the contract?

4 Was the agreement subject to any implied terms? (You may have to come back to this question.)

5 Exactly what was the consideration – on *both* sides?

6 If you are under 18, were any of your personal contracts for things other than necessaries?

7 Was 'undue influence' used to obtain your consent to any of the agreements?!

8 Did you or the other party break the contract in any way? If you did, what was done/can be done about it?

Key words ─────────────────────────

Contract
An agreement which the courts will enforce. Viewed in commercial terms, a simple bargain but in legal terms often a complicated arrangement.

Contract law
A framework of rules which regulates the making of commercial arrangements. These rule in practice become important when agreements start to go wrong.

Freedom to bargain
The basic principles of contract law were developed on the theory that the parties to the contract were free to negotiate their agreement. In practice this theory is subject to economic forces and statutory intervention.

Elements of a valid contract
Essentially there must exist an *agreement*, a *bargain* and an *intention to be legally bound*. Other factors are relevant to the subsequent enforceability of the contract.

─────────────────────────

Organisations, consumers and the law

Consumer law in context

You have already seen in this chapter that the concept of freedom to bargain is usually rather illusory when an individual consumer enters into a contract with a large organisation. A large organisation will usually conduct its business according to set procedures and on prescribed terms of business contained in standard form contracts. Ally this to the increased standardisation in methods of production and distribution and the average consumer's lack of financial resources and unwillingness (often inability) to pursue a claim through the courts, and you have a compelling case for the law to recognise and to attempt to remedy the inequality in bargaining power between consumers and producers and distributors of goods and services. In particular, consumers need protection from misinformation, unfair influence and unfair limitations on their range of choice – economic exploitation in general. As you will see in the rest of this chapter, the principle of *caveat venditor* (let the seller beware) has now made significant inroads into the 19th century *laissez-faire* approach of *caveat emptor* (let the buyer beware).

In this context the framework of consumer law provides the corresponding responsibility and accountability of an organisation in relation to its products as that discussed in Chapter 12 in relation to its resources. Once again, responsibility is both economic and social: a trading organisation must make sufficient profit to continue in business and it cannot grossly exploit the market to the detriment of the community at large. Legal accountability to consumers is clearly inherent in the framework but in recent years a comprehensive structure of administrative accountability has been created, primarily through the Office of Fair Trading. However, administrative accountability is in reality an amalgam of legal, economic, political and social forms of accountability.

The common law has played only a limited role in consumer protection. It has concerned itself more with specific aspects of consumerism, for example the interpretation of clauses excluding a supplier's liability for supplying defective goods, rather than with general policy. Consumer law is therefore largely statutory and the product of government intervention in both the common law principle of 'freedom of contract' and in the free working of the economy. This intervention can be considered as a political response to some of the socially unacceptable characteristics of a capitalist economy.

Who is a consumer?

A consumer is defined for the purposes of the Fair Trading Act 1973 as a person:

(a) to whom goods or services are supplied, or sought to be supplied, in the course of a business carried on by the supplier; and

(b) who does not receive or seek to receive them in the course of a business carried on by him.

However, while we are concerned here with the consumer as defined by the 1973 Act, you have already seen that organisations 'consume' goods and services in a similar way to individual consumers. Therefore, the law is not based upon the nature of goods or services supplied but upon the *status* of the recipient and the *use* to which the goods or services are put. Thus, a distinction can be drawn between 'consumer' goods and 'producer' goods, the latter being goods that are used in the creation of further wealth. This corresponds to the legal distinction between persons dealing as consumers and those who do not. For example, a computer would be classed as a consumer good and the sale would be a consumer sale when sold to a private individual, but would be a producer good sold in a non-consumer sale when sold to a trading organisation of any kind. A formal definition of 'dealing as a consumer' is given by the Unfair Contract Terms Act 1977. A person deals as a consumer if:

(a) he neither makes the contract in the course of a business nor holds himself out as doing so;

(b) the other party does make the contract in the course of a business; and

(c) the goods passing under or in pursuance of the contract are of a type ordinarily supplied for private use or consumption.

Governments have used the law to distinguish between what can be termed 'domestic consumers' and 'business consumers' primarily because the latter are considered better able to appreciate the law and to be in a position to enter contracts on more equal terms with suppliers of goods and services than the former. They do, of course, have the protection of the general law but some specific statutory protection, e.g. relating to exclusion clauses, does not apply to business consumers. Continuing our example of the computer, you will see later in this chapter that the Sale of Goods Act 1979 implies into every contract for the sale of goods a condition that the goods must be of 'merchantable quality', e.g. that the computer works properly. In a sale to a person dealing as consumer this implied condition cannot be excluded at all but where a person deals other than as consumer, i.e. a sale to a trading organisation, an exclusion of the implied condition of merchantability will be legally effective if it is reasonable in the circumstances of that particular transaction. (*See* the Unfair Contract Terms Act 1977.)

On the face of it, organisations may seem to be unfairly treated in the realm of consumerism. On the one hand, their freedom to bargain with their customers has been greatly reduced, while on the other they do not receive the same protection as their own customers when they in turn enter into contracts for the supply of goods and services. However, experience has shown that positive discrimination in favour of consumers is necessary to counter-balance the control over prices, output and terms of business which large organisations can exert. As you saw in the previous chapter, organisations in an imperfect market are able to use their position in it to maximise profits to the detriment of consumers. While consumer law cannot hope to make imperfect markets perfect, it can at least mitigate the worst excesses of unfettered economic might.

The legal framework of consumer protection

The object of this section of the chapter is, as the heading suggests, to describe the legal framework of consumer protection and only general references will be made to the working of the actual law involved.

The law protecting consumers may be either civil law or criminal law and the relevant rights, duties or liabilities may in turn be created or imposed by the common law or by statute. The nature of these different types of law is discussed in Chapter 25 but each may be described briefly as follows.

1 Civil law. The body of law concerned with the rights and obligations of individuals (and organisation) towards each other. Unlike criminal law, the injured party, and not the state, must initiate legal proceedings and compensation, not punishment, is the object of court action.

2 Criminal law. This consists of rules protecting society which are enforced by the state on pain of punishment. A criminal conviction for a 'consumer offence' does not necessarily mean that the injured consumer will receive compensation; they may have to bring a separate civil action to obtain this. They may, however, use the trader's criminal conviction as evidence in their civil action.

3 *Common law.* The body of law consisting originally of customs but now consisting of case law.

4 *Statute law.* This consists of Acts of Parliament and Orders and Regulations (Statutory Instruments) made under them. Since the passing of the original Sale of Goods Act in 1893 there have been a considerable number of statutes passed to protect consumers, giving them civil remedies where there has been misrepresentation, misleading advertisements and the like. Additionally, Parliament has employed the criminal law to stop such trade malpractices as the use of false trade descriptions and the sale of adulterated food.

In reality, of course, this strictly legal framework cannot be divorced from the administrative safeguards which exist to protect consumers. In particular, the Office of Fair Trading exercises a variety of quasi-judicial functions (*see* page 320) based upon the general legal framework of consumer protection.

It is worth noting before we begin a detailed look at the legal framework that the aim of the law is prevention rather than the punishment of 'consumer offences'. In relation to the number of consumer transactions, the number of civil actions brought by consumers is very small, the vast majority of business organisations fulfilling their legal obligations. Similarly, prosecutions of traders are fairly rare. Trading standards officers prefer to warn rather than prosecute where the law is infringed.

The common law

The *law of contract* and the *law of torts* are the two most important branches of the common law. The former, as you have seen in this chapter, regulates business agreements. If either party fails to perform their side of the bargain the other can sue for breach of contract. The latter protects the rights of individuals (and organisations) by imposing duties on other individuals (and organisations). A breach of duty entitles the injured party to an action for damages (a payment of money). For example, if you take your car to a garage to be repaired you are entitled to a reasonable standard of workmanship. Similarly, if you hire tools or equipment to repair your car yourself they must be of reasonable quality and reasonably fit for the job. In both cases failure to measure up to the standard of 'reasonableness', a question of fact, amounts to a breach of contract. However, should you buy tools, equipment or any other product which injure you or somebody else, or damage property, their manufacturer could be sued for damages in the tort of negligence. (You, as purchaser, could of course also sue the retailer under the Sale of Goods Act 1979 for the injury *you* have suffered.)

The liability of manufacturers to the ultimate consumer in tort for injury caused by their negligence was established in *Donoghue v Stevenson* (1932), an extremely well-known House of Lords decision which is also the foundation of the modern tort of negligence. In that case the plaintiff's friend had bought her some ginger beer in a dark opaque glass bottle. She drank some. When the remainder was poured, out flowed the remains of a decomposed snail. The plaintiff suffered shock and gastroenteritis as a result of the impure ginger beer.

The plaintiff had not bought the ginger beer herself and consequently could not sue the retailer under the Sale of Goods Act 1893. However, the House of Lords held that the manufacturer owed a duty of care to the plaintiff. The liability of manufacturers to ultimate consumers is called the 'narrow principle' of *Donoghue v Stevenson*; there is also a 'broad principle'. This states that 'You must take reasonable care to avoid acts or omissions which you can reasonably foresee would be likely to injure your neighbour' (Atkin). A 'neighbour' is anyone whom it could reasonably have been foreseen would be affected by the act or omission in question. This 'broad principle' is important in consumer law. For example, a repairer of goods owes a duty of care to their users and a provider of a service is liable if goods left with them are misappropriated by an employee, a fur coat left with a dry cleaners for cleaning being an example.

Perhaps we should make two points at this stage. First, you may consider it somewhat remarkable that a manufacturer was *not* liable to the ultimate consumer until 1932. Pause to think what the implications of that position were. We surely take a maufacturer's legal responsibility for granted today. Second, consumers who suffer any form of damage caused by a faulty product no longer have to rely on *Donoghue v*

Stevenson (1932), they can take action under the Consumer Protection Act 1987 (*see* below) which imposes *strict liability* on manufacturers of faulty goods.

The problem with the common law action was that you not only had to show that the defect *caused* the damage – this is still required by the 1987 Act – but also that the manufacturer, was at *fault*. Besides the understandable tendency of manufacturers to deny fault, there were often major problems in proving it, particularly where scientific or technical knowledge were involved. The 'Thalidomide children', for example never won compensation in a court of law. The substantial compensation they *eventually* received under an out of court settlement resulted from the pressure of public opinions against the manufacturers of the drug and the willingness of a wealthy parent of one of the children to risk his fortune in a court case. At the time the balance of opinion was that, had the case gone to trial, they could not have been certain of proving negligence. You will read below, however, that a 'state of the art' or 'development risk' defence has been included in the Consumer Protection Act 1987 and it would certainly be raised if another tragedy such as the Thalidomide case ever happened. At the end of the day the law is not about knee-jerk or emotional responses to sometimes horrific and heart-rending events. While it is always a matter of *policy* what the level of protection is and a matter of *opinion* what it should be, through the law the protection provided must be applied objectively. Obvious damage and moral responsibility of themselves do not constitute causation and 'fault/strict liability' at law.

'Change' is directly and indirectly a theme of this book. The evolution of the present statutory strict liability under the Consumer Protection Act 1987 is an excellent example of change in the law from common law liability to purchasers in contract law, through common law fault liability in tort, through an EC directive – partly 'organic', partly 'institutional'. Only Parliament was capable of making the jump from fault to strict liability in this context.

While the common law offers some general protection to consumers, it is obvious that it is not an adequate means of consumer protection. In particular, its basic *freedom of contract* approach allowed traders to exclude or limit both their duties and consumers' rights and the common law's intervention was limited to interpreting such exclusions in favour of the consumer (where possible). The bulk of the law protecting consumers is therefore to be found in Acts of Parliament and Orders and Regulations made under them.

Statute law

Legislation on consumer protection unfortunately does not fall into neat categories for text book purposes. A particular Act may cover more than one aspect of 'consumerism' and may employ both the criminal and civil law to achieve its objectives. Thus, it is best to list the legislation grouped according to general areas and then consider each alphabetically (*see* Table 17.1).

Competition Act 1980

Under this Act the Director General of Fair Trading is able to investigate the trading practices of individual business organisations to see whether they are operating an *anti-competitive practice*. The Act defines this as 'comprising a course of conduct which has, or is intended to have or is likely to have the effect of restricting, distorting, or preventing competition in the UK'. If the DGFT makes enquiries and finds such a practice, he can try to obtain an undertaking from the trader concerned to stop it. If he will not give one, or will not abide by this undertaking, the DGFT can refer it to the Monopolies and Mergers Commission and the Secretary of State for Trade can then prohibit that person from operating that practice. The Act extends this possible action to monopoly situations arising in the remaining nationalised industries as these organisations are not covered by the Fair Trading Act.

Consumer Credit Act 1974

The Act is a framework into which detail can be written by the Secretary of State for Trade by means of Statutory Instruments. Its basic aims are to:

(a) remedy the inequality in bargaining position in consumer credit transaction;
(b) control trading malpractices;
(c) regulate remedies for failure to comply with the Act.

The Act covers all credit agreements where no more

Table 17.1 Legislation on consumer protection

Area involved	Main relevant legislation
Business practices against consumer interests	Restrictive Trade Practices Act 1976, Resale Prices Act 1976, Fair Trading Act 1973, Competition Act 1980
Compensation for injury suffered by consumers as a result of a criminal offence	Powers of Criminal Courts Act 1973
Credit	Consumer Credit Act 1974
Dangerous goods	Consumer Protection Act 1987, Sale of Goods Act 1979
False or misleading descriptions	Trade Descriptions Act 1968, Misrepresentation Act 1967, Theft Act 1968, Food and Drugs Act 1955, Sale of Goods Act 1979
Faulty goods	Consumer Protection Act 1987, Sale of Goods Act 1979, Supply of Goods and Services Act 1982
Faulty services	Supply of Goods and Services Act 1982, Unfair Contract Terms Act 1977
Prices	Prices Act 1974, Consumer Protection Act 1987
Quantities for sale	Weights and Measures Act 1985
Short measure	Weights and Measures Act 1985, Theft Act 1968, Trade Descriptions Act 1968, Sale of Goods Act 1979
Unordered goods	Unsolicited Goods and Services

than £15,000 (at present) is advanced to private individuals, sole traders and business partnerships; it does not apply to limited companies and other incorporated bodies, e.g. public corporations. Also covered are agreements for the hire of goods where the agreement may be for more than three months and no more than £15,000 will be involved.

This stricter control of the credit industry is achieved administratively by a system of licensing and by law through the creation of several criminal offences and civil rights and duties. The Director General of Fair Trading is responsible for licensing credit organisa-tions and administering the Act generally.

First and foremost, it is a *criminal* offence to trade as either a provider of credit or as a credit broker, e.g. a shop that introduces customers to finance houses, without a licence. Unlicensed traders are unable to enforce their credit agreements without the Director General's consent. Further offences include sending credit cards to people without being asked to do so and sending documents to minors (persons under 18) inviting them to borrow money or obtain other credit facilities. Prosecutions are brought by either the Office of Fair Trading or, more usually, by the trading standards departments of local authorities.

A variety of *civil* law rights are given to consumers. They may complain to the court if they think that the terms of the credit agreement are extortionate and the court has the power to order repayment if it agrees with the complaint. They have the right to the name and address of any credit reference agency consulted about them and further rights to obtain a copy of the reference and have corrected any mistakes that it may contain. Another important provision is that a provider of finance other than the actual seller, e.g. a finance house or credit card company, is equally liable with the seller for any breach of contract or misrepresenta-tion by the seller unless the cash price is less than £100 or more than £30,000.

Consumer Protection Act 1987

This major Act deals with three different aspects of consumer protection: product liability, consumer safety and misleading pricing.

Part I of the Act introduced *product liability* into the UK, thereby implementing an EC directive of 1985. The Act makes producers of goods *strictly liable* for damage caused by defects in their products, i.e. they are liable whether or not they were negligent or realised that the goods were defective.

Liability is imposed on not only the actual producer but also any person who puts his own name on a product produced by someone else (an 'own brander') and anyone who imported the product into on EC member state from outside the Community. Suppliers are also liable if they are asked to identify the producer, own brander importer or their own supplier and unreasonably fail to do so. The intention of the Act is quite simple – to make producers liable to end users with whom there is no contractual relationship.

Liability under the Act is strict, not absolute, and it is a defence to show that the product complied with any mandatory statutory or EC requirements, e.g. it had to be manufactured in a particular way. However, merely complying with a recommended standard, e.g. a British standard, is no defence. It is also a defence to show that the product was not supplied in the course of business or that the defect did not exist when the product was supplied. Most important is the 'state of the art' or 'development risk' defence which member states have the option of including in their domestic legislation. Here it is a defence to show that given the state of scientific and technical knowledge at the relevant time the producer could not have been expected to discover the defect in the product. This may prove particularly useful to the pharmaceutical industry. Finally, a producer of a component has a defence if it can be shown that the defect was solely due to the design of the product in which the component was incorporated or through complying with instructions given by the producer of the finished product. It is not possible to exclude liability under the Act but contributory negligence can be pleaded against the injured party, e.g. where they continued to use the defective product knowing of the defect, and all rights of action are lost 10 years after the producer supplied the product to another.

The Act undoubtedly represents a major step forward for consumer protection although it is argued by some that the 'development risk' defence takes away with one hand what is given with the other. The defence was included by the Government after lobbying by the CBI that not to do so would stifle innovative research and harm Britain's competitiveness. Nevertheless, even seen at its worst the Act does mean that people suing for injury or death caused by defective products no longer have to prove negligence, the onus is on the producer to prove the defence applied.

Part II of the Act deals with *consumer safety*. It enables the Secretary of State to regulate the composition, design and construction of certain goods in order to prevent risk of death or personal injury caused by them. Examples include oil heaters, electric blankets and flexes on domestic appliances.

Infringement of the regulations is a *criminal* offence and consumers who have suffered loss or injury caused by such infringements are given a right of action for damages at *civil* law. (In addition, actions under the Sale of Goods Act 1979 may be available.) The Secretary of State may also make prohibition orders and notices under the Act. These prevent the sale or supply of goods which are considered unsafe. It is a *criminal* offence to disregard prohibition orders and notices.

Misleading pricing is covered in Part III of the Act. It embraces goods, accommodation (including new houses and flats), services (banking, parking, electricity supply etc) and facilities and makes it an offence to mislead any consumer as to the price of any good, service or facility. 'Price' means the total payment and any method of determining the total.

Two examples to illustrate: first, it would be an offence to advertise something for sale at, say, £1,500 and then tell a potential buyer that VAT must be added. It would also be an offence to use a price ticket on which a higher price and lower price are shown, but with the former crossed out, unless the goods have been sold at the higher price for at least 28 consecutive days in the last six months (as required by the Trade Descriptions Act 1968) or, if not, that this is made clear.

Fair Trading Act 1973

This Act established the Office of Fair Trading, which is now the main institution of consumer protection, granting wide-ranging powers to its Director General. The Office of Fair Trading is considered in more detail below but one of its powers is that traders who persist in breaking the *criminal* law or flout their *civil* obligations can be asked to sign an undertaking promising to stop doing so. If they refuse to give such an undertaking or do not abide by an undertaking previously taken, the Director General can bring a *civil* action for an injunction against them in the Restrictive Practices Court.

The Act also gives the Secretary of State the power to make orders outlawing undesirable trade practices following the recommendation of the Director General or the Consumer Protection Advisory Committee. Two such orders are the Consumer Transactions (Restrictions on Statements) Order 1976 (considered below) and the Business Advertisements (Disclosure) Order 1977. The latter order seeks to ensure that consumers are not misled about the status of the seller of goods advertised for sale. It requires all advertisements by persons seeking to sell goods *in the course of a business* to make this fact clear. Failure to comply with either order is a *criminal* offence.

Misrepresentation Act 1967

Consumers are able to bring a *civil* action for damages under the Act for any loss they suffer as a result of false statements of fact made by the seller or provider of goods or services which induce them to enter into a contract for those goods or services. An attempted exclusion of liability under the Act is ineffective unless it is fair and reasonable in the circumstances. This is for the court to decide.

Powers of Criminal Courts Act 1973

One provision of this Act enables courts to award compensation to anyone who has suffered loss as a result of a criminal act. At present the power of the magistrates' court to award compensation is limited to £2,000. While the Act is of general application, it has quite frequently been used to compensate consumers for loss suffered through offences under the Trade Descriptions Act 1968.

Prices Act 1974

The Act enables the government to make Orders and Regulations governing prices, particularly their display but also maximum price levels. For example, Orders have been made requiring that the price per weight of food is given, that pubs and other licensed premises must display the prices of their drinks and that garages must not display their petrol prices in a misleading way.

The Price Marking (Bargain Offers) Order 1979 only allows a price display stating that an article is worth, say, £100 but that the price charged is only £75 if the seller, or someone specified by them, has charged, or will charge at some future specified time, the higher price for the article.

Resale Prices Act 1976

This Act prohibits 'resale price maintenance' in order to encourage competition in the interests of consumers. Although 'recommended' prices can still be laid down by manufacturers, any pressure on retailers to sell at a minimum price, e.g. threats to withhold supplies of goods, is a *civil* offence and an action can be brought against them by retailers and consumers who have suffered from this price-fixing, or by the Director General of Fair Trading.

Restrictive Trade Practices Act 1976

Under this Act, agreements by traders to restrict competition among themselves, e.g. by fixing prices, must be registered with the Office of Fair Trading. A registered agreement may be referred to the Restrictive Trade Practices Court to determine whether it is in the public interest. Any agreement found to be contrary to the public interest is prohibited.

The Act applies to both goods and services and the Office of Fair Trading can bring a *civil* action in the Restrictive Practices Court against anyone who operates a restrictive agreement which has not been registered. A consumer who has been affected by an unregistered agreement can also bring a *civil* action for damages.

A possible way of avoiding the Act is for companies to merge but the Monopolies and Mergers Commission (considered below) protects the public interest by investigating potentially undesirable mergers.

A government Green Paper published in 1988 doubted the effectiveness of the existing Act and is likely to lead to legislation in 1990. The main criticism is that the Act looks to the *form* of the agreement rather than its *effect* on competition. This allows damaging agreements to be drafted which do not require registration. Furthermore, many economic sectors and professional services are not covered by the Act. The Green Paper proposes abolition of the present registration system in favour of a general prohibition on agreements, concerted practices between undertakings and decisions and recommendations by associations of undertakings which restrict or distort competition. This would bring the UK in line with the EC approach to competition law. A new competition authority would be established based on the Office of Fair Trading to enforce the prohibition.

Sale of Goods Act 1979

The original 1893 Act was the first great landmark in consumer protection and as amended and re-enacted is still the foundation of all protection relating to the purchase of goods. The Act automatically implies certain conditions into every contract for the sale of goods when they are bought from someone who sells in the course of a business, namely: that the goods must be of 'merchantable equality', i.e. new goods must not be broken, damaged and must work properly; they must be 'fit for their purpose', i.e. they must do what they are supposed to do; and must correspond to their description, whether on the *article* itself, its packaging or by any other sales description. Remember, these implied conditions *cannot* be excluded in a consumer sale.

Furthermore, the Consumer Transaction (Restrictions on Statements) Order 1976 makes it a *criminal* offence to attempt to exclude these implied conditions by notice or other document, e.g. a 'no money refunded' notice. In addition, any statement on the goods, their container or in any document relating to the consumer's rights or obligations where the goods are defective, or are not fit for a particular purpose or do not correspond with their description, must be accompanied by a clear and conspicuous notice informing the consumer that his statutory rights are not affected. The order is necessary because unscrupulous traders could purport to exclude their liability and rely on the ignorance of the law on the part of customers to render a legally ineffective exclusion effective in practice.

The Act is part of the *civil* law and failure to comply with these implied conditions is a breach of contract entitling the buyer to return the good and receive a full refund. Although a repair, an exchange or a credit note may be acceptable alternatives to the consumer, the buyer cannot be compelled to accept one of these in lieu of a complete cash refund. In addition, a buyer of faulty goods can also claim damages for other loss, e.g. damage to property, personal injury and the cost of hiring a replacement.

The economic effects of poor quality are enormous. Poor quality has been partly responsible for British goods losing their competitive edge in export markets and in the home market Office of Fair Trading statistics show that poor quality is overwhelmingly the greatest source of consumer dissatisfaction. Part of the problem is the fact that many consumers with legitimate grounds to set aside a contract and demand their money back choose to accept a lesser remedy such as a repair. Usually the reason is (understandably) unwillingness to take legal action and a wish to avoid general inconvenience. This means that the influence of the law as it is practised is towards a repair or replacement policy rather than stringent quality control.

Supply of Goods and Services Act 1982

The Sale of Goods Act 1979 does not apply to absolutely all contracts under which the ownership of goods is transferred. An example would be a repair of an article where spares are supplied. Here the substance of the contract is doing work rather than selling goods. Another example is where goods are exchanged. This is not a contract of sale under the 1979 Act because money is not involved. In all such contracts, the Act implies the same conditions in the same circumstances as those implied by the 1979 Act.

The Act also implies certain conditions into contracts for the supply of a service. Specifically, where suppliers act in the *course of a business* they must carry out the service with reasonable care and skill and within a reasonable time where a specific time was not stated in the contract. The conditions are implied whether or not goods are also transferred and any attempted exclusion of them is subject to the provisions of the Unfair Contract Terms Act 1977 (*see* below).

Theft Act 1968

It is a criminal offence under the Theft Act 1968 to 'obtain property by deception'. Thus, for example, a car salesman who deliberately falsifies the distance recorded on a car's odometer has committed an offence. The Act is of general application rather than specifically designed to be part of the machinery of consumer protection.

Trade Descriptions Act 1968

It is a *criminal* offence under the Act for traders to misdescribe goods or to make false statements about services if they know that they are false or if they do not care whether their statements are true or false. Under the Act traders can be fined on summary conviction and/or imprisoned after conviction on indictment. In addition, the local authority trading standards or consumer protection officers have the power to enter premises and seize and inspect goods if traders are suspected of contravening the Act.

The Act does not apply to private sales and any descriptions of houses or land.

Unfair Contract Terms Act 1977

This Act, part of the *civil* law, is another landmark in consumer protection. It restricts the extent to which liability can be avoided for breach of contract and negligence. You have already seen that this Act is sufficiently wide in its scope to cover attempted exclusions of liability under the Occupiers' Liability Act 1957 (but not the 1984 Act) for death or personal injury arising from negligence in connection with the occupation of premises used for the business purposes of the occupier. In fact, with the exception of liability for breach of implied obligations in sales of goods and hire-purchase contracts, the Act regulates only *business liability*, i.e. liability arising from activities in the course of a business premises. However, the term 'business' includes professions, and the activities of government departments and local or public authorities.

Basically, it is not possible to exclude or restrict liability for death or personal injury caused by negligence. Liability for other loss or damage caused by negligence can only be excluded or restricted in so far as the term or notice used satisfies a test of 'reasonableness'. Where one party deals as a consumer or deals on the other's written standard terms of business, *any* exclusion of liability for breach of contract or any term allowing the other party to substantially vary their contractual obligations is ineffective unless the 'reasonableness' test is satisfied. Since business organisations frequently buy their resources on the standard terms of others, they, as well as 'consumers', are protected by the Act.

Unsolicited Goods and Services Act 1971

The main way in which this Act affects the consumer is to make it a *criminal* offence for traders to demand payment for goods which they have sent to persons who have not ordered them. The teeth of the Act are in the *criminal* liability that it imposes. A person would not be legally bound to pay for the goods sent in any case because no contract exists: the essential ingredient of 'agreement' is totally absent.

Furthermore; if unsolicited goods are sent to you, they become your property after six months, or 30 days if you write to the sender giving your name and address and stating that the goods were unsolicited, providing of course that you agree neither to keep them nor to send them back.

Weights and Measures Act 1985

This Act does two main things. First, it provides a system for the *uniformity and control* of weights and measures. Second, it uses the *average contents system* in the application of this system.

More specifically, it provides a uniform system of weights and measures, controls weighing and measuring equipment used for trade purposes, protects the consumer against short weight and measure in commodities, and requires certain pre-packed items to bear an indication of the quantity of the contents.

The average contents system removes criminal liability from retailers who blamelessly sell short weight. The system means that an offence arises only where a batch of packages falls below the stated weight on averaging their actual contents, or where more than a specified number of packages in a batch fall below a specified tolerance level. The Act imposes the duty of compliance with the system on packers and importers, not on retailers. However, where a retailer *knowingly* sells an inadequate package, i.e. one where the shortfall is more than twice the permitted tolerance, the retailer commits a criminal offence.

1 Make a file of leaflets on the rights of the consumer. The Office of Fair Trading, for example, publish a considerable number. You might find these in Citizens Advice Bureaux, Law Centres, Consumer Advice Centres, or you could contact the Office of Fair Trading direct.

2 Do you consider a court to be the most appropri-

ate forum for consumers to enforce their rights? Give your reasons.

Business practices, the consumers and the law

In a mixed economy such as ours, the best way to protect the interests of consumers is generally considered to be by encouraging and maintaining free and undistorted competition. However, you have seen in previous chapters that totally free competition is unattainable.

Indeed, the existence of large business organisations distorts competition producing imperfect markets. Such distortion is always to the possible detriment of consumers and often and unfairly to the actual detriment of smaller business units.

Once again the common law has made only a very small contribution to the present legal framework and the relevant law is almost entirely statutory. The principal statutes are the Fair Trading Act 1973, the Restrictive Trade Practices Act 1976, the Resale Prices Act 1976 and the Competition Act 1980, all of which were mentioned in the previous section of this chapter. In addition, the competition rules of the EC, based on Articles 85 and 86 of the Treaty of Rome 1957, embody the philosophy of competition more strictly than our own domestic law.

The main agency for implementing government policy on competition is the Office of Fair Trading. Under the Fair Trading Act 1973, its Director General must keep under review commercial practices in the UK and collect information about them so that he can discover monopoly situations and uncompetitive practices. Under the Restrictive Trade Practices Act 1976 he has a major role in the regulation of restrictive trading agreements.

Monopolies

At its simplest, a monopoly arises when one trading organisation alone supplies an entire market. This, however, is very rare (nationalised industries are an exception) and the Fair Trading Act 1973 defines a monopoly as being where one person, company or group of related companies supplies or acquires at least 25% of the goods or services in question in the UK – a 'scale monopoly situation'. A 'complex monopoly situation' exists if at least 25% of the goods or services of a particular description are supplied in the UK as a whole by two or more persons, unconnected companies or groups of companies who intentionally or otherwise conduct their affairs in such a way that they prevent, distort or restrict competition in the supply of the goods or services, e.g. refusing to supply goods or services to particular customers.

'Complex monopoly situations' are far more common than 'scale monopoly situations' for there are many cases where particular industries are dominated by a small number of suppliers, each of whom holds a very large share of the market, e.g. detergents, where there are two major suppliers. The Director General of Fair Trading may refer what he considers to be a monopoly to the Monopolies and Mergers Commission for investigation.

The main inherent dangers of a monopoly are restriction of output, price fixing, regulation of terms of supply and removal of consumer choice. Additionally, free competition may be stifled by preventing competitors from entering the market and a monopolist may use his monopsonic buying powers (monopsony is a situation where one buyer dominates the market) to dictate terms to his suppliers. The government uses the law to forbid or regulate these practices.

Restrictive trade practices

The Restrictive Trade Practices Act 1976 is concerned with any agreement or arrangement between suppliers of goods or services, particularly concealed agreements but including recommendations made by trade associations, which restrict competition. Examples include agreements between suppliers to charge the same prices, to divide up the market, to trade on the same terms of business, or to restrict supply. The airline industry is an excellent illustration. High prices can be maintained on transatlantic routes by agreements to peg prices or to restrict flights. It was no coincidence perhaps that the price of air fares fell when Laker Airways were in business but rose again after they went out of business.

Such practices are unlawful and the object of the Act is to ensure that only such agreements, arrangements and recommendations as are in the public interest are allowed to continue. To achieve this, full details of *registrable agreements* must be sent to the Office of Fair Trading for entry in a public register. The Director General then has the power to refer the practice to the Restrictive Practices Court to consider whether or not it is against the public interest. The proceedings are part of the *civil* law.

There are a number of grounds (often called 'gateways') on which the practice can be upheld as being in the public interest, for example, where it is necessary to protect the consumer, as when certain patent medicines are only supplied to qualified pharmacists, or where removal of the restriction would prevent fair competition between producers, e.g. small businesses could be allowed to combine to avoid being driven out of the market by the business giants.

Under the Act the Director General may instigate a *civil* action for an injunction to prevent an unlawful restrictive practice from being continued or repeated. A consumer directly affected by it may bring a *civil* action for damages.

Unfair trading practices

The powers given to the Director General of Fair Trading under the Competition Act 1980 to investigate and control the anti-competitive practices of single firms and the abuse of monopoly power in the public sector supplements the existing powers to investigate monopolies and restrictive agreements among firms. The purpose of the Act is to promote competition and efficiency in industry and commerce.

Under the Act, the Secretary of State has power to investigate prices which he considers to be 'of major public concern having regard to whether the supply, or acquisition, of the goods or services in question is of general economic importance, or the price is of special significance to consumers'. No direct sanctions are possible but it could be treated as an anti-competitive practice.

EC rules on competition

EC competition policy is designed to ensure that trade between member states take place on the basis of free and fair competition and that *state* barriers to trade between member states, when totally dismantled by the end of 1992, are not replaced by *private* barriers which would fragment the single market. This policy

is based on Articles 85 and 86 of the Treaty of Rome 1957.

Article 85 prohibits all agreements between business organisations, decisions by trade associations and concerted practices which may affect trade between *member states* and which have as their object or affect the prevention, restriction or distortion of competition. Article 85 would include fixing buying and/or selling prices or other terms of business, discriminating in favour of certain business organisations giving them a competitive advantage and sharing markets. If, for example, a manufacturer appointed a sole distributor of its products in each EC country, and each distributor agreed not to export to other EC countries, the 'common market' would be divided into separate markets and competition among member states would be effectively distorted.

Article 86 declares that the abuse of a dominant position in the market structure is incompatible with the EC, e.g. imposing buying or selling prices or other trading conditions which are unfair, limit production, markets or technological development to the prejudice of consumers.

Practices infringing Articles 85 and 86 must be notified to the EC Commission by the Director General of Fair Trading. The question of possible infringement of these Articles can be decided by domestic courts as well as by the Commission and the European Court of Justice.

Articles 92-94 forbid government subsidies to industries or individual firms that distort or threaten to distort competition. However, aid to depressed regions and to promote new economic activity is allowed. Unfortunately it is not unknown for the Commission to find out about illegal aid after it has been given and therefore had the desired effect. By this time, of course, it is too late to do anything about it.

Resale price maintenance

The enforcement of minimum selling prices by manufacturers or distributors of goods, either individually or collectively, is illegal under the Resale Price Act 1976 unless held to be in the public interest by the Restrictive Practices Court. At present only minimum prices for books and proprietary medicines have the Court's sanction. Any person adversely affected, or the Director General of Fair Trading, may take *civil* proceedings against those who seek to re-impose minimum resale prices.

Resale price maintenance poses an economic dilemma to governments. On the one hand consumers benefit and efficient organisations are rewarded by allowing free pricing of commodities. On the other, consumers can suffer because many small businesses will be unable to compete with large multiple retailers in price cutting and may be forced to close down, thereby reducing retail service to the public. A good example at the present time is the decline of independent chemists since supermarkets have been allowed to sell patent medicines. Indeed, indiscriminate promotion of competition may have the effect of operating to the detriment of the very consumers it seeks to protect.

In practice, however, this effect is partially mitigated by 'consumer loyalty' to local traders. In return for slightly higher prices, they can provide a level of personal service and convenience which large retailers cannot.

It is perhaps worth noting that it is often the less fortunate, those who are unable to travel to shopping centres or buy in bulk for example, who patronise the local corner shop which in turn may even begin to provide a kind of community service. This 'class distinction' in consumerism will surely become even more marked with the continued development of out-of-town hypermarkets.

Mergers

The Fair Trading Act 1973 covers mergers involving the acquisition of gross assets of more than £15m, or where a monopoly, i.e. 25% or more of the relevant market in the UK or a substantial part of it, would be created or enhanced. Also included are situations where one company acquires the ability to control or materially influence another company without actually acquiring a controlling interest.

The Director General of Fair Trading is responsible for keeping a watchful eye on possible mergers within the Act but his role is only to advise the Secretary of State as to whether a reference should be made to the Monopolies and Mergers Commission; he may not make a reference directly. This contrasts with his powers relating to monopolies. The Secretary of State has power under the 1973 Act to order that the merger shall not proceed or to regulate any identified adverse effects of a merger or proposed merger, e.g. the effect on labour relations.

Each reference is considered on its own merits and on the criterion of the 'public interest', the latter encompassing the maintenance and promotion of competition, consumer interests, effects on employment and, in some cases, the possibility of 'asset stripping' or tax avoidance.

The Treaty of Rome makes no reference to mergers as such but the Commission of the EC has sought to encourage mergers which lead to improved competition throughout the Community.

Advertising

Advertising is a multi-million pound industry. It is a perfectly acceptable, indeed necessary, way to bring particular goods and services to the notice of consumers. But it can be used as a device for persuading consumers to buy things they neither want, need nor can afford by methods which are unacceptable. The power and effectiveness of advertising is recognised by the state and the practice is controlled by many criminal statutes, numerous voluntary codes of practice produced by trade associations and an EC directive requiring all members states to ban unfair and misleading advertisements.

Day-to-day control over all advertising, except that on radio and television, is exercised by the Advertising Standards Authority. The Authority draws up and enforces its own codes, ensuring that advertisements are: legal, decent, honest and truthful; consistent with principles of free competition; prepared with a sense of responsibility to consumers; and do not bring the advertising industry into disrepute. For example, in 1985 it held that the slogan 'Guinnless isn't good for you' did not amount to the same as saying 'Guinness is good for you', one of the most famous advertising slogans of all time which is now banned under the rule that forbids claims that drinking is good for your health. Radio and TV advertising is controlled by a code drawn up by the Independent Broadcasting Authority. It recently decided, for example, that an advert portraying 'the hero' jumping from a cable car on the way to presenting his lady friend with a box of chocolates was 'most unlikely' to encourage dangerous imitation by children.

The Trade Descriptions Act 1968 makes its a *criminal* offence for traders to describe inaccurately the goods they are selling or the services they are offering and any person induced to enter into a contract by a false advertising claim can rescind the contract and claim damages in a *civil* action under the Misrepresentation Act 1967. In addition, the Director General of Fair Trading has a general responsibility under the Fair Trading Act 1973 to ensure that all trading practices, which includes advertising, do not adversely affect consumer interests and local authorities are empowered under the town and country planning legislation to control the extent of outdoor advertising.

Obtain copies of codes published by the Advertising Standards Authority and/or Independent Broadcasting Authority, or by an individual newspaper. Select one or more advertisements from newspapers or magazines, or on TV to which you object. Explain precisely why you do and consider whether or not the advertisements could possibly infringe the codes. Do you consider that the codes need amending – if so how and why?

Draft a suitable amendment of or addition to the code.

Administrative agencies of consumer protection

The Office of Fair Trading

You will have already gained a general idea about the working of the Office from the previous section of this chapter but, as its work is crucial to consumer protection, a more specific summary is necessary.

The Office was established in November 1973 following the passing of the Fair Trading Act earlier in that year. It describes its job as keeping watch on trading matters in the UK and protecting the consumer against unfair practices. It does not handle individual complaints from consumers (except about monopolies and restrictive and unfair trade practices) but acts as a central bureau for collecting and disseminating information, taking general action when necessary.

At its head is the Director General of Fair Trading who is responsible for the administration and enforcement of the laws designed to foster competition,

protect consumers and regulate the credit industry. He can act independently of the government for he is neither a civil servant nor a politician. Ultimately, however he has political masters. The Secretary of State for Trade has ministerial responsibility for the working of the Office of Fair Trading, Parliament makes the laws which he administers and enforces, and the Office is both a government agency and a quasi-governmental body financed wholly from public funds with clearly defined statutory powers and duties.

There are six main ways in which the Director General is active in protecting consumers.

1 He collects information on business activities which are harmful or potentially harmful to consumers, which restrict or inhibit competition and which are against the public interest in general. He can refer such activities to the Consumer Protection Advisory Committee, Monopolies and Mergers Commission or Restrictive Practices Court as the case may be.

2 He publishes information explaining to consumers their rights.

3 He encourages trade associations to prepare and publish codes of practice which include explanations of how consumers can make complaints. These codes invariably raise standards of service.

4 He takes action against organisations which commit 'consumer offences' or infringe the competition laws. Usually the organisation involved is asked to give a written undertaking that it will cease the offence or restrictive practice but a civil action for an injunction restraining a restrictive practice, or prosecution of organisations which persistently commit consumer offences, may be necessary.

5 He licenses businesses which give credit or hire goods, as well as credit brokers, debt collectors and credit reference agencies. He is also responsible for the general regulation of the credit industry.

6 He proposes new laws to put an end to unfair business activities by plugging loopholes in the existing law. The Consumer Protection Advisory Committee (a body appointed by the Secretary of State and operating independently of the Office) plays an important role in such proposals. It reports to the Secretary of State on the Director General's proposals after having had a particular matter referred to it by the Director General.

The Monopolies and Mergers Commission

The Commission is an independent body whose membership includes industrialists, trade unionists and academics. It is supported by a staff of civil servants including economists and accountants.

As its name suggests its function is to investigate monopolies or possible monopolies referred to it by the Director General of Fair Trading and mergers referred to it by the Secretary of State for Trade on the advice of the Director General. Its role is then to assess whether such monopolies and mergers do or would operate against the public interest. The Secretary of State may make Statutory Orders to remedy the adverse effects identified by the Commission. More usually the Director General is asked to obtain written undertakings from the business organisations involved to remedy such effects themselves.

Local authorities

1 Trading standards or consumer protection departments. These departments work very closely with the Office of Fair Trading in watching for unfair trade practices. They have the task of ensuring that local consumer laws are obeyed and complaints from individual consumers investigated.

2 Environmental health departments. These departments deal with consumer complaints about health matters such as unfit food and drink and dirty shops or restaurants.

The National Consumer Council

This independent Council was set up by the government in 1975. It does not deal directly with consumer complaints but seeks to further consumer interests by its representation on public and other bodes.

Consumer and consultative councils of nationalised industries

The remaining nationalised industries are public corporations which often have a complete monopoly of their own particular economic activity. The apparent contradiction of their existence amid extensive law promoting free competition can be partly explained by the enormous capital investment that they require and the important role that they play in the economy (*see* Chapter 3).

The control of nationalised industries has already been discussed, but the monopolies they have in basic social and economic resources nevertheless put the consumer in a uniquely weak position. For this reason it is generally accepted that it is appropriate to represent consumers in an advisory capacity in the policy-making of the nationalised industries with the aims of helping to prevent the misuse (perhaps quite unintentional) of monopoly power and of bridging the technological gap between the industry and its customers. The creation of consumer and consultative councils has been the Government's chosen method of protecting consumer interests in the activities of nationalised industries. They deal with all matters of consumer interest (including complaints) and the industries are bound to consult them before taking major decisions.

The work of the councils does not meet with universal acclaim, in particular their effectiveness is frequently doubted. Four main criticisms are made:

(a) that their close links with the industries affect their role as consumer champions;
(b) that the public is unaware of their existence and hence does not use their services;
(c) that they have inadequate resources to face the corporate might of the industry; and
(d) that the Secretary of State's power of appointing members prevents them from being true grassroots representative bodies.

The European Consumer

The promotion of competition between member states is fundamental to the philosophy of the EC and the increasing remoteness of producers from consumers, partly fostered by this philosophy, means that there is a need for Community action on consumer protection.

In 1975 the Community adopted a programme for consumer information and protection embodying five basic consumer rights:

1 the protection of health and safety;
2 the right to protection of the consumers' economic interests;
3 the right to redress;
4 the right of information and education; and

5 the right to consumer protection.

By the use of Directives to member states, the EC Commission can implement the programme throughout the Community. Examples to date include bans on certain ingredients in foods and cosmetics, listing of dangerous substances which can only be marketed subject to specific conditions, and the introduction of 'sell by' dates on food.

The Consumers' Consultative Committee, established in 1973, is the most important consumer protection body within the Community. It ensures that the Commission is aware of consumers' interests when taking policy decisions. The Committee consists of 25 members, ten of whom must be 'persons particularly qualified in consumer affairs' and the remainder representatives of consumer associations.

Conclusion

This chapter has two distinct parts: the first outlines the essentials of a contract, the second discusses the wider rules of trading practice within which business contracts are made. The chapter taken as a whole endeavours to show how the law is used to realise business objectives while at the same time protecting consumer interests. It does the latter by banning or regulating unacceptable business practices and by reducing the inequality in bargaining power between producers or suppliers and their customers. Few would doubt the efficacy of most consumer legislation but anti-monopoly legislation poses a problem. It should be judged in terms of economic gain and not from the belief that competition is by definition beneficial. Unfortunately, any benefits could also be the result of other factors, such as changes in tax rates or currency values. The benefits are therefore hard to assess.

Only the administrative safeguards provided by the

Key words

Consumer
Both individuals and organisations consume goods and services but at law a consumer is a person who does *not* acquire or use the goods acquired in the course of a business activity.

Consumer law
A body of very largely statutory law which has the simple central aim of protecting the individually weak consumer.

Fault liability
The common law approach to injuries not arising from a breach of contract. Sometimes there is serious difficulty in proving fault.

Strict liability
An approach to legal liability which makes causation, not fault, the key issue. Under the Consumer Protection Act 1987, for example, a manufacturer is liable for injuries caused by a defective product without proof of fault.

Competition law
Statutory law is used to lessen the undesirable consequences of imperfect markets. Competition law has both a national and, increasingly, a European dimension.

Consumer protection
A framework of legal rules (both common law and statutory) and administrative agencies which prohibits or lessens the effects of undesirable business activities and practices.

main official administrative agencies of consumer protection have been covered. No attempt has been made to analyse the many voluntary codes of practice produced by trade associations, or the official and unofficial sources of consumer advice available, e.g. the Citizens Advice Bureau. Had this been done, you, as consumers (of this book), would probably have felt in need of protection from our product!

Learning projects

1 A commercial contract is the means by which a business organisation pursues its objectives. The terms it contains are therefore most important. Working in small groups, discuss the terms you would need to include in a contract for the supply of a simple service, e.g. a video rental shop or a copy bureau, to ensure that you traded on terms which protected your interests.

Having done this, individually draft a suitable contract containing appropriate terms.

2 Table 17.1 – Legislation on consumer protection –

lists the main areas of consumerism regulated by statute. Choose one of these areas to research further. Having done this, prepare a leaflet suitable for the 'typical consumer' explaining the nature of the statutory regulation, the specific protection given, what administrative agencies may or may not be involved, and what avenues are open to the consumer whose rights have been infringed. The emphasis of your work should be in the communications and presentation of this information in a suitable form

3 Consumers are comprehensively protected but are they aware of their rights? Use your text book and any leaflets you have collected to devise a questionnaire suitable for street interviews with shoppers or, perhaps, students studying non-business studies courses.

Working as a group carry out a survey, collate your results (preferably using a database/statistical program) and report your findings and any recommendations you consider you can make.

4 Proposed takeovers and mergers are frequently covered in the newspapers. As and when a suitable example happens, maintain a file of press cuttings covering the takeover/merger and write an informal report on it. Your report should cover the nature of the businesses involved, the arguments for and against the takeover/merger (as appropriate), whether or not it was caught by the Fair Trading Act 1973 (and with what result) and whether the takeover/merger was successful.

18

Theory and practice

CHAPTER OBJECTIVES

After studying this chapter you should be able to:

Examine critically the importance of objectives, policies and structures to organisations;
Appreciate the implications of equal opportunities policies, change and technological progress;
Explain the significance of market theory;
Evaluate freedom to bargain as the basis for contract law;
Assess the effectiveness of state intervention as a regulator of the market-place;
Appreciate the problems posed by economic inefficiency, profit and ignorance;
Appreciate and account for the differences between theory and practice in the market-place.

Introduction

In this chapter we are not going to tell you that everything you have learnt so far does not apply in the *real world* but we are going to point out some ways in which practice *appears*, at least, to differ from theory and how the differences may possibly be reconciled. For example, few, if any, small businesses will determine their prices by directly referring to pricing theories and few consumers will consider everyday purchases in terms of contract law.

If this is so, you may ask why we have spent so much time explaining the theory. Well, there are perhaps three main reasons. First, it is by studying the theory that we can best try to understand the practice. Practice would be too confusing for most of us to use as the starting point since it would need considerable case study to determine the principles involved. At a basic level most things can be understood using

common sense but this soon ceases to be adequate as the complexities of human, organisational and market behaviour are encountered and the scale of activities increase. Second, while many organisations can carry on business without a great deal of theoretical knowledge while things are going well, an understanding of the theory becomes very useful when things do not go so well. There is no need to understand the technicalities of contract law when a contract is being performed according to its terms, for example, but this may become all important if a dispute arises over its meaning or performance. Third, and probably the most important reason in the short term, your course assessment will require you to show an understanding of and the ability to apply theory to practice!

We are primarily concerned in this chapter with the problems of theory and practice in the market-place but we can usefully begin by briefly reconsidering a few topics we covered in the first two parts of this book which are relevant to the operation of the market-place and which should present you with a few new ideas to think about. Let us first reconsider organisations.

Organisations

Objectives and policies

In Chapter 2 we considered objectives and policies in some detail. We explained that while there are practical problems associated with them they are crucial to the successful operation of an organisation. But are you familiar with the 'This applies to other organisations, ours is different' attitude? Perhaps we should have treated determining objectives and policies as an interesting aside, something which most managers and supervisors learn about but never have the need nor opportunity to try.

This may be going too far but consider carefully what organisational objectives and policies mean to you in practice. If you cannot write down the main objectives of the organisation in which you work or study, can your immediate boss or tutor? Should they be able to? Is it important anyway? These are questions that you may best be able to answer, or at least form an opinion on, after a few years' work experience.

Structures

We also discussed functions and structures within organisations. These are more readily understood than organisational theory because you can actually see what people do and relate this to a name, e.g. 'finance.' However, while it may be relatively simple to draw an easily understood diagram of how an organisation is structured, in reality the diagram may obscure the practice or merely be one way among several of depicting the organisation. For example, many organisations are apparently structured on fairly traditional departmental lines but have some cross-departmental functions. This being so, it would be possible to draw two very different diagrams according to whether you wished to highlight the departmental or the functional elements of the structure. You might have concluded that the *systems approach* (*see* page 38) is the best representation of practice, but how many people really understand its implications and operation?

Committees and agendas for meetings illustrate well specific differences between theory and practice. Both apparently promote involvement and democracy but there is an alternative view. If you recall your school physics you will remember that electricity has to be transmitted at high voltage over long distances to overcome resistance in the cable. In other words, what goes in at one end does not necessarily come out of the other! Can the same be said for committees? Can they be used by senior management to kill off effectively (in a democratic way) issues which they do not support?

Similarly, agendas for meetings can be used, even at the very highest levels of discussion and decision-making, to divert attention away from issues which the 'boss' does not want discussed. Some would say that many managers spend too much time trying to determine the *hidden agenda* of meetings and pursuing their own personal or departmental objectives to the detriment of the central corporate objectives. However, if this is the practice, should we accept it and spend time studying it? Would the 'powers that be' wish it to be studied?

Equal opportunities

Equal opportunities is generally understood to mean equality in such things as education and employment regardless of a person's race, culture, religion, sex, sexual orientation or disability. As such it asks fundamental questions about the nature of our society and our own personal *value systems*.

As institutions, do our employers or colleges discriminate consciously or unconsciously against certain groups? Consider the following questions.

(a) Is it easy for persons with disabilities to get into the college? Are the health and safety regulations infringed when they do because the building was never designed to cater for them?
(b) Does the timetable discriminate against women with children by starting at the same time as the children are due at school? Is there a creche?
(c) What is the percentage of students from ethnic minorities on part-time 'professional' courses compared with those on full-time general education or vocational courses?
(d) To what extent do our employers or colleges

consider alternatives to formal educational qualifications for entry to different grades or courses?

(e) What are your own value systems? Are these shared by your colleagues and managers? How do you react to working or studying with 'gays', 'lesbians', 'people with disabilities' or 'blacks/whites'? Do you find the question disturbing?

Equal opportunities can easily become the 'flavour of the month' because it is fashionable and talking about it can be a convenient alternative to actually doing something. There is much *tokenism* when personal or institutional gestures in favour of equal opportunities fail to grapple with basic inequalities.

The law is often an ineffective way of dealing with problems of inequality. It is difficult to change people's attitudes through legislation. Perhaps you would like to reflect on the idea put forward in Chapter 25 that law can and will only promote *justice* when it is itself the product of a just society.

Consider the organisation for which you work or in which you study. List the factors which contribute to greater: *(a)* equality, *(b)* inequality.

What means do you consider would most actively promote greater equality?

Change

We devoted the first chapter to aspects of change. Change is usually very real and can have enormous effects on individuals and organisations. Here, however, we want you to think about two ideas. First, the possibility that change in organisations can be *tokenism*. In other words, the organisation fails to comprehend the true nature of the change and preoccupies itself with cosmetic responses. Second, that such responses may well frustrate and disable the organisation. As *Caius Petronius* remarked in AD 66:

We trained hard, but it seemed that every time we were beginning to form up into teams we would be reorganised. I was to learn later in life that we tend to meet any new situation by reorganising, and a wonderful method it can be for creating the illusion of progress, while producing confusion, inefficiency and demoralisation.

Technology

There is a widely held view that technological progress is by definition both useful and good. Undoubtedly, sophisticated technology now enables us to do things as a matter of course which only a few years ago were quite beyond our imagination. However, technological progress does not always translate into benefits for the user. Many organisations that invested in computers have found that they either did not really need them at all or that the system bought was not the most suitable. Employing another clerk might have been cost-effective, besides creating a job.

What is the relevance of sophisticated technology to Third World countries? Very often the level of development prevents technology from being either understood or exploited. If there are enormous pools of unused labour, is it perhaps better, at least initially, to utilise them? In recent years there has been increased interest in *intermediate technology* of a kind more suitable to the needs of such societies; an example being simple but highly efficient wind-machines to pump water and generate electricity.

Technological progress can also bring its own problems. As happened with the *Spinning Jenny* in the 18th century, computers in the latter part of the 20th century have put people out of work with, as yet, no real sign of the great wealth and alternative employment that their introduction is meant to create. Progress in the Industrial Revolution left permanent scars on the landscape. Today planning regulations are much stricter but the disaster at the Russian atomic power station at Chernobyl in 1986 indicates that while precautions against environmental damage are far more stringent, the magnitude of the risk is often proportionally greater.

Finally, what of the ethical questions raised by spending colossal sums on technological research, much of it military, while most of the Third World starves for the want of basic technology with which to establish just a subsistence economy?

Keywords _____

Theory and practice
There is often a world of difference between theory and practice but it is by understanding and applying theory that we can best understand and debate the practice.

Hidden agenda
What is really to be discussed although it never features on the formal agenda.

Tokenism
By saying or doing something which *appears* to come to terms with a difficult issue, often one involving our personal attitudes or change, we avoid actually doing so and continue with the same attitudes as before.

Intermediate technology
Technology which is half-way between the capital intensive technology of the Western World and the indigenous techniques of the Third World. The development of intermediate technology may well have involved applying sophisticated techniques and processes to produce a very simple device or system.

Problems of the market-place

The significance of theory

Now let us turn our attention specifically to the working of the market-place and attempt to synthesise our knowledge in all its aspects: economic, legal, political and so on. In order for us to do this, you must have thoroughly understood the material in the previous chapters of this part of the book.

As we have said, you may well object and say that business people know little about the finer points of contract law and have little knowledge of concepts such as marginal cost and marginal revenue. Not only this, more advanced texts will tell you that such costs are all but impossible to calculate anyway.

The problem of scale may also give rise to further difficulties when assessing the relevance of theory. When trying to explain concepts it is convenient for us to use small businesses because they are more easily understood. It is also the case that we indulge in a great deal of mathematical simplification for the same reason. Thus, for example, we might say 'Suppose the business is producing 5 units per week' when we know perfectly well that an output of 50,000 is more realistic. We also tend to use familiar activities such as farming in our examples because they are readily understood and fit in well with theory.

Two points should be made when considering these problems. First, we are *not* trying to make the real world conform to the theoretical but rather we are trying to understand simple examples so that we can later understand the complex ones. Second, although the small business may have little use for theory, this is not true of the large business. For example, when computers are used in the management of the firm, it is at once apparent that we must have definite ideas on the nature of costs and revenues for these are the basis of the software used. This, however, brings a countervailing problem. People who are very sceptical of theory often have great faith in the output of computers. They forget that the output is only as good as the theory on which it is based.

But the significance of theory is much more important than this. It is the theory of the market-place that lies at the heart of our *political* understanding of the capitalist system. Both those that defend the free enterprise system and those that attack it do so in terms of the theories that we have discussed. This is because theory forms the only *common ground* that can be understood and argued about by the various parties.

At the core of the defence of market economics lies the idea of competition. Those that defend the system argue that competition provides both freedom of choice and optimum efficiency in minimising costs.

The Chicago School

Until recently the free enterprise economy has been under attack. The state has interfered in the economy both by taking over industries and by regulating the market-place through legislation and by specialist government agencies such as the Monopolies and Mergers Commission.

Since the mid 1970s Western economies have tended to try to re-introduce market economics. This we saw with the election of the Thatcher government in the UK and the Reagan government in the USA, both committed to rolling back the frontiers of state intervention in the economy. The dramatic events in Eastern Europe in 1989 and 1990 seemed to underlie the collapse of collectivist ways of running an economy. Intellectually, the belief in free market policies is associated with the *Chicago School* of economics. The name comes from the Chicago Business School which has played an important role in the revival of these ideas. Among the chief advocates of the free market are Milton Friedman and Friedrich Hayek.

It is the contention of the Chicago School that free

market economics is the optimal way of regulating the economy. State intervention, its followers argue, has both restricted the growth of economies and brought with it problems such as inflation. More specific to our purposes here, it is also argued that the consumer is best protected by the market-place. By this they mean that if consumers are not satisfied with the goods or services they buy, the best guarantee of redress is their ability to buy from another supplier. This, the argument goes, will keep all businesses on their toes and therefore benefit the consumer. Furthermore, specialist consumer legislation is seen not only as being unnecessary but also as harmful because it increases inefficiency in the market-place. (Much the same argument was used to justify the proposed abolition of wages councils, *see* Chapter 8.) The free marketeers argue that consumers who have a legitimate grievance, say, because they have bought shoddy goods, can find suitable redress in basic contract law; a branch of the common law which itself is a product of the free market system and the legal means of supporting the process of exchange.

Inequality in the market-place

The argument for the free market system is severely weakened by the glaring inequality in bargaining power that exists in the market-place. Be it different organisations competing for resources or markets, or consumers entering into contracts with or seeking redress from organisations, it is clear that some are better equipped than others to compete in the market-place. If these inequalities were removed, which they realistically could never be, the theory would be more attractive.

Think back to Chapter 17: *Law and the market-place.* Contract law is said to be based on the notion of *freedom to bargain.* This assumes that the parties bargain from positions of equal strength and have complete freedom in their decision-making. But is any bargaining actually involved? Certainly not in the commercial sense in an ordinary consumer contract. We have a system where the seller fixes the price and the terms of business and the buyer's freedom is essentially to accept or reject this. Often, of course, the consumer is not in a position to reject. He needs the goods or services and no suitable alternative source of supply may be available. If one is, the consumer is likely to be presented with much the same terms of business. (This, incidentally, seems strangely at odds with the concept that in a retail sale it is the buyer who makes the offer to the shop, the display being merely *an invitation to treat.*)

Standard form contracts

Perhaps the whole emphasis of conventional contract law theory is wrong. How often do business people analyse their contracts in terms of 'offer and acceptance'. They are concerned with concluding a mutually satisfactory *bargain* by negotiation, often over a considerable period of time, and protecting their interests if the other side does not keep its side of the bargain. On many occasions, a contract in the strictly *legal* sense is never concluded. The legal technicalities are often regarded as matters of little relevance to modern commercial practice and business and commercial exchanges frequently fail to conform to the conventional theoretical model of a contract. Where a formal contract is used in a commercial exchange, a business will always try to use a standard form – its own of course – wherever possible. A standard form contract provides a simple, proven and cost-effective way of doing business.

The position may become interesting from a theoretical viewpoint when both sides use standard forms in their negotiations, i.e to use conventional legal terminology, the 'offer' contains standard terms and conditions and so does the 'acceptance' – different ones. This is referred to as a *battle of the forms* and it becomes difficult to determine which of the two sets of standard terms and conditions is the basis of the contract. How can the parties be said to have concluded the all important *agreement*? The practice is clearly at odds with the theory. Of course the parties have reached an 'agreement' if they are doing business with each other, the theoretical problems only surface on the relatively rare occasions when a dispute arises. Interestingly enough, theory finds it hard to cope with such situations. While the conduct of the parties clearly suggests an agreement was made, there is equally clearly no agreement on the terms and conditions. Perhaps arbitration by specialists rather than the judicial process is better equipped to resolve such disputes.

Does intervention produce equality

Whatever the theoretical niceties involved, there is no doubt that economic inequality combined with the use of standard form contracts, particularly in consumer sales, seriously undermines 'freedom to bargain' as the basis of contract law. Arguably it also justifies state intervention in the market-place through such statutes as the Consumer Credit Act 1974, the Unfair Contract Terms Act 1977, and the Consumer Protection Act 1987.

The position is mirrored in resource markets where the inadequacies of contract law have led to some of the more important employment rights having nothing whatever to do with the contract of employment. Protection against unfair dismissal and redundancy, both provided by interventionist legislation (*see* Chapter 8) would hardly be the product of a voluntary agreement between a profit maximising employer and his individually weak employee. Interestingly, this would not be true in all societies. For example, in Russia and Japan we would see a very different picture. In Russia we would see state paternalism and in Japan, corporate paternalism.

Yet, does such intervention produce equality? Can the average consumer be expected to understand the information which by law must be given to him? What would the average consumer do if a supplier offered a repair, an exchange, or to give a credit note but not to make a refund when they returned a faulty article? In all probability, one of the alternatives offered would be acceptable but what if it was not? The supplier would be acting illegally but how many consumers would feel equal to the task of and be prepared to face the hassle involved in taking out a county court summons? How many would be prepared to pay a solicitor to do this for them? The consumer is faced with problems of both *substantive law*, i.e his actual rights, and *procedure*, i.e the machinery by which he can *attempt* to enforce those rights. It is probable that the difficulty would lie with the latter. And even where a consumer succeeds in court, an award of damages, the only remedy that the court is likely to grant, may not be what the consumer wants. Usually, the consumer wants defective goods repaired or replaced and shoddy workmanship made good, the courts can not order these. Business people may ignore the legal process

and its remedies entirely, preferring to come to informal arrangements or make provisions for bad debts. So much so that there is the theory that business practice is non-contractual, or is it that contract theory is irrelevant to business?

Some organisations operate a trading policy at the opposite end of the spectrum. They are prepared to refund the purchase price on perfect goods just because, in practice, the purchaser changes his or her mind. Here, legal theory is being stood on its head, the organisation is under absolutely no obligation to give a refund. Interestingly enough, such a trading policy is an effective way to compete in the market-place and one organisation which operates such a policy, Marks and Spencer, is reputed to drive extremely hard bargains with its own suppliers, using its superior bargaining position (monopsony) to good effect.

Perhaps we can conclude this section with the general proposition that if a society is ignorant of legal rights, there will always be some who will exploit that ignorance.

Do you consider that you have freedom to bargain in contracts which you make? List the changes in the law or in institutions which you think would do most to reduce inequality in bargaining power.

Economic inefficiency

If you turn back to Fig. 16.7 on page 286, you will find the general conclusion that in the imperfect market-place (remember that all markets are imperfect) the business will restrict its output, thereby increasing both its *prices* and *costs*. It is only in near perfect markets, such as agriculture, that cost minimisation is maintained. Such is the standard economic conclusion.

You may argue that there are many industries where competition is fierce and cost-cutting all important. This is to misunderstand the nature of the problem. Businesses compete by product *differentiation* and it is that which is wasteful. Consumers are often very happy with this situation and support it by being willing to pay high premiums to own designer jeans, use the latest cosmetics, drive a BMW and so on. Part of the attraction of, for instance, a BMW is that it is so expensive! (*See* page 251.) But are you equally happy that the same is true for electricity, telephone calls, detergents, processed food, housing, etc?

An additional argument is involved when we consider very large-scale operations. If you look at the Toymota and Kruks example on page 292, it becomes apparent that the costs of manufacturing a car are much lower where the industry is dominated by a few large firms. The conclusion you might be tempted to draw from this is that monopoly or oligopoly is to the advantage of the consumer. However, it should be equally apparent that, unrestrained, the monopolist is likely to exploit the consumer even if the product is being produced efficiently. There is also likely to be much product differentiation. Let us continue with the example of car manufacture. It is the case that people will often pay several thousand pounds more for the top-of-the-range car, for example, a Ford Escort XR3i, when the extra manufacturing cost is only a few pounds. Is there a role here for the government in protecting consumers or should they by ignorance or by choice be free to spend their own money as they wish?

The problem of profit

The problem of theory and practice is illustrated well by the concept of profit. The economist happily defines *normal* and *abnormal profit* (*see* page 220) while at the same time admitting that they are virtually impossible to quantify! The accountant would possibly argue that a precise figure can be arrived at. Consider the following however. The economist would insist that normal profit is a legitimate cost of the business while the accountant would never regard profits as costs. On the other hand, the economist would take a jaundiced view of the cost of advertising and product differentiation as, for example, when a monopolist furiously pits one of its brands in competition with another. This latter problem also afflicts the government when it tries to restrict or tax profits. The business can choose to 'lose' its profits in advertising campaigns, promotions, sponsorships and the like rather than pay them out in tax.

Ignorance

The ignorance of consumers poses a special problem when we come to assess the market-place. To some extent there is nothing that can be done for the consumer who appears intent on buying inferior goods and paying superior prices. Problems are raised, however, by a number of factors.

1 The growing technical complexity of products. People are increasingly buying products, the working of which they understand only imperfectly. What should producers be required to tell consumers?

2 Consumers' rights. People are often ignorant of their legal rights – a point we have made several times before. For example, a person may take faulty sale goods back to the shop to be confronted by a notice saying 'No money refunded on sale goods'. To what extent should the government educate consumers as to their rights in such situations?

3 Product liability. Despite legislation designed to prevent it, products may still be sold that are downright dangerous. Hairdryers that catch fire or cars that explode when involved in collisions are obvious cases for intervention but what about furniture that catches fire easily and gives off fumes which kill in seconds? Before answering this question, pause to consider that the furniture in your home is probably like this. Truly safe furniture would most likely cost you two or three times as much as the best selling lines.

You saw in Chapter 17 that Britain has now implemented the EC directive on product liability by the Consumer Protection Act 1987. However, both the European and domestic political processes, having been lobbied by powerful pressure groups, held up its introduction for a considerable time.

4 Search theory. Knowledge is a resource and resources cost money. The problem and cost of obtaining information applies to both the consumer and to the firm. For example, if you are trying to buy the best hi-fi at the cheapest price, this may involve you in spending a lot of time reading magazines and going to different shops. There will come a time when the cost of the *search* will exceed the saving and is no longer worthwhile. When we apply this principle to the firm, it is given the grand name of *search theory*. The theory proposes that the cost of search may oblige a business to settle for second or even third best.

Consider two examples. First, suppose that a business wants to appoint a new accounts manager, there being no suitable person within the firm. The business must advertise, interview applicants and in the meantime go without the services of the accountant it needs. There must, therefore, be a limit to the money and time that the firm can spend searching for the best person. Second, if we assume that firms are profit maximisers, then they will wish to save every penny they can in manufacture. However, at some stage the cost of tracking down savings will exceed the savings made and the firm will therefore settle for some inefficiencies. This principle largely explains why firms only start to become concerned when individual departmental or project budgets are overspent and are relatively unconcerned with spending within the budget.

Demonstrate that a firm producing at the output at which AC = AR is more efficient than one producing at the output at which MC = MR.

Keywords

Chicago School
Believes in neo-classical free market economics. Led by Milton Friedman, the Professor of Economics at the University of Chicago, 1948 –

Freedom to bargain
A basic assumption of the common law approach to making contracts. From a practical perspective you may care to question the appropriateness and validity of this assumption.

'Battle of the forms'
A situation which arises when the parties to a contract base their 'agreement' on an exchange of incompatible standard forms. But problems arise only if there is a dispute between them.

Economic inefficiency
The misuse of resources so that the producer of a product uses up a greater amount of factors of production.

Ignorance
Not stupidity but sheer lack of knowledge is one of the greatest causes of inequality and imperfection in markets.

Product liability
Producers are strictly liable for the damage caused by defects in their products.

Conclusion

It should be apparent from what we have said that there is a case for specialist consumer legislation. We argued in Chapter 16 that governments will need to intervene to prevent excessive profits from being made and to try to ensure that the monopolist and oligopolist produce nearest the point where AC = AR rather than where MC = MR. In the wider frame, the aim of intervention in the market-place is to eliminate the *economic inefficiencies* which imperfect markets bring with them. This, as we have seen above, is complicated by the difficulty of determining such costs and revenues accurately and of defining what constitutes excessive profit.

We have also considered the problems of *ignorance* and of *inequality in bargaining power*. From this we can argue that there is a need not only for legislation to protect consumers but also for specialist agencies, such as the Office of Fair Trading, to actively promote the rights of consumers. There are, however, psychological limits to this. If, for example, a consumer buys a product such as an expensive perfume, knowing that it is over-priced, what can or should the law do to protect such a person? If we argue for legislative controls on such behaviour we are arguing for a change in the whole nature of our society rather than just for regulation of the market-place.

The role of the state

We hope that we have demonstrated the main possibilities.

1 Competition is the best regulator of and safeguard in the market-place.
2 The government should intervene to regulate the market-place.
3 The market-place is by definition inefficient and state provision is the alternative.

In this we touch on fundamental questions about the nature of society. To what extent can and should people be the judge of their own best interests? To what extent should one person be allowed to exploit another?

One aim of this chapter has been to show that many

of these questions are only accessible through theory. That is to say, what we know and believe about the nature of the market-place is a *product* of our theoretical understanding.

Learning project

'People of the same trade seldom meet together, even for merriment and diversion, but the conversation ends up in a conspiracy against the public, or in some contrivance to raise prices.'

Adam Smith in *The Wealth of Nations* 1776

'Fundamentally, there are only two ways of co-ordinating the economic activities of millions. One is central direction involving the use of coercion – the technique of the army and the modern totalitarian state. The other is voluntary co-operation of individuals – the technique of the market place.'

Milton Friedman 1970

1 Both Smith and Friedman are great advocates of free market economics. Analyse these seemingly contradictory statements.

2 Under what circumstances might law be necessary to redress inequality in the market place?

How Britain is governed

CHAPTER OBJECTIVES

After studying this chapter you should be able to:

■ Describe the four elements of central government;
■ List the forms of local government;
■ Explain the finance of local government;
■ Define and describe the role of quasi-governmental bodies.

Throughout the book we have made reference to 'the government'. In this section we examine the influence of the government upon organisations and the community. First of all we will examine the organisation of government.

Central government

Central government has four elements, the *legislature*, the *judiciary*, the *executive* and the *Civil Service*. The judiciary is considered in Chapter 26 and therefore in this chapter we will consider the other elements of government.

Parliament: the legislature

Parliament consists of the Queen, Lords and Commons and is the supreme legislative authority in the UK. To some extent this ancient and fundamental principle has been modified by our membership of the EC (*see* page 347).

Discover the following:

(a) **the name of your local parliamentary constituency;**
(b) **the name of the sitting MP;**
(c) **the political party to which they belong;**
(d) **their majority at the last election.**

In practice the House of Commons is the most important part of the legislature, for it is the political party which controls the Commons which, in turn, forms the Government. Since the Government can almost invariably muster an overall majority in the Commons, and also controls the timetable, it has very considerable power over what is discussed.

Fig. 19.1 traces the progress of a typical Bill through Parliament. Most Bills which run the full course and become law are government-sponsored and start off along the 'Green Paper, White Paper' trail. There is only a small amount of time for *private members' Bills* and it is a lottery that decides who will be allowed to introduce one. Nevertheless, private members' Bills have often introduced important legislation, for example homosexual law reform.

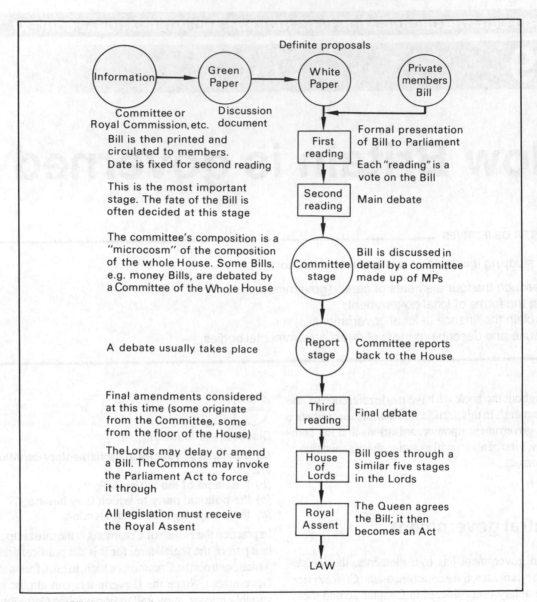

Fig. 19.1 How a Bill becomes an Act

Private members' Bills should not be confused with *private Bills*. The latter apply only to a group or section of the community or to a particular geographical area, e.g. British Rail promoting a new stretch of railway line. Such Bills are deposited in the private Bill Office and usually go through Parliament unopposed.

The amount of time it takes for a Bill to pass through Parliament varies enormously. In the 1970s The Prevention of Terrorism Act 1974 was introduced into Parliament on the morning of 27 November and received the Royal Assent at 9.40 am two days later. On the other hand, the Scottish Devolution Bill had to be introduced in several separate sessions of Parliament before it was finally agreed in a much amended form. (In fact Scottish devolution was not achieved because it failed to gain the necessary percentage support in a referendum. Such was also the fate of devolution for Wales.) The speed with which a Bill passes through Parliament will be determined by whether or not it is opposed and the degree of urgency which the government places upon it.

1 Do you consider that the House of Lords should be reformed? Give reasons for your answer and put forward proposals for an alternative second chamber.

2 Choose an Act of Parliament which has become law recently. Use the newspapers and journals in your library to trace the progress of this legislation up to the point when it became law. (You can find a useful summary of the progress of current Bills in the *New Law Journal*.) You should include reference to the source of the Proposal – Government manifesto commitment, Royal Commission Report, Green Paper, etc – and indicate the ways in which the original proposals were modified as a result of the legislative process. Were there, for example, any significant amendments made as a result of pressure from interest groups?

The Prime Minister and the Cabinet

The Prime Minister, or First Lord of the Treasury, to give the official title, has many powers: appointing and dismissing ministers and determining the membership of Cabinet committees; deciding what the Cabinet will discuss and chairing the meetings; summarising the discussions of the Cabinet and sending 'minutes' to ministers which are, in effect, directives. In addition to this, the Prime Minister dispenses a great deal of patronage in both government and non-government posts as well as the honours list, bishops in the Church of England and certain judicial posts. The Prime Minister can also ask the Monarch to dissolve Parliament. This is a considerable power as a time can be chosen which is considered the most favourable to the re-election of the government.

Discover three recent occasions in which the Government was defeated on its legislative proposals. (Hint: Do not forget the House of Lords.)

These many powers have led many people to suggest that we now have government by Prime Minister. In other words, the Prime Minister acts more in the manner of an American President rather than as a 'first' minister. Lord Hailsham, the former Lord Chancellor, has suggested that, with a secure majority, the Government is in effect 'an elected dictatorship'. While there may be much truth in this, Prime Ministers are still subject to serious constraints for they must secure the agreement of Parliament and also command the loyalty of the Cabinet. In practice, Prime Ministers are particularly dependent upon the support of the *inner cabinet*, a small group of senior colleagues who are capable of commanding the support of the party and Parliament.

In recent years the *kitchen cabinet* has become more important. This is a small group of advisers on whose loyalty the Prime Minister can totally rely. They may be colleagues from Parliament or they may simply be advisers appointed by the Prime Minister. As a result Downing Street has come to look more like the White House. This was well-illustrated in 1989 with the resignation of the Chancellor Nigel Lawson who objected to the Prime Minister preferring the advice of her personal adviser Sir Alan Walters to his own.

The word cabinet was originally a term of abuse used to describe the clique which advised Charles II. Today the composition of the Cabinet depends upon the preferences of the Prime Minister although it must, of course, include the most senior ministers such as the Chancellor of the Exchequer, the Foreign Secretary, the Home Secretary and the Minister of Defence. It will also include those responsible for the running of Parliament such as the Leader of the House of Commons. The Prime Minister and Cabinet constitute the *executive* branch of government for it is they who decide upon policies and implement them.

An important aspect of the Cabinet is the doctrine of *collective responsibility*. That is to say, the Cabinet should always appear to speak with one voice. If a member of the Cabinet is in serious disagreement with a policy then they should resign. On the other hand, the Cabinet takes responsibility for the actions of its members collectively, so that an attack upon one is an attack upon all. In recent years, the disagreements of cabinet ministers have become more public. The Thatcher Government began to turn 'semi-official' leaks of Cabinet transactions into a regular occurrence. The dangers and pitfalls of this practice were well illustrated by the *Westland Affair* when the substance of leaks became the occasion for the resignation of two Cabinet ministers.

Government departments

The Government of the country is divided between different departments of state: at the head of each is a *minister* or *secretary of state*. They are political figures and are termed *members of the Government*. Most senior posts are filled by members of the House of Commons. The minister or secretary may, or may not be, a member of the Cabinet. Each minister is assisted by a *Parliamentary secretary*, while secretaries of state are assisted by *Parliamentary under-secretaries*. These people are known as *junior ministers* and receive a salary for their job. This is in contrast to Parliamentary *private secretaries* who receive no remuneration other than their salaries as MPs and usually undertake the task in hope of future advancement. There seems to have been a proliferation of secretaries of state recently as large composite ministries have appointed secretaries to be in charge of particular functions; examples of this are Defence and the Department of the Environment which are subdivided into smaller sections such as transport and local government..

The three great departments of state, the Treasury, the Foreign and Commonwealth Office, and the Home Office, tend to remain the same, but the duties and titles of the other departments are often changed by the Government of the day.

The Civil Service

The Civil Service is the *secretariat* which has to translate the policy of the Government into action. Although legally civil servants are servants of the Crown, they are in practice employed by the separate departments of state and responsible to the minister in charge. If the Government changes, civil servants do not. This gives continuity to the departments but it also tends to give a great deal of power to civil servants. It is perhaps another example of the growth of the 'techno-structure' (*see* page 99.)

Each departments usually has a *permanent secretary* (Sir Humphrey in 'Yes Minister' is a permanent secretary). He is the minister's adviser and he is also responsible to the *Public Accounts Committee* of Parliament. Do not confuse the permanent secretary, who is professional administrator and civil servant, with the Parliamentary secretary, who is a political

figure often without expertise in the work of his department. The permanent secretary and his deputies are often referred to as 'mandarins' and are thought to wield enormous power. The administrative class of the Civil Service still tends to be made up of 'Oxbridge' graduates.

Although the permanent heads of the Civil Service may have great power, it is the ministers who must accept the political and legal responsibility for the acts of departments. Beneath the administrative class of civil servants are the thousands of other civil servants: executive class; clerical class; the professional, and the technical and scientific class, who carry out the work of the department.

Local government

The structure of local government

Local authorities are responsible for a wide range of services from education to refuse collection. The structure of local government has been the subject of much revision in recent years. The *London Government Act* 1963 brought the Greater London Council (GLC) into existence in 1965. This replaced the London County Council. The local government of London was sub-divided between the GLC and 32 London boroughs and the City of London. The *Local Government Act* 1972 created the system of counties and districts which became the pattern of local government outside London in 1974 (1975 in Scotland). The predominantly rural areas of the country (often called the *shire counties*) were run by *county councils* which were subdivided into *district councils*. The chief urban areas of the country were covered by six *metropolitan counties* which were sub-divided into *metropolitan districts*.

This pattern was modified in 1986 when the GLC and the metropolitan counties were abolished. Some of their functions were devolved to metropolitan districts and the London boroughs while others, such as police, fire and public transport, were to be controlled by newly created *joint boards*. These boards were made up of members nominated from the various district and borough councils within the area. As an interim measure *residuary bodies* were appointed to wind-up the affairs of the defunct authorities.

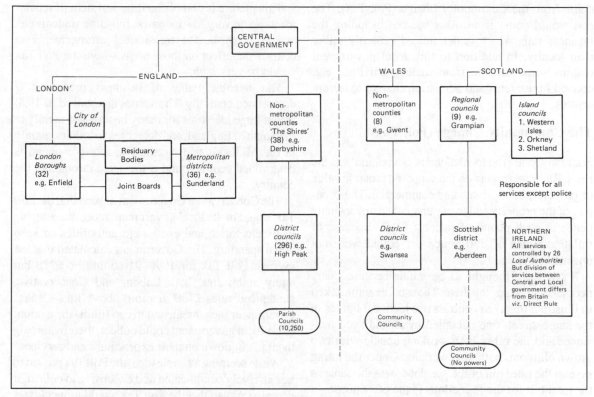

Fig. 19.2 The organisation of local government in the UK. There are ministers with special responsibility for Scotland and Wales. Northern Ireland is governed direct from Westminster.

The *parish councils*, in some cases dating back to 1086, still continue in non-urban areas. Despite being criticised for the last 200 years they have proved the most durable unit of local government, although they possess few powers today.

To add to the confusion of local government some local authorities cling to titles such as borough, city or town councils. This is usually because they acquired this title by Royal Charter. These are, however, merely courtesy titles and in the case of borough and city councils they are, in fact, district councils. Their Charter usually gives them the right to have a mayor or a lord mayor. Town councils are a curiosity; they are parish councils which have been granted the right to call themselves town councils. Examples of this are Ely and Wells. Their chairman therefore becomes a city mayor. The structure of local government is summarised in Fig. 19.2.

There is no common pattern to the division of responsibilities between the local authorities. For example, education is provided by the metropolitan districts and by the outer-London boroughs but elsewhere in the country it is provided by the county councils.

Discover the following:

(a) the name of your local authority ward (constituency);
(b) the name of your local councillor and their party;
(c) do you elect more than one local councillor and if so why?
(d) which party controls your local government.

Finance of local government

It is a common misconception that local government is financed by local taxes. Figure 19.3 shows that this is not so. For the year 1990–91, it was estimated that only 19.5% of local government revenues would come from the Community Charge (Poll Tax). The rest would come from other sources including the business rate, which is determined centrally rather than locally. In addition to this, local government obtains some income from trading activities, e.g. council house rents and admission charges to leisure centres.

The Community Charge (Poll Tax)

For many years the local element of taxation was the rates. Rates were a tax on the supposed rentable value of property, both private and commercial. The occupier of the property had to pay annual rates of so many pence in each pound of rateable value. Because of inflation, rates of 350 pence per pound were not uncommon.

Rates were thought to be unfair because many people escaped paying them. The usual example taken to illustrate this is to contrast two identical homes in the same street, one occupied by an old-aged pensioner and the other by a working couple with two grown children, both also working. Under the rating system the rates bill of the pensioner was the same as the total bill for the four adults in the other house.

The Conservative Government replaced the rates with the Community Charge, which came into effect in April 1990 (earlier in Scotland). This is a flat rate tax on everyone over the age of eighteen. Thus, it corresponds to the electoral register of those eligible to vote, hence its usual name of 'Poll Tax'. The picture is modified by the fact that those with two properties pay two lots of Poll Tax, but do not get two votes!

The method of determining the total amount of Poll Tax to be raised by a local authority and the total amount they used to raise by rates are similar. The local authority determines how much it is to receive from central government and other sources and compares this with its estimated expenditure. The difference between the two is the amount to be raised by Poll Tax. For example, consider the following for the County of Eastmoreland.

Total expenditure for Eastmoreland	£350m
Total income from central government etc	£250m
To be raised by Poll Tax	£100m

If there are 250,000 people liable to pay the poll tax in Eastmoreland, this means that each person has to pay £400, i.e. £100m ÷ 250,000 = £400.

This picture is complicated by a system of rebates for those on very low incomes, full-time students etc, and by complicated transitional arrangements to counter the effect on those areas where the Poll Tax would be very high.

The rateable value of business properties is determined centrally. The values announced in 1990 meant large increases for many businesses, mainly in the South of England, and decreases for others, mainly in the Midlands and North. The rate per pound is determined centrally and is the same throughout the country.

The Conservative Government argued that the Poll Tax would make local government more accountable to its electorate and encourage authorities to keep down spending. The Government calculated that the average Poll Tax for 1990–91 should be £278 but many authorities, both Labour and Conservative, announced rates £100 or more above this. Central government then threatened to cap (limit) the amount of tax local government could collect, thereby forcing them to cut down on their expenditure and services.

While seeming a simple idea, the Poll Tax proved to be extremely complicated and expensive to collect. It was also argued that the Poll Tax would more closely match what people paid to the services they received – consider the example of the pensioner and the four adults mentioned above. However, it has never been a fiscal principle that you should pay taxes according to the services you receive – this would make school children the biggest taxpayers of all! Also, the idea that taxes should be uniform throughout the country is suspect. A poor inner-city borough is likely to have very high expenses but few people who have high incomes to pay the tax. By contrast, a 'shire' county may have low expenses but a generally wealthy population.

It has been argued that there is little to recommend a tax which 'taxes a duke the same as a dustman'. You might find it useful to consider see how it accords with the canons of taxation (*see* page 433). The last time the country had a poll tax was in 1381 and this caused the Peasants' Revolt! Of this tax the historian J R Green wrote:

To such a tax the poorest man contributed as large a sum as the wealthiest, and the gross injustice of such an exaction set England on fire from sea to sea!

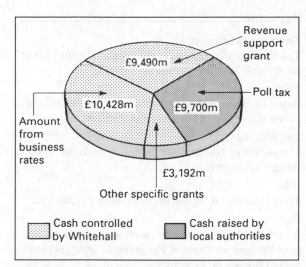

Fig. 19.3 Local government revenues 1990–91

The only concession to modernity in the Community Charge is that it falls not only on the poorest man but also on the poorest woman!

Construct a diagram to illustrate the pattern of income of your local authority. Compare this with the national pattern shown in Fig. 19.3. What differences exist and why?

Other local authorities

Since 1974 health services have been controlled by regional and area health authorities. These organisations are better described as types of *quasi-governmental bodies*. To these we may add the joint boards set up after the abolition of the metropolitan counties. Although they are controlled by nominees from elected authorities, they are not directly responsible to the electorate and may therefore be classed as quasi-governmental bodies.

Quasi-governmental bodies

Any organisation which is neither a private business organisation nor an elected body but which fulfils an executive or administrative function designed to implement or further Government policy can be de-

scribed as a *quasi-governmental body* today. In our complex society hundreds of such bodies exist because Government departments cannot or do not wish to allocate directly their own resources to the organisation and control of certain specific activities within the economy.

Some *quasi-government bodies* implement Government policy directly, e.g. the Monopolies and Mergers Commission, the Training Agency and the Office of Fair Trading. Indeed, in so far as their commercial policy is to some extent determined by the Government, the remaining nationalised industries and other public corporations can also be considered *quasi-governmental bodies*.

Others are concerned with matters which are generally considered to be outside the mainstream of Government policy and decision-making. Such bodies are frequently referred to as *quangos* – quasi-autonomous non-governmental organisations. Quangos operate in the administrative grey areas between central government on the one hand and local government and organisation in the private sector of the economy on the other. Most are established by an Act of Parliament or by an Order made under an Act. Some, however, have been established by a minister's administrative act. Their chairpersons are appointed by the minister responsible for their establishment and the Prime Minister has personal patronage of some.

The phrase 'government at arm's length' has been used to describe their activities since they enjoy considerable autonomy from their parent department. Each was created following a policy decision to remove a specific governmental function from the direct control and responsibility of a minister. In consequence, the minister ceases to be answerable to Parliament for their day-to-day activities. Important examples of quangos include the BBC and the IBA under the Home Office; the Industrial Training Boards under the Department of Employment, and the National Economic Development Office (NEDO) and the Review Board for Government Contracts under the Treasury.

Depending on how you define a quango, there are somewhere between 400 to 3,500 of them. Many have purely advisory functions, some distribute large sums of public money, e.g. the Arts Council, and some, like the regional and district health authorities, are policy-making bodies.

List five quangos other than those mentioned in the text.

Quangos undoubtedly serve very useful purposes. They are an excellent way of getting things done, allowing government departments to concentrate on broader policy issues. In their own policy-making they are free from the sensitivities of the political world and can maintain a long-term plan and exercise broader discretion than a government department ultimately dependent on public support. Above all, perhaps, they are free from direct political control in their day-to-day decision making.

However, four main criticisms are levelled against them. First, there are simply too many of them; second, they give government ministers an undesirable power of patronage – 'jobs for the boys' is the expression often used; third, they are not sufficiently accountable to Parliament, particularly in their spending; and fourth, many question whether they should have the power to determine policy.

Conclusion

Thus, we can see that the Government of the UK is not vested solely in Westminster and the town hall but in an amalgam of many diverse organisations and institutions. Three factors should be borne in mind when assessing these organisations. First, they are in a constant stage of change; their responsibilities, powers, and often their geographical definition are subject to frequent revision. Second, many powers are vested in non-elected bodies which may have implications for the democratic control of society. Third, the scope of the public sector itself changes. In recent years

Keywords

Central government
The national government of the country. In the case of the UK it is Westminster and Whitehall.

Parliament
In the UK this consists of the House of Commons, the House of Lords and the Queen in Parliament.

Legislature
The person or body entitled to pass laws. In the UK this is Parliament.

Bills
The proposals for legislation debated in Parliament.

Acts
A proposal for legislation becomes an Act when it has gone through all stages of Parliament. An Act is then part of the law of the land.

The Cabinet
The inner-circle of senior Ministers of State controlling Government policies. Members of the Cabinet are always named but the Prime Minister may change them.

Civil Service
Permanently employed members of Government departments concerned with the implementation and operation of Government policy.

Local government
Many important services, such as education, are supplied and directed by locally elected bodies such as County Councils. The main outline of policy is still controlled by central government.

Community Charge (Poll Tax)
A flat rate tax levied by local authorities.

Quangos
Many important national and local functions and services are controlled by quangos.

many things for long seen as part of the public sector have passed to the private sector, as was the case with the water and sewerage authorities.

Learning project

The Poll Tax

Read the following article which appeared in *The Observer*, 18 February 1990 and answer the questions which follow.

Political disaster with no chance of an early escape
Adam Raphael

The poll tax is a political disaster which has been waiting a long time to happen. After three

Government enquiries and numerous White and Green Papers spanning nearly a generation, the Community Charge has finally arrived.

Yet with 35 million demands due to drop through letterboxes in a few weeks' time, there is hardly any member of the Cabinet, apart from Mrs Thatcher, who regards it with any enthusiasm. For ministers now know that the poll tax will fall far short of achieving either of its principal aims – controlling local expenditure and making local authorities more responsive to their electorates.

The probable decision of many councils, Labour and Conservative, to levy community charges hugely above the official guidelines has already prompted Government threats of retaliation by central capping, bringing the accountability argument full-circle. As for the voters, even Conservative Central Office is in no doubt that retribution will be visited on the Tories rather than on high-spending Labour Councils in this year's local government elections.

The unfairness of a flat-rate tax on individuals, combined with the horrendous administrative problems of levying it, are defects which will exert a high political price. The opposition parties are understandably dancing for joy on this particular grave. What is not yet appreciated, however, is that, like it or loathe it, poll tax is likely to be a part of British life for at least a decade. Even if Labour wins the next election with a working majority, it is unlikely to be able to introduce its alternative scheme, an income-linked property tax based on capital values, within the lifetime of a single Parliament.

Evidence by Inland Revenue officials to the Environment Select Committee in 1982 suggested that it would take 'four full years' to prepare capital valuations on every property in England and Wales.

Quite apart from the administrative complications of switching to capital value taxation, there are a number of other formidable hurdles. Some house owners could face very large increases in both their present rates bill and their future poll tax assessments. The Institute of Revenue, Rating and Valuation said in a report published last year that one in seven households might face increases of 50% or more.

The huge rise in capital values in the South compared with the North would cause painful regional impacts unless central government undertook to cushion this affect. If Labour wants to win the next election, it might have to do just that.

The heart of the problem is not the tax system, but how we elect local authorities and what powers we give them. In brief, rotten boroughs produce rotten levels of taxation. So long as one-party fiefdoms flourish under our current first-past-the-post electoral system, and so long as the responsibilities of local authorities bear no relation to their taxing powers, the attempt to reform local government finance will be a continuing nightmare.

1 Investigate the revenues of your local authority. Present these in diagrammatic form.

2 Adam Smith said that a good tax would be one that was *equitable*, *economical*, *convenient* and *certain* (*see* page 433). Assess how well the poll tax meets these criteria.

3 Advance arguments for and against the poll tax.

4 Assess the following as alternatives to the poll tax: *(a)* a tax on the value of property, *(b)* a local income tax, *(c)* a local purchase tax.

5 Is the poll tax likely to make local authorities more or less accountable to central government?

6 Besides the poll tax, 1990 saw the introduction of a standard business rate throughout the country based on new valuations. Assess the effects of this business rate both locally and nationally.

7 The article makes reference to central capping of local authorities. What is meant by this and what are the consequences for local government?

8 The article mentions a Select Committee. What is a Select Committee and what is its function?

20

The European Community

CHAPTER OBJECTIVES

After studying this chapter you should be able to:

☐ Describe the origins of the European Community;
☐ Explain the meaning of the term 'common market';
☐ Evaluate the importance of the Single European Act;
☐ Explain the structure of the EC and functions of its Institutions;
☐ Analyse the importance of the EC to the British economy and society;
☐ Describe the nature of EC law and its relationship with UK law.

The origins of the EC

A plaque in Strasbourg marks the spot where Winston Churchill made a speech on European unity in 1945 but successive British governments turned their back on European co-operation. The origins of the EC are to be found in the European Coal and Steel Community (ECSC) set up in 1952 by France, Italy and the Benelux countries; West Germany joined later. The objective of the ECSC was to abolish trade restrictions on coal and steel between member countries and to co-ordinate production and price policies. The ECSC proved such a success that the members decided to investigate the possibility of the greater co-operation. The result of negotiations was the Treaty of Rome, signed in 1957. On 1 January 1958 the EC (often called the 'Common Market') came into existence. Britain was invited to participate in both the ECSC and the EC but declined to do so due to worries about the potential loss of sovereignty.

Britain eventually joined the EC in 1972, together with Ireland and Denmark. The membership of the Common Market was increased to ten by the accession of Greece in 1981 and to 12 in 1986 by the accession of Spain and Portugal. It is now a Community of some 323 million people.

What is a common market?

The establishment of the EC involved the setting-up of both a customs union and a common market.

Customs union

The establishment of a customs union involves both the *abolition of tariffs* between members and the levy of a *common external tariff* to the rest of the world. If each country does not have the same external tariff then imports will simply flood into the member country with the lowest import duties and then spread out to the rest of the customs union. The general policy which the EC used in arriving at its common external tariff was to take an arithmetic mean of the previous six duties. In some cases, e.g. the import of produce from France's tropical ex-colonies, the lowest duty was used, since this involved no disadvantage to members. Several of the old colonial states have special arrangements with the EC.

When Britain joined it was particularly difficult for her to agree to the common external tariff because she formerly enjoyed duty-free imports from Australia, Canada and New Zealand. The products of these temperate countries were, however, in direct competition with those of European farmers and Britain was not allowed in until she had agreed to raise import duties against her Commonwealth partners.

Arrangements with a number of African, Caribbean and Pacific (ACP) states were formalised by the Lomé Convention in 1975. This gives free access to the EC for ACP exports on a non-reciprocal basis. The EC also gives aid to the ACP countries from the European Development Fund and the European Investment Bank. This agreement was due to run out in February 1990.

Common market

The EC is known colloquially as the Common Market but this is only one aspect of it, although potentially the most important. It refers to the organisation of the economies of the members as if they were one country. This implies the free movement of labour, capital and enterprise within the EC. So far it is only in agriculture (the Common Agricultural Policy – CAP, *see* page 246) that there has been a truly common policy (but *see* below). The achievement of European monetary union (EMU), however, would lead to a much greater integration of the economies.

List five possible consequences if the Channel Tunnel operates successfully.

The structure of the Community

The Treaty of Rome envisages that the EC will eventually lead to European political union. This seems distant at present, economic and monetary union will come first, but the four main institutions of the EC provide the four essential components of a state.

1 The Council of Ministers – the executive or Cabinet.

2 The European Commission – the secretariat or Civil Service.
3 The European Parliament – the legislature.
4 The European Court of Justice – the judiciary.

The first three of these institutions are examined in this part of the chapter, while the Court of Justice is examined in the next.

The Council of Ministers

This is the EC's decision-making (executive) body. It consists of 12 members, one minister from each country. Determining which minister attends will depend upon the matter being discussed. If, for example, it is agriculture, then it will be the minister for agriculture of each country. In turn each member state assumes the Presidency of the Council for six months.

On the basis of Commission proposals, the Council frames the major policies and decisions of the Community. It also has the power to make new community law. Such law is known as *secondary legislation*, the *primary legislation* being that of the Treaty of Rome.

On most aspects of the 'Single Market' (*see* below) decisions of the Council are taken by majority vote, 54 votes (out of a total of 76) are required. However, unanimity is required on items relating to taxation, the free movement of persons and the rights and interests of employees. Unanimity is also required for a decision on the entry of new members to the EC and on an item which Parliament has opposed, the trend being away from consultation and towards co-operation in

Table 20.1 Voting power of the Council of Ministers

Country	No of votes
France	10
Italy	10
United Kingdom	10
West Germany	10
Spain	8
Belgium	5
Netherlands	5
Greece	5
Portugal	5
Denmark	3
Ireland	3
Luxembourg	2
Total	76

the relationship between Council and Parliament. The Council usually tries to reach a decision without taking a vote.

Which member state currently holds the Presidency of the Council? What are the main political and other objectives of the current holder and what support for and opposition to these objectives is there among the other member states?

COREPER

As ministers continue with their responsibilities in their own countries, they meet irregularly. Because of this a *Committee of Permanent Representatives* (COREPER) exists. This consists of an ambassador from each of the 12 countries. COREPER meets weekly and is able to take decisions on many of the proposals springing from the Commission. In this way it leaves only the most important or controversial issues to be decided by the ministers themselves.

The European Commission

The Commission is the EC's secretariat or 'civil service'. It comprises 17 Commissioners, two from each of the five largest countries and one from the seven others (*see* Table 20.1). Each is appointed for four years and each is completely independent of their country of origin. Behind the Commission and the other institutions is a staff of many thousands, working mainly at the EC headquarters in Brussels. The staff are of various nationalities and successive presidents of the Commission are selected from different countries.

It is the job of the Commission to undertake the day-to-day administration of the EC. They are supposed to do this in a European manner without national bias. It involves monitoring the activities of member states to see that they do not conflict with community policy. In addition to this, they implement community policies such as the CAP.

The Commission also tries to develop EC policy by formulating policies for economic co-ordination for consideration by the Council. It is proposals by the Commission on such things as food hygiene which

provoke outbursts in the British Press about 'the European sausage' or 'the European chicken'. Similarly, issues such as the introduction of tachographs into lorry cabs originally provoked great opposition from many people in Britain.

There are 17 Commissioners each with a different responsibility. List these responsibilities and what each embraces; name the Commissioner responsible and state which country he or she is from. Who is current President of the Commission?

The European Parliament

The European Parliament meets in Strasbourg. The UK elects 81 MEPs out of a total of 518 (*see* Table 20.2). In Parliament members are seated according to party allegiance, not according to nationality. Thus, for example, Labour MEPs sit with the SPD members from West Germany.

Discover the identity of your MEP. What party do they belong to? Which of the European political groupings in Strasbourg are they associated with? What is the date of the next elections to the European Parliament?

Unlike national parliaments the European Parliament has no legislative powers although it can and frequently does propose legislative action to the Commission, most of its proposals being acted upon. Its main function is to monitor the activities of other community institutions although, under the 'co-operation procedure' introduced by the Single European Act it gives opinions when the Commission makes a proposal about the Single Market and again when the Council has reached an agreement in principle. The aim is to allow the Parliament to propose amendments to a Commission proposal after the Council has formed a view on it but before the Council has formally adopted it as Community law. It must also consent to the accession of new members to the Community.

To achieve *authority* the Parliament will have to gain the ability to initiate and enact legislation. To gain *power* the Parliament will have to obtain control of the EC budget. At the moment it only has power to amend,

Table 20.2 Composition of the European Parliament 1986. Number of MPs per state

Country		No of seats
UK		81*
England	66	
Scotland	8	
Wales	4	
N. Ireland	3	
France		81
W Germany		81
Italy		81
Spain		60
Netherlands		25
Belgium		24
Greece		24
Portugal		24
Denmark		16
Ireland		15
Luxembourg		6
Total		518

* Average size of UK constituency is 514,000 electors.

adopt or reject the Community budget and it is required to give its opinion on Commission proposals. It also watches over the Commission and Council and can, theoretically at least, vote to sack the Commission. If European union is to be achieved, arguably the development of the European Parliament is essential.

Collect newspaper and journal articles on how the EC Institutions have dealt with specific issues. What do these tell you about the relationship between the Institutions and the wider national political factors which have to be taken into account.

Community law

You have already seen in this chapter how the secondary legislation of the Community is made by the Council of Ministers but drafted by the Commission after consultation with the advice from the European Parliament. Remember, however, that unlike our own Parliament, the European Parliament is not a legislative body. Nor does it, at present, exert more than a modest degree of democratic control over the Commission and Council of Ministers. Its only major

weapons are drastic ones – rejecting the Community budget or sacking the entire Commission. This relationship between national governments, Community institutions and Community law is shown in Fig. 20.1.

Community law consists of Community legislation and judgments in disputes concerning it that have been referred to the European Court of Justice. It is mainly concerned with customs duties, agriculture, free movement of labour, services and capital, transport, restrictive trade practices and the regulation of coal, steel and nuclear energy industries.

Community legislation

There is a basic distinction between *primary* and *secondary* legislation and a further distinction between legislation which is *directly applicable* to the population of each member state and legislation which requires *further action* by the member states for its implementation.

Primary and secondary legislation

Primary legislation is Community law contained in the Articles of the main treaties. It takes precedence over domestic law, although domestic legislation may sometimes be required to implement it. *Secondary legislation* is the law made by the Council of Ministers and the Commission under the authority conferred on them by the Treaty of Rome. The Treaties themselves are not open to review by either the Court of Justice or domestic courts, although both may interpret them. Secondary legislation is open to review on the grounds that it is *ultra vires* (beyond the powers of) the Council of Ministers or the Commission, or because the proper procedures have not been followed.

Secondary legislation takes three forms.

1 Regulations. These apply directly to the population of the Community. They automatically form part of the law of member states and confer individual rights and duties which the national courts must recognise. if there is a conflict between a regulation and an existing national law, the regulation prevails.

2 Directives. These are binding instructions to member states but they are not directly applicable. The member states must take appropriate steps to implement them. The Companies Act 1981, for example,

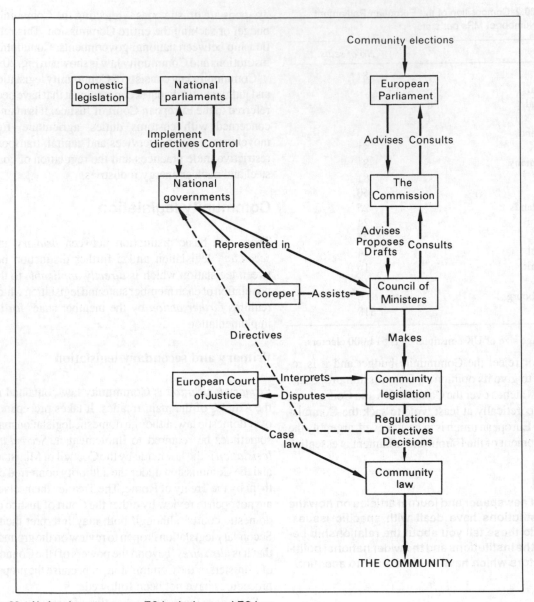

Fig. 20.1 National governments, EC institutions and EC law

implemented the EC's fourth directive on company accounts by reducing the amount of information required from small and medium-sized companies in accounts filed with the Registrar of Companies. The directive's aim was the harmonisation of company accounting throughout the Community. In Great Britain directives are normally implemented by statutory instrument.

3 Decisions. These are directly binding but they are addressed to specific individuals or organisations within the member states and not to the population generally.

Discover at least two examples of each kind of secondary legislation which directly affect the organisation for which you work or an organisation with which you are familiar. In particular, consider the specific ways in which the legislation has affected its activities.

Interpreting community legislation

The European Court of Justice is the final arbiter on all questions of law arising from the Community Treaties, in particular questions of *interpretation*. Any court or tribunal of any member state can ask the Court for a preliminary ruling on a question which concerns the interpretation of the Treaties. Where such a ruling is considered necessary for a decision and no appeal lies from the court or tribunal hearing the case, reference *must* be made to the Court of Justice. Hence, in Great Britain the High Court and Court of Appeal have a discretion whether to allow an appeal to be made to the Court of Justice but the House of Lords (being the final appeal court in the UK) must allow such an appeal if requested to do so.

In *Bulmer v Bollinger* (1974) the Court of Appeal laid down guidelines to help judges decide whether or not to refer a case to the Court of Justice. The English court must consider the delay involved; the danger of overloading the Court of Justice; the expense to the parties involved; the importance of referring only problems of interpretation and not issues of fact or application of the Treaties; the practical advantages of deciding all but the most important and difficult questions of interpretation itself; and, to some extent, the wishes of the parties.

Community case law

Community case law consists of judgements of the European Court of Justice in disputes involving interpretation or breach of the Treaties and the review of secondary legislation. Like Community legislation, it is binding on member states and their courts. Should our own case law conflict with it, Community case law will prevail.

The effect of Community law in the UK

You have seen that by the European Communities Act 1972 the UK acceded to the Treaties constituting the European Communities. By doing so a system of supranational law, often binding upon organisations and individuals without further Parliamentary enactment, was introduced into this country. Law which was inconsistent with Community law was repealed by implication, e.g. laws relating to trade tariffs and custom duties, for the Act provides that all rights, powers, liabilities, obligations, restrictions, remedies and procedures under the European Treaties are to be given immediate effect in English law. As Lord Denning (then Master of the Rolls and head of the Civil Division of the Court of Appeal) somewhat metaphorically put it: 'The courts will graft the new law on to the old as a gardener does a shoot. The sap from our main stock will circulate through the shoot and make all one.'

Parliamentary supremacy

The supranational structure of Community law clearly affects the principle of the Parliamentary supremacy. This declares that within the UK only Parliament has the right to make law and that no single Parliament can bind its successors, i.e. any Act passed can by repealed. However, for three reasons this effect is not as drastic as it may seem. First, Community law does not affect any of the matters which concern solely England and the people in it, i.e. domestic law is unaffected. Second, the supremacy of Parliament must be seen in political as well as legal terms. Thus, while the repeal of any Act, including the European Communities Act 1972, is legally possible, political considerations may make it impossible. Britain could hardly repeal the various Acts giving Commonwealth countries their independence and it would be a politically extreme step, and very probably disastrous to the economy, to repeal the 1972 Act. Third, Community law affects the sovereignty of all member states and not just the UK.

Activity

To what extent do you think that Parliamentary Supremacy has always been a theoretical concept rather than a practical reality?

Problems?

Community law and the decisions of the European Court of Justice can, nevertheless, put domestic governments into difficult positions. In February 1986, for example, the Court ruled that where men retire at

65 it is a breach of the EC's directive on equal treatment of men and women in employment to force women to retire at 60. The ruling had significant social and economic implications. It was estimated that about 300,000 women retire at 60 each year and if only a third chose to work to 65 this would result in 100,000 jobs being unavailable to other people. Nevertheless the Sex Discrimination Act 1986 now prevents different compulsory retirement ages from being set (see page 160). Removing the difference in pensionable ages, which treats men unfairly and does not reflect women's changed role, let alone their longer life expectancy, could prove enormously costly and would be a completely different matter. Any government that attempted it would be courting political disaster.

The European Court of Justice

Functions

Under Article 164 of the Treaty of Rome, the role of the Court is to 'ensure that the law is observed in the interpretation and implementation of the Treaty'. It is the final arbiter on all questions involving *interpretation* of the Community Treaties and it deals with *disputes* between different member states, between member states and the Commission (as Community watchdog), and between the Commission and business organisations, individuals or Community officials. Although the court can condemn violations of the Treaty by member governments, it has no sanctions against them except goodwill.

The Court also has *review powers*. These enable member states to question the legality of acts of the Council of Ministers and the Commission, e.g. a member state may ask the Court to investigate its complaint that the Commission has: acted outside the powers allocated to it; failed to follow proper procedures; or misused its powers. If the complaint is upheld, the Commission's act will be annulled.

Composition

The Court of Justice comprises 13 judges with at least one from each member state. The president of the Court is elected by the judges from among their own number. Judges hold office for a renewable term of six years. Unlike the British practice, an academic lawyer or a lawyer in private practice can be appointed a judge of the Court. Their independence is protected by the fact that judges can only be removed by unanimous votes of their colleagues.

The judges are assisted by six advocates general, an office modelled on the *Commissaire du Gouvernment* of France's *Conseil d'Etat* (Administrative Court) and without a British equivalent. An advocate general will sum up impartially at the end of each case, looking at the issues involved from the point of view of Community law. They are not members of the court and take no part in the judges' discussions or drafting of judgments. The judges do, however, pay great attention to the submissions in court of the advocates-general.

Practice and procedure

The Court's practice and procedure are based on a code of rules of procedure drawn up by the Court and there are four main ways in which it differs from that of British appellate courts. First, proceedings are *inquisitorial* as opposed to the adversary or contest system of procedure found in British courts. Basically, this means that the judges of the Court of Justice investigate the dispute, or questions, themselves. British judges, on the other hand, are essentially umpires between two contesting parties. Second, the Court does *not sit in divisions* and all cases brought before the Court are heard by all the judges. Third, one *collective judgment* is made, dissenting judgments are not given. Fourth, it is *not bound by its previous decisions* although it will follow them where possible to achieve consistency.

There is no appeal from a decision of the European Court of Justice and the decision cannot be challenged by a national court when called upon to enforce it.

The Court of First Instance

In September 1989 The Court of First Instance of the European Communities was established because the Court of Justice was unable to keep up with the number of cases being referred to it, a situation made worse by the many cases resulting from moves to complete the Single Market. For example, in 1988,

373 cases were brought before the Court of Justice but it delivered only 238 judgments. The aim of establishing the new Court is therefore to provide for quicker and better justice within the EC by cutting the workload of the main court by about a third.

The Court of First Instance consists of 12 judges selected on the same criteria as judges of the Court of Justice. A judge may also be called upon to act as an advocate general. Unlike the Court of Justice, it sits in divisions of three or five judges. A right of appeal to the Court of Justice exists on points of Community law. Because of this last point, it remains to be seen whether the new court will significantly speed up the EC's judicial process.

The Court of First Instance has jurisdiction over disputes between the Community and its employees and over applications for judicial review in relation to the implementation of the EC's competition rules. It does not have jurisdiction in cases brought by member states or the Community institutions, or on questions referred by national courts for a preliminary ruling on the interpretation or validity of Community law.

The 'Single Market' – 1992

By signing the Single European Act in February 1986 the EC member states committed themselves to progressively completing the single 'common' market, envisaged in 1957, by the end of 1992. The Act, which came into force in July 1987, defines the Single Market as 'an area without internal frontiers in which the free movement of goods, persons, services and capital is ensured in accordance with the provisions of this Treaty.' At present, for example, (a) the free movement of goods is impeded by technical barriers, such as differing product standards; (b) a free and competitive market for services is blocked by a range of national restrictions; (c) competition in the market as a whole can be distorted by national public purchasing and subsidy policies; and (d) substantial differences in indirect taxes such as Excise Duty distort the pattern of trade.

Eliminating trade restrictions

The completion of the Single European Market will mean that people and goods can move freely any-

Keywords _____

European Community (EC)
An organisation of, at present, **12 states** set up by the Treaty of Rome which consists of a customs union and a common market for goods and services.

Council of Ministers
The executive body of the EC. It consists of one minister from each member state.

COREPER
The Committee of Permanent Representatives; this body takes many non-controversial executive decisions on behalf of the Council of Ministers based on Commission proposals.

European Commission
Consisting of 17 Commissioners, the Commission is the EC's Secretariat. It is responsible for day-to-day administration but also formulates policy for consideration by the Council.

European Parliament
An elected assembly of 518 members (MEPs) which debates European issues and proposes legislation but which, unlike national parliaments, has no power to legislate.

Community legislation
This consists of *primary* legislation contained in the main treaties and *secondary* legislation – regulations, directives and decisions – made by the Council and Commission under the authority given to them by the Treaty of Rome.

Supremacy of Parliament
EC law overrides the national law of the member states and therefore affects the principle of Parliamentary supremacy, i.e. that only Parliament has the power to make law for the UK and that no one parliament can bind its successors.

European Court of Justice
The final arbiter on questions of European law. In 1989 the Court of First Instance was established to assist the Court of Justice.

where in the EC. In theory you should be able to drive from Glasgow to Rome without having to stop at customs, produce documents, etc. Britain, however, insists that border controls should remain as protection against terrorism, drug trafficking and rabies.

In more detail, the elimination of trade restrictions to achieve the Single Market will cover the following specific areas.

• European regulations and standards will mean that products approved in any one Community country can be freely marketed throughout the Community.

• The progressive opening up of government and other public body contracts to all Community contractors on an equal basis.

• More competitive and efficient services in telecommunications and information technology.

• Greater competition on air routes, shipping services between member countries on equal terms and the elimination of most red tape on road haulage – plus, of course, the Channel Tunnel.

• All restrictions on the movement of capital will be removed. Banks and securities houses authorised in their home country should be free to provide banking and investment services anywhere in the Community. Insurers will have greater freedom to cover risks in other member states.

• Protection of industrial property will become easier through harmonisation of national laws on patents and trade marks (*see* pages 213–7).

• Professional qualifications obtained in one country will be acceptable in all other countries.

It should be clear to you that the removal of such barriers to trade presents both opportunities and threats.

The benefits of the Single Market

Most economists advocate the benefit of free trade. It is argued that, in the long run, everyone will be better off. This is based on the theory of *comparative advantage*.

It is obvious that if the product you wish to buy is cheaper in another country then it is to your advantage to buy it from there. You will obtain the product more cheaply, which will leave you with money left to spend on other things. However, you may be prevented from doing this by taxes which make the product *seem* more expensive or by transport costs. The abolition of tariffs is an attempt to increase the trade and wealth of the members.

But not everyone benefits in the short-run. Suppose the product we are considering is cars and they are more cheaply produced in Spain and Germany. The result of free trade will be unemployment for British car workers.

To illustrate the long-term advantages let us consider a historical example. In the late nineteenth century British agriculture experienced what became known as the Great Depression. This was brought about by the import of cheap food from the USA and Australia which was made possible by the development of rail transport and improvements in shipping and refrigeration. If this cheap food had been kept out by barring imports or by placing huge taxes on it, consider what might have happened. Today, instead of working in an office, driving a car, living in a centrally heated house etc, the average Briton could still be working 15 hours a day in the fields, earning a wage of £15 a week, living off a diet of bread and cheese, etc. The resources freed by the decline of agriculture gave Britain the ability to staff industry, to build roads and schools and to construct our modern economy.

It is salutory to consider the present state of British manufacturing industries. Their present situation may not be unlike that of agriculture in the Great Depression. This has become known as 'deindusrialistation' (*see* page 20) and some commentators maintain that Britain may be likely to experience a prolonged period of heavy unemployment. On the other hand, taking the optimistic view we may be evolving into a richer, high-tech economy.

Either way, for those made unemployed life will indeed be hard but this seems to be an argument for making adequate transitional arrangements and giving compensation rather than saying to our European partners 'No! We don't want your products – and certainly not those from Korea and Taiwan – because they're much better value than ours!'

Trade diversion

There is free trade only *within* the EC. To the rest of the world the EC presents a common external tariff, in many cases quite high. Because of this tax Europeans may prefer to buy, say, German goods rather than American and Japanese even though these are produced more cheaply. Thus, we deny ourselves the benefit of free trade. This distortion of the pattern of trading through the imposition of taxes is known as *trade diversion*.

Activity

Study the information in Table 20.3

Table 20.3 Index of GDP per head (adjusted for relative purchasing powers)

	1982	1987
Belgium	104.0	100.7
Denmark	110.9	113.7
France	114.4	109.2
Germany	112.7	113.6
Greece	57.4	54.3
Ireland	66.3	64.2
Italy	103.2	104.4
Luxembourg	116.3	125.4
Netherlands	107.0	104.5
Portugal	54.9	53.6
Spain	72.7	74.0
United Kingdom	100.8	105.3

Source: Eurostat

1 Which country showed the greatest relative increase in GDP per head and which showed the greatest relative decline?

2 With respect to the EC averages, Ireland's GDP per head seems to have declined from 66.3 to 64.2 between 1982 and 1987. Does this mean that real income per head has necessarily declined? Give reasons for your answer. What other information would you need to know to give a more definite answer?

3 These figures assume that Spain and Portugal were both members of the EC in 1982, which they were not. How would the figures differ in 1982 if they were excluded?

4 The figures in Table 20.3 are adjusted to take account of relative purchasing powers. How do you think the figures might differ if GDP per head were measured in US dollars or Deutschmarks?

Fiscal harmonisation

Although 1992 should see the end of tariffs it still leaves the problem of other taxes. Consider the information in Table 20.4.

The EC believes that VAT and excise duty must be brought more into line throughout the Community. If everyone charges the same rates of excise duty and VAT, there will be no need for elaborate calculations of tax payable on goods moving between countries.

The EC proposes two VAT bands – a high and a low band – and the same goods will be in the same band throughout the EC. Britain objects strongly to this. Excise duty presents an even bigger problem. To average out duty, Britain would have to reduce the

Table 20.4 Indirect taxes in the EC

	Excise duty – wine (pence per 75cl bottle)	Excise duty – spirits (pence per 75cl bottle)	VAT per cent	Tax on cigarettes (£s per pkt of 20)
Belgium	15	228	25	0.55
Denmark	69	735	22	1.76
France	1	172	18.6	0.33
Germany	0	217	14	0.82
Greece	0	12	36	0.17
Ireland	112	436	25	1.20
Italy	0	62	19	0.47
Luxembourg	6	153	12	0.60
Netherlands	16	239	18.5	0.62
Portugal	0	34	30	0.32
Spain	0	72	12	0.08
UK	74	473	15	1.12

Source: Which?

duty on spirits by 50%. This would be a massive loss of revenue to the Exchequer and is also firmly opposed on health grounds. The Greeks, meanwhile, would have to multiply their duty 39 times!

Indirect taxes such as VAT and excise duty are an obvious problem. No less so is the problem of direct taxes. If there are large differences between income tax or the taxes on companies, the people or companies will move to minimise their tax burdens. Imagine, for example, that income tax is 40% in Denmark but only 25% in Germany. Those living in southern Denmark might well move to northern Germany and commute to their jobs in Denmark. It is also quite possible that companies might move their main offices to those countries with the most favourable tax regimes.

Thus, we can see that a truly single market must have taxes that are roughly in line with one another. This is called *fiscal harmonisation*. Without it there can be no true Single Market.

Employment problems

In many industries there is excess capacity in the EC. The Community, for example, is capable of producing much more steel and many more cars than it needs. Rationalisation of output could lead to the loss of millions of jobs. As you can see, if you remember the section above on the benefits of the Single Market, putting these people back to work depends upon there being other expanding industries.

Industrial combination

In terms of its purchasing power, the Single European Market is the largest market in the World. For example, car sales at 13 million per year, are greater than those of any other nation. This is why so many companies are keen on the Single Market. it also means, however, that companies will have to be suitably large to compete with other world giants. It is inevitable, therefore, that there will be many takeovers and amalgamations. For example, Siemans and GEC pooled their defence electronics businesses in 1989 to compete with their American rivals.

The existence of large monopolistic or oligopolistic companies has implications for EC law on competi-

tion. An example of the operation of this was the case of the Distillers Company Ltd who, in 1977, were ordered to stop selling the same brand of whisky at different prices in the Community. (*See* discussion in Chapter 17.)

The Social Charter

In May 1989 the Commission put forward its proposals for a 'Community Charter of Fundamental Social Rights', usually referred to as the 'Social Charter'. The proposals cover the rights to:

(a) improvements in living and working conditions;
(b) freedom of movement;
(c) fair remuneration in employment;
(d) social protection;
(e) freedom of association and collective bargaining;
(f) vocational training;
(g) equal treatment for men and women;
(h) information, consultation and worker participation;
(i) health protection and safety at the workplace;
(j) protection for children and adolescents;
(k) protection of elderly and disabled persons.

Most of these 'rights' are not controversial and are necessary if a true common market is to emerge. For example, a higher level of social protection in one country increases its costs and therefore distorts the market to its disadvantage. It may also be a factor in attracting movement of labour to that country. Conversely, a lower level of social protection could present a barrier to the movement of labour to that country. Others, for example *(e)* and *(h)* are seen by the present Conservative government as 'socialism by the back door' and the present government is therefore opposed to the 'Charter'.

The EMS

One of the objectives of the EC is European monetary union (EMU), that is to say one currency for the entire Community. So far this has not proved possible but in March 1979 the European Monetary System (EMS) was set up.

The ecu

The EMS is based on an artificially created unit of account – the European currency unit (ECU). The value of an ecu is determined by combining the value of the members' national currencies according to their relative importance. Their values are shown in Table 20.5.

Table 20.5 The ecu 1989

Currency	Relative weighting in EMS basket (%)
Belgium franc	8.5
Deutschmark	34.5
Greek drachma	0.7
Danish krona	2.7
Irish punt	1.1
French franc	18.5
Italian lira	9.2
Luxembourg franc	0.3
Dutch florin	10.8
UK pound	13.7

In 1989 one ecu cost 66 pence in sterling. The ecu is now the unit of account for EC transactions. In other words, our contribution to or payments from the EC are counted in ecus.

The Exchange Rate Mechanism

All the countries in Table 20.5 except Greece are members of the Exchange Rate mechanism (ERM). They have agreed not to let the value of their national currencies fluctuate by more than 2.25% (6% in the case of the pound and the peseta) above or below its agreed value against the ecu. Thus, there is stability in the value of EC currencies. The value of the ecu itself, however, may rise or fall against other world currencies. Negotiations began in 1989 to bring the Spanish and Portuguese currencies into the value of the ecu. (*See* discussion of exchange rates in Chapter 21.)

A common currency?

Despite the fact that the ecu has no concrete identity in the form of notes and coins (there have been special commemorative issues of gold ecus), it is being used for an ever-increasing number of international economic and financial transactions. Furthermore, the ordinary individual can use ecu travellers' cheques for holidays abroad (even outside the Community), buy bonds in ecus, invest in ecus and, in certain countries, obtain bank loans and mortgages in ecus.

Belgium and Luxembourg were the first countries to authorise the opening of bank accounts in ecus and from 1 July 1990 this was possible in eight of the 12 Member States.

First and foremost an instrument of finance, the ecu is the fifth most widely-used currency in issues of international bonds (*see* discussion of Eurocurrency markets on page 272) and is becoming firmly established as an international currency.

Although at present it is used in a limited number of international transactions, it is gaining ground. The advantage of the ecu to businesses both within and outside Europe is principally its relative stability, which is better than that of most national currencies.

Effective progress in the use of the ecu has been made in:

● short-term financial transactions;
● invoicing for the sale of goods and services leading to the calculation of a price index in ecus which private firms use in certain international contracts;
● international payments.

A European central bank?

Will the ecu one day become a common currency for the EC countries? It would offer a new facility for European companies and private individuals, who would benefit from its stability and who would no longer have to change money at every border. It is estimated that if you took £100 and changed it from one EC currency to the other currencies in turn (pounds to francs, francs to lire and so on), at the end of the operation you would have only £32!

The implication of a common currency, however, is that there would have to be a central monetary authority to issue and control it. Thus, the UK's monetary policy would no longer be determined at the Bank of England but in Brussels. The proposals for this were put forward by the President of the EC, Jacques Delors, in the Delors Plan. This has been firmly resisted by Margaret Thatcher.

Table 20.6 The economies of the EC members compared

	Gre	Bel	Den	Germ	Fra	Ire	Italy	Lux	Neths	UK	Spain	Port	Eur 12
Population													
millions (1986)	9.9	9.9	5.1	61.0	55.4	3.5	57.2	0.4	14.6	56.7	38.7	10.2	322.8
Employment (% 1987)													
Agriculture	26.9	2.7	6.4	5.2	7.1	15.3	10.5	3.5	4.7	2.4	15.1	22.2	7.9
Industry	27.9	28.7	26.5	40.5	30.8	28.1	32.6	32.5	27.2	30.1	32.3	34.9	32.9
Services	45.2	68.6	67.1	54.3	62.1	56.6	56.9	64.0	68.1	67.5	52.6	42.9	59.1
GDP													
Av annual growth (1982–87 %)	1.4	1.5	2.7	2.1	1.6	1.8	2.6	4.0	2.1	3.2	2.9	2.1	2.3
Per inhabitant in 1987 PPS*	7,928	14,712	16,606	16,580	15,951	9,381	15,242	18,313	15,258	15,383	10,807	7,838	14,605
Standard of living													
Private consumption per head: 1986 (ecu)	2,695	7,380	8,902	9,154	8,017	3,989	6,488	7,312	7,296	6,096	3,837	1,982	6,681
Telephones per 1,000 inhabitants in 1986	338	420	730	600	560	247	420	603	397	540	361	169	466
Doctors per inhabitants in 1987	2.5	2.6	2.4	2.4	2.1	1.3	3.2	1.7	2.0	1.7	2.5	1.8	2.3
Cars per 1,000 inhabitants in 1986	136	346	—	441	388	202	—	421	337	323	249	221	—

* PPS = Purchasing power standard

— = Figures not available

Source: Eurostat

Some figures

A comparison of the economies of the members of the EC can be made by studying the figures in Table 20.6. When the EC was first formed the UK had a strong economy and felt confident staying outside the Community. As Britain's economy declined relative to that of the members of the EC, so Britain felt more and more constrained to join.

1 What other international units of account are there besides the ecu? (*See* page 369 if you are unsure.)

2 Most international comparisons are still done in US dollars. Why is this so?

3 Use the information in Table 20.6 to comment upon the relative standards of living of the various EC members.

Conclusion

Much is likely to change in Europe in the next few years. The arrival of the Single European Market could bring huge upheavals. In addition to this we must consider the implications of changes on the world scene. The peaceful revolutions in Eastern Europe could profoundly affect the EC. The reunification of Germany also poses questions for the EC and for NATO. There is enormous potential for change, both for better and for worse.

The Thatcher government distanced itself from many of the more radical suggestions of European unity. The danger for the UK is that it becomes marginalised as France and Germany proceed with their plans and ignore Britain.

Keywords

Common market
The treating of the economies of several different countries as if they were one.

'Single Market'
The name given to the EC's commitment to eliminate all restrictions on the free movement of goods, persons, services and capital within the Community by the end of 1992.

Comparative advantage
A theory first explained by David Ricardo suggesting the benefit of free trade.

Harmonisation
The term used within the EC to describe the close approximation of policies in member countries so that there are no great differences between taxes etc

The 'Social Charter'
Proposed in 1989 by the Commission and correctly titled the 'Community Charter of Fundamental Social Rights', this embodies declarations on living and working conditions, fair pay and social protection, equality, training, and health and safety, etc.

Ecu
Artificially created unit of account used in the EC.

Exchange Rate mechanism (ERM)
The tying of the value of members' currencies to the value of the ecu.

European Monetary System (EMS)
Together the ERM and the ecu comprise the EMS.

European Monetary Union (EMU)
The goal of only one currency for the entire EC.

Learning project

A single market?

Read the following article taken from *The Guardian*, 12 January 1990 and complete the following tasks.

Car prices in Britain top EC by 40 pc
Alan Hope in Brussels

Car prices in Britain cost up to 40% more than in most other European Community countries, according to a report from a European consumer organisation which says that dealers are depriving buyers of their legal right to bring cheaper cars in from abroad. The Bureau of European Consumer Unions found June 1989 prices for 18 models varied widely across Europe. In many cases, British buyers pay more.

Denmark is the cheapest country in the EC for cars, according to a comparison of tax-free prices. For Danish residents, the advantage is largely wiped out by the heavy tax on new cars. But Denmark should offer substantial savings to buyers from other countries.

An Audi 80E which cost £10,350 pounds tax free in the UK can be bought for £6,880 in Denmark. Only Portugal is more expensive than Britain. A Peugeot 405 which costs £7,240 tax free in Britain costs £4,200 in Denmark.

In Belgium prices on average are now 31% lower against 19% in 1987. For the Audi 80E the margin

was 43% with the Citroen AX costing 38% more in Britain.

The Bureau condemns the continuing wide difference in prices. 'If this situation evolves, the car market in 1992 will be neither a true Common Market nor a competitive one.'

A spokesman said: 'EC Institutions must put an end to illicit practices by member states whose sole intention is the partitioning of their national markets. Consumers should be free to choose their cars where the prices are lowest'.

The right of buyers to purchase their cars abroad is guaranteed by European law, but dealers and manufacturers, as well as national authorities, put up barriers to make parallel imports more difficult.

Manufacturers apply sanctions against dealers who sell to foreigners and so undercut dealers elsewhere, although this practice is illegal.

National authorities often raise administrative obstacles to the registration of imported cars.

In Britain, the report says, the licensing authority refuses to register cars brought in by professional importers, although private individuals have no problem.

Car makers such as Nissan and Isuzu refuse to honour car guarantees on parallel imports while Volkswagen and Rover dealers in Ireland have refused to sell cars intended for export to the UK.

The Society of Motor Manufacturers and Traders said yesterday that if the survey was carried out more than about six months ago, the current picture could be very different with Sterling down by about 10% today – a factor which would reduce the alleged price gap correspondingly.

Discounting, which was very prevalent in Britain, was 'certainly far less common elsewhere in Europe.'

1 The article describes a situation of price discrimination. State the conditions which must exist for such discrimination to be worthwhile to the manufacturer. Also analyse how the manufacturer might set about deciding the price and output of cars in each particular market.

2 Explain how car manufacturers separate the British market from the rest of Europe. Will the advent of the Single European Market eliminate price discrimination? Explain your answer.

3 What other goods and services are also subject to this type of price discrimination in the EC?

4 What measures has the Commission taken to prevent the illegal practices described in the article relating to cars and other goods and services and how successful have these measures been?

5 Explain how price discrimination conflicts with the Treaty of Rome.

6 The article suggests that a fall in the value of Sterling would reduce the price differentials. With the aid of a diagram, explain why this might be so.

7 Do you consider that the EC needs to introduce more legislation to protect consumers from abuses like the one described in the article? Alternatively, do you consider that competition is the consumers' best protection? Give reasons for your answer.

Further ideas for learning projects

1 Consider arguments for and against increasing the powers of the European Parliament.

2 Do you fancy a subsidised visit to Brussels? The EC provides funds for educational visits. Organise one.

3 On the basis of the material in this chapter and elsewhere which you may be able to discover, assess the relative living standards of the members states of the EC. (Do not forget qualitative criteria such as 'sunshine' and the environment generally.) Which country would you most like to live in and why? Support your arguments with statistical, graphical and descriptive justifications.

4 Consider Table 20.4.

(a) If taxes on alcholol and tobacco were harmonised, what would be the effect on exchequer revenues? Illustrate your answer with a demand and supply diagram. How would the situation differ in Greece? What conclusions do you draw about the nature of demand for these products in the two countries?

(b) The differences in the pattern of indirect taxes illustrated in Table 20.4 reflect more than purely fiscal considerations. What other factors may explain this pattern of taxation?

21

International trade and institutions

CHAPTER OBJECTIVES

After studying this chapter you should be able to:

List the main components of Britain's overseas trade;
Describe the distribution of Britain's trade;
Identify the most common types of export contracts;
Explain methods of payment in export sales;
Explain how the balance of payments balances;
State the problems posed by multinational companies;
Describe and explain the IMF system;
State the advantages and disadvantages of floating exchange rates.

Increasingly there is an international dimension to the dealings of organisations. For example, foreign countries offer potential markets while at the same time representing competition in the domestic market-place. We also need to consider those international organisations that affect businesses and governments.

One of the complications we face when studying the international aspect of organisations (as well as exchange rates, languages, customs, etc) is the *bias of nationalism*. By this we mean the tendency to believe that anything produced or done by our own country is automatically better or right. For example, successive governments (and now the EC) have supported agriculture. The result of this is higher incomes for farmers and greater self-sufficiency for the economy. But looked at the other way round, it means that you, as a consumer, pay over twice as much as you need to for dairy products and considerably more for bread, meat and so on. We can therefore conclude that it is costing us dear to eat our own food! On the other hand, we see it as entirely desirable that foreigners should buy our exports. 'The notion dies hard' said Lord Harlech 'that

in some sort of way exports are patriotic but imports are immoral.'

The pattern of Britain's overseas trade

The importance of trade

Of all the nations in the world, few are as dependent as the UK upon foreign trade. The UK depends upon imports for half of its food requirements and for most of the raw materials needed by its industries. Equally, the continued well-being of the economy depends upon exporting a large proportion of the national product each year. In 1988, imports of goods and services were equivalent to 31.8% of the GDP while exports of goods and services accounted for 26.0%. This large discrepancy between imports and exports is the cause of much trouble to the UK.

Table 21.1 Value of UK exports and imports 1988

Commodity	Value of exports £ million	%	Value of imports £ million	%
Food, beverages and tobacco	5,489	6.8	9,926	9.79
Basic materials	2,134	2.6	5,452	5.37
Oil	6,018	7.5	3,231	3.18
Other mineral fuels and lubricants	242	0.3	1,476	1.45
Semi-manufactured goods	24,091	29.9	27,915	27.52
Finished manufactured goods	40,640	50.4	51,646	50.92
Miscellaneous	1,988	2.5	1,782	1.76
	80,602	100.0	101,428	100.0

Source: United Kingdom Balance of Payments, HMSO

International trade is also a vital component of national income (*see* page 399). An adverse movement in trade has a depressing effect upon the level of income and employment in the economy. Britain suffers from the recurrent problem that as soon as the economy begins to expand it draws in increased imports of raw materials which are necessary to our manufacturing industries. This, however, causes a payments crisis which brings the expansion to a halt. In recent years a disturbing trend has been the tendency for the expanding economy to draw in manufactured goods which the domestic economy is failing to produce.

Which products are traded

Table 21.1 summarises the main categories of products which are traded. The traditional pattern has been for the UK to export substantially more manufactured goods than it imports. However, in 1983 imports of manufactured goods exceeded exports for the first time. This disturbing trend is associated with the *deindustrialisation* of the economy and the collapse of manufacturing industries. The potentially disastrous effects of this were offset by the export of North Sea oil. The problem of the relative decline of manufactured exports and its effects upon the economy are further complicated by the collapse of oil prices in 1986 and the fact that reserves of North Sea oil are becoming depleted.

Exports

The competitiveness of Britain's exports has been badly affected by rates of inflation much higher than those of her trading partners. To some extent this was offset in the mid-1970s by the fall in the value of sterling. The recovery in sterling in the late 1970s had an adverse effect upon exports. This supposes that price is a major factor in determining the volume of export sales. It is possible to suggest, however, that other factors, such as poor marketing, inferior design, bad after-sales service, low quality and, perhaps most important of all, long delays and unreliable delivery, are at least as important as price disadvantage in impeding sales of British exports.

Imports

There was a huge growth in the value of imports in the early 1970s because of the rise in the price of oil and other commodity prices. Britain was protected from the worst rigours of the 1978 rise in the price of oil because of her own earnings from North Sea oil. Depression of the home market also helped to restrict imports but, despite this, foreign manufacturers continued to capture an increasing share of the market for such products as automobiles and electronics. Uncertainty about exchange rates also had unsettling effects. In the early part of 1985 the exchange rate declined so much that it was thought that we would reach a rate of £1 = $1. The subsequent recovery of the rate to around

Table 21.2 The UK's ten leading trading partners (by value) 1987 and 1974

		Trade 1987 Imports (cif) £ million	%	Exports (fob) £ million	%	Trade 1974 Imports %	Exports %	
Position								Position
1	West Germany*	15,783.9	16.8	9,404.3	11.8	8.2	6.3	2
2	USA	9,136.0	9.7	11,014.2	13.8	9.8	10.9	1
3	France*	8,382.0	8.9	7,781.5	9.7	5.8	5.6	4
4	Netherlands*	7,148.0	7.6	5,856.2	7.3	6.9	6.1	3
5	Italy*	5,216.8	5.5	4,145.7	5.2	3.1	3.1	8
6	Belgium/Luxembourg*	4,362.5	4.6	3,857.7	4.8	3.2	4.1	7
7	Ireland*	3,488.4	3.7	3,831.7	4.8	3.5	5.0	6
8	Japan	5,463.1	5.8	1,495.1	1.8	2.5	2.0	14
9	Sweden	2,952.5	3.1	2,322.2	2.9	4.0	4.4	5
10	Switzerland	3,298.0	3.5	1,835.9	2.3	1.8	2.1	15
Total of these ten		65,230.4	69.2	48,094.5	64.4	48.8	49.6	
Total of all trade		94,015.7	100.0	79,851.4	100.0	£23,138.9	£16,309.2	

* Members of EC
Source: Compiled from the Annual Abstract of Statistics

£1 = $1.50 did little to help exports while the collapse of oil prices to 1973 levels decreased export earnings. It is true, of course, that the UK exports more than ever before; the trouble is that it also imports much more. For many years the growth of imports has outstripped that of exports and has therefore caused an even wider trade gap.

Trading partners

In Table 21.2 you can see that more than 65% of Britain's overseas trade is with ten countries. Despite this, you should not form the impression that Britain's pattern of trade is narrow, for the UK continues to have a more worldwide pattern of trade than any other nation except the USA.

Traditionally, Britain drew her imports of raw materials from the Commonwealth and Empire to whom, in return, she exported her manufactures. Since 1945 there has been a growing dependence on North America and Europe. This trend was quite apparent before Britain joined the EC and, indeed, was one of the reasons why it was essential for Britain to join. Since joining the EC, Britain has become much more dependent upon European-produced food and less dependent upon Canadian and Australasian produce, for

example, Canada dropped from second trading partner in 1967 to fifteenth in 1987. There has also been a marked decrease in the percentage importance of trade with the USA.

The oil price rises of the 1970s dramatically increased the value of trade with the oil exporting countries. This was shown by the arrival of Saudi Arabia in the list of top ten trading partners. Saudi Arabia has since dropped back to around fourteenth place as oil prices have fallen and as the UK has become an oil exporting nation. The trading surplus which the UK now has with the oil exporting nations helps to counterbalance the deficit with other leading trading partners. In Table 21.2 you can see that there is a considerable adverse imbalance with Germany, Japan and Switzerland.

Activity

1 Explain why there is such an adverse trade balance with *(a)* Germany, *(b)* Switzerland, and *(c)* Japan.

2 List three products which are imported from each of these countries.

Table 21.3 shows the proportions of British exports and imports going to different parts of the world. You

Table 21.3 Geographical analysis of UK's visible trade 1977 and 1987

Area	1977 Exports £m	%	Imports £m	%	1987 Exports £m	%	Imports £m	%
European Community*	11,848	37	14,160	39	39,416	49	49,557	53
Other W Europe	4,734	15	5,083	14	7,621	10	12,869	14
North America	3,905	12	4,983	14	12,993	16	10,781	11
Other developed countries	2,088	7	2,846	8	4,045	5	7,282	8
Oil exporting countries	4,323	14	3,703	10	5,222	7	1,699	2
Other developing countries	4,201	13	4,258	12	8,514	11	9,285	10
Centrally planned economies	906	2	1,125	3	1,538	2	2,097	2
Total	31,990	100	36,219	100	79,851	100	94,015	100

* Figures relate to all 11 countries
Source: Annual Abstract of Statistics: HMSO

can clearly see the substantial rise in the importance of trade with the EC. The majority of the growth in value of trade between 1977 and 1987 is accounted for by price rises. Whereas the *value* of exports had risen by 481% in this time, the *volume* had risen by only 41%; similarly while the value of imports had risen by 465% the volume of imports had risen by 61%. Again, note the discrepancy in the growth of exports and imports.

If we remove oil from the import/export figures some even more disturbing trends are highlighted. In the period 1971–86 the volume of non-oil exports grew by only 24% while our non-oil imports grew by no less than 65%! This is dramatic evidence of the massive import penetration of our domestic markets and the collapse of our manufacturing industries.

Consider the following industries.

- **Automobiles**
- **Nuclear engineering**
- **Silicon chip manufacture**
- **Shipbuilding**
- **Aircraft manufacture**
- **Petrochemicals**
- **Steel**
- **Cotton textiles**

1 **Which of these industries are at present located only in advanced industrial economies?**

2 **Which are in the process of transferring to less developed economies or have already done so?**

3 **The consequences of such transfers might well be unemployment for the advanced economy. What type of unemployment would this be and how might government policy reduce it?**

Keywords _____

Balance of trade
The relationship between exports and imports – also termed the visible trade balance. It is said to be *favourable* if exports are greater than imports.

Terms of trade
An index of the relative prices of exports and imports.

Balance of payments
An account of all the transactions of everyone living and working in the UK with the rest of the World. It is recorded in £s.

The direction of trade
Which nations exports go to and come from.

The components of trade
An analysis of trade in terms of the products and services which it comprises. For example, what proportion of imports are raw materials.

Bias of nationalism
The belief in 'my country right or wrong' which may obscure the benefits of international trade.

Export sales

It is possible to sell goods overseas by four main methods.

1 By setting up a subsidiary business organisation overseas.
2 By setting up a joint venture or other collaborative arrangement with a business overseas. (Such an arrangement is, perhaps, particularly important to smaller businesses wishing to take advantage of the Single Market to be established by the end of 1992.)
3 By appointing agents overseas.
4 By concluding an exclusive sales agreement with an importer based in each of the foreign countries to which the exporter hopes to sell. Such agreements must not infringe either domestic law or international agreements, e.g. Article 85 of the Treaty of Rome, relating to restrictive practices.

Types of contracts

A number of standardised contracts exist from which the exporter and importer may choose the one which best suits their requirements. The following are well-known and important terms in such contracts. They primarily indicate the price basis of the contract, although other important legal consequences follow, e.g. at what stage the *risk* of accidental loss of, or damage to, the goods passes from the seller to the buyer.

Ex works

Under this type of contract the exporter's obligation is to have the goods available at the agreed time and place. It is the buyer's duty to collect them and the price is normally payable on delivery. The seller must assist the buyer in obtaining any documents which are required in the transaction and available in the seller's country, e.g. an export licence.

FOR (free on rail)

At their own expense, sellers are responsible for the packing and delivery of the goods to the nearest railhead or goods depot. If the contract is expressed to be FOT (free on truck) their obligations extend to loading the goods on to the railway truck. The price becomes payable when the goods are delivered to the railway authority; at the same time the *risk* passes to the buyers.

FAS (free alongside ship)

Sellers' obligations extend one stage further. They must transport the goods at their own expense alongside ships nominated by the buyers.

FOB (free on board)

Under an FOB contract, sellers must pack, transport and place the goods on ships nominated by the buyers. The buyers are responsible for the cost of the freight and insurance.

As soon as the goods pass over the ship's rail the *risk* passes to the buyers, although the Sale of Goods Act 1979 requires sellers to give buyers sufficient notification of this to allow them time to insure the goods.

Ex ship

Here sellers must transport the goods at their own expense to a port named by the buyers. During transit the goods are the sellers' responsibility and they must bear the *risk* of them being accidentally lost or damaged.

CIF (cost, insurance, freight)

The essential feature of CIF contracts is that they are performed by the delivery of the shipping documents, i.e. the bill of lading, the invoice and a certificate or policy of insurance. The goods are at the buyers' *risk* as soon as they are shipped and they are bound to pay the price when the documents are tendered to them, even though the goods may already have been lost. If this should happen, they will be able to claim under the insurance policy.

The sellers' obligations may be summarised as shipment of the contract goods within the agreed time, making the contract for their carriage, insuring the goods, and tendering the shipping documents to the buyers.

When sellers are responsible for the cost of the carriage but not the insurance, the goods are said to be sold CF (cost and freight). As with FOB contracts they must notify the buyers of the shipping so that the buyers may effect insurance cover.

FOB and CIF contracts are the most important contracts in export sales and, as Tables 21.1 and 21.2 show, for UK statistical purposes, imports are calculated on their CIF values and exports on the FOB values, i.e. their respective values at UK ports. Thus, a small proportion of an adverse balance of trade is accounted for by the cost of transporting goods from abroad.

Export documents

Bills of lading

Bills of lading are really three documents in one: a receipt for goods upon shipment; a contract for the carriage of goods; and a document of title which enables an exporter to transfer ownership or possession of the goods. They usually include a brief description of the goods, state the terms on which they are carried, the name of the carrying vessel and the port of destination. They are signed by the master of the ship or by some other person authorised by the shipowner. As they prove ownership, bills of lading are very important documents and the carrier will deliver the goods to the buyer against a signed copy.

If a bank is financing the export sale, the bill of lading is normally handed to the bank together with a bill of exchange or letter of credit, the seller's invoice and the certificate or policy of insurance.

Invoices

The seller's *commercial invoice* describes the goods, states their price and names the buyer. It will generally also include quantities, weights, packing details, etc, and a statement of the nature of the contract, e.g. FOB or CIF. Several copies are prepared, some for the buyer's use and some for the information of various authorities in their country, e.g. customs and bankers.

Consular invoices are mandatory when exporting to certain parts of the world such as South America. They are specially printed invoices issued in the exporter's country by the consulate of the importing country. Their purpose is to corroborate the details of a particular shipment for the authorities in the importer's country.

A *certificate of origin* is a declaration by the exporter stating the country of origin of the goods shipped.

Insurance

Insurance cover against loss or damage during shipment is essential. In the case of regular exporters, it is now far more common to issue insurance certificates, based on the overall policy, than individual policies for each shipment. As you have seen, in terms of the contract determine whether it is the buyer or seller who must effect insurance cover. (See also the section on the ECGD on page 364.)

Methods of payment

A major concern of exporters is to find a secure but simple method of ensuring payment for goods shipped to buyers in a foreign country. The principal difficulty is that of *control* of the goods and payment for them. If exporters allow importers to obtain control of the goods before they have been paid for, they are taking a risk that the goods may not be recoverable at a later date if payment is not made. As you will see, much depends on how the *documentation* relating to the shipment is dealt with.

Cash with order

This is the most desirable method of payment from the exporter's point of view. It is, however, rare and some form of credit for the importer is an accepted part of export sales.

Open account

This method is very simple; the documents of title are sent direct to the importer who then pays by cheque or by money transfer. However, it is only common where there is an established trading relationship between exporter and importer because the exporter takes a considerable financial risk. They lose control of the goods once they are despatched while the buyer may not pay for them, through either lack of funds or regulations restricting the transfer of money.

Documentary collections

Where the exporter is satisfied with the integrity of the importer, the transaction may be completed on a collection basis. The exporter despatches the goods and sends the documents to their bank who will forward the documents to a bank in the importer's country (preferably the importer's bank or an overseas branch of the exporter's own bank) for collection by them.

Included with the shipping documents is a *bill of exchange*, i.e. a demand for the payment of a certain sum of money at a specified date, drawn by the exporter on the buyer, and settlement is made by the importer paying the bill of exchange. The bill must be paid according to its tenor, i.e. immediately if payable on demand ('sight bills'), or at a fixed or determinable future date (usually 30, 60 or 90 days) after the bill is presented to the buyer for acceptance, i.e. after sight, or after the date on the bill itself. When the bill is not payable on demand the importer must *accept* the bill (by signing it) after which they are bound to make payment when the bill matures, i.e. on the date specified in the bill. The documents are then released to the importer and they are able to obtain possession of them from the master of the ship.

This method protects exporters in so far as the documents of title are only released against payment or acceptance of the bill by the importers, although payment is neither immediate nor guaranteed in the latter case. If the bill is payable after *sight*, importers benefits from having a period of credit in which to pay for the goods while exporters can obtain their money immediately if they are able to *discount* the bill with their banks. This involves selling a bill to the bank at slightly less than its face value, i.e. at a discount. The bank credits the customer's account with the agreed sum immediately and then collects the full proceeds of the bill on the due date, taking its profit from the difference between the amount paid for the bill and the amount realised.

Documentary credits

Documentary credits are a method of financing overseas trade by inserting in the contract of sale a provision that payment shall be made by a bank. In a *letter of credit* the bank in effect undertakes to pay the price for the goods upon delivery of the export documents to the bank. It is the surest and quickest method of obtaining payment.

The importer agrees with their bank (the issuing bank) to instruct a bank in the seller's country to make payment on the presentation of documents which conform *exactly* to the instructions and descriptions specified in the documentary credit.

Credits may be available for payment at sight (on demand), or for acceptance (at a fixed or determinable future date). In the latter case a bill of exchange will be drawn by the seller and accepted by the issuing bank. After payment or acceptance of the bill the documents are sent to the issuing bank for processing and then to the importer to enable them to take possession of the goods on arrival.

Credits can either be *revocable* or *irrevocable*. The former are now rare because they can be cancelled or amended by the importer at any time without the prior knowledge of the exporter. The latter are the most widely used method of payment in export sales. Under irrevocable credits the issuing bank gives its irrevocable undertaking and guarantees payment if all the terms of the credit are met. Should the exporter require greater security than that afforded by the name of the issuing bank, the irrevocable credit can be confirmed (including the acceptance of the bill of exchange) by one of the leading UK banks (the advising bank). This means that the letter of credit will be honoured irrespective of what might happen either to the importer or to the overseas issuing bank.

A bill of exchange is a negotiable instrument. What is meant by the word 'negotiable' in this context? Bills of exchange can be endorsed. What is meant by the word 'endorsed'? (Remember, a cheque is a type of bill of exchange.)

The Export Credit Guarantee Department (ECGD)

The ECGD is a government-backed body of great importance in export sales. It offers two main services; insurance and guarantees for bank finance.

ECGD *insurance covers* two broad categories of risk. These are:

(a) the *creditworthiness* of the importer;
(b) the *political and economic risks* of the country concerned, for example, war, civil disorder and the imposition of exchange control restrictions. It does not cover risks normally insured by commercial companies, e.g. fire and marine accidents.

Most exporters selling on credit will need the help of banks to bridge the credit period. However, an exporter is usually able to obtain this at a preferential rate if the ECGD *guarantees* the advance because the guarantee is government-backed and consequentially carries very little risk for the bank.

Overall, the ECGD enables exporters to conduct their business with greater security. They are able to adopt a more aggressive sales technique, selling to new customers and offering large amounts of credit on longer terms in order to match or defeat their competitors.

The export and import of goods is only one part of international commerce, there is also the sale of services and the movement of money and capital to consider. To do this we must consider the *balance of payments*.

For each of the following types of contracts:

- Ex works
- FOR
- FOT
- FAS
- FOB
- Ex ship
- CIF

1 Give the meaning of the initials.

2 State:

(a) the seller's responsibility for delivery;
(b) where the price is payable;
(c) when risk passes to the buyer.

Keywords

Export contracts
A variety of standard export contracts exist, e.g. *ex works*, *FOR*, *FOB* and *CIF*. These will determine, among other things, the price to be paid and who bears the risk of accidental loss or damage to the goods.

Bills of lading
Documents used in international trade which serve as: *(a)* a receipt, *(b)* a contract of carriage, and *(c)* a document of title.

Documentary collections
A method of payment used in international trade whereby exporters forward bills of exchange with the shipping documents via their banks to the importers' banks for later payment by the importers.

Documentary credits
A method of payment used in international trade whereby importers instruct their banks to issue letters of credit in favour of the exporters to banks in the exporters' country.

ECGD
A government agency which *(a)* insures against insolvency of importers and political and economic risks in the importers' countries, and *(b)* guarantees advances by banks to exporters.

The balance of payments

The balance of payments is an account of all the transactions of everyone living and working in the UK with the rest of the world. It is always recorded in £s. While many different currencies are involved, these are converted into £s at the current exchange rate. If anyone normally resident in the UK sells goods or services to someone abroad, this creates an inflow (+) of money, while anyone in Britain buying goods or services from abroad causes an outflow (−) of money from the country. Not so obviously, if anyone in Britain invests abroad this will cause an outflow (−), while if a foreigner invests in Britain, e.g. an American company takes over a British company, then an inflow of currency (+) is created. When all these transactions are recorded we arrive at the balance of payments, as in Table 21.4.

Items in the account

Current account

The current account has two components: *visible trade*, which is the export and import of goods (from which we get the *balance of trade*), and *invisible trade*, which is the sale and purchase of services. Invisible trade is vitally important to Britain. The balance of trade is often confused with the balance of payments. In Table 21.4, you can see that the balance of trade is only a part of the balance of payments, albeit an important part. It is therefore possible to have a deficit on the balance of trade and surplus on the balance of payments. Britain is usually in deficit on the balance of trade but until recently made it up with invisible earnings. It is regarded as very important to have a surplus on the balance of payments current account.

Activity

Distinguish between the balance of trade and the balance of payments and discuss the relationship between the two.

Transactions in external assets and liabilities

This involves the movement of capital (money) rather than goods and services, i.e. it is concerned with international loans and investment. It includes such items as:

- UK investment services;
- overseas investment in the UK;
- borrowing and lending overseas by UK banks;
- other items such as government loans to foreign countries
- changes in official reserves.

The last item refers to the increases or decreases in reserves of gold and foreign currency held by the Bank of England. Increases in reserves create a minus (–) and drawings on (running down the reserves) a plus (+). This point is perhaps made clearer if you remember that the balance of payments is recorded in £s and, therefore, if reserves of foreign currency increase it

must be because foreigners have been buying sterling and £s will therefore have left the country (–).

Table 21.4 Balance of payments of the UK 1988

Current account	£ million
Visible trade:	
Exports (FOB)	80,602
Imports (CIF)	101,428
Visible balance (balance of trade)	–20,826
Invisibles	
General government	–1,833
Private sector	
Sea transport	–576
Civil aviation	–862
Travel	–2,042
Financial and other services	9,478
Interest profit and dividends	
General government	–837
Private sector	6,456
Transfers	–3,575
Invisible balance	6,209
Current account balance (1)	–14,617
Transactions in external assets and liabilities	
Investment overseas by UK residents	–24,937
Investment in the UK by overseas residents	11,985
Net foreign currency transactions by UK banks	14,595
Net foreign currency transactions by other UK residents	3,443
Official reserves (additions to (–), drawings on (+))	–2,761
Other	9
Net transactions in assets and liabilities (2)	2,334
Balancing item (3)	12,283

Source: UK Balance of Payments, HMSO

The balancing item

This amount is necessary to arrive at a correct balance and makes up for anything which has been left out, or for errors. It can be either positive or negative.

State where in the balance of payments (exports, investment profit and dividends etc) the following items would appear and whether they would cause a minus (–) or a plus (+).

1 Dividend paid to US shareholders in Ford UK.

2 Sales of Scotch whisky to Japan.

3 Britons taking holidays in Greece.

4 Price support to UK farmers paid by the EC.

5 A Briton buys shares in Air France.

6 Foreign currency reserves at the Bank of England increase.

7 Barclays Bank writes off its Third World Debt.

8 Credit Suisse buys a UK stockbroking firm.

9 UK government expenditure on the British Army of the Rhine.

10 Sales of Phil Collins records in the USA.

Prior to 1986 there was a section of the Account known as *official financing*. In this section were recorded the changes in official reserves and borrowing and lending with such official bodies as the IMF. It used to be said that the overall deficit or surplus on this section was needed to balance the overall deficit or surplus on the rest of the account. The government balanced the books, so to speak, by its borrowing and lending and by changes in the reserves.

This section was discontinued because it had become dwarfed by the transactions in the private sector, i.e. private borrowing and lending being many times greater than public. Therefore, it was regarded as unrealistic to speak of official financing balancing the books. There is, of course, still massive government intervention from time-to-time but other measures are needed such as changes in interest rates.

Cures for balance of payments problems

Balance of payments problems can arise out of either deficits or surpluses. Similarly, a balance of payments problem can be accompanied either by a high level of economic activity at home or a low level. For many years Britain was faced with recurrent balance of payments deficits accompanied by inflation. The late 1970s and early 1980s saw some handsome balance of payments surpluses but these were accompanied by such a low level of economic activity in the domestic economy, i.e. heavy unemployment, that they seemed equally undesirable. The late 1980s saw massive deficits on the current account. There are many actions the government might take to combat a balance of payments problems; which the correct one is will depend upon the reasons for the problem.

Some of these measures are considered below.

1 Increasing productivity. If a country is facing massive current account deficits as the UK did in the late 1980s due to failure to export sufficiently, increasing productivity is the best cure. Failure to export could be caused by prices being too high and through poor marketing. One of the chief reasons why Japanese car exports are so successful is that it takes only one quarter of the labour to produce a car in Japan as it does in the UK. Under these circumstances, if the UK wishes to compete it must become more efficient. The government, therefore, needs to take *supply side* measures (*see* page 397) to increase efficiency in the economy.

If increasing productivity is the best long-term measure, there are still many short-term measures which can be used and these we will now consider.

2 Borrowing/increasing reserves. Faced with a deficit, a government could borrow or run down its reserves. Conversely, faced with a surplus it could lend or increase its reserves. This should only be done for a short-term disequilibrium – it is not a long-term solution.

3 Exchange control. A government could regulate its payments position by imposing restrictions on the exchange of its currency; this tends to annoy trading partners. Britain used this measure in 1967 (in order to support the pound at the time of devaluation) but in 1979 all exchange controls were abolished.

4 Deflation. If a deficit is caused by inflation at home a credit squeeze or a tight fiscal policy might cure it. However, this is hardly the measure to use if there is unemployment at home. This has been tried many times by British governments.

5 Devalue/revalue. A nation could try to cure a deficit by devaluation and a surplus by revaluation. This will only work if the demand for exports and imports is elastic. If the demands are inelastic these measures will exacerbate the situation. Britain devalued in 1949 and 1967 and the pound floated in 1972. Since that date there have been great variations in the exchange rate, as there have been in many other countries. These are discussed later in this chapter.

 Activity

1 **In order for devaluation to work as a method of helping a balance of payments deficit, is it necessary that the elasticity of:**

(a) Demand for imports be elastic/inelastic?
(b) Demand for exports be elastic/inelastic?

Assuming that you got the answer right, consider this further problem.

2 **Suppose that the balance of payments is in equilibrium. What values of the coefficient of elasticity are required if devaluation is to produce a surplus on the balance of payments?**

6 Reflation. This would only be seen as a solution when there was a deficit on the balance of payments coupled with domestic unemployment. Britain has been prevented from doing this by the danger of worsening inflation.

7 Reduce expenditure abroad/overseas aid. A major world power such as Britain or the USA might reduce military expenditure overseas as a method of reducing a deficit. Conversely, the giving of overseas aid could reduce a surplus.

8 Protectionism. A traditional way to restrict imports has been to impose tariffs (import taxes) or quotas (a restriction on the quantity of a product that may be imported). Although most nations have signed treaties (*see* page 373) designed to reduce tariffs, more subtle forms of protectionism have been found. For example, countries impose strict safety regulations on imported goods in order to keep them out of the country. At the Tokyo Summit in 1986 the leading industrial nations pledged themselves to fight the rising tide of protectionism in the world but little progress has been made.

9 Change in investment. A country in deficit could sell off its overseas investments or receive investment from abroad. Conversely, a creditor nation could eliminate its surplus by investing overseas. Curiously, Britain continues to be a net investor overseas despite

(or perhaps because of) its problems.

10 Interest rates. If the government raises interest rates this should attract funds into the country, thereby helping to balance the books in times of deficit. Unfortunately, this also means that more interest must be paid out. It is estimated that each 1% on the interest rate costs £1 billion in foreign exchange.

Interest rates also affect the domestic economy. If high interest rates decrease domestic demand they will also decrease the demand for imports. Since one third of all goods are imported, this should have a beneficial effect upon the balance of payments. At the same time high interest rates make exports expensive by keeping the external value of the pound high and increase the costs of production. Despite these reservations, it was on interest rates that the government was relying to rectify the deficit at the beginning of the 1990s.

 Activity

1 **List six measures which a nation might take to rectify a *surplus* on its balance of payments.**

2 **Why might a nation consider a surplus to be a problem?**

Multinational companies

We tend to think of the business organisation as a national entity, perhaps with interests overseas, while economies are in fact becoming dominated by large multinational companies. These pose special problems, for government, law and economics. It is not just that such companies are large but that they are truly multinational. In 1988 about 27% of British industry was foreign owned. Britain nevertheless continues to be a major overseas investor. By 1990 the UK was the World's second largest creditor nation after Japan. Among the many multinational companies operating in Britain are Ford, General Motors, Rank Xerox, IBM, Phillips, Michelin, Alcan, Nestlé and Ciba-Geigy.

Some of the problems posed are:

1 Host and hostage. A company may often pursue policies which are not in the best interest of its host state but equally it may find its assets held hostage to

368 PART 4 THE ORGANISATION IN ITS NATIONAL AND INTERNATIONAL CONTEXT

the particular demands of a country.

2 *Taxation.* It is often difficult to stop companies avoiding tax by switching their revenues.

3 *Legal.* The company may find itself having to comply with different regulations in different countries. However, it may in turn be able to avoid onerous regulations by having offices registered overseas, e.g. flags of convenience.

4 *Statistical.* One of the greatest problems posed by the multinational is one of information. Statistics are compiled in different ways in different countries and many of them take no account of the ultimate ownership of capital.

The conventional Marxist picture of *economic imperialism* is of companies investing overseas to exploit cheap labour. This seems to be borne out by the shift of the manufacturing base of the world away from Europe and North America towards the Pacific Basin. While some high-tech and much military production is still concentrated in the West, much of the basic manufacturing of clothing, footwear, electronics, motor vehicles etc is now in countries such as Japan, South Korea and Taiwan.

Theory seems to lag behind practice in that when we analyse organisations we tend to do so in a national context but, increasingly, the important business organisations are multinational. In addition to our difficulties in analysing the behaviour of multinational companies, there is no generally accepted body of international law to regulate their activities. We do not know whether these large companies will become the basis of a more rational international behaviour or become a source of friction and conflict.

The International Monetary Fund

Having examined the international dimension of the UK economy, we now turn to look at *international organisations.* As you will recall from Chapter 2, an international organisation is one which is *constituted* internationally, whereas multinationals are simply businesses which operate in many countries.

Keywords

Exchange control
Placing limits on the amount of foreign currency which may be bought or sold.

Official reserves
The amount of gold and foreign currency held by central banks and other monetary authorities.

Protectionism
The use of tariffs, quotas or other measures to restrict the amount of imports.

Devaluation or depreciation
A fall in the external value of a nation's currency. It makes exports cheaper and imports dearer.

Revaluation or appreciation
A rise in the external value of a nation's currency. It makes exports dearer and imports cheaper.

Multinational companies
A business operating in many different countries. Multinationals are very difficult for national governments to control.

Bretton Woods

In July 1944 a conference took place at Bretton Woods in New Hampshire to try to establish the pattern of post-war international monetary transactions. The aim was to try to achieve freer convertibility, improve international liquidity and avoid the economic nationalism which had characterised the inter-war years. The conference was chaired by the Secretary of the American Treasury, Henry Morgenthau. The conference was dominated, however, by the great English economist, John Maynard Keynes, and the American, Harry Dexter-White.

Keynes had the idea that an international unit of currency should be created. This he called *bancor.* It was to be a hypothetical unit of account against which all other currencies would be measured. This would be administered by a world bank with which all countries would have an account. In effect, this bank would perform the tasks of an ordinary bank, except its customers would be nations: cheques could be written out to settle bills; money would be created to finance trade and overdrafts could be given to those countries which required them. It was essential to the concept of the bank, however, that it be allowed to determine each country's exchange rate and adjust it to ensure that nations did not fall hopelessly into debt. The plan foundered because nations, none more so than the UK, were unwilling to allow an international institution to determine the value of their currency.

The result was that two compromise institutions were established in 1947: the International Monetary Fund (IMF) and the International Bank for Reconstruction and Development (IBRD). The latter is usually called, misleadingly, the World Bank, for it is the IMF which contains the remains of Keynes' idea for the *bancor*, not the IBRD.

It was the IMF system which dominated the pattern of international monetary payments from 1945–72. The objectives of the Fund were to achieve free convertibility of all currencies and to promote stability in international money markets. It has not achieved the first of these but, until the late 1960s, there was comparative stability of exchange rates accompanied by economic prosperity for many of its members.

Quotas

Each of the 141 members of the IMF is required to contribute a quota to the fund. The size of the quota will depend upon the national income of the country concerned and upon its share of world trade. The quota used to be made up of 75% of the country's own currency and 25% in gold. In this way it was hoped that there would be enough of any foreign currency in the pool for any member to borrow should it get into balance of payments difficulties. The gold part of the quota is now subscribed in reserve assets, not in gold. In addition to its quota, members have an allocation of SDRs (*see* below).

Voting power in the IMF is related to the size of quota and in this way the USA and the other industrialised nations have managed to dominate the Fund for most of its life. The relative importance of countries has obviously changed since 1947 but member countries have resisted upward revisions of their quotas since it would involve contributing more to the Fund. Britain's quota was originally 14.9% and it now stands at 7.2%. The USA's quota is 20.8% and that of the combined oil exporting nations 11%. The total quotas have been revised upwards seven times since 1947 and an eighth review seems likely. All quotas are now expressed in SDRs.

Borrowing

Originally each member of the Fund could borrow a 25% slice (tranche) of its quota in a foreign currency for up to five consecutive years, i.e. it was possible for a member to borrow the equivalent of 125% of its quota. Today it is possible to borrow up to the equivalent of 450% over a three-year period. This is not, however, an unconditional right to borrow, for the Fund may, and usually does, impose conditions of increasing severity upon a member as it increases its borrowing.

The methods of borrowing from the Fund have received several modifications.

Stand-by arrangements

Devised in 1952, this method has become the most usual form of assistance rendered by the Fund. Resources are made available to a member which may be drawn if required. Attaining a stand-by facility is often enough to stabilise a member's balance of payments situation without it actually drawing upon the Fund. Stand-by facilities are similar to a bank overdraft. It is still necessary for a member to agree to conditions for each tranche.

General agreement to borrow (GAB)

In 1961 the ten leading members of the IMF agreed to make a pool of £6 billion available to each other. Although channelled through the IMF, the Group of Ten would decide itself whether or not to give assistance. They now offer aid to less developed countries. At present, GAB has funds of SDR 17 billion available. In 1984 this was supplemented by the membership of Switzerland and Saudi Arabia.

Special drawing rights (SDRs)

In 1967 it was decided to *create* international liquidity for the first time. This was to be done by giving members an allocation of special drawing rights which could be used in settlement of an international debt if the creditor nation was willing to accept them. SDRs were first made available in 1970.

SDRs are the nearest equivalent so far to Keynes' idea of *bancor*. Originally calculated as 1 SDR = $1, the value of SDRs is now calculated by combining the value of the five leading currencies in the following proportions: US dollar 42%; Deutschemark 19%; French franc 13%; pound sterling 13%; Japanese yen 13%. This gives a value of approximately 1 SDR = $1.15.

To what extent might SDRs and ecus be regarded as money?

The adjustable peg

The members of the IMF originally agreed to fix or 'peg' the value of their currencies by defining them in terms of gold, thus re-establishing a type of gold standard. This could be done directly or indirectly by defining the value of a currency in terms of one of the two reserve currencies, the dollar and the pound.

The pegged value of currency was permitted to vary within a margin of 1%. If, for example, the exchange rate of the pound was £1 = $2.80 (1949–67), then its value could fluctuate within the limits £1 = $2.78 – $2.82

Beyond these limits, adjustment of the pegged value of a currency required the permission of the Fund. The permission was to be virtually automatic for changes of up to 10% but more conditional beyond this.

Convertibility

It was the aim of the Fund that any currency should be freely convertible into any other. This would mean the abolition of all exchange controls but not the controls on the movement of capital funds. The Fund was fairly successful in improving convertibility. The pound became freely convertible in 1958 and in 1979 all exchange control measures were abolished by the UK.

Discipline

A country which wants to borrow from the Fund is likely to have to agree to conditions before the loan is granted, e.g. the implementation of domestic deflation and credit control. In 1976, for example, Dennis Healey, the Labour government's Chancellor of the Exchequer, had to provide the Fund with a 'letter of intent' stating the limits to the expansion of the money supply.

A country which is in continual balance of payments surplus could also cause severe embarrassment to the international scene. In such circumstances the Fund can, under Article Seven, declare as 'scarce' the currency of the country in surplus. This scarce currency provision would then allow other members to take exchange control sanctions against that country. The provision has never been used but its threat may have been instrumental in bringing about revaluations of the yen and the Deutschemark.

List three main functions of the IMF.

The era of floating exchange rates

Although the IMF is still in existence, the system of fixed exchange rates, the basis of the Bretton Woods Agreement, has been swept away. Following the abandonment of the gold standard by the Americans in 1971 and the failure of various attempts to return to an adjustable peg system, most of the World now operates on a system of floating exchange rates. An exception to this is the EMS of the EC discussed in the previous chapter.

Floating exchange rates

After Britain 'floated' the pound in 1972, it was not long before most other currencies, including the USA, followed suit.

When a country has a floating, or freely fluctuating, exchange rate, it means that it is determined by the forces of demand and supply in international markets. This is illustrated in Fig. 21.1. In this diagram all foreign currencies are considered together and are measured in terms of dollars. The supply of pounds (SS) in this market is the result of the British desire to import goods. Pounds are not acceptable to foreigners

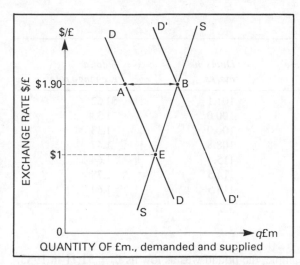

Figure 21.1 The determination of the price of the pound sterling. the figures used are for illustration only.

What would be the likely effect of the following upon our exchange rate?

1 **An increase in the rate of inflation.**

2 **Increased government spending overseas.**

3 **A rise in domestic interest rates.**

4 **A surplus on the balance of payments current account.**

5 **An increase in the demand for Jaguar cars in the USA followed by the UK's purchase of Trident missiles.**

In each case attempt to illustrate your answer with the correct graph.

and they will demand payment in their own currency. The demand for pounds comes from the desire of foreigners to buy British goods. To do this, however, they must obtain pounds and so they demand British currency by offering their own money. Where the demand and supply are equated is the equilibrium price (E) or the exchange rate. The exchange rate is thereby determined by the interaction of import demand and export supply. It should be clear from this why a failure to export goods can have a disastrous effect upon the exchange rate.

Although most exchange rates are nominally floating, virtually all governments intervene either openly or covertly to try and stabilise their exchange rate, or to manipulate it to their advantage. In Fig. 21.1 the move to D'D' illustrates the exchange rate for the pound being driven up to $1.90 by the Bank of England buying pounds, thereby increasing the demand for them and putting up their price. The distance AB represents the quantity of pounds which the Bank would have to buy to maintain the exchange rate at $1.90. When the government intervenes in this manner there is said to be *dirty floating*. *Clean floating* would occur if the government took no part but allowed the exchange rate to be fixed by the unrestricted forces of demand and supply. The movement from DD to D'D' could also be brought about by market forces. For example, in 1980 the effect of North Sea oil drove up the exchange rate as foreigners demanded pounds to buy our oil exports.

Britain: floating or sinking?

A floating exchange rate should bring about automatic rectification of any balance of payments disequilibrium. This comes about because a deficit on the balance of payments would cause the exchange rate to depreciate, thereby making exports cheaper and imports dearer so that the deficit is turned into a surplus. Conversely, a surplus would cause the exchange rate to appreciate, thereby making imports cheaper and exports dearer. Advocates of floating exchange rates, or *managed flexibility* as dirty floating is politely called, claim several advantages for it.

(a) There is an absence of crisis meetings because imbalances sort themselves out.
(b) Because of *(a)* there are no disputes of the 'You should devalue', 'No, you should revalue' kind between nations in payments imbalance.
(c) Internal economic policy is freed from the constraints of the external payments position, e.g. the economy does not have to deflate to protect an unrealistic exchange rise.

Has this worked for the UK? When Britain floated in 1972 the exchange rate was £1 = $2.60; it reached an all-time low of £1 = $1.10 in January 1985, an effective devaluation of 58%. Since this time it has climbed back up again being £1 = $1.64 in 1989. Now that the dollar is also floating, the exchange rate is quoted not only against the dollar but also as a weighted

Table 21.5 Changes in exchange rates

Effective exchange rate indices (1985 = 100)					
	Sterling	US dollars	Japanese Yen	Deutsche-marks	£/dollar exchange rate
1983	105.3	89.8	91.8	101.1	$1.52
1984	100.6	96.9	97.9	100.0	1.33
1985	100.0	100.0	100.0	100.0	1.33
1986	91.5	80.2	124.5	108.8	1.47
1987	90.1	70.3	133.1	115.4	1.64
1988	95.5	66.0	147.3	114.5	1.78
1989	92.6	69.4	141.9	113.5	1.64

Source: Bank of England Quarterly Review

index against a 'basket' of 16 leading currencies.

The drop in the value of the pound in the 1970s was not altogether unwelcome to the British government, who believed it would make exports competitive. The success or otherwise of this would depend upon the relative elasticities of demand for exports and imports. It should be remembered, however, that increasing the price of imports will also increase inflation. It is reckoned that a 4% rise in import prices causes 1% domestic inflation. The British government, however, seemed happy to settle for a rate of about $1.70, but no sooner was the rate stabilised around this level that the prospects of North Sea oil brought money flooding into London and the exchange rate soared, much to the displeasure of the government. It appeared that a pound that floated upward was almost as difficult to live with as a sinking one.

Table 21.5 shows the indices of various currencies since 1983. You can see from this that the average value of the pound has fallen steadily, that the dollar has fluctuated while the Yen and the Deutschemark have both risen considerably.

The strength of sterling in the beginning of the decade when it reached £1 = £2.38 reflected the importance of oil and the consequent strength of the UK's balance of payments. The subsequent decline reflects the gradually deteriorating position of the UK's balance. It is estimated that the current account deficit for 1989 was over £20 billion. The pound was only kept from falling still further by the very high interest rates prevailing at the time. The fluctuations in value are even greater than suggested by Table 21.5 since the table only shows annual averages. For ex-

ample, the pound was as low as £1 = $1.11 in 1985. Whatever the merits of floating exchange rates, such great variations can only be harmful.

List three advantages and three disadvantages of floating exchange rates.

The Eurocurrency markets

One reason for the instability in currency markets is the growth of eurocurrencies. These are nothing to do with the EC or EMS and are in fact dealings between banks and other financial institutions. A Eurocurrency is any deposit in a financial institution which is not denominated in the national currency. For example, deposits of sterling in a French bank which continue to be counted as sterling and not as francs are Eurocurrency – in this case Eurosterling. Most Eurocurrency deposits are in dollars.

London is the chief centre of the Eurocurrency market but tthere is nothing exclusively European about Eurocurrency markets: the American dollar is the chief currency traded and centres outside Europe such as Tokyo and Hong Kong are important. Enormous sums of money are traded ($150 billion per day in 1989) both for trading purposes and for speculation.

We mentioned earlier in the chapter that governments would find it difficult to intervene to either balance their payments or to stabilise currencies. When you realise the amount of dealings in Eurocurrency, it is easy to see why this is so.

Other international organisations

The IBRD (International Bank for Reconstruction and Development)

The IBRD (or 'World Bank') was set up as a sister organisation to the IMF in 1946. Its aim was to make loans to help to redevelop war-shattered economies. The IMF, you will remember, does not make loans for capital projects, only to help alleviate payments difficulties. The World Bank derives its funds from three sources.

1 Quotas. Members make contributions in relation to their IMF quotas, 10% of the quota being paid while the other 90% acts as guarantee for the Bank's loans.
2 Bonds. The World Bank sells bonds on the capital markets of the world.
3 Income. A very small proportion of the Bank's funds comes from the Bank's earnings. As it progressed, the World Bank turned its attention from Europe to the poorer countries of the world. Today it is almost wholly concerned with helping LDCs. It is a valuable source of advice and information besides making loans.

The World Bank has also increased its operations by forming new organisations. These are:

1 The International Finance Corporation (IFC, 1956). This was set up to enable the Bank to give loans to private companies as well as governments;
2 The International Development Association (IDA, 1960). The objective of the IDA was to make loans for longer periods and on preferential terms to LDCs. The IDA has become known as the 'soft loan window';
3 'The third window'. In 1976 the IBRD announced its intention of making loans available to LDCs on even more favourable terms in order to try to relieve them of the enormous burden of debt interest. This has become known as 'the third window'.
4 The Multilateral Investment Guarantee Agency (MIGA). This agency was set up in 1988 by the seven leading industrial nations (G7) and is operated by the World Bank. The object of the agency is to guarantee long-term private investment in developing countries against political risks.

In the 1990s one of the greatest problems facing the international community is that of Third World debt. By 1989 this was estimated to be approaching $700 billion. The repayment of this is such a burden that the Third World is sending money to the rich nations of the World rather than vice versa, i.e. even considering all the foreign aid and extra loans given, more money still reverts to the industrialised nations than flows from them. The World Bank's funds are totally inadequate to deal with the problem of international debt which is because official lending to the Third World is dwarfed by that of commercial lenders such as the banks. This is a problem for both the poor nations, desperate for money but ground down by debt, and for creditor nations who are having to write off debts which will never be repaid.

GATT (the General Agreement on Tariffs and Trade)

The 23 signatories of the Havana Charter 1948 had intended to set up a worldwide trading organisation (ITO). In the event, however, they could not reach an understanding and so instead came to a general agreement on tariffs and trade. The main parts of this agreement were as follows.

1 Tariffs. All the signatories agreed not to increase tariffs beyond their existing level.
2 Quotas. The signatories agreed to work towards the abolition of quotas.
3 'Most favoured nation'. Every signatory was a 'most favoured nation', i.e. trading privileges could not be extended by one member to another without extending them to all. Existing systems of preferences, such as Commonwealth Preference were allowed to continue.
4 Trading blocs. The establishment of common-market type agreements such as the EC and EFTA were allowed but were encouraged to be outward-looking rather than insular.

Several rounds of talks succeeded in reducing tariffs and virtually abolishing quotas. The most famous of these was the *Kennedy Round* of the 1960s. GATT members now account for about 80% of international trade.

In recent years emphasis has shifted to the gap between the rich northern countries and the poor southern countries. This has become known as the north-south dialogue. This has mainly been conducted through the United Nations Conference on Trade and Development (UNCTAD). The poor countries are mainly producers of primary commodities but they are unable to trade freely with the rich northern countries because they are discriminated against by protectionist policies such as those of the EC. The poor countries insist that they must have freer access to markets and better prices for their products if they are to progress. So far, little progress has been made.

OECD (the Organisation for Economic Co-operation and Development)

The OECD was originally called the *Organisation for European Economic Co-operation*. It was set up in 1947 to administer the USA's *European Recovery Programme ('Marshall Aid')*. By 1960 it was considered that it had achieved its objective and so it became the OECD with the objective of turning its attention to the less developed countries of the world. The OECD now has 21 members which are most of the European countries, the USA, Canada and Japan, who joined in 1965. The methods of the OECD are to try to co-ordinate the economic policies of its members, to co-ordinate economic aid and to provide specialised services, one of the most important of which is information.

OPEC (the Organisation of Petroleum Exporting Countries)

The domination of the rich industrialised nations in world trade has done little to help the producers of primary products (mainly the poor countries) because it has prevented them from uniting to obtain good prices for their products. The one exception to this was OPEC. It consists of a group of Arabian, African and South American countries who *export* oil. (America is still a great producer of oil but is a net importer.) The OPEC countries were able to combine successfully for three main reasons: geographically they are relatively concentrated; the demand for their product was highly inelastic; and they were united by a common political hostility to Israel. The 1973 fourfold increase

in the price of oil must be one of the most successful coups of all time. The further attempt by OPEC to raise prices in 1978 had far reaching consequences. It was sufficiently large to help plunge the world into depression. The worst hit nations were the poor Third World countries who were oil importers. The depression therefore led to a decline in the demand for oil. This came at a time when world oil supplies had been increased, e.g. by North Sea and Canadian oil. Thus, OPEC was no longer able to control the market and the price collapsed.

The policy of OPEC, which had seemed like a beacon of light to other primary producers, was now in ruins. The problems of primary producers and the difficulties of trying to control markets were further illustrated by the collapse of the tin market in 1986.

Keywords

International Monetary Fund (IMF)
An organisation designed to give short-term help to nations in balance of payments difficulties and to stabilise exchange rates.

Bretton Woods Conference
The meeting which set up the IMF.

Tranche
A French word meaning slice – often used in financial jargon to denote a portion of a quota or allocation. For example, the 25% of quota paid to the IMF in gold was called the gold tranche.

General Agreement to Borrow (GAB)
Set up in 1967, this is an agreement among the ten richest nations to help each other with foreign exchange borrowing. The facility is now available to other nations.

Adjustable peg
The system of fixed exchange rates operated by the IMF up to 1971.

Convertibility
The ease with which one currency can be changed (converted) into another. A non-convertible currency is one which it is very difficult to change into another, e.g. the rouble.

Floating exchange rates
This is where the external value of a currency is set by the forces of demand and supply in international markets.

Dirty floating
This is where the government intervenes to

manipulate a floating exchange rate. A *clean float* is when it does not interfere.

Effective exchange rate index

The value of a currency expressed as an index against a basket of other currencies. The UK's present index is based on 1985 = 100 and is calculated against the value of 16 other currencies.

US dollar

Still the most widely used unit of international account reflecting the USA's dominance of world trade since 1945.

Pound/dollar rate

In the UK this is still the most widely quoted and understood measure of the external value of the pound, e.g. £1 = $1.60, meaning that one dollar costs 62.5 pence. The pound/Deutschemark rate is now also widely quoted.

Eurocurrency

A deposit in a financial institution which is denominated (counted) not in the currency of the institution's country but in some other, e.g. US dollars in a British bank still accounted for in dollars. Leading Eurocurrencies are the US dollar, the Deutschemark, the Yen, the Swiss franc and sterling.

World Bank

The International Bank for Reconstruction and Development (IBRD) – set up in 1946, its objective is to give loans to nations for long-term capital development. It has too few funds.

GATT

General Agreement on Tariffs and Trade – set up in 1948 to promote world trade and reduce tariffs and quotas.

OECD

Organisation for Economic Co-operation and Development – an organisation of the 21 leading industrial nations set up to promote trade and development.

OPEC

The Organisation of Petroleum Exporting Countries – a cartel of mainly Arabian, African and South American countries which attempts to fix the price and output of oil. OPEC was successful in the 1970s but less so in the 1980s as other nations outside OPEC began to export oil.

Learning project

Rouble devalued by Soviet Union

Read the following article by Jonathan Steele which appeared in the *Guardian* on 26 October 1989.

The Soviet Union has dropped the rouble to one-tenth of its previous value against the dollar in some transactions, in a sweeping attempt to defeat the flourishing black market.

The massive devaluation, which comes into effect on November 1 is a blow to Soviet citizens who need hard currency to go abroad.

It is not yet clear how it will benefit tourists coming in or the resident foreign community.

A terse four-paragraph notice from the official newsagency, Tass, said that the USSR State Bank had taken the decision 'to serve Soviet and foreign citizens'. But the notice made no further reference to visiting or resident foreigners.

Soviet citizens going abroad will have to pay 6 roubles 26 kopeks for a dollar, instead of the 60 to 65 kopeks that they pay at the moment.

They used to be allowed to get up to $200 at the favourably high rate of the rouble.

With so many Soviet citizens travelling abroad since President Gorbachev started his reform programme, there has been a serious drain on the country's hard currency reserves.

The new rate makes foreign travel more of a luxury and will soak up more of the population's spare cash.

For foreigners holding hard currency, the official rate was absurd, as a brief commentary in the government newspaper, *Izvestia*, accepted last night.

'If a businessman could unofficially get 10,000 roubles for $1,000 instead of 600 roubles at the official rate, the temptation to change on the black market was too high,' the newspaper said.

The devaluation was a 'more than decisive measure' against the black market, it added.

Senior officials at the State Bank were unavailable for comment last night, but it was assumed that the new exchange rate would work for cash transactions for foreigners as well as for Soviet citizens.

It was not clear whether it would change the

system whereby foreigners have to make certain purchases in roubles, exchanged at the present high rate, such as hotel rooms and rents. Nor is it clear how it affects foreign trade. Tass said that two rates for the rouble would apply in future.

'The rouble's special rate will be published monthly, along with the official rate of the USSR State Bank, in the newspaper *Izvestia*, before the two rates come into force,' Tass said.

The devaluation is a partial step towards the full convertibility of the rouble which President Gorbachev has put forward as his eventual goal.

It is the first official admission that the present exchange rate was unrealistic.

Complete the following tasks.

1 With the aid of a demand and supply diagram explain the existence of a 'black market' in foreign currency in Russia prior to the changes mentioned in the article.

2 Assume that the exchange rate before the devaluation was 60 kopeks to the dollar and also assume that the new rate of 6 roubles 26 kopeks is the correct exchange rate. Demonstrate the proposed changes with the aid of a diagram.

3 What measures might a government take to maintain an exchange rate above the free market equilibrium rate, i.e. that the currency is overvalued.

4 What effect do you expect the 1989 changes in Eastern Europe to have upon the exchange rate regimes there.

5 Assess the success of interest rates as a method of influencing exchange rates.

Further ideas for learning projects

1 The following information contains all the figures that are needed to calculate a summary balance of payments statement for country X.

	$million
Services	+2,435
Exports	55,565
Net increase in external assets	30,831
Transfers	−1,809
Net increase in external liabilities	28,569
Interest, profits and dividends (net)	+1,078
Imports	53,234

(a) Prepare country X's balance of payments statement.
(b) Confirm that the balancing item is $−1,773 million.
(c) Do these figures suggest that country X is a developed or a less developed nation? Give reasons for your answer.

2 Prepare an information sheet outlining the full range of services of the ECGD.

3 Compile a chart or table of Britain's 15 most important trading partners showing the volume of exports and imports in £m. Then express the importance of trade with the EC as a percentage share of exports and imports.

22

The working of the economy

CHAPTER OBJECTIVES

After studying this chapter you should be able to:

- List and define the main components of national income;
- Define and calculate the propensities to save and to consume;
- Calculate the size of the multiplier;
- Describe the operation of the accelerator;
- Explain the main propositions of monetarism;
- Understand the composition of national income accounts.

Introduction

Most of the economics with which we have concerned ourselves so far is termed *microeconomics*. By this we mean the functioning of individual parts of the economic system, e.g. the price of a particular product or the behaviour of an *individual* firm and so on. The part of economics which is concerned with the functioning of the *whole* economy is termed *macroeconomics*. In this we are no longer concerned with individual organisations but with broad aggregates. Therefore, it is not, for example, the demand for an organisation's product we consider, but the total demand for all goods and services within the society. Similarly, we are not concerned with individuals' incomes but with the total of all incomes in the economy.

The level of national income is of critical importance to the well-being of the economy for on this depends the level of employment. If, for example, there is a decline in national income the result will be unemployment. What follows in this chapter might be regarded as 'models' of the economy.

Models are a simplified and formalised series of ideas and assumptions which help us to increase our understanding of the economy. There is no true model of the economy but a whole series of them which help to advance our understanding. As Professor Lipsey says in his book *An Introduction to Positive Economics*, 'the student should beware of the essentialist belief that there is one true model and that debates between two theories should be settled according to which theory best approximates to the true model. Different theories and models may be best for different uses.'

We will first examine the Keynesian and neo-Keynesian view of the economy. We will then consider other *models*: monetarist and neo-classical.

The Keynesian model

The general theory

An organisation is one of hundreds of thousands which make up the *macroeconomy*. In the same way that the organisation can be analysed in terms of cost structures, revenues and market behaviour, so the whole economy can be examined in terms of its various *components*. Much of our present understanding of the economy is based on the work of J M Keynes. His most famous work *The General Theory of Employment, Interest and Money* was published in 1936. The economic theories of the 'classicists' had proved inadequate to deal with the Great Slump. Keynes believed that the economy was not self-regulating and that it was up to the government to intervene to ensure the economic welfare of society. This is so commonly accepted today that it is difficult to realise what a radical idea this was. Many people would argue that we have enjoyed economic prosperity since 1945 by adopting Keynesian ideas. The present difficulties which Western economies are suffering are partly because Keynes did not foresee the economic problems of today and we await someone whose vision is as profound as Keynes to explain these new problems.

Many Keynesian ideas are now regarded as common sense even by those economists who are not Keynesian. Today, many of these ideas are amalgamated with older concepts to form what is known as the *neo-classical synthesis*.

The circular flow of income

As we go on to examine an economy in more detail, we might begin by identifying two main sectors – that is households and firms. Firms produce goods and services. Households buy them. These sectors are therefore identified not by who they are but by what they do; that is to say, firms *produce* while households *consume*. Everyone in the economy belongs to a 'household' since everyone must consume. The households also own the factors of production. Thus, in order to produce, the firms must buy *factor services* from households. This is illustrated in Fig. 22.1. Here you can see that goods and factor services flow one way around the diagram while money flows the other way so that the flow of goods and money are always *counter-cyclical* to one another. The money paid by households for goods purchased from the firms is termed *consumption* (C) while payments for factor services such as wages, rent, interest and profit are collectively referred to as *income* (Y). Money flows from households to firms and from the firms back to households; this is referred to as the *circular flow of income*.

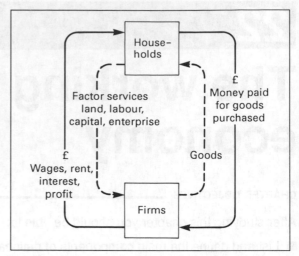

Fig. 22.1 Flow of money and goods between households and firms

Since there is always a corresponding counter-cyclical flow of goods, it is convenient to leave this out of a circular flow diagram and just include the *money flows*. It is possible, therefore, to construct a simple circular flow diagram showing the movement of money and using the abbreviations noted above. This is illustrated in Fig. 22.2.

Savings

If the value of consumption (C) were equal to the value of income (Y) it would appear that there would be no

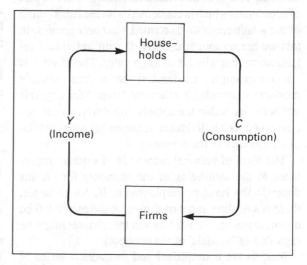

Fig. 22.2 The circular flow of income

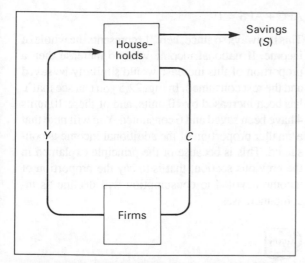

Fig. 22.3 Savings are a withdrawal from the circular flow of income

tendency for the level of income to change. Households, however, do not spend all their income, a proportion is saved. Savings may be defined as *money not spent*. It is, therefore, money taken out of the circular flow and can be described as a *leakage* or *withdrawal* from the circular flow of income. Although most money saved is put into institutions such as banks and therefore becomes available for other people to spend, it does not follow that people will necessarily, or immediately, borrow it from the bank. So, when we speak of savings we are talking of the function of not spending. This is illustrated in Fig. 22.3. Here you can see that saving leaves less money for consumption and therefore decreases the circular flow of income. Savings are represented in the diagram as being carried out by households. Saving may, in fact, take place at any point in the circular flow. In the diagram we have reduced it to one point in the system for the sake of simplicity.

The prime determinant of savings is the level of income. As national incomes rises so does the level of savings. There may be variations in this from time to time but in general this is so. There are many reasons why people save, some of these are listed below.

(a) Deferred purchase – saving up for a holiday or car, etc.

(b) Contractual obligations – mortgage repayments, insurance premiums, etc.

(c) Precautionary motives – money put by for a 'rainy day'.

(d) Thriftiness – some people, or societies, are much thriftier than others as a result of habit or custom.

(e) Age – people tend to save different proportions of their incomes at different times of their lives.

The amount which people wish to save is also influenced by such things as *taxation, government policy* towards savings, the availability of *credit* and *expectation of price changes.*

The classical economists believed that savings were determined by the rate of interest. If the interest rate went up then people saved more to gain the higher rate of interest and vice versa. Today it can be seen that people will save whatever the rate of interest. In recent years saving has still taken place even when the rate of inflation was higher than the rate of interest. The rate of interest may be important, however, in deciding how people save, for example in choosing between banks and building societies, but the reasons for saving would appear to be primarily non-economic.

Hoarding

Although saving is money not spent, most saving is done through institutions so that the money is not lost to the economy but is available for other people to borrow. If, however, people *hoard* money, e.g. put it under a mattress or bury it in the ground, then it is lost to the economy until it reappears. If a lot of hoarding takes place this can have a detrimental effect on the economy. Fortunately, hoarding is not a problem in the UK although it may be a problem in some Third World countries.

Consumption and savings

If saving is money not spent it is clear that the determinants of saving and consumption are closely interrelated. It is, therefore, possible to conclude that consumption is also determined by income. As income increases so does consumption. The proportion of income devoted to consumption, however, decreases as income increases. Thus, although a greater amount is consumed at higher levels of income, this represents a smaller percentage of income. The reason for this is fairly obvious. When an economy is very poor virtually everything must be devoted to con-

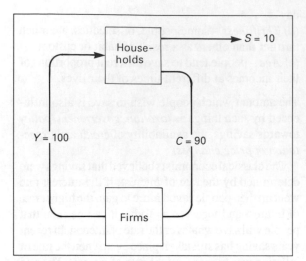

Fig. 22.4 The average propensity to consume

sumption. At very low income levels consumption can even exceed income and in such a situation there would be a negative saving (or *dissaving*). As income rises so more material wants can be satisfied and the economy can 'afford' to save. To take an analogy with individual incomes, it is obvious that the rich are able to save a greater proportion of their income than the poor.

Propensities to save and to consume

If we take the amount saved and the amount consumed and express them as proportions of income, we arrive at the propensities to consume and to save. In Fig. 22.4 you can see that of 100 units of income 10 are saved and 90 are consumed. Therefore, the average propensity to consume (APC), which is the proportion of income devoted to consumption, is 9/10. This is expressed in the following manner:

$$APC = \frac{C}{Y}$$

The average propensity to save (APS) is the proportion of income which is devoted to saving and is expressed as:

$$APS = \frac{S}{Y}$$

In our example above it is therefore 1/10. It follows that:

$$APC + APS = 1$$

This is always so since, here, 1 represents the whole of income. If national income were to increase then a proportion of this increase would similarly be saved and the rest consumed. In Fig. 22.5 you can see that Y has been increased by 10 units, and of these 10 units 4 have been saved and 6 consumed. You will note that a smaller proportion of the additional income is consumed. This is because of the principle explained in the previous section; that is to say the proportion of income devoted to consumption will decline as income increases.

What is the APS for the UK economy at present? How did you determine this?

The marginal propensity to consume (MPC) is defined as the proportion of any addition to income which is devoted to consumption. This is calculated as the increase in consumption divided by the increase in income.

$$MPC = \frac{\Delta C}{\Delta Y}$$

In the above example this would be:

$$MPC = \frac{6}{10}$$

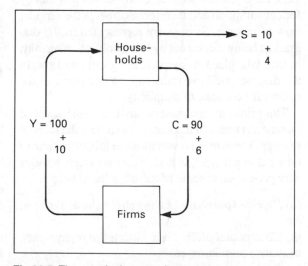

Fig.22.5 The marginal propensity to consume

Table 22.1 Income determination (all figures £ billions).

	Levels of national income (Y) (1)	Planned consumption (C) (2)	Planneed savings (S) (3)	Planned invcestment (I) (4)	Average propensity to consume (APC) (5)	Marginal propensity consume (MPC) (6)
A	£10	£20	£–10	£20	2.00	
B	40	40	0	20	1.00	0.66
C	70	60	10	20	0.86	0.66
D	100	80	20	20	0.80	0.66
E	130	100	30	20	0.77	0.66
F	160	120	40	20	0.75	

The marginal propensity to save (MPS) is the proportion of any addition to income that is devoted to savings and is calculated as:

$$MPC = \frac{\Delta S}{\Delta Y}$$

In the above example this would be:

$$MPC = \frac{4}{10}$$

It also follows that

$$MPC + MPS = 1$$

because, here, 1 represents the whole of the addition to income. We would normally assume that the APC is greater than the MPC. This is because a greater portion of income is consumed at lower levels of income.

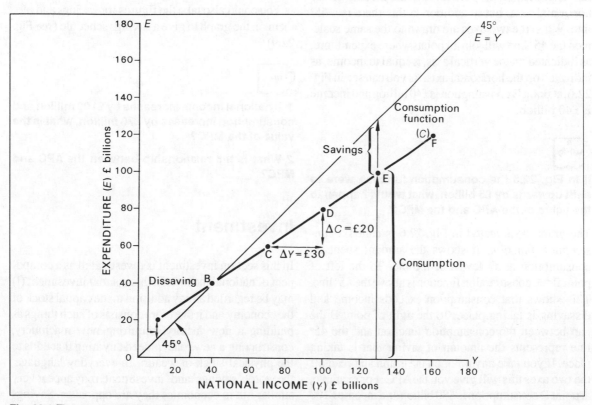

Fig. 22.6 The consumption function

If consumption (C) is 2,000 units and income (Y) is 3,000 units, assuming there are no other leakages and withdrawals, what is the value of the APS?

The consumption function

Table 22.1 consists of some data relating to a hypothetical economy and shows the amount of income that is devoted to consumption at several levels of income. At point B dissaving has ceased and all of the income is devoted to consumption. As income continues to rise so the proportion going to consumption declines. This is shown in column (5) which gives the APCs. In this example the MPC appears to be constant. As you can see, this is because every time income increases by £30 billion, consumption goes up to £20 billion. These figures can be plotted as a graph. National income graphs are rather special. Expenditure is plotted on the vertical axis and income on the horizontal axis, but in addition to this there is a 45° line. When the two axes are drawn to the same scale, then the 45° line will join all points where expenditure, as indicated on the vertical axis, is equal to income, as indicated on the horizontal axis. As you can see in Fig. 22.6, at point B consumption is £40 billion and income is £40 billion.

If in Fig. 22.6 the consumption function were to shift upwards by £5 billion, what would happen to the value of the APC and the MPC?

The graph constructed in Fig. 22.6 is called a *consumption function*. It shows the amount spent on consumption at all levels of income. To the left of point B the consumption function is above the 45° line. This shows that consumption exceeds income and dissaving is taking place. To the right of point B the gap between the consumption function and the 45° line represents the amount of saving that is taking place. If you take any point on the graph and read off the two axes this will give you the APC. For example, at point D consumption is £80 billion and income £100 billion. If we arrange them according to the formula:

$$APC = \frac{C}{Y}$$

then we obtain:

$$APC = \frac{80}{100}$$

$$APC = 0.80$$

If we consider a movement between two points on the graph, for example from C to D, then we will obtain the MPC.

$$MPC = \frac{\Delta C}{\Delta Y}$$

$$MPC = \frac{20}{30}$$

$$MPC = 0.66$$

In this example the consumption function is a straight line. This has been done for simplicity. You will note, however, that when the consumption function is a straight line the MPC remains constant while the APC decreases from left to right.

You could also take the figures for savings and plot them on the graph to give a savings schedule (*see* Fig. 22.9).

1 If national income increases by £100 million and consumption increases by £70 million, what is the value of the MPC?

2 What is the relationship between the APC and MPC?

Investment

In this section investment is investigated as a component of national income. In this context investment (I) may be regarded as any addition to the capital stock of the economy and it therefore consists of such things as building a new factory, acquiring new machinery, constructing a new road, indeed anything that adds to the physical stock of wealth. In everyday language, the words 'savings' and 'investment' may appear very similar but in economics they are opposites. Savings means not spending and is mainly undertaken by indi-

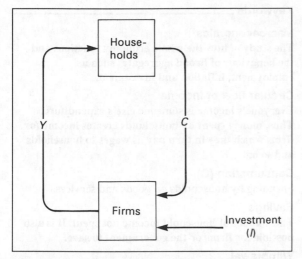

Fig. 22.7 Investment is an injection into the circular flow of income

viduals for non-economic motives, whereas investment is spending and is mainly undertaken by firms in the expectation of economic gain. Also, in saving, a person is nearly always *lending* money whereas firms *borrow* money to invest. (Buying shares on the Stock Exchange is not investment in this context because all that is happening is that the ownership of the shares is passing from one person to another.)

Investment is an *injection* or an *addition* to the circular flow of income. It may be incorporated into our circular flow model as in Fig. 22.7. Here investment is represented as being undertaken by firms. You can see that it will have the effect of increasing the circular flow of income.

What do you consider would be the effect on the level of investment of the following:

(a) **An improvement in technology;**
(b) **Government increasing the tax threshold on capital relief for new investment;**
(c) **An increase in the level of saving;**
(d) **A new issue of shares on the Stock Exchange;**
(e) **An increase on the rate of interest?**

Gross and new investment

The capital stock of the country is constantly depreciating. This is due both to physical decay and to

obsolescence. Therefore, in order that the economy remains at its present level of wealth, a good deal of investment must take place simply to replace existing capital. This may be termed 'replacement investment'. In order for an economy to grow, the capital stock of the country must be increased. Any addition to the capital stock is called net investment, thus:

Gross investment = Replacement investment + Net investment

The determinants of investment

When firms undertake investment they will almost certainly do so in the expectation of gain. Whether or not they expect to gain will depend on their calculation of the cost of investing compared with the expected return. This is sometimes referred to as the *marginal efficiency of capital* (MEC). This will be influenced by several factors, one of which is the *level of technology*. If this is increasing it will make investment more worthwhile since it will increase the net productivity of capital (*see* page 206). Another factor is *business people's expectations*, if they believe prospects are good then this will encourage investment. One of the prime determinants of business optimism is the current state of *income and consumption*. Investment will also be influenced by the *government's taxation policy* towards both depreciation and profits. Although firms frequently finance investment from their own savings, they must also calculate the return on their money if they placed it elsewhere.

The cost of borrowing is obviously an important factor but if businesses are optimistic about the future they will tend to borrow even when interest rates are very high. Conversely, if businesses are pessimistic about the future they will not borrow even if money is very cheap. This was well illustrated in the 1930s when the government tried to eliminate the slump by making money cheap. This did not encourage many people to invest and certainly did not get rid of the depression. The schemes that are most likely to be affected by the cost of borrowing are long-term schemes because in these the interest payments will be a much greater proportion of the capital cost. To understand this you need only to consider taking out a mortgage for 25 years. There is a relationship between the level of economic activity and the level of investment. This is called the *accelerator* and is dealt with later in this chapter.

The classical economists believed that investment was almost entirely determined by the rate of interest. If the rate of interest went up then the level of investment would decrease and vice versa. The failure of this argument was amply demonstrated during the 1930s. For much of this chapter we will make the simplifying assumption that investment is constant. In reality this is not so but it allows us to consider the interrelationships of the components of national income more easily. It is an assumption that can be dropped later.

The Keynesian equilibrium of national income

The significance of the equilibrium

We have examined the main components of national income and we can now begin to discuss how they interrelate. Although there are withdrawals other than savings and injections other than investment we can, by examining these two, lay down the principles. At a later stage we can introduce the other injections and withdrawals.

There is a tendency for the level of national income to reach an equilibrium, i.e. a level at which, other things being equal, it will remain stable. The equilibrium will be reached where the total of spending in the

Keywords _____

Macroeconomics
The study of how the whole economy functions and the behaviour of broad aggregates such as employment, inflation and investment.

Circular flow of income
Everyone's income is someone else's expenditure. Thus, money spent by households creates income for firms which they in turn pay as wages to households and so on.

Consumption (C)
Spending by households on goods and services.

Savings
The amount of household income not spent. It is also possible for firms or the government to save.

Withdrawal
Any leakage of money from the circular flow which results in money not being passed on.

Average propensity to consume (APC)
The proportion of income devoted to consumption.

Marginal propensity to consume (MPC)
The proportion of any addition to income devoted to consumption.

Consumption function
The relationship between consumption and the level of income.

Investment
Any addition to the real capital stock of the nation.

economy is equal to the total income. The significance of the equilibrium is that the level of employment depends upon the level of income. If the equilibrium is at too low a level of income, the result will be unemployment. If the equilibrium level is too high, there will be other unpleasant consequences such as inflation.

The equality of savings and investment

If the injections into the circular flow are greater than the withdrawals then, other things being equal, national income will rise. Conversely, if withdrawals are greater than injections, then national income will fall. If, as in Fig. 22.8, injections (I) are equal to withdrawals (S), then there is no tendency for the level of national income to change and it is in equilibrium.

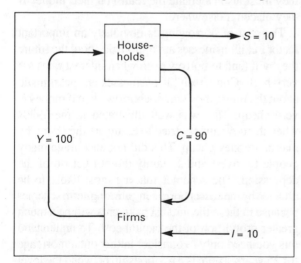

Fig. 22.8 The circular flow of equilibrium S = 1

We may summarise the situation like this.

(a) I > S then national income will rise.
(b) S > I then national income will fall.
(c) S = I then national income is in equilibrium.

Thus, S = I is the equilibrium condition for the economy. It would also follow that if there is a change in either S or I we will be returned to an equilibrium situation when $\Delta S = \Delta I$. Bearing in mind that the level of savings is directly determined by the level of income, the equilibrium of national income can be explained in the following way:

(a) if investment were greater than savings then national income would rise;
(b) if national income rises then savings rise;
(c) this would continue until the increased savings equalled the original increased investment ($\Delta S = \Delta I$);
(d) the economy is returned to equilibrium at a *higher* level of income where once again S = I.

Conversely:

(a) if savings were greater than investment then national income would fall;
(b) if national income falls then savings fall;
(c) this would continue until savings were reduced to such a level that they once again equalled investment;
(d) the economy is returned to equilibrium at a *lower* level of income where once again S = I.

Thus, you can see that savings will always equal investment. This, however, is a *post factum* equilibrium. This means that although savings and investment may not equal each other at any particular moment, they will, when considered over a period of time.

The graphical analysis of national income

We have seen that savings and investment are dependent on quite different factors; savings tend to depend on the level of income while investment depends upon such things as the MEC. In this example the simplifying assumption has been made that investment is constant at £20 billion. This means that when it is plotted as a graph (see Fig. 22.9) it is a horizontal straight line (I). The consumption function utilises the data from Table 22.1 and Fig. 22.7. If we subtract the

amount of consumption from the level of income, we obtain the amount of savings. This can be plotted as a separate savings line (S). The savings line starts below the horizontal axis because at very low levels of income consumption exceeds income and therefore dissaving is taking place. Where the savings line crosses the horizontal axis (£40 billion) the whole of income is devoted to consumption so that we see the consumption function crossing the 45° line at the same level of income.

So far in this chapter we have assumed that there are two types of spending in the economy, spending on consumer goods (C) and spending on investment or producer goods (I). If these two are added together, they will give the total of spending on all types of goods and services in the economy. This is called aggregate demand or *aggregate monetary demand* (AMD). In Fig. 22.9 this is shown by the line C + I. The C + I line is parallel to the consumption function since investment is constant. (Students often believe that the savings line is also parallel to the consumption function. This is not so as you will see if you examine the diagram.)

As we stated in the previous section of this chapter, the equilibrium level of national income is where the total of spending in the economy is equal to total income. Since the C + I line represents total spending, the equilibrium level of income will therefore be where the C + I line crosses the 45° line (£100 billion). You will see from the diagram that this is also the level of income at which savings equals investment. The diagram therefore demonstrates, once again, that the equilibrium level of national income is where S = I. To explain this further we will simplify the diagram. Examine Fig. 22.10 and you will see that at point R the total withdrawals from the economy are equal to total injections (S = I) and the equilibrium level of national income is therefore D. If income were lower, for example B, then investment would be greater than savings and hence the tendency would be for national income to rise. On the other hand, if income were F then savings would be greater than investment and national income would therefore tend to fall.

It is worth reiterating that there is nothing necessarily desirable about the equilibrium level of national income. In Fig. 22.10 it could be that the level of income which is necessary to maintain full employment is F but equilibrium level is lower than this, at D. There

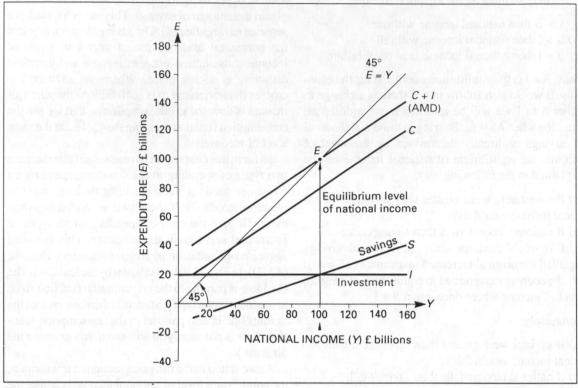

Fig. 22.9 The equilibrium of national income

will therefore be unemployment. (We develop this point more fully on page 394.)

In Fig. 22.9, what would be the effect if the investment line were to shift upwards?

The paradox of thrift

Thriftiness is usually regarded as desirable. However, changes in the overall thriftiness of an economy can have some unusual consequences. If there is an autonomous increase in the level of savings, e.g. if for some reason households decide to devote a larger proportion of their incomes to savings but investment remains unchanged, then the savings line will move upwards. This is illustrated in Fig. 22.11. Here you can see that as the savings line shifts from S to S' so the equilibrium changes from R to R'. The effect of increased savings, therefore, is to *decrease* the equilibrium level of national income. This comes about

because, if at a given level of income, people save more, they will automatically consume less. Therefore, there is less demand for goods and services.

Since most incomes are derived, directly or

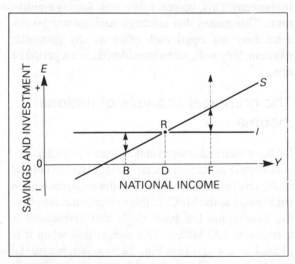

Fig. 22.10 Savings equalling investment is the equilibrium condition for the economy

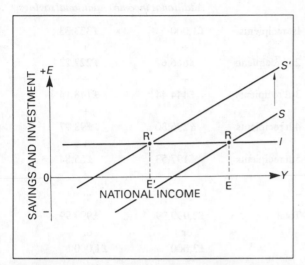

Fig. 22.11 The paradox of thrift. Increased savings cause the equilibrium level of national income to fall

indirectly, from the sale of goods and services, it follows that there will be less income. This is what brings about the paradox of thrift. The paradox can be further illustrated if we dispense with the assumption that investment is constant. We will now assume that investment is related to income. This is a fairly realistic assumption in that the production of more goods and services at a higher level of income will demand a greater capital stock and vice versa. The investment line now slopes upward from left to right. In Fig. 22.12, we again consider the effect of an upward shift in the savings line. Here the paradox is fully illustrated in that not only does increased saving bring about a lower level of income and investment but it also leads ultimately to less being saved. This effect comes about because there is a lesser ability to save at the lower level of income.

The effect of increased thriftiness also depends upon the state of the economy. In times of inflation an increase in savings might reduce the inflationary pressure in the economy and therefore would be a desirable thing. If, however, we have an economic depression with high unemployment an increase in thriftiness could be quite disastrous, taking us into a vicious deflationary spiral. It would appear, therefore, that if we 'tighten our belts' in times of economic depression, the depression is likely to be made even worse. This is what Keynes meant when he said 'every time you save five shillings you put a man out of work

for a day'. The high propensity to save in the late 1970s and the early 1980s contributed to the worsening of the recession in the economy.

The investment multiplier

One of the most famous theorems put forward by Keynes is that of the *investment multiplier*. In doing this he was building on the work of *Kahn* from whose name the abbreviation for the multiplier (K) comes. The multiplier is concerned with the effects of changes in investment upon the equilibrium level of national income. In Fig. 22.13 you can see the effect of an upward movement in the investment line. Here you can see that the equilibrium has moved from R to R' and that the equilibrium level of income has risen from D to E. You can also see that the rise in income D to E appears to be greater than the rise in investment I to I'.

This is indeed so. If you turn back to Fig. 22.9 and imagine that investment were to increase by £10 billion, from £20 billion to £30 billion, you will see that the new equilibrium level of income would be £130 billion. In this case a rise in investment of £10 billion has caused an increase in income of £30 billion. This is known as the *multiplier effect*. If we measure the ratio of one to the other, that is the change in investment to the change in income, we obtain a figure known as the *multiplier* (K).

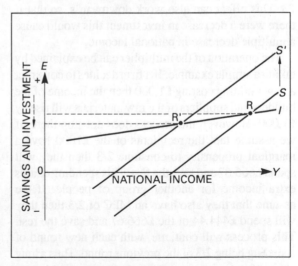

Fig 22.12 The paradox of thrift. Increased savings eventually lead to less being saved

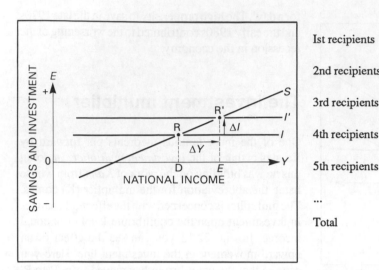

Fig. 22.13 The multiplier effect

	Additional income	Additional savings
Ist recipients	£1,000	£333.33
	+	+
2nd recipients	£666.67	£222.22
	+	+
3rd recipients	£444.44	£148.14
	+	+
4th recipients	£296.30	£98.77
	+	+
5th recipients	£197.53	£65.84
	+	+
...	...	...
Total	£2,999.99	£999.99
	or	or
	£3,000	£1,000

$$K = \frac{\Delta Y}{\Delta I}$$

$$K = \frac{30}{10}$$

$$K = 3$$

In this case the multiplier is 3. This means that every extra £1 of investment that is injected into the economy will eventually cause national income to rise by £3. This effect can also work downwards, so that if there were a decrease in investment this would cause a multiple decrease in national income.

The operation of the multiplier can be explained by taking a simple example. If a firm decides to construct a new building costing £1,000 then the income of the builders and suppliers of the raw materials will rise by £1,000. However, the process does not stop there. If we assume that the recipients of the £1000 have a marginal propensity to consume 2/3 then they will spend £666.67 and save the rest. This spending causes extra income for another group of people. If we assume that they also have an MPC of 2/3 then they will spend £444.44 of the £666.67 and save the rest. This process will continue, with each new round of spending being 2/3 of the previous round. Thus a long chain of extra income, extra consumption and extra saving is set up.

The process will come to a halt when the additions to savings total £1,000. This is because the change in savings is now equal to the change in investment and, therefore, the economy is returned to equilibrium because S = I once again. At this point the additions to income total £3,000. Thus, £1,000 extra investment has created an extra £3,000 income, demonstrating that, in this case, the value of the multiplier is 3.

It would be rather cumbersome to work things out in this manner every time. Fortunately, the figures above represent a well-known mathematical principle called an *infinite geometric progression* which has the value of $1/(1 - r)$. In this case r represents the MPC. Thus, we can derive a formula for the multiplier, which is:

$$\text{the multiplier (K)} = \frac{1}{1 - \text{MPC}}$$

This can also be written as:

$$K = \frac{1}{\text{MPS}}$$

This is because MPC + MPS = 1.

If the value of the MPC is 2/3, then:

$$K = \frac{1}{1 - 2/3}$$

$$= 3$$

Table 22.2 A model of the accelerator. Capital-output ratio = 2. Capital is replaced over a five year period

Year (1)	Aggregate demand £m (2)	Capital stock required £m (3)	Investment Replacement £m (4)	Net £m (5)	Total £m (6)
1	100	200	40	—	40
2	120	240	40	40	80
3	130	260	40	20	60
4	140	280	40	20	60
5	120	240	—	—	—
6	120	240	40	—	40

Determine the value of the multiplier (K) if the MPC is:

(a) **0.66;**
(b) **0.75;**
(c) **0.8.**

The accelerator

Induced and autonomous investment

So far in this chapter we have maintained that investment is determined by factors such as technological change, business expectations and the rate of interest. This investment is often termed *autonomous investment* because it is not determined by the working of the rest of the system in the way that, say, saving is determined by income. Indeed, for most of the chapter we have assumed that investment is constant. There is a theory, however, which maintains that *new* investment is determined by changes in the level of demand. Such investment is termed *induced investment* since it is induced by changes in the system. The relationship between the level of demand and the level of investment is called the *accelerator principle*. The level of aggregate demand in the economy may of course be equated with the level of income. The accelerator principle is that small changes in the *rate of change* of aggregate demand bring about much larger changes in the absolute level of investment demand. This is best explained by using a simple model of an economy.

A model of the accelerator

In this economy the initial capital stock is valued at £200m. When fully employed, this stock is just adequate to produce the £100m of goods which constitute the aggregate demand in the economy for a year. That is to say, there is a capital-output ratio of 2 which means that a capital stock of £2 is necessary to produce a flow of output of £1. The capital in this economy has a life of five years and is replaced evenly so that a replacement investment of £40m is needed to maintain the capital stock. This is illustrated in Year 1 in Table 22.2.

In Year 2 demand rises by 20% to £120m. To meet this demand the economy will need a capital stock of £240m. This is £40m more than it has. Therefore, in Year 2 the economy's demand for capital will be £40m for replacement and an additional 40m to meet the new demand. Thus, the total demand for capital is £80m. Between Year 1 and Year 2 a 20% rise in aggregate demand has brought about a 100% rise in investment demand. This is an illustration of the accelerator principle.

Now assume that in Year 3 demand rises to £130m. The capital stock required is now £260m. Therefore, there will be a demand for £20m of extra capital but the total demand for capital will have *fallen*. The capital demand is now £40m for replacement and £20m for the new capital. The £40m of extra capital last year will not need replacing for a further five years. Therefore, although aggregate demand was still rising, capital demand has fallen. This is because when the *rate of increase* of aggregate demand falls the *absolute* level of induced investment will decline. This is further illustrated between Years 3 and 4 where the demand for capital is constant because the rate of increase is constant. Between Years 4 and 5 aggregate demand drops from £140m to £120m and the capital stock required, therefore, decreases from £280m to £240m. There is therefore no need to replace the £40m of capital stock which has worn out. Thus, capital demand, both replacement and net, is eliminated. Finally, in Year 6 demand is stabilised at £120m; it therefore becomes necessary to replace the £40m of capital stock that will have worn out.

From this example you can see that the accelerator principle links the rate at which aggregate demand is changing to the absolute level of investment demand. It is because of this principle that the capital goods industries, such as shipbuilding, construction and iron and steel, tend to suffer from much more severe ups and downs in their fortunes than other sectors of the economy. For these industries it is often a case of 'famine or feast'.

Suppose that an economy has an initial capital stock of £600 million. When fully employed, this stock is just adequate to produce the £200 million of goods which constitute the aggregate demand in the economy for a year. That is to say, there is a capital:output ratio of 3. The capital in this economy has a life of 10 years and is replaced evenly. The table below illustrates the changes in the level of aggregate demand over six years. Assuming all other things remain equal, complete the remaining four columns of the table to show the effect of the accelerator.

A modified accelerator

From the example above it might be inferred that the capital goods sector of the economy is subject to massive reverses of fortunes. It should be remembered, however, that the accelerator principle only refers to induced investment. There is an addition to this autonomous investment. This is determined by other factors. Furthermore, we assumed that the capital stock of the country was fully employed and, therefore, that the additional demand could only be met by increasing investment. If there was unemployed capital in the economy, a rise in demand could be met by utilising the spare capacity. However, even if all the capital in the economy were fully employed, there are several factors which moderate the effect of the accelerator.

First, businesses learn from experience. This means that they are unlikely to double their capacity on the strength of one year's orders. Conversely, if demand is dropping, they might be willing to increase their inventories against a rise in demand in subsequent years. It may also be the case that the capital-output ratios are not as constant as suggested by our example. In the example it was assumed that £2 of capital was necessary to produce £1 of goods. If demand rose it might, however, be possible to obtain more output from the existing capital stock by varying the other factors of production. For example, the workforce might undertake shift work or overtime to meet the extra demand.

Finally, the depreciation and replacement of capital might be a function of factors other than time. In our example it was assumed that the capital wore out after five years. If there was an increase in demand it might

The accelerator. Capital – output = 3. Capital is replaced over a 10-year period. (All figures in £ millions.)

year (1)	Aggregate demand (2)	Capital stock required (3)	Replacement (4)	Investment Net (5)	Total (6)
1	£200	£600			
2	220				
3	230				
4	240				
5	220				
6	200				

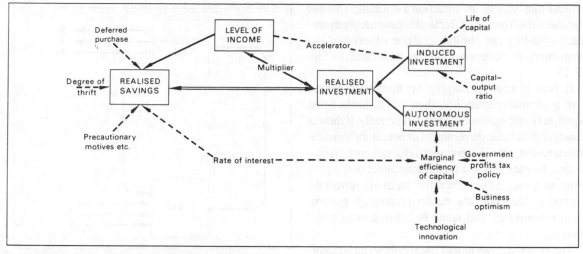

Fig. 22.14 The determination of national income

be possible to continue using old capital equipment after it was planned to scrap it. Often the period over which capital is depreciated is an accounting convenience and does not correspond to the physical life of the capital. Conversely, capital may become technologically obsolete long before it has physically depreciated.

The multiplier and the accelerator

Students frequently confuse the multiplier with the accelerator. From the above explanations of these two principles you can see that there is no direct relationship between them. Indeed, there is a great contrast between them in that for the accelerator to expand output it is necessary for the economy to be operating at or near capacity, whereas for the multiplier to affect output it is necessary that there be unemployed resources. Fig. 22.14 summarises the main factors in the determination of the equilibrium level of national income which we have considered so far.

Other components of national income

The economy we have been considering so far has been a closed economy with no government intervention, i.e we have not considered the effects of the

government and foreign trade upon national income. To obtain a full picture of the economy we must do so.

Government fiscal policy in income determination

The government's budget used to be regarded simply as a method of raising taxes to meet necessary expenditure. Since Keynes' analysis of national income we realise that the budget has other important effects. This is because taxation (T) is a withdrawal or leakage from the circular flow of income while government

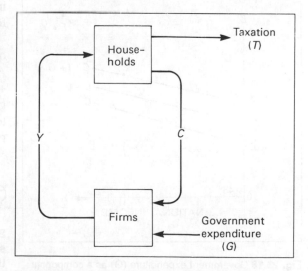

Fig. 22.15 Fiscal policy in the circular flow of income

expenditure (G) is an injection or addition to the circular flow. Thus, the effects of taxation and government spending are similar to those of savings and investment respectively. This is illustrated in Fig. 22.15.

If there is a *budget surplus*, i.e. taxation is greater than government spending, then, other things being equal, national income will fall. Conversely, if there is a *budget deficit*, i.e. government expenditure is greater than taxation, then the tendency is for national income to rise. Keynes realised that management of the government's budget could therefore be used to direct the economy. Directing the economy through government expenditure and taxes is referred to as *fiscal policy*.

The effect of government fiscal policy can be incorporated into the graphical analysis of national income. This is illustrated in Fig. 22.16. In the diagram you can see that in addition to consumption spending and investment spending we now add government spending (G). Thus, total demand in the economy is now C + I + G. You should also note that there is a multiplier effect from government spending.

Other things being equal, if there were unemployment in the economy, the correct government policy would be to run a budget deficit, thereby increasing aggregate demand. Conversely, if there were too much spending in the economy, i.e. inflation, then the correct fiscal policy would be to run a budget surplus.

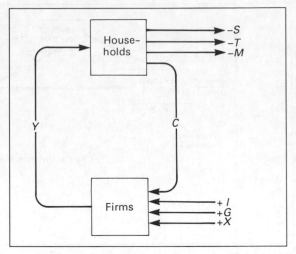

Fig. 22.17 The components of national income

Foreign trade in income determination

Exports (X) may be regarded as an injection into the circular flow of income. This is because money will flow into the country in return for the goods exported, thereby creating additional income. Imports (M), on the other hand, are a leakage since we must send money out of the country to pay for them. If there is a *trade surplus*, i.e. exports are greater than imports, the tendency will be for national income to rise. A *trade deficit*, however, will decrease the level of national income. Hence the external trading position is crucial for the health of the economy.

We now have a complete picture of the components of national income. This is illustrated in Fig. 22.17. Aggregate demand for the economy is now C + I + G + (X - M). Foreign trade may be incorporated into the graphical analysis of national income in a similar way to fiscal policy. There will therefore also be a multiplier effort from foreign trade.

Study the diagram on the next page, which represents a development of the circular flow model of the economy illustrated in Fig.22.17, and complete the following tasks.

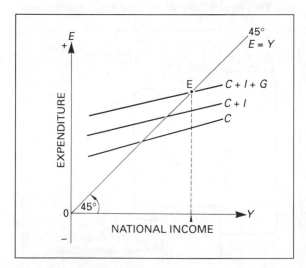

Fig. 22.16 Government expenditure (G) as a component of aggregate demand

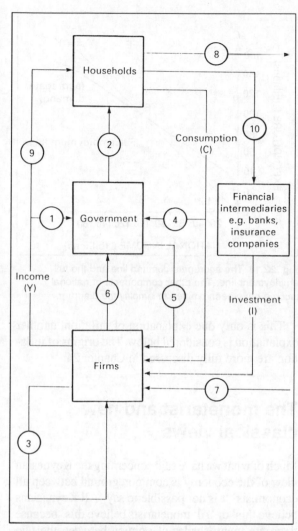

1 **Match the following items with the numbered flow which best illustrate it.**

(a) Government payments of civil servant's salaries.
(b) A British householder's purchase of a Volkswagen.
(c) Old age pensioners' deposits in a building society.
(d) A British firm's sale of goods to a West African firm.
(e) Income tax.
(f) The government's purchase of arms from a munitions firm.
(g) Disposable incomes.
(h) A firm ploughing back profit by purchasing new equipment.

(i) **VAT.**
(j) **Corporation tax.**

2 State which of the above items are:

(a) **withdrawals;**
(b) **injections;**
(c) **neither.**

A combined multiplier for the economy

Earlier in this chapter we derived a formula for the multiplier:

$$K = I \div MPS$$

It is now apparent that savings is not the only leakage from the circular flow of income. A formula for the whole economy must also take account of taxation (T) and imports (M). If we total the leakages we would therefore obtain a formula:

$$K = \frac{1}{s + t + m}$$

where s is the marginal propensity to save, t is the propensity to pay taxes and m is the marginal propensity to import. If, for example, $s = 0.15$, $t = 0.10$ and $m = 0.25$ then the value of the multiplier would be:

$$K = \frac{1}{0.15 + 0.10 + 0.25} = 2$$

The figures below show what happened to each additional £100 of notional income generated in the period 1989–90.

Increase in income	£100
of this direct taxes	£9
Consumption =	......
of this imports	£10
Consumption of domestic product at market prices =	......
of this indirect taxes	£21
Consumption of domestic product =	......

1 **Fill in the missing values.**

2 On the basis of these figures, determine the value of the multiplier.

3 What would be the effect upon the size of the multiplier if:

(a) VAT were cut to 8%;
(b) the propensity to import were to increase?

Inflationary and deflationary gaps

At any particular time there is a level of national income which, if attained would be sufficient to keep all resources in the economy fully employed. In Fig. 22.18 this is represented by the vertical line FE, the full employment line. In this diagram the equilibrium level of national income, £100 billion, corresponds with the full employment level. It has already been stressed, however, that the equilibrium level of national income is fortuitous.

If there is insufficient demand in the economy the equilibrium will occur at a lower level of income and to the left of the FE line. This is illustrated in Fig. 22.19*(a)*. Here you can see that the equilibrium level of national income is £40 billion and there is, therefore, severe unemployment in the economy. The distance between the 45° line and the C + I line at the full employment level of national income is referred to as a *deflationary gap*. In order for unemployment to be eliminated, the C + I line must be moved up by £20 billion? Why would extra spending or £20 billion raise national income by £60 billion? The answer is that in this case the multiplier is 3. In Fig. 22.19*(b)* the equilibrium level of national income appears to be to the right of the FE line at £160 billion. This is because people in the economy are trying to buy more goods and services than can be produced at full employment. There is 'too much money chasing too few goods'. The result of this is that excess demand forces up prices and there is inflation. The demand for goods and services has thus been met but only in money terms. The vertical distance between the C + I line and the 45° line at the full employment level of income is referred to as an *inflationary gap*. In this example it would be necessary to lower the C + I line by £20 billion to eliminate inflation. Again note that, because of the multiplier, cutting expenditure by £20 billion causes income to decline by £60 billion.

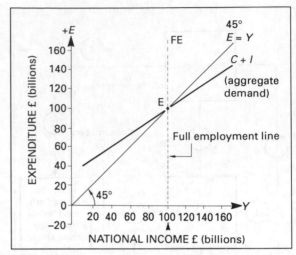

Fig. 22.18 The aggregate demand line and the full employment line. The other components of national income have been omitted to simplify the diagram.

This is only one explanation of inflation, another explanation is considered below. The origins of inflation are more fully discussed in Chapter 24.

The monetarist and new classical views

Much of what we have said concerning the Keynesian view of the economy is common ground between all economists. It is not possible to say 'All Keynesians believe this' or 'All monetarists believe this' because there are many shades of opinion between the two views. In addition to this, there are other models of the economy such as the New Classical School and the Rational Expectations School. Then there are, of course, totally different views such as the Marxist view.

However, in modern political/economic debate it has been the Keynesian–monetarist argument which attracted most attention in the 1970s and early 1980s. During the late 1980s, monetarism was less in favour and the new classical argument came to the fore. There is, however, much common ground between the two views. Let us first consider monetarism.

Monetarism

The leading figure in monetarism is the American

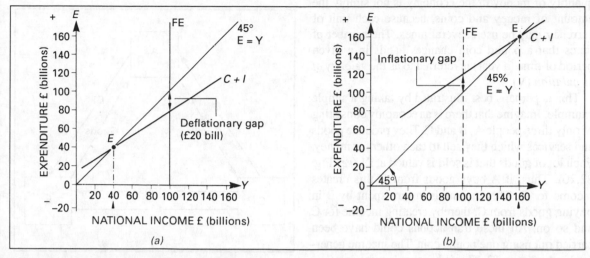

Fig. 22.19 (a) Deflationary gap (b) Inflationary gap

Keywords

Equilibrium of national income
The level of national income which if reached would not tend to change. It occurs when injections are equal to withdrawals.

Aggregate demand
The total of all spending in the economy. It is given by the expression C+I+G+(X–M).

Paradox of thrift
A theorem which suggests that a rise in the propensity to save might actually result in less savings.

The multiplier
The tendency for small increases in the level of injections into the economy to cause a greater rise in the level of income. Originally stated by Keynes as:

$$K = \frac{I}{I - MPC}$$

Combined multiplier
Given by the formula

$$K = \frac{I}{s + t + m}$$

The accelerator
Small changes in the level of aggregate demand in the economy cause *accelerated* changes in the level of investment demand.

Budget surplus
If government revenues are greater than taxation,

then this decreases national income in a multiple manner.

Trade surplus
If exports are greater than imports, then this increases national income in a multiple manner.

Inflationary gap
The inflationary tendency in the economy caused by an equilibrium in the national income above that corresponding to full employment.

Deflationary gap
Unemployment in the economy caused by an equilibrium below the level of full employment.

---

economist Milton Friedman. In order to understand the argument we must first investigate the quantity theory of money.

The quantity theory of money

In any economy, goods and services are constantly being exchanged for money. At the same time organisations are buying the services of factors of production. Every time a person buys a commodity from someone else this creates income for the seller. It is impossible to spend money without creating income for someone else. Thus everyone's income is someone else's expenditure and vice versa. Exchange is carried out through the medium of money. However, the quantity of money in the economy is not simply the amount of money and coins, because each unit of currency may be used several times. The number of times that a pound coin changes hands in a given period of time (a year) is referred to as the *velocity of circulation* (V).

This is perhaps best illustrated by taking a simple example. Imagine that there is an economy consisting of only three people A, B and C. They produce goods and services which they sell to each other for money. Each lot of goods that is sold is valued at £1 (*see* Fig. 22.20). Thus, if A buys goods from B this creates income for B. This income is in turn spent by B in buying goods from C, thereby creating income for C and so on. All these transactions could have been carried out using one pound coin. The income generated is, however, £3. This is because income is a *flow* of money with respect to time, while the amount of money is a *stock*. An analogy might be a central heating system. The quantity of water in the system is the stock, which is constantly being circulated around. The quantity of water passing through any particular part of the system is the flow. The stock may remain constant while the flow becomes greater or smaller as the system is speeded up or slowed down. Similarly, the amount of income in an economy does not solely depend upon the stock of money but also upon how quickly it is being used. The quantity of money is calculated as the stock of money (M) multiplied by the velocity of circulation (V).

Quantity of money = M x V

In the above example this would be £1 x 3 = £3. Since everyone's income is someone else's expenditure this could also be looked at in another way. It is possible to take the *general price level* (P) of the goods, in our example £1, and multiply it by the number of transactions (T), in our example 3. This would give the same figure £3. So that we derive the formula

MV = PT

This is known as the quantity equation of money. It was first developed by the American economist Irving Fisher in the 1930s. The quantity equation has been revived by Friedman (and others) and modern monetarism is based on a restatement of the terms in the equation.

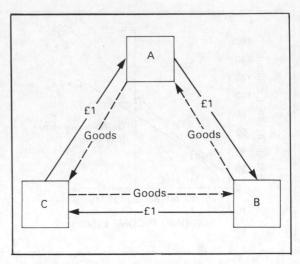

Fig. 22.20 The counter-cyclical flow of goods and money between three individuals

Consider the following information about a hypothetical economy: The money stock (M) = £30 million; the velocity of circulation (V) = 4 and the number of transactions (T) = 20 million per year.

1 What is the general level of prices (P)?

2 If the stock of money were to increase to £40 but the velocity of circulation (V) and the number of transactions (T) were to remain constant, what would be the new level of prices (P)?

3 If in the original situation the velocity of circulation were to rise to V=5 and the number of transactions were to rise to T=25 million, what would be the new general level of prices?

Monetarist propositions

1 Probably the most important assertion of monetarists is that the velocity of circulation (V) is constant, or at least, predictable. This being the case, it follows that any change in M must lead to a change in money national income (PT). This seemingly abstract proposition translated rather crudely means that inflation is caused by changes in the money supply *and by nothing else*. Critics of monetarism argue that the causation is the other way round; that is to say that the money supply adjusts to the level of economic activity. We can re-translate this argument to say that it is a debate between whether inflationary pressures in the economy cause the money supply to change or whether changes in the money supply cause inflation.

2 It is argued that if the government does not intervene in the economy, there will be an automatic tendency towards the 'national level of unemployment'. Put another way; that government attempts to eliminate unemployment by managing aggregate demand (as suggested on page 392) are more likely to cause inflation than they are to create 'real' jobs.

3 Monetarists also maintain that, left to itself, the economy will reach an equilibrium at, or near, full employment, i.e. the natural level of unemployment, and that any government interference is likely to cause instability in the economy.

Monetarist policy recommendations

Unlike Keynesians, monetarists are against the use of fiscal policy to manipulate the level of aggregate demand. Instead, they recommend a 'fixed throttle' approach of limiting the growth of the money supply to that consistent with the growth of the 'real' economy. No attempt should be made to use monetary policy to offset short-term disturbances in the economy because such efforts are likely to make matters worse because of the difficulties of predicting short-term changes and because of the time-lags which occur in the implementation of policies. Monetarists also oppose the use of fiscal policy because they argue that any increase in public expenditure will increase the demand for funds in the economy and so *crowd out* private investment.

We can summarise the monetarists' major policy recommendation as: maintain a steady growth in the money supply and otherwise leave things well alone.

New classical economics

Much of what has just been said about monetarism is also true for new classical economics.

New classical economics is the application of classical economics, i.e. theories of market price, applied to the macroeconomy. This means that the economy is

governed by prices and this results in the most efficient running of the economy. In turn, this automatically ensures that all resources in the economy are used.

Thus, new classicists argue, like monetarists, that unemployment will settle at the natural level and attempts to reduce it below this natural level will fail. Any attempt to stabilise output or unemployment below or above the natural rate by fiscal or monetary policies will prove ineffective and will not alter the value of real variables in the long-run.

The new classical macroeconomists therefore attempt to show that the economy is essentially self-regulating. This is in opposition to the central Keynsian idea of managing the level of aggregate demand. Instead, new classical economics focuses on supply-side economics.

Supply-side economics

The apparent failure of Keynsian demand-management policies in the 1970s made economists and politicians turn to examine the supply side of the economy. Supply-siders maintain that the principle determinant of the rate of growth of natural output is the allocation and efficient use of the real resources in the economy such as labour and capital. This means that supply-siders are concerned with the shape of the *aggregate supply curve*.

Much concern is therefore given to those factors which impede the free and efficient use of the factors of production. Chief among these are believed to be disincentives to work and invest as a result of the structure of taxes and also the restrictive practices of trade unions. Thus, supply-siders would recommend lowering taxes and decreasing union legal rights and immunities.

Supply-side based policies were followed by the Reagan government in the USA and the Thatcher government in the UK.

National income accounts

Whatever theory of national income we adopt we have the problem of measuring what is going on in the economy. In this last section of the chapter we con-

Table 22.3 Gross national product by category for expenditure (expenditure method) 1988.

Category of expenditure	£ million
1 Consumers' expenditure (C)	293,569
2 General government final consumption (G)	91,847
3 Gross domestic fixed capital formation (I)	88,751
4 Value of physical increase in stocks and work in progress (I)	4,371
5 Export of goods and service (X)	108,533
6 *less* imports of goods and services (M)	−125,194
Gross domestic product (GDP) at market prices	461,877
Factor cost adjustments	
7 *less* taxes on expenditure (T)	75,029
Subsidies	5,883
Statistical discrepancy	2,056
Gross domestic product (GDP) at factor cost (average estimate)	394,787
Net property income from abroad	5,619
Gross national product (GNP) at factor cost	400,406
less capital consumption	−54,769
8 National income (Y) (i.e. net national product (NNP)	345,637

Source: United Kingdom National Accounts, *CSO*

sider how the national accounts are arrived at. The figures are published annually every September by HMSO as the *United Kingdom National Accounts*, this publication usually being known as the 'Blue Book'. The figures are also to be found in the *Annual Abstract of Statistics* and the *Monthly Digest of Statistics*.

National income is measured in three different ways: as national *income*, national *output* and national *expenditure*. The idea of this is to give a measure of all the wealth produced, distributed and consumed in the economy over the period of a year. Since 'everyone's income is someone else's expenditure', it should be clear that these are three different ways of arriving at the same figure. Hence, we can arrive at the statement:

National income = National output = National expenditure

That is to say, national income is the total of the incomes of the inhabitants of the country which should be equal to the value of all the goods and services in the economy (the production of which gives rise to incomes). This, in turn, should be equal to the value of all expenditure on goods and services, both consumer goods and capital (investment) goods. Because of the

enormity of the task of calculating these values, an average figure from all three measures is regarded as the current value. The difference between this average value and that obtained by the income, output and expenditure methods appears in the accounts as the item *statistical discrepancy*.

National expenditure method

The national expenditure method of calculating national income is the method which most closely corresponds with the way in which we have examined the components of national income. If you examine Fig. 22.21 and Table 22.3 together you will see this correspondence. Thus, if we consider items (1) to (7) we arrive at a total for the gross domestic product (GDP) in the same way that the total C + I + G + (X - M). However, much of the investment that has taken place has been to cover depreciation and therefore we must subtract *capital consumption*. After the minor adjustment for *net property income from abroad* we arrive at the figure for the national income (net national product). Thus, we have demonstrated that national income (Y) = C + I + G + (X − M).

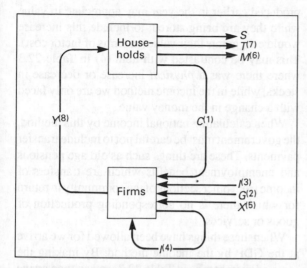

Fig. 22.21 The components of national income. The numbered items correspond to items in Table 22.3. *See* also Fig. 22.17.

We will consider some of the items in the account in more detail.

Consumers' expenditure

This includes all the consumers' expenditure on goods and services except for the purchase of new houses, which is included in 'gross fixed capital formation'.

General government final consumption

The main portion of this is the provision by the government of public and merit goods such as defence and education. Since these are not 'sold' to consumers at an economic price, they are, here, calculated at their cost of production.

Gross domestic fixed capital formation

Fixed capital formation is the major portion of *investment* in the economy. It is shown in Fig. 22.21 as being carried out by firms. But investment is in fact undertaken by firms, government and households and it includes such things as the construction of new factories, hospitals and houses.

The value of physical increases in stocks and work in progress

It is quite likely that the stock of goods held by businesses at the end of the year will be different from that at the beginning. The value of the physical difference in the size of the stocks is counted as part of investment in the economy. It is possible, however, for this figure to be positive or negative.

Exports and imports

Exports create income for persons in this country and are therefore added to national income whereas imports create income for persons overseas and are therefore subtracted from national income.

Foreign trade is extremely important to the UK. In 1988 26.3% of our resources were taken up in producing goods and services for export. On the other hand, we also imported goods and services to the value of 31.7% of our GDP.

Gross domestic product (GDP)

When we total all the above amounts we arrive at a figure known as the *gross domestic product at market prices*. This is the value of national income (net of foreign trade) in terms of money actually spent. This, however, is misleading since the price of many articles includes taxes or subsidies. To obtain the value of national income in terms of the resources used to produce it, we must subtract the taxes on expenditure levied by the government and add on the amount of subsidies. When this has been done we arrive at a figure known as the *gross domestic product at factor cost*. This is the most commonly used measure of national income and you will see that it appears in all three modes of measurement.

Gross national product (GNP)

The GDP represents the extent to which resources (or factors) are used in the economy. National income can, however, be affected by rent, profits, interest and dividends paid to, or received from, overseas. This is shown in Table 22.3 as *net property income from abroad*. This figure may be either positive or negative.

When this has been taken into account we arrive at the *gross national product at factor cost*.

Net national product (NNP)

The capital stock of the country such as roads, factories, machines, etc., gradually wears out. Part of the gross fixed capital formation is, therefore, to replace worn out capital and this is referred to as *capital consumption*. When this has been subtracted we arrive at a figure known as the *net national product*. The NNP gives the measure of national income in that it represents the most important determinant of the standard of living. The GDP, on the other hand, gives a measure of the extent to which resources are being utilised in the economy.

National income method

Table 22.4 illustrates the second method by which national income is measured. Here you can see that income from all different sources is totalled to give the GDP.

The imputed charge for the consumption of non-trading capital is principally the imputed rent for owner-occupied houses. To arrive at the GDP an amount of stock appreciation must be deducted. Goods produced earlier in the year may appreciate in value while they are being stored; to include this increase would exaggerate their value (in terms of factor cost). This may be contrasted with item (4) in Table 22.3 where there was a *physical* increase or decrease in stocks, while in the income method we are only faced with a change in the money value.

When calculating national income by this method, the government must be careful not to include transfer payments. These are things such as old age pensions and unemployment benefits which are transfers of income from other sections of the community in return for which there is no corresponding production of goods or services.

When these things have been allowed for we arrive at the GDP by the income method. By making the same adjustments as in Table 22.3 we can then arrive at the figures for GNP and NNP.

National output method

The final method by which national income is calculated is to total the contributions made by the various sectors (industries) of the economy. This is illustrated in Table 22.5 where, as you can see, the largest contribution comes from the manufacturing sector. This is hardly surprising in a highly industrialised

Table 22.4 Gross national product by category of income (income method) 1988.

Category of income	£ million
Income from employment	249,775
Income from self-employment	42,617
Gross trading profits of companies	70,242
Gross trading surpluses of public corporations and government enterprises	7,216
Rent	27,464
Imputed charge for consumption of non-trading capital	3,408
less stock appreciation	−6,116
Gross domestic product (GDP) (income based)	394,606
Statistical discrepancy	181
Gross domestic product (GDP) (average estimate)	394,787
Net property income from abroad	5,619
Gross national product (GNP)	400,406
less capital consumption	−54,769
National income (Y) (i.e. net national product NNP)	345,637

Source: United Kingdom National Accounts, CSO

Table 22.5 Gross domestic product by industry (output method) 1988.

Industry	£ million
Agriculture forestry and fishing	5,625
Energy and water supply	21,845
Manufacturing	93,433
Construction	25,745
Distribution, hotels and catering; repairs	55,131
Transport and communication	28,657
Banking, finance, insurance, business services and leasing	76,922
Ownership of dwellings	21,407
Public administration, national defence and compulsory social security	27,023
Education and health services	35,237
Other services	25,785
Total	416,810
Adjustment for financial services	−22,204
Gross domestic product at factor cost (income based)	394,606
Statistical discrepancy	181
Gross domestic product (average estimate)	394,787

Source: United Kingdom National Accounts, *CSO*

economy such as the UK although this is declining in relative importance and service industries, such as banking, are becoming more important. When calculating the GDP in this manner the government must be useful to avoid *double counting*. To do this, only the value added by each business should be included. For example, the value of the steel in motor vehicles should not be included if it has already been counted in the steel industry. In Table 22.5 the figures for the various sectors are shown before allowance has been made for the net interest payments on the borrowing. This is allowed for as the composite figure *adjustments for financial services*. After this has been allowed for, we arrive at the GDP at factor cost. By then making adjustments for net property income from abroad and for capital consumption we can arrive at the GNP and the NNP.

The table on the next page presents all the figures necessary for the calculation of the Gross National Product by the expenditure method. It also contains some figures only relevant to other methods of calculation.

1 Prepare a statement of national product by the expenditure method. This should show:

(a) GDP at market prices;
(b) GDP at factor prices;
(c) GNP at factor cost;
(d) Net national product.

2 Discuss the difficulties involved in compiling national income accounts.

Conclusion

This has been a mainly theoretical chapter and, as you have seen, there are disagreements about the theory. If we take Keynesianism and new classical macroeconomics as being the two poles of the debate we could summarise the differences as follows. The Keynesian school argues that the economy is not self-regulating. Left to itself the equilibrium level of national income will not necessarily be that which is best for the welfare of society. It is, therefore, up to the government to intervene in the economy and, by fiscal policy, make sure that the level of aggregate demand is appropriate. New classicists, on the other hand, argue that the economy automatically tends towards an equilibrium, at the *natural level of unemployment*.

Figures for calculating GNP	£ million
Value of physical increase in stocks and work in progress	+562
Gross trading profits of companies	3,730
Export of goods and services	5,156
Net property income from abroad	233
Adjustment for financial services	−158
Consumers' expenditure	16,939
Subsidies	493
Stock appreciation	−122
General government final consumption	4,224
Subsidies	2,885
Import of goods and services	5,549
Imputed charge for consumption of non-trading capital	160
Gross domestic fixed capital formation	4,190
Taxes on expenditure	3,378
Capital consumption	2,047

Further, it is said that government intervention to alter this is likely to cause inflation. Therefore, the best policy prescription is to leave the economy well alone.

You should not draw from this the conclusion that it is just an academic debate between economists which has no relevance to the 'real' world. Even the briefest glance at the economy, which still has nearly two million people unemployed, shows us that both what we understand and what we do not understand about the economy is of profound importance. Is the unemployment due to a deficiency of aggregate demand as Keynesians argue or is there something fundamentally wrong with the *supply side* of the economy as new classicists maintain? Still worse – could this be the natural level of unemployment?

Having found that there are such differences over theory it is hardly surprising that there are equal differences over policy. The operation of government economic policy is discussed in Chapter 24.

Keywords

Monetarism
A school of economic thought which argues that

disturbances in the money supply are the principal cause of instability in the economy.

Quantity equation
MV=PT: in which M is a measure of the money stock, V is the velocity of circulation, P the general level of prices and T the number of transactions in the economy.

New classical economics
The school of thought based on classical economics which believes that the economy is run by prices and is self-regulating.

National income accounts
Various measures of economic activity in the economy published annually in the 'Blue Book'.

National expenditure method
National product calculated by totalling all spending in the economy.

National income method
National product calculated by totalling all incomes in the economy.

National output method
National product calculated by totalling the contribution made by each industry to the economy.

Learning project

The components of national income

Table 22.6 gives the consumption function for a closed economy with no government intervention. Having studied the information in the table, complete the tasks which follow.

1 Redraw and complete the columns for savings and the APC and MPC.

2 Draw a graph using the figures in the Table 22.6 to

Table 22.6 The determination on national income (all figures £ billions)

Income (Y)	Consumption (C)	Savings (S)	Investment 1 (I¹)	Investment 2 (I²)	Average propensity to consume (APC)	Marginal propensity to consume (MPC)
0	25					
50	62.5					
80	85					
100	100					
120	115					
140	130					
160	145					
180	160					
200	175					
220	190					
240	205					

show the consumption function and the savings line (do not forget the 45° line).

3 Assume that in the first instance investment is £20 billion at all levels of income. Determine the equilibrium level of national income and demonstrate it graphically.

4 Assume that investment now rises to £30 billion at all levels of income. Determine the new equilibrium level of national income and demonstrate it graphically.

5 Explain the principle that is at work in moving between the two equilibrium levels of national income as investment changes.

6 Update the Table 22.7.

7 Construct a table similar to the Table 22.6, but omitting the investment columns, and enter the information you have obtained in it.

8 Calculate consumption, the APC and the MPC and enter them in the table.

9 With this information construct a consumption function similar to the one you drew for task two.

10 In about 200 words, account for the observed variations in the size of the APC.

Table 22.7 Personal disposable income and savings in the UK (figures in £ millions).

	1978	1979	1980	1981	1982	1983
Disposable income	113,422	136,137	160,733	177,324	192,055	206,162
Savings	12,575	16,621	21,717	22,623	22,239	20,267
	1984	1985	1986	1987	1988	
Disposable income	221,463	239,581	259,333	278,966	307,170	
Savings	22,568	22,558	20,177	17,268	13,601	

Source: National Accounts, *HMSO*

Further ideas for learning projects

1 Prepare a table to compare the percentage of GDP devoted to gross fixed capital formation of four different countries with which you are familiar, e.g. the UK, the USA, Nigeria and Malaysia. Suggest reasons for the observed differences.

2 Suggest the correct Government policies to eliminate:

(a) an inflationary gap;

(b) a deflationary gap.

3 'Nobody doubts that monetarism will stop inflation if it is practised long enough and hard enough. At some point high interest rates stop all economic activity as well as inflation. But the price is very high, not equally distributed across the population and not endurable in a democracy.'

Critically evaluate Lester Thurrow's statement in the light of the last 15 years' experience here and abroad.

23

Financial organisations

CHAPTER OBJECTIVES

After studying this chapter you should be able to:

State the attributes and functions of money;
Explain the process of credit creation;
Describe the structure of British banks;
Describe the organisations which make up the money market;
List the functions of the Bank of England;
Explain the operation of monetary policy and analyse its shortcomings.

The role of banks

Banks are the most important of all the financial organisations. They provide several essential services to both business organisations and individuals. Banking services sold overseas are also one of Britain's main export earners.

Banks act like *ledger clerks*, providing a record of financial transactions. A bank statement is the closest the average individual gets to a statement of their personal finances. Banks constitute the most important *channel for the settlement of debts* and they are also a *source of finance* and a place where *cash can be readily and easily deposited* to gain interest. In addition to this, banks today provide many *other services*: tax advice, executor and trustee services, stockbroking, insurance, etc. However, if we look at the bank's place in the whole economy we will see that its most vital function is none of these; its function is in fact the *creation of money*. We will, therefore, first have a look at money and then go on to see how banks set about creating it.

Money

What is money?

Anything that is readily acceptable as a means of payment is money. Many different things have been used as money – cowrie shells, camels, cigarettes, pigs' teeth – but the most common form of money throughout most of history has been precious metals. Only one civilisation, the Incas, has flourished without some form of money. Today, bank notes, coins and bank deposits all from part of our money supply. Only notes and coins, however, are *legal tender* and yet they do not constitute the major part of the money supply. A contrast between modern money and the forms of money, for example gold or livestock, is that the old forms had *intrinsic value* while money today, almost exclusively, has only *exchange value*. Also, money is today created by governments or business organisations so that in examining these organisations we are also examining the creation of the money supply.

The attributes of money

Listed below are some of the attributes that are necessary for an asset to function as money. From this you should appreciate not only why camels ceased to be used as money but also why such items as cigarettes have functioned as money at times when paper money lost some of these important attributes, as was the case in Germany 1945–7.

1 What is meant by the acronym EFTPOS? Give two examples of this.

2 Do you think that it is likely that we shall move to a 'cashless society'? If not, why not?

3 Consider your own expenditure pattern. What proportions are in cash, direct debit, cheques etc? How do you think your pattern will differ in ten years' time, and why?

1 Acceptability. The most important attribute of money is that it is readily acceptable. It does not, however, have to be universally acceptable.

2 Difficult to counterfeit. It is no good using something as money which people may readily forge.

3 Durability. Money should not wear out quickly. This was the major factor in the replacement of the pound note with the pound coin.

4 Stability of value. Inflation affects the acceptability of money. In 1923 hyperinflation made it completely unacceptable in Germany.

5 Portability. It would not be very convenient to use coal as money as we would have to take a tonne of it to do the week's shopping!

6 Uniformity. Money should be uniform so that we may divide it into smaller amounts, e.g. the pound coin into 100 pence. In addition one form of money should not differ from another. For example, if gold coins circulated today everyone would be tempted to hold the gold thereby pushing it out of circulation. This illustrates *Gresham's law*, 'bad money drives out good'.

1 How much do you know about your own currency? Examine a £1 coin. Explain all the inscrip-

tions on it.

2 Pound coins are legal tender. How large a transaction can be paid for in coins?

What does money do?

Money is so much part of our lives today that we perhaps fail to recognise the *functions* which it performs..

1 A medium of exchange. Its most vital function is to act as a medium of exchange, i.e. the means by which we swap one lot of real goods or services for another. The alternative, barter, is very restrictive because it depends upon the *double coincidence of wants*. That is to say, if you have chickens and you want shoes then you must find someone who wishes to exchange shoes for chickens. It is much easier if we sell the chickens for money and then exchange the money for shoes. This vastly increases the possibilities for trade.

2 A unit of account. All the many disparate commodities which make up the economy – suits of clothes, litres of oil, visits to the cinema – can be reduced to a common unit of account and hence compared in value by giving them a price. Of course, one might argue that many things on which one places great value command little or no price. However the accountant, the banker, the lawyer, the economist and the business organisation are interested only in exchange value, i.e. the price. Perhaps at this stage we might recall Oscar Wilde's famous comment: 'What is a cynic? A man who knows the price of everything and the value of nothing.'

3 A store of wealth. If we did not have money and we wished to save, we would have to stockpile the things which we thought we would need in the future. This would be most inconvenient and we might find our requirements changing. Money allows us a convenient means of saving up for any requirement.

4 A standard of deferred payment. Money is the means by which we are able to settle debts in the future. Hence, we can agree to work for so many pounds a year or the bank can agree to pay us a percentage interest on each pound we deposit with it.

It hardly needs saying that without the medium of money the economy would not have developed and would not continue to develop. It is important to note that bad management of the country's money supply can hinder the development of the economy since the functions which money carries out are essential to the economy's well-being.

Consider the following list of assets.

- Land
- Diamonds
- Share certificates
- Cars
- National Savings Bonds
- Coins
- Sight deposits
- Postal orders

1 Arrange these in order of their liquidity, starting from the most liquid through to the least liquid.

2 Of the assets which *you* possess, which do you consider the most liquid and which the least?

3 Which item(s) on the above list might be considered money? Which are legal tender?

4 There is one item on the list which used to be legal tender but is not now. Which is it?

Where does money come from?

Both paper money and modern banking practice originated from the activities of goldsmiths. Goldsmiths used to accept deposits of gold coin for safe-keeping and in return issue a receipt which was in effect a *promissory note*. As time went by these notes began to be passed around in settlement of debts, acting as bank notes do today. Goldsmiths also discovered that they need not keep all the gold they had on deposit in their vaults because at any particular time only a small percentage of their customers would want their gold back. They discovered that they could lend out, say, 90% of their gold deposits keeping only 10% to meet the demands of their depositors. This relationship of the cash kept to liabilities to pay is known as the *cash ratio*. Because they had put most of the gold they had accepted on deposit back into circulation and also circulated promissory notes for the amount of gold they had accepted, the goldsmiths could be said to have increased the money supply. The completion of this process occurred in the 1680s when Francis Childs became the first banker to print bank notes.

Some of the gold which the goldsmiths had lent out would be used to pay bills and then the recipient would redeposit it with the same or another goldsmith. Then the process would be repeated, writing out more promissory notes and re-lending the gold. The limit to this process was that goldsmiths always had to keep the equivalent of 10% of their liabilities in gold. The bankers, for this is what goldsmiths had become by this time, did not really create money in the sense that they personally could not spend it. However, they could lend it out at interest and so they are said to have *created credit*.

Today this process of credit creation lies at the heart of our money supply. Originally the gold had intrinsic value and the paper money was issued on the faith in the bank. Any currency issued that was not backed by an equal amount of gold was called a *fiduciary issue*. Today, banks create credit in the form of cheque money against the security of Bank of England notes in the same manner that the old banks created bank notes on the security of gold. Today, however, the whole edifice of money rests on confidence in the banking system because all bank notes are now fiduciary issue. The creation of credit is kept under control by the Bank of England since it issues the bank notes and insists upon the banks maintaining specific ratios of assets to liabilities.

There are a number of different institutions in the UK which issue bank notes and coins. Name four of them.

Changes in the value of money

While a bank note was backed by a specific quantity of gold, its value could not change unless the value of gold changed. Today money has value only in so far as it can be exchanged for goods. Changes in the value of money adversely affect some of its most important functions.

The most common acceptable measure of the value of money is the *index of retail prices* (RPI). In this the prices of 3500 goods are sampled and their importance *weighted* in eleven major categories. All these items are then combined to give one index number. Thus, if we start off in 1974 at 100 and in 1984 discover that the index is 351 this means that on average prices have gone up by 251% or, alternatively, that the pound in 1984 is only 28% of its 1974 value. (The present index

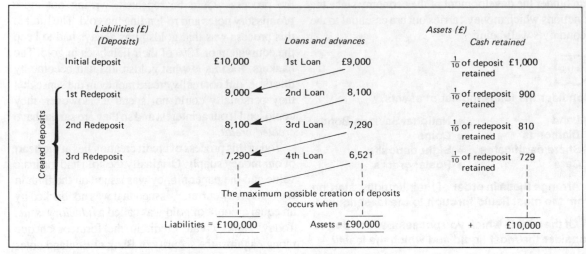

Fig. 23.1 Deposit creation in a single bank system with a 10% cash ratio

is based on 1987 (13 January 1987 = 100) and in October 1989 it stood at 117.5.)

The following information about four married couples was obtained in December 1989.

Family	A	B	C	D
Age of parents	35, 32	36, 28	60, 58	45, 42
Total income	£7,000	£28,000	£45,000	£60,000
Ages of children	2, 5, 10	—	32, 28	8, 12, 15
Residence	Rented	Owned	Owned	Owned
Changes in cost of living over previous 12 months	+9%	+15%	+6%	0%

1 Give possible reasons why the change in the cost of living varied so much among these families.

2 Give three reasons why you think that the RPI may not give an accurate measure of the cost of living.

How banks create money

A single bank system

Let us imagine there is only one bank – a large bank with which everyone in the country does business. This bank has initial deposits of £10,000 in cash so that its balance sheet would be:

Liabilities (£)		*Assets (£)*	
Deposits	10,000	Cash	10,000

The bank knows from experience that only a tenth of this money will be demanded at any particular time and so it is able to lend out £9000 at interest. The people who borrow this money use it to buy various goods and services. The shopkeepers, etc., who receive this money then put it into the bank and the bank finds the £9000 it lent out has been redeposited. This could be described as a *created deposit*. It is then able to repeat this process lending out nine-tenths of this £9000 and retaining £900. The 8100 it has lent out will find its way back to the bank again when it can again lend out nine-tenths of it and so on. This is illustrated in Fig. 23.1.

Thus, at the end of the process, with total cash of £10,000 in the system and a cash ratio of 10%, the bank is able to make loans amounting to £90,000. Although so many more deposits have been created, you will see that everything balances out because the bank still has the necessary 1/10 of its assets in cash to meet its liabilities. You can also see that each horizontal line in Fig. 23.1 balances assets against liabilities and, therefore, at no stage are accounting principles infringed. The bank's balance sheet at the end of this process would appear:

Liabilities (£)		Assets (£)	
Initial deposits	10,000	Cash	10,000
Created deposits	90,000	Loans and advances	90,000
	£100,000		£100,000

NB: The bank itself cannot distinguish between initial deposits and created deposits. The limit to credit creation in this manner is the cash ratio – here it is 10%. If it were 5% created deposits could amount to £190,000 whereas if it were 20% they could only be £40,000.

A multi-bank system

If we consider a system in which there are many banks, credit creation will go on in the same manner, except that money which is loaned out may find its way into a bank other than the one which made it. This is illustrated below where we assume that there are two banks in the system. Here each bank has raised the cash ratio to 12.5% to guard against the possibility of losing potential deposits to the other bank. The initial £10,000 is divided equally between them and with a cash ratio of 12.5% they are able to create deposits of seven times this amount.

Bank X

Liabilities (£)		Assets (£)	
Initial deposits	5,000	Cash	5,000
Created deposits	35,000	Loans and advances	35,000
	£40,000		£40,000

Bank Y

Liabilities (£)		Assets (£)	
Initial deposits	5,000	Cash	5,000
Created deposits	35,000	Loans and advances	35,000
	£40,000		£40,000

Thus, the initial £10,000 is used to support £80,000 or, put another way, each £1 of cash the bank holds secures £8 of liabilities. Regarded in this way we can see that each extra £1 cash the banking system is able to acquire enables it to expand its loans in this multiple manner. However, it is also true that if the system loses £1 cash then it must also contract its loans and deposits in a multiple manner in order to maintain its cash ratio.

If the reserve (or liquid asset) requirement of a bank is 20% and it receives additional deposits of £1 million, what amount of additional loans will it be able to make?

Modern ratios

The cash ratio was abolished in 1971 and was replaced by a 12.5% *reserve assets ratio*, although the clearing banks were expected to keep 1.5% of their assets in cash at the Bank of England. In August 1981 the *reserve assets ratio* was abolished. From this date members of the monetary sector (see page 413) are required to keep the equivalent of 0.4% (originally 0.5% and then 0.45%) of their *eligible liabilities* in cash at the Bank of England. This is held in non-operational accounts, i.e. the banks may not use this cash. The object of these non-operational, non-interest bearing accounts is to supply the Bank of England with funds. In addition to this money, banks will have to keep cash at the Bank of England for the purpose of settling inter-bank indebtedness.

Although there is no cash or reserve assets ratio, banks need to keep a minimum level of cash and liquid assets, i.e. assets that can quickly be turned into cash, in order to meet their obligations on a day-to-day basis. The Bank of England has laid down guidelines for banks to assess the volume of liquid assets which they need. The asset cover varies according to the kind of deposits (liabilities) the bank has accepted. Thus, it is not possible, at present, to state this as a simple ratio. The composition of banks' assets and liabilities is discussed in detail below.

The balance sheet of the commercial banks

The nature of banking business

Banks act as *financial intermediaries*, accepting money on deposit from one group of people, who may want it back on demand or at very short notice, and lending it out to other people for periods of time – often several years. The banks' function then is to convert short-run deposits into longer-run loans. On one side stand people who have money which they would like to lend but who would also like to be able to get it back any time they wish. On the other side are people who wish to borrow but who may not wish to pay the money back for several years. They obviously cannot do business with each other. The bank acts as *financial intermediary* accepting deposits and giving a rate of interest, and making loans and charging the borrowers a higher rate of interest. The bank manages to do this by conducting its business in such a way that it always has enough cash in hand to meet the claims of depositors wanting their money back. The bank's object in this, like any other business organisation, is to make a profit.

There are many banks in the country but by far the most important are the eight groups of 'high street' banks which make up the Committee of London and Scottish Clearing Banks. We can learn a great deal about how banks conduct their business by examining their balance sheets. An actual combined balance sheet for the clearing banks is presented in Table 23.1.

The banks' liabilities

The liabilities of the banks are mainly the deposits it has accepted. Previously there were only two main types of account. *Current* accounts consisted of money which could be withdrawn on demand and which were operated by a cheque book. They did not, usually, earn interest. *Deposit* accounts usually needed seven days notice of withdrawal if the depositor was not to lose interest. Since then, however, new kinds of accounts have been developed as banks and building societies have competed for business. Thus, for example, it is now possible to have a high interest current account which combines the benefits of both current and deposit accounts. Normally customers have to agree to keep a minimum deposit, e.g. £100, in the account to take advantage of such schemes. The rate of interest on deposit accounts is usually several per cent below the *base* rate.

Eligible liabilities

A certain portion of banks' liabilities are classified as *eligible liabilities* for the purposes of monetary control. These comprise, in broad terms, *sterling* deposit liabilities, excluding deposits having an original

Table 23.1 Balance of London & Scottish banks' groups as at 20 February, 1990.

		£ million
Liabilities		
Sterling deposits		263,144
of which sight deposits	103,257	
Foreign currency deposits		71,924
Other liabilities		61,996
Total liabilities		397,064
Assets		
Sterling		
Cash and balances with Bank of England:		
Cash ratio deposits		866
Other deposits		2,457
Market loans:		
Discount houses		7,460
Other UK monetary sector		39,204
UK certificates of deposit		5,692
Local authorities		385
Other		6,440
Bills:		
Treasury bills		1,628
Other bills		8,328
Special deposits with Bank of England		—
Investments:		
British Government stocks		2,476
Other		9,429
Advances:		
UK private sector		195,196
UK public sector		315
Overseas residents		6,272
Other sterling assets		20,805
Foreign currencies		
Market loans		52,631
Bills		471
Advances		27,237
Other		9,773
Total assets		397,064
Eligible liabilities		206,721

Source: The Committee of London and Scottish Bankers' Statistical Unit.

maturity of over two years, plus any sterling resources obtained by switching foreign currencies into sterling. The banks are allowed to *offset* certain inter-bank and money market transactions against their eligible liabilities. The changes of August 1981 widened the scope of these offsets. In February 1990 52% of the clearing banks' total liabilities were classified as eligible liabilities.

Consider the effect upon the banking system if the Bank of England were to reclassify 'eligible liabilities' so that all bank liabilities were to be considered 'eligible'.

The banks' assets

The structure of a bank's assets is most important. It illustrates the constant conflict in banking between *profitability* and *liquidity*. To earn profits banks would like to lend as much money as possible at as high a rate of interest as possible. On the other hand they must always be able to meet depositors' demand for their money (liquidity). Although most business is carried out by cheque and credit transfer, the bank must always be prepared to meet depositors' demands for notes and coins.

The assets which a bank has will have differing maturity dates. For example, the bank might be able to turn a short-run loan to another bank into cash overnight but a loan to a customer given over a five-year period will be much more difficult to liquefy. The Bank of England has therefore laid down that banks should have *liquid assets* to cover their liabilities in proportions which are related to maturity dates of their liabilities. Thus, much greater cover would be expected for short-run liabilities than for long-run ones. For example, liabilities with a maturity of over one year might require only 5% liquid asset cover while short-run money market deposits might require 100% cover. Thus, the liquid asset cover which a bank requires will depend upon the type of deposits it has accepted. It is therefore no longer possible to state this as a simple ratio; it will differ from bank to bank and from time to time. The clearing banks whose activities are relatively stable might have a predictable ratio but this will differ from other members of the *monetary sector*.

Coins and notes

These are reserves of cash kept by the banks. Since 1971 there has been no requirement to keep a specific percentage. The amount of cash which a bank has to keep in hand will depend upon the type of business it does. All banks will naturally want to keep as small a proportion of their assets in cash as possible because holdings of cash do not earn income.

Balances with the Bank of England

These are deposits of cash made by the banks at the Bank of England. They now take two forms, the *non-operational accounts* equivalent to 0.45% of the banks' *eligible liabilities* and the *operational balances* kept to operate the *clearing house* system. All cheques drawn by customers on their bank accounts go through the Clearing House at 10 Lombard Street. Here they are totalled so that at the end of each day the indebtedness of one bank to another can be settled by one transaction. This is done by the debtor bank transferring money from its Bank of England account to that of the creditor bank. The eight banks which operate this system are known as clearing banks.

If we consider the balance sheet of the clearing banks then it becomes apparent that the proportion of coins and notes and balances with the Bank of England to eligible liabilities is about 1.2%.

In recent years there have been attempts to control the activity of banks by controlling the amount of cash and the amount of bankers' balances with the Bank of England. This is known as *money base control (see page 423).*

Market loans

The market referred to is the *London money market* (which we describe in detail later in this chapter). The loans consist of money lent to other banks or to the discount houses. The money is usually lent *at call* (for one day at a time) or *short notice* (usually seven days). All banks must now agree to maintain an average of 5% of their *eligible liabilities* in the form of secured loans to a defined section of the money market.

Certificates of deposit (CDs)

If a company agrees to deposit cash with a bank for, say, two years, it will receive a high rate of interest. However, it may want its money back before then. It can have the best of both worlds by accepting a *certificate of deposit* which is *negotiable*, i.e. it can sell it on the money market if it wants its cash before the two years are up. CDs can be in sterling or in other currencies.

Local authority deposits

These are loans made through the money market to local authorities. Local authorities also issue bills and bonds in a similar manner to central government.

UK Treasury bills

These are Treasury bills which are bought by the banks from the discount houses, usually when they have only five or six weeks left to maturity.

We have considered Treasury bills and commercial bills. From your own research or elsewhere in this book, consider what is meant by a bill of exchange.

1 There is a special type of bill of exchange with which you are undoubtedly familiar. What is it?

2 If you were buying a house, you would employ a solicitor who would check whether the seller had a good title to the house. What would be the effect on commerce if the same procedure was necessary to establish title to a bill of exchange?

3 How does the law deal with this problem?

4 Describe what is meant by a negotiable instrument. To what extent does the acceptability of cash depend upon its being a negotiable instrument?

Other bills

There are commercial *bills of exchange* issued by companies who wish to borrow money for a short period.

Special deposits

If the Bank of England wishes to control the banks' lending it may call upon them to make special deposits

of cash with it. This would reduce bank lending in the multiple manner described on page 424. Usually the Bank of England calls for special deposits in amounts of 0.5% or 1% of the bank's assets. As you can see from Table 23.1, at this particular time the Bank had not called for any special deposits, nor did it during the entire 1980s.

British government stocks

These are loans to the British Government other than Treasury bills. The bank will always try to ensure that it has a *maturing portfolio* of bills, stocks, etc and that a quantity of these mature each week so that the bank has the option of liquidating its asset or re-investing.

Advances

These are bank loans and overdrafts to customers. Usually they earn a rate of interest at least 3% higher than base rate and constitute the chief earning asset of the bank. In our example they constitute 63% of sterling business. This is a typical ratio.

Liquidity

Until August 1981 banks were required to keep 12.5% of their assets in the form of *reserve assets*. As explained above, this requirement has now been dropped and the liquidity required of a bank now depends upon the type of business it does. Banks must always maintain liquidity for *prudential* reasons and the assets which banks considered liquid before 1981 were around 33%, i.e. considerably greater than the *reserve assets ratio*.

The post 1981 integrated approach to banks' liquidity does not closely define which assets are acceptable, as the old ratio did. However, the assets which the Bank of England considers as liquid are very similar to the old *reserve assets*. These are:

(a) balances with the Bank of England;
(b) money at call with the London money market;
(c) UK Treasury bills;
(d) local authority and bank bills eligible for re-discount at the Bank of England;
(e) British government stocks with less than one year to maturity.

The regulation of financial services

Until relatively recently there was little *statutory* regulation of banking in the UK. The Bank of England exercised control through *moral suasion* and through the operation of monetary policy. This was partly changed by the Banking Act 1979 but the Bank still tends to proceed by laying down guidelines which it expects the banks to follow. From 1971 to 1981 the Bank's guidelines were known as *competition and credit control*. The main change brought in by competition and credit control in 1971 was the dropping of the old *liquid assets ratio* of 28% and its replacement by the 12.5% *reserve assets ratio*. This brought about a massive expansion of bank credit which was one of the major causes of the high rates of inflation in the early and mid-1970s.

The 1970s saw great upheavals in the financial world. In 1973 there was the secondary banking crisis which forced the Bank of England to organise the 'lifeboat' operation in order to save a number of fringe banks from collapse. Another factor was the oil crisis which vastly increased the amount of money in the money markets. The 1970s also saw a great influx of foreign banks into London. It is hardly surprising, therefore, that the government and the Bank of England have found it necessary to bring in new regulations for banks.

The Banking Act 1979

On 1 October 1979 the Banking Act and the Credit Unions Act came into force. The Banking Act gave the Bank of England statutory powers to supervise banks and other 'deposit-taking institutions'. These powers brought the UK into line with the EC banking directive that all member states must have a system of authorising banks by mid-December 1979. There were three main parts of the Act.

1 Licensing of banks. It became an offence for any institution to accept deposits unless it was licensed by the Bank of England.
2 The deposit protection scheme. The aim of the scheme was to give protection to small depositors in the event of a bank failure. This part of the Act was a response to the secondary-banking crisis of 1973 and

the 'lifeboat' operation which had to be mounted to protect depositors. The scheme is similar to the Federal Deposit Insurance Corporation (FDIC) in the USA.
3 Banking names and advertisements. Only recognised banks and certain other named institutions may use the title bank or banker. The other named institutions include the Bank of England and the National Savings Bank. Foreign institutions may use the name they operate under in their home state provided that it is accompanied by an indication that the institution is formed under the law of that state. The Bank also has powers to regulate the form and content of any advertisement inviting the making of deposits.

The reasons for passing the Act were the need to comply with EC directives and also the desire to avoid another banking crisis like that of 1973. However, the failure of Johnson Matthey Bankers in 1984 showed that supervision was far from perfect and led to the Banking Act 1987 (*see* below).

Monetary control provisions 1981

These are set out in the Bank of England paper *Monetary control – provisions*. The main points of the provisions are as follows.

1 Each institution in the monetary sector was required to keep 0.45% of its *eligible liabilities* in a non-operational account at the Bank of England.
2 A new 'monetary sector' somewhat broader than the old 'banking sector' was defined. It included:

- all recognised institutions;
- National Girobank;
- some banks in the Channel Isles and Isle of Man;
- the trustee savings banks (TSBs);
- the Banking Department of the Bank of England.

3 Eligible liabilities were to be calculated in an integrated uniform manner for all institutions (*see* above, page 410).
4 The special deposit scheme was retained.
5 The list of institutions whose acceptances were eligible for discount at the Bank was widened.
6 The *reserve assets ratio* was abolished.
7 The Bank of England discontinued the regular 'posting' of the *minimum lending rate*. Instead it

operates within an unstated band of interest rates. However, it retains the right to announce the rate at which it will operate if it thinks this necessary. Such was the case in January 1985 when the Bank re-introduced minimum lending rate for one day in order to try to stop the panic on foreign exchange markets.

The Banking Act 1987

The aim of this Act was to improve the Bank of England's supervision of the monetary system. Deposit taking by banks is regulated and supervised by the Bank of England and by a committee set up by the Bank known as the Board of Banking supervision.

The Act laid down that in order to be recognised as a bank by the Bank of England, an institution must have at least £5 million paid-up capital (i.e. shares). Other financial institutions with at least £1 million paid-up capital may be allowed to provide financial services and accept deposits, but cannot use the word 'bank' in their business name.

The Building Societies Act 1986

In the UK building societies are outside the control of the Bank of England. This may seem a little curious when you consider that they take in more deposits than banks and that these deposits are included in some definitions of the money supply (*see* page 421).

During the 1980s banks and building societies became more like each other and competition between them has greatly increased. For example, banks now give mortgage loans for house purchase and most building societies will provide members with cheque books.

At law, however, building societies are friendly societies and are owned by their members, i.e. the depositors. The aim of the Building Societies Act 1986 was to allow building societies to provide a wider range of services such as personal loans. The Act also allows building societies to become plcs, which means that they can become banks.

In 1989 the Abbey National became the first building society to become a plc. It is now the fifth largest *bank* in the UK (although it avoids using the term in any description of its activities) but is not, as yet, a member of the Committee of London and Scottish Clearing Banks.

The Financial Services Act 1986

The Conservative Government of the 1980s pursued policies of liberalising financial dealings. This, however, meant that consumers needed to be protected from reckless businesses which might lose depositors' money, as was only too well illustrated by the failures of Johnson Matthey and Barlow Clowes.

The Financial Services Act 1986 was based on the principle of *self-regulation*. It set up the Securities and Investment Board (SIB) which oversees the work of a number of Self-Regulating Organisations (SROs) such as FIMBRA. Self-regulating means that these boards are nominated by the businesses which they oversee. In order for any business to offer financial services, it must be recognised by the appropriate SRO. The SROs have the power to disqualify and discipline businesses if they act in an irregular manner.

The system of SROs is illustrated in Fig. 23.2.

Activity

Which SRO do the following organisations belong to:

- Halifax Building Society
- Legal and General Assurance Co
- NatWest Bank plc
- Barclays Bank plc
- Buckmaster & Moore (stock brokers)
- Mercantile Credit (finance house)
- Bank of Cyprus
- S & G Unit Trust

Problems with the new technology

The financial service industries are particularly susceptible to the impact of the new technology. Some of the applications may be obvious to you, for example, cash machines and computerised bank statements. However, the changes are more fundamental. In Chapter 1 we discussed how the new technology is eliminating many of the middle order skills in banking. In addition to this, there are the new services such as EFTPOS (electronic funds transfer at point of sale). This will allow a customer's account to be debited directly as a sale is made in a shop. As building societies begin to compete more directly with banks, they may utilise the new technology more fully, leav-

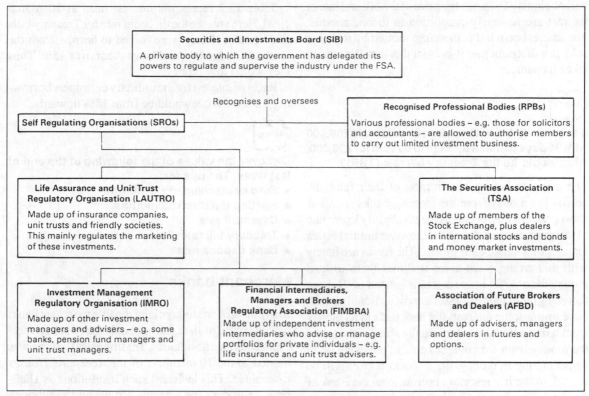

Securities and Investments Board (SIB)

A private body to which the government has delegated its powers to regulate and supervise the industry under the FSA.

Recognises and oversees

Self Regulating Organisations (SROs)

Recognised Professional Bodies (RPBs)

Various professional bodies – e.g. those for solicitors and accountants – are allowed to authorise members to carry out limited investment business.

Life Assurance and Unit Trust Regulatory Organisation (LAUTRO)

Made up of insurance companies, unit trusts and friendly societies. This mainly regulates the marketing of these investments.

The Securities Association (TSA)

Made up of members of the Stock Exchange, plus dealers in international stocks and bonds and money market investments.

Investment Management Regulatory Organisation (IMRO)

Made up of other investment managers and advisers – e.g. some banks, pension fund managers and unit trust managers.

Financial Intermediaries, Managers and Brokers Regulatory Association (FIMBRA)

Made up of independent investment intermediaries who advise or manage portfolios for private individuals – e.g. life insurance and unit trust advisers.

Association of Future Brokers and Dealers (AFBD)

Made up of advisers, managers and dealers in futures and options.

Fig. 23.2 The provisions of the Financial Services Act 1986 (FSA) established a pattern of self-regulation for the financial markets.

ing the banks with the antiquated cheque clearing system. (You will find the learning project at the end of Chapter 7 informative in this regard.)

The new technology brings with it problems of control. There are new possibilities for fraud and for financial institutions to operate unrestricted by the present system of control. So far, apart from the Data Protection Act 1984, the authorities have not really addressed themselves to these problems. Indeed, it is true to say that there is no legislation or case law which deals specifically with automated payment systems.

Other financial organisations

Discount houses

The discount houses are a group of 10 financial organisations which originally made their income from discounting commercial bills of exchange and

Treasury bills. Treasury bills are sold every week by the Bank of England on behalf of the government. They are a method of borrowing and constitute part of the national debt. A Treasury bill is a promise by the Government to pay a specific sum (£50,000) 91 days after the date the bill is issued. A discount house might offer to buy the bill for, say £48,750, in which case it has cost the government £1,250 to borrow £48,750 for 91 days. This is equivalent to an annual rate of interest of just over 10%. The Treasury bill rate is, however, not a true interest rate; it is the rate of discount and is calculated in the following manner:

$$\left(\frac{1,250}{50,000} \ \text{x} \ \frac{100}{1} \right) \text{x} \ \frac{365}{91} \ = \ 10\%$$

The discount houses often resell these bills to the clearing banks before maturity. The nearer the bill is to maturity the closer the price will be to £50,000.

If interest rates are falling this will cause discount houses to tender at a higher price. Conversely, if interest rates rise the price the Government can expect will obviously fall since the price of the bill and rate of interest are inversely proportionate to one another. The interest on a bill is therefore formed by its being sold at a discount and it is from this that the market takes its name.

If a Treasury bill with a maturity value of £100,000 with 91 days to maturity were to be sold for £96,000, what would be the Treasury bill rate (TBR)?

The discount houses obtain most of their funds by borrowing money from the clearing banks at call or short notice. Thus, they borrow at a slightly lower rate of interest than they charge the Government and in this manner they make their profits. The banks are happy with this arrangement since it allows them to lend money for only 24 hours at a time instead of 91 days, thereby giving them an asset almost as liquid as cash but earning some interest. If a bank calls in its money from a discount house it is usually able to re-borrow the money from the creditor bank. In the event of all banks calling in money, the discount houses will be forced, in the last resort, to borrow from the Bank of England. The rate at which the Bank was willing to lend used to be announced every week and was termed the minimum lending rate (MLR). From August 1981 the Bank ceased to announce the rate at which it was willing to lend but it still determines rates of interest through its actions in the money markets. The rate at which the Bank is willing to lend is always higher than the Treasury bill rate, which means the discount houses will lose money. It is this fear of losing money which ensures that market rates of interest move in sympathy with the Bank's interest rate, thereby enabling the Bank of England to control market rates.

Table 23.2 Selection of interest rates at 10 March 1990

	%
Clearing banks base rate	15.0
Clearing banks deposit rate	5.0
Clearing banks overdraft rate	18–20
Discount market deposits (overnight)	14.94
Eurodollars (3 months)	8.5
Treasury bill rate (3 months)	14.625
Eligible (commercial) bills (3 months)	14.75
Sterling certificates of deposit (3 months)	15.125

Table 23.2 represents interest rates at 10 March 1990. Here you see the discount rate for Treasury bills of 14.625%. If they were forced to borrow from the Bank of England it would cost them over 15%. Thus they would lose money.

Rates of interest for the ordinary customers borrowing from the bank would be from 18% upwards.

Discover the values of the following at the end of last week. The rate for:
● **Euro deutschemark: 3 months**
● **Sterling interbank: 3 months**
● **Overdraft rate**
● **Treasury bill rate: 7 days**
● **Bank deposit rate**

Merchant banks

Many institutions today claim the title merchant bank; indeed, some of the clearing banks have set up merchant banking subsidiaries. Traditionally the term was limited to the 16 members of the *Accepting Houses Committee*. This included such institutions as Hambros, Schroders and Lazards. Rothschild's, although not a member of the Committee, has always been classed as a merchant bank. Accepting is a process whereby the accepting house guarantees the redemption of a commercial bill of exchange in the case of default by the company which has issued the bill. For this they charge a commission. A bill which has been accepted by a London accepting house becomes a *fine bill* or a *first class bill of exchange*. This makes it much easier to sell on the money market and it may make it eligible for re-discount at the Bank of England. In order to be able to guarantee bills in this way, accepting houses have to make it their business to know everyone else's business. A merchant banker may therefore specialise in certain areas of business or in certain areas of the world. (Companies from all over the world raise money on the London money market.) Hambros, for example, specialise in Scandinavian and Canadian companies. These days there are many more merchant banks than in the Accepting Houses Committee. As mentioned above, the clearing banks usually have a merchant bank subsidiary and many foreign banks in London undertake merchant banking business.

In addition to accepting bills of exchange, merchant banks undertake many other functions. They might undertake to raise capital for their clients or even invest in the company themselves. They often act as agents in takeover bids and in the issue of new shares. In recent years many merchant banks have become involved in unit trusts and investment trusts.

The traditional distinction between banks, merchant banks, building societies, etc is increasingly breaking down. The clearing banks now compete in the mortgage market, merchant banks compete with unit trusts and so on. It is therefore increasingly difficult to define precisely the categories of financial institutions.

Finance houses

These are the institutions which provide hire purchase finance. Before 1971 they were subject to general regulations on the amount of loans, size of deposits and repayment periods. In 1971 they became subject to controls similar to those on banks, except that they had to keep a 10% reserve assets ratio. Although they attract deposits on the money market at rates of interest similar to those of other institutions, compared with the banks they charge much higher rates of interest on loans to their customers.

Local authorities

Local authorities became involved in the money market during the 1950s raising money by the issue of both bills and bonds. Local authority bills now form an important part of banks' liquidity.

The capital market and the money markets

The classical and parallel markets

The money markets are those institutions and arrangements concerned with the short-term wholesaling of money, i.e. lending and borrowing large sums for short periods of time. Most money market dealings are for no longer than three months. The *classical money market* is the expression used to describe the traditional arrangement which existed between the dis-

count houses, the clearing banks and the Bank of England for discounting bills of exchange. Today there are several other markets, such as the local authority market, the finance houses market and the Eurocurrency market. These are known as the *parallel markets* (*see* Fig. 23.3).

The capital market

The *capital market* refers to the people and institutions who are concerned with the raising and subscribing of capital for longer-run investment in companies. Some of the participants in this market are as follows.

1 Merchant banks. They act as issuing houses and arrange *underwriting* for new issues.

2 Insurance companies. The insurance companies have enormous funds at their disposal and a look at the ownership of many large companies would show that insurance companies have become the major institutional investor (*see* page 201).

3 Unit trusts. In recent years unit trusts have become a popular avenue for the funds of small investors. They buy units in the trust which uses the money received to buy shares in a number of other companies, thereby spreading the risk.

4 Investment trusts. These are joint stock companies whose business is investing in other companies. Shares are bought in them in the normal way, not as units on sale to the general public as with unit trusts. They therefore do not tend to attract small investors.

5 Government sponsored institutions. Two government sponsored organisations were created in 1945, the Industrial and Commercial Finance Corporation and the Finance Corporation for Industry. In 1973 a merger to the two corporations was proposed and in 1975 Finance for Industry Ltd (FFI) was formed. Its shareholders are the clearing banks (85%) and the Bank of England. FFI has access to funds of £1,000 million and is intended to give medium-term assistance to industry. In 1982 this was renamed 'Investors in Industry' and is popularly known as the *3is*.

Keywords ⎯⎯⎯⎯⎯⎯⎯⎯⎯⎯⎯⎯⎯⎯⎯⎯

Money
Anything which is readily acceptable in the settlement of a debt.

Functions of money
Money acts as a medium of exchange, a unit of

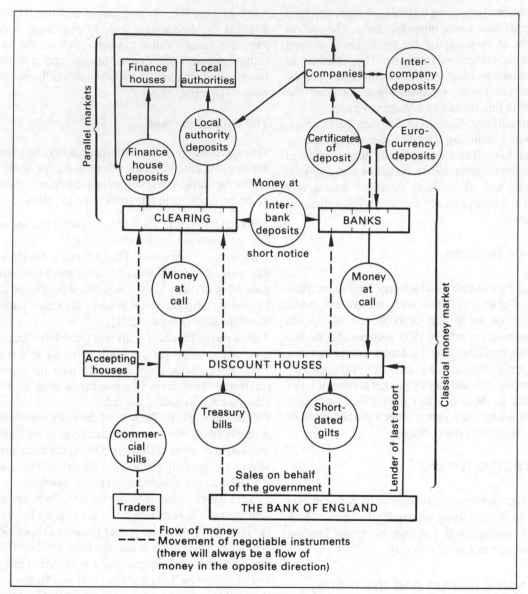

Fig. 23.3 The main participants in the London money markets. The part labelled 'classical money market' is often termed the money market, while the 'parallel markets' are more recent developments

account, a store of wealth and a standard of deferred payment.

Attributes of money
For an asset to function as money it should be acceptable, durable, stable in value and homogeneous.

Credit creation
Banks create credit by giving loans and accepting the redeposit of money. The extent of credit creation is governed by the liquidity ratio which banks maintain.

Financial intermediation
Banks and some other institutions are financial intermediaries. They act as go-betweens channeling funds from lenders to borrowers. They also transform the risk and maturity characteristics of the loans they accept.

Index of retail prices (RPI)
An index used to measure inflation in the retail sector of the economy. The present index is based on 1987.

Liquidity ratio
The percentage of its assets which a bank keeps in cash or highly liquid forms to be able to meet any demands upon it for cash.

Liquidity
The ease with which assets may be turned into cash. Money itself is totally liquid.

Eligible deposits
The part of banks' assets taken into consideration for control purposes by the Bank of England – in general, all sterling deposits with an original maturity of less than two years.

Money markets
Those institutions and arrangements involved in the borrowing and lending of large amounts of money for short periods of time.

Classical market
The arrangement existing between the discount houses, the clearing banks and the Bank of England for the discounting of bills of exchange.

Parallel markets
The 'newer' money markets such as the local authority market and the eurocurrency market.

Table 23.3 Balance sheet of the Bank of England as at 27 December 1989

Liabilities	£m	Assets	£m
Issue Department			
Notes in circulation	17,071	Gov't securities	13,961
Notes in Banking	9	Other securities	3,119
	17,080		17,080
Banking Department			
Capital	15	Gov't securities	1,306
Public deposits	62	Advances and other accounts	526
Special deposits	—		
Bankers' deposits	1,644	Premises, equipment and other securities	2,680
Reserves and other accounts	2,800	Notes and coins	9
	4,521		4,521

The functions of the Bank of England

The Bank of England is the *central bank* of the UK. Most countries have central banks but not all are responsible for the issue of notes as the Bank of England is. In the USA, for example, notes are issued by the *US Treasury* while the *Federal Reserve Banks* together form the central bank. Central banks have many functions. These can be understood more fully if we examine the balance sheet of the Bank (Table 23.3). The Bank has published a weekly return since the Bank Charter Act of 1844; this Act also divided the Bank into two departments. You can see in the balance sheet below that the *Issue Department* is solely responsible for the issue of notes, while the *Banking Department* carries out the other banking functions of the Bank.

Items in the balance sheet: Issue Department

Notes in circulation

This item illustrates the Bank's function as the *sole issuer of notes* in England. The Scottish banks were at this date responsible for the issue of £538 million of notes and the Northern Ireland banks for £60 million of notes. Beyond £4.3 million, all Scottish and Northern Irish notes must be fully backed by Bank of England notes. Therefore there is very little effect upon the volume of notes in circulation.

Notes in Banking Department

These are notes which have been created by the Issue Department and sold to the Banking Department where they are kept ready for distribution to the banks. You will see that this item appears on the assets side of the Banking Department as 'notes and coins'. Thus, since the two departments are separate, Bank of England notes are a liability to the Issue Department but an asset to the Banking Department.

Government securities

The main backing for the currency is British government securities. Thus, one piece of government paper secures the other. The real backing of the currency comes from the fact that it is both readily acceptable and legal tender.

Other securities

These consist of securities other than those issued by the British government. They also include the government debt dating back to 1694 and coins bought from the Royal Mint but not yet put into circulation.

The liabilities of the Banking Department

Capital

This represents the ownership of the Bank in the same way as the capital of any other company. This was taken over by the government in 1946.

Public deposits

Public deposits are the British government's deposits at the Bank and represent the Bank's function as the *government's banker*. The figure is sometimes surprisingly small. This is because the government balances its revenue and expenditure through the sale and purchase of Treasury bills. This item also includes the dividend accounts of the commissioners of the national debt for the Bank is also responsible for *servicing the national debt*.

Special deposits

The existence of this item illustrates the Bank's function as the operator of government monetary policy.

Bankers' deposits

These are the deposits of the main English banks. The main function of these deposits is to operate the clearing house system. This demonstrates the Bank's role as the *banker's bank*.

Reserves and other accounts

This item consists of undistributed profits and the accounts of other persons at the Bank. These fall into three categories: the bank's employees; private customers who had accounts at the bank in 1946; and other persons having a special need to bank with the Bank, such as foreign banks. This illustrates that the bank also functions as an *ordinary bank*.

The assets of the Banking Department

Government securities

Like the Issue Department, the main assets of the Banking Department are British government securities.

Advances and other accounts

These are loans which the Bank has made mainly to institutions such as discount houses. This illustrates the Bank's function as *lender of last resort*. By always being prepared to lend money, the Bank ensures that the major financial institutions never become insolvent.

Premises, equipment and other securities

As well as its well-known Threadneedle Street site the bank also has branches, e.g. in Birmingham and Manchester.

Notes and coins

The Bank is responsible for supplying the clearing banks with the new bank notes and coins that they require.

Other functions of the Bank of England

There are several functions of the Bank of England which are not apparent in its balance sheet. First, since 1946 it has had the responsibility for 'disposing of the means of foreign payment in the national interest'. That is to say all *foreign exchange transactions* in Britain are controlled by the Bank. In addition to this, it operates the *Exchange Equalisation Account*. This is a fund, established in 1932, the purpose of which is to buy and sell currency on the foreign exchange market with the object of stabilising the exchange rate. The Bank also *sells stock* on behalf of the government. It advises the government on the issue of new securities, it converts and funds existing government debt, it publishes prospectuses for any new government issue and it deals with the applications for them and apportions the issue. The Bank is also responsible for giving the government more *general advice on the monetary system* and publishes large quantities of *statistical information* on the monetary system along with studies of various sectors of the economy. The effect of the Banking Act and the monetary control-provisions has been to greatly widen the scope of the statistics which the Bank publishes.

Finally, an important function of the Bank is to *represent the government* in relations with foreign central banks and also in various institutions such as the Bank for International Settlements (BIS) and the International Monetary Fund (IMF).

Monetary policy

What is monetary policy?

Monetary policy is the direction of the economy through the supply and price of money. However the supply of money is defined, bank deposits form the major part of it. Generally it is assumed that increasing the supply of money will stimulate the economy while restricting it will restrict the economy. Similarly, monetary policy is based on the premise that raising the price of money (the rate of interest) will discourage borrowing, and hence depress demand in the economy, while lowering the rate of interest will encourage borrowing, thereby stimulating the economy. We might summarise the options as in Table 23.4.

Table 23.4 Monetary policies

Name of Policy	Action	Effect
Tight money	Restrict money supply	} Deflationary
Dear money	Raise interest rates	
Easy money	Expand money supply	} Inflationary
Cheap money	Lower interest rates	

Thus, it would seem that if we are faced with unemployment we need only adopt an 'easy money, cheap money' policy to reflate the economy. However, the economy may be faced with several problems simultaneously, for example unemployment *and* inflation. This means that monetary policy is usually used in conjunction with other things, such as fiscal policy.

The money supply

Earlier in this chapter we defined money as anything that is readily acceptable in settlement of a debt. In Chapter 22 we looked at the theoretical concept of the quantity of money in circulation. We will now examine the practical measurement of the money supply.

There are several measures in common use at the moment. The narrowest (or smallest) definition is M0. It is also termed the *wide monetary base*. M0 consists of notes and coins in circulation and bankers' operational deposits with the Bank of England (*see* Table 23.5) and is the most recent of the definitions of the money stock. The government has placed great faith in controlling M0 as a way of controlling the whole money supply and thus inflation. However, it will be apparent to you from what we have said that many other things besides cash can constitute money, for example bank deposits, because they are 'readily acceptable in settlement of debts'.

The measures that calculate money as being cash and bank deposits are the M1 to M5 definitions. (*See* Tables 23.6–8.) Nib M1 constitutes cash plus private sector non-interest bearing (Nib) deposits. Traditionally this has meant current accounts since these do not normally earn interest.

The M2 measure attempts to assess all the money in the economy that is available for more or less immediate spending. By adding to Nib M1 all other retail deposits in banks, building societies and the NSB, i.e. those held by the general public rather than by companies etc, we arrive at the M2 measure. This can also be termed the *transactions balance* because it is said that all this money is available for transactions purposes. This measure corresponds with the monetarist definition that money is 'anything which is the temporary abode of purchasing power'.

M4 is arrived at by totalling notes and coins in circulation, all sterling bank and building society deposits plus sterling certificates of deposit. If foreign

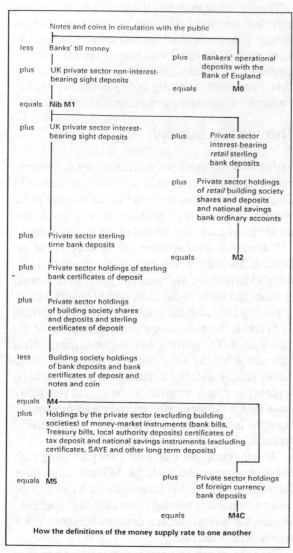

Fig. 23.4 How the definitions of the money supply relate to one another.

currency deposits are added to this it gives M4c, the 'c' standing for foreign currency. The broadest definition of the money stock is M5 which includes M4 and certain money market instruments. The relationship of these various definfintions is shown in Fig. 23.4.

The studious reader might well ask what became of M1 (as opposed to Nib M1) and to M3. The publication of these ceased after the Abbey National became a bank because the addition of its deposits to these definitions made them appear to grow rapidly. This was unacceptable to the government which had for so long made control of M3 a central target of policy. Figures for M0, Nib M1, M4 and M5 are shown in Tables 23.5–8.

Activity

1 Consider the effect upon the money supply if a number of large building societies were to become plcs.

2 Many of the definitions of the money stock (M2, M4 etc) show that bank deposits are a major part of supply. Name three advantages and three disadvantages of bank deposits as money as opposed to being notes and coins.

3 State two assets which are in the M4 definition of the money stock but not in the M2 definition.

Table 23.5 M0, the wide monetary base as at December 1989

	£ million
Notes and coins in circulation outside the Bank of England	18,820
Banks' operational deposits with the Bank of England	186
M0	19,006

Table 23.6 Nib M1 December 1989

	£ million
Non-bank private sector's holdings of notes and coins	15,578
Non-bank private sector's holdings of non-interest bearing deposits	32,370
Nib M1 (Money stock)	47,948

Table 23.7 M2:December 1989.

	£ million
Nib M1	47,948
Interest bearing bank retail deposits	92,718
Building society retail deposits	96,222
National Savings Bank ordinary accounts	1,576
M2	238,464

Source: Bank of England Quarterly Bulletin (all tables)

Table 23.8 M4, M4c and M5: December 1989

	£ million
Notes and coins	15,297
Banks' retail deposits	125,088
Building society shares and deposits	142,115
Other interest bearing bank deposits (inc CDs)	135,985
Other building society deposits (inc CDs)	4,441
M4 (money stock)	422,926
Private sector holdings of foreign currency deposits (not included in M5)	45,950
M4c (money stock)	468,876
Money market instruments	5,164
Certain National Savings Schemes	11,697
M5 (money stock)	439,787

Source: Bank of England Quarterly Bulletin

The weapons of monetary policy

Although monetary policy may be decided by the Government, it is implemented by the Bank of England. The Bank has a variety of measures it can use to implement a policy. These are usually referred to as the weapons of monetary policy and are mainly aimed at affecting the level of bank deposits and the rates of interest.

The issue of notes

Theoretically the Bank could influence the volume of money by printing more or less. In practice it is very difficult for the Bank not to supply the notes which banks are demanding, so that it is not too effective as a restricting mechanism. The reverse is not true, however, for expanding the issue of notes could expand the money supply. Indeed many people would argue that the over-printing of bank notes was one of the causes of inflation in the mid-1970s. Table 23.9 traces the growth of the fiduciary issue in the 1970s and 1980s.

Liquidity ratios

For many years banks were obliged to keep a certain portion of their assets in a particular form. In 1981 the Bank of England abandoned the reserve assets ratio. The only requirement now is that banks should keep 0.45% of their eligible liabilities with the Bank. However, this does not mean that no control exists over banks' assets. As we have discussed (*see* page 411), although there is no stated ratio, banks are still required to order their assets in particular ways. As the Bank of England is able to influence the supply of liquid assets, it is therefore still able to influence bank lending. In addition to this, the Bank has stated that it regards the funds which banks voluntarily retain with it for clearing purposes as 'the fulcrum for money market management'.

If the banking system was working to a liquidity ratio of 12.5% and this was raised by the monetary authorities to 20%, what would be the effect of this on the monetary system. Illustrate your answer with a numerical example.

Table 23.9 The growth of the fiduciary issue

Years to mid-August	Fiduciary issue (£m.)	Percentage increase over preceding year
1972	4,052	—
1973	4,545	12.2
1974	5,109	12.4
1975	5,902	15.5
1976	6,674	13.1
1977	7,314	9.6
1978	8,512	16.4
1979	9,305	9.3
1980	9,798	5.3
1981	10,256	4.5
1982	10,745	4.7
1983	11,611	8.0
1984	12,185	4.9
1985	12,148	–0.3
1986	12,824	5.5
1987	13,592	6.0
1988	14,755	8.6
1989	15,578	5.6

Interest rates

The Bank of England as the central bank guarantees the solvency of the financial system by always being willing to lend money. The way in which this is done is that the Bank re-discounts (buys) *Treasury bills* or other *first class bills of exchange*. However, the rate (of interest) at which it is willing to do this is always higher than the rate which the bill would earn if it ran to maturity. Thus, it involves the borrower in a loss. But since the Bank is the only institution which guarantees to lend money, the rate at which it does so is extremely important and all other rates of interest tend to move in line with it. Until 1981 this rate used to be announced every week as the minimum lending rate (MLR). Now, however, the Bank of England works within a 'band of interest rates' which are not announced. Nevertheless the clearing banks set their *base rate* at, or near, the rate at which the Bank of England is currently willing to lend.

In the late 1980s the government was relying on high interest rates to restrain inflation. List three other policy methods it might have used to achieve the same objective.

Open-market operations

These are the sale or purchase of securities by the Bank on the open market with the intention of influencing the volume of money in circulation and the rate of interest. Selling bills or bonds should reduce the volume of money and increase interest rates, while the re-purchase of, or the reduction in sales of, government securities should increase the volume of money and decrease interest rates.

Open-market operations affect the liquidity ratio of a bank and can therefore bring about a multiple expansion or contraction of banks' deposits.

Let us consider a bank whose assets and liabilities are arranged in the following manner conforming with a 25% ratio (*see* below).

Let us now assume that the Bank of England *sells* £1,000 of securities to the general public. The public pays for these by drawing cheques on their banks. The Bank of England collects the money by deducting the

Bank X before open-market sales

Liabilities (£)			Assets (£)	
Deposits	100,000	25% (ratio)	Liquid assets	25,000
			Securities	25,000
			Advances	50,000
	100,000			100,000

Bank X after open-market sales

Liabilities (£)			Assets (£)	
Deposits	99,000	24.2% (ratio)	Liquid assets	24,000
			Securities	25,000
			Advances	50,000
	99,000			99,000

£1,000 from the clearing bank's balance at the Bank. Thus, after open market sales the bank's balance sheet will be as above.

The Bank of England's actions will have reduced the amount of money in circulation by the amount of sales and may have increased the interest rate by depressing the price of securities. More importantly, however, it has disturbed the bank's liquidity ratio, reducing it to 24.2%. It is the bank's actions in restoring its liquidity ratio which brings about the most important effect of open-market operations.

Final Position of Bank X

Liabilities (£)			Assets (£)	
Deposits	96,000	25% (ratio)	Liquid assets	24,000
			Securities	24,000
			Advances	48,000
	96,000			96,000

In order to restore its liquidity ratio it has had to reduce its deposits to £96,000. It has done this by selling off securities, thereby depressing their price and raising the rate of interest, and by reducing its advances, thereby making money both harder to obtain and more expensive.

Thus, £1,000 of open-market operations has reduced the volume of money in circulation by £4,000. The magnitude of the effect is the reciprocal of the liquidity ratio. The effect would work in reverse if the Bank of England were buying back securities.

If the Bank of England were to undertake open market sales of securities of £5 million this would immediately reduce the volume of commercial bank deposits with the Bank of England by £5 million. Suppose that the banking sector was working to a reserve requirement of 5%, what would be the maximum possible *additional* contraction in the money supply which could result from banks adjusting their assets and liabilities to meet the ratio? (Hint: it isn't £100 million!)

Funding

This is the conversion of short-term government debt into longer term government debt. It will not only reduce liquidity but also, if the Bank is replacing securities which could be counted as liquid assets with ones which could not, it could bring about the multiple contraction of deposits described above.

Special deposits

The calling for special deposits will bring about a multiple contraction in bank lending and will also be less expensive than either open market operations or funding.

Special directives

The Bank of England used to issue directives on both *how much* banks should lend (quantitative) and *to whom* they should lend (qualitative). Since 1971 it has ceased to make quantitative directives and makes only qualitative ones, such as the one in the 1980s that mortgages should only be given for house purchase or improvement and not, as had been the case, in order to let people buy cars or flats in Cyprus.

Criticisms of monetary policy

The weapons of monetary policy might be criticised as being either ineffective or as having the wrong effect upon the economy.

1 Interest rates. Raising the interest rate should discourage investment and consumption. Most investment decisions, however, are *non-marginal*, i.e. the

entrepreneur will be anticipating a sufficiently great return on their investment so that small changes in the interest rate are unlikely to make a potentially profitable project unprofitable. If interest rates do affect investment schemes, they are much more likely to affect long-run ones than short-run ones. This is because interest charges form a much greater percentage of the capital cost in the former schemes. This is the opposite of the desired effect, i.e. the government would like to leave long-run capital projects unaffected while cutting back on short-run consumer projects. One might draw an analogy with the individual consumer and ask which borrowing would be most influenced by a rise in the interest rate, borrowing to buy a car or to buy a house?

In September 1989 newspapers reported that high interest rates were depressing the demand for and the price of houses. At the same time reports showed that new car sales in August were at an all time high. Explain these, seemingly contradictory, phenomena.

2 Liquid assets and the multiple contraction of deposits. The efficacy of open-market operations will depend upon two factors.

(a) Who buys the securities which the Bank of England is selling. For open-market operations to work they must be purchased by the general public. If the securities are bought by the banks, they will have little effect upon the banks' liquidity, since most of them count as liquid assets.

(b) How near the banks are to the liquidity ratio. For the multiple contraction of deposits to come about, the banks' liquid assets must be reduced below the appropriate level. If, however, the banks are operating well above this, as they often do, open-market operations will have to be massive before they are effective.

3 Funding. This may indeed be effective in bringing about a multiple contraction of bank deposits but it is expensive since the rate of interest the government must pay on long term debt is much higher than on short term.

4 Special deposits and directives. Both these methods are simple, cheap, effective and quick-acting. The disadvantage they have is that they may annoy the clearing banks. This factor is important since the willing co-operation of the banks is necessary for the effective implementation of monetary policy.

During the early 1980s the Government concentrated on control of the money supply. It believed that if it controlled M3 it would control inflation – this it saw as the chief problem (*see* pages 441). However, it proved very difficult to control the money supply. In the mid-1980s M3 was abandoned as a target and, and as we have seen, even its measurement was discontinued in 1989. The one remaining money supply target was M0.

In the later 1980s the Government relied on the control of interest rates as almost its only weapon of policy. By 1989 short-term interest rates were so high for so long that long-term rates such as the mortgage rate inevitably followed. The Government reasoned that this would take money out of people's pockets , thereby leaving them less to spend, so that the expansion of credit would be controlled. It was also relying on this weapon to redress the current account deficit and to restrain inflation. It was a great deal for one instrument to achieve!

Conclusion

This has been a wide ranging chapter taking in the nature of money and its creation, a description of the major financial institutions and finally a discussion of monetary policy. There is, therefore, a lot to understand. Remember also that banking is one of the UK's premier growth industries and also one which is dramatically affected by the new technology. In addition to this, the practices of financial institutions are going through some of the most profound changes this century.

Keywords

Central bank
The institution responsible for controlling the nation's money supply and banking system. In the UK this is the Bank of England.

Fiduciary issue
An issue of bank notes not backed by gold. Today all of our currency is fiduciary issue.

Lender of last resort
Central banks agree to lend money to the banking system if it is short of cash.

Monetary policy
The direction of the economy through the supply of and price of money.

Money supply
The amount of money in the country. There are various different measures: M0, M2, M4 etc.

Weapons of monetary policy
The various different devices the monetary authorities use to implement monetary policy.

Interest rates
An important weapon of policy – set by the Bank of England through its role as lender of last resort.

Open market operations
Attempts by the monetary authorities to influence the interest rate and the volume of money in circulation through the sale and purchase of securities on the open market.

Learning project

MidWest plc

The table on the next page provides all the figures that are necessary for the presentation of MidWest Bank plc's balance sheet. MidWest is a recognised bank and all its business is in sterling. The distribution of its assets is in accordance with the regulations of the Bank of England.

Complete the following tasks.

1 Present these figures as a balance sheet laid out in the conventional manner for a bank (*see* Table 23.1) and determine the overall balance for MidWest Bank Plc.

2 If the whole of the items marked * in the table are regarded as liquid (or reserve) assets, determine the liquid assets ratio on which MidWest is operating.

3 Outline the factors which determine the distribution of a bank's assets and liabilities.

4 Examine the consequences of there being a signifi-

MidWest Bank plc	£ million
Advances	14,367
Special deposits with The Bank of England	Nil
Other bills*	602
Coins and notes	451
Money at call and short notice*	650
Certificates of deposit	729
Loans to UK banks*	531
Investments	3,732
Balances with The Bank of England	563
Government stock with less than one year to maturity*	206
UK Treasury bills*	326
Current accounts	9,922
Local authority bills*	279
Deposit and investment accounts	12,628
Non-operational deposits with The Bank of England	114

cant decline in the required liquid assets ratio.

5 Contrast MidWest's balance sheet with that of a typical clearing bank.

Further ideas for learning projects

1 Prepare a report on the effects of the introduction of the new technology on the banking system.

2 Investigate the relationship between changes in the money supply and the rate of inflation over the last ten years.

3 Examine the effects of the introduction and expansion of credit cards on the British economy.

4 Analyse the structure of expenditure in retailing as between cash, cheques, credit cards and hire purchase finance.

24

Directing the economy

CHAPTER OBJECTIVES

After studying this chapter you should be able to:

Define fiscal and monetary policy;
List and explain the main taxes;
Describe the pattern of government expenditure;
Analyse the shortcomings of fiscal policy;
List and describe the causes and consequences of inflation;
Explain the importance of economic growth.

The government and the economy

Methods of control

Adam Smith believed that the economy would run itself admirably if the government did not interfere but allowed the 'invisible hand' of self-interest to guide the economy. The new classical school, as we have seen (page 397), argues for a self-directing economy. However, when Smith was writing, the role of government was very limited. Today, in every industrialised country, governments are responsible for large slices of the economy; the Japanese government disposes of about 30% of its GDP while in Sweden it is over 60%.

Today, therefore, most people realise that the prime responsibility for the well-being of the economy rests upon the government's shoulders. The actions of the government now affect almost every aspect of the life of both individuals and organisations. The direction of the economy is not so much a legal process as an economic one, i.e. the government cannot pass a law to get rid of inflation or to decree that there must be economic growth. There are three main ways in which

the government controls the economy: fiscal policy, monetary policy, and direct intervention.

Activity

Consider the following countries:

● UK;
● Japan;
● Germany;
● France;
● Sweden;
● Switzerland;
● Netherlands.

1 Which country is the most heavily taxed and which the least heavily taxed?

2 Why do the inhabitants of some countries pay a much smaller proportion of their income in tax than the inhabitants of other countries? Does this imply that they have a higher income?

Fiscal policy

This is the direction of the economy through taxation and government expenditure. In the UK the way in which the Government spends money is obviously very important since it is responsible for disposing of over 40% of the *gross domestic product* (GDP). Even more important, however, is the relationship between taxation and Government spending, i.e. whether the Government is running a budget deficit or surplus, (*see* page 391).

Monetary policy

This involves direction of the economy through the supply of and price of money. The Government can try to influence the economy through varying the quantity of money in the economy and by raising or lowering interest rates (*see* Chapter 23).

Direct intervention

Both monetary and fiscal policy aim at *inducing* the economy to conform to the government's wishes. The government could, however, intervene directly to see that its wishes were carried out. Perhaps the most obvious example of this is a *prices and incomes policy*, the operation of which also illustrates that direct intervention in the economy is as difficult as trying to induce people and organisations to do the right thing.

Which of the following are examples of monetary policy and which are examples of fiscal policy:

(a) The Bank of England raises interest rates;
(b) there is a cut in the rate of income tax;
(c) open market operations;
(d) medium-term financial strategy;
(e) an increase in excise duty?

Government policy objectives

Even within one political party opinions differ on the correct objectives of policy but it is possible to discern four general objectives which are the aim of every political party.

1 The control of unemployment. During the 1950s and 1960s, levels of unemployment were usually less than 300,000. Many people believed that the spectre of mass unemployment had been banished forever. Unemployment, however, began to increase in the 1960s and had reached one million by 1979. Unemployment then 'took-off' in the recession of the early 1980s, reaching 3.3 million, (13.5% of the working population) in 1986. By the end of the 1980s unemployment had fallen to 1.8 million but still remained a major problem. Control of unemployment is clearly an important objective of policy.

2 The control of inflation. The worst year for inflation was 1975 when prices rose by 26%. The rate had fallen to under 10% by 1979 but rose again to 18% in 1981. During the mid-1980s the rate fell to 3.5%. However, by the end of the decade inflation was around 8%. The Government continued to regard the control of inflation as its most important policy objective.

3 A surplus on the current account of the balance of payments. This has proved to be the most intractable problem of the post-war years. The revenues from North Sea oil returned the UK to surplus in the early 1980s. However, the late 1980s saw the current account deteriorate rapidly so that by 1990 the deficit was over £20 billion (*see* page 364).

4 Economic growth. The final object of all economic policies is a growth in the real national income of the country so that everyone may enjoy a better standard of living. The boom years of the 1950s and early 1960s gave way to stagnation and even to decline in the early 1980s. The middle years of the 1980s saw the beginning of rapid economic growth. For a number of years the UK's rate of growth of real GDP exceeded that of most other industrialised nations. However, this gave rise to inflation and to a worsening balance of payments situation, forcing the Government to halt growth in order to deal with these other problems. Economic growth must be achieved if people's standards of living are to increase.

There is no disagreement about these objectives of policy. The disagreement arises out of how to achieve them and which are the most important. Given just one problem, such as inflation, any government could solve it but it must also try to achieve the other objectives at the same time. It is not just a question of priorities but also of conflict because curing one problem often aggravates another. For example, eliminating unemployment might well increase inflation.

Table 24.1 Receipts of the public sector 1989–90

	£ billion
Inland Revenue	
Income tax	46.9
Corporation tax	22.4
Petroleum revenue tax	1.4
Capital gains tax	2.1
Inheritance tax	1.1
Stamp duties	2.4
Total Inland Revenue	76.3
Customs and excise	
Vale added tax	30.0
Petrol etc duties	8.8
Tobacco duties	5.1
Alcohol duties	4.7
Betting and gaming duties	1.0
Car tax	1.4
Customs duties	1.8
Agricultural levies	0.1
Total Customs and Excise	52.9
Vehicle excise duties	2.9
Oil royalties	0.6
Gas levy	0.4
Local authority rates	20.6
Other taxes and royalties	3.3
Total taxes	156.9
National insurance contributions	34.0
Interest and dividends	7.0
Gross trading surpluses and rent	3.3
Other receipts	5.2
General government receipts	206.4

Source: Financial Statement and Budget Report, HMSO

Work your way through the list of the objectives of policy and discover what has happened to each of them over the last 12 months. What is the rate of inflation etc?

Fiscal policy: raising money

The most important aspect of fiscal policy is the relationship between the Government's revenues and expenditure, i.e. whether it is running a budget deficit or surplus. Before considering this we must examine some of the items which make up the two sides of public finance. Table 24.1 shows government income for 1989–90.

Direct taxes

Direct taxes are those which are levied on the income or earnings of an individual or an organisation. These are the most important revenue raisers for the Government and can be considered under three headings.

Taxes on income

Before taxing an individual's personal income, allowances are made for such things as children and mortgage interest. The remaining taxable income is referred to as the *legal tax base*. For example, if a man had an income of £8,000 pa and allowances of £3,500 then his legal tax base would be £4,500. The *marginal rate of tax* is the amount of tax a person would pay on each successive unit of legal tax base. In 1989–90 a person would pay 25% on the tax base up to £20,700 and 40% on any income over this. Such a tax is said to be *progressive* because it takes proportionately more off people with higher incomes. If one takes gross income and expresses the actual tax paid as proportion of it we arrive at the *effective rate of tax*. (*See* Table 24.2.)

Table 24.2 The effective rate of tax

For example, suppose a married man whose wife did not work had an income of £39,000 per year. Then, in terms of the 1989–90 tax arrangements, his situation might work out like this:

Total income	£39,000
Less married person's allowance	£4,375
Less other allowances, e.g. mortgage interest tax relief	£3,000
Equals legal tax base	£31,625
Tax on first £20,700 @ 25%	£5,175
Tax on remaining £10,925 of legal tax base @ 40%	£4,370
Equals total income tax paid	£9,545

The effective rate of tax is therefore:

$$\frac{£9,545}{£39,000} \times \frac{100}{1} = 24.5\%$$

Corporation tax

This is a tax levied on the profits of companies. In 1989–90 it was levied at the rate of 25% for small companies and 35% for large ones. It can be argued that corporation tax is a disincentive to enterprise. On the other hand, the possibility of offsetting the tax against capital expenditure has meant that many of the largest profit earners in the UK have paid little or no tax at all in recent years.

Taxes on capital

Capital as such is not taxed but increases in the value of capital are taxed when it is sold or inherited. *Capital gains tax* is paid when an asset is sold at a profit, for example the sale of stocks and shares. In 1989–90 an individual could make capital gains of £5,000 before paying the tax. Beyond this stage there was a tax of 30% on gains. 1986 saw the replacement of *capital transfer tax* by *inheritance tax*. This, like income tax, is progressive and is paid on inheritances of over £118,000.

A disincentive to work?

It has been argued that direct taxes are a disincentive to work and effort. This is difficult to assess as far as companies are concerned but when individuals are considered it will depend upon the person's *target level of income*. If a person is earning less than they would like (i.e. less than their target level), then increasing income tax decreases their income and causes them to work harder or longer to make up their income. If a person is above their target level of income, increasing income taxes makes it less worthwhile for them to work harder and hence leisure appears to be a cheaper alternative. From this it has been argued that it is those on a very high income that find taxes a disincentive. It was for this reason, among others, that Conservative Chancellors in the 1980s cut the rate of income tax. In 1979 the highest band of tax was 83%! In addition to which, there could be an investment income surcharge of 15%, bringing the highest rate of income tax to 98%. By 1989 the highest rate of income tax was only 40%. Despite these cuts, the amount of income tax collected went up rapidly. This could be evidence of lower tax rates giving

people the incentive to work more – they keep more of what they earn but, at the same time, the Government's total tax revenue increases. On the other hand, it could be because the Inland Revenue became more efficient at collecting taxes and because, with lower rates of tax, rich individuals no longer went to elaborate lengths to avoid paying it.

Examine the Laffer curve in the figure below.

1 Describe what it shows.

2 Do you think that this implies that the Chancellor should raise taxes or lower them? Give reasons for your answer.

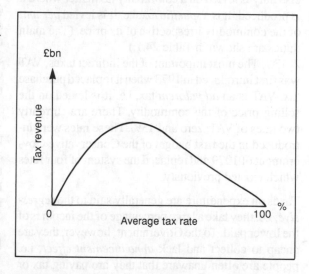

Direct taxes and inflation

Where progressive taxes are concerned, inflation will mean that the Chancellor takes a bigger and bigger proportion of a person's income as increased money wages raise him from a lower to a higher tax bracket. This tendency is known as *fiscal drag* and it is to offset this that the Chancellor frequently raises the tax thresholds, i.e. the levels at which people pay the various rates of income tax.

Indirect taxes

Indirect taxes are usually taxes on expenditure. They

are so called because the tax is paid *indirectly*, the consumer pays the tax to the shopkeeper who in turn pays it to the government. For example, in the case of the duty on whisky it is the distiller who must pay the tax, this being referred to as the *impact* (or *formal incidence*) of the tax. The tax is then 'shifted' down the chain of distribution until the *burden* (or *effective incidence*) of the tax falls upon the consumer. (We explain the determination of the incidence of tax on page 260.)

The following are the main forms of indirect tax in the UK.

1 Customs and excise duty. Customs duty may be levied on goods coming into the country but this only accounts for about 1% of Government revenues. Excise duty is levied on a commodity no matter where it is produced. It is a *specific tax*, i.e. it is levied *per unit* of the commodity irrespective of its price. (The main duties are shown in Table 24.1.)

2 VAT. The most important of the indirect taxes, VAT was first introduced in 1973 when it replaced purchase tax. VAT is an *ad valorem* tax, i.e. it is levied on the selling price of the commodity. There are currently two rates of VAT: zero and 15%. These rates were introduced in the first budget of the Conservative Government of 1979 and replaced the system of four rates which existed previously.

Taxes on expenditure are generally said to the *regressive*, i.e. they take a large percentage of the incomes of the lower paid. To the Government, however, they are cheap to collect and lack *announcement effect*, i.e. people are often unaware that they are paying tax or how much they are paying. For example, over £5 of the price of a bottle of whisky is excise duty.

Other indirect taxes include car tax, road fund and television licences and stamp duty.

What effect does inflation have upon taxes? Contrast the effect of inflation upon direct and indirect taxes.

National insurances, etc.

This used to be paid as a fixed price 'stamp' with contributions from employer, employee and Govern-

ment. Today, the contributions are still tripartite but employers now pay 9% of their income in contributions. You will see from Table 24.1 that National Insurance contributions are a massive source of revenue for the Government and, to all intents, may be regarded as another form of income tax.

Borrowing

For many years a shortfall between the Government's expenditure and income was a frequent occurrence. This was made up by borrowing, i.e. the Government increased the size of the National Debt. If we consider the borrowing both by central and local government this gives the *public sector borrowing requirement* (PSBR). This is where fiscal policy spills over into monetary policy because a large PSBR would expand the banks' credit base, thereby pushing up the money supply. (This does not happen if foreign investors buy the government bonds; on the contrary, this restrains the money supply.)

However, at the end of the 1980s cutbacks in government expenditure and increased tax revenues meant that instead of borrowing the Government was actually paying back some of the national debt. It was therefore possible to speak of the Public Sector Debt Repayment (PSDR) rather than PSBR. In 1989–90 the PSDR was estimated to be £13.8 billion.

Local authority revenues

Table 24.3 shows local government revenues for 1989–90. You will see how relatively unimportant rates were to local government. 1990 saw the replacement of rates by the Community Charge (Poll Tax). This is examined in Chapter 19.

Table 24.3 Local authorities income 1989–90

	£ billion
Current grants from central government	28.0
Rates and Community Charge	26.6
Other	6.6
Total receipts	55.2

Source: Financial Statement and Budget Report, HMSO

Is there such a thing as a good tax?

No-one likes paying taxes but if taxes are necessary then what makes one tax better than another? In the 18th century Adam Smith laid down four *canons* (criteria) *of taxation*. Although taxes have changed a great deal the principles still remain good today.

1 Equitable. A good tax should be based upon the ability to pay. Today, progressive income tax means that those with high incomes not only pay a large amount but also a greater proportion of their income in tax.

2 Economical. A good tax should not be expensive to administer and the greatest possible proportion of it should accrue to the government as revenue. In general, indirect taxes are cheaper to collect than direct taxes but they are not, however, so equitable.

3 Convenient. This means that the method and frequency of the payment should be convenient to the taxpayer. The introduction of PAYE made income tax much easier to pay for most people.

4 Certainty. The tax should be formulated so that taxpayers are certain of how much they have to pay and when. This information is widely available today although it is often badly understood.

A good system of taxation should also be one which is readily *adaptable* to changing circumstances. A fiscal system might also be judged on the *welfare principle*, i.e. the extent to which the taxes are received back by the taxpayers as services and on the principle of *least aggregate sacrifice*, i.e. that inconvenience to taxpayers is minimised. If sacrifice is minimised and welfare maximised, the fiscal system is running on the principle of *maximum social advantage*.

The objectives of taxation

1 To raise revenue. The chief reason for taxation is to raise revenue for the Government but in addition to this there are many secondary purposes which a tax may serve.

2 Redistribution of income. The Government taxes those with high incomes heavily so that it may use this money to redistribute income towards the poorer section of society.

3 Discouraging consumption. High rates of indirect tax might be placed on certain goods with the object of discouraging their consumption. This could be done, for example, to discourage imports. It is often argued that high excise duty on tobacco and alcohol serves to discourage consumption but since the demand for these products is highly inelastic this is arguable.

4 Influencing the location of industry. Differences in the rate of tax and in tax reliefs in different parts of the country might be used to persuade business organisations to locate in development areas.

We will now consider the effect of taxation on the general level of demand for goods and services in the economy.

Keywords

Prices and incomes policy
Attempts by the Government to impose norms for increases in the level of prices and of people's incomes.

Direct taxes
Those which fall chiefly on people or companies, e.g. income tax.

Indirect taxes
Taxes on expenditure such as VAT.

Marginal rate of tax
The tax paid on each extra pound of income.

Effective rate of tax
Total tax paid expressed as a percentage of total income.

Progressive tax
One which takes a greater percentage off those with high incomes.

Regressive tax
One which takes a greater percentage off those with low incomes.

Fiscal drag
The effect of inflation upon the amount of tax paid.

PSBR
Public sector borrowing requirement.

Disincentive effect
The tendency for raising or lowering taxes to discourage people from working.

Table 24.4 Distribution of income in the UK

Each group is 20% of households and shows its percentage share of total income

	Poorest fifth	Next fifth	Middle fifth	Next fifth	Richest fifth	Total
Income before taxes and benefits						
1976	0.8	9.4	18.8	26.6	44.4	100.0
1983	0.3	6.7	17.7	27.2	48.0	100.0
1986	0.3	5.7	16.4	26.9	50.7	100.0
Income after taxes and benefits						
1976	7.0	12.6	18.2	24.1	38.1	100.0
1983	6.9	11.9	17.6	24.0	39.6	100.0
1986	5.9	11.4	16.9	23.9	41.8	100.0

Source: Social Trends CSO

Fiscal policy: spending money

The provision of goods and services

As the Government disposes of over 40% of the GDP it is obvious that the most important effect of Government expenditure is its influence on the general level of demand in the economy. The Government, however, has other objectives. Governments, both central and local, provide *public goods*, perhaps the best example of this being defence. Armies are probably the oldest form of public expenditure. Today, there are many other public goods paid for from taxation such as the police service and street lighting. These are commodities which have seldom been provided in any other way. Over the last century, however, governments have stepped in to provide such things as education and health services which were formerly sold to the public.

Goods and services are also supplied by the nationalised industries but these should not involve government expenditure since they should be self-supporting. On many occasions, however, the Government has had to give financial assistance to nationalised industries.

Activity

1 Distinguish between a public good and a merit good.

2 Which of the following (if any) are public goods:

(a) clean air;
(b) defence;
(c) light houses;
(d) higher education;
(e) street lighting;
(f) council houses;
(g) the National Health Service?

3 Give reasons why you consider that university education should be treated as a merit good? Then give reasons why you think university students should pay the full cost of their own education.

The redistribution of income

We saw how it could be argued that the rich should pay more taxes. To complete the redistribution of income, Government spending must benefit the poor. Those on low incomes benefit from the consumption of public goods in the same way as anyone else although they may have contributed little towards them. They may also benefit by way of *transfer payments* such as unemployment benefits and old-age pensions. They are called transfer payments because money is transferred from one section of the community to another without the recipient providing any corresponding product or service. Table 24.4 illustrates the distribution of income in the UK. As you can see, income is very unevenly distributed but this is mitigated by the effects of progressive taxation and the redistribution of income through transfer payments such as old age pensions. It is the case, however, that whether we consider pre- or post-tax incomes, the distribution has become more uneven in recent years. Table 24.5 shows similar information for the distribution of wealth. Again, you can see that, in the UK, wealth is most unevenly divided. Whatever year we select, the richest 1% of the population enjoy 20% of the total wealth while the poorest 50% have only about 7% of total wealth between them.

Examine the information in Table 24.4. What factors do you think account for the increased imbalance in the distribution of income?

Table 24.5 The distribution of wealth in the UK

Marketable wealth (% of pop)	1976	1983	1985
Most wealthy 1%	24	20	20
Most wealthy 2%	32	27	26
Most wealthy 5%	45	40	40
Most wealthy 10%	60	54	54
Most wealthy 25%	84	78	76
Most wealthy 50%	95	96	93
Total marketable wealth (£s billion)	263	745	863

Source: Social Trends CSO

Prices support policies

If a government subsidises the cost of producing something, it may do this either with the object of supplying it to the consumer at a lower price or in order to prevent the producer from going out of business. The old farming support programmes in the UK did both. People enjoyed cheap food and farmers were maintained in business. The conflict between these objectives has become apparent since we joined the EC because the CAP supports agriculture by guaranteed high prices, to the disadvantage of the consumer. The government has not yet resolved this conflict and still continues to subsidise some food prices.

What is meant by the expression 'free goods'? Is primary education a free good in this sense? Are economists correct when they say 'There's no such thing as a free lunch'?

Table 24.6 Public expenditure 1989–90

Expenditure	£ billion
Department	
Social security	51.0
Health	23.2
Defence	20.0
Education and Science	19.6
Home Office and legal departments	8.0
Transport	5.4
Scotland	9.0
Wales	3.8
Northern Ireland	5.5
Other departments	23.1
Privatisation proceeds	–5.0
Reserve	3.5
Public expenditure planning total	167.1
General government gross debt interest	17.1
Other adjustments	10.1
General government expenditure	194.3

Source: Financial Statement and Budget Report, HMSO

The pattern of government expenditure

Table 24.6 shows the different programmes on which the Government planned to spend money in 1989–90. It is important to distinguish between *current expenditure on goods and services* and *transfer payments.* Health, education and defence, for example, are examples of current expenditure. This is because in these cases the government is *buying* the use of factors of production from the economy. Thus, for example, it is buying labour by paying the salaries of teachers and its is buying products when it purchases drugs for the National Health Service or aeroplanes for the RAF. It is thus a measure of the Government's involvement in the economy. The total of all Government current expenditure corresponds to the item *general government final consumption* to be found in Table 22.3 on page 398.

Table 24.6 also records the amount spent on transfer payments. This comprises things such as unemployment benefit and old age pensions. These are termed transfer payments because there are no services or products changing hands. It is just money being *transferred* from one section of the community to another. In Table 24.6 this is chiefly represented by the item Social Security. That this figure is so large should not surprise you when you consider the number of old age pensioners and unemployed.

Debt interest

In 1989–90 the percentage of public expenditure going in debt interest was £17.1 billion. There was a dramatic rise in the size of the national debt in the 1970s following the oil crisis and the 'three-day week'. This increase slowed in the mid-1980s and in the late 1980s the size of the national debt actually decreased. If we examine the nominal value of the national debt in 1989–90 and compare it with the national income, it represents the equivalent of 22 weeks as compared with 61 weeks of the national income in 1962. This spectacular fall in its relative size is partly offset by the enormous increase in interest rates.

People often believe that increasing the size of the national debt is a bad thing but all that happens is that wealth is transferred from private control to public control. If the Government uses the money wisely, increasing the debt may well benefit the community. In addition to this, inflation and growth of the economy will reduce the burden of interest and repayment. On the other hand, interest payments are *regressive*, i.e. they transfer money from people with low incomes to the wealthy and, if the interest is paid overseas, they represent a real drain on the economy.

Activity

Examine Table 24.6. There you can see that general expenditure on defence was 10.3% of the total. What percentage of expenditure went to overseas aid? Do you consider this latter amount too much and does it contribute to the balance of payments deficit.

A balanced budget?

It was Keynes who first pointed out that the budget could be used as a method of directing the economy. The budget is a method of managing the level of aggregate demand in the economy. A budget deficit would mean that the level of aggregate demand was increased while, conversely, a budget surplus would reduce the level of aggregate demand. In theory, a balanced budget should not affect the level of economic activity (*see* Chapter 22).

This ought to mean that if the Government is faced with an inflationary situation it should run a budget surplus to restrain the level of demand and therefore take the heat out of the economy. This is unlikely to work by itself and the Government would usually try to use it in conjunction with monetary policy. Orthodox economics suggests that the Government should be able to cure unemployment in the economy by running a budget deficit. There are, however, several types of unemployment.

1 Frictional. People displaced by the normal working of the economy, for example people between jobs.
2 Seasonal. People being made unemployed because their job depends upon the time of year. It is most significant in the construction industry.
3 Structural. This is unemployment caused by a change in the structure of the economy, e.g. the decline of one industry and (hopefully) the rise of another. In Britain this has manifested itself as *regional unemployment*. Originally this was associated with the decline of the *old staple industries* such as shipbuilding and textiles. However, in recent years this has been added to by the decline of other newer industries such as motor vehicles.
4 Technological. The recent advances in technology have had the effect of eliminating many jobs.
5 General or cyclical unemployment. Originally taking its name from the trade cycle, this is unemployment associated with a general depression in the economy.

It is only the last of these types of unemployment which a budget deficit would cure. Running a deficit to cure structural unemployment tends to cause inflation by increasing demand in the already fully employed sectors of the economy. Structural unemployment is best dealt with by regional policy or by a policy aimed at a particular sector of the economy. (*See* Chapter 9.)

The difficulties of fiscal policy

Fiscal policy would seem to be a straightforward way of directing the economy. Certainly, most governments since 1945 have relied on it as a major weapon of policy. In practice, however, its operation is subject to a number of difficulties.

The net effects of the budget

The effect of a budget will depend not only upon the amount of taxes and the amount of spending but also upon who is taxed and on what the government spends money. If we imagine a very simple budget in which all the taxes were raised as capital transfer tax, while all the expenditure was on unemployment benefits, the amount paid could be less than the amount collected so that the budget was ostensibly in surplus. However, the money that has been collected in taxes is money that would not have been spent, i.e. people with high incomes would probably have saved a good deal of it. On the other hand we can be reasonably certain that all the unemployment benefit would be spent. Thus, the Government has moved the money from non-spenders to spenders, and, therefore, the effect on the economy would be that of deficit, although the budget was in an accounting surplus.

This would also work the other way round. If, for example, a government's budget were in deficit but its revenue had been raised mainly from taxes on expenditure, such as VAT, and spent mainly on paying interest on the national debt, the effect of the budget would be that of a surplus. This is because the government has, effectively, transferred money from spenders to non-spenders. Thus, when the government announces a deficit or surplus a much more careful examination of its plans will be necessary before we can decide what the net effect on the economy will be. Put into economists' language, the effect of the budget will depend upon the *marginal propensity to consume* of those being taxed and of those receiving the government's expenditure. You will recall that there will also be a multiplier effect from any budget deficit or surplus (*see* Chapter 22).

The inflexibility of government finance

Adjusting the Government's level of economic activity to suit changing circumstances is not as straightforward as it may seem. Much of the Government's

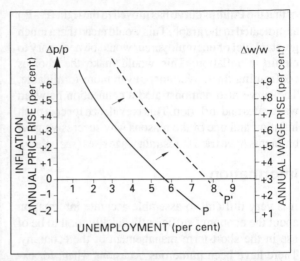

Fig. 24.1 A Phillips curve. The Phillips curve is used as evidence for cost push inflation

finance is inflexible. One of the reasons for this is that the major portion of almost any department's budget is wages and salaries and it is not possible to play around with these to suit the short-term needs of the economy. In addition to this, for example, it would be impracticable to build a power station one year because more demand was needed or, conversely, to stop the construction of a half-built motorway because less expenditure was needed. Much of the Government's expenditure involves long-term planning.

Conflicts of policy

In devising its budgetary policy, the Government must try to reconcile conflicting objectives of policy. In 1986, for example, the Government might have liked to reflate the economy to try to cure unemployment but it was loth to do this in case it caused more inflation. The most famous conflict of different ends of policy is illustrated by the *Phillips curve* (*see* Fig. 23.1). By plotting figures for unemployment, inflation and wage rises in the British economy 1862–1958, Professor Phillips derived this relationship.

Professor Phillips' research appeared to show that the nearer the economy was a full employment the greater would be the rate of inflation. When he wrote (1962) it seemed that if there were 5.5% unemployment then inflation would be zero. It would appear in the 1980s that either this relationship ceased to operate or that the Phillips curve has moved to the right $(P - P')$ as indicated in the graph. This would mean that a much greater level of unemployment would be necessary to eliminate inflation. This would make the choices confronting the Government even more formidable. The curve also demonstrated a connection between wage rates and inflation. This is evidence for cost push inflation and one of the reasons why successive governments have tried to restrain wage rises (*see* below).

Information

It is very difficult to assemble accurate information about the economy sufficiently quickly for it to be of use in the short-term management of the economy. There have been numerous occasions when, for example, the balance of payments has been declared to be in deficit in one quarter but a few months later, when more information is available, it has been discovered that the quarter was in fact in surplus. It is difficult, therefore, for a government to be sure about the accuracy of the information. Even if the figures are accurate, the Government still has to decide what they mean. For example, if the balance of payments is suddenly in deficit, is this the beginning of a long-term trend or is it just a freak result of that month or quarter?

Time lag

One of the chief objectives of fiscal policy is stability, i.e. the Government tries to avoid violent fluctuations in the level of economic activity. One way to do this is for the Government to have a *counter-cyclical* policy so that if, for example, the level of economic activity were low, government activity would be high, i.e. they would have a budget deficit. Conversely, if there were a high level of activity then the Government would budget for a surplus.

Unfortunately, it takes time for a government to appreciate the economic situation, then to formulate a policy and then to implement it. This may mean that the Government's policy works at the wrong time. For example, if the Government decided to reflate the economy during a recession, it could be that by the time the policy worked the economy would have recovered anyway! Thus, Government's actions have the effect of boosting the economy to an undesirable degree. At this time the Government decides to clamp

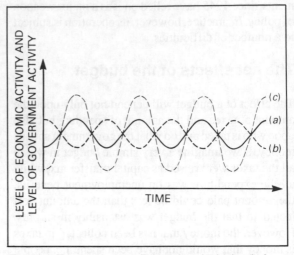

Fig. 24.2 The time lag. *(a)* Fluctuations in the level of economic activity without government intervention. *(b)* Proposed pattern of government counter-cyclical activity. *(c)* Worsened fluctuations in the level of economic activity caused by government policy acting at the wrong time.

down on the economy but by the time the policy acts, the economy has naturally returned to recession. The Government's action therefore makes the slump worse and so on. This pattern will be familiar to anyone who lived through the *stop-go* policies of the 1950s and 1960s (*see* Fig. 24.2).

Thus, while fiscal policy appears at first sight to be an attractive way of running the economy it is subject to many shortcomings. As far as such things as information, time lags and inflexibility are concerned, these may be offset by the use of *built-in stabilisers*. These are fiscal weapons which would automatically dampen the economy when it was overheating and boost it when it was in recession. Two such measures are progressive income tax and unemployment benefits. Progressive income tax automatically takes money out of the economy as incomes increase while, conversely, unemployment benefits put extra money into economy as unemployment increases. It would appear, however, that their effect is not great enough.

Monetary policy

Monetary policy is the direction of the economy through the supply and price of money. The shortcomings of monetary policy were discussed in Chapter 23.

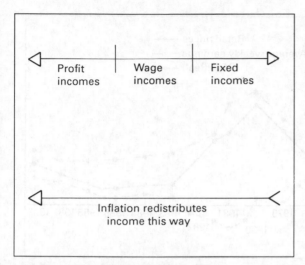

Fig. 24.3 Inflation redistributes incomes

It would appear that, like fiscal policy, there are problems involved in using monetary policy. Politically speaking, the use of monetary policy has been considered a right-wing method of directing the economy. Despite this, controlling the money supply as an object of policy can be said to date from the sterling crisis of 1976 when the Labour Party formed the Government.

During the early 1980s, the Conservative Government became pre-occupied with control of the money supply as one of the chief objectives of policy, believing that this was essential to control inflation. This was because it believed in the monetarist explanation of inflation, i.e. that inflation is *only* caused by increases in the money supply (*see* page 395–7). The control of the money supply was part of the Government's *medium-term financial strategy* (MTFS). The MTFS, which is announced each year at the time of the Budget, is a set of targets for the growth of such aggregates as the money supply, Government expenditure and inflation. The hope was that by announcing firm and reducing targets for these it would reduce people's *expectations* of inflation and, therefore, help to restrain it.

Targets for the money supply were consistently overshot and had to be constantly redefined. At the same time inflation declined, being only 3.3% in the mid-1980s. Thus, it became increasingly apparent that the relationship between the money supply and inflation is more complex than suggested by monetarists.

Keynesians might argue that inflation was being restrained by the huge rise in unemployment rather than by any action of monetary policy. Whatever the correct explanation, the government abandoned all targets for money supply except that for M0.

In 1987 the Stock Exchange 'crash' rocked the economies of the industrialised nations. To restore confidence, the British, and other governments, lowered interest rates. Partly as a consequence of this, inflation in the the UK began to increase again as people borrowed relatively cheaply to buy consumer goods. This forced the Government to raise interest rates. By 1990 the banks' base rate was 15%. Thus, by 1990, we can say that the Government was using interest rates as the chief weapon of monetary policy. (Monetary policy is more fully discussed in Chapter 23.)

Inflation

The effects of inflation

Inflation is, quite simply, a rise in the general price level and therefore a fall in the value of money. Although there are several ways of measuring inflation, the most common in the UK is the Index of Retail Prices. Inflation has several unpleasant consequences.

1 Effect on the balance of payments. Inflation will make our exports dear to foreigners while imports become cheaper. Other things being equal, this will cause a deficit on the balance of payments. This will not happen, of course, if other countries are inflating at a more rapid rate than the UK. What is important, therefore, is the relative rate of inflation between countries. Unfortunately for the UK, the rates of inflation of most of our trading partners have been less than our own.

2 Effect on savings. Saving is rendered less attractive because at the end of the year the money saved will buy less goods. (Money put by for a rainy day only buys a smaller umbrella!) This could mean, therefore, that insufficient funds are released for investment, which in turn would mean that the economy's development would be threatened. However, in recent years the high level of inflation has increased people's uncertainty about the future and thereby caused them to increase their *precautionary* saving. This increase

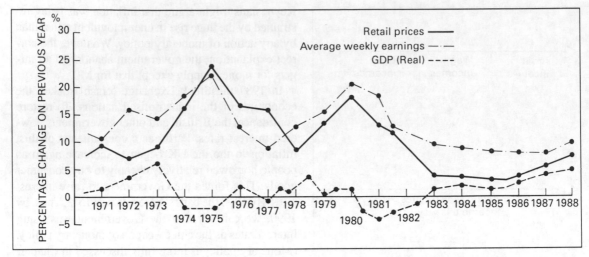

Fig. 24.4 Wages, prices and growth, 1971–89

in the *propensity to save* has, unfortunately, had the effect of further reducing the level of *aggregate demand* in the economy and therefore increased the level of unemployment.

3 Redistribution of income. A fall in the value of money will remove purchasing power from those living on fixed incomes, such as pensioners, and redistribute it towards those who draw their living from prices. This is illustrated in Fig. 23.3. Wages are seen as being in the middle of the spectrum, their ability to keep up with or ahead of price rises will depend upon the wage-earners' bargaining power. This will tend to mean that those whose skills are in great demand will succeed in keeping pace with inflation while those who are poorly unionised, such as shop workers, agricultural workers and bankers, or in declining industries lose out. Generally speaking, however, the general level of wage rates has kept ahead of inflation (*see* Fig. 24.4).

4 Instability. A high rate of inflation might very possibly cause a crisis of confidence in the monetary system and a consequent breakdown of the economic order. Although we have so far avoided *hyperinflation* like that in Germany in 1923, we have experienced rates of inflation which have caused economic disruption. As inflation continues at a high rate and business organisations allow for it and predict it in their accounting systems, there may be a danger of building inflation into the economic system.

There are several arguments to be made in favour of

inflation. First, a little inflation is conducive to growth. This is because it makes it easier to make profits. The business's costs are historic, i.e. it has hired the factors of production at an agreed price sometime in the past, while its revenues automatically increase with inflation. This, therefore, encourages investment. Second, it would appear that eliminating inflation causes very high levels of unemployment.

The causes of inflation

There is no universal agreement among economists about the causes of inflation. To make matters more complicated, political viewpoints enter into the judgement. For example, right-wing opinion would blame inflation on greedy trade unions while the unions blame it on inept management. Three explanations of inflation are considered below.

Cost-push

This view of inflation maintains that inflation is a supply phenomenon with increased costs of production pushing up prices. Some of the factors which contribute to cost inflation are said to be the following.

1 Powerful trade unions that push up wage costs without any corresponding increase in productivity. This is one of the most widely held views of inflation. Although there is an undoubted connection between wage rates and inflation (see Fig. 23.4), the precise nature of it remains unclear.

2 *Import prices* undoubtedly play a part in inflation. To a country like the UK, which imports over 33% of all the goods it consumes, it is obvious that if prices overseas increase we will, in effect, import inflation. This was clearly illustrated by the oil price rises of the 1970s. However, while this point is correct, we must also consider that the countries from which we buy most of our imports have *lower* rates of inflation than the UK.

3 A *fall in the exchange rate* is inflationary because it puts up the price of imported goods. It has been estimated that a fall in the exchange rate of 4% adds as must as 1% to the rate of inflation. This undoubtedly contributed to inflation during the 1970s following the floating (sinking?) of the pound in 1972.

4 *Mark-up pricing*, i.e. the method by which firms fix their prices on a unit cost plus profit basis (*see* page 289). This means that prices tend to go up automatically with rising costs whatever the state of demand in the economy.

Demand pull

Inflation occurs when people try to buy more goods and services than the economy is capable of producing, thus pulling up prices. This is the Keynesian view of inflation (*see* page 394). Evidence for it is said to be a *wages drift*, i.e. the tendency of earnings to rise faster than wage rates. Thus, a 5% rise in wages may lead to an 8-9% rise in earnings when overtime, bonuses, etc., are considered. This puts extra demand in the economy which will pull up prices. On many occasions the government has tried to restrain demand through fiscal and monetary policy as a way of combating demand inflation.

The money supply

At its simplest, the monetarist view of inflation maintains that inflation is caused by the Government creating too much money. In Britain (1965–89) the average annual growth of GDP (in constant prices) has been only 2.0%. If the money supply is allowed to grow more than this it must, so the argument goes, cause inflation. The evidence for this is an observed tendency for any rise in the money supply to be followed by a rise in prices a year or so later. Certainly the 1970 Conservative Government's large increase in the money supply (1971–3) was followed by massive inflation (*see* Fig. 24.4). It is, as we have seen, very difficult to discover the causal mechanism which links these two. In addition to this the money supply is difficult to define. Is it M5, M3, or M0? Another problem is the control of the money supply. Together with control of the money supply, we must consider other factors, such as the velocity of circulation and banks' lending policies, which enter into it and which make it difficult to adjust the total quantity of money with any accuracy.

Incomes policy

The seeming inability of fiscal and monetary policies to deal with inflation led successive Governments to introduce incomes policies. An incomes policy tries to ensure that incomes do not rise faster than the increased wages costs can be absorbed by rising productivity. If incomes can be kept below this level there is the added bonus of extra resources which are free for investment. These simple aims have been very difficult to achieve.

Incomes policies are of two main types: *voluntary*, where the co-operation of employers and unions is sought; or *statutory*, where the Government imposes its will by legislation. Just freezing wages or prices is not enough; the Government must also take measures to alleviate the pressures which are causing inflation, otherwise price control is simply like breaking a thermometer to try to cure a temperature.

Which is correct?

You may legitimately ask 'Which explanation is correct?'. It could be that they all are! That is to say that inflation is brought about by a compound of these causes or that one factor causes inflation at one time and another factor causes inflation at a different time. High levels of wage settlements, for example, have often contributed to inflation. On the other hand, there was demand-pull inflation in the late 1980s as high house prices enabled people to use their houses as security and borrow large sums of money from banks to spend. To this the monetarists might argue that this borrowing expanded the money supply and that it was this that caused inflation.

Control of inflation must therefore depend upon the type of inflation which we are considering. If there are a number of causes for inflation then we probably need a number of policies to control it.

It is a depressing thought that we may not have a great deal of control over inflation. Inflation went up in the UK as it went up in the rest of the world and came down as rates declined overseas. However, this still does not explain why the rate in Japan and Germany is typically half that of the UK.

Economic growth

We have seen that there are four main objectives of Government policy: stable prices, full employment, a sound balance of payments and economic growth. But the first three of these are only means to an end. The increased wealth and welfare of the economy is almost entirely dependent upon economic growth. It is no good having a large surplus in the balance of payments if the national income is declining and it is no use curing inflation by depressing everyone's living standards. The UK's economic growth since the end of the Second World War in 1945 has been disappointing

when compared with other European states, and disastrous when compared with some far eastern states such as Japan and South Korea.

The Conservative Government's policy for both promoting growth and reducing unemployment was founded on *supply-side economics*. This leads to policy prescriptions such as tax cuts to encourage greater enterprise and the reduction of restrictive practices in the labour market, e.g. by weakening trade unions. Such policies have been successful in the USA. However, they have been accompanied there by massive budget deficits so that it may be possible to argue that the expansion is due to an orthodox Keynesian fiscal boost. Research published by the National Institute for Economic and Social Research (NIESR) and also by the London Business School (LBS) suggested that tax cuts were a much less efficient way to create jobs than increasing Government expenditure. They estimated that it took £32,000 in lost Government revenue to create a job by tax cuts but only £12,000 to create one by direct Government expenditure. However, what supply-side economics has done is to emphasise the importance of improving the efficiency of supply. By this we mean increasing productivity on which depend both economic growth and, ultimately, jobs.

Keywords

National debt
The total amount of money owed by the government to citizens in *this* country.

Net effect of budget
The overall effect of the budget on the economy having considered the effect of different MPCs on spending and raising money.

Phillips curve
A graph showing the supposed trade-off between inflation and unemployment.

Stop-go policies
Rapid changes in the direction of government policy alternating between promoting growth and

controlling inflation or the balance of payments.

Inflation
A rise in the general level of prices and a fall in the value of money.

Cost-push inflation
Rises in prices caused by increases in the costs of supply.

Demand-pull inflation
Rising prices caused by excess demand in the economy.

Monetary inflation
Rising prices caused by over-expansion of the money supply – 'Too much money chasing too few goods.'

Learning project

UK economic indicators

Examine the information in Table 24.7 which is taken

from various publications, including the *Annual Abstract of Statistics, National Accounts* and *The Employment Gazette*.

Table 24.7 UK Economic Indicators 1976–89.

Year	Unemployed (%)[1]	Real GNP[2]	Earnings (£s)[3]	Inflation (%)[4]
1976	4.8	85.7	79.8	23.4
1977	5.2	86.9	91.0	16.6
1978	5.1	89.8	101.2	9.9
1979	4.6	92.4	119.3	9.3
1980	5.6	89.8	129.4	18.4
1981	9.0	89.4	138.2	13.0
1982	10.3	91.0	151.5	12.0
1983	11.2	94.8	163.8	4.9
1984	11.1	96.9	174.3	5.1
1985	11.5	100.0	192.4	5.0
1986	11.6	104.1	207.5	5.5
1987	10.3	108.5	224.0	3.9
1988	8.0	113.4	239.0	3.3
1989	7.4	—	—	7.8

[1] Unemployed: % of workforce, OECD definition.
[2] Real GNP at factor cost: 1985 = 100.
[3] Earnings: full-time males, arithmetic mean.
[4] Inflation: year on year change.

1 Update the information.

2 Construct a graph with the rate of inflation on the vertical axis and unemployment on the horizontal axis. On this graph plot the rate of inflation against the rate of unemployment. This will produce a series of points; label each of these points with the year to which it applies.

3 On the basis of the diagram you have constructed for task 2, is it possible to support the idea of a Phillips curve (*see* Fig. 24.1)? Support your answer by suggesting what relationship does exist between inflation and unemployment.

4 On a larger scale, construct a graph similar to Fig. 24.4 with percentage change on the vertical axis and time (1976–to date) on the horizontal axis. On this plot curves to show inflation, the change in earnings and the change in real GNP.

5 Annotate this graph to show:

(a) periods of different governments;
(b) events that you consider to be significancant to it.

6 The figures given for earnings relate to the *arithmetic mean*. how would you expect the *median* figure to differ from this and why?

7 On the basis of the information you have presented in this learning project:

(a) do you consider that there is a relationship between earnings and prices; and
(b) which government policies do you think would be most effective in dealing with inflation?

In both cases give reasons for your answers.

Further ideas for learning projects

1 Consider Table 24.8.

(a) Examine the basis and methods of calculation of the various taxes in this table.
(b) Comment upon the changing distribution of these two types of tax revenue as fully as possible and upon their relationship to other taxes.
(c) How is the Single European market ('1992') likely to affect these taxes?

2 In what ways will government policy be changed by entry into the Single European Market?

Table 24.8 Shares of total UK government revenue raised by Customs and Excise.

Type of tax	Name of tax	1963–4 (%)	1983–4 (%)	1988–9 (%)
Specific tax				
	Tobacco	13.0	2.8	3.9
	Alcohol	7.0	2.9	3.5
	petrol etc	8.5	4.2	6.5
	Total of these	28.5	9.9	13.9
Ad-valorem taxes				
	Purchase tax	7.5	—	—
	VAT	—	11.5	20.4
	Other	6.5	2.0	3.0
	Total of these	14.0	13.5	23.4
Total Customs and Excise		42.5	23.4	37.3

25

The legal background

CHAPTER OBJECTIVES

After studying this chapter you should be able to:

- Discuss the nature of law;
- Explain and discuss the role and functions of law with particular reference to business organisations and the government;
- Define and distinguish between different types of legal rights and duties;
- Explain the nature of forms of legal liability;
- Outline the origin and sources of English law;
- Discuss the role of legislation and outline the rules of statutory interpretation;
- State the functions of the law commission.

The idea of law

Any attempt to define and explain the 'idea of law' in a book of this nature can do no more than give a very limited introduction to an important philosophical subject. Unlike scientific laws, *the law* cannot be objectively defined, let alone proved. It is the product of man, not of nature, and it means different things to different people according to their time, culture and the social structure in which they live.

The greatest of the world's philosophers have considered the 'idea of law', but no single definition has been universally accepted. There are, however, three main kinds of *jurisprudence* (legal theory): first *historical*, which studies the growth of law, particularly in connection with the development of the state; second *analytical*, which studies the concepts and structures of the law as they actually are; and third *sociological*, which considers how the workings of the law affect society.

To a greater or lesser extent, all jurisprudence attempts to answer the following four questions:

1 What is law?
2 Why is law necessary?
3 What is the purpose of law?
4 How just is the law?

We will suggest answers to these questions, but you should always remember that different theories attempt to answer different questions. Some are concerned with the *form law takes*, some with its *concept* and others with law's *function*.

Similarly, methods of enquiry differ. An *inductive* approach produces definitions and answers from the observations of actual situations and legal phenomena, while a *deductive* approach involves formulating definitions and answers based on initial assumptions about the nature of law. In our own legal system the common law follows an inductive approach but legislation is often the result of a deductive process of lawmaking. Of greatest importance, perhaps, is the fact that all definitions of law are to a greater or lesser extent, consciously or subconsciously coloured by value systems and ideological factors – social, economic or political.

Our objective is not to attempt definitive answers to such questions but to stimulate further thought, discussion and argument.

What is law?

Although there is no universally accepted definition of 'law', we can usefully begin our discussion of this question by quoting three well-known jurists.

'The body of principles recognised and applied by the State in the administration of justice ... In other words the law consists of rules recognised and acted upon by courts of justice.' (Salmond)

'A law is a general rule of external human action enforced by a sovereign political authority.' (Holland)

'A social process for settling disputes and securing an ordered existence in the community.' (Paton)

In all three definitions two ideas are either expressly or impliedly involved. First, that law is a *set of rules* by which human conduct within society is ordered and controlled. Second, there is reference to the *state* or other sovereign power within society. The first of these ideas is largely self-explanatory and uncontentious but reference to the state raises fundamental issues about the nature of our law.

Is law imposed?

Laws are certainly enforced by the state but does the state impose its own corporate will on its members or is law essentially the will of the people recognised and adopted by the state? Clearly, an individual or business organisation is unlikely to volunteer money to the state to finance its activities, and taxation by law is therefore a necessary imposition. Apart from such examples, however, which is true? Perhaps the truth lies somewhere in between. Primitive law consists of basic social norms and customs which evolve spontaneously through an unspoken consensus based on the needs of physical survival. In so far as modern law still reflects these basic social norms and customs, it comes from the people. However, factional interests very soon emerge in a society as it becomes more complex and in the past our law has been imposed blatantly to serve class or factional interests, for example, those of landowners. Yet in pre-industrial Britain, as in other

countries at a similar stage in their economic development, this basic *consensus* and *conflict* could co-exist. On the one hand all classes shared the common need to survive, while on the other the basic conflict between the landed classes and the peasantry remained through the inability of the latter to challenge the position of the former.

Today the law is sometimes used equally boldly by governments to fulfil their policies and serve their political philosophy. To this extent, the law is imposed on the majority by an elite and conflict may follow. Many would argue, however, that given our sophisticated industrial society, today's changes in the law are usually the result of competition between different groups, each group competing to achieve change in line with their individual interests. This is referred to as *pluralism* (*see* Chapter 27). You must decide for yourself the extent to which the law exists for the benefit of society as a whole, for the benefit of the ruling elite (whatever political party they may or may not belong to), or for the benefit of any group that can successfully use it.

Law and politics

On the assumption that a great deal of our contemporary law is imposed upon us by the government of the day, politics must be involved in its formulation, and any attempt to view law as a self-contained discipline is unrealistic. Indeed, *government* can be viewed as a composite of both the political and legal processes. Such matters as industrial and welfare law frequently raise issues of straight party politics. Furthermore, there is the view that we are governed by an 'elected dictatorship' which, providing it can command a majority in the House of Commons, can quite lawfully use the political process and the supremacy of Parliamentary legislation to realise its political aims for up to five years without effective restraint. Consequently, some argue that there should be a 'bill of rights', which would be above the normal political processes and legislative repeal or amendment, allowing the courts to protect basic constitutional rights from dictatorial and arbitrary use of political power. While it is true that politics and government are carried on within a framework of law, it is essential to remember that this framework is itself the product of the political process. Hence, we could argue that it is the political process rather than law which actually rules us.

Law and morality

The concepts of morality and law are clearly closely linked. Virtually all serious crimes are immoral acts, e.g. murder and theft, and some essentially immoral acts are crimes, e.g. perjury (lying on oath) and libel may both be the subject of criminal proceedings; but a vast number of criminal acts committed each year, minor motoring offences in particular, are not usually considered immoral acts but are nevertheless punished. Conversely, many moral offences, adultery for example, go unpunished by the criminal law. The difference between them in legal terms is that law is enforced by the state while morals are not, except when law and morality coincide.

The legal distinction between law and morality raises an important issue about the purpose of law: should law be used to enforce morals? Recent examples of the law venturing into this difficult area include the Video Recordings Act 1984, which established a censorship and classification system for video recordings; the Surrogacy Arrangements Act 1985, which prohibits the operation of commercial surrogacy agencies and advertising of surrogacy services; and the 'Gillick Case', where the House of Lords (by a majority of three to two, thereby reversing the Court of Appeal's decision which had earlier reversed the High Court judgment) upheld DHSS guidance that doctors could in exceptional cases prescribe contraceptives to girls under 16 without their parents' consent.

Each of you will have your own views on this, but it is worth remembering that many would say that the law is inherently conservative and tends to reflect the views of an atypical elite from a previous generation, lagging behind contemporary social norms. Leading lawyers themselves tend to be conservative (with a small 'c') by virtue of their socio-economic background and status, and sometimes seem to be out of touch with the 'real' world. In the celebrated *Lady Chatterley's Lover* Case in 1961, prosecuting counsel asked the jury, 'Is this a book that you would ever wish your wife or your *servants* to read?'. In 1985 a rapist was fined £2000, after the judge branded his victim guilty of 'contributory negligence' for hitch-hiking alone at night.

In 1989 a difficult situation arose which encompassed almost everything you could think of: law morality, culture and religion. Salman Rushdie's book *The Satanic Verses* was construed by most Muslims in the UK – indeed worldwide – as a blasphemous libel against Islam. The demonstrations and threats on Rushdie's life which followed do not concern us here, only the book's legal position. Quite possibly the book was 'blasphemous' but the common law offence of blasphemous libel only protects Christianity. Furthermore the offence is virtually obsolete, only six successful prosecutions have been brought in England this century – four against one particular active atheist – and none between 1922 and 1972 when a private prosecution was brought against *Gay News* for publishing a poem which suggested, among other things, that Christ was a promiscuous homosexual. No successful prosecutions have been brought in Scotland since 1840!

In a multi-cultural society there is an argument for extending blasphemy to cover other religions but doing so would pose insurmountable problems of definition and selection – what about the 'Moonies' and even more extremist sects? – besides requiring what most people would surely regard as totally unacceptable restrictions on free speech. Besides, the existing laws against public order offences, indecency and obscenity are adequate to cover truly gross excesses.

Given that most people in this country hold only token religious beliefs, what purpose does the offence serve? Should anyone be punished for expressing an opinion or describing a situation which a particular group finds offensive? Perhaps a much stronger argument, exists for abolishing blasphemous libel altogether. And yet, can the value systems (*see* page 117) of the 'white, Protestant British' fully cope with the views of those who felt so aggrieved?

Why do we need law?

All except anarchists would agree that the existence of law is necessary. A society presupposes order and it would seem that the natural order usually to be found in small primitive communities breaks down as the society becomes larger and more complex. It is clear that controls on powerful bodies and individuals are necessary if the interests of the majority are to be protected. For example, experience has shown that the absence of health and safety, employment protection and monopoly legislation can have harmful social and economic effects on a society.

1 (a) Law and morality are linked but separate ideas. For example, murder is both immoral and illegal, exceeding the speed limit probably just illegal and committing adultery just immoral. List five other activities which are just illegal, five which are just immoral, and five which are both illegal and immoral.

(b) Do you agree that the law should/can be used to uphold moral values in a society?

2 Consider the 'Rushdie Affair' and answer the following questions.

(a) What would be the wider implications of extending blasphemy to religious (and other) beliefs apart from Christianity?

(b) Should a minority ethnic group within a society have to accept the moral, cultural and religious values of the majority?

(c) How best can the law deal with a group of several hundred, even several thousand, people who openly call for the death of an individual?

What is the law's purpose?

The law's purpose is usually considered to be the general regulation and control of society, the criminal law in particular providing and enforcing minimum standards of social behaviour. The legal system complements legal principle by providing means of resolving conflicts and dealing with those who infringe legally enforced social and commercial norms. However, on the assumption that it is only a small minority of individuals and organisations in society that the law has to positively control, law can equally well be considered as an *enabling medium* for the majority. For example, individuals are able to use and enjoy their land because the tort of nuisance restrains the few who would interfere with it, and companies could not exist or function as they do without the basic concept of juristic personality (*see* page 50) and the framework of commercial and industrial law in general.

Other more specific views of the purpose of law do, of course, exist, for it is the servant of economic and

political forces and it is used by powerful pressure groups to achieve their objectives. Even Bentham's 'greatest good for the greatest number' philosophy of 'utilitarianism' and Pound's view of law as a process of 'social engineering' (a sociological approach) must be seen in this context and not in isolation.

It is not within the scope of this book to argue the validity of different legal theories but one well-known example will illustrate how economic and political ideology can determine theories of the nature and purpose of law. In classic Marxist philosophy, law is viewed as the institutionalisation of the prevailing ideology. The socio-economic elite of a society then use this to coerce the masses into obedience in order to preserve their privileged position. Thus, the purpose of the law is seen here in terms of achieving social, economic and political objectives. This may be an unsophisticated and rather extreme view of the nature and purpose of the law but many of you may have often considered that the government uses the law to impose its will upon the individual and that large organisations of all kinds are able to use the law to further their commercial (or other) interests at your expense.

It is clear from this single example that it is difficult to discuss the ultimate purpose of law without asking fundamental questions about the nature of society as it is and as we might wish it to be. Such questions merit a book to themselves but we shall examine later in this chapter the specific functions and uses of the law in relation to organisations and the government, the nature and sources of legal rights and duties and forms of legal liability.

Law and justice

The ultimate aim of all law should surely be to promote justice. But any attempt to define law in these terms meets two serious obstacles. First, 'justice' is a vague concept, meaning different things to different people. Second, law must be considered within its socio-political context and, assuming that law exists to serve society, what may be justice with regard to one individual may not be useful to society. Theft, for example, is a serious crime and it is right that it should be punished. What, however, of the mother who steals food from a supermarket because she cannot afford to feed her children? Is justice served by her imprisonment? You might consider the argument that law will always produce occasional injustice unless it is the product of a socially and economically just society.

It is possible, however, to talk in more objective terms about the distinction between procedural justice and substantive justice. The former is concerned with the legal process and the latter, justice in particular cases. At one time the common law was concerned almost solely with procedure. Even today the apparent complexity of the legal process seems to act as a positive deterrent to the ordinary person who seeks redress at law. It is probably not unfair to lay most of the blame for this at the door of lawyers themselves. A sociologist might further argue that lawyers have a vested interest in preserving the mystique of the law for by this they preserve their status in society. In this, of course, lawyers are no different from other professional groups who similarly use language, conventions and procedures which only they fully understand.

Justice at law can be assessed in terms of *natural justice*, the assumption being that there exists a perfect code of rules to which human law should aspire. Two basic principles of natural justice are that a man must be allowed to speak in his own cause and that conflicts must be resolved by an impartial judge. These are, of course, completely acceptable. However, the weakness of natural justice as an objective criterion for comparison lies in its own human philosophical origins unless, of course, you believe in divine intervention and guidance! Perhaps all that we can say is that some laws and some legal systems promote justice more than others.

Organisations and the law

Law *regulates* the activities of organisations by providing a framework of rules governing their formation and dissolution; their use of resources and other activities; and their responsibility and accountability to providers of finance, employees, customers and the community and environment in general. At the same time, however, the regulatory nature and the inherent certainty of this framework *enable* organisations to plan their activities to achieve their commercial and other objectives. Let us consider some specific examples.

Key words _____

Law
A set of rules enforced by the State which regulates conduct within society.

Enabling medium
Law does not necessarily state 'Thou shalt not . . .' Law more commonly facilitates organisations' and individuals' pursuit of activities designed to achieve their objectives. Where the law forbids an activity it does so in order to enforce generally accepted norms of social and commercial behaviour.

Justice
Fairness in a given situation. Conventionally a function of the law is to promote justice but law – a set of practical rules, and justice – an ideal state, are certainly not the same thing.

_____

1 Legal status. You saw in Chapter 3 that the law recognises various types of business organisation and in particular draws a distinction between corporations and unincorporated associations. Thus, the form of organisation most suitable to the specific business unit can be chosen. Each offers its own advantages, operates within its own framework of legal rules and has its own specific methods of creation and dissolution. Corporate status is sought in order to give the business unit an existence independent from its members. This enables it to own property, enter contracts and pursue legal actions in its own right.

2 Agency. To cope with the increasingly specialised nature of modern commercial activity, an organisation frequently needs the services of outside specialists; or alternatively it is employed to use its own specialised facilities or expertise on behalf of other individuals or organisations. The relationship created is that of principal and agent. The use of the law of agency is vital to economic activity as we know it.

3 Contract. The rules of contract law are basic to the activities of organisations. It is by making contracts that they are able to acquire raw materials and sell their finished products and services. (The principles of contract law are discussed in Chapter 17.) In addition, specific aspects of contract law are used by organisations to regulate their relationships with their employees, the methods by which they pay and are paid for goods and services, e.g. by bill of exchange or cheque, their responsibilities to those who provide their finance and their rights as the creditors of others.

4 Property. By using the law, organisations can acquire property and protect their interests in it. This may be land, premises, plant and machinery, or it may be industrial property such as copyrights, patents and trademarks. The latter in particular need protection at law because by their very nature they cannot be physically protected.

Governments and the law

Any government that can maintain a majority in Parliament is virtually an 'elected dictatorship' lasting up to five years. During this time the supremacy of parliamentary legislation gives a government largely unfettered power which it can use to try to achieve its social, economic and political objectives. In addition, the government can sometimes curb the dissemination of information about its activities by invoking the Official Secrets Acts and the Attorney-General (a minister in the government and its chief legal adviser) and the Director of Public Prosecutions (an officer working under the general supervision of the Attorney-General) will sometimes exercise a measure of control over the use of the judicial process, although both should fulfil their functions free from political influence and considerations. Certain criminal offences, e.g. those under the official secrets legislation, can only be prosecuted by or with the consent of the Attorney-General or Director of Public Prosecutions and the Attorney-General exercises (albeit rarely) the Crown's prerogative power to stay criminal prosecutions on indictment by the entry of a *nolle prosequi*. In addition, the Attorney-General sometimes acts as a barrier between the individual and the courts in so far as there is a wide and growing range of laws which cannot be enforced without his consent. For example, there can be no prosecutions under the Race Relations Act 1976 or the Theatres Act 1968 (involving censorship) unless the Attorney-General agrees to associate himself with a private individual in the public interest. Similar consent is also necessary before actions to restrain a public nuisance or other interference with the public interest can be brought. These are known as *relator* actions and the Attorney-General has an absolute discretion whether or not to initiate such proceedings when requested to do so by an individual. He is accountable only to Parliament for his decision.

This is, of course, a rather simple and cynical view of a government's use of law but it is entirely valid in so far as it reflects both the important interrelationships between law, politics and the political process and the weakness of legal controls over the Executive (*see* page 335) under our system of government. While the law continues to have an important regulatory function with regard to the exercise of executive power, and without a written constitution to protect the rights of the individual by placing limits on the power of the Legislature and Executive, 'government according to the law' is *theoretically* open to whatever interpretation the government of the day wishes to put upon it. The courts may interpret legislation and review both quasi-judicial and administrative government decisions for possible illegality but they cannot challenge government policy nor Parliament's power to legislate. Indeed it is possible (although unusual) for a statute to exclude all judicial review of government decision-making in matters covered by that particular statute. In other words, so long as a government does not exceed the power given to it by legislation (often its own), its activities and decisions are not open to judicial review and it is possible for even this power of review to be excluded.

Checking the Executive's power

Some people argue that the courts should be given a much greater role in checking executive power. This is reflected in three separate but related developments. First, the increasing use of *judicial review* to challenge government decisions. In 1985, for example, the Secretary of State for Transport was defeated three times in the courts. In the first case an order raising tolls on the Severn Bridge was held to be 'null and void' because an inspector had not considered all the objectors' points at a public inquiry; in the second it was held that he could not stop the GLC's night and weekend ban on lorries; and in the third a demand for £250 million from the GLC (now disbanded) in connection with the transfer of London Transport from the Council to a new regional authority was 'unlawful, irrational and procedurally improper.' Such use of judicial review introduces a new level of accountability to supplement what many see as much weakened political parliamentary accountability.

The second development is the proposal to incorporate the provisions of the *European Convention on Human Rights* into English and Scottish law. The third is pressure to replace the Official Secrets Act by a *statutory right to information*.

Central to these developments is the balance of power and the relationship between a Parliament perceived to be increasingly weak, an executive which appears to be enjoying increasing administrative discretion, and the individual. Traditionally, Parliament (the *Legislature*) has been seen as the check on the possible excesses of the government (the *Executive*) while the *Judiciary* ensured that both abided by the *rule of law*. As we have seen, the recent rise of the Executive has threatened this balance.

Whether or not you feel that stronger legal curbs are necessary on the power of the executive, the law is the basic medium through which governments implement their policies. Acts of Parliament and delegated legislation directly give effect to government policies, while ministerial decisions (made under statutory authority) and the activities of quasi-governmental bodies (established by legislation) are indirect methods of using the law to implement policy. The quasi-governmental functions of the Monopolies and Mergers Commission and the Director General of Fair Trading are particularly important to trading organisations, while public corporations are both trading organisations and quasi-governmental bodies in so far as their economic activity is partly dictated by government policy.

The role of legislation

A government's ultimate objectives will always be the subject of political debate and the content of the legislation promoted by the government of the day will nearly always reflect its economic and political beliefs. However, all British governments use legislation for three main purposes.

1 To regulate and control society. In particular, it controls antisocial behaviour and protects an individual's basic social rights, e.g. to education, to welfare services and to freedom from discrimination. To a lesser extent it also protects some basic traditional 'legal' rights of the individual, e.g. the Criminal Law Act 1977 supplements a residential occupier's common law rights to possession of their property by making 'squatting' a criminal offence in certain circumstances.

2 To raise by taxation the necessary finance for its activities, thereby implementing its fiscal policies.

3 To create or repeal, revise or reform the law. New principles can be introduced into the body of the law by legislation, e.g. the concept of 'unfair dismissal' by the Employment Protection Act 1975, while bad, unpopular or unworkable law can be removed, e.g. the Trade Union and Labour Relations Act 1974 repealed the Industrial Relations Act 1971, an attempt to control industrial relations by law which simply did not work and caused great resentment.

Consolidating and codifying Acts are sometimes passed. The former re-enact a number of statutes on the same subject with little amendment but in a rationalised and therefore simpler form, e.g. the Companies Act 1985 collected into one Act all the previous legislation on registered companies. (However, it has already been substantially modified by the Companies Act 1989!) The latter (codifying Acts) seek to rationalise both statute and case law on a given subject into one coherent code, although it is the expression rather than the content of the statute which usually differs substantially from the previous law. The Sale of Goods Act 1893 (now the Sale of Goods Act 1979) was a particularly good example of a codifying Act. The Insolvency Act 1986 is a recent example and one where the law was changed in substance to bring it into line with contemporary commercial practice. (It also repealed and replaced important sections of the Companies Act 1985 which became law only a few months earlier!)

The need to revise substantive rules of law ('lawyers' law') by statute may become apparent through the working of the doctrine of binding judicial precedent. This is particularly true following an unpopular (and perhaps politically unacceptable) decision of the House of Lords, e.g. the Race Relations Act 1976 which was passed partly as a response to the decision in *Dockers Labour Club and Institute Ltd v Race Relations Board* (1974) (*see* below). Since its creation in 1965, the Law Commission has been the major influence on a government's use of legislation to revise substantive rules of law.

1 List *five* ways in which law enables business organisations to achieve their objectives.

2 Consider the three main functions of legislation listed above. Which of these do you consider the most important and why?

3 Collect a file of cuttings on an example of government power being challenged by judicial review. Write a short report which examines the issues involved and the outcome of the case and its significance.

Key words

'Elected dictatorship'
The term which has come to be used for a government which commands a large overall majority in the House of Commons and which *appears* not to take into account the views of others.

Judicial review
A legal process by which government ministers (and others) can be called to account for their actions before the High Court. When a government's large Parliamentary majority weakens political accountability, such legal accountability can be an effective check on unauthorised use to the government's executive power.

Society and the law

Within society in general, law is used as a method of organising, regulating and controlling activities in order to protect and preserve social norms. This is achieved:

(a) through a system of largely correlative (corresponding) legal rights and duties;
(b) by imposing criminal or civil liability and enforcing sanctions or remedies against those who infringe legally recognised social norms; and
(c) by providing methods of resolving conflict where the existence of a right or duty is disputed, or where conflicting rights must be reconciled. (Conflict resolution is discussed in depth in the next chapter.)

Rights and duties

A *right* can be said to be a legally protected interest, and a *duty* a legal obligation to respect such an interest. The obligation may involve either positive action or the avoidance of conduct which would infringe the right. In the strict sense, rights are protected by correlative duties, i.e. the existence of a particular right involves the existence of a corresponding duty, enforceable by the owner of the right, to respect that right. However, in a wider sense a right includes any legally recognised interest irrespective of the existence of a correlative duty. Thus, the term includes all legally conferred benefits and advantages. For example, neither the right of landowners to walk on their land, nor the right of people to make wills controlling the succession to their estate (property) involves the imposition of a duty upon anyone else.

Rights can be classified in various ways, e.g. into proprietary or personal rights, into rights *in rem* or rights *in personam*, and into public or private rights. There is, of course, overlap between the classifications.

A *duty* may be *correlative* or *absolute* to a right i.e. owned directly to the state in the interests of the members of society generally. The duty not to interfere with a landowner's right to possession of their land is an example of the former and the duty of an individual to refrain from breaking the criminal law is the primary example of the latter. In addition, many social, welfare and other public duties are absolute.

Any violation of a right or breach of a duty is a legal wrong which results in the state imposing some sanction against the wrongdoer and/or ordering the payment of compensation or the granting of some other form of legal redress to the injured party.

Proprietary and personal rights

The distinction between proprietary and personal rights is based upon the object or subject-matter of the right. Proprietary rights are rights to property, either material property – personal possessions or land – or intangible property such as the goodwill of a business, trade-marks and debts. Personal rights are a matter of an individual's status or condition, e.g. the right to your reputation, protected by the tort of defamation, is of general application, while the right to vote is restricted to persons over eighteen years of age and the right to social security payments is restricted to persons who satisfy certain socio-economic criteria.

Rights *in rem* and rights *in personam*

A right *in rem* corresponds to a duty imposed on persons in general, while a right in *personam* corresponds to a duty imposed on specific individuals. (We have already explained the origin of these terms on page 169). The right of a freeholder to the occupation of his land is a right *in rem*, a right to the land itself which is enforceable against anyone. The owner of a trade-mark or registered design also has a right *in rem*. Conversely, the right of a creditor to be paid a debt is a right in *personam*, a right exercisable only against the debtor himself. This distinction explains why a bank (or other lender) will usually take a legal mortgage over property when making a substantial advance to an organisation or individual. The contract of loan gives the bank a right *in personam* to recover the money from the borrower while the legal mortgage gives a right *in rem* to sell or otherwise deal with the property charged as security if the borrower cannot make repayment.

Public rights and duties

There is a basic distinction between public and private law and hence between public and private rights. Basically, *private law* relates to rights and duties among individuals, e.g. those protected and enforced by the law of contract and the law of torts. *Public law* comprises those branches of law in which the state has a direct interest, mainly administrative, constitutional, criminal, and revenue law. There is, of course, some overlap; an individual may bring a private prosecution against another individual, e.g. for assault, and a public authority may be sued in contract and tort in much the same way as an individual.

Public rights and duties are mainly created and regulated by statute, although some basic principles of the criminal law and some traditional freedoms are still partly embodied in the common law. Statute imposes a wide range of public duties on an equally wide range of individuals and public bodies, e.g. an individual's duties to refrain from breaking the criminal law and to make a tax return, and the duties owed

by public bodies to provide health care and education.

Public rights range from an individual's right to various social security and welfare benefits, to the exercise of basic constitutional rights and freedoms, e.g. the right to vote and the freedoms of person, speech, association, worship, and meeting and procession; and from the right of a local authority to make by-laws and compulsory purchase orders, to the right of the Attorney-General to refuse his consent to a *relator* action (*see* above).

Private rights and duties

Private rights and duties are derived from the common law rather than from statute and comprise the theoretical basis of the civil law, e.g. the law of contract protects rights and enforces obligations on the basis of the agreement reached between the individuals involved. Thus, each party has a right to expect the other to perform his contractual obligations, and each has a correlative duty to do so. It is the law of torts, however, which is the source of most important private rights and duties. You have already seen in Chapter 9 that a tort is a legal wrong against an individual which gives a right of action at civil law for damages, the purposes of the law of tort being to regulate and defend the rights and interests of individuals against certain types of wrongful conduct. It also decides in what cases compensation should be awarded for damage suffered by their infringement. The rights and interests protected and enforced by the law of contract differ in that their basis is the agreement between those involved and not a set of legal rules imposed on society in general as is the case in the law of torts.

For historical reasons each tort protects a particular private right or interest and does so by imposing a correlative private duty. This is probably best explained by a brief survey of the more important torts.

The tort of *trespass to land* protects an individual's possession of land by imposing a duty on others not to intentionally and directly interfere with it without lawful authority. By imposing similar duties, *trespass to the person* (assault, battery and false imprisonment) protects an individual's right to be free from intentional interference with their person or freedom of movement and *trespass to goods* protects both an individual's right to possession of their goods and their interest in their physical condition. However, the tort of *conversion*, which also protects an individual's right to possession and control of their goods (but not their physical condition), is usually relied on where an intentional interference amounts to a denial of title to them, e.g. by stealing goods or by selling goods without title to them.

The tort of *nuisance* protects a person's right to use or enjoy their land or some right over or in connection with the land of another, e.g. a right of way or fishing rights, free from interference. Nuisance and trespass to land differ in two ways. First, nuisance protects interests in land against indirect interference, e.g. by noise, vibrations and smells, or interference by pollution of a river in the case of fishing rights, and not against direct interference. Second, damage must be proved for an action in nuisance to succeed while *all* forms of trespass are actionable *per se* (without proof of damage).

The tort of *defamation* protects the personal right of an individual to their reputation, while the tort of *negligence* protects an individual's right not to suffer injury to their person or property through the negligent act or omission of another. The correlative duty of reasonable care to *neighbours* formulated in *Donoghue v Stevenson* (1932), is the best known and most important legal duty imposed by the law of torts.

The tort of *passing-off* protects proprietary rights in industrial property, e.g. the goodwill of a business and trademarks. As such, this particular tort has more relevance to business organisations than to ordinary individuals.

Some rights and duties protected and imposed by the law of torts have a statutory origin. These too affect organisations more than individuals, e.g. the 'common duty of care' owed by an occupier of premises under the Occupiers' Liability Act 1957. Indeed some are specifically designed to apply to organisations, e.g. the duties imposed upon employers by the Health and Safety at Work, etc Act 1974 (*see* Chapter 9).

Balancing conflicting rights

In a complex society, one function of law is to balance and reconcile conflicting rights. Hence it follows that virtually all rights, be they proprietary or personal, *in rem* or *in personam*, public or private, are qualified, not absolute, and therefore subject to some restriction. For example, the public right of freedom of speech is restricted by the private right to reputation and public duties relating to national security and obscenity. The right of a local authority to make by-laws is similarly not absolute for it is subject to a correlative duty not to exceed the powers given to it by statute – a duty enforced by the *ultra vires* rule.

Private rights are similarly qualified. The rights of a landowner to possess and use his land are restricted by public duties imposed by planning legislation and by statutory public rights of compulsory purchase. Again, the right of an individual to his reputation is also restricted in several ways, e.g. Members of Parliament enjoy an absolute privilege (a right) to say whatever they like during Parliamentary debate even though it may be defamatory.

Different forms of legal liability

It is partly according to the type of legal liability involved that one workable distinction can be drawn between various types of legal wrongs. This is because a particular act or omission may constitute more than one type. For example, taking property belonging to another is both a crime (theft) and a tort (conversion), and negligent driving by a taxi-driver which causes injury to his passenger is a breach of contract in addition to being both a crime and a tort.

Workable distinctions can also be drawn on the basis of the different functions, procedures and consequences involved in different branches of the law. Under the English legal system the basic distinction affecting individuals and organisations alike is that between criminal and civil law. We will therefore discuss the nature and function of criminal and civil law and then, more specifically, criminal and civil liability. Having done this we will consider the different concepts of *fault*, *strict*, and *vicarious* liability, and their relevance to criminal and civil law.

Criminal and civil law

A *crime* is a breach of a public duty, a legal wrong which affects society in general. The state uses the criminal law to regulate the conduct of its citizens and to protect society. This it endeavours to do by prohibiting certain types of conduct and imposing sanctions upon those members of society that disregard the prohibition.

A *civil wrong* is a breach of a private duty which may arise from an agreement between individuals, as in the law of contract, or be imposed by a rule of law, as in the law of torts (the two areas of civil law with which we have been concerned in this book). Thus, the *civil law* is concerned with protecting and enforcing legal rights and duties between individuals and ordering the payment of compensation for damage suffered when they have been infringed or broken.

Since it is impossible to distinguish between crimes and civil wrongs (torts in particular) purely on the basis of the act or omission involved, we must use various other criteria.

1 A *functional* distinction. This distinction has already been made but you will no doubt have appreciated that the criminal law indirectly protects private rights by its deterrent effect.

2 The *consequences* of a successfully brought action. A successfully brought prosecution results in conviction of the accused and the imposition of *sanctions* upon them, either conventionally in the form of a fine or in a term of imprisonment. A successfully brought civil action, however, usually results in the defendant paying damages to the plaintiff, although other remedies may be granted by the court, e.g. an order for the specific performance of a contract or for an injunction to restrain the commission of a tortious (wrongful) act.

3 The *different purpose* of these sanctions and remedies. Criminal sanctions are intended to punish and reform the criminal and deter them and others from similar activities, thereby protecting society. Civil remedies are designed to compensate the individual for the damage suffered as a result of the interference with their private rights. In an action for breach of contract an award of damages is generally intended to put the injured party into the financial position they could reasonably have expected to have enjoyed had the defendant fulfilled their contractual obligations, e.g. the loss of profit on a cancelled order. In an action in tort, damages are designed to restore, as far as this is possible, the injured party to the position enjoyed before the right was infringed. It is obvious, however, that money is poor compensation for many kinds of personal injury and even where business interests are injured, e.g. goodwill, it is often difficult to estimate the financial loss accurately.

However, civil proceedings may result in 'punish-ment' and criminal proceedings in 'compensation' but these are always ancillary to the primary purpose of the proceedings. In exceptional circumstances exemplary or punitive damages may be awarded in civil actions, e.g. for defamation. Here the award exceeds the plaintiff's actual loss and it is designed to satisfy wounded pride and to act as deterrent to others. Under the Powers of Criminal Courts Acts 1973 a criminal court may make a compensation order against a convicted criminal ordering them to pay compensation for personal injury, loss or damage resulting from the offence. In addition, the Crown Court can make a criminal bankruptcy order.

4 There are *different courts* which deal with different infringements of the law. However, as you will see in the next chapter, most courts exercise both civil and criminal jurisdiction. Nevertheless, there are real differences in the form of trial, procedure and rules of evidence. In particular the burden of proof differs. In a criminal case the prosecution must prove the accused's guilt 'beyond reasonable doubt', while the plaintiff in a civil action must prove an infringement of their rights by the defendant 'on the balance of probabilities', a lighter burden of proof.

5 The role of the *state*. In effect, criminal proceedings are initiated and controlled by the state whereas civil proceedings are initiated and controlled by individuals. Only the state can stop a criminal prosecution (by entering a *nolle prosequi*) once it has begun, while a civil dispute is often resolved by the parties before judgment. However, in so far as the stability of our society depends largely on the protection of private rights, the state has an interest in seeing that they are protected. Thus, it provides a means of conflict resolution and enforces civil judgments.

Criminal liability

There are two distinct elements in criminal liability:

(a) a specified act or omission (the *actus reus* or 'guilty act'); and

(b) a specific state of mind (the *mens rea* or 'guilty mind').

For example, under the Theft Act 1968 the *actus reus* of theft is the appropriation of property belonging to another, and the *mens rea* is a dishonest intention to permanently deprive the other of that property. Similarly, the *actus reus* of burglary is entering a building as a trespasser, and the *mens rea* is the intention to commit certain offences inside, e.g. theft. It follows that it is merely the *tort* of trespass and not the crime of burglary to unlawfully enter a building without the required unlawful intention.

Both elements are necessary for criminal liability, for where punishment is involved the mere breach of a prohibition should not be a crime. You will see later, however, that there are a range of statutory criminal offences where a 'guilty mind' as such is not required. These are crimes of strict liability.

The *actus reus* embraces not only the the specific act or omission required for the offence but also the wider circumstances (if any) which may be specified in the definition. In theft, for example, the property taken must 'belong to another'. Hence, taking abandoned property cannot be theft, no matter how dishonest the intention.

It is common to translate *mens rea* as the 'guilty mind' but this translation is somewhat misleading. A person may quite possibly commit a crime without any sense of guilt and even in the belief that their conduct is justified at law. It is more correct to explain the *mens rea* as one of four possible mental attitudes in relation to the *actus reus*. In order of culpability these are:

(a) intention – a person both foresees and desires the consequences of their act or omission;

(b) recklessness – a person foresees the probable consequences of their act but does not desire them, i.e. they take a deliberate risk;

(c) negligence – a person does not foresee the consequences of their act that a reasonable and prudent person would have foreseen, they do not, therefore, desire them;

(d) blameless inadvertence – a person neither foresees nor should have foreseen the consequences of their act.

The law must distinguish between these mental attitudes. Clearly, an intention to commit the *actus reus* should result in conviction and punishment while blameless inadvertence should not. But to what extent should recklessness and negligence warrant punishment? As a generalisation, we can say that a reckless person is usually convicted and punished while a negligent person is not. Thus, *mens rea* can be ac-

ceptably defined as intention or recklessness with respect to the circumstances and consequences of the *actus reus*.

Civil liability

We have already said a considerable amount about the nature of torts and breaches of contract, the *civil wrongs* with which organisations are most likely to be involved, and you have seen that they are both infringements of private rights.

Civil liability clearly requires an act or omission but, because the essence of civil law is the protection of rights, it is neither realistic nor necessarily productive to attempt to list and define specific acts or omissions which infringe these rights. In contrast, the criminal law specifically defines the acts or omissions which it prohibits. In short, only acts or omissions within the definition of a particular crime can be prosecuted while any act which unlawfully interferes with a private right gives grounds for an action at civil law.

The importance and relevance of mental attitudes in civil liability varies but far less emphasis is generally placed upon it than is the case in criminal liability. This is because the purpose and consequences of a civil action is compensation of the injured party and not punishment of the wrongdoer. For example, while a breach of contract may have been *committed* intentionally, recklessly or negligently, the reason for awarding compensation to the plaintiff is the infringement of their private right by the breach itself. The wrongdoer's liability does not differ, whether they intended to break the contract, were negligent in their conduct or acted with blameless inadvertence.

In the law of torts mental attitudes are more important and most torts require *intention*, although *culpable inadvertence* (negligence) is the essence of negligence, the most important tort. However, while most people who commit torts other than negligence desire the consequences of their act or omission, *intention* as the required mental attitude usually has a more technical meaning and relates to the act or omission and not to its consequences. For example, people who walk over another's land, believing reasonably but wrongly that they are entitled to do so (they may believe that they are following a public right of way), have committed trespass because they intended their actions, even though they did not intend to interfere with the landowner's right of possession.

If the law is going to protect private rights effectively, the mental attitude of the defendant towards the act or omission which infringed the plaintiff's right must be a lesser consideration than the infringement itself.

Answer the following questions about criminal and civil liability.

1 In what ways is it possible to draw valid distinctions between crimes and civil wrongs?

2 What is meant by the *actus reus* and *mens rea* of a crime?

3 Is the mental element more or less important in civil liability as compared with criminal liability?

Fault liability

Liability based upon *fault* is primarily associated with the tort of negligence, for here people incur civil liability for failure to exercise reasonable care in their activities. Expressed formally, the tort of negligence is committed by the breach of a legal duty of care owed to another person which causes that other person foreseeable damage. With a few important exceptions, e.g. manslaughter and causing death by dangerous driving, negligence is rarely the gist of a criminal offence and, therefore, people are rarely criminally liable if they are merely at 'fault'.

It is perfectly proper that anybody who is injured by the fault of another should be able to recover compensation from that person. However, fault liability is widely and seriously questioned, particularly in relation to road traffic accidents and industrial injuries. 'Product liability' (*see* page 312) now covers injuries caused by defective goods, an area of law where statute has actually replaced fault liability by strict liability.

The principle of fault liability suffers from two important practical weaknesses. First, it assumes that people at fault have sufficient financial resources to compensate those that they have injured. Second, in reality compensation is frequently paid by an insurance company or by the employer of the people at

fault. Taken together, these defects significantly reduce the validity of fault as a basis for civil liability. Indeed this supports the argument for further extending the principle of strict liability (discussed below) in combination with various techniques of compensation through insurance. This would relegate legal proof of fault to a position of secondary importance behind the basic right to receive compensation for injury caused by another.

Strict liability

Where criminal or civil liability is *strict*, the wrongdoer's mental attitude is irrelevant, i.e. proof that they acted intentionally or were at fault in their conduct is unnecessary. They are liable merely because they have committed the *actus reus* of the particular criminal offence or have caused the plaintiff harm by breaking a legal duty owed to him.

The scope of strict liability in *criminal law* is limited because it is generally wrong in principle that people who neither intended their actions nor acted recklessly should be punished. However, many offences of strict liability have been created by statute because they are an effective means of social regulation; almost invariably they involve only a small degree of 'wrong'. Nevertheless, as you have seen, there is a legal presumption that *mens rea* is always necessary for criminal liability. Therefore, the statute must expressly or impliedly exclude it. Statutes creating road traffic offences and offences relating to the sale of food and drugs are good examples of this having been done.

In the *law of contract* a civil wrong is committed merely by breaking a contractual obligation. Civil liability for breach of contract is therefore strict. This applies even where a business organisation sells 'unmerchantable goods' in breach of s.14 of the Sale of Goods Act 1979 without the slightest idea or opportunity to find out that the goods were unmerchantable.

Strict liability in *tort* is found in the Consumer Protection Act 1987 (product liability – *see* page 312) and in the rule in *Rylands v Flectcher* (1868), where a particular activity is inherently dangerous to the community. The rule in *Rylands v Flectcher* applies where a 'dangerous thing' which a person has brought on to his land and which is not naturally there, e.g. water, gas or fire, escapes from the land and causes damage. The mere fact that damage occurs in such circumstances makes the occupier of the land liable in tort. However, liability is *strict* and not *absolute* and the occupier can plead certain defences, e.g. that the escape occurred through the unforeseeable 'act of a stranger' or that the occupier was acting under statutory authority in the use of the land.

Quite clearly the rule cannot apply to every non-natural user of land otherwise all industrial activity would be subject to it. Thus, strict liability is imposed on those who pursue activities which involve an unreasonable risk to the community or an extraordinary use of land. It is for the court to decide on the facts of the case whether an activity falls within the rule and it is clear that a judge will balance the magnitude of the risk against the defendant's interest in the activity and its benefit to the community.

While the rule in *Rylands v Fletcher* cannot be allowed to interfere with necessary industrial activity, it is equally clear that the community must be protected from dangers inherent in the industrial use of certain materials. Consequently a number of statutes impose strict liability for damage caused by 'environmental hazards'. Examples are the Nuclear Installations Act 1965, dealing with nuclear incidents, the Merchant Shipping (Oil Pollution) Act 1971, dealing with escape or discharge of oil from a merchant ship, and the Control of Pollution Act 1974, dealing with unlawful deposits of poisonous, noxious or polluting waste.

Liability in the tort of nuisance is probably strict if the plaintiff only seeks an injunction, for here the defendant is merely forbidden from commencing or continuing a wrongful activity. (An action for damages in nuisance probably requires proof of fault.) More generally, liability for breach of a duty imposed by statute, e.g. under the Factories Act 1961, is usually strict on the grounds of public policy.

Vicarious liability

Liability is said to be *vicarious* where one person is liable for the actions of another. In so far as vicarious liability is independent of intention or fault, it is similar to strict liability.

Vicarious liability in *tort* often arises under a contract of insurance but it is more usually associated with employment because the common law imposes liability on employers for the torts committed by their employees in the course of their employment. It follows that the principle of vicarious liability is directly relevant to most organisations.

It is important to distinguish between employees (servants) and independent contractors for employers are only liable for the tortious acts of independent contractors in certain circumstances, e.g. where they expressly or impliedly authorises the tortious act, where an independent contractor creates a danger on the highway, where the rule in *Rylands v Fletcher* applies, and where employers delegate duties imposed upon them by statute or common law to independent contractors.

At law an employee (a servant) is employed under a contract *of* service while an independent contractor is employed under a contract *for* services. However, it is far easier to recognise than to define a contract of service and, therefore, it is difficult to distinguish satisfactorily between an employee and an independent contractor. For example, the 'control' test, i.e. that a master (an employer) is able to tell the servant what to do and also how to do it while the independent contractor can only be told what to do, cannot be realistically applied today to many skilled employees. Other tests are somewhat involved and may still give an inconclusive result. The best general approach would seem to be that employees and their work are an integral part of the business whereas independent contractors and their work, while playing a part in the business, are not integrated into it.

It is similarly difficult to define 'course of employment'. While it certainly embraces an employee's negligence and mistakes, its scope must ultimately depend on the circumstances. The well known legal cliché that an employer is liable unless an employee is 'on a frolic of his own' tends to restate the problem reversed and in rather more obscure language!

Vicarious liability in tort can be explained and justified in two main ways. First, employees' work benefits the employers and they should therefore answer for the damage which occasionally results from the employment. Second, organisations (the employers) will almost certainly be better able to pay compensation than individuals (its employees). Indeed, the Employers' Liability (Compulsory Insurance) Act 1969 *requires* employers to insure themselves against vicarious liability for injuries caused by employees to their *colleagues* and most will choose to extend the insurance to persons other than employees.

In *criminal law* a person is not generally liable for the criminal acts of another. This is because criminal liability at common law requires intention or recklessness with respect to the *actus reus*. A person clearly cannot have this if they knew nothing of the other's action. Conversely, a person who authorises or commands another to commit a criminal offence will be liable as a *participant* in the crime.

There are, however, a considerable number of offences created by statute where the courts have held that the statute imposes criminal liability on one person for the acts of another. Such interpretations can be justified because they are necessary if the will of Parliament is to be implemented and the object of the legislation achieved. As in tort, vicarious liability in criminal law is almost solely concerned with employers and their employees.

Vicarious liability in criminal law arises *(a)* where a person is under a statutory duty but delegates this to someone else, e.g. under the Licensing Acts only the licensee can commit the offences; and *(b)* where one person's acts are in law those of another, e.g. where an employee sells goods, the sale is deemed to be the employer's act for the purposes of such statutes as the Trade Descriptions Act 1968.

1 Compare and evaluate the following statements.

'If A is at fault and injures B, A should compensate B.'

'If A injures B, B should be compensated.'

'If B is injured by A, B should be compensated by A's employer.'

2 Assess the economic consequences of substituting strict liability for fault liability in industrial injury and road accident cases.

Organisations and legal liability

The civil liability of the members of a *non-corporate organisation* is the same as that of an ordinary individual. They are liable for breaches of contract and may be sued for their own tortious acts and those committed by their employees in the course of their employ-ment. Special procedural rules apply in actions against both partnerships and trade unions, however, and considerable immunity from legal liability is enjoyed by the latter, their officials and members for any tortious acts committed in furtherance of a trade dispute. There is also a presumption that collective agreements made between trade unions and employers are not legally enforceable. The members of a non-corporate organisation are also in a similar position to private individuals as regards the criminal law. Nevertheless, a statute may sometimes provide for the criminal liability of an unincorporated organisation and proceedings are then taken against the organisation in its own name and not in that of its members.

Corporate organisations pose a theoretical problem in this context. As they have no physical existence and cannot be formed to pursue an unlawful activity, they logically cannot commit an unlawful act or form any unlawful intention. However, such a theory put into practice would give a totally unacceptable result and corporate organisations do incur both civil and criminal liability.

Since a corporation can only act through its directors and employees, both its criminal and civil liability must be vicarious. It is vicariously liable for the tortious acts of its employees committed in the course of their employment in exactly the same way as any other employer. If any particular mental attitude is required this is supplied by the employees concerned and attributed to the corporation on the basis that it has a fundamental responsibility for their acts or omissions.

In criminal law a corporation's vicarious liability extends beyond that of an individual. This must be so if it is to be subject to the same public duty as that imposed on a natural person by the criminal law. It commits the *actus reus* of an offence and has the required *mens rea* through the acts or omissions and mental attitudes of those persons who control and direct its activities: usually its directors. Their acts, omissions and mental attitudes are considered at law to be those of the company itself. It is, therefore, liable for its own acts and not for those of its servants. Despite this reasoning, however, its liability is still in reality *vicarious*.

A corporation cannot be imprisoned, and therefore can only be convicted of offences punishable by fine – in fact most offences are punishable in this way. There are, of course, certain offences which a corporation cannot commit, e.g. indecent exposure!

Key words

Rights and duties

A *right* is a legally protected interest, a *duty* a legal obligation to respect that interest. This framework of legally recognised rights and duties provides the basis on which behaviour in a society is regulated.

Public and private law

Public law is law in which the state has a direct interest, *private law* concerns rights and duties among individuals.

Law of torts

This branch of law is the main source of private rights and duties. Each tort protects a specific right and compels anyone who infringes it to compensate the owner of the right. Examples include the torts of nuisance and negligence.

Crimes and civil wrongs

A particular action can easily be both, e.g., theft is also an example of the tort of conversion. A *crime*, however, is a breach of a public duty usually resulting in punishment of the offender; a *civil wrong*, e.g. a tort or a breach of contract, is a breach of a private duty which usually results in the payment of compensation.

Fault liability

Liability at law based on the plaintiff being caused injury by the fault of the defendant.

Strict liability

Liability at law based, in civil law, merely on the breach of a legal duty owed by the defendant to the plaintiff. Proof of negligence is unnecessary.

Vicarious liability

Liability for the acts of another. Most commonly associated with employment where an employer is liable for the wrongful (tortious) acts of an employee committed in the course of latter's employment.

The origin and sources of English law

Introduction

Law has its origins in *custom*, a far cry from the sophisticated statutory law of today. A custom is nothing more than a group of people doing something in a particular way. It evolves spontaneously and becomes the accepted social norm followed by the members of the community. Failure to observe social norms endangers society and breaches of the customary law would be punished. Today we can define a custom as usage recognised by law.

Originally, customs controlled the basic aspects of life necessary to preserve and protect a simple society. Custom would regulate marriage, provide a simple criminal law, e.g. 'thou shalt not kill', 'thou shalt not steal'; and, somewhat later, a method for determining property rights, particularly rights over land and its inheritance. Primogeniture (inheritance by the eldest son) is both an early example of the quest for status in society and recognition that it was economically undesirable to divide land into tiny units. Hence, land passed from father to eldest son without division among others.

In the earliest communities, as with animal groups, customary rules would be enforced by the physically strongest. Gradually more sophisticated ideas of government and law-making would evolve. In many communities, rule by the eldest or group of elders, or by a 'wiseman' of some kind, emerged. In time certain families might attain supreme power and the idea of 'kingship' evolved. Perhaps the final stage in the evolution of law enforcement to date is to be found in a free and democratic system of government, although it is debatable whether a truly democratic system can ever be achieved.

The English legal system is unique in having followed the highly idealised process outlined above more closely than any other system. There has been very little external interference in our legal development; even the laws and legal system left by the Romans were almost totally destroyed during the Saxon age which followed and in contemporary times joining the EC has had little effect on our purely domestic law.

The term 'source' has a number of different meanings in the context of English law. It is to this and the different sources that we now turn.

The formal source

This means the formal authority which gives a particular rule the force of law. Under the UK's constitution, the *Queen in Parliament* is the formal source of law and supreme power in the state. While legislation originates in Parliament, it must receive the Royal Assent before it is enforceable. In theory, the Sovereign could refuse her consent to a particular piece of legislation but in practice it is highly unlikely that this would ever be done. In addition, the judges are the Sovereign's judges, deriving their authority from the Royal prerogative and making decisions in the Sovereign's name.

Legal sources

These may be defined as the ways in which ideas and principles become recognised as law. In chronological order, these are custom, case law and legislation. They are the sources of all public and private rights and duties.

Custom

Before the Norman conquest in 1066 there was no centralised English state, let alone a UK. The Normans began a process of creating a single nation under a centralised government but built upon the existing Saxon institutions. The *feudal system*, for example, predated the conquest but the Normans refined it into an efficient system of social, economic and political organisation and control, served by a developing *common law*.

From time to time the Norman kings would send tax officials and government administrators around the country to collect the King's revenues and to look after his interests. It became common for these royal officials, who were not trained lawyers, to resolve local disputes and try those accused of crimes. It became the practice for their decisions to be based on the customs of the locality.

Over the years a body of customs emerged which were either to be found in all parts of the country or which the royal officials, or justices as they began to be called, thought should be applied everywhere. Such customs became known as *common customs* or *customs of the realm* (as opposed to local customs), and formed the basis of the common law which was enforced in the common law courts (the King's courts). The basic principles of contemporary criminal law can be traced back to such common customs and some crimes, murder for example, are still common law

offences, i.e. not defined by statute. Similarly, the basic principles of the law of torts and the law of contract are to be found in customs of the realm as refined by judicial decisions and the legal process.

Today, common customs have long since been absorbed into case law and statute and are only of historical interest. However, local customs (applying to a particular place, group of people, or both) which satisfy a number of legal requirements are occasionally recognised as exceptions to the general law and enforced accordingly. A particularly well-known example was the custom of *Gavelkind* which was still found in Kent in the 19th century. Under this, land was inherited by all sons in equal shares and not by the eldest son alone. A recent example occurred in Windsor in 1975 when the customary use of a piece of land called Bachelor's Acre by local residents for lawful sports and pastimes was upheld by the Court of Appeal, preventing New Windsor Corporation from using part of this land as a car park.

Case law

As soon as Royal courts were established in England, common custom became the basis of their decisions. From the earliest times judges have always referred to the decisions in previous cases for guidance but the present system of case law or *judicial precedent*, as it is technically called, dates from the later part of the 19th century and two events in particular. To base decisions on previous cases it is essential to have accurate records and this was made possible in 1865 by the establishment of the Incorporated Society for Law Reporting. Similarly, it is necessary to have a rational court structure so that the avenues of appeal and the authority of each court are settled. The reorganisation of the court structure by the Judicature Acts 1873–5 brought this about.

Case law is based on the rule that previous decisions of a higher court are followed by lower courts. Basic to the system is the concept of the *ratio decidendi* (the legal reason for deciding). This consists of three things: first, the judge's statement of the relevant facts, this being used for comparative purposes in later cases; second, an account of the way in which the decision was reached, e.g. which cases and statutes were referred to as 'authority', in other words the process of legal reasoning that was employed; and third, the decision made to resolve the dispute between the parties. The *ratio decidendi*, particularly the legal reasoning employed by the judge, becomes part of the common law and can be used as the basis on which to make later decisions.

The English legal system divides precedents (previous decisions) into those which have binding authority and those which have only persuasive authority. The idea of being *bound* by previous decisions is a principle only found in countries which operate a system of law based upon our own, e.g. the Commonwealth countries.

Binding precedents are decisions of the House of Lords and the Court of Appeal which have not been overruled by a later case or by legislation. Such decisions must be followed whether the judge in the later case approves of them or not. This gives an important element of certainty to the system but may at times make it rather rigid and inflexible.

There are three kinds of *persuasive precedents*.

1 Decisions of lower courts.
2 Decisions of Commonwealth and American Courts, and the recommendations of the Privy Council.
3 Obiter dicta. These are statements of law made by the judge when giving judgment which are not strictly relevant to the decision before the court but which must be treated with respect in later cases. In some instances important principles have been introduced into the law through *obiter dicta*. The *obiter* statements made by the House of Lords in *Hedley Byrne & Co Ltd v Heller & Partners Ltd* (1963) are examples which directly affect business organisations. They established that in certain circumstances a person can be liable for making negligent statements which cause purely financial loss to a person who relies on them.

The operation of the system of judicial precedent is very closely tied to the court structure (*see* Chapter 26). Basically, higher courts bind lower courts. The House of Lords binds all other courts and, except in exceptional circumstances, is bound by its own previous decisions. Below this the Court of Appeal binds the High Court and County Court but is itself bound by the House of Lords and its own previous decisions. However, in all matters relating to the interpretation of the EC treaties and subsidiary legislation made under them, *all* English courts must follow the decisions of the European Court of Justice.

Legislation

The common law – the system of judge-made law originating in custom – was designed to order a socially simple, economically underdeveloped and politically uneducated society. It existed largely to serve the interests and needs of the ruling élite (the nobility and landed gentry) from whose number almost all the judges were drawn. Consequently, the common law clearly reflected their interests in preserving property rights and the social *status quo*, for these were the bastions of their privileged position.

Such a system, reflecting interests and values perfectly typical of underdeveloped societies both before and since, could not survive the tremendous social and economic upheavals brought about by the Industrial Revolution. The population dramatically increased, new towns grew up almost overnight and completely new problems of government associated with urban living and an industrialising society arose. A new, creative type of law-making was needed: Parliamentary legislation.

While there are a number of well-known statutes from earlier centuries, legislation only became an important source of law in the second half of the 19th century. In particular, the basis of modern commercial law affecting business organisations was codified into statutory form in this period. Examples included The Bills of Exchange Act 1882, The Factors Act 1889, The Partnership Act 1890, and The Sale of Goods Act 1893. Since 1945 legislation has been totally dominant as the main source of law and the annual output of Acts and Orders made under their authority has reached staggering proportions. The structure and regulation of modern British society is now very heavily dependent on legislation.

Legislation takes two forms.

1 Acts of Parliament. These may be defined as the will of a democratically elected assembly confirmed by the Sovereign. Acts of Parliament are the supreme form of law in this country and they can change, repeal or create law. Since the Bill of Rights 1688, the judges have recognised the supremacy of Parliament and, while they are able to interpret an Act when its meaning is ambiguous or obscure, they have no right to challenge the Act itself.
2 Delegated Legislation. As the common law was too

unwieldy and too unsophisticated to serve the rapidly changing socio-economic needs of the 19th century, so Acts of Parliament by themselves are inadequate to cope with modern society's demands on law. Governments have increasingly looked to delegated legislation as a means of implementing their policies. Delegated legislation is law made by a body to which Parliament has given limited powers of law-making. It follows that the *ultra vires* rule applies to such legislation and it may be challenged in court and declared void if, in making it, the law-making body exceeds the power granted to it by Parliament.

In Chapter 9 you saw that the Health and Safety at Work, etc Act 1974 enables the Secretary of State for Employment to make regulations altering, amending or repealing previous relevant legislation. These ministerial regulations and orders made under the authority of 'parent' Acts are known as *statutory instruments*, and are a type of delegated legislation. They are of crucial importance to the process of government for it is largely by statutory instruments that the Government's policies are implemented. Parliament itself would certainly not be able to afford the time, and would probably lack the technical expertise and knowledge, to deal with the minutiae of policy implementation.

Parliament is ultimately able to control the use of statutory instruments by government ministers since important regulations and orders may have to be submitted to both Houses for approval and others are laid before Parliament and a resolution rejecting them may be passed within forty days. A great many are not laid before Parliament, however, but are subject to committee scrutiny in both Houses. Thus, Parliament should be informed if ministers exceed the authority granted to them by parent Acts. Local authority by-laws are the other best known example of delegated legislation.

In addition to the two forms of domestic legislation, the UK is subject to the supra-national legislation of the European Communities. This has already been discussed in Chapter 20.

The interpretation of statutes

In a classic 'David and Goliath' confrontation in *Daymond v S W Water Authority* (1973), Mr Day-mond achieved a notable victory for the individual consumer against a (then) large public utility corporation. The House of Lords held that the Water Act 1973 did not give a water authority power to charge (in Daymond's case £4.89) an owner or occupier of premises not connected to the main drainage for sewerage and sewage disposal services, even though s.30 of the Act gave authorities 'power to fix, and to demand, take and recover such charges for the services performed, facilities provided ... as they think fit.' Consequently, the statutory orders which prescribed the charges (an example of delegated legislation) made under the Act were *ultra vires*. Mr Daymond's property was not connected to main drainage and was 365m away from a sewer. As a result of the decision, water authorities found themselves many millions of pounds worse off and this meant that all owners and occupiers of premises connected to main drains had to pay more.

A somewhat unusual situation came before the court in *Bourne v Norwich Crematorium Ltd* (1967). It had to be decided whether a crematorium was an 'industrial building' within the meaning of the Income Tax Act 1952 because the company which operated it was entitled to a tax allowance if it was. An 'industrial building' was defined by the Act as a building in use 'for the purpose of a trade which consists of . . . the subjection of goods or materials to any process'. The Court was unable to accept the argument that cremating human remains fell within the definition!

The Race Relations Act 1968, which made it unlawful '. . . for any person concerned with the provision to the public or a section of a public . . . of any goods, facilities or services to discriminate against a person seeking to obtain or use those goods, facilities or services by refusing or deliberately omitting to provide him with any of them . . .', had to be interpreted by the House of Lords in *Dockers Labour Club and Institute Ltd v Race Relations Board* (1974). It was decided that refusing to serve a black associate member (there were about one million associate members of about 4000 clubs) at the club's bar was not unlawful discrimination within the meaning of the Act because the club operated in the 'private sphere' while the Act was designed to stop discrimination in the public sphere. The decision was correct at law but was politically and socially unacceptable and the Race Relations Act 1976 repealed the 1968 Act, one of its provisions making it unlawful for clubs of 25 or more members to discriminate on racial grounds.

Parliament makes the law but the Courts enforce it and it is sometimes necessary to ascertain the intention of Parliament before this can be done. The three cases above are all examples of statutes where this was necessary because particular words or phrases used in them were unclear or ambiguous when applied to the facts. However, you must remember that the courts cannot challenge Parliament's authority to legislate. If the words of the statute are clear and unambiguous the need for judicial interpretation does not arise.

A thorough study of statutory interpretation uncovers a considerable diversity of rules, judicial attitudes and precedents, so much so that at times it seems that there are no real rules of interpretation at all. Nevertheless, a general summary should always be included in any consideration of legislation for, through their power of interpretation, the courts may be able to affect the meaning and application of some statutes. In a few cases Parliament has passed an amending Act nullifying the judicial interpretation of the previous Act. The passing of the Race Relations Act 1976 is a good example.

It is presumed that an Act of Parliament does not bind the Crown and that it applies only to the UK. Similarly, it is presumed not to be retrospective (have any application to past events) nor to alter the common law. As you have seen, the common law is the fundamental law of the land and if Parliament wishes to alter it then it must do so in very clear terms. A well-known example of this is *Sweet v Parsley* (1969). At common law, *mens rea* (*see* page 456) is always required for criminal liability but this is not always the case with offences created by statute. The defendant was charged with being concerned in the management of premises used for the purpose of smoking cannabis contrary to the Dangerous Drugs Act 1965. The Act made no mention of *mens rea*. At the time of the offence the defendant had let the house that the police raided and was living a long way away, only visiting the house to collect the rent. The House of Lords allowed her appeal against conviction on the ground that where Parliament creates an offence without any reference to a *mens rea* one will be presumed. Knowledge of the smoking of drugs was necessary for her to have committed an offence under the Act.

Conventionally there are said to be three basic judicial approaches to statutory interpretation: the 'literal' rule, the 'golden' rule and the 'mischief' rule.

1 The literal rule. The role of the judges is to ascertain the intention of Parliament from the Act itself. Thus, if the words of the statute are capable of only one meaning, this is the meaning the court will take and the statute will be enforced accordingly, even if the result is unlikely or harsh. The remedy for a harsh law lies in an amending act and not with the courts. However, in the great majority of cases a literal interpretation of the statute produces the desired result.

A somewhat harsh yet perfectly correct decision, based on a literal interpretation of the Agricultural Holdings Act 1948, occurred in *Newborough v Jones* (1974). A notice to quit had been served on a tenant by pushing it under his door. Unfortunately, it was also pushed under the floor covering and remained there for some months undiscovered. The Act started that a notice was 'duly served if left at the tenant's proper address'. Thus, the Act had been fully complied with and the notice was effective even though the tenant was unaware of its service.

2 The golden rule. This is said to be a modification of the literal rule. It is used either where a literal interpretation would produce an obviously absurd or unwanted result, providing a reasonable alternative interpretation is possible, or where the statute is capable of more than one literal meaning, i.e. it is ambiguous. In the latter situation the literal rule has no place and the golden rule is applied to effect the most reasonable of the alternative meanings possible. This latter use of the rule is more common than the former. If the converse was true, the court would be usurping Parliament's function and exceeding its constitutional role as the interpreter and enforcer of legislation.

Both *Daymond's Case* and *Bourne's Case* are examples of the golden rule being applied.

3 The mischief rule. This rule has a long history and dates from *Heydon's Case* (1584). It can be applied where the statute under consideration was passed to remedy a defect or 'mischief' in the law, most commonly where the statute passed to do this is ambiguous. The rule is used to promote the interpretation which remedies the defect. Occasionally, however, it is applied in preference to the literal rule where an application of the latter would not remedy the defect in the law. However, in *Docker's Labour Club and*

Institute Ltd v Race Relations Board (1974), where the mischief in the law was (before the Race Relations Act 1968) that there were inadequate means of controlling racial discrimination in *public*, the House of Lords allowed an appeal by the club against a declaration that it was guilty of unlawful discrimination on the grounds that associate members of the appellant club were not 'a section of the public' and so not within the 'mischief' that the 1968 Act was meant to remedy.

The mischief rule is notable for providing the sole exception to another basic principle of statutory interpretation: that the intention of Parliament is to be ascertained only from the words of the Act itself and not from external sources, e.g. Parliamentary debates or reports of Royal Commissions. When applying the mischief rule the court can look outside the statute to discover the defect in the law which the statute was designed to remedy and hence interpret the statute to 'suppress the mischief and advance the remedy'.

EC Legislation

You have already seen that the legislation of the European communities is somewhat different from our own. In particular, community legislation tends to enact broad principles rather than detailed provisions. Consequently, English courts must play a far more active role to affect the aims of Community legislation than they need or can do with our own domestic legislation. They must look to the intent and purpose of the legislation and not be concerned to examine the words in meticulous detail or argue about their precise grammatical sense. If there is a gap in the legislation they must fill it as they think the European legislators would have wished. This is in sharp contrast to domestic legislation where any gap must be filled by Parliament.

Thus, in following the European pattern far more use will be made of the golden and mischief rules than the literal rule. In addition, statements made on behalf of the Community, and Community publications which reflect the substance of the attitudes in the negotiations which led to the conclusion of the treaties (the *travaux préparatoires*), may be consulted to resolve any ambiguity or uncertainty in an enactment. This again is in sharp contrast with English principles of interpretation.

Conclusion

Organisations are affected no more and no less than individuals by legislation and its interpretation. However, *Daymond's Case* (1973) shows that a large organisation can suddenly find basic assumptions of its operation swept away or undermined by a single interpretation of a single statute. More generally, the interpretation and application of the various Companies Acts and detailed tax legislation can fundamentally affect organisations both large and small. Occasionally, judicial interpretation of statutes can have repercussions which directly affect important social and political issues, e.g. the *Dockers Labour Club Case*.

Before moving on, remember that in general it is a very small number of men and even fewer women from a narrow and rather atypical socio-economic background, holding traditionally conservative views and appointed from the ranks of a small elite profession, who have some power to affect the enacted will of a democratically elected Parliament. In 1988 more than 30% of judges were over 65, they were almost exclusively white and only 4% were women. In addition, of the 10 law lords (the judges who hear appeals in the House of Lords) only one had been educated at a state school.

Notwithstanding these facts it is surely equally true to say that vigilance and positive intervention by the judiciary acts as a deterrent to and safeguard against possible abuse of statutory power by the government or other public bodies.

1 The Times carries law reports nearly every day. Over a period of time collect cuttings of cases (or take photocopies) which involved the court in interpreting Acts of Parliament. Read the reports carefully to see how they went about the interpretation and decide which basic rule of interpretation the court employed.

Do you think the result was a 'fair' one? Why? Was a different outcome possible? How?

2 Will the male, middle-aged, middle class, public school and Oxbridge educated judge soon become a thing of the past or is such a background a qualification for the job?

The literary sources

These are the written records of the law. There are three main literary sources.

The statute books

These contain the Acts of Parliament. Two original copies of each Act are signed by the Sovereign or her representative, one being kept at the Public Records Office and the other in the House of Lords. However, for all practical purposes the Queen's Printer's copies are acceptable.

The law reports

These contain records of the facts, legal arguments and decisions in important court cases. Today, nearly all important cases are reported. However, the courts have never created a methodical system of producing reports and it has been left entirely in the hands of private organisations. Consequently, there is still an element of chance and individual preference as to whether a case is reported or not.

In 1865 the Incorporated Council of Law Reporting in England and Wales was founded and by convention since then its *Law Reports* are always cited in court when they contain a report of the required case. A few series of private reports are still published, of which the best known and most comprehensive are the *All England Law Reports*. (You are quite likely to have these in your college library.) In addition, *The Times* newspaper carries reports of the previous day's cases and these are sometimes cited in court when the decision is too recent to have been published in the more formal series.

New technology has had an impact on law reporting and the preparation of cases. LEXIS, a computer data base of leading cases, including some unreported in the conventional reports, and statute law is now fairly widely used. It can drastically reduce the time taken to find a relevant legal authority merely by inputting details of the issue concerned. However, some leading judges have seen it as a mixed blessing. Sir John Donaldson (the Master of the Rolls – head of the Civil Division of the Court of Appeal) said in one 1983 case that 'the profession was afflicted, or assisted, as the case may be, by electronic data processing appliances.' The problem he foresaw was of judges being bombarded with numerous unnecessary and often otherwise unreported decisions just because the database had produced them. Later the same year, the House of Lords stated that unreported decisions could generally not be cited in an appeal to the House. This was a significant change to ancient practice where any decision could be cited which was vouched for by a barrister.

Textbooks

Modern textbooks, no matter how well respected, are not authority for legal rules until and unless a particular passage or passages have been accepted and adopted by the court as true statements of the law. This happens infrequently. Nevertheless, textbook writers influence successive generations of judges and lawyers and in this way they are an influence on the evolution of the law.

However, a few 'classical texts' from the seventeenth century and earlier are accorded the status of legal sources of law because they contain the only reliable written record of the law as it was in the writer's time. Bracton's 13th century treatise *De Legibus et Consuetudinibus Angliae*, the main literary source of the medieval common law, and Coke's *Institutes*, the contemporary authoritative work on early 17th century law, are good examples.

The historical sources

Custom

English law has its origin in custom and even today a local custom may very occasionally be established as an exception to the general law. To this extent custom is a legal source of law. However, custom has long since ceased to be an important creative source, and it is far more realistic to classify custom as the major historical source of the common law. Its role in the evolution of the common law has already been discussed.

Equity

English law is unique in having had two distinct systems of law operating side by side for at least four centuries, *common law* and *equity*. This dual jurisdiction was ended by the merger of the administrations of the two systems under the Judicature Acts 1873–5.

All actions at common law were begun by a writ (a written command in the name of the Sovereign) and by the 14th century its procedure had become so rigid that no action could be brought unless one of a fixed number of writs fitted the plaintiff's claim. This inflexibility was the main reason for the evolution of equity. It became the practice for those with sufficient influence, money and determination to petition the King when the common law offered them no satisfaction in their claim. In time, petitions began to be heard by the Lord Chancellor instead of the King. Finally the Court of Chancery, presided over by the Lord Chancellor, was established to administer the rules of equity. The present Chancery Division of the High Court is a direct descendant of this early judicial function of the Lord Chancellor.

At first the Lord Chancellor decided disputes brought before him purely on the facts of each individual case but gradually a body of case law evolved in the Court of Chancery which was applied almost as strictly as the common law in the common law courts.

Equity's growth in the late middle ages depended above all else on its recognition and protection of one particular interest in property, that of a beneficiary under a trust. A *trust* is an arrangement whereby legal title to property is given by one person to another (a trustee) with the latter promising to use the property for the benefit of a third person (the beneficiary).

Trusts originated in the Middle Ages. Some of the earliest examples were the arrangements made by knights when they went to fight overseas and wished to ensure that their estates would be maintained and their families provided for, or when a person wished to provide for a monastic order which was forbidden to own property. As neither the knight's wife, nor his heir under 21, nor the monks could, for different reasons, own land, a straightforward transfer of ownership was impossible and a trust had to be employed. Hence, legal title was vested in the trustee(s) but the benefit of the property was vested in the knight's family or monastery.

The common law only recognised the basic transaction – the transfer of the legal title to the trustee(s) – and would neither recognise nor protect the beneficiary's interest, e.g. where the trustee used the property for his own benefit. This was clearly unfair and the Lord Chancellor would intervene to compel the trustee, the legal owner of the property, to act according to his conscience and use the property for the benefit of the beneficiary, the owner in equity.

Trusts became increasingly common. They provided a way of avoiding some feudal payments and soon became a basic device for property settlements in landowning families. Today they enable people (or organisations) who are, for one reason or another, unable to hold legal ownership of property to enjoy the benefit of it. For example, minors cannot hold legal estates in land but the land can be held in trust for them. (It is possible that you, or one of your fellow students, is a beneficiary under a family trust.) Similarly, since a partnership has no corporate existence, it cannot own property itself and the partnership property of a large firm is usually held by four of the partners (as trustees) on trust for the partners generally.

Equity ceased to be a separately administered system of law in 1875. Consequently it is best considered as a historical source of law. However, the principles of equity have still retained their identity in the modern system. A good example of equity's contemporary vigour is the *High Trees Case* (1947) (*see* page 304) and the subsequent development of the principle of promissory estoppel in contract law. The common law, even in full evolution, had serious deficiencies and equity always aimed to supplement the common law to remedy these weaknesses. Promissory estoppel mitigates the rigidity of the common law's approach to *consideration*, holding a person to his promise when it would be inequitable for him to go back upon it, irrespective of whether consideration was given for it.

Perhaps the best practical example of equity's role is to be found in its remedies. If Jack repeatedly trespasses on your property, the common law remedy of damages may achieve little. The amount received will probably be small and he may very well continue to trespass. However, the equitable remedy of an injunction will, if awarded, order Jack not to repeat his illegal interference. Should he do so he will be in contempt of court and ultimately liable to imprisonment.

The law merchant

This is a historical source of English law and its legacy directly affects business organisations. Much of our present law on the sale of goods and bills of exchange, e.g. cheques, has its origin in the customs brought to England by foreign merchants in the days when England's economy was based almost entirely on agriculture and the production of raw materials. These customs were based on the law of the Italian commercial cities in which Roman law was naturally a strong influence. From the 17th century onwards many of these customs became judicially incorporated into the common law and were eventually codified as the Bills of Exchange Act 1882 and the Sale of Goods Acts 1893 in the period of legislative law reform at the end of the 19th century.

The government and law reform

In 1974 Lord Scarman, the first Chairman of the Law Commission (from 1965 to 1972), warned that our legal system failed to meet the challenge of today's society because it had not adjusted to the social, political and economic changes of the post-war world. In particular he questioned the ability of the *common law* system, moulded in very different times, to cope with modern socio-legal problems, e.g. 'A law of torts, a land law, and a family law conceived on common law principles, however admirable in substance, cannot effectively protect the general public or the weak, the poor, the aged and the sick.'

He chose five areas where he saw the present law as being particularly inadequate: human rights; matters arising from membership of the EC; the environment; industrial relations; and constitutional devolution to the regions. Scarman's conclusion was that if the influence of law and the *rule of law* continued to decline, the administrative authorities would become dominant. Control over their decisions would be exercised by the Government itself and not by the courts. The citizen would have no effective way to challenge governmental or administrative acts. We have discussed most of these points elsewhere in the text.

Among other cures for these consequences, Scarman proposed a new constitutional settlement, with provisions protecting it from administrative power and legislation by bare Parliamentary majority; a new supreme constitutional court; and immediate study of the possibility and problems of further statutory codification of the law. 'Look to the new sources and fields of law and endeavour to retain the spirit of the old while abandoning habits of thought and action from a society that no longer exists.' It is a truism to say that the law must adapt to meet the needs of a changing society for 'if the law does not adapt and adjust it will be rejected'.

The power to change the law to resolve new socio-legal problems and more effectively protect and enforce existing rights and duties lies with Parliament, or more correctly perhaps, with the government. While judges may mould and modify particular aspects of the law, sometimes in effect 'creating' new principles, e.g. the 'neighbour' principle of *Donoghue v Stevenson* (1932), they cannot nor should not openly affect fundamental changes either in principles or procedures.

Each Government will undertake general law reform according to its own ideology. This it will do by legislation, which it will then use to pursue its objectives. However, in those areas of law which are not openly political, the Government now looks mainly to the Law Commission to propose reform. Examples of statutes mentioned in this book which were the direct result of Law Commission proposals are the Town and Country Planning Act 1971 and the Unfair Contract Terms Act 1977. Important areas of the Commission's current work are the reform of the conveyancing and child care laws and possible codification of contract law. In October 1989 it proposed the introduction of three new criminal offences to combat computer 'hacking'.

The Law Commission was established by Act of Parliament in 1965 as a permanent full-time law reform agency. Its task is to keep the law under review with the aim of systematic development and reform, including, in particular, codification, the elimination of anomalies, the repeal of obsolete enactments, consolidation and generally the simplification and modernisation of the law. To do this it has the authority to prepare programmes of consolidation and statute law revision and to undertake the preparation of draft

Bills. It may also advise Government departments and other organisations at the instance of the Government, and propose reform of any branch of the law.

In addition to the Law Commission, there are several other standing bodies concerned with law reform, for example, the Criminal Law Revision Committee which was responsible for the Theft Act 1968. Over the years there have also been innumerable departmental committees and royal commissions to look at particular aspects of law and the machinery of justice. However, of greater interest perhaps is the work and activities of the many 'legal' *pressure groups* such as 'Justice' (the British section of the International Commission of Jurists), 'LAG' (the Legal Action Group), the Society of Labour Lawyers; and the Inns of Court Conservative and Unionist Association.

Effective agencies of law reform exist and informed discussion takes place. However, you should remember that law reform agencies tend to be dominated by senior lawyers (part of the 'establishment') who may not reflect the views of the 'rank and file', and that effective reform depends upon the government's willingness to give Parliamentary time to the proposals.

Key words

'Sources' of law

This term can mean a variety of things: formal source, legal sources, literary sources, and historical sources. It usually means a way in which ideas and principles become recognised as law, i.e. a legal source – custom, case law and legislation.

Case law

Often termed *judicial precedent*, case law is a system of judge-made law which for our present purposes is more or less synonymous with the term *common law*.

Ratio decidendi

The process of legal reasoning by which a court case is decided. This process is central to the system of case law/judicial precedent.

Legislation

Law made by Parliament, often referred to as statute law. Legislation has only been important since the latter part of the nineteenth century but now the regulation of society, in all its respects, is largely dependent upon it.

Delegated legislation

Law made by a body or an individual to which Parliament has given limited powers to legislate.

Interpretation of statutes

Parliament makes the law but the courts interpret and enforce it. It becomes necessary to interpret legislation when its meaning is uncertain or ambiguous when applied to a specific situation. Fortunately, however, this is fairly rare.

Common law

A system of law based originally on custom but now consisting of case law. Before 1875 the common law was administered exclusively in the common law courts.

Equity

A system of law based originally on principles of fairness and natural justice which before 1875 was administered in the Court of Chancery quite separately from the common law.

Law Merchant

Much modern commercial law has its origins in the Law Merchant – commercial customs which foreign merchants brought to this country and which gradually became absorbed into the common law and, later, statute law.

Learning project

Choose an Act of Parliament or, possibly, a court case in the last 20 years and assess its effect on the organisation for which you work or, perhaps, the college in which you study.

1 Write a short report on:

(a) the aims of the act,

(b) its main provisions, and

(c) its specific effects on the organisation chosen and, if possible, your own work.

2 Produce a leaflet suitable for use at work which explains the main provisions of the Act and the procedures which must be adopted to comply with them. (This may involve discovering the organisation's policy on how to comply with the Act.)

26

Conflict resolving

CHAPTER OBJECTIVES

After studying this chapter you should be able to:

■ Explain judicial and quasi-judicial processes of conflict resolving;
■ Outline the jurisdiction of the superior courts and the most important inferior courts;
■ State the advantages and disadvantages of administrative tribunals as a means of conflict resolving, and account for their increasing use;
■ Explain the methods by which quasi-judicial and administrative decision-making is supervised and controlled.

Introduction

It is a common misapprehension that trial by judge and jury is the typical conflict resolving process of the English legal system. This is far from the truth. Of the approximately two million people convicted of criminal offences each year in England and Wales, only about 100,000 are tried by judge and jury in the Crown Court and about 50% of these plead guilty! The remaining 1.9 million or so are tried by magistrates, most of these in turn pleading guilty. In civil cases the use of the jury is extremely limited. Nearly all civil disputes *must* either be tried by a judge sitting along, or be submitted to arbitration, or be resolved by an administrative tribunal.

The judicial process remains central to the trial of criminal cases and the jury will no doubt continue to be used in certain civil disputes as well as in criminal trials where a person is accused of a serious offence. However, civil disputes are increasingly being resolved by arbitration and administrative tribunals rather than by the formal judicial process. Administrative tribunals and formal arbitration bodies are *quasi-judicial bodies*. These may be defined as public bodies

which have the power by law to establish facts and apply legal rules without being constituted as parts of the ordinary court system or following the strict rules of evidence and procedure which the courts must follow.

To some extent the decline of the judicial process in civil disputes is inevitable. Quasi-judicial conflict resolving is far better suited to some increasingly important branches of the law, such as welfare and employment law, and could be usefully extended into other areas where wider discretionary powers would be an advantage. Welfare law is largely determined by socio-political policy, and while tribunals must reach their decisions judicially, i.e. according to the relevant law and procedure and not purely on policy, their composition and informal procedure make them far better able to deal with the often complicated combination of factual circumstances, policy and socio-legal problems involved.

Employment law and the judicial process have traditionally had a rather strained relationship, and the quasi-judicial conflict resolving system in this field – ACAS, industrial tribunals and the Employment Appeal Tribunal – appears to work much better. In the commercial world quasi-judicial processes are far from new and for centuries arbitration has been used to resolve disputes between business people. Perhaps above all else it is the informality in procedure and the relevant expertise of the decision-makers involved that has brought quasi-judicial conflict resolving processes to a position of such prominence in the legal system.

The judicial process, whether with or without a jury, is better suited to the criminal law, where the full 'majesty of the law' is probably an advantage, and to civil disputes involving questions of 'pure law' where little discretion is needed. Examples here would be the construction of an Act of Parliament, conflicts involving an alleged breach of contract or the protection of an individual's legal rights. To some extent, such purely legal issues (if there can ever be such a thing) can be considered in a legal vacuum; but even here *public policy* is being more openly considered in judicial decisions, e.g. in actions brought under the tort of negligence.

In addition to this natural process, it can be argued that lawyers themselves have been partly responsible for the increased use of alternatives to judicial conflict resolving. In so far as lawyers have created procedures which leave 'mere laymen' confused and trembling at the portals of justice, the law all too often seems to presuppose the existence of lawyers, which is surely wrong. In particular, it usually follows that the poorer and less well-educated members of society are least able to cope with bemusing procedural technicalities. In consequence, they are most in need of expert advice and assistance. However, lack of money and lack of education are often very effective barriers to obtaining proper assistance, although it is true to say that the modern legal aid scheme can, to some extent, raise these barriers.

Lawyers and the courts frequently seem isolated from both the problems of ordinary men and women and the actual day-to-day workings of the business world. Many lawyers are far more familiar with conveyancing than with anything else. However, welfare law may be equally, if not more, technical. It is certainly as important. The entitlement to income support, for example, is vital to satisfy many a family's material needs. Fortunately, in recent years there has been pressure to broaden the hitherto narrow, legalistic education and training of lawyers. It now often en-compasses sociological perspectives and sometimes the study of welfare law. In addition, a few organisations willing and able to advise on such matters now exist, e.g. neighbourhood law centres. However, by themselves they can never hope to solve the problem; most lawyers will, unless forced to do otherwise, sell their services to the highest bidder.

If it was just a matter of money, one would expect business people to use lawyers and the judicial process whenever they encountered a legal problem or became involved in a legal dispute. However, business people may prefer to take their legal problems to accountants rather than to lawyers because accountants are perceived as being more in tune with the realities of the business world. Thus, while lawyers and judges may epitomise the middle classes and have at times alienated the working classes, particularly by their apparent hostility to trade unions, the isolation of the courts from social and economic conflict situations cannot be explained purely in class terms. The judicial process appears to be its own prisoner, its prison being its own procedure and its gaoler its own isolation from social, economic and political realities.

We will now examine the work of the courts and the nature of the judicial process, and quasi-judicial conflict resolving by arbitration and administrative tribunals.

The courts and the judicial process

Historically, the administration of justice is a prerogative of the Crown, but the Crown has long since ceased to play an active role in this function of the state. Nevertheless, all English courts derive their jurisdiction directly or indirectly from the Crown and the administration of justice is still formally undertaken in the Sovereign's name. For example, writs in civil actions are issued in the Queen's name and all criminal proceedings are taken on her behalf, the judges are 'Her Majesty's Judges' and they sit in the 'Queen's Courts'.

Classifying the courts

English courts may be classified in various ways. One possible classification is into those which have *crimi-

nal and those which have *civil* jurisdiction. Unfortunately, this simple functional distinction is unsatisfactory; while some courts may have exclusively civil or exclusively criminal jurisdiction, most exercise both. A functional classification according to *original* (trial) or *appellate* jurisdiction is unsatisfactory for the same reason.

The one valid classification of practical importance is according to status and not jurisdiction. English courts can be divided into *superior* and *inferior* courts, the two characteristics of the latter being:

1 that their jurisdiction is limited both by the value of the disputed subject-matter and geographically; and
2 that they are subject to the supervisory jurisdiction of the High Court (*see* below).

The *superior* courts are the House of Lords, Court of Appeal, High Court, Crown Court, Employment Appeal Tribunal and the Restrictive Practices Court.

The European Court of Justice, which has jurisdiction in this country in disputes involving Community law, clearly does not fit into even this classification. Fig. 25.1 shows the structure of the courts, including the European Court of Justice, in terms of their primary functions as criminal or civil, trial or appellate courts. (Refer to Fig. 25.1 as you read through the text.)

The work of the courts

Appeal Courts

The House of Lords, the Court of Appeal (Civil and Criminal Divisions) and the Employment Appeal Tribunal have only appellate jurisdiction. In matters involving purely domestic laws, the House of Lords is the final appeal court in the UK for both civil and criminal cases.

High Court

The High Court sits in three separate divisions, Queen's Bench, Chancery and Family, and has virtually unlimited original jurisdiction in civil matters. Trial is by a single judge, although a jury will sometimes sit in the Queen's Bench Division to hear actions involving defamation or fraud.

Queen's Bench is the largest of the three divisions and deals mainly with disputes involving the law of contract or the law of torts. The Division also exercises the criminal jurisdiction of the High Court. This latter jurisdiction is entirely appellate and consists of deciding points of law stated to it from magistrates' courts and from the Crown Court when it hears appeals against summary conviction or sentence. It also has minor appellate jurisdiction in some civil matters originally heard in the magistrates' courts or certain tribunals. In addition, the Division exercises the supervisory jurisdiction of the High Court over quasi-judicial decision-making (*see* below) by the issue of the prerogative orders of *certiorari*, *mandamus* and prohibition.

The Division also operates the Commercial Court of the High Court staffed by judges with extensive commercial knowledge and experience, to hear cases of a commercial nature, e.g. insurance disputes. The Court uses a simplified procedure which, together with the commercial experience of the judge, is designed to overcome the traditional reluctance of business people to resort to court action instead of arbitration. Indeed a judge of the Court can sit as an arbitrator in a private arbitration and a majority of the Court's work is now in this field rather than in cases heard by the Court itself.

In 1987, 228,687 proceedings were commenced in the Queen's Bench Division. In 104,967 cases, judgment was given without trial and there were only 14,278 hearings listed. In fact, only 19,21 disputes (0.84%) had to be resolved by an actual trial, leading to a judgment.

The *Chancery Division* exercises original civil jurisdiction in matters which were originally heard in the Court of Chancery (abolished in 1875), e.g. over trusts, mortgages, specific performance of contracts concerning land, and partnership actions. The division has statutory jurisdiction in company liquidation, bankruptcy, tax cases, town and country planning matters, and probate disputes. In addition, it has minor appellate jurisdiction, e.g. income tax appeals from the Commissioners of Inland Revenue.

The *Family Division* has exclusive original jurisdiction over matrimonial disputes and conflicts involving children. It has limited appellate jurisdiction from the magistrates' courts and country courts in similar civil matters.

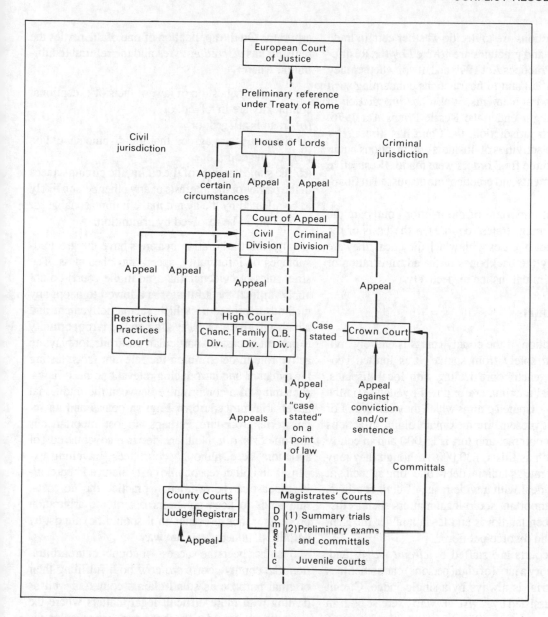

Fig. 26.1 The principal civil and criminal courts and the system of appeals

You can see from this outline of their jurisdiction that much of the work of the Queen's Bench and Chancery Divisions of the High Court is of direct relevance to business organisations.

Crown Court

The Crown Court has exclusive original jurisdiction to try all indictable offences, i.e. offences, generally of a serious nature, where the trial *must* be by judge or jury, and jurisdiction to hear appeals against summary conviction or sentence from a magistrates' court. In addition, High Court judges may sit in the Crown Court to exercise the High Court's civil jurisdiction outside London.

Restrictive Practices Court

The Restrictive Practices Court exercises jurisdiction outside the scope of the ordinary civil and criminal law. Its functions are to decide whether certain trade agreements and practices are covered by the Restrictive Trade Practices Act 1976 and, if so, whether they can be justified and to hear actions concerning such practices and agreements. It also has jurisdiction in actions brought under the Resale Prices Act 1976. Having such jurisdiction, the Court has direct relevance to the activities of business organisations but in 1987 only three final orders were made. (Restrictive trade agreements and practices are discussed in Chapter 17.)

The most important of the inferior courts are the county and magistrates' courts. On the basis of the sheer number of cases with which they deal, they are undoubtedly the backbones of the administration of civil and criminal justice respectively.

County courts

The jurisdiction of the county courts is entirely civil and derived solely from statute. It is limited geographically, each court dealing with local disputes, and financial maxima are imposed by statute on the value of the disputed claims which they can hear. For example, at present the maximum claim in actions founded on contract and tort is £5,000 and in equity matters, such as trusts, £30,000. Although they may seem to operate as judicial debt-collecting agencies at times, they deal with a wide range of civil conflicts, including important socio-legal matters such as disputes between landlords and tenants under the Rent Act 1968 and divorce petitions.

County courts are staffed by *circuit judges* and, while in theory a jury (of eight persons) can sometimes be called, trial is always by a single judge. Circuit judges are assisted by *registrars* who exercise both an administrative and a judicial function, the former of which is largely delegated to subordinates. Unless the parties object, a registrar may try actions where the claim does not exceed £500 or any other actions with their consent. Appeal lies from the decision of the registrar to the judge.

Claims involving £500 or less, i.e. 'small claims', are automatically referred to arbitration in the county court by the registrar as soon as a defence to the claim has been received. Normally, the registrar will be the arbitrator but, if either of the parties ask, he can refer the dispute for arbitration by the judge or by an outside

arbitrator. On the application of one of the parties the registrar has *discretion* to rescind the referral to arbitration where:

(a) a difficult question of law, or facts of exceptional complexity are involved: or

(b) fraud is alleged; or

(c) the parties are agreed that the dispute should be tried by the court; or

(d) the subject matter of the claim, the circumstances of the parties or the interests of any other person likely to be affected by the award make it unreasonable for the dispute to be resolved by arbitration.

County court arbitration hearings have the great advantages of informality, speed and cheapness. The strict rules of evidence (as used in the court) do not apply. In fact, the arbitrator is allowed to adopt any method of procedure which seems convenient and which will give each party a fair and equal opportunity to present its case. In particular, the arbitrator plays an active role in determining the relevant facts, testing the evidence and introducing relevant points of law – something of a compromise between the traditional adversarial procedure of English courts and an inquisitorial procedure. Perhaps of most importance is the 'no-costs' rule. Neither side can recover the cost of solicitors' fees, although court fees, travelling expenses and other reasonable costs incurred in preparing the case can be awarded. In practice, the 'no-costs' rule tends to keep solicitors out of the arbitration procedure; their presence in it should be, almost by definition, unnecessary anyway.

Such has been the success of county court arbitration, the county courts are now both fulfilling their original purpose as small claims courts as well as dealing with more difficult legal matters where the amounts involved are not that great. In particular, the county court arbitration procedure recognises that the fundamental problem with small claims is one of economics. To enable consumers (most arbitration hearings concern consumer matters) to pursue their claims on relatively equal terms against organisations requires the system to exclude bought legal expertise and familiarity with legal procedures. While there is nothing to stop anybody employing a solicitor, the 'no-costs' rule and the registrar's discretion over procedure go a long way towards ensuring equality between the parties.

In 1987, 2,375,431 proceedings were commenced in the county courts. However, in only 161,401 cases (6.8%) was judgment entered at a court hearing. Of these in turn, 142,528 were tried by registrars and not by judges and in 57% of them judgment was entered after the defendant had failed to appear in court! A further 28.5% were settled by arbitration. Thus, only in some 23,000 cases was there an actual trial. The figures clearly show that in the vast majority of cases merely commencing proceedings is enough to achieve the plaintiff's objectives.

The Courts and Legal Services Bill 1989 proposes a massive shift of work from the High Court to the County Court, leaving the High Court to deal with the complex cases. Monetary limits on jurisdiction will be increased, the arbitration limit is expected at least to be doubled, and non-lawyer representatives are likely to be given rights of audience in certain other proceedings.

Magistrates' courts

Magistrates' courts have both criminal and civil jurisdiction, although the importance of the former far outweighs that of the latter. Magistrates have jurisdiction to try summary offences, i.e. those which do not have to be tried by jury, and certain other offences which may be tried either by judge and jury in the Crown Court or by summary procedure in a magistrates' court. In 1988, in England and Wales, about 1.86 million defendants were proceeded against in the Magistrates Courts of which 800,000 were charged with minor motoring offences. Indeed, even this figure is not a true reflection of the importance of magistrates' courts, for a magistrate will have conducted a preliminary examination (*see* below) of the evidence before committing an accused person to stand trial at the Crown Court for an indictable offence.

From the above you can see that magistrates' courts have two quite separate functions in relation to criminal cases. First, they conduct preliminary examinations of indictable offences in order to establish whether or not the prosecution has sufficient evidence to justify the accused being committed on bail or in custody to stand trial before judge and jury in the Crown Court. Second, they try a vast range of summary offences (all created by statute) and some hybrid offences (where trial may be either on indictment or by

summary procedure), and offences committed by children and young persons under the age of 17 years.

The civil jurisdiction of the magistrates' courts is very varied and includes the recovery of certain debts, e.g. unpaid income tax and rates, and the renewal and revocation of licences. Of greatest importance is its domestic civil jurisdiction. For example, it can make orders that one spouse need no longer live with the other and that the defendant must pay a reasonable weekly sum to the complainant as maintenance.

1 Using Fig. 25.1 as your basis, draw two diagrams to show separately those courts which exercise civil jurisdiction and those which exercise criminal jurisdiction.

2 For civil and criminal actions separately, list those courts which have *(a)* original jurisdiction, and *(b) appellate* jurisdiction.

3 In which court(s) would the following matters be dealt with:

(a) an appeal on a point of law from a magistrates' court;
(b) an action for specific performance of a contract;
(c) a claim for £50,000 in damages for breach of contract;
(d) an appeal from the Queen's Bench Division;
(e) a civil dispute where the parties have agreed to arbitration;
(f) an indictable offence.

The judicial process

The judicial process consists of an independent adjudicator (a judge) making a reasoned decision according to known rules of law on the basis of the evidence available to both parties and offered to the court. Each party, usually through their legal representatives, can test the evidence offered by the other and each may put forward factual or legal arguments. In conflicts where a jury sits with a judge, i.e. on the trial of indictable offences in the Crown Court and in some civil actions tried in the Queen's Bench Division of the High Court, the judge decides disputed points of law and the jury determines questions of fact. If the plaintiff succeeds in his action, a civil jury will also determine the amount of damages (if any) that the defendant may pay him. It is worth noting here that the colossal, many would say outrageous, damages paid to successful plaintiffs in libel actions in recent years has completely discredited the jury's role in this respect. For example, an award of £600,000 was made to Sonia Sutcliffe, wife of the 'Yorkshire Ripper', against *Private Eye* in 1989 – an award which was subsequently reduced to £60,000 by the Court of Appeal!

The judicial process assumes that there is an applicable legal rule which will resolve the conflict and that this can be discovered by a rigorous examination of *authority*, i.e. statutes and cases. As a consequence of this, judges can very seldom exercise completely unfettered discretion and in most cases they are bound to follow *precedent*.

By tradition, the English judicial process is an adversarial and not an inquisitorial system (in contrast to the European Court of Justice). Hence, the court plays a largely passive role and the case is conducted by the parties (usually through their lawyers) with the judge as 'umpire' to ensure that the procedural rules are observed and to adjudicate in the dispute at the end of the process.

The main advantages of the judicial process are said to be:

(a) an independent adjudicator with an open mind;
(b) a clearly determined issue to be decided;
(c) a full and equal opportunity for both sides to present their case;
(d) the production of the best available evidence;
(e) the exclusion of all irrelevant material;
(f) the application of known legal rules to resolve the dispute; and
(g) a statement of reasons for the decision made.

Impressive though these advantages undoubtedly are, the process does have a number of disadvantages. These can seriously detract from its benefits. Many would argue that the process resembles a gladiatorial combat where might – in the form of superior legal representation – can overcome right. Inherent in this particular criticism is the high cost of the process, perhaps its major detraction. Laypeople will usually find that the technicality of legal procedure and the formality of the process effectively bar their access to the courts unless they employ a professional lawyer and yet the sheer expense which this involves may

cause them to abandon all hope of redress at law. Even where legal representation and legal aid are readily available, considerable delay is inevitable before the conflict is resolved. In addition, the adversarial system allows the parties to control the process and the truth may not be fully uncovered because the court is unable to enquire into the facts. Finally, it is argued by some that the isolation of judges from the 'real world' makes it difficult for them to fully appreciate the background to many of the conflicts that they must resolve.

Legal aid

Legal aid is a scheme which pays or contributes to the cost of a litigant's legal fees. It is funded by the State and administered by the Legal Aid Board. The scheme is designed to enable a person unable to pay legal fees to obtain legal representation in court proceedings. To the parties involved it probably seems part and parcel of the judicial conflict-resolving process.

Legal aid in both criminal and civil cases is governed by the Legal Aid Act 1988. The Act, as periodically amended, determines applicants' eligibility to legal aid and any contribution that they must make to the court costs.

Legal aid in civil court proceedings

Legal aid will be granted if applicants fulfil two conditions.

1 They must be in receipt of income support or satisfy a means test. At present, an applicant with a disposable income, i.e. gross income less rates, rent, mortgage repayments, tax, allowances for dependents, etc, of less than £2,515 a year and disposable capital of less than £3,000 will not be required to make a contribution to the costs of the case if legal aid is granted. Persons with a disposable income in excess of £6,035 are ineligible, and legal aid may be refused to a person with disposable capital of over £6,000. In between these maximum and minimum figures a successful applicant may be required to pay a proportion of the costs.

2 The applicant must satisfy the Board that there are reasonable grounds for taking or defending the action.

Two main criticisms are made of the present scheme. First, with the exception of the Employment Appeal Tribunal and the Lands Tribunal, legal aid is not available in cases heard by administrative tribunals, even though the use of the tribunals in conflict resolving is steadily increasing. It is never available for arbitration hearings. Second, too many people are excluded from the scheme on financial grounds; in particular, the means test is unfair to the prudent saver.

Legal aid in criminal court proceedings

An application for legal aid in criminal cases is made to the appropriate court and applicants must include a statement of means with their applications. Legal aid in criminal cases differs in two further ways from the civil scheme. First, a criminal legal aid order is made before any possible contribution has been assessed. The need to expedite the trial of criminal cases explains this difference. Second, it is rarely refused, except on financial grounds, where the applicant is charged with a serious offence and it must be granted on a murder charge. The grant of civil legal aid is far more discretionary.

After the conclusion of the case, the court may order any assisted person to make a contribution to the costs according to their financial commitments and resources.

Key words

Superior and inferior courts
The one valid classification of the courts, an inferior court having limited jurisdiction and being subject to the supervisory jurisdiction of the High Court. Classifications based on functional criteria, e.g. into civil and criminal courts, do not work.

Judicial and quasi-judicial processes
The *judicial process* is where a judge makes a decision in a dispute according to rules of law on the basis of the evidence produced in court. A *quasi-judicial* process differs in that the strict rules of procedure and evidence characteristic of the judicial process, are relaxed to a greater or lesser extent.

Legal aid
A means tested contribution to legal expenses incurred in court proceedings.

Arbitration

Arbitration is a quasi-judicial process used in civil disputes where the parties involved agree to allow a third to resolve the dispute between them. It is an alternative to the judicial process – it is quite separate from the county court arbitration procedure discussed above – and not a replacement for it. Most arbitration agreements are in writing and the arbitration process is regulated either by one of a number of specific statutes, which provide for disputes arising out of their provisions to be settled by arbitration, or by the Arbitration Acts 1950 and 1979.

Referring disputes or arbitration

A dispute can be referred to arbitration under the provisions of a specific statute or in accordance with a term contained in the contract between the parties in dispute. Since the Middle Ages the courts have recognised such contractual terms and enforced the arbitration awards made. Today, provision for disputes to be referred to arbitration is frequently found in partnership agreements, insurance and building contracts and in industrial relations.

It is not possible for an arbitration agreement to prevent access to the courts because such an agreement would be void on the grounds of public policy. However, a suitably worded provision will generally prevent one of the parties proceeding with court action until after the dispute has been referred to arbitration.

Arbitration procedure

Normally one arbitrator is appointed, often selected by a trade or professional body, but each party has the right to appoint an arbitrator of their own choice. Where this is so, an umpire must be selected whose function is to decide the dispute, should the arbitrators fail to agree. A judge of the Commercial Court, part of the Queen's Bench Division of the High Court, may sometimes sit as a sole arbitrator providing they can be released from their judicial duties.

The arbitration follows normal judicial procedure but by agreement it is possible to relax strict procedural rules and, in particular, to dispense with the rules of evidence. For example, while witnesses are often cross-examined and can be ordered to attend (by *subpoena*) by the High Court, evidence is frequently submitted by affidavit (a written statement made on oath).

The arbitrator's decision is in the form of an award. This may include the payment of money or costs and an order to perform the contract (specific performance). The award prevents the parties taking the issues decided to court and unless the arbitration agreement provides for an appeal, e.g. to an appeal committee or tribunal, the arbitrator's decision on the facts is final.

The role of the court

The role of the court is to ensure that the arbitrator process is conducted fairly, so as not to restrict its use. For example, it can revoke the authority of an arbitrator or umpire and set aside the award for delay or improper conduct, stay proceedings by injunction and enforce the arbitration award in the same way as its own judgment. But it cannot hear appeals against the award except where a judge of the Commercial Court sits as arbitrator. If this last rule were reversed, reference to arbitration would be pointless. However, the Arbitration Act 1979 provides that there may be an appeal to the High Court on a question of *law* providing both parties consent or the court gives permission. Where, however, the parties have entered into an agreement which excludes the right to appeal, this is binding upon them. In any event the court will give permission to appeal only if it considers that the determination of the question of law could substantially affect the rights of one or more of the parties. This procedure means that business people can ensure that their disputes are decided solely by the method of their choice, without any review by the courts on questions of law, and that costly and protracted delays by (unnecessary) references of points of law to the court are prevented.

An arbitrator acts in a quasi-judicial capacity and therefore no legal action can be taken against him for negligently conducting the arbitration. Negligence would, however, provide grounds for the High Court to set aside his award.

Advisory Conciliation and Arbitration Service (ACAS)

Arbitration has always been an important way of resolving conflicts in industrial relations and, because its activities are directly relevant to business organisations, ACAS must be discussed further. Indeed, besides making arrangements for arbitration in industrial disputes, the Service plays a much wider role in industrial relations generally.

The Service is run by a Council consisting of a chairman and nine members – three nominated by the CBI, three by the TUC and three independent members – with a staff of civil servants experienced in industrial relations. Its main functions are to provide:

(a) advice on industrial relations and the development of modern personnel practices;
(b) conciliation in industrial disputes;
(c) conciliation in certain disputes between individual employees and their employers, e.g. disputes under the Equal Pay Act 1970 and, in particular, cases of alleged unfair dismissal, thereby avoiding the need to take the dispute to an industrial tribunal;
(d) help in improving collective bargaining.

By its very nature, industrial relations is a subject where a variety of issues may be involved in any one problem and the Service's functions are therefore closely integrated.

Arbitration arranged by ACAS can either be by a single arbitrator appointed by ACAS or by an *ad hoc* board of arbitration specially appointed to deal with a particular dispute. ACAS appoints an independent chairman, who acts as an umpire if required, with the other members nominated by the parties to the dispute. Unlike other forms of arbitration, an ACAS award is not legally binding. However, since the arbitration normally presupposes the parties' joint desire to resolve the dispute between them, such awards are normally implemented.

Advantages and disadvantages of arbitration

The advantages of arbitration can in some ways be considered to be the opposites of the disadvantages inherent in the judicial process. To the business world in general these advantages are attractive.

Arbitration takes place in private and while counsel may appear for the parties, the rules of evidence are relaxed and the process is relatively informal. In consequence, it is argued that disputes can be decided in a less emotionally charged and tense situation.

The resolution of many commercial disputes requires expert knowledge, and a major advantage of the process is that a person with the necessary expertise can be appointed as arbitrator. In fact trade and professional associations maintain lists of suitably qualified persons. Many commercial arbitration agreements also leave the appointment of an arbitrator to the relevant trade or professional body.

Arbitration is not, however, necessarily cheaper nor quicker than a court action. Experienced arbitrators can command high fees and lawyers will charge the same fees as for litigation in court. Delays can easily occur while an arbitrator is agreed upon by the parties and even then the arbitrator is unlikely to be free to resolve the dispute immediately. Another drawback is that legal aid is unavailable. This can be unfair where there is a marked imbalance in the financial resources of the parties in dispute, particularly if the arbitration agreement is used to stop a claim being pursued in court where legal aid may have been available to the financially weaker party.

Administrative tribunals

Since the end of the Second World War in 1945 there has been a great increase in socio-legal problems, many of which the ordinary courts are ill-equipped to deal with. These problems are mainly associated with the tremendous expansion of social and welfare services. To resolve the inevitable conflicts which arise in such matters, increasing use has been made of administrative tribunals.

Administrative tribunals fall outside the ordinary court system and yet they have extensive powers of decision-making which directly affect the private rights of individuals. In fact, adjudication in civil disputes between the individual and the State by a court rather than by a tribunal is the exception rather than the rule and the use of tribunals to resolve disputes between individuals is becoming steadily more common. Although they will usually have a legally qualified chairman, they are normally staffed by non-lawyers.

They may have original or appellate jurisdiction.

Their functions and procedures are regulated by the Tribunals and Inquiries Act 1971. This makes provision for a statutory right of appeal on a point of law from a tribunal to the Queen's Bench Division of the High Court, provides for considerable uniformity in standards and procedures, e.g. chairmen are selected by the appropriate government minister and appointed by the Lord Chancellor, and has established the Council on Tribunals to oversee the constitution and functioning of the most important administrative tribunals, including the work of the Director General of Fair Trading. The Council makes an annual report to the Lord Chancellor.

The work of administrative tribunals

There are some 2,000 individual tribunals dealing with a wide variety of socio-legal matters, their only common element being that they are all statutory bodies which exercise functions laid down by particular Acts of Parliament. For example, the lands tribunals deal with disputes over compensation paid to owners of land which has been compulsorily purchased by government departments or local authorities, and the Registered Designs Appeal Tribunal hears appeals from the Comptroller-General of Patents, Designs and Trade-marks. However, they play their most important roles in welfare and employment law. The national insurance tribunals decide disputed claims to unemployment and sickness benefits and appeals against the withdrawal of income support are heard by a social security appeal tribunal. Industrial tribunals deal with a wide range of disputes arising from employment. In most cases appeal lies to the Employment Appeal Tribunal.

The Employment Appeal Tribunal

The Employment Protection Act 1975 created the Employment Appeal Tribunal. This Tribunal hears appeals on points of law from industrial tribunals in disputed claims concerning redundancy, discrimination (including equal pay), and disputes under the Trade Union and Labour Relations Act 1974 (as now amended), the Employment Protection Act 1975 and the Employment Protection (Consolidation) Act 1978 (as now amended). It also hears appeals on points of both fact and law arising from proceedings before the trade union Certification Officer. In 1987, 673 appeals were disposed of.

The Tribunal occupies a somewhat anomalous position in that it operates as a tribunal but has the status of a superior court. Its procedure is designed to be cheap and informal and the parties may appear in person or be represented by anyone they wish, e.g. a barrister or solicitor, or trade union or employers' association official. Strict rules of evidence need not be observed and costs are not normally awarded. However, the Tribunal can order the attendance and examination of witnesses, the production and inspection of documents and it can enforce its orders.

The Tribunal is staffed by judges from the Court of Appeal and High Court, nominated by the Lord Chancellor, including one from the Scottish Court of Session, and lay members with expertise in industrial relations sitting as representatives of either employers or workers. The Tribunal may sit anywhere in Great Britain and it must consist of one judge sitting with either two or four lay members (chosen to give equal representation to employers and workers), or one judge and one lay member where the parties consent. A decision of the Tribunal on a question of fact is final, but an appeal on a point of law can be made to the Court of Appeal or Court of Session.

As a superior court, the Employment Appeal Tribunal is not subject to the supervisory jurisdiction of the High Court (*see* below).

Advantages and disadvantages of administrative tribunals

Administrative tribunals are vital to the resolution of conflicts of a socio-legal nature. They are usually staffed by expert laymen and they are able to consider policy criteria far better than judges. They are relatively cheap, legal representation is unnecessary and costs are not usually awarded, a decision is reached relatively quickly, they are flexible in that they are not bound by precedent, and they are relatively informal.

However, the increasing use of administrative tribunals has its own disadvantages. Arguably, there are too many kinds of tribunals and they often have overlapping jurisdictions. More fundamentally, they are said to infringe the *rule of law* – which aims to protect the individual from arbitrary government – in that they are run by government departments with an interest in the dispute.

Though administrative tribunals are relatively informal when compared with the courts, most of the applicants to them tend to be very much out of their depth in any situation involving 'officialdom'. This being so, expert advice is often required in their applications but this is usually very hard to obtain. Legal aid is not available for such applications although the Council on Tribunals in its 1987/8 report, repeating a call first made in 1974, asks for legal aid to be introduced as a matter of urgency. However, if it was, it could be argued that the involvement of lawyers could detract from the significant advantages that administrative tribunals offer as a means of conflict resolution. Above all else, perhaps, they can never hope to solve the problems created by bad government.

Compare and contrast the advantages and disadvantages of the courts, arbitration and administrative tribunals as means of resolving civil disputes.

Domestic tribunals

These are mainly disciplinary bodies which regulate certain trades and professions. Some have been established by statute but the authority of many derives entirely from the contracts between them and their members. Examples include the General Medical Council, The Law Society, and the Securities and Investments Board (SIB).

Domestic tribunals are not subject to the prerogative orders (*see* below) because they are not public bodies, but the courts can intervene to ensure that the rules of such bodies are correctly interpreted and that natural justice is observed in their application, e.g. in connection with admission to and expulsion from the trade or profession, and restriction on members' activities.

Administrative decision-making

A statute frequently gives a minister the power to resolve disputes arising under its provisions, e.g. a disputed route for a new major road and the compulsory acquisition of land for it. These powers are necessary if government policy is to be implemented, for any independent quasi-judicial body might make decisions which would frustrate this. Such powers may be either original or appellate, and with or without a right of appeal. Similar powers are given to local authorities, e.g. in relation to the control of development under the Town and Country Planning Acts, public bodies and office-holders, e.g. the Monopolies and Mergers Commission and the Director General of Fair Trading.

Administrative decisions are made by an *administrative process*. This entails the collection of information and expert opinions, the preparation of analyses and summaries and the taking of a decision based upon them, the whole process rarely being open to public inspection. The administrative process is mainly used for matters that are to be decided on *policy*, i.e. decisions which can be based on any grounds or reasons which appear appropriate. In contrast, the judicial and quasi-judicial processes involve the application of given rules to resolve disputes. However, whenever an administrative decision presupposes the existence of a dispute and parties to it, the decision-maker is fulfilling a *quasi-judicial function* and his decision will be subject to judicial review accordingly (*see* below).

In some cases a minister is required to hold a public inquiry before making his decision. Such public inquiries are purely investigatory and some would say that they are little more than public relations exercises which have very little effect on the actual decision-making process except to delay it.

Control and supervision of quasi-judicial and administrative decision-making

Judicial control

Unless granted by statute there is no right of appeal to the ordinary courts against the *decisions* of administrative tribunals, for such a right would nullify most of the advantages that they possess as a means of resolving disputes. However, it is essential that administrative justice should exist within a framework of effec-

tive legal controls and safeguards.

Judicial control takes two main forms:

(*a*) the supervisory jurisdiction of the High Court; and
(*b*) any statutory rights of appeal which exist from a tribunal to the High Court. Appeal must usually be on a point of law.

The supervisory jurisdiction of the High Court is exercised by a Divisional Court of the Queen's Bench Division through the issue of the prerogative orders of *certiorari*, prohibition and *mandamus*. They can be used to challenge any decision which involves a *judicial element*, even though it is reached by an administrative rather than a judicial or quasi-judicial process. Consequently, they are available against ministers of the Crown and other administrative bodies besides inferior courts and administrative tribunals. They are issued following an *application for judicial review*, a procedure which encompasses applications for an injunction or declaration, the other remedies available in administrative law, and any consequential claim for damages. The leave of the High Court is required before an application for judicial review can be made.

Tribunals are kept within their jurisdiction by the orders of *certiorari* and prohibition. An order of *certiorari* brings a dispute, already resolved or still under the process of adjudication, before the High Court for the Court to consider whether the tribunal has acted in excess of its jurisdiction and whether the rules of natural justice have been broken. If such is found, the High Court will quash the decision made or send the matter back to the tribunal with a direction to reconsider and reach a decision in accordance with the findings of the Court. It is also used to correct errors of law apparent on the record of the proceedings. It *cannot* be used to challenge the merits of the decision.

An order of *prohibition* is issued to prevent something from being done. It can be used to prevent inferior courts, tribunals, other public bodies and public office-holders exceeding their jurisdiction when exercising judicial or quasi-judicial powers.

Mandamus is an order to perform public duties or to exercise statutory powers. It may be issued against inferior courts, tribunals and public office-holders where they wrongfully refuse to deal with a dispute within their jurisdiction or fail to fulfil other statutory duties.

In addition, the courts will assume, in the absence of express provisions to the contrary, that any powers conferred by statute, whether quasi-judicial or purely administrative, must be exercised reasonably, without negligence, after taking into account all relevant matters and following any conditions and procedures which may be specified. Thus, while a judicial element must be shown before the High Court can exercise its supervisory powers by prerogative order, purely administrative governmental decisions are also, to a limited extent, open to judicial review. However, in the final analysis the courts cannot nor should not control policy decisions to any greater extent. As Professor Jackson says in his book *The Machinery of Justice in England*, 'It is quite as necessary to provide against being ruled by judges as it is to guard against being judged by ministers.'

Administrative supervision

Responsibility for supervising parts of the machinery of government and administrative tribunals is shared between the Council on Tribunals and the Parliamentary Commissioner for Administration (the 'Ombudsman').

The Council on Tribunals

The Council on Tribunals was established in 1958 to review the constitution and working of tribunals and inquiries. It must be consulted about procedural rules relating to them and it can make recommendations on its own Initiative to the Lord Chancellor. Although its investigations rarely have any effect on decisions already made, substantiated complaints generally lead to improvements in procedure for the future. The raising of procedural standards is, therefore, the main function of the Council.

The Ombudsman

The office of Parliamentary Commissioner for Administration (the 'Ombudsman') was established by statute in 1967. He is appointed by the Crown and investigates complaints of injustice caused by malad-

ministration, in particular the failure of government departments to observe proper standards of administration where this falls shorts of actual illegality. He has no direct powers in relation to tribunals and cannot entertain complaints about the way they reach decisions but he can investigate complaints of maladministration which prejudiced a case which went to a tribunal. In addition he can refer complaints concerning them to the Council on Tribunals of which he is a member.

The Ombudsman's jurisdiction is limited to complaints of maladministration in central government, excluding public corporations and the armed services, and he will only deal with complaints brought to him by Members of Parliament. Most of the relatively few complaints upheld have been cases of unjustifiable delay.

He has no power to annual decisions which have been made but by making representations he may obtain forms of redress which no court could give. For example, he may be able to persuade a government department to reconsider a particular case, such as reopening a planning inquiry, or possibly obtain an *ex gratia* payment where an administrative decision is irrevocable. In most cases investigation of a complaint has resulted in the proceedings at fault being improved.

Ombudsmen have also been appointed to investigate complaints of maladministration in the national health service and local government. In the latter case the complaints must be made through local councillors. This could be seen as reducing the effectiveness of the supervision in that the complaints are essentially against the work or the responsibilities of the councillors themselves.

It is perhaps interesting to note here that Ombudsmen have been established by the banking, insurance and building society industries to deal with customer complaints, and by the Council of the Stock Exchange to deal with disputes between investors and stockbrokers. Although they have no 'official' or statutory status, they fulfil a useful role when disputes cannot be resolved privately between the parties and redress at law is not an attractive or feasible option. Furthermore, the Courts and Legal Services Bill published in late 1989 proposes to establish a Legal Services Ombudsman to monitor the way the professional bodies investigate complaints.

Key words ————————————————

Arbitration
A quasi-judicial process used to resolve civil disputes.
It is very common in the commercial world.

Administrative tribunals
Quasi-judicial bodies which resolve a wide range and
a great number of civil disputes.

Domestic tribunals
Disciplinary bodies which regulate the activities of
members of certain trades and professions. The courts
are not concerned with the rules that they operate,
merely that these rules are applied correctly and
fairly.

Administrative decision-making
Decision-making based on the analysis of information
and opinions and not rules of law. Most administrative
decision-making is ultimately based on policy
considerations.

Judicial review
A legal procedure which enables the High Court to
investigate quasi-judicial and administrative decision-
making to ensure the decision-makers acted fairly and
within their legal powers.

Conclusion

In this chapter we have discussed judicial and quasi-
judicial conflict resolving processes and, to a lesser
extent, administrative decision-making. While the
discussion has been general, organisations are directly
affected by these processes as much if not more than
private individuals.

Arbitration, both in its traditional form and in its
modern 'official' role in the county courts and by
ACAS, is without major critics. The judicial process
of the courts, the quasi-judicial process of administrative tribunals, administrative decision-making and
their inter-relationship are, however, the subject of
some controversy.

The distinction between courts and administrative
tribunals is one of age rather than function. The
deficiencies apparent in the former when faced with
the socio-legal conflicts of a complex industrial society led to the growth of the latter. While it is wrong in
principle to be either ruled by judges or judged by
administrators, an element of discretion is sometimes
essential in resolving disputes and a judicial element
is sometimes necessary in administrative decision-
making. The courts, bound by precedent, are rarely
able to exercise any real discretion but most tribunals
are able to consider *policy* alongside rules of law to
some extent. In contrast, administrative decisions are
based on policy rather than rules of law and, while any
judicial element in such decisions is subject to judicial
review, policy decision-making is, and indeed should
be, ultimately controlled through the ballot box.

A valid distinction can be drawn between judicial
and quasi-judicial conflict resolving by courts and tribunals, and administrative decision-making by the
government or its agents. The former presupposes a
dispute between two parties and the resolution of it,
according to rules of law, by a third. The latter primarily involves policy decisions taken to achieve social,
economic or political objectives, although they may
also involve a conflict between individuals and organisations, or between the government and individuals or organisations. For reasons of principle and
practice, administrative decision-making must remain
separate from judicial and quasi-judicial conflict resolving processes. However, can the same be said for
the latter? Tribunals can be considered a more modern
form of court, differing from traditional courts more in
procedure than function.

Learning projects ————————————————

1 The most accessible court is the magistrates' court.
Arrange to visit your local magistrates' court and makes
notes on;

(a) the kind of cases dealt with;
(b) whether or not you considered that the defendants
understood and fully appreciated the proceedings;

(c) the role of the police, the lawyers, the justices' clerk
and the magistrates themselves;
(d) the justice administered.

Note: If you intend to visit as a group you should liaise
with your tutors and contact the court first. It may be
possible to arrange for a court official to talk to you
about the work of the court.

2 Arrange for a solicitor, in private practice or employed by a company, to talk to your group about the nature of legal services required by a company.

Note: You may need to use your college to make the initial contact for you or, perhaps, make an approach to your local Law Society. Remember, whoever comes to talk to you will be giving up valuable time to do so – do not waste it!

3 (a) Draft an information sheet fully explaining eligibility for legal aid.
(b) Examine the likely affects of making legal aid available in disputes referred to arbitration or heard by tribunals.

27

Government policy formation

CHAPTER OBJECTIVES

After studying this chapter you should be able to:

☐ Understand and apply political and social models to government policy formation;
☐ Describe how policies are formed within government departments;
☐ Explain the paradox of party difference;
☐ Explain how pressure groups influence government policy-making;
☐ Outline the reasons for the growth in the political power of trade unions;
☐ Explain the importance of the media;
☐ Identify external influences on government policy.

R A Butler defined politics as the 'art of the possible'. Therefore, when we examine the formulation of government policy, we will find that it is a combination of what the government would like to do, what it is persuaded to do and what is practicable.

Another way of putting this is to say that politics is the process by which conflicting interests among individuals and groups are recognised and resolved, although in an ever-changing environment that resolution may only be temporary. It follows that rather than being the cause of conflicts in society, politics is a response to them, providing a means of keeping them within manageable and reasonable limits. Fig. 27.1 represents the political process in a very simplified diagrammatic form.

Politics is a universal activity. While we normally associate it with national and international matters, it takes place in each and every organisation. In Chapter 2, for example, we described how different groups in an organisation will have conflicting objectives and policies. The process by which the conflicts that arise are resolved is *political*, whatever other name may be given to it.

Political and social models

Government policy-making and social change is frequently analysed according to theoretical 'models'. This of course means that a particular decision or policy may be interpreted quite differently according to the model used. Clearly, this is not a book on government and policies or sociology and just a very basic explanation is given of some of the best known models. Still, they should enable you to view a given policy or instance of change from a number of contrasting perspectives.

In our discussion of the models we will refer to the idea of *power*. Power is an aspect of a relationship, it has no abstract meaning. When we talk of power, we are talking of power *over others*. A practical definition would be that power is the degree to which an individual or a group can get their own way in a relationship.

Elite theory

Elite theory basically argues that power is concentrated in the hands of a dominant minority, i.e. that all

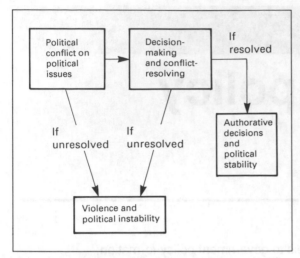

Fig. 27.1 A simplified model of the political process

societies are divided into the ruling minority and ruled majority. It all also argues that this situation is inevitable. It differs from *Marxist* theory in that Marx argued that it is the forces of production that divide society into dominant and subordinate groups. Elite theorists argue that it is personal qualities, such as intelligence and organisational ability, and the hierarchical structure of organisations that enable a minority to achieve, exercise and maintain power. Indeed, if the Marxist proletarian revolution should occur, elite theorists argue that this will merely succeed in replacing one elite with another.

A central element of the elite model is the cohesiveness and organisation of the elite minority in contrast to the disorganised majority. This enables the elite, even in what appears to be a democratic system, to ensure that government decisions and policies usually reflect its own interest while the largely apathetic majority is persuaded that these are also in *its* best interests by the elite's own propaganda.

Studies in western democracies have argued the case for the existence of a *power elite*, essentially a close liaison between those that control major companies, the armed forces and the government. Critics of the theory argue that this is based more on theory than on observation of actual decision-making. Nevertheless, there is ample evidence that the captains of industry, senior officers in the armed forces and many leading politicians share similar socio-economic and educational backgrounds. In addition, direct family or marriage connections often exist. It is perhaps in communist societies, however, that the elite theory is best illustrated.

Pluralism

The pluralist model sees power in a liberal democracy as being fragmented and residing in many competing social and economic interest groups, both inside and outside of Parliament. Examples of extra-Parliamentary groups are large companies, trade unions, the mass media, the Stock Exchange and the banks. These groups constantly struggle to further their own interests and governments must, according to the model, respond to their demands. Politics is therefore seen as a process of bargain and compromise. *Pressure groups*, which we discuss below, are examples of extra-Parliamentary pluralism in action.

The pluralist model can accommodate the concept of elites in so far as most, if not all, of the competing interest groups are headed by a small elite, so much so that the term *elite pluralism* is sometimes preferred. Indeed, seen as a continuum, it merges with consensus theories at one end and conflict theories at the other (*see* below).

Although pluralism merely describes and does not attempt to justify the distribution of power in society, its critics argue that fundamental questions such as the distribution of wealth are rarely the subject of practical policy-making and that pluralist debate never seriously threatens the interests of the elites which hold effective political, economic and social power. While it may appear that all interests in society are represented in the pluralist model, society is full of inequalities and this is reflected in the differing influence and power of interest groups. In fact, its critics argue that powerful groups can use a pluralist system to promote 'non-decision making'. It follows that the privileged are able to use a pluralist system to preserve their privileges and the *status quo*. Pluralism tends to foster 'liberty' rather than 'equality'.

Consensus

Consensus theory sees society as a generally cohesive, stable, integrated whole. Broad agreement on basic values which determine its objectives, a society's *value system*, is the main feature that in turn dictates its structures, holds it together and keeps it orderly, the different parts of the society being interdependent. For example, materialist values produce objectives such as economic expansion and higher living standards and a structure of commercial organisations designed to achieve them.

The integrated nature of society is seen as influencing and often coercing individuals in society to conform to these broadly shared values, objectives, behavioural norms and structures, for it is the shared belief in these things that keeps society cohesive. But consensus theory also demands that a society must adapt to its environment, it must meet the physical needs of its members if it is to survive and it must always return to a stable equilibrium.

In consensus theory, politics is the process by which, and political institutions the structure through which, society's goals or objectives are determined and policies for their attainment formulated. Society strives to achieve an *equilibrium* in which there is no conflict, in which individuals know what is expected of them in any role and in which these expectations are constantly being met. Change is seen as reflecting public opinion. Such a total equilibrium is impossible to achieve but processes of *socialisation*, through which individuals learn what is expected of them in a given role, and *social control*, systems of rewards and punishments, are well developed. So too is the judicial system which generally ensures that conflicts are resolved according to the prevailing norms and that they do not lead to a breakdown of the system.

Perhaps the major criticism of consensus, as put forward by theorists such as Talcott Parsons, is that it is naive. As we have seen, many argue that power is frequently used to further sectional interests rather than to benefit society generally. Other criticisms are that the sophistication of industrial societies reduces consensus to the level of extremely broad and superficial generalisations and that research has failed to prove conclusively the existence of the presumed consensus in the first place.

Conflict

Consensus theory sees conflict as a minor strain in the system which is kept in check by the structure of the system itself. Conflict theory, on the other hand, sees conflict as a central and integral part of the system itself since it involves competition for scarce resources and the conflict of interests which this will generate. Thus, instead of seeing society as a cohesive whole, agreed on values and goals, it is seen in terms of divisiveness, conflict, hostility and coercion. The different interests lead to the formation of groups seeking to preserve, extend or realise their own interests against other groups. Change results from their activities.

As such, conflict theory can be viewed at one end of a continuum with consensus at the other and pluralism (or elite pluralism) occupying the middle ground. Nevertheless, both the consensus and conflict approaches see society as a *system* and are commonly referred to as *structuralist* theories. The difference lies in their views of the nature and working of the structure.

Karl Marx, whose writings are central to conflict theory, saw conflict in society as being polarised into two groups: those who have a strong interest in maintaining the existing system and those with a strong interest in changing it. Social change comes about as a result of the struggle between these two groups. Marx saw the composition of these groups in economic terms: those who exploited and those who were exploited, those who oppress and those who were oppressed.

Max Weber, on the other hand, considered status and party as well as economically defined 'class' as important in the concept of power. *Status* refers to the way the organisation of society accords different degrees of prestige or social honour to different groups of individuals. This derives from a style of life practised by a group and their attempts to develop practices which preserve and distinguish them from other groups. A simple example of this would be attempting directly or indirectly to ensure the marriages of their children to the right kind of partners. *Party* refers to the way groups organise themselves to achieve goals. These may be positions, honours or complete control of the social order. Parties may clearly be formed on the basis of class or status group, or on combinations of the two.

Some modern theorists, notably Ralf Dahrendorf, see the conflicts in 'post-capitalist' society as having become institutionalised: they are orderly, structured and controllable. For example, there are now well-developed channels for collective bargaining through which 'workers' are able to express their interests. Social and structural change in society has given everyone at least some stake in the system and so conflict is now less bitter and takes place according to the 'rules of the game'. In addition, a steadily growing 'middle class' has emerged between the capitalists or bourgeoisie (as Marx called them) and the workers or proletariat. Marx's interpretation of economic class conflict is seen as having been superseded by conflict based on *authority*, conflict between those who exercise it and those who are subject to it. On this basis, conflict cannot be seen as being between only two opposing groups, as Marx saw it, but between many interest groups. In other words, pluralism becomes the basis for conflict.

Keywords

Politics
The science and art of government, political affairs or life.

Political model
A formal or informal framework of analysis which seeks to abstract from the complexities those characteristics of the political system which are crucial to an understanding of the behavioural, institutional and technical relationships which underlie that system.

Elite theory
This argues that political power is concentrated in the hands of a dominant minority.

Pluralism
The idea that in a liberal democracy policy and power is fragmented between many different groups. This contrasts, say, with the communist or fascist system where all power rests with one party.

Consensus
This exists where there is broad agreement about the nature and goals of society even though there may be disagreement over policies and priorities.

Conflict theory
This sees society in terms of divisiveness, conflict, hostility and coercion. Fascism is a good example of this.

Policy formation

Within government departments

The Treasury is usually considered the most important of the departments of state, the *primus inter pares*, as Professor Hood Phillips described it. The Treasury supervises and controls all public finance. It regulates taxation and controls government expenditure. This fiscal policy we often regard as the most important of its functions. As well as this supervision of the economy, it has to arrange the day-to-day financing of the public services. In addition to this, it is also responsible for the establishment, i.e. the staffing, of all other departments. Most other departments try not to upset the Treasury, although they are often engaged in battles with it about their budgets.

There is no Department of Economics in Britain, i.e. no department responsible for the formulation of plans for the whole economy. Such a Department was formed in 1964 and was headed by Lord George Brown. Three years later it had been wound up and the residue of its functions transferred to the Treasury. Many people would argue that the Treasury is ill-suited to this role. By its very nature the Treasury is a watch-dog ministry, always trying to cut down on the other departments' expenditure. This is, of course, a vital task but on the other hand it can be argued that we need a ministry to push for expansion and to act in the Cabinet as a lobby for growth. No individual minister at present can stand up to the Chancellor of the Exchequer other than the Prime Minister.

A government is, supposedly, elected to implement the policies it fought the election on. In practice they may be very vague and unformulated. Even when a government has a clear idea of what it wishes to do, it is the Civil Service that has to formulate the detail of the legislation and implement it. How successful a minister is will to some extent depend upon the relationship between himself and his civil servants. It could be argued that civil servants have helped to prevent a lot of damage to the economy by protecting it from the vacillation of government policies. This continuity of policy is a good thing. On the other hand, a minister who is trying to implement a radical policy is almost bound to encounter opposition from the Civil Service whatever the merits of the policy. This is not helped by frequent changes of minister within a government and by the fact that most ministers are not experts in the area which they are supposed to govern.

A new aspect of the role of the civil servant was raised by the Clive Pontin affair in 1984. Pontin, a senior civil servant, deliberately leaked information

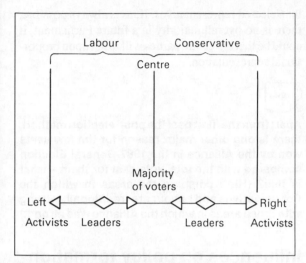

Fig. 27.2 The paradox of party difference

about the sinking of the Argentinian cruiser *Belgrano* during the Falklands War when he became convinced that ministers were misleading the public. This raised the question of how far a civil servant is the servant of the government (party) in power and how far the servant of the country. It also illustrated the fact that when civil servants are pushed too far they may react against the government.

We have, so far, supposed that a government has come to power with a policy formed by discussion and decision by its party conferences etc. However, there are often abrupt changes of direction in policy as a government encounters new or recurring problems. Under these circumstances policy is going to be determined at cabinet level, by the interplay of personalities within the cabinet, their party advisers and senior civil servants. The Government, however, is also subject to pressures from outside, not least from its own party.

Political parties

If we assume that it is the political party in power which governs the country, then we could say that there are four possibilities for control of the party: First, that it is controlled by the leader; second, by Members of Parliament of that party; third, by party activists; or finally we could imagine that it is controlled by voters.

This picture may well be modified if there is ever a breakdown of the traditional two-party system. In the mid-1980s this seemed possible but now seems far less so. The domination of politics by the two major parties since the Second World War has given rise to what David Butler has termed the *paradox of party difference*. He argued that party leaders are more extreme than electors but much less extreme than the activists in their own party (*see* Fig. 27.2). The democratisation of party structure in recent years has tended to make policies more extreme, as has the decline in party membership. Thus, party leaders are usually pulled towards the centre to please voters but to extremes to please their parties.

While in opposition a political party will tend to become more extreme because it relies heavily on its party activists and also, perhaps, because it does not have to implement its policies. It is also more difficult for the leader to keep the party in line. Once a party is in office much greater power is conferred upon the leadership because the leader is the bestower of government posts and patronage, and because the policy must be made acceptable to the electorate.

The same principle applies to MPs. While out of office the party leadership is much more amenable to MPs' opinions but once in power the leader is in an almost unassailable position. Thus, while a government is in power the decision-making ability tends to move from the party in general towards its leaders, centring upon the Prime Minister and the 'inner Cabinet'. This, Butler argued, brings it more to the *consensus* view of the voters. In opposition, power passes back the other way towards the party but this takes the party away from the average voter. This could be seen as highly desirable for it seems to leave power with the middle of the road consensus. It could not be argued, however, that this was the case during the Thatcher administrations. Certainly the Labour party initially became more extreme in opposition. Such was the bitterness of the debate within the Labour Party that a number of MPs eventually broke away and formed the Social Democratic Party (SDP) which later entered into an alliance with the Liberal Party. However, tensions within the Alliance caused it to fragment after the 1987 election in which it gained few seats. The defeat of the Labour Party at the poll in 1987 caused it to alter course and become more middle of the road in its policies.

It has often been the case that changes in government have led to great fluctuations in policy. This, everyone admits, has a deleterious effect upon the economy. These fluctuations could be as a result of *adversary politics*, the tendency for one party to automatically assume the opposite point of view to the other. Over an issue like Northern Ireland both major parties agree that dispute would be a bad thing and both parties therefore support Government policy. We do not seem to be able to agree that the management of the economy is a question of equal seriousness. Whatever one's politics, it must be admitted that frequent changes in policy towards investment, inflation, employment and economic growth are the worst of both worlds. It could be argued that one way to avoid this would be to abolish the present 'first past the post' method of elections to Parliament and replace it with some form of *proportional representation*. Both the Labour and Conservative parties, however, are resolutely opposed to this.

Since 1951 the percentage of votes cast for the two major parties has declined from 96.8% to 73% in 1987. On the other hand the seats they control in Parliament have only declined from 99% to 93%. In the 1987 General Election the Conservatives won a substantial victory; they won 57.8% of the seats although they polled only 42.3% of the vote. The Alliance Parties polled 23.1% of the votes but only won 3.5% of the seats. Another way to look at this is to say that it took only 36,600 votes to elect a Tory but 333,700 to elect an Alliance MP! Under proportional representation on the same voting figures the Alliance would have won 149 seats instead of 22, the Conservatives 279 instead of 375 and Labour 202 instead of 229 – a very different story! With the voting system so heavily favouring the two major parties, it seems unlikely at present that a third force will emerge in British politics. It is possible, however, that a small party might hold the balance of power in a Parliament in which there is no overall majority – a 'hung' Parliament. This being the case, a change in the voting system to some form of proportional representation would possibly result as the price demanded by the small party for supporting one of the major parties. It is possible that this could lead us to some sort of consensus policy-making and the elimination of dangerous vacillations in policy. On the other hand, it could lead to a permanent stalemate which would tend to place more power in the hands of bureaucrats rather

than elected representatives. If, as is always possible, there is no overall majority in a future Parliament, it could be that the centre parties will insist upon proportional representation.

Apart from the 'first past the post' election method, there is one other major reason for the few seats won by the Alliance in the 1987 General Election compared with the total vote cast for them – what is this? (Hint: compare the areas in which the Conservatives and Labour are traditionally strong with those areas in which the Alliance was strong.)

Influences on policy formation

Pressure groups

Pressure (or interest) groups number many thousands and exist in all areas of society. While their specific objectives and activities are probably incapable of definitive classification, they all exist to articulate ideas, interests and values and by so doing hope to influence the government's decision and policy-making processes. They are a medium through which the government is made aware of the views of a section of the public or of organisations and exemplify pluralism in practice. Some, like the TUC and CBI, are of national importance and their activities can be seen to have a direct effect on the government and other organisations; others achieve temporary prominence and sometimes resounding individual success, e.g. the 'anti-airport' groups in the Wing and Foulness areas. Most, however, pursue their own interest quietly and steadily, relatively unnoticed by the public.

Pressure groups may be distinguished from political parties in that they do not seek 'office' in order to acquire political power, do not present a programme covering a wide range of political issues and may exist to exert their influence against non-governmental organisations. In addition, a major function of many, e.g. trade unions, is the provision of services for their members.

The role of pressure groups

While Parliament is the real main formal institution

for the representation of interests, MPs have become increasingly unable to represent and reconcile the ever more diverse and often conflicting interests present in modern society. The two major political parties are each traditionally identified with sectional interests but these interests are often too general. Pressure groups provide continuous protection of far more specific interests which a government, constrained by wider political considerations and a maximum term of office, cannot. In particular, many pressure groups are a response to increasing government intervention in the economy and they seek to influence government policy to their own advantage.

Governments are usually happy to consult with pressure groups for three reasons. First, consultation is seen as part of the democratic process; second, pressure groups can contribute expertise on particular issues which may not be readily available to governments; third, they can help with implementing a policy, e.g. by publicising a government initiative or regulation.

Types of pressure groups

Pressure groups are most easily classified on functional criteria. *Sectional groups* exist to promote the common economic interests of their members, e.g. trade unions and employers' associations are sectional groups. In addition, they will normally provide a range of services for their members. *Promotional groups* are established to fight for particular causes, e.g. the various anti-airport or motorway groups and other environmentalist groups such as Friends of the Earth. Most are short-lived.

Many other organisations, ranging from a local youth club to a large company, may find themselves fulfilling the functions of a pressure group through circumstances rather than choice. For example, they may be forced to promote their interest where limited resources are being allocated or where a local planning enquiry directly threatens them.

Pressure groups and the policy formation process

At the risk of over-simplifying the policy formation process, we can represent it as a series of stages.

1 Getting an issue on the policy agenda. A government must first be persuaded that there is a policy problem which should be addressed. This may be the most difficult stage to achieve.

2 Preliminary consultations. These precede the issue of a green or white paper. Pressure groups have an excellent opportunity to promote their interests at this stage because the government is looking at various options for dealing with the issue. A Royal Commission may be established if the issue is sufficiently important, more usually a civil service committee will be used.

3 Issue of a green or white paper. These contain the government's proposals.

4 Parliamentary procedures. When a government has a large majority, the opportunities to affect proposals at this stage are limited.

5 Implementation. Since many Acts are implemented by detailed statutory instruments at a later stage, pressure groups have a major opportunity to exert their influence at this stage.

How pressure groups operate

The initial task of any pressure group is to *determine the interest* which it will promote and protect. It generally follows that the difficulty in doing this increases in proportion to the size of the group. Indeed, there may be directly conflicting interests to be resolved within a group. The CBI, for example, must reconcile its support for members in difficulty, and who may therefore need government assistance, with its basic philosophy of free enterprise. So too must the TUC, e.g. excessive pay rises now may mean unemployment later.

A pressure group will partly determine the interests to promote by collecting information from its members. This in turn can be used to support its representations at a later date. The information will be collected in four main ways.

1 Case studies – these are particularly common in trade union activities;

2 Specialist publications, in particular their correspondence columns – publications such as the *British Medical Journal* of the British Medical Association are extremely influential;

3 Surveys; and

4 Requests for information from local and central government.

The second task is the *transmission* of their interest into the political or decision-making process. The target will depend upon the nature of the interest. Nationally it would be aimed at the EC, the government and the central administration, Parliament, or the public. Locally it would be aimed at the council or the management of a company, e.g. one involved in a pay or redundancy dispute with its employees.

Three main techniques exist for this transmission of ideas.

1 Propaganda. This could take the form of public meetings, publicity exercises, advertising, etc. It will have three main objectives:

(a) to increase public awareness of, and interest in, the group;

(b) to influence public opinion; and

(c) to increase membership of the group itself.

The ultimate aim of all propaganda is to increase the political influence of the pressure group.

2 Representation This technique consists of direct communication with decision- and policy-makers. It is usually more effective than propaganda (which will tend to be used by groups without 'contacts') and the relevant authorities are often receptive to representations which they consider could prevent problems or confrontations arising in the future.

Organised links exist between nationally important groups, such as trade unions and employers' associations, and government, Parliament and administration. Indeed, relatively obscure groups may be able to acquire such links either by direct retainers to MPs or buying the services of specialist public relations organisations. The extensive links between the Association of Metropolitan Authorities and central government and administration are a prime example of how such links may effectively promote group interests.

For pressure groups 'recognised' and regularly consulted by government, achieving direct communication is not a great problem but other groups can only do this through giving evidence before Royal Commissions and inquiries and by lobbying Parliament and individual MPs (although the last technique is often more effective as a propaganda exercise). Undoubtedly, the most effective lobbying is done behind the scenes.

While its structure and methods of operation are hard to define, the diverse but regular system of contacts among the government, administration, business organisations, trade unions and other well-organised pressure groups, is often termed the *Establishment*.

3 Supply of information This technique increases public awareness of the group's interests and usually has a valuable propaganda function. In particular, a pressure group can seek to influence MPs' opinions by supplying information which they have insufficient time and resources to acquire themselves.

How successful are pressure groups?

Pressure groups are rarely successful if their interest is contrary to the wider political interest. Sometimes opposing pressure groups seem to counteract each other, the CBI and the TUC being the classic examples. The CBI urges the government to restore the profit incentive to the economy as a means of regenerating economic activity and the TUC promotes policies designed to create more jobs and curb price rises. Such giants are well-matched. In other areas of conflict the pressure group with the better organisation, finance, economic and social leverage, political contacts and public support will normally win.

The 1980s saw a decline in the importance of pressure groups as an influence on the fundamentals of government policy. A number of reasons can be identified. Governments were elected with large Parliamentary majorities and even controversial legislation had an easy passage through Parliament; they believed in conviction rather than consultative politics; their policies were highly ideological, which brought them into direct conflict with many pressure groups; and their policy of reducing the importance of the public sector made them far less dependent on the consent, goodwill and support of many pressure groups such as trade unions and welfare groups.

However, despite this, by 1990 the activities of pressure groups and of lobbyists generally were at an all-time high. By acquiring political power and influence in policy and decision-making, they are able to affect the day-to-day activities of both the government and other organisations. Although this effect may be difficult to quantify, the very fact that so many pressure groups exist and that so much time and money is put into their work is surely proof that a great many people believe their effect to be considerable. In fact in recent years pressure groups have been successful despite government opposition, e.g. the defeat of the Shops Bill in 1986 (which would have legalised Sunday trading), the nurses' pay award and the ban on the use of certain types of foam in furniture in 1988.

Cause for concern?

The existence of powerful and successful pressure groups raises important questions about the nature and equality of representation in the UK. Should MPs be allowed to accept fees for acting on their behalf and should professional public relations organisations be able to use their Parliamentary contacts to further commercial interests by getting clauses inserted into a Bill already allocated Parliamentary time? Do government departments accept the advice of powerful pressure groups too uncritically, possibly at the expense of the wider public interest, and should they take such notice of the views of bodies which may be inherently undemocratic? Perhaps above all else, given that pressure groups cannot actually control policy and decision-making, the fact that so much representation goes on behind the scenes gives some cause for concern.

The political power of trade unions

A feature of politics since the 1939–45 war has been the increase in trade union power and consequently in their influence over political policy and decision making processes. The clash between the Conservative Government and the miners in the winter of 1973–4 was the climax of this growth and, in the general election of February 1974, led to the election of a Labour Government which was more sympathetic to union objectives. However, even the Labour Government discovered that the need to gain the co-operation of the unions in economic policy gave the unions new and unprecedented influence over Government policy and decision-making. For these reasons, the Conservative Government, elected in 1979, determined to reduce the influence of the trade unions.

Since 1979 the unions have seen many of the powers and privileges that they acquired taken away

from them (*see* Chapter 8). In addition, a high level of unemployment and changing patterns of work have combined to greatly reduce trade union influence. This was underlined by the Miners' Strike of 1984–5 in which the NUM was substantially defeated.

Most major unions are affiliated to the Labour Party and it is within the Party that they exercise their *direct* political influence. Their political levies provide most of the Labour Party's funds (even though most union members are politically apathetic) and trade unions also have great influence on the National Executive Council of the Labour Party and control many votes at the Party Conference. However, neither the NEC nor the Party Conference control the Parliamentary Labour Party. The party leaders are elected by an electoral college consisting of the trade unions, the constituency parties and the MPs. There have also been attempts to make Party Conference decisions binding upon the Parliamentary Labour Party. Within Parliament, unions sponsor about 40% of Labour MPs and give financial assistance to many others, although they have not, as yet, sought to control their votes. Since 1972 direct links have existed between the Party and the TUC through the TUC-Labour Party Liaison Committee. The Trade Union and Labour Relations Act 1974 was a product of this link.

The Conservative government of 1979 sought no co-operation with the unions; rather it began to attack the privileges and influence they had acquired in the previous five years. The government skilfully avoided conflict with the more powerful unions, such as the miners, for the first two years of its office. In addition to this, unemployment escalating beyond three million dampened wage demands, reduced trade-union membership and decreased the willingness to strike. Following a further victory at the poll in 1987, the Conservative Government continued to confront unions and to attack the legal protection enjoyed by trade unions.

The media

When you watched the 'news' or a current affairs programme on TV last night, or listened to a news broadcast or read your newspaper this morning, you were receiving neatly packaged information likely to affect your views on contemporary political issues. It follows that the *media* – the press, TV and radio – not only spread awareness of political issues by reporting them but also influences policy and decision-making by manipulating public opinion. Deliberate mis-reporting is unnecessary to achieve this; careful selection of news and views is quite sufficient to influence public opinion and promote certain causes. In turn, the media can be used as effective propaganda organs by policy and decision-makers themselves.

In party political terms, radio and TV must, by law, endeavour to remain neutral in their coverage of political events and issues. Nevertheless, the BBC tends to be a mouthpiece for the 'Establishment' and commercial broadcasting companies must take into account the views of their advertisers. Despite this, in the late 1980s the Conservative Party began to regard the BBC as being anti-government in its reporting. It is difficult to determine whether this view is sincerely held or simply an attempt to influence the content of reports. Much depends on your point of view.

Newspapers are often openly partisan. Among the 'popular' press, the *Daily Mail* and the *Sun* are Conservative while the *Daily Mirror* usually supports Labour policy. The same is true of the 'quality' papers; the *Daily Telegraph* is openly right-wing, *The Guardian* espouses Liberal policies and *The Times*, while perhaps being the most objective, still tends to be conservative with a small 'c'. Among the weeklies, the *Spectator* is Conservative, the *New Statesman* socialist and the *Economist* supports policies which further the interests of 'big business'.

A wide range of extreme partisan publications also exist, e.g. the *Morning Star* and *Socialist Worker*, but because they have small circulations and usually preach to the converted, they tend to have little impact on 'opinion'.

Political partiality in reporting is not necessarily undesirable, but there is a danger in the frequency with which it is reported as hard fact. You should always remember this particularly when reading political comment in newspapers.

Select one of the political news stories of the week and contrast the way in which it is reported in different newspapers.

The media's influence on public opinion is recognised and exploited by politicians, in part as a response to the potential power of the media to undermine the politicians' own positions. Suitable images for party leaders are projected via professional public relations organisations and the effect of news reports can be influenced through carefully calculated disclosures of information. The 'lobby correspondent' system is one of the best ways of doing this. Under this system certain correspondents have free access to the Members' Lobby in Parliament and receive briefings from members of the government. Providing they do not quote their sources they can use this information in their reports. In turn, politicians gain much of their own information from the 'quality' newspapers and weeklies. Thus, influence exists in both directions.

Perhaps the power of the media is best demonstrated by the extreme censorship it suffers in many undemocratic states and how, in any political coup, control of the media is always one of the first objectives, witness the State TV station as the focus of the Romanian Revolution in 1989–90 .

External influences

In the 19th century, Great Britain 'ruled the waves' and governments could formulate policies without taking much notice of influences outside the UK itself. Today, the situation is very different: the UK is just one industrialised country among many and the Government and other organisations are increasingly influenced by bodies external to the economy. Particularly good examples include the EC, NATO and the IMF. Indeed, the move towards the Single Market could see domestic policy formation increasingly subordinated to decisions taken in Brussels.

1 List three examples of the EC influencing the policy of the British Government.

2 If we are more fully integrated with the EC after 1992, what new areas of domestic policy do you expect Brussels to start influencing?

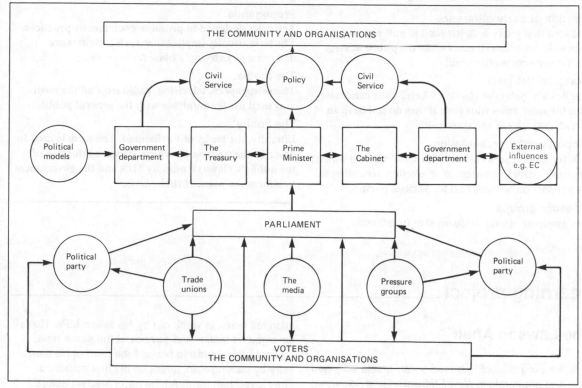

Fig. 27.3 The policy machine: from the community and back again

The organisation, the state and the community

We have endeavoured to show in this book that the organisation is not a passive bystander, waiting to have government policy imposed upon it, but a cog in the machine which determines that policy. The primary factor which will influence the economic well-being of the business organisation is the general state of the economy. These days this is acknowledged to be the responsibility of the Government, and, in addition, business organisations receive much direct help and benefit from the Government. Examples of this include the ECGD, regional development grants and ACAS. In a sense, the State could be said to provide an organisational framework within which organisations can operate. On the other hand, the health of the economy also depends upon the enterprise and initiative of organisations, their efficiency and profitability, and their ability to respond to change and utilise new technology.

This illustrates a basic argument of this book: organisations cannot be viewed as individual economic phenomena nor studied in academically isolated disciplines. The market economy as envisaged by Adam Smith is no longer, business organisations operate in a mixed economy which is not so much a compromise between, but rather a compound of, collectivism and capitalism, possessing its own separate character and properties. Within the mixed economy an amalgam of diverse social, economic and political forces determines government policy (*see* Fig. 27.3). Organisations are both the subject of government policy and a factor in its formation. In the words of Galbraith, organisations 'influence government, influence the consumer. Only the textbooks hold otherwise.'

Keywords

Paradox of party difference
The idea that party activists tend to pull policy outwards towards extremes while the public at large push it towards moderation.

First past the post
The British system of election whereby the candidate with the most votes wins even if they do not have an overall majority of the votes cast.

Proportional representation
This term embraces various systems of election which attempt to distribute seats in an election according to the proportion of votes cast for various parties.

Pressure groups
Any group or organisation seeking to influence government policy for their own purpose.

Propaganda
Activities designed to promote doctrines or practices. The term usually implies that such activities are dishonest or extremely biased.

The media
The newspapers, television, radio etc – all the mediums used to communicate with the general public.

The 'lobby'
Literally, the lobby of Parliament. The term is used to describe the process by which MPs are informed of the public's views or used by MPs and the government to inform the press of their views.

Learning project

The Lawson Affair

This learning project is based on an article abridged from one appearing in *New Statesman and Society* on 3 November 1989 by Sarah Benton. It concerns the resignation of Nigel Lawson as Chancellor of the Exchequer. This was over the issue of Margaret Thatcher preferring the advice of her 'guru' Sir Alan Walters to that of her Chancellor. The dispute was over whether or not the UK should enter the Exchange Rate Mechanism of the EMS. The arguments in Parliament and in the media, however, soon developed into disagreements about the style of Government policy formation.

The Avenger

In the five days following his resignation Nigel Lawson made three of the most astute moves in his political life. He resigned, he kept quiet about why until he addressed the House on Tuesday, and he chose that occasion to produce with a flourish, after weeks of flat assertions that he had nothing up his sleeves except high interest-rates, a new option: an independent central bank to ensure monetary stability.

This triple display of his unassailable brilliance ensured that he was lovingly welcomed into the House. One minute he was the imperious Chancellor, the next, a mascot of the impotence and humili-ation felt week in week out by his fellow MPs. He re-emerged as victim and saviour at the same time.

Nigel Lawson made himself the hero of his own story by picking Parliament as his first audience. They loved him for it. All the other leading actors were off stage. Sir Alan Walters chose to emerge in front of the TV cameras, Bernard Ingham skulked as usual. As for a whimsical and tyrannical creature called The Pound, she was gossiped about endlessly by the servants downstairs, aka the Members of Parliament.

The Prime Minister chose to commune with us through the spirit mediums of Jean Rook and Brian Walden. She has made no statement to the House of Commons at all. She did slip into the Commons on Tuesday night but then slipped away, probably to get advice from her ouija board. Despite the world triumph of Thatcherism, she can still learn a thing or two from the Reagans.

The point, for Parliament, is that for a decade the Prime Minister has made it quite clear that she does not feel herself accountable to them.

When the story actually began, we shan't know until all the actors have leaked their accounts. On the Tuesday before Lawson resigned, a day chosen by Labour for a debate on the economy, Smith and Brown stepped smartly out, all guns firing. Their cruel lampooning was, if not the proximate cause of Lawson's resignation, astonishingly percipient for a pair of economic spokesmen. Sir Alan Walters had worked for an Institute financed by the Moonies, Gordon Brown told the Commons. 'Many lonely, sad and embattled people labour under the delusion that their thoughts are being influenced by the Moonies next door – but for the Chancellor at Number 11 Downing Street, sadly, such fears may be thoroughly well-grounded. I assure the Right Honourable Gent that he is not paranoid, they really are out to get him.'

If Smith and Brown can claim credit for driving Lawson to the end of his tether, until, like a desperate scapegoat, he broke free and fled, that is an exceptional display of Parliamentary power. The resignations of Michael Heseltine and Leon Brittain oozed a tangle of intrigue behind closed doors. The change after three years, is that the Labour party has now got the measure of how Mrs Thatcher governs. Her persona has become such a material factor in government, that by contemplating it, they have a window into the Cabinet. It was their portrayal of a shady, back-stairs world, where disloyalty breeds, which hit home rather than their assault on economic policy.

Between the opening and closing speeches of Big Debates there is a long interlude of three or four hours, a sort of extended playtime in the House, when the juniors can take part too. It is a procedural anachronism, a hangover from the time when MPs, if no one else, believed what they said mattered. Now most of them don't believe it either and if there are two dozen in the Chamber on even major occasions like this Tuesday's, that's a good show.

Graham Allen, MP for Nottingham North, said that this week will be remembered not as an economic crisis but as a constitutional one. We have a twisted, presidential system in which the Cabinet and Parliament can be disregarded. We are impotent and decorative; we can't even get access to Bernard Ingham and Alan Walters.

Ironically, the man who would agree with him is Nigel Lawson. What you know about Sir Alan Walters so far, he said, is just the tip of an iceberg. He thus suggests his fourth but most deadly move of

the week. The Prime Minister is dependent on the tiny cabal of hand-picked, unaccountable men, whom she trusts. She doesn't trust anyone else. She would rather lose her Chancellor than one of them. She can weather resignations and any number of direct attacks. But to oppose and destroy her links with the trusted few would be more than she could bear. Her personality is going to remain at the heart of the political debate.

Complete the following tasks.

1 The article mentions the word 'cabal'. What is the origin of this term and what does it mean?

2 It is apparent from the article that even on important occasions there are often very few MPs in the House. This may also be apparent to you if you have watched televised debates from Parliament. Do you think that the televising of parliament will alter the way business is conducted? Give reasons for your answer. What suggestions would you make for improving television coverage of Parliament?

3 The article seems to suggest that backbench MPs have very little power. Why is this? Under what circumstances would their power be increased? Give an example of when the action of backbench MPs have been important in the formation of policy.

4 Graham Allen describes MPs as 'impotent' and 'decorative'. Explain what you think is meant by these terms. By what methods might MPs get access to non-elected advisers such as Bernard Ingham and Alan Walters?

5 Examine the role which the media played in the Lawson resignation crisis.

6 What is meant when the article says 'The Prime Minister chose to commune with us through the spirit mediums of Jean Rook and Brian Walden'? Why do you think Margaret Thatcher 'preferred' these mediums of communication?

7 Examine the extent to which the British voting system leads to a presidential style of government.

Further ideas for learning projects

1 Compile a file of newspaper cuttings to illustrate the progress of a local dispute concerning an issue such as the proposed construction of an airport, power station, motorway etc.

(a) Identify the different groups and interests involved

in the dispute.

(b) List the arguments for and against the project as presented by the protagonists.

(c) Outline ways in which the dispute could have been or was resolved.

2 Each year, Parliament passes a new Finance Act. The passing of the Finance Act is the culmination of a long process which includes the presentation to Parliament by the Chancellor of the Exchequer of the Government's proposals – the Budget. But the process of policy formation has, of course, begun long before budget day.

(a) For the most recent Budget, find out as much as you can from newspapers and periodicals about how the Chancellor's proposals were influenced.

(b) Budgets are supposed to be very closely guarded secrets. Nevertheless, each year astonishingly accurate 'predictions' are made about the content of the Budget speech. Compare the predictions in the newspapers before Budget day with the actual Budget. How accurate were the predictions? If you suspect that there might have been leaks, suggest reasons why it might be in the Government's interest to allow them.

3 The table at the top of the next column shows the votes cast in the General Election of 1987 and the resulting number of MPs for each party.

3 The table below shows the votes cast in the General Election of 1987 and the resulting number of MPs for each party.

(a) Say whether or not you consider this to be a 'fair' distribution of seats. Give reasons for your answer.

(b) Explain how the results might have been different under different electoral systems.

Votes cast in the 1987 General Election

Party	Votes for	% of total votes	Nos of seats in Parliament
Conservative	13,763,066	42.3	376
Labour	10,029,778	30.8	229
Alliance	7,341,290	22.6	22
Others	1,402,005	4.5	23

4 The table below gives the results for a hypothetical parliamentary constituency. In the constituency an experiment was tried using the *alternative vote system*. In this the voters marked (1) at the side of their first choice, (2) against the name of their second choice and so on.

After the election it was discovered that no candidate had an overall majority, therefore the candidate with the fewest votes (Solidarity with Albania) was eliminated and his 27 votes distributed according to his supporters' second preferences. This process continued until one candidate obtained an absolute majority of votes cast. After four such redistributions it was found to be unnecessary to worry about the third and fourth preferences because a candidate had an overall majority. State:

(a) which candidate was elected;

(b) what was his or her majority over his or her nearest rival;

(c) the strengths and weaknesses of this method of election.

Votes cast in the Northgate constituency by-election 1990

Candidate	First preference	First redistribution	Second redistribution	Third redistribution	Fourth redistribution
I Bunting (Liberal)	13,062	3	12	1,270	—
C Faux (Green)	1,990	9	—	—	—
B O'Sullivan (Labour)	15,089	2	27	502	9,427
K Hyndman (Conservative)	18,427	6	310	74	3,426
A Rethil (National Front)	502	—	—	—	—
G Woolf (Solidarity with Albania)	27	—	—	—	—

Total electorate 59, 874
Electorate voting = 82%

Index